FRANCIS PICABIA

FRANCIS PICABIA

HIS ART, LIFE AND TIMES
BY WILLIAM A. CAMFIELD

PRINCETON UNIVERSITY PRESS
PRINCETON, NEW JERSEY

Copyright © 1979 by Princeton University Press
Published by Princeton University Press, Princeton, New Jersey
In the United Kindom: Princeton University Press,
Guildford, Surrey

All Rights Reserved
Library of Congress Cataloging in Publication Data
will be found on the last printed page of this book

Publication of this book has been aided by a grant from
the Institute of the Arts at Rice University

This book has been composed in Bodoni Book with
Busorama display type

Clothbound editions of Princeton University Press books
are printed on acid-free paper, and binding materials are
chosen for strength and durability.

Printed in the United States of America by
Princeton University Press, Princeton, New Jersey
Color plates are printed by Village Craftsmen,
Rosemont, New Jersey
Black-and-white plates are printed by Meriden Gravure Company,
Meriden, Connecticut

Designed by James Wageman

To Ginny, John and Dominique

CONTENTS

ACKNOWLEDGMENTS

I CANNOT imagine this book without the support of Picabia's family, above all his widow, Olga Picabia, and his former wives, Gabrielle Buffet-Picabia and Germaine Everling-Picabia. The insights, the documents and the introductions they provided were indispensable. Each is an extraordinary woman in her own right, and I cherish their friendships. Picabia's half sister, Mme Yvonne Gresse-Picabia, and his children—Marie, Pancho, Salvador and, especially, Jeannine Bailly-Cowell—have also contributed.

It was my good fortune to have begun this study at Yale University under the guidance of Professor George Heard Hamilton. His example as a teacher-scholar and his quality as a man have been lasting influences.

Four libraries and their staffs merit special gratitude: the Collection of American Literature in the Beinecke Rare Book and Manuscript Library, Yale University (Curator Donald Gallup); the Bibliothèque Littéraire Jacques Doucet, Paris (Conservateur François Chapon); the library at the Museum of Modern Art, New York (Librarians Bernard Karpel and Inga Forslund); and the Humanities Research Center, The University of Texas at Austin (Curator Carlton Lake).

Essential financial support has been provided by the American Council of Learned Societies (Fellowship, 1973–1974, and Grant-in-Aid, 1967); the American Philosophical Society (Penrose Fund, 1965); research and travel grants from Rice University and the University of St. Thomas and grants for color reproductions from the Institute for the Arts at Rice University and William N. Copley.

A handful of individuals, museums and art galleries have contributed so much to this study that they must be singled out for special thanks. I name with abiding fondness and respect Marcel Duchamp, Yves Poupard-Lieussou, Arturo Schwarz, Mme Simone Collinet, Henri Goetz and Christine Boumeester, and Mr. and Mrs. John de Menil.

From the beginning two galleries were crucial for research on Picabia, the Galerie Furstenberg, Paris, and the Galleria Schwarz, Milan. More recently the Galleria Notizie, Turin, and the Galerie des 4 Mouvements, Paris, have been leading galleries for Picabia's work. Other galleries especially supportive of this study include the former Rose Fried Gallery, New York; the Galerie de L'Ile de France, Paris; Galerie A.F. Petit, Paris; Galerie Cavalero, Cannes; Galleries Maurice Sternberg, Chicago; Galerie Jacques Tronche, Paris; Galerie Agora, Paris; Galerie Mona Lisa, Paris.

Among the museums which have responded to my endless requests with extraordinary kindness and professional skill, I count the Solomon R. Guggenheim Museum, especially Thomas M. Messer (Director), Angelica Rudenstine (Research Curator) and Linda Shearer (Assistant Curator); the Museum of Modern Art, New York, especially William Rubin (Director of Painting and Sculpture) and his entire staff, including Betty Jones, now at Smith College; the Musée National d'Art Moderne, Paris, especially K.G. Pontus Hultén (Director), Michel Hoog (Librarian) and Hélène Seckel and Jean-Hubert Martin (Curators); the Philadelphia Museum of Art, especially Anne d'Harnoncourt (Curator); and the Musée Cantini, Marseille, especially Mme Jacques Latour (Director).

I also wish to underscore the cooperation of Picabia's older friends and colleagues who granted invaluable interviews and, in a few instances, written statements when an interview was impossible: Tristan Tzara, Man Ray, Hans Arp and Marguerite Arp-Hagenbach, Georges Ribemont-Dessaignes, Philippe Soupault, Richard Huelsenbeck, Hans Richter, Serge Charchoune, René Clair, Georges Christian, Amédée Ozenfant, Suzanne Duchamp-Crotti, Mme H.P. Roché, Georges Hugnet, Pierre de Massot, Max Ernst, Alexandre Archipenko, Alice Halicka (Mme Louis Marcoussis), Mme Albert Gleizes, Beatrice Wood, Christian Schad, Paul-Emile Pissarro, Edith Clifford Williams, Mrs. Edgar Varèse, Jacques-Henri and Angelica Lévesque, E.L.T. Mesens, René Magritte, Otho St. Clair Lloyd, Mme Pierre Albert-Birot and Marcel Janco.

Having pursued Picabia's enormous production into hundreds of collections, there are numerous individuals, museums, galleries and institutions still to be acknowledged. I deeply regret that, owing to your number, recognition must be reduced to a few words and a long list. For this study I depended in part on all of you; many went beyond the simple call of duty in terms of time, photographs, documents and introductions to other collectors; some provided even food, shelter and friendship. Thank you all:

Rodrigo de Zayas and Mrs. Marius de Zayas, Robert Lebel, Mlle Germaine Henri, Pierre André Benoit, Georgia O'Keeffe, Mme Suzanne Romain, Mr. and Mrs. Herbert Rothschilde, M. and Mme Saint-Maurice, M. and Mme Michel Perrin, Mrs. Leonard Brown, M. and Mme Lionel Cavalero, William N. Copley, Dr. and Mrs. Barnett Malbin, Dr. Luigi Campi, Mr. and Mrs. Charles D. Clark, Señor Ramon Julia, Mrs. Georges Marci, Mr. and Mrs. Luciano Pistoi, Mr. and Mrs. Ippolito Simonis, M. and Mme Montet, Robert Motherwell, Mme Jean Krebs, André Buckles, Mrs. Maurice Buckles, George Bennett, Paride Accetti, Enrico and Roberta Baj, M. and Mme Funck-Brentano, the Honorable David Montagu, Malitte Matta, M. André Napier, Mr. and Mrs. E.S. Power, M. and Mme Michel Périnet, Arnold A. Saltzman, M. and Mme Trésar, M. Christophe Tzara, M. and Mme François Baron, Benjamin Bernstein, Mme G. Cavaillon, M. Patrick Bokanowsky, Frances Oertling-Reynolds, Mr. and Mrs. Neil Reisner, Dorothy Norman, Mr. and Mrs. Morton G. Neumann, Mme R. Gasquel, Mme Méraud Guevara, Ann de Journo, Mr. and Mrs. Barnet Hodes, Jean Whitehill, Prince Troubetzkoi, Dr. Beppe Sesia, Jasper Johns, Robert Rauschenberg, Mr. and Mrs.

Jack Josey, Mr. and Mrs. Turhan Taner, Robert Greene, Dr. Robert Lesmale, Marietta von Meyenberg, M. Pierre Granville, Mme Francine Kapferer, Mme I. Solomon, Mr. and Mrs. Roland Penrose, Rosamund Bernier, Mr. and Mrs. Alvin Romansky, Mlle Cécile de Rothschild, Michel Seuphor, M. Henri Parisot, William Benenson, Charles Benenson, Mme Odette Rosenberg, M. and Mme C. Pomaret, Mrs. Morton G. Schamberg, Dr. Ira Leo Schamberg, Mr. and Mrs. Edward E. Voynow, Mme Huguenin, Mrs. R. Cochrane, Mrs. William Sawyer, Prof. Guido Rossi, Mrs. William Sisler, M. Henri Daher, Arthur A. Cohen, M.J. Dumas, Norma Copley, Mr. and Mrs. David T. Schiff, Giovanni Traversa, M. René Jean Ullmann, Mr. and Mrs. Sidney M. Ehrman, Mme Landau Fischer, F. Mendel, Corrado Levi, Mrs. Harris Weston, Cesare Tosi, Mrs. Charles Roberts, M. and Mme F. Aladjem. M. Robert Altmann, Roberto Crippa, Nancy Cunard, M. Romanens, M. G. Waisman, Mrs. M. Victor Leventritt, Steingrim Lauursen, Dr. Eliot Corday, Celia Ascher, Mme Jean Peysson, Dr. Robert Schnell, Richard Smart, Sam Wagstaff, Jr., Mme J. Schulman, M. Roger Delpech, Mme Eva Fischer, M. Filiberti, M. Gilbert Boudar, M. Drevet René, Mrs. Gabriel François Picabia, Ron Padgett, Jim Dine, M. Simonet, Claudio Bruni, J.W. Gillon, Dr. Richard E. Gibbons, M. Fernand Graindorge, Joseph Weissman, M. and Mme Maurice Weinberg, Dr. Robert Pfeffer, Dr. F.J. Bossard, M. and Mme H. Bouvard, M. Emil Jean Bomsel, M. Adrien Dubucq and M. Marcel Dubucq, M. Raymond Erny, Mme Illa Knina, Mr. and Mrs. Arnold Maremont, M. Jacques Antoine Legrain, Hugh Ford, M. Simon Bilew, Bureau de Maire, Lisieux, Mr. and Mrs. Charles Park, M. Armand Charles, M. Joseph Lafosse, Frederick Shore, Mme Lucienne Radisse, M. and Mme J.P. Normand, M. René Cavalero, Dr. and Mme Colin, M. Edouard Dermit, M. L.R. Pissarro, Orovida Pissarro, Mme Jean Baumel, E.A. Bergman, Dr. Franco Camerini, M. A. Faurie, Peggy Guggenheim, Solomon Ethe, M. Jacques Bouillat, Henry Leffert, Enrico Matta, M. André Peeters, M. Lucien Vallet, M. Charles Lavergne, Richard Karasik, Alfredo Taglia, Dr. D. Hannema, M. H. Picard, M. Félix, John M. Fink, Mr. and Mrs. Andrew Fuller, M. A. Vallens, M. and Mme Lundberg, John Levy, M. Jean-Jacques Lebel, Mrs. John Fabick, Dr. Colette Jéramec Tchernia, Hubertus Wald, Jane Harper, J. Marion Gulnayer, M. Lamothe Fenelon, Lillian Florsheim, R. Morone, M. J.L. Merckx, M. Léon Jérusalmi, Dr. Max Welti, Mme Jeanine Schulman, M. Albert Lazaroo, M. X. Larmurier, Prince Serge Lubomirski, Timothy Baum, Jack C. Massey, Mme L. Landry, William Stix Wasserman, Lewis Robbins, Pierre Soulages, Louise Bruner, Mme Cécile Eluard Valette, Gordon Page Williams, Philip Pearlstein, Erwin D. Canham, M. Robert de Charnacé, Mrs. Henry Epstein, Mr. and Mrs. Lewis Fine, Melvin Jacobs, M. R. Maake, Herbert Schimmel, Dr. Alex B. Stone, Mlle Anne-Marie Ronchèse, Count Boël, Carl Frederick Reutersward and Mr. and Mrs. Kolodny.

I gratefully acknowledge the cooperation of the following museums, libraries, universities and other institutions: The Metropolitan Museum of Art, New York; The Art Institute of Chicago; Musée d'Art Moderne de la Ville de Paris; Yale University Art Gallery and the Collection of the Société Anonyme, Yale University, New Haven; Museo de Arte de Cataluña, Barcelona; The Tate Gallery, London; The National Gallery, London; Uffizi Gallery, Florence; The Baltimore Museum of Art; The Arts Club of Chicago; Galleria d'Arte Moderne, Turin; The Louvre, Paris; The National Gallery of Art, Washington, D.C.; Museo del Prado, Madrid; The Tyringham Institute, Tyringham, Mass.; The Francis Bacon Foundation, Claremont, California; The New York Public Library; Frick Art Reference Library, New York; Archives of American Art, Washington, D.C.; Bibliothèque Nationale, Paris; Oeffentliche Kunstsammlung, Basel; Museo Nazionale, Naples; Museo e Galleria Nazionali di Capodimonte, Naples; Accademia Carrara, Bergamo; Museo delle Terme, Rome; Musée de Peinture et de Sculpture, Grenoble; Musée d'Art et d'Industrie, St.-Etienne; Fogg Art Museum, Cambridge, Mass.; Albright-Knox Art Gallery, Buffalo, New York; Seattle Art Museum; New York University Art Collection; Carnegie Institute, Pittsburgh, Pa.; The Berkshire Museum, Pittsfield, Mass.; Rhode Island School of Design Museum of Art, Providence; U.C.L.A. Art Galleries, Los Angeles; Moderna Museet, Stockholm; Silkeborg Kunstmuseum; The Petit Palais, Geneva; Koreografiska Institutet, Stockholm; Société des Gens de Lettres, Paris; Hannema de Steurs Foundation, Heino, The Netherlands; Stedelijk Museum, Amsterdam; Institute Français au Portugal, Lisbon; Musée de Libourne; Caisse Nationale des Monuments Historiques et des Sites, Paris; San Francisco Museum of Art; Phoenix Museum; Kunsthalle Bern; Musées Royaux des Beaux-Arts de Belgique, Brussels; Wallraf-Richartz Museum, Cologne; Temple Newsam House, Leeds; The Art Gallery of Toronto; The Detroit Institute of Arts.

I wish to thank personnel with the following galleries and auction houses for their help, without which no serious study of Picabia's work could have been achieved: Galerie Henri Bénézit, Paris; Galerie Berri-Lardy, Paris; Fourcade and Droll, Inc., New York; Hilde Gerst Gallery, New York; Galerie Jacques Benador, Geneva; Krugier et Cie, Geneva; Galerie d'Elysée, Paris; Galerie Jean Chauvelin, Paris; Galerie des Etats-Unis, Cannes; Cordier and Ekstrom, New York; Tarica, Ltd., Paris; Galerie Denise René, Paris; Galerie Chevalier Charley, Paris; Gertrude Stein Gallery, New York; Kaplan Gallery, London; Tooth and Sons, Ltd., London; Speiss S.A.R.Z., Paris; Galerie Lorenceau et Brame, Paris; Galerie Sept, Paris; Galerie Louis Carré, Paris; Galerie Berry St. Honoré, Paris, Galerie de Seine, Paris; Galerie 22, Paris; Galerie M. Rousso, Paris; Richard Feigen Gallery, New York; Robert Elkon Gallery, New York; B.C. Holland, Inc., Chicago; Acoris Gallery, London; Marlborough Fine Art, Ltd., London; Robert Fraser Gallery, London; Galerie Diderot, Paris; La Cour d'Ingres, Paris; Galleria d'Arte del Naviglio, Milan; Galerie Hasenklever, Munich; Hella Nebelung Gallery, Dusseldorf; Alan Auslander Gallery, New York; Sidney Janis Gallery, New York; Leo Castelli Gallery, New York; Maryna Kaston Gallery, New York; Matthiesen Gallery, London; Roland, Browse and Delbanco, London; Everett Ellin Gallery, Los Angeles; Gallery M.A. Gribin, Los Angeles; Commissaires Priseurs au Département de la Seine, Paris; Kornfeld and Klipstein, Bern; Sotheby's, London; Parke Bernet, New York.

A number of colleagues have also contributed to this study, and I thank them warmly for their help: Peter Bunnell, Lucy Lippard, Robert Herbert, Michel Sanouillet, Edward Fry, Rafael Santos Torroella, Robert Rosenblum, Virginia Spate, Linda Henderson, Daniel Robbins, Bill Kane, Amy Vandersall, L.C. Breunig, Jacques de Caso, Maurizio Fagiolo dell'Arco, John Rewald, M. Marcel Adéma, Leo Steinberg, Helen Winkler, Rainer Michael Mason, M. François Daulte, Patrick Gowers, Mme Volta, W.S. Meadmore, Thomas F. Barrow, Dr. H.M. Barzun, Joost Baljeu, M. Henri Béhar, Margaret Blum, Mlle Dominique Bouissou, Harald Szeemann, John J. McReavy, C.S.B., Roland Hunt, Richard E. Spear, David Sylvester, Charles Talbot, Mlle Babette Hallberg, M. Jean-Albert Cartier, William C. Agee, Standish Lawder, Bert Edmundson, Joe Guerinot, Josué Seckel and Jack Burnham. I thank Allen Mewbourn and John Lee Simons for their painstaking work with many of the photographs and Karen Coffey for her sensitive translations and thoughtful editing of my own translations. Joanne Greenspun has been an ideal copy editor, contributing substantially to this publication owing to her thoroughness and thoughtfulness.

I conclude with a tender recollection of the professional and personal qualities of Harriet Anderson, Mary Laing and Margot Cutter at Princeton University Press, and, last but hardly least, recognition for my wife—beloved typist, critic, editor and companion throughout it all.

INTRODUCTION

WHEN I undertook this study of Picabia fifteen years ago, one might have identified him briefly as one of those intriguing artists who appear in all the history books but about whom little of substance is known. There were no books of any kind devoted to him; the literature consisted of articles, homages, exhibition prefaces and passages in books on Cubism, Dada and modern art in general. Save for a handful of writings by Picabia's wives and a few perceptive individuals, the commentary tended to be repetitious and superficial, frequently characterizing him as a secondary cubist (who never really understood what it was about) and a major dadaist who scandalized the public with paintings of preposterous machines that were wholly nonsensical and antiart. On the surface of it, such assessments appeared inadequate, particularly the latter—an example of what I call the "dada syndrome," which discouraged serious study by implying that it was somehow futile or inappropriate to analyze the mocking, antiart of a dadaist. The desire to learn more led to a work of unforeseen duration, dimensions, difficulties and delights.

Since that beginning fifteen years ago, conditions have changed; much more is known about Picabia and his milieu. Nevertheless, this is still the first comprehensive art-historical study of Picabia, and, as such, it addresses much the same need for facts and interpretations present at its birth.

Little wonder no one rushed to produce a thoughtful, comprehensive study of Picabia. For the entire first half of this century, this painter, poet, polemicist and bon vivant lived in a whirlwind of activity. His production was enormous, bewildering in its variety and scattered around the world, much of it in unknown collections. And then, as now, that work competed with Picabia's extravagant life-style, which generated fabulous tales and a credulous audience more absorbed with the myth than with the man or his work.

Though short in stature and stout, Picabia was a striking man—dark, vaguely foreign and exotic in appearance; intense, unpredictable, enchanting; one who animated every gathering. He was an utter hedonist who pursued a life unfettered by any sort of restrictions or responsibilities which might thwart his freedom and well-being. He had a flair for one-liners expressive of that life-style:

Taste is fatiguing like good company.

There is only one way to save your life; sacrifice your reputation.

It is easier to scratch one's ass than his heart. St. Augustine.

If you want to have clean ideas, change them as often as you change your shirts.

Picabia possessed the wealth and, in his own way, the "moral" will to pursue his ideal life with remarkable effectiveness. Institutions and individuals alike paid a price for it—church, state, artists' groups, family, friends and, above all, Picabia himself. Needless to say, he was rarely viewed with indifference. Many adored him; many were hurt and infuriated by him; those closest to him experienced all those emotions. Women, in particular, found him irresistibly attractive. According to his widow, Olga Picabia, he possessed in his lifetime 7 yachts and 127 automobiles, and that was "little compared to his women." But the range of his friendships was extraordinary, a veritable international who's who—Marcel Duchamp, Alfred Stieglitz, Tristan Tzara, André Breton, Guillaume Apollinaire, Gertrude Stein, Erik Satie, Jean Cocteau, Mistinguett and Isadora Duncan, to name only some of the most illustrious. And no study of Picabia can be complete without consideration of some of those relationships.

Picabia's work is equally complex and fraught with controversy. Though primarily known as a painter, he wrote poetry, polemical articles, dadaist manifestos and at least one novel; he edited dadaist magazines, helped to establish two avant-garde art galleries and did costumes, scenery and scenarios for everything from the Swedish Ballet to dada spectacles and nightclub skits. All that notwithstanding, the variety of his painting alone was too much for most people. From about 1900 to 1950, his work ranged over styles related to Impressionsim, Neo-Impressionism, Fauvism, Cubism, abstract art, figurative art, Dada and Surrealism. Major stylistic periods started and stopped with apparent abruptness and unpredictability; alien styles coexisted, and, in every phase of his career, Picabia's work was totally erratic in quality. Occasional works now count among the masterpieces of modern art, but others seem to reflect utter indifference to time, taste and technical proficiency. Early in his career, Picabia was labeled a millionaire joker.

The variety and controversy in Picabia's life and work extended to his audience. A few people accepted virtually everything he produced; many scoffed at the lot of it; most embraced one or two styles in his oeuvre, but recoiled from other styles which seemed contrary to everything they esteemed. As far as some were concerned, Picabia's career ended when he abandoned Impressionism in 1908. In the eyes of the majority, that impressionist period was of no consequence; for them Picabia's importance in the history of art stopped about 1922 when he forsook Dada. A small but ardent minority hails the very works which succeeded Dada— the so-called monsters—as the best of his career. Other minority groups are equally fervent in their love for the transparencies of ca. 1930, or the realist paintings of the early 1940s, or the late abstract compositions, while those later styles are dismissed by many critics as inexplicable aberrations which have nothing whatever to do with the rest of Picabia's career.

Inevitably, this book enters that stream of controversy. Some readers will rail that no critical judgment was exercised, that everything was accepted, burdening the book with unnecessary attention to insignificant periods. Other readers may be angered by critical passages or by what strikes them as prejudiced judgment which eviscerates those very periods some critics deem dispensable.

To those anticipated critics of both schools let me say that, in my opinion, Picabia's work needs no special pleading or protection. His work has indeed kindled my respect and abiding pleasure, but, regardless of personal taste or feelings, Picabia is an artist who counts in the twentieth century; his work merits the respect of full exposure without anxiety over the praise or criticism which may follow. However, for those who would disown entire periods of Picabia's oeuvre, I do extend an invitation to read with special care the chapters which deal with those periods they would discard. Severe editing of entire styles or "ugly" works would be a disservice and a distortion of Picabia—just as would the history of anything (Christianity, Communism, a political leader) which excludes dark episodes or questionable characteristics.

Surface appearances to the contrary, Picabia's art was of a piece and at one with his life. Indeed, his art functioned with a responsiveness approaching that of speech. It was called up to express his thoughts, emotions and reveries without distinction between those which were grand or trivial, simple or complex, urgent or enduring. And, in terms of that analogy with speech, one encounters Picabia making serious public statements and whispering secrets; lashing out in social protest; telling dirty jokes; and merely passing the time of day. To function in that manner, Picabia's work could not be burdened by commercial need, by desire for fame or by ambition to produce something important or beautiful. Spontaneity and flexibility were necessarily vital (though not exclusive) elements in Picabia's art as they were in his life. Accordingly, the wholeness one finds is not so much one of style as one of personality and content. Within that realm of content reside profound continuities and modulations of a unique sense of humor and irreverence, of bitterness, melancholy and an implacable demand for personal freedom.

In terms of style, Picabia's work seems less original, more dependent on other visual sources—but he contributed important innovations of his own, and, in the final analysis, all that he borrowed was so thoroughly transformed to his own ends that the result was a new entity unmistakably Picabian in form and content. William Copley, in reference to Picabia, remarked that the "greatest achievement for any creative person is to arrive where his personality, his life, is synonymous and indistinguishable from his work." Picabia could not have agreed more, and in his ability to make his art an intimate extension of his whole life, Picabia became an outstanding example of a central aspect of modern art, namely, art as individual self-expression.

I did not possess this view of Picabia at the outset. It developed gradually over the years, shaped by hundreds of interviews with his family, friends and adversaries; by visits to over 300 private and public art collections; by sifting through thousands of documents on Picabia and his associates. The revelations of that research suggested, finally, not only a wholistic view of Picabia, but the shape of this book.

As an art historian, I had intended to produce a traditional monograph concentrating heavily on Picabia's career as a painter. When it became evident that basic historical data for the paintings (titles, dates, media and dimensions) was in a state of chaos, a reliable chronology had to be established and integrated into the text. Likewise, as it became clear that Picabia's life and art were inseparable, this study was enlarged to include consideration of his writings and more biographical information than one normally encounters. However, in the last analysis, this book is primarily a study of Picabia's art, not a biography, nor a catalogue raisonné, nor a thorough review of his writings. Each of those areas merits separate study—acknowledgment that this book, despite its size and relative comprehensiveness, is hardly the last word on Picabia. His work is rich enough to sustain a variety of studies.

ABBREVIATIONS

B.D.	Bibliothèque Littéraire Jacques Doucet in the Bibliothèque Ste.-Geneviève, Paris
C.T.	Collection Tzara, B.D.
D.P.	Dossiers Picabia, B.D.
Yale	Collection of American Literature, Beinecke Rare Book and Manuscript Library, Yale University, New Haven, Conn.
A.S.A.	Alfred Stieglitz Archive, Yale
G.S.A.	Gertrude Stein Archive, Yale
M.D.L.A.	Mabel Dodge Luhan Archive, Yale
M. de Z.A.	Marius de Zayas Archive, Paris; xerox copies in Butler Library, Columbia University, New York, and the Collection of American Literature, Beinecke Rare Book and Manuscript Library, Yale University, New Haven, Conn.

FRANCIS PICABIA

1. CHILDHOOD AND EARLY CAREER

FRANÇOIS MARIE MARTINEZ PICABIA was born on or about January 22, 1879, in Paris. He was the only child of a Cuban-born Spaniard, Francisco Vicente Martinez Picabia, and his French wife, Marie Cécile Davanne (illus. 1, 2). Both parents came from wealthy, distinguished families, and young Picabia was raised in an affluent bourgeois household that included his maternal grandparents, Alphonse and Cécile Davanne, and an uncle, Maurice Davanne.[1] The deaths of his mother and grandmother in 1886 and 1887, respectively, left a headstrong lad in the care of his father, grandfather, uncle and doting servants.

Francisco took a second wife in 1891—a ballerina, Blanche Patouillard, who bore him a daughter, Yvonne, in 1902. But prior to that remarriage the Picabia household was referred to as the house of *quatre sans femmes* ("four without women"), a designation which friends later noted suggested a pun appropriate to Picabia—*quatre cents femmes* ("400 women"). The father perhaps contributed most to his son's life-style; Picabia's uncle and grandfather offered more for his interest in art. Francisco Vicente had no need to work, but occupied himself quietly with the pleasures of life and between about 1902 and 1914 served in a largely honorary position as chancellor to the Cuban Embassy in Paris. Picabia retained a great fondness for his father and expanded spectacularly the family tra-

1. Picabia's birth was declared in the second arrondissement of Paris on January 24, 1879 (letter to the author from the Archives du Département de la Seine et de la Ville de Paris, September 10, 1963). His paternal grandfather, Juan Martinez Picabia (1798–1858) of La Coruña, Spain, married Josefa Delmonico (1818–1880) of Switzerland in New York in 1840. That grandfather prospered as a planter in Cuba before returning to Spain, where he became a principal figure in the construction of the Madrid–La Coruña railroad, a service for which he was honored by the Spanish government (data based on information supplied by Picabia's half sister, Mme Yvonne Gresse-Picabia, and on unpublished legal documents in her possession drafted by an agent of the Colegio de Notarios Escribanos R de Madrid for Picabia's grandmother, Josefa Delmonico, on December 7, 1860).

Picabia's father, Francisco Vicente Martinez Picabia (1847–1929), moved from Havana to Paris, where in 1878 he married the daughter of Alphonse Davanne, a wealthy businessman linked to the Charcot and Waldeck-Rosseau families (Michel Sanouillet, *Francis Picabia et "391,"* II, Paris, 1966, 17). Davanne was also a distinguished amateur photographer who reportedly worked with Daguerre.

dition for gratifying personal pleasures. Most tales of Picabia's youth stress a boy spoiled beyond measure, with irrepressible energy and imagination, a facility for art and a reputation at the lycée for feats of strength and precocious experiences with the night life of Paris. Almost overlooked among accounts of his audacious conduct is one story of a toy scale with which he weighed the light and shadow falling on his windowsill.[2] He never forgot that in that childhood experiment darkness was heavier than light—and throughout his life there was within Picabia's intense élan an underlying, profoundly pessimistic and tragic view of life. Those characteristics, as well as his physical appearance, prompted many friends to comment on the peculiarly Spanish qualities of the man.

Picabia's uncle, Maurice Davanne, was a cultivated professional— conservator of the Bibliothèque Ste.-Geneviève, a collector of art and rare books, and a great music lover. His collection was dominated by the paintings of Félix Ziem and Ferdinand Roybert, and family tradition records that young Picabia earned money by selling some of his uncle's paintings, concealing their absence with convincing copies of his own.[3] Such exaggerated stories notwithstanding, Picabia did win drawing prizes as a schoolboy at the Collège Stanislas (illus. 3) and probably took his first "art lessons" from Ziem's landscapes in his uncle's collection.[4] Thanks also to that uncle, he may have discovered the philosophy of Nietzsche which nourished him all his life. And from his grandfather, Alphonse Davanne, Picabia acquired—via reaction—the guiding principle of his future art. Davanne, an ardent amateur photographer, taught his grandson how to operate a camera and talked at length about the relation of art and photography. Convinced that the perfection of color photography would make painting obsolete, he advised Picabia to abandon his interest in painting, but Picabia later recalled his instinctive resistance to that advice: "You can photograph a landscape," he said to himself, "but not the forms that I have in my head."[5] A decade passed, however, before Picabia began to work with those forms in his head. In the meantime, he began a conventional study of art and even used a camera as an aid in his work.

In 1895, with his resistance to an academic education firmly established, Picabia was permitted to enter the Ecole des Arts Décoratifs.[6] According to traditional accounts, his studies there were interrupted in 1897 when, as a youth of

2. Reported by Picabia in "Jusqu'à un certain point . . . ," *Comoedia* [Paris], April 16, 1922, 1.

3. Galerie René Drouin, Paris, *491, 50 ans de plaisir*, March 4–26, 1949, statement by Michel Tapié. Both Ziem (1821–1911) and Roybert (1840–1920) were well-known conservative artists. Roybert was primarily a painter of genre scenes, while Ziem excelled at landscapes, many with striking sunset effects.

4. After beginning professional art studies, Picabia frequently worked in Martigues, where as late as 1905 he paid his respects to Ziem in a painting of that artist's house (private collection, Beverly Hills, Calif.).

5. Gabrielle Buffet-Picabia, "Picabia, l'inventeur," *L'Oeil*, no. 18 (Paris, June 1956), 32.

6. Picabia entered this school on November 1, 1895 (letter to the author from the Ecole des Beaux-Arts, Paris, January 14, 1966). According to Sanouillet *(Francis Picabia et "391,"* II, 19) he also had previous training at the Ecole du Louvre.

eighteen, he embarked on his first of many amorous adventures—fleeing to Switzerland with Mme Orliac, mistress of a well-known journalist in Paris. By those same accounts, the sojourn in Switzerland was crucial; Picabia supposedly supported himself by selling landscapes painted on smooth lake stones, met Nietzsche and members of the Pissarro family and began painting in the impressionist manner. In fact, the earliest phase of Picabia's career was hardly so flamboyant as claimed in those romantic tales that have been elaborated over the years thanks to Picabia's faulty memory and the tendency of others to embroider. He did go to Switzerland with Mme Orliac, but the date of his conquest is unknown. Moreover, during 1897–1898 he met neither Nietzsche nor members of the Pissarro family, and he did not produce impressionist paintings.[7] Instead, Picabia made a quiet debut at the conservative Salon des Artistes Français in 1899, and his first knowledgeable critic, L. Roger-Milès, recorded that despite a favorable mention of his work, Picabia realized "the effort still to be made in order to become master . . . of his craft; . . . he went to the atelier of Cormon and Humbert. . . . six years, day and night, he attended diligently the courses of study."[8]

For six years he did indeed list himself as a student of Humbert, Wallet and Cormon. Moreover, until the winter of 1902–1903, he exhibited only at the Salon des Artistes Français and produced just two types of work—delicate watercolors of Spanish figures and modest landscapes in a post-Barbizon manner.

At present, the earliest known painting (fig. 1) bears a date of 1893 and has been described as the product of a bored teen-ager during his summer vacation.[9] The beginning of Picabia's career, however, remains cloudy, for no other dated paintings have come to light prior to 1898–1899, and the first of those (fig. 2) are darkly painted, moody landscapes less impressionistic and sometimes less accomplished than the work attributed to 1893. By 1900, such paintings as *The*

7. Following a total breakdown in 1889, Nietzsche was paralyzed and secluded from the public; from 1897 to his death in 1900, he lived with his sister in Weimar.

Scholars and descendants of the Pissarro family all agree that Picabia did not meet any member of the family during 1897–1898 in Switzerland (letters to the author from Mme L.R. Pissarro, February 22, 1963; Miss Orovida Pissarro, February 1963; Paul-Emile Pissarro, December 7, 1963; W.S. Meadmore, September 25, 1963; and John Rewald, February 4, 1963).

8. Galerie Haussmann, Paris, *Picabia*, February 10–25, 1905, preface by L. Roger-Milès. Roger–Milès attributed the date of Picabia's first Salon to 1898.

Contrary to numerous reports that Picabia exhibited at the 1894 Salon des Artistes Français, his name does not figure in any Salon catalogue or other reliable document until 1899. Through 1901 Picabia listed himself as a student of Albert Charles Wallet (1852–1918) and Ferdinand Humbert (1842–1934), and until 1905 he gave his address as the Villa des Arts (15, rue Hégésippe-Moreau), where studios were maintained by Wallet, Humbert, Fernand Cormon and Eugène Carrière. Georges Braque and Marie Laurencin were fellow students at Cormon's studio (Henry Hope, *Georges Braque,* New York: The Museum of Modern Art, 1949, 15), and Picabia was proud of having won a drawing competition between the students of Cormon and those of the Académie Julien.

9. Letter from Lionel Cavalero to the author (July 18, 1972), reporting information from Mme Olga Picabia.

Roofs of Paris (fig. 4) exhibit greater interest in natural light and atmosphere, but there is still no suggestion of Impressionism in either the brushwork or the gray, blue and brownish tones of this humble work. Not until 1902 can one perceive in dated paintings a shift from the solid forms and earthen hues of a Barbizon tradition to such paintings as *The Banks of the Loing* (fig. 5), where the brushwork indicates some impressionist influence.

This sequence of canvases permits attributions of an early date to other paintings such as *Sunset at St.-Tropez* (fig. 3). This landscape also resembles the composition of Goya's *The Executions of May 3, 1808*, without the foreground figures, and serves to introduce Picabia's lifelong practice of referring to models of one kind or another, including old masters.

In addition to such landscapes and a few student sketches labeled "atelier Cormon" (see fig. 7), Picabia's early work concentrated on Spanish subjects—particularly Spanish women and toreadors, who fascinated him all his life (see fig. 8). These facile pencil sketches, overlaid with delicate color washes, tend toward "type" portraits that are concerned with their subjects primarily as romantic motifs. Nonetheless, these portraits are fetching for their simplicity and freshness, and some of them register not only distinctive physical features but a variety of subtle expressions—overtones of sensuality and languor, of melancholy and haughtiness, and the ability to generate an ambiguous, provocative relationship between subject and beholder that is intrinsic to much of Picabia's work.

Again and again during his career, Picabia executed Spanish figures with modest changes in style, but in the fall of 1902 his landscape painting—and the basic course of his career—was radically altered. About November, Georges (Manzana) and Rodo Pissarro met Picabia in the Midi (see illus. 4) and described that encounter to their father, who passed it on to his son Lucien:

> We have just received a letter from Rodo [who is with Georges in Martigues]. . . . he tells me that they go around with a pupil of Cormon; this youth is extraordinary, he makes many studies from nature using the methods taught in the schools. In this way he is able to cover endless quantities of canvas without taking into account the air or the light, and he paints everything a uniform brown! And that in the south! When he has made enough sketches this way, he addresses himself to his painting, for the official Salon, a canvas of more than six feet, after having established his motif by means of photographs![10]

Though Georges and Rodo Pissarro were contemptuous of Picabia's work, they found him to be a fascinating companion.[11] Moreover, he soon became an

10. Camille Pissarro, *Camille Pissarro, Letters to His Son Lucien*, 2nd ed., ed. John Rewald, trans. Lionel Abel (London: Kegan Paul, Trench, Trubner and Co., Ltd., 1950), 352. In the original French edition (Paris, 1943, 496–97), Rewald identified Picabia as the Cormon student.

11. Paul-Emile Pissarro recalled with pleasure the carefree conduct of Picabia and described his disastrous attempt in a Montmartre nightclub to duplicate the feat of a Cirque Medrano juggler who had yanked off a restaurant tablecloth without spilling the contents of the table (letter to the author, December 1, 1963).

ardent convert to Impressionism—and the last of several famous "students" of that grand teacher, Camille Pissarro. He met and sketched the aged Pissarro in 1903 and maintained contact with the sons for a number of years, particularly with Manzana, who became a painting companion and possibly the agent for important contacts later in Picabia's career.

2. CATCHING UP WITH MODERN ART: IMPRESSIONISM, NEO-IMPRESSIONISM, FAUVISM AND EXPERIMENTS, 1903-1909

PICABIA'S image has been so dominated by his dada activities that even some friends have found it difficult to believe he once was an impressionist. Their surprise notwithstanding, virtually every artist who contributed to "modern" art during the first decades of the twentieth century passed through an impressionist or neo-impressionist phase early in his career; Picabia is exceptional only in the fact that for him Impressionism was not merely a passing phase but a major period.

Over the winter of 1902–1903, the paintings of Monet, Sisley and Pissarro redirected his vision, and he soon encountered still more recent art and aesthetic theories which served him the rest of his life. For the first time, he also began to exhibit in the liberal Salons of Paris—the Salon des Indépendants and the newly opened Salon d'Automne—and he worked prodigiously, producing well over 300 paintings in about six years.[1] These paintings brought him critical acclaim and financial success. He signed a contract with a fashionable gallery, exhibited throughout Europe and counted among his patrons some of the most distinguished public figures in France. Years later, as a crusty old man who had participated substantially in Cubism, Dada and abstract art, he worked again briefly in a quasi-impressionist idiom, and was wont to linger in the impressionist galleries of the Jeu de Paume, musing fondly over that period of his youth.

Picabia's first efforts at Impressionism were somewhat stiff until his technical development caught up with his emotional conversion. In *View of St.-Tropez* of 1903 (fig. 9), for example, the brighter palette and broken brushwork of Impressionism are simply applied to the more firmly defined forms and stable com-

1. About 250 paintings can be accounted for in exhibition catalogues of 1903–1909; many others, not identifiable through early exhibitions, steadily appear on the market. Because most of these paintings entered private hands and were not favored by subsequent collectors, they have been little known and seldom exhibited.

positional conventions of an older tradition. Within a year, however, such paintings as *Les Saules, effet de soleil d'automne* (*Willows, Effect of Autumn Sun*, fig. 10) and *Le Soleil d'avril* (*April Sun*, fig. 11) mark the conclusion of his apprenticeship. He selected simple, but charming and specific sites, framed them informally and used an impressionist palette and brush technique to capture the fleeting qualities of those scenes. Space and time are open; the spectator is invited to savor the passing of the day and to explore the riverbank beyond the frame. Nature seems to be neither ordered nor dramatized but recorded by an appreciative and relatively objective observer.

By working in that manner, Picabia remained faithful to Impressionism as it had developed in the 1870s, but his better paintings were not dull, derivative essays. In contrast to the original impressionists, Picabia displayed less concern for optical properties and a greater interest in form and composition, plus a technical assurance that caught the eye of Berthe Weill. However, after just one group exhibition at her struggling avant-garde gallery, Picabia was lured away by the director of the fashionable Galerie Haussmann.[2]

His first one-man exhibition at the Galerie Haussmann opened in February 1905 with sixty-one paintings and a substantial catalogue prefaced by L. Roger-Milès.[3] The critical acclaim was overwhelming. Virtually every Parisian newspaper and magazine with a column on the arts reviewed the exhibition and, as reported by the critic of *Le Figaro*: "The exhibitions multiply, but none has the good fortune to attract the multitude like the exhibition of landscapes by M. Picabia, which is taking on the proportions of a major event. . . . everyone wants to see it, many pretend to have predicted it."[4]

Once catapulted into public attention, Picabia remained there. His work followed seasonal campaigns—two or three winter months in the Midi with the remainder of the year in and around Paris. One of Sisley's haunts, Moret, became a favored site, but he also worked in Paris, Montigny and Villeneuve-sur-Yonne; in Martigues, Cannes, Antibes and St.-Tropez. Those campaigns provided a flow of canvases for numerous group shows, salons and one-man exhibitions in Paris, London and Berlin.[5] These paintings generally received favorable criticism and

2. Berthe Weill opened her gallery in 1901 and by 1902 was handling the work of such artists as Picasso and Matisse. Picabia was included in a group exhibition of October 1904 along with Picasso, Raoul Dufy, Pierre Girieud and Gaston Thiesson. Picabia's enticement to M. Danthon's Galerie Haussmann is described in Berthe Weill's *Pan! dans l'oeil!* . . . (Paris, 1933), 105–106.

3. Galerie Haussmann, Paris, *Picabia*, February 10-25, 1905.

During his career, L. Roger-Milès (Léon-Octave-Jean Roger; 1859–1928) wrote poetry, directed magazines and published numerous books, articles and catalogues on art including the preface for Sisley's large one-man exhibition at the Galeries Georges Petit in 1897. He may have contributed much to Picabia's knowledge of modern art and aesthetics.

4. G. Davenay, "La Vie artistique; les paysages de Monsieur Picabia," *Le Figaro* [Paris], February 14, 1905, 5.

5. Picabia had one-man exhibitions in his own studio, at Caspar's Kunst-Salon (Berlin, April 1906) and at the Cremetti Gallery (London, March 1907). He also continued to exhibit at the Independent and Autumn salons, at the Société des Artistes Français and at the Salon de la Gra-

found ready buyers, including the French government and such prominent men as Raymond Poincaré, Julien Benda and Pierre Lafitte.[6]

It is difficult for today's sophisticated audience to understand this reception of Picabia's work, aware as it is that the original impressionists had realized their vision over thirty years earlier and had spawned a generation of post-impressionists who in that very year of 1905 were eclipsed by a new movement dubbed Fauvism. In 1905, however, a survey of exhibitions and art journals reveals that only the small avant-garde community was familiar with contemporary art. The work of Puvis de Chavannes and the impressionists constituted the aesthetic frontiers for the general art public, and Picabia seems to have come along at the right time with a charming, conservative brand of Impressionism perfectly suited to the taste of many critics and to M. Danthon's distinguished bourgeois clients.

Such, at least, is the suggestion of the prominent critic, Louis Vauxcelles, who underscored Picabia's draftsmanship and knowledge of old masters as laudable features: "Finally, what I also wish to praise in this young impressionist is the sureness of the drawing, the solidity of the construction; merits disdained by many virtuosos, but which veritable masters . . . have never neglected."[7] This critic, notorious for his opposition to most modern art, later had occasion to change his opinion about Picabia.

Many of Picabia's paintings were indeed distinguished from the work of his impressionist masters by firm drawing, harmonious compositions and occasional references to old masters. If one compares paintings by Sisley and Picabia of the river mill at Moret (figs. 12, 13), Sisley's composition seems tense, arbitrarily framed and active in both the thrust of the bridge and in the agitated brushwork of the water. Picabia's brushwork is more uniform and bound to the forms; he chose to exclude the dynamic diagonal of the bridge and to bring into equilibrium the distant trees and middle-ground millhouses. The final effect is ordered and self-contained in contrast to the more spontaneous, open quality of the Sisley.[8] Even more conservative qualities characterize Picabia's annual entries to the stodgy Salon of the Société des Artistes Français. His canvas at the 1906 Salon, *Les Pins, effet de soleil à St.-Honorat, Cannes* (*Pine Trees, Effect of Sunlight at St.-Honorat, Cannes*, fig. 15), is a very large, firmly composed landscape—so large in fact that it could not have been painted on the site. It must have required laborious work in

---

vure Originale en Couleurs. In December 1906, his work was included in an exhibit of art purchased by the State.

6. Raymond Poincaré (1860–1934), lawyer and politician elected president of the French Republic in 1913, purchased *Le Soleil d'avril* (fig. 11). Julien Benda (1867–1956) was a philosopher and novelist; Pierre Lafitte (1872–1938) was an editor and the primary developer of the modern illustrated magazine in France.

7. Louis Vauxcelles, "Notes d'art," *Le Gil Blas* [Paris], February 10, 1905, 1.

8. The first extensive exposure of Sisley's paintings occurred between 1902 and 1908 (François Daulte, *Alfred Sisley*, Lausanne, 1959, 34, 342). Accordingly, Picabia's work was seen in direct competition with that of his most influential model.

the studio where impressionist freshness and informality were sacrificed for grandeur and studied composition. Picabia's 1907 Salon entry, *Port de mer dans le Midi, effet de soleil* (*Seaport in the Midi, Effect of Sunlight*, fig. 16), painted in the winter of 1906–1907, not only bears a similar studio quality, but immediately brings to mind the harbor scenes of Claude Lorrain.

In all likelihood, Picabia produced these big paintings specifically for that conservative Salon, but comparison of modest-sized paintings and drawings suggests that he simply may not have been as devoted to working spontaneously on the site as Sisley and Monet. A 1905 drawing of *Le Pont du chemin de fer, Moret* (*Railroad Bridge, Moret*, fig. 17) is so finished that one is inclined to view it as an independent work rather than as a study. Nonetheless, it is so close to a contemporary painting (fig. 18, and color pl. I)—including cloud formations and the figures in the boat—that one must consider the possibility of a painting finished in the studio with the aid of a detailed drawing. These drawings—perhaps more clearly than the paintings—also reveal Picabia's reluctance to permit dissolution of form by light and movement. The same is true of the etchings (see fig. 19) and lithographs in his little-known production as a printmaker.[9] Only his work in watercolor (see fig. 20) consistently possesses more fully impressionist qualities of spontaneity and movement. There are witnesses, of course, to vouch for the fact that Picabia did some work out-of-doors, and he adopted another habit identified with Impressionism, namely, the practice of painting the same scene several times in different seasons and light conditions, as in *Le Pont de Villeneuve, effet de neige* (*Bridge at Villeneuve, Snow Effect*, fig. 21) and *Le Pont de Villeneuve-sur-Yonne, effet de soleil* (*Bridge at Villeneuve-sur-Yonne, Sunlight Effect*, fig. 22).[10] Ironically, it is this traditionally impressionist practice that also records the transformation of Picabia's Impressionism into two other modes of painting which, though thoroughly indebted to Impressionism, are, in effect, revolutions against it.

Lever du soleil dans la brume, Montigny I and II (*Sunrise in the Mist, Montigny* I and II, figs. 23, 24) depict exactly the same site, but the latter is so abstracted that the spectator's attention is initially absorbed by its pervasive blue tonality and succulent pigment rather than by identification of the scene. One might suppose that it was a study for the larger, more finished painting, but that "more finished" canvas is signed and dated 1905 while the small, sketchy canvas is a dated work of 1906. Apparently it is—in its own way—a finished painting, representative of Picabia's development of a subjective mode of Impressionism, that is to say, a mode of painting in which the relatively objective recording of

9. Nothing is known of Picabia's training in printmaking, but from ca. 1905 to 1908 he produced competent etchings and lithographs and participated in the Salon de la Gravure Originale en Couleurs. The Société de la Gravure Originale en Couleurs was founded in 1903 with J.F. Raffaëlli as its president. Annual Salons were instituted in 1905 at the Galeries Georges Petit.

10. *Le Pont de Villeneuve, effet de neige* was purchased by the State in 1906 or 1907. Most of Picabia's paintings of Villeneuve-sur-Yonne date from 1906, but one exists from 1900 (formerly Galerie Brame et Lorenceau, Paris).

optical data gave way to a sensuous manipulation of colored pigment in order to express a mood generated by nature.[11]

Picabia suggested as much in a contemporary statement: "Craft in any fashion must not be the quest of the painter; he must reproduce the emotion which nature made him feel without the least care for technique."[12] Roger-Milès provided still more insight for Picabia's new mode of Impressionism in a preface to his second one-man exhibition at the Galerie Haussmann in 1907.[13] After some effort to refute past criticism of Picabia's dependence on Sisley's work, Roger-Milès concentrated on the artist's new aesthetic concerns. Nature, he wrote:

> presents itself to us with successive and infinitely varied harmonies; one must trap its character in a synthesis both lifelike and expressive; . . . And in order to reveal all of this to us, the landscapist must be one who is moved by feeling; he must "interpret," not "copy"; his work must reflect his own sensation, and not just the image of what strikes his retina without having a reverberation in his soul![14]

Roger-Milès employed musical analogies to justify Picabia's departure from literal realism, referring to the artist as a "virtuoso, seated at his clavier, plucking scales," who "launches into an escalade of arpeggios, or preludes at random, according to his psychic disposition, spontaneous improvisations which he will forget tomorrow."

Picabia no longer conceived art as the representation of the appearance of nature, but as the equivalent of one's emotional experience of nature—an equivalent realized by orchestrating the autonomous, expressive properties of form and color. There was nothing original about that concept of art. It was "in the air" of the artists' studios, derived from late-nineteenth-century symbolist-synthesist theories on the *correspondance* of colors, forms, rhythms, sounds, etc., with mental and emotional experiences. For Picabia, however, this concept of *correspondance* was crucial. For the remainder of his life, his work was nourished by

11. Studies of perception indicate that, in the strictest sense, there can be no "objective" art because there can be no seeing without feeling and no feeling without thought. However, this does not preclude the existence of approaches to art which, for want of more subtle terms, can be called "objective" and "subjective." Such distinctions in Impressionism have been analyzed by George Heard Hamilton in *Painting and Sculpture in Europe, 1880–1940* (Baltimore, 1967), 7–8, 15–19, and in *Claude Monet's Paintings of Rouen Cathedral* (London, 1960).

The Roman numerals used in conjunction with *Lever du soleil dans la brume, Montigny* were not employed by Picabia, but have been used by this author throughout the book to identify different works bearing the same title.

12. Francis Picabia, in response to a poll, "Le Paysage contemporain: L'Opinion de quelques paysagistes. M. F. Picabia," *Le Gaulois du dimanche* [Paris], February 9–10, 1907, 2. Picabia's statement also bore conservative admonishments at odds with popular notions about his revolutionary traits: "The first thing for a landscapist to be is a conscientious artist. . . . One should not want to bowl over the public as many young people do; the Salon d'Automne is a very unhappy example of that."

13. Galerie Haussmann, Paris, *Picabia*, February 1–15, 1907.

14. Ibid.

one or more of the liberating characteristics of that aesthetic—its celebration of individualism, its compatibility with the notion that spontaneous expression is a more effective, "truthful" means of rendering one's sensations, and, finally, its concept of autonomous and associative values for color and form which was open to the development of abstract art.[15]

Through mid-1908, Picabia oscillated between objective and subjective modes of Impressionism, but in the autumn of 1908 both were supplanted by a third mode (figs. 25, 26) which may be described as neo-impressionist. As was his custom, Picabia revisited his old sites (compare to figs. 9, 11), this time reducing the compositions to more simplified forms which are ranged in planes parallel to the picture surface and rendered with a system of uniformly sized, bricklike brushstrokes. These features, reminiscent of the contemporary work of that proselytizing neo-impressionist Paul Signac, transmit a stronger sensation of structure, order and permanence. But in contrast to Signac, Picabia remains more concerned about the specific site, and his bright palette suggests less interest in neo-impressionist color theory than a concern for the blazing, natural light of the Midi and the influence of Fauvism, which he had also tested by that date.

Like his preceding objective and subjective modes of Impressionism, Picabia's neo-impressionist style was presented in a one-man exhibition—this time at the Galeries Georges Petit in March 1909. The indefatigable Roger-Milès again provided a preface which contrasted the new work to its predecessors:

> In his first joy of production . . . he [Picabia] had not taken time to reflect on his "writing"; he expressed himself without effort and felicitously. . . .
>
> Then he returned to the places he had previously interpreted, and he studied them more stringently. He searched for their significance within form; . . . he applied himself to presenting his new insight in a formula in which no touch would be a virtuoso's arpeggio thrown in a burst of inspiration, but in which each brushstroke corresponded to an essential orchestration of the *euchromatisme*. No more superfluous embroideries or excessively summary notations. The clear idea expressed in a simple verb: the synthesis more and more concentrated toward an art more and more explicit and united, more and more considered as decor.[16]

Picabia and his historians have been blessed by Roger-Milès's articulation of verifiable modes within the artist's impressionist period, but caution is advisable in face of the implication of an overly simple, logical development. The neo-impressionist canvases are easily recognized and confined to a brief phase from the fall of 1908 to the early spring of 1909. But the objective and subjective modes do not seem completely adequate or pertinent for the remainder of Picabia's impressionist oeuvre, and no chronological guide is possible beyond the

15. For a concise statement on Symbolism and symbolist aesthetics, see Hamilton, *Painting and Sculpture in Europe, 41–43*.

16. Galeries Georges Petit, Paris, *Exposition de tableaux par F. Picabia*, March 17–31, 1909.

observation that a more analytical approach dominated during 1903–1905 while the subjective approach was more common in 1906. Finally, Picabia's impressionist period is sprinkled with more daring experiments which point toward a second turning point in his career during the winter of 1908–1909.

One such experiment was recorded as early as 1905 by Roger-Milès, who said that Picabia, while playing hooky one day from the classes of Cormon and Humbert "grew drunk on nature . . . and brought back a violent study which his comrades regarded with surprise and which the master examined with regret."[17] Positive identification of that study cannot be made, but *Tree* (fig. 27), long attributed to ca. 1903–1904, merits consideration. It is compatible with Roger-Milès's comments, and its abstractness is derived from a sensuous manipulation of pigment different only in degree from Picabia's near-contemporary paintings.[18] More surprising than the possible early date of *Tree* is the fact that—whatever its date—Picabia left it as a solitary venture. His career harbors a baffling number of such unique experiments. Some were never pursued; others, after a quiet gestation period, reemerged in a new form.

Picabia's early experiments also included two curious "abstract" sketches, one dated 1908 (fig. 28), which may be related to the much-discussed *Caoutchouc* of ca. 1909 (fig. 38). Equally solitary and problematic is the *Portrait of Mistinguett* (fig. 29), queen of the Paris revues and one of the first of many prominent entertainers befriended by Picabia during his lifelong fascination for music halls, nightclubs, circuses and the cinema. Both the subject and the date of this painting have been questioned, but, under any circumstances, it remains an early, attractive example of Picabia's experiments with decorative compositions and simplified color planes derived from such varied sources as Gauguin, Toulouse-Lautrec, Japanese prints and Fauvism.[19]

Picabia's essays with Fauvism are documented at the end of 1908, and, characteristically, they began not as wholehearted emulations of Matisse, but as conservative syntheses of Fauvism and older styles. In *Port of St.-Tropez* (fig. 30) he combined intense, decorative color with some neo-impressionist brushstrokes and an ongoing concern for specific features of the site. *La Femme aux mimosas* (*Woman with Mimosas*, fig. 31) is equally conservative but important for its early date and its subject, a young music student named Gabrielle Buffet who exercised

17. Galerie Haussmann, Paris, *Picabia*, February 10–25, 1905.

18. On the stretcher of this painting there is a faint pencil inscription, "Mougins mars 1925." This inscription does not appear to be in Picabia's hand, but the date indicated should not be dismissed as a possibility.

19. As observed by Angelica Zander Rudenstine (*The Guggenheim Museum Collection: Paintings 1880-1945*, II, New York, 1976, 590), this portrait is an evocative likeness rather than an explicit one, but Mme Gabrielle Buffet has verified that Picabia knew Mistinguett before 1908, and both Mme Buffet and a daughter-in-law of Mistinguett have identified the subject.

Microscopic examination of the signature and date reveals that they are painted over cracks in the original paint and must, therefore, have been added well after completion of the painting (Rudenstine, op. cit., 589). Given the evolution of Picabia's work, a date of ca. 1908–1911 is most plausible, but the 1907 figure will not be completely discarded here.

a critical role at this turning point in Picabia's life over the winter of 1908–1909. While studying music in Berlin, Gabrielle had seen Picabia's paintings at Caspar's Kunst-Salon, but she did not meet the artist until September 1908, when he appeared at her family home in one of his grand automobiles after a day of painting in the country with her brother, Jean Buffet.

Signs of a break in Picabia's career had been accumulating. The theory of *correspondance* had served to quicken and articulate his inclinations in a theoretical way; exposure to revolutionary developments in art all about him provided visual suggestions for an art more intimately responsive to the artist, and, finally, given his restless, egocentric temperament, a substantial shift in his career seems to have been inevitable.[20] Gabrielle Buffet has recalled that when she first met Picabia, he was bored with his past work; small drawings of monstrous figures and abstract designs flowed from his pen, and he talked animatedly about liberating art, about producing "painting situated within pure imagination which re-creates the world of forms according to one's desire and imagination."[21] Though initially astonished by Picabia's application of that idea to painting, her study with Vincent d'Indy had already exposed her to similar theories in music.[22] That fostered a stimulating intellectual rapport between Gabrielle and Francis which flourished alongside a headlong romance.

As his personal and artistic aims became focused, Picabia took dramatic action to cast off the past and set out anew. In the course of a few months he broke with the Galerie Haussmann, auctioned off all his older paintings, jilted a mistress of long standing and married Gabrielle Buffet. Their marriage took place in January 1909, and it was during their honeymoon in the Midi that Picabia painted many of the neo-impressionist and fauvist canvases which were exhibited at the Galeries Georges Petit in March 1909. Just prior to that exhibition, Picabia disposed of over 100 impressionist works in an auction at the Hôtel Drouot. Despite an apparent boycott by Paris art dealers, that sale was a success, adding to the coffers of an artist beginning to acquire a reputation as a wealthy playboy and maverick in art.[23] Picabia's commitment, however, was utterly serious, and his

20. In addition to contact with avant-garde art through colleagues and the Salons, Picabia assembled an important collection of modern and primitive art. The date and identification of his acquisitions are poorly documented, but by 1913 the collection included major works by Picasso, Braque and Duchamp, African sculpture and probably a still-life painting attributed to Cézanne (Montreal Museum of Fine Arts).

21. Gabrielle Buffet-Picabia, "Picabia, l'inventeur," *L'Oeil*, no. 18 (Paris, June 1956), 32. The drawings cited in this statement are no longer extant save perhaps the two remaining in the Succession Picabia (see fig. 28).

22. Gabrielle, a member of a cultivated family linked to Jussieu and Lamartine, had studied music with Gabriel Urbain Fauré (1845–1924), Vincent d'Indy (1851–1931) and Ferruccio Busoni (1866–1924). Early in his career, d'Indy had been influenced by Wagner. He was acquainted with many of the French symbolists, shared their aesthetic convictions and passed those concepts on to his students. See Norman Demuth, *Vincent d'Indy, 1851–1931* (London, 1951), 55, 83–85, passim.

23. The auction of Picabia's work was held at the Hôtel Drouot on March 8, 1909. An un-

proclivity for change amounted to much more than the inconstancy of a playboy artist; it was a profound element of his character which became increasingly evident in his life and in his career after this date. In Picabia's art, no synthesis was ever a stable compound. His career became an erratic course of conflicts between "significant form" and "emotional truth," between spontaneous painterly instinct and deliberate craftsmanship, between sensuous indulgence with the visible world and private emotional-intellectual concerns that would seem to be inexpressible in terms of the visible world.

---

signed notice about that auction supports a family tradition that Picabia broke a lucrative contract with M. Danthon and was boycotted at the Hôtel Drouot sale: "Curious thing, everything was bought by amateurs and not a single number was knocked down to a dealer" (*New York Herald* [Paris], March 9, 1909, 5).

3. SEARCH FOR SELF-EXPRESSION: FAUVISM, CUBISM AND ORPHISM, 1909-1912

Initial Essays and Formation of La Section d'Or Artists

THE CRISIS in Picabia's career over the winter of 1908–1909 marked the beginning of a four-year search for self-expression in the visual vocabulary of avant-garde art. That period of search was framed by two important voyages, a honeymoon trip to Spain during the spring of 1909 and a visit to New York for the Armory Show early in 1913. For much of the time between those voyages, Picabia seemed literally adrift, lurching unpredictably between figurative and quasi-abstract art superficially related to Fauvism, Futurism, Cubism and an impulse of abstract art dubbed Orphism by the poet-critic-impresario of that epoch, Guillaume Apollinaire. A single constant underlay the baffling tacks and uneven quality in Picabia's work, his fixation on an art that dealt not with the appearance of the world but with one's inner experience of life. By the end of 1912 he realized his goal with paintings that synthesized abstract forms and highly personal content. Those paintings were still nourished by the old symbolist theory of *correspondance* and by several movements in modern art, especially Cubism. But Picabia knew his work was a bold departure related to a new wave of avant-garde art, and he embarked for the Armory Show as a zealous missionary for that "new art."

Francis and Gabrielle had taken a brief honeymoon jaunt to the Midi in January 1909, but that trip had been interrupted by the need to return to Paris for the auction of his impressionist canvases at the Hôtel Drouot and the exhibition of his new paintings at the Galeries Georges Petit. That accomplished, they departed anew in April for Spain, where Picabia had relatives in Seville and a cousin,

Pepe, who owned a hacienda in the rugged Sierra Morena.[1] Ironically, Picabia's interest in more abstract art was stimulated by natural forms in the Sierra Morena, notably the gnarled, stunted oaks whose form seemed more important than their identity as trees.[2] That particular experience was recorded in a drawing (fig. 32) whose flat curvilinear color planes suggest the continuing influence of Gauguin and Fauvism; other experiences on that honeymoon would reemerge unexpectedly in some of Picabia's major cubist paintings of 1912 and in the "transparencies" of ca. 1928–1932.

It was probably after his return to Paris in the late spring or early summer of 1909 that Picabia first experimented with some superficial aspects of Cubism. Earlier dates have been attributed to that work, but the only documents presently available are the paintings and drawings themselves, primarily landscapes dated 1909–1910. They bear summer and fall foliage, and, in all likelihood, date from mid-1909 onward, perhaps after a visit to the Salon des Indépendants (March 25–May 2), where he could have seen some early cubist paintings by a former fellow student at Cormon's studio, Georges Braque.

With his own initial venture into Cubism, Picabia suddenly acquired a more modern look, but he worked conservatively, blending superficial aspects of Cubism with characteristics of his earlier fauve style. *Landscape* (color pl. II) transmits an immediate impact by means of simple forms, strong colors and impetuous brushwork, but it owes little to Cubism beyond the simple faceting or "cubifying" of form reminiscent of Derain's paintings in 1907–1908.[3] There is nothing of Braque's restrained palette and cubist ambiguity of form and space. Instead, we are shown a specific site with intense colors serving both decorative and descriptive ends, and heavily outlined forms that recede plane by plane from the foreground river with its sprinkling of neo-impressionist brushstrokes to a distant blue sky. At that time, Picabia may have looked upon Cubism simply as a concern for basic form complementary to the *orchestration essentielle* of fauve color.

In *Houses* (fig. 33), that superficial synthesis of Fauvism and Cubism was expressed in a more abstract and aggressive manner. As crudely applied pigment, garish colors and roughhewn planes battle each other in a compressed space, one wonders whether Picabia was working out of indifference, passion or conviction about the virtues of spontaneity. In contrast to this raw painting, *Paysage à Cassis*

1. For an account of this trip see Gabrielle Buffet-Picabia, "Picabia, l'inventeur," *L'Oeil*, no. 18 (Paris, June 1956), 32–33. Picabia's relatives in Seville were the Abreu y Picabia; other family members with the name Martinez lived in Barcelona.

2. Conversation with Mme Buffet-Picabia, Paris, January 14, 1974.

3. When this author first examined and photographed *Landscape* in the mid-1960s, it was signed and dated in Picabia's hand in the upper right corner of the canvas, "Picabia 1909." Sometime prior to its accession at the Musée National d'Art Moderne, Paris, in 1970, the date was changed by an unknown hand to read "1906." A recent suggestion for a date as late as 1910 is not supported by Picabia's signed and dated canvases (Françoise Nora, "Picabia Fauve et Dadaïste," *La Revue du Louvre*, no. 3, Paris, 1973, 189–92).

(*Landscape at Cassis*, fig. 34) is a composition of softer forms, controlled brushwork and harmonious colors. A black-and-white reproduction also makes it appear more abstract than it is, for the colors are essentially descriptive and a patch of light blue sky facilitates perception of overlapping landscape forms that recede to a horizon.

Picabia's drawings of 1909 tend to be more consistent in quality and exhibit a greater range of abstraction. One typical drawing (fig. 35) incorporates not only a synthesis of bright colors and faceted forms but also the use of visible portions of the textured paper to create a sensation of flickering light. Another characteristic drawing—perhaps slightly later in the year (fig. 36)—is more highly abstracted. Though it depicts a specific site and receding space exists in the drawing, its faceted forms are more independent of nature and stress the two-dimensional surface of the paper. *Abstract Landscape* (fig. 37) represents the extent of this early trend toward abstraction. The landscape motif is discernible, but flat, faceted and brightly colored shapes, locked together like a jigsaw puzzle, are so independent of nature that Picabia was on the threshold of "pure" abstract art, that is, art whose forms and colors bear no recognizable reference to other forms but instead compel the spectator to regard them only in relation to themselves as forms and colors, as "pure painting" rather than as a "painting of something." A point of decision confronted Picabia; the slightly awkward, unresolved effect of this drawing could be dealt with only by eliminating the last vestiges of nature or by backing off from abstract art.

The same issue was posed by *Caoutchouc* (fig. 38), probably at about the same time, although both the date and abstraction of this work are debatable. Since its first recorded exhibition in 1930, many authors have hailed this somber-toned gouache as one of the first abstract paintings in the twentieth century. Others have insisted that imagery lurks in the cluster of circular forms, but their identification of those forms ranges from bouncing balls to bouquets. Mme Buffet-Picabia has written that *Caoutchouc*, so named years after its execution, was a still life of ca. 1909, and her claim is supported by two other paintings (figs. 39, 40).[4] *Still Life with Pitcher and Peppers* (fig. 39), signed and dated 1909, is

4. In conversations with this author and others (Marc Le Bot, *Francis Picabia*, Paris, 1968, 97), Mme Buffet-Picabia claimed that *Caoutchouc* was a still life of oranges on a table. Philip Pearlstein ("The Paintings of Francis Picabia," M.A. thesis, New York University, Institute of Fine Arts, 1955, 24) interpreted *Caoutchouc* as a bouncing rubber ball.

Since the first known exhibition of *Caoutchouc* by that title (Chez Léonce Rosenberg, Paris, *Exposition Francis Picabia*, December 9–31, 1930, no. 4), it has been referred to as either one of the first abstract paintings or as *the* first abstract painting by such authors as Christian Zervos (*Histoire de l'art contemporain*, Paris, 1938, 31), Jean Cassou et al. (*Gateway to the Twentieth Century*, New York, 1962, 155), Bernard Dorival (*Twentieth Century Painters*, New York, 1958, 116), Michel Seuphor (*L'Art abstrait*, Paris: Maeght, 1949, 33), Le Bot (*Francis Picabia*, 93) and Michel Sanouillet (*Francis Picabia et "391,"* II, Paris, 1966, 23).

In all published accounts of *Caoutchouc* it has been attributed dates of 1907, 1908 or 1909 with most authors favoring 1909. Guy Habasque found that date on the reverse of the gouache, but implied that it was added later (Galerie Knoedler, Paris *Les Soirées de Paris*, May 16–June 30,

particularly helpful. Excepting the angular background planes, it resembles Picabia's fauvelike work over the winter of 1908–1909. Those curious background planes are (in reverse) almost identical to the corresponding planes in *Caoutchouc*, and further comparison tempts one to draw more associations. The shape and decoration of the pitcher seem related to the clustered circles in *Caoutchouc*, and those circles are framed on the left by a sweeping curve which has a counterpart in the paper that enfolds the flowers in *Still Life with Pitcher and Peppers*. Another *Still Life* (fig. 40) is unmistakably related to *Caoutchouc* and verifies the subject matter, but it is not dated and raises difficult questions of its own. Is it contemporary with *Caoutchouc*, or, as the dry, machinelike forms suggest, a reinterpretation done during Picabia's machinist period of ca. 1915–1922? At first glance one may be inclined to the latter period, but on stylistic grounds it finally does not reside there comfortably, and Picabia himself seems to have remembered it as an early work. For a 1947 reedition of Gleizes's and Metzinger's *Du Cubisme*, he made a drypoint etching after *Still Life* and dated it 1907 (fig. 41), presumably reflecting his memory of the original.[5]

While caution is in order for the subject and date of *Caoutchouc*, on balance our information suggests a still life of ca. 1909, highly abstracted from nature in the manner of Picabia's contemporary landscapes. And like those landscapes, *Caoutchouc* embodies an awkward, unresolved tension between abstraction and suggested imagery. Picabia was one of the first twentieth-century artists to confront on canvas the leap into "pure painting." For students of modern art, aware of a fifty-year development toward abstract art, that leap into "pure" abstraction seems like a logical, inevitable step. But in 1909 it was a leap, and Picabia, like so many other pioneers in abstract art, eased into it a few years later. In 1909 he backed way off. During 1910 his work evolved from cubist landscapes slightly less abstracted from nature (figs. 42, 43) to scenes characterized by a vapid, simplified naturalism (see fig. 44). Other canvases of 1910 indicate a resumption of fauve interests which were to dominate Picabia's work during 1911. But the abstract possibilities of his venturesome paintings of 1909 were not pursued, and *Caoutchouc* became another of the one-of-a-kind works that thwart efforts to construct simple, logical developments in his career.

Scant information exists for Picabia's life during 1910; few works are known and his participation in exhibitions dropped off sharply. However, Francis and Gabrielle began their family with the birth of Marie in 1910 and that of Gabriel (Pancho) in 1911. Picabia also joined an organization which was to be of conse-

---

1958, no. 24). Mme Buffet-Picabia (*Aires abstraites*, Geneva, 1957, 26–27, and "Picabia l'inventeur," *L'Oeil*, 32) claimed Picabia was drawing monstrous figures and abstract compositions like *Caoutchouc* when they met in 1908. On stylistic grounds I have considered and decided against substantially later dates ("Francis Picabia [1879–1953]. A Study of His Career from 1895 to 1918," Ph.D. diss., Yale University, 1964, 77).

5. Albert Gleizes and Jean Metzinger, *Du Cubisme* (Paris: Compagnie française des arts graphiques, 1947); original edition, Paris, 1912.

quence for his career and the history of Cubism. That organization, the Société Normande de Peinture Moderne, was largely composed of belated fauve and post-impressionist artists preoccupied with the theory of *correspondance* and the inter-relationship of all the arts. It was founded in Rouen in 1909 by Pierre Dumont, supplanting an earlier organization, Les XXX, also chartered by Dumont in emulation of the Belgian symbolist association of the 1890s, Les XX. Annual exhibitions of the Société Normande deliberately combined diverse styles of painting and decorative arts with evening concerts and lectures.[6] Their first program in December 1909 included a soprano from Vincent d'Indy's *Schola cantorum* interpreting works by d'Indy and Debussy, and lectures on Romain Rolland and P.N. Roinard, the latter a symbolist poet of Normandy. Such programs paralleled the aesthetic interests of Picabia and his wife, and he joined the first exhibition in December 1909, invited perhaps by an old friend, Manzana Pissarro, or by the proselytizing Pierre Dumont, who eventually welcomed so many Parisians and foreigners into the association that it had little to do with Normandy.[7] Picabia may have met at that time a Parisian from Normandy who contributed in a major way to the Société Normande and to his life—Marcel Duchamp.

The exact date of their meeting is unknown, but by the fall of 1911 they had established a friendship which was to provide a lifetime of mutual stimulation and droll adventures.[8] Duchamp has given unequivocal witness that "the spirit of Picabia was astonishing,"[9] though Duchamp himself has come to be recognized as the more challenging, influential artist. And during 1910 it was Duchamp who developed the most noteworthy paintings—chiefly nudes and portraits in a style

6. The membership of Les XXX at its first exhibition (Galerie Legrip, Rouen, October 29–November 12, 1907) numbered eleven writers, one sculptor, one composer and twenty painters, including André Derain, Raoul Dufy, Othon Friesz, Albert Marquet, Henri Matisse and Maurice de Vlaminck. Despite those prominent fauve members, diversity of styles was stressed as a characteristic of the organization in the catalogue of that exhibition.

7. For accounts of this exhibition (Salle Boieldien, Rouen, *Exposition de peinture moderne*, December 20, 1909–January 20, 1910) and the accompanying program, see the *Journal de Rouen* ("Exposition de peinture moderne," December 20 and 28, 1909, 2).

8. In a conversation with this author (May 21, 1962), Duchamp said he and Picabia first met before the latter's painting *Sur la plage* at the 1911 Salon d'Automne. With Pierre Cabanne (*Entretiens avec Marcel Duchamp*, Paris, 1967, 52), he recalled that Pierre Dumont introduced them at the 1911 Salon d'Automne before Picabia's large painting of *Bathers*. Mme Buffet-Picabia has written that Dumont introduced them in the 1910 at the Hedelberg Gallery, also known as the Galerie de l'Art Contemporain or the Galerie d'Art Ancien et d'Art Contemporain, 3, rue Tronchet, Paris ("Some Memories of Pre-Dada: Picabia and Duchamp" in Robert Motherwell, ed., *The Dada Painters and Poets*, New York, 1951, 256). Picabia did participate in an exhibition at the Galerie de l'Art Contemporain in 1910 (*Exposition de sculpture, peinture, art décoratif*, November 18, 1909–January 15, 1910), but it had no relation to the Société Normande and Duchamp did not figure in it. Mme. Buffet-Picabia may have confused that event with the contemporary opening of the Société Normande exhibition in Rouen. In another article ("La Section d'Or," *Art d'aujourd'hui*, IV, Paris, May 1953, 74–75) her efforts to establish a correct series of exhibitions are not wholly successful, but her description of the meeting of Duchamp and Picabia matches what is known of their paintings at that first exhibition of the Société Normande in December 1909.

9. Cabanne, *Entretiens avec Marcel Duchamp*, 52.

indebted to Fauvism and Symbolism—which may have caught the eye of Picabia as he worked out of his doldrums of 1910 in a renewed fauve manner. Landscapes continued to dominate his work, but subject matter became more varied and may have reflected his association with Duchamp in several instances.

Regattas (fig. 46), which exemplifies Picabia's renewed fauve landscapes, was perhaps executed early in 1911, since he maintained the practice of painting in the Midi during the winter months. Space has been compressed and pigment and brushwork stress the surface, yet that surface gives way to a distant view of sailboats; colors are bright and decorative, though still descriptive; forms are reduced to Gauguinesque curvilinear shapes, but only some patches in the foreground seem liberated from description of specific forms.

Several undated paintings may be situated chronologically on the basis of their relationship to *Regattas* and earlier documented works. *Le Torrent* (*The Torrent*, fig. 45) is similar in style but more muted in color and possibly earlier in date. *Dolls* (color pl. III) is more abstract but basically compatible with the style of *Regattas*; moreover, it is an engaging painting whose rounded forms and bright colors evoke a joyous, childlike sensation even before one discovers toys and teddy bears in the lower portion of the composition.

Picabia chose major exhibitions for the presentation of two new themes, both of them dealing with nudes and exactly contemporary in date with works by Duchamp on similar subjects. In *Adam and Eve* (fig. 47), exhibited at the second Salon of the Société Normande in May 1911, renewed tension between figuration and abstraction appears in the contrast of the figures and their more schematic setting, although that contrast is diminished by uniformly sensuous pigment and lush colors which also enhance the sexual content of the subject. Picabia returned to Adam and Eve in every style of his long career, and his interpretations of the subject were as diverse as those styles, but erotic-psychological motives prevailed, as here where Eve, seemingly amused by her power, poises herself and the forbidden fruit tantalizingly above the hapless Adam. This interpretation of the temptation is compatible with the attitude of Picabia, who, in his own affair-studded life, often saw himself as a subject or (generally willing) victim of women and the sexual nature bestowed on man by God.

Printemps, unrecorded since its exhibition at the 1911 Salon des Indépendants, is presently known only through a faded newspaper reproduction and contemporary criticism as a "canvas where M. Picabia evokes, in fantastic colors, spring symbolized by four nymphs in diverse attitudes and fatigued poses."[10] It was included in salle 41 of the Salon des Indépendants, where Gleizes, Metzinger, Léger, Delaunay and Le Fauconnier had organized what is considered to

10. René Jean, "Le Salon des Artistes Indépendants," *Gazette des Beaux-Arts*, 4th period, VI (Paris, July 11, 1911), 56. Five rather than four figures are discernible in the reproduction published by Jean. *Printemps*, or a study for it, is also known by a photograph of Picabia's studio in which it appears as the small painting (resting on it side) to the upper right of Picabia (illus. 5).

be the first public manifestation of Cubism. Some members of the Société Normande were deeply impressed by the cubist works there. Picabia was not one of them—he continued to work in a fauve idiom—but Marcel Duchamp, Jacques Villon and diverse artists within and without the Société Normande affirmed the relevance of Cubism for their interests by beginning explorations in that style. Common interests led to personal contacts that multiplied over the summer. By the fall of that year there was forming around a core of "salle 41" cubists and Société Normande members a loose confederation of artists who were in frequent contact at the studios of Gleizes (Courbevoie) and Villon (Puteaux), the apartment of Alexandre Mercereau and the Closerie des Lilas, the latter a traditional gathering place of the symbolist poets. The diversity of the artists who eventually participated cannot be conveyed by a simple descriptive name, but "Section d'Or" artists is employed here because the 1912 exhibition by that name was their climactic activity.

The stylistic influence of the cubists gradually prevailed among this group, but other styles were never entirely excluded, and a variety of interests set these artists apart from Braque and Picasso. The revolutionary work of those two creators of Cubism developed in a private, intuitive and largely formal manner. They had ceased public exhibition of their paintings and were disdainful of both the activities and much of the art produced by those attracted to the cubist movement. In contrast, the Section d'Or artists were publicly concerned about the intellectual, social and aesthetic characteristics of a new art for a new era. They engaged in a steady round of exhibitions, publications and meetings, where conversations ranged from developments in science and technology to the writings of Leonardo da Vinci, the concept of *correspondance*, the fourth dimension and the philosophies of Nietzsche and Bergson.

As a student of the Académie Ranson, Roger de La Fresnaye had been exposed to symbolist theories of a more mystic bent than those common among the Société Normande members. Gleizes's background included participation in a utopian-socialist colony of artists and workers, the "Abbaye de Créteil" (1906–1908), which published Jules Romains's *La Vie unanime* and other writings focused on the qualities of modern life, particularly its speed, science, simultaneity and industry.[11] Dumont, Gleizes and Metzinger did critical writing, and the latter two began their booklet *Du Cubisme* around the winter of 1911–1912.[12] The oft-

11. See the Solomon R. Guggenheim Museum, New York, *Albert Gleizes*, September 15–November 1, 1964, catalogue by Daniel Robbins; Daniel Robbins, "From Symbolism to Cubism: The Abbaye of Créteil," *Art Journal*, XXIII, no. 3 (New York, winter 1963–1964), 111–16; and Marianne W. Martin, "Futurism, Unanimism and Apollinaire," *Art Journal*, XXVIII, no. 3 (New York, spring 1969), 258–68.

12. Pierre Dumont wrote art reviews for *Les Hommes du jour* during part of 1912. The idea for Gleizes's and Metzinger's influential book *Du Cubisme* (Paris, 1912) probably arose in 1911, but the book was written during 1912 and published by November of that year (see the book review of Arsène Alexandre, "La Semaine artistique," *Comoedia* [Paris], November 30, 1912, 3).

cited but mysterious actuary, Maurice Princet, fanned an interest in mathematics and geometry whose dimensions are just beginning to be realized.[13] Contemporary editions of Leonardo's *Treatise on Painting* became another source for discussions about proportion, order and, surprisingly, an emerging interest in "pure painting."[14] Given such interests, it is no surprise that only a few Section d'Or artists followed docilely in the wake of Picasso and Braque. Some found Cubism too radical or alien for their tastes and turned to more naturalistic idioms; others found Cubism not radical enough and led important new developments out of that style.

The cubist-oriented members of this amorphous association exhibited together that fall of 1911 in salle 8 of the Salon d'Automne, thanks to the persuasive efforts of La Fresnaye, Duchamp-Villon and Georges Desvallières, all members of both the Salon d'Automne hanging committee and the Société Normande. The temperamental Delaunay had already withdrawn, but newcomers swelled the ranks, and still more adherents appeared a month later for the first exhibition of the entire association at the Galerie d'Art Ancien et d'Art Contemporain on the rue Tronchet, Paris.

The latter exhibition, appropriately entitled "Exposition d'art contemporain," was organized by Pierre Dumont under the auspices of the Société Normande. Consistent with the traditions of that organization, Dumont assembled paintings, sculpture and decorative arts representing a variety of contemporary trends and organized a series of lectures headed by Apollinaire.[15] The continuation of those practices in the association's second exhibition, "La Section d'Or," accounts for some of the features of that 1912 exhibition which have befuddled students of Cubism. The 1911 exhibition, neglected in some studies of Cubism, attracted considerable contemporary attention, and it is thanks to the critics that something of Picabia's role is known, since his paintings there and at the contemporary Salon d'Automne have not come to light. Hostile critics lamented his bizarre colors and deformed figures, but one sympathetic writer hinted at Picabia's

13. Linda Dalrymple Henderson, "A New Facet of Cubism: 'The Fourth Dimension' and 'Non-Euclidean Geometry' Reinterpreted," *The Art Quarterly*, XXXIV, no. 4 (Detroit, winter 1971), 410–33. Mrs. Henderson has expanded that work in an important Ph.D. dissertation, "The Artist, 'The Fourth Dimension' and Non-Euclidean Geometry. 1900–1930: A Romance of Many Dimensions," Yale University, 1975; see pp. 128–35 for Princet.

14. Villon has stressed the influence of Leonardo's *Treatise* (Dora Vallier, *Jacques Villon*, Paris, 1957, 117–18), an edition of which was published by Péladan in Paris in 1910. The theft of the *Mona Lisa* from the Louvre in August 1911 (and Apollinaire's false implication in the theft) focused still more attention on Leonardo.

15. Galerie d'Art Ancien et d'Art Contemporain, Paris, *Exposition d'art contemporain*, November 20–December 16, 1911. Informative reviews appeared in *Paris-Journal*, November 17 (announcement of lectures by Apollinaire, René Blum, Louis Nazzi and Gabrielle Reuillard); *Paris-Journal*, November 22; *Mercure de France* (Paris, December 16), 844–47; and *La Côte* [Paris], November 25 (Roger Allard's comments on Apollinaire's lecture). See also Guillaume Apollinaire, *Chroniques d'art*, ed. L.C. Breunig (Paris, 1960), 204, 461–62. Breunig's annotated collection of Apollinaire's writings as an art critic is a useful reference which will be cited instead of the original source, except in instances where knowledge of the original source is essential.

continued aesthetic interests by praising "superbly ordered gardens which give a sensation akin to a *musical emotion*" (author's italics).[16]

Those paintings of gardens have not been securely identified, but the comments of that critic seem relevant to another painting apparently exhibited there (fig. 49).[17] The ostensible subject, horses, is readily identified but of secondary importance; Picabia's primary concern was the orchestration of strong blue, black, brown, green and gray colors, here rendered in patches of thick, impetuously brushed pigment which tend to disintegrate into autonomous color forms. A notable advance in that direction is exhibited in *Landscape* (fig. 48, and illus. 5) and in *Souvenir de Grimaldi* (*Memory of Grimaldi*, illus. 8, upper center). The latter, probably a product of Picabia's traditional winter campaign in the Midi, was exhibited at the 1912 Salon des Indépendants and at the Armory Show.[18] Subsequently, all trace of it has been lost, but Armory Show installation photographs are good enough to document its greater degree of abstraction, and the title itself indicates Picabia's shift from dependence on models in nature to a method based on memories of places and experiences.

These limited remains from the latter half of 1911 and early 1912 do not provide grounds for assured evaluation of Picabia's oeuvre, but two contemporary critics—one friendly and one not so friendly—may guide us. André Salmon, in his slender book *La Jeune Peinture française*, could not say enough bad things about Picabia's work. "The disaccord between his color and his drawing is complete"; he "is a belated Fauve; . . . wanting in taste"; and on and on. But Salmon grudgingly conceded that it was necessary to consider Picabia "because he plays an important role in the young groups and because, despite his faults, he has this quality of being himself."[19] Salmon was correct in his assessment, for in the gatherings of the avant-garde painters Picabia did enjoy a prominence that exceeded the intrinsic interest of his painting. In part that position derived from his personality. He was a stimulating man with countless entertaining, influential friends and money enough of his own to finance some of his colleagues' projects. But his position also depended on his work and his ardent advocacy of "pure painting." Even at their most slapdash, Picabia's paintings projected something of his vital spirit, and of all the artists under discussion, including those Apollinaire later designated orphists, Picabia was the one repeatedly cited in articles of 1911–early 1912 as the advocate for an art liberated from nature in a manner

16. Anon. review, "Exposition de peinture," *Le Journal* [Paris], November 22, 1911, 3.

17. This painting does not appear in the exhibition catalogue, but the art critic for *La Côte* [Paris], November 1911 (attrib.), referred to Picabia's painting of *Les Chevaux* there. This is the only painting of that subject known in Picabia's oeuvre, and it is a compatible in style to his work of late 1911–early 1912.

18. Salon des Indépendants, Paris, March 20–May 16, 1912, no. 2559. Association of American Painters and Sculptors, *International Exhibition of Modern Art* [The Armory Show], New York, February 17–March 15, 1913, no. 418; Chicago, March 24–April 16; Boston, April 28–May 19.

19. André Salmon, *La Jeune Peinture française* (Paris, 1912), 82–83.

analogous to music. The second critic (and friend), Pierre Dumont, best expressed Picabia's situation on the occasion of the 1912 Salon des Indépendants:

> . . . Parallel to the Cubists, M. Francis Picabia wants to communicate to us a new artistic emotion by expressing himself through harmonies of colors and quests for ordered forms, a sensation . . . closely related to that which comes to us from an audition. It is now almost two years since he declared his search for this goal; and if he has not yet reached a complete realization, it is clear that he has taken a big step with the canvases exhibited here [among them *Souvenir de Grimaldi*, illus. 8]. He will attain his ideal . . . and soon, for he knows where he is going, he possesses within himself an imperious force which propels him to the end of his desire.[20]

Dumont was also correct in his assessment and in his prophecy, for as the possibility of "pure painting" became more imminent during 1912, Picabia was becoming an able practitioner of it as well as one of its first and most outspoken advocates.

Pure Painting, La Section d'Or and Orphism

The development of abstract art in Paris from late 1911 to 1913 is a complex matter under any circumstances, and prospects for its clarification are not enhanced by the prominence of Apollinaire's writings, which reflect his numerous, constantly evolving interests. It is evident, nonetheless, that over the winter of 1911–1912 a concern for "pure painting" was "in the air," nourished by a rich array of visual and theoretical stimuli. In the realm of theory, developments in the most diverse fields were appropriated if they supported the artists' quests for a new expression of life liberated from the naturalistic, materialistic thrust of the nineteenth century. In the visual arts, Cubism was the primary vehicle, but Fauvism, Expressionism, Symbolism, Cézanne and Neo-Impressionism all contributed to the immediate background of those artists most relevant to the development of abstract art—Picasso and Braque, Delaunay, Kupka, Picabia, Mondrian, Kandinsky and the futurists, to name only the most important.

Public proclamation of "pure art" was made by Apollinaire in the lead article of his magazine *Les Soirées de Paris* (February 1912).[21] With customary exuberance he announced that some young artists were making paintings where there is

20. Pierre Dumont, "Les Indépendants," *Les Hommes du jour* (Paris, April 20, 1912).

21. Guillaume Apollinaire, "Du sujet dans la peinture moderne," *Les Soirées de Paris*, no. 1 (February 1912), 1–4.

no *sujet véritable*. Though they may observe nature, he wrote, they do not imitate it for:

"Verisimilitude no longer has any importance . . . everything is sacrificed by the artist to the composition of his painting.

"One is thus led toward an entirely new art, which will be to painting, as one has previously envisioned it, what music is to literature.

"It will be a kind of pure painting just as music is a kind of pure literature."

He concluded more soberly that the young artists have not yet abandoned nature and that the new art, "only at its beginning . . . is not yet as abstract as it would like to be."

The wording of that article resembles the aesthetic convictions of Picabia, whom Apollinaire had met in 1911,[22] but many artists must have contributed to Apollinaire's concepts, above all Picasso and Braque, whom he instinctively embraced as the creators of the primary movement in contemporary art. Those two creators of Cubism finally rejected abstract art, always preserving in their work a balance between reality and abstraction. But over the winter of 1911–1912 that balance had become tenuous as identifiable subjects almost vanished from their paintings, and just a suggestion of an object here or a fragment of a word there maintained a toehold on reality (see fig. 50). When the Italian futurists stormed into Paris for their important exhibition in February 1912, Apollinaire, consistent with his esteem for Cubism, found their work weak in plastic invention and excessively concerned with literary subject matter and "soul states."[23] At the same time, however, Apollinaire reserved his warmest praise at the contemporary 1912 Salon des Indépendants for Delaunay's *City of Paris*—a painting epic in theme but conservatively cubist in style—while according scant attention to Delaunay's friend and pioneer abstractionist, Wassily Kandinsky, and ignoring completely František Kupka, the only artist who may have produced abstract art in Paris by the spring of 1912.[24]

22. The exact date of their meeting is unknown, but there is a portrait drawing of Apollinaire by Picabia, signed and dated 1911 (formerly collection of the Galleria Schwarz, Milan).

23. Galerie Bernheim Jeune, Paris, *Les Peintres futuristes italiens*, February 5–24, 1912. A considerable stir was created by the Italian artists, their works and the "Technical Manifesto of Painting" in the catalogue. See Marianne Martin, *Futurist Art and Theory* (Oxford, 1968), 120–26. For Apollinaire's criticism see *Chroniques d'art*, 212–17, 462–63.

24. For Apollinaire's comments on Delaunay and Kandinsky at the 1912 Salon des Indépendants see *Chroniques d'art*, 224–25, 227. Kupka never figured in Apollinaire's writings, and his name has not yet appeared in a single exhibition catalogue or review concerning the Section d'Or artists. Some authors persist in the opinion that Kupka participated in the 1912 exhibition of La Section d'Or (the issue is unresolved), although their arguments tend to strengthen the opposing viewpoint. For the most thorough account see Margit Rowell, "František Kupka: A Metaphysics of Abstraction" (*František Kupka*, New York: The Solomon R. Guggenheim Museum, 1975, 47, 74, 79, 310–11). Kupka produced what may be considered abstract art by late 1911, and he exhibited two abstract paintings at the 1912 Salon d'Automne, *Amorpha, fugue à deux couleurs* and *Amorpha, chromatique chaude*. His *Plans verticaux I* was also painted during 1912. See the Guggenheim Museum catalogue above, nos. 86, 92 and 96.

Kandinsky and Delaunay had corresponded since late 1911, when the latter was invited to

These seemingly contradictory positions of Apollinaire during the early months of 1912 defy resolution, but two suggestions will be offered. First, despite his announcement of pure art, Apollinaire was not really ready for it or was not inclined to perceive much substance in a brand of it which—like Kupka's—derived from Symbolism rather than Cubism. Second, the subject matter and content of highly abstracted art might be—like Picasso's— a subtle, integral part of a composition with profound formal properties or—like Delaunay's—a heroic, self-evident subject having no need for a program. But, contrary to his view of futurist paintings, Apollinaire thought that subject matter should not be excessively literary.[25] Apollinaire's thoughts and tastes are perhaps more comprehensible by 1913 and will be reconsidered toward the end of this chapter. But throughout 1912–1913 suffice it to note that his apparent inconsistencies were the product of both complex interests and his effort to cope with basic questions posed by the serious prospect of abstract art. Might artists eliminate all identifiable reference to the phenomenal world, and, if so, what then would be the subject and content of art? Or should one retain recognizable references to nature, and, if so, in what manner?

Needless to say, such questions were even more pressing for a number of artists. In the spring and summer of 1912 Picasso and Braque reasserted their contact with reality by one of the most influential innovations of modern art, the introduction of actual objects in their works by means of collage. Most cubists followed suit insofar as they stopped short of abstraction. Gleizes and Metzinger, for example, insisted on retaining grand, human social themes and were disturbed by colleagues who seemed to be going too far too fast with abstraction. Duchamp's *Nude Descending the Staircase* fit that category, and before the installation of the 1912 Salon des Indépendants, Gleizes (a member of the hanging committee) asked Jacques Villon and Raymond Duchamp-Villon to persuade their younger brother to withdraw his painting.[26] Delaunay shared Gleizes's interest in epic themes, but from about April 1912 through the winter of 1912–1913 he developed an important form of abstract art which Apollinaire placed at the head of the movement he called Orphism. At the same time in the spring of 1912, Duchamp began paintings and drawings on the theme of the king and queen, which, though not

exhibit at the Blue Rider exhibition in December 1911. See Delaunay's *Du Cubisme à l'art abstrait* (Paris, 1957), 178–83. Other contracts existed through the visit of Franz Marc and Paul Klee to Paris (April 2–18, 1912) and Kandinsky's book (*Ueber das Geistige in der Kunst*, Munich, 1912), which could have have reached Paris early in 1912. Duchamp has stated that Kandinsky's book was not known among the Section d'Or artists, and that he personally encountered it in Munich during July 1912 (conversation with the author, December 16, 1963).

25. In a letter to Kandinsky, Delaunay makes an intriguing, mysterious reference to subject matter: "I will speak to you sometime about the subject in painting, about the palpitating conversation at Apollinaire's, who begins to believe in our researches" (Delaunay, *Du Cubisme à l'art abstrait*, 179). This letter is undated but attributable to early 1912, given references to the futurists and Kandinsky's book, which Delaunay had seen but could not read.

26. Robert Lebel, *Marcel Duchamp*, trans. George Heard Hamilton (New York, 1959), 9.

abstract, were unidentifiable and were breaking out of the cubist orbit. And Picabia, with such paintings as *Tarentelle* and *Port de Naples* (figs. 51, 52), took a stride toward pure painting which put his work on a par with his theorizing.

Those two paintings, exhibited in June at the third Salon of the Société Normande, were the first of Picabia's works described by Apollinaire as cubist.[27] With their earthen color harmonies, angular planes and advanced degree of abstraction, they do reveal a definite shift toward the trappings of Cubism, but they also embody distinct personal aims alien to the Cubism of Braque and Picasso. *Tarentelle* (fig. 51) retains a balance between abstraction and realism insofar as it is possible to discern in it human figures and a village setting referring to the Italian settlement by that name. However, that balance is tipped toward abstraction as the ragged color patches refuse to remain fixed as solid and void or as light and shadow, but shift into unpredictable new combinations or revert to mere planes of colored pigment. Thick impasto and agitated brushwork emphasize the materiality of the painting, while the colors, a range of buff, cream, rose, gray and brown, are both harmonious in themselves and evocative of a parched Mediterranean village. *Port de Naples* is more abstract—a welter of ragged, brownish color planes which suggest no immediate association with the title, originally printed in bold letters in the upper right corner.[28] Picabia's practice of painting titles on the canvas itself was often taken as a joke or as public mockery, but there is no evidence that he began it for any other reason than as a straightforward identification of the subject in paintings which had become increasingly abstract. The same was probably true of Duchamp, although the nature of his subjects lent the titles a more cryptic, poetic existence parallel to the paintings.

Hen Roost (color pl. IV) is a particularly handsome painting which suggests the transition between Picabia's essentially fauve works of late 1911 and the cubist qualities of *Tarentelle* and *Port de Naples*. It retains the curvilinear planes and more readily identified subject matter of the earlier fauve compositions, but also exhibits Picabia's thrust toward pure painting by a masterly composition of harmonious tan and gray color forms which is more important than the ostensible subject of chickens.[29]

27. Apollinaire, *Chroniques d'art*, 281. The *Salon de Juin* of the Société Normande was held in a large skating rink (Rouen, June 15–July 15, 1912). Elie Faure and Maurice Raynal provided prefaces for a substantial catalogue (see Edward Fry, ed., *Cubism*, New York, 1966, and Georges Dubosc, review in the *Journal de Rouen*, June 17, 1912, 3). Conflicting contemporary reports on the lectures are resolved by accounts of four lectures in the *Dépêche de Rouen* (see Jeffrey J. Carre, "Guillaume Apollinaire à Rouen," *La Revue des lettres modernes*, [no. 4], Paris, 1964, 157–59).

28. The title *Port de Naples* is evident in the upper right corner of a 1913 reproduction (Albert Gleizes and Jean Metzinger, *Cubism*, Eng. trans., London: T. F. Unwin, 1913, 133). At an unknown date that title was removed or painted over and no longer appears on the canvas.

29. Galleria Schwarz, Milan, *Picabia: Le Poulailler*, October 1974, essay by William Camfield. During 1912 Picabia conceived and then abandoned a project to raise chickens in a thirteenth-century Benedictine monastery in southern France (see Mrs. André Roosevelt, "Recollections of Mrs. André Roosevelt, Stories and Anecdotes About Some Early Cubists," unpublished memoirs, Archives of American Art, Smithsonian Institute, Washington, D.C.).

Apollinaire's genuine interest in Picabia's new paintings probably had a great deal to do with the transformation of their acquaintance into a memorable friendship. Apollinaire was in need of a lively friend at that time, for in June 1912 he was crushed by the departure of Marie Laurencin after their long and troubled liaison. Picabia has recounted how he and Apollinaire were together almost every evening for awhile, absorbed in animated conversation on every imaginable subject, drinking, smoking opium, and roaring about Paris in his magnificent automobiles (illus. 9).[30] All their legendary capers seem to have begun at that date—painting ties on Apollinaire's shirtfront, abandoning lecture audiences, and probably their attendance—along with Marcel Duchamp—at a performance of Raymond Roussel's fantastic *Impressions d'Afrique*.[31] The staging of Roussel's bizarre episodes dealing with preposterous rituals, physical prowess, art, sex, science and Rube Goldberg machines was a delight to all three men and a lasting influence on Duchamp at a critical point in his career. He went to Munich in July, just to work quietly, he has said, and produced the astounding series of drawings and paintings of the *Virgin* and *The Bride* (fig. 62). Delaunay also left for the summer, to La Madaleine in the valley of the Chevreuse, where he produced a group of paintings entitled *Windows* and notes which later exerted considerable influence on Apollinaire. In Paris, Picabia and Apollinaire played, talked and worked—the latter on his book *Les Peintres cubistes* and Picabia on a dozen or so major paintings.[32]

One evening around late July, after numerous cocktails with Claude Debussy

30. The most informative accounts of this friendship have been provided by Picabia ("Guillaume Apollinaire," *L'Esprit nouveau*, no. 26, Paris, October 1924), and Gabrielle Buffet-Picabia (*Aires abstraites*).

During the early twentieth century, smoking clubs were not uncommon for the "social" use of opium among well-to-do Parisians, and both Picabia and Apollinaire participated in them (conversations with Mme Buffet-Picabia, October 1962). That practice was apparently more important for Picabia and continued by him until ca. 1918–1919. Efforts by this author to detect an influence of the drug in Picabia's art have failed to isolate any demonstrable feature in either the conception or execution of his paintings.

The effect of opium on artistic creation is largely unexplored. Most authors from the late nineteenth century onward have disputed Thomas De Quincy's description of the effect of the drug on his poetry. Meyer Howard Abrams (*The Milk of Paradise*, Harvard Honors Thesis in English, Cambridge, Mass., 1934) is an exception, as is Jean Cocteau in some respects (see his *Opium*, trans. Ernest Boyd, London, 1933). For descriptions of the mental and physiological aspects of opium and other drugs, see Bernard Finch, *Passport to Paradise . . . ?* (London; 1959).

31. The premiere of *Impressions d'Afrique* occurred at the Théâtre Fémina aux Champs-Elysées on Setptember 30, 1911. It was produced again at the Théâtre Antoine from May 11 to June 5, 1912 (John Ashbery, "Les Versions scéniques 'd'Impressions d'Afrique,' et de 'Locus Solus,' " *Bizarre*, nos. 34–35, Paris, 2nd quarter, 1964, 20–21). Since Apollinaire's cordial relations with Duchamp and Picabia developed only in 1912, they probably attended a 1912 performance at the Théâtre Antoine as Duchamp has acknowledged in conversations with this author (December 16, 1963).

32. Apollinaire began the book around May or June, and on August 28, 1912, he wrote Serge Férat, "I have done a little book on the cubists" (Apollinaire, *Les Peintres cubistes*, eds. L.C. Breunig and J.-Cl. Chevalier, Paris, 1965, 18).

at the Bar de la Paix, Picabia proposed to Apollinaire that they drive to Boulogne and take the boat to England, where Gabrielle was vacationing.[33] The poet immediately agreed, noting that they should have no trouble since he spoke English. The next morning they arrived, famished owing to the inability of English waiters to understand Apollinaire's particular dialect, which he described as "ancient Irish." After an amusing adventure or two in English nightclubs, Apollinaire and the Picabias returned to France, pausing for dinner in Boulogne where Gabrielle recalls a serious discussion about "pure painting." In her memory, Apollinaire recoiled from the prospect of totally abstract art, calling it "an inhuman art, unintelligible to the sentiment which risks remaining purely decorative." "Are blue and red unintelligible?" responded Picabia; "Are not the circle and the triangle, volumes and colors, as intelligible as this table?"[34]

Although Mme Buffet-Picabia was writing many years after that conversation, her recollection of it confirms what appears to have been Apollinaire's ambivalence toward abstract art several months earlier, and she bears witness to one of several influences on Apollinaire's notion of "pure painting" and the subject matter or content of art by the winter of 1912–1913. Picabia's influence was not limited to conversations; his prodigious production of documented paintings from June to September came very close to realizing a form of abstract art expressive of "soul states," and the intrinsic interest of a number of those canvases was sufficient to lend credibility to the aesthetic aims he pressed on Apollinaire over the summer.

Danses à la source I (*Dances at the Spring* I, fig. 56) was probably one of the first canvases completed that summer.[35] This painting has long been one of Picabia's most popular cubist pictures—purchased out of the Armory Show and from then onward frequently cited and reproduced. It is also one of the most resolved paintings of this period in his career, balancing abstraction and figuration and the formal properties of light and dark, straight and curved lines, two- and three-dimensional space, stability and motion. At the same time, scholars of Cubism have tended to see it as an unsophisticated, derivative painting—lacking the subtle and demanding formal properties of a Braque or a Picasso and marked by the influence of both futurist motion and Léger's "tubular" mode of Cubism. Such criticism is essentially accurate from the viewpoint of the mainstream Cubism of Picasso and Braque, but it is handicapped by neglecting viewpoints more relevant to Picabia. Despite obvious dependence on cubist ambiguities of

33. Picabia, "Guillaume Apollinaire," *L'Esprit nouveau*. A slightly different account was published by Mme Buffet-Picabia (*Aires abstraites*, 47–51). The date of the trip is verified by an unsigned note, "Les Arts, villégiature," *Le Gil Blas* [Paris], August 14, 1912.

34. Buffet-Picabia, *Aires abstraites*, 54–57.

35. A drawing for *Danses à la source* was reproduced in the catalogue of the Société Normande de Peinture Moderne, Rouen, *Salon de Juin*, June 15–July 15, 1912. The painting was exhibited at the Salon d'Automne (Paris, October 1–November 8, 1912, no. 1351) and reproduced in a review by Claude-Roger, "Au Salon d'Automne, maîtres cubes," *La Comoedie artistique* (Paris, October 5, 1912), 62–65.

space, light and faceted form, Picabia was not really a cubist any more than he had been a fauve. He was adapting stylistic elements to his own ends—here the evocation "of an observation during his honeymoon journey of two peasant girls dancing" in the rugged, sunbaked countryside near Seville or Naples.[36] The earthen palette and ponderous rhythms in this painting seem determined more by a concern for aesthetic harmony and the evocation of that experience than by the classic monochrome canvases of Braque and Picasso.

Other experiences called for different palettes, as in *Figure triste* (*Sad Figure*, fig. 58), where a chord of blue, black and gray corresponds to the quality of "sadness" struck in the title. In comparison to *Danses à la source* I, the relation of *Figure triste* to Cubism is already more tenuous, and its handling of figuration and abstraction quite unsettled. *Procession Seville* (color pl. v) is more striking, an ominous mass of faceted color forms suggesting a cubist version of Goya's sinister *Pilgrims of San Isidro*. *Procession Seville* was in fact based on Picabia's memory of a religious procession in Seville in 1909—with perhaps a glance at Goya. And his palette of blue, gray, ochre and black successfully combines both formal harmony and a symbolic-psychological use of color to suggest the barren Spanish terrain, black-frocked religious figures and the mysterious, foreboding qualities of their procession.[37]

Paris (fig. 55) unites new architectonic forms, possibly influenced by Kupka's *Vertical Planes I*, and a skittering patchwork of angular color planes reminiscent of *Tarentelle* and *Port de Naples* (figs. 51, 52). Those same paintings are recalled by the thickly brushed forms in *The Red Tree* (fig. 53), a painting keyed to an earlier fauve landscape entitled *Grimaldi après la pluie* (*Grimaldi After the Rain*).[38] *Landscape, La Creuse* (fig. 54) has not been identified with works exhibited in 1912, and its outlined forms are unusual for that date. Nonetheless it is compatible in brushwork, color harmony and degree of abstraction with such paintings as *The Red Tree* and *Danses à la source* I, and it appears in a photograph of Picabia's studio (illus. 5), dated many years later "Thursday July 9, 1913" and

36. Apollinaire ascribed to Picabia the statement that *Danses à la source* was "the expression of a natural plastic emotion experienced near Naples" (*Les Peintres cubistes*, Paris, 1913, 71). Mme Buffet-Picabia states that she and Picabia never visited Naples (conversation with the author), and that this painting was inspired by Picabia's memory of a young shepherdess dancing beside a stream during their 1909 honeymoon in Spain ("Picabia, l'inventeur," *L'Oeil*, 33). The discrepancy of these claims is less important than the fact that Picabia was working from his memory of events rather than from models. Nevertheless, evidence of a trip to Naples some time early in Picabia's career continues to appear as late as the 1930s.

37. The source of this painting, another experience during the Picabias' honeymoon in Spain, was noted by Mme Buffet-Picabia, "Picabia, l'inventeur," *L'Oeil*, 32–33.

38. *Grimaldi après la pluie* is presently known only from a faded newspaper reproduction in the *Nebraska State Journal* [Lincoln], February 9, 1913, sec. B, 7. It appears to be a landscape of 1911 that is based on the landscape setting for *Adam and Eve* (fig. 47). *The Red Tree* is probably identical with the *Paysage* (*Landscape*) attributed to 1911 in the original edition of Apollinaire's *Les Peintres cubistes* (Paris, 1913) and printed upside down both there and in a reedition (Geneva: Pierre Cailler, 1950, fig. 35).

subsequently corrected to read "1911." Given the fact that Picabia is shown in the midst of fauve paintings from late 1911 and cubist works in progress, a further correction to read "1912" is in order.

The themes of two key works, *Danses à la source* I and *Procession Seville* (fig. 56; color pl. v), were continued in three other paintings probably finished late in that summer of 1912—*Musique de procession* (*Procession Music*, fig. 59), *La Source* (*The Spring*, fig. 60) and *Danses à la source* II (fig. 57). *Musique de procession*, known only from a deteriorated newspaper reproduction, reaffirms Picabia's use of musical analogies to indicate his creation of harmonies of color and form liberated from the representation of nature. *La Source* and *Danses à la source* II, which were recently discovered, count among Picabia's best paintings of that epoch.[39] *Danses à la source* I and II were exhibited simultaneously during the fall of 1912, the former at the Salon d'Automne and the latter at the Section d'Or. It is evident that they are closely related, but their differences may be more revealing for the direction of Picabia's work at that date. *Danses à la source* II is twice the size of its counterpart, more abstract, and rendered in a different color chord (a high-keyed, energized red-orange)—features which suggest the variations, ambition and confidence of a later version. *La Source* (fig. 60) is an equally large, highly abstracted version of the same theme, here composed in a striking harmony of grays and browns which, however, did not protect it from some of the most unfavorable criticism aimed at entries to the Salon d'Automne. A contemporary wag caricatured it (see fig. 61), while other critics caviled that Picabia had set "the year's record for fantasy" with "ugly" works that "evoke incrusted linoleum."[40]

With fortunate timing, Picabia's election as an associate of the Société du Salon d'Automne shortly preceded his emergence as a controversial member of the avant-garde. As an associate he could not be excluded from the annual Salons, an immunity which he exercised to the fullest during the dada epoch, although it did not spare him the barbs of predominantly hostile critics from 1912 onward. He shared in the general rage ignited that fall by the cubist paintings clustered in room 11, *la salle infernale*, of the Salon. Mounting reviews and letters bristled with hostility, while disgusted deputies made threatening speeches about government censure of the Salon and attacks on the budget for the Beaux Arts: "Liberty for art, yes, but when it becomes a lamentable license, outside the national

39. Four major paintings by Picabia, *Danses à la source* II (1912), *La Source* (1912), *C'est de moi qu'il s'agit* (1914) and *Mariage comique* (1914) (figs. 57, 60, 98, 99) figure in a recent gift to the Museum of Modern Art by the children of Eugene and Agnes E. Meyer—Elizabeth Lorentz, Eugene Meyer III, Katharine Graham and Ruth M. Epstein. I am grateful to personnel of the Museum of Modern Art for permission to reproduce these paintings, which have not been exhibited in over sixty years and were thought to have been lost or destroyed. A full account of their discovery and history will be published by the Museum once restoration of the paintings has been completed. Inasmuch as restoration could not be achieved prior to the publication of this book, the reproductions printed here represent the paintings prior to restoration.

40. Jean Claude, "La Vie artistique. Le Salon d'Automne," *Le Petit Parisien*, September 30, 1912, 2.

palace, that is to say, the Grand Palais [will be] closed to the Salon d'Automne if it persists in its aims."[41]

Apollinaire, on the contrary, was at last genuinely enthusiastic about the new stirrings within Cubism. After exposure to Picabia's paintings and aesthetics throughout the summer, he was further stimulated by the works which Duchamp and Delaunay brought back to the capital (see fig. 62). Obviously something new had emerged from Cubism; earlier hesitation gave way and he proclaimed the new tendency in two special forums available that fall—the Salon of the Section d'Or in October and his booklet, *Les Peintres cubistes*. These events are complex and fraught with unknowns, but must be considered because of their importance and Picabia's substantial role in them. He was a principal organizer of the Section d'Or, one of the ten new artists featured in *Les Peintres cubistes* and host to the famous Jura trip, long considered important for both activities.

The Jura trip was a madcap week shared by the Picabias, Duchamp and Apollinaire in Gabrielle's family home near the Swiss border, a remote site reached after a wild night ride in one of Picabia's famous automobiles. For many years it was believed that the sojourn there occurred in September 1912 and was instrumental in the planning of the Section d'Or and Apollinaire's booklet on *Les Peintres cubistes*. That could not have been the case since both projects were under way long before September, and, more recently, scholars have been inclined to a date of late October or November. Marcel Adéma's research has finally resolved the question of time; the Jura trip occurred about October 20–26, but the significance of that trip remains open.[42] It probably contributed to changes Apollinaire soon made in *Les Peintres cubistes*, and it was reportedly the occasion on which he first read his epic poem "Zone." Duchamp returned with a project for the Jura-Paris road which is suffused with the mechanical-human analogies, eroticism, symbolism, intellectualism and punning identified with him for the remainder of his life.[43] In the last months of 1912, Picabia went on to produce his first wholly abstract paintings (see fig. 65).

More is known about the Salon de La Section d'Or at the Galerie La Boétie (October 10–30). From the beginning it has been considered an important exhibi-

41. Reported by Raphaël Mairol, "Le Grand Palais fermé au Salon d'Automne?" *Comoedia* [Paris], October 13, 1912, 2. Extensive coverage of this scandal appears in *Comoedia*; see especially articles on November 25 and December 4, 1912.

42. I am indebted to M. Adéma for the following sequence of events. Apollinaire was with Picabia in Levallois (Paris) on October 17, 1912. On October 22, André Billy received a postcard from Apollinaire and Picabia postmarked in Etival. Louis Marcoussis received a postcard from Apollinaire mailed from Avallon on October 26 during the return to Paris.

43. For Duchamp's "Jura-Paris Road" project see Duchamp, *The Bride Stripped Bare by Her Bachelors, Even* (trans. George Heard Hamilton, typographic version Richard Hamilton, London, 1960); Arturo Schwarz, *The Complete Works of Marcel Duchamp*, 2nd. rev. ed. (New York, 1970) and Lebel, *Marcel Duchamp*, 25–26. For Apollinaire and "Zone" see Michel Décaudin (*Le Dossier d'alcools*, Geneva, 1960, 35, 37, 39, 41, 83, 85), Scott Bates (*Guillaume Apollinaire*, New York, 1967, 112, 181–82) and Pär Bergman ("*Modernolatria*" et "*Simultaneità*," Stockholm, 1962, 375–86).

tion; in fact, many believe it was the climactic exhibition of Cubism. It seems to have been that, yet as noted by René Blum in the catalogue preface, it was also the scheduled successor to the 1911 Exhibition of Contemporary Art, and it celebrated the fission, or "quartering" of Cubism as Apollinaire described it in his famous lecture in the gallery.

In accord with traditions of its Société Normande heritage, the Section d'Or, though dominated by Cubism, included diverse styles, decorative art, a series of lectures, and, for the first time, a bulletin.[44] The curious title of the exhibition, claimed by Jacques Villon, has never been satisfactorily explained. Contrary to the implications of that title, many of the thirty-one participants had no particular interest in mathematics, much less the "mystic ratio" of the golden section. However, Juan Gris did employ that ratio in some compositions, and its use as a title does reflect the widespread interests of many cubists in mathematics, proportion systems, non-Euclidean geometry and the fourth dimension.[45]

Such features of the Section d'Or were no more significant, however, than Apollinaire's baptism of the new tendency that had emerged from Cubism. In his gallery talk, "The Quartering of Cubism," on October 11, he divided Cubism into four categories—scientific, physical, orphic and instinctive, with emphasis on "orphic cubism," later called Orphism.[46] The text of the talk has not survived, but

44. For the single issue *Bulletin* of the Section d'Or, see Fry, ed., *Cubism*, 97–101. More detailed considerations of the exhibition are available in the Albright-Knox Art Gallery, Buffalo, *Painters of the Section d'Or*, September 27–October 22, 1967, catalogue by Richard West; Leonard Hutton Galleries, New York, *Albert Gleizes and the Section d'Or*, October 28–December 5, 1964, essays by Daniel Robbins and William A. Camfield; and William Arnett Camfield, "La Section d'Or," M.A. thesis, Yale University, 1961.

45. For non-Euclidean geometry and the fourth dimension see n. 13. For the golden section see William Camfield, "Juan Gris and the Golden Section," *The Art Bulletin*, XLVII, no. 1 (New York, March 1965), 128–34.

Villon claims he suggested the title "La Section d'Or" because he was interested in proportions and realized while reading Leonardo's *Treatise on Painting* the importance that Renaissance master attached to the golden section (Vallier, *Jacques Villon*, 118). Leonardo had made illustrations of the golden section for Luca Pacioli's book, *De Divina Proportione* (1509), but that ratio is not specifically discussed in the many references to proportion in his own treatise. It seems more likely that Villon and his colleagues encountered the golden section in the work of Seurat, an artist they admired for his "reasoned" paintings, or through the Académie Ranson, where Paul Serusier had taught the golden section and other proportional theories to at least two Section d'Or artists, Roger de La Fresnaye and Paul Véra. Meda Mladek has Kupka as another possible source ("Central European Influences," *František Kupka*, New York: The Solomon R. Guggenheim Museum, 1975, 32).

Daniel Robbins's proposal to include the "Section d'Art" and the *Bandeaux d'Or* in the geneology of La Section d'Or (Leonard Hutton Galleries, *Albert Gleizes and the Section d'Or*) further enriches our consideration of this critical exhibition.

46. The term "orphism," ultimately derived from the legendary Greek poet-musician Orpheus, was probably inspired by Apollinaire's association of the new painting with his concept of poetic Orphism as the creation of the artists' own world independent of the natural world. In his *Bestiaire ou cortège d'Orphée* (Paris, 1911) he had associated "pure poetry" and painting in a poem entitled "Orphée." It has also been sugggested that Apollinaire may have seen a pertinent article by Auguste Joly ("Sur le futurisme," *La Belgique artistique et littéraire*, XXVIII, no. 82, Brussels,

it is reflected in various articles and in drafts of *Les Peintres cubistes*. In the first of these, an article in mid-October,[47] the new art was linked to the "pure painting" that had preoccupied him earlier in the year; he still spoke of analogies to music and cited three familiar artists, Delaunay, Duchamp and Picabia. The oft-quoted definition of orphic cubism in *Les Peintres cubistes*, essentially completed in November 1912, maintained the emphasis on "pure art": "Orphic cubism is . . . the art of painting new structures with elements which have not been borrowed from visual reality, but have been created entirely by the artist and have been endowed by him with a powerful reality. The works of the orphic artists must simultaneously give a pure aesthetic pleasure, a structure which is self-evident and a sublime meaning, that is, the subject. This is pure art."[48]

Picasso and Léger were added to the orphist ranks in this statement, but as early as October 1912 Delaunay clearly enjoyed Apollinaire's favor. By "his own choice" the proud and temperamental Delaunay had not figured in either the Section d'Or or *Les Peintres cubistes*, but his paintings and theories increasingly dominated Apollinaire's concept of Orphism. Particularly influential was Delaunay's aesthetic statement entitled "Réalité, peinture pure" in which he dwelled on sensations of light, beauty, harmony, proportion, dynamism and simultaneity transmitted by the eye to the soul, the supreme sense.[49] These qualities, mirrored in his most recent paintings by luminous discs of color that created simultaneous effects of light, movement, form, space and content, were fully compatible with Apollinaire's long-standing poetic preoccupation with light and his burgeoning interest in simultaneity. During November–December 1912, Apollinaire adopted Delaunay's ideas, even his phraseology, and offered in the poem "Les Fenêtres"

July 1912, 68–74; reprinted as a futurist broadsheet). Joly regarded the futurists as descendants of the ancient Orphics and mystics who also sought "the 'sens direct' of things, of life and of thought." See Virginia Spate, "Orphism" (Ph.D. diss., Bryn Mawr, 1970, 99–100), and Martin, *Futurist Art and Theory*, 122.

47. Apollinaire, "Art et curiosité; les commencements du Cubisme" (*Le Temps* [Paris], October 14, 1912; *Chroniques d'art*, 263–66).

48. Apollinaire, *Les Peintres cubistes* (Paris, 1965), 57. According to the chronology established by Breunig and Chevalier ("Apollinaire et 'Les Peintres cubistes,' " *La Revue des lettres modernes*, nos. 104–107, Paris, 1964, 89–112), Apollinaire: 1) wrote Serge Férat on August 28, 1912, that his book [*Les Peintres cubistes*] was done; 2) corrected the first galleys in September; 3) received the second [Tzara] galleys on October 8 and corrected them during November while living with the Delaunays; and 4) corrected a third set of galleys before publication on March 17, 1913.

Most changes in the galleys occurred in pages based on Apollinaire's lecture at the Section d'Or, namely, chapter seven with its four categories of Cubism and statements on individual artists. Picabia was grouped with the "instinctive" cubists in the first galley but designated an "Orphic" cubist in the second galley—after the Jura trip.

The remainder of the book was composed of writings published from 1905 to 1912 and was intended to carry the title *Méditations esthétiques* with *Les Peintres cubistes* as a subtitle.

49. As noted by Virginia Spate ("Orphism," 97–99), this passage is similar to Leonardo da Vinci's comments on harmony, simultaneity and proportion in his *Treatise on Painting*. Delaunay took notes on Leonardo from *Textes choisi* (Fr. trans., Paris: Péladan, 1907, 174–80) and probably knew the 1910 French translation of *Tratatto delle Pintura* (*Traité de la peinture*, Paris: Péladan, 1910).

(Windows) tangible evidence of the resonance of all those qualities in painting and poetry.[50]

As Apollinaire's enthusiasm expanded, he extended Orphism's heritage to include Impressionism, Divisionism and Fauvism as well as Cubism; he opened its ranks to "instinctive" associates among the contemporary German expressionists and the Italian futurists; and he claimed the existence of Orphism in poetry.[51] By March 1913, Orphism, like Cubism before it, was beginning to strain under Apollinaire's propensity to find relationships in all the art which seemed new and vital to him. Chief among those new interests was a rapprochement to Futurism and a growing fascination with simultaneity as a central feature not only of some modern painting, but of poetry, drama, music and contemporary life. As those new interests first colored and then displaced Apollinaire's enthusiasm for Orphism, one loses track of the definition of it offered in *Les Peintres cubistes*. As early as March 1913, in his reviews of the Salon des Indépendants, Apollinaire no longer stressed pure art. Regarding Orphism he wrote instead of "simultaneity," of "suggestive painting which acts on us in the manner of nature and poetry," of "a vision more interior, more popular, more poetic of the universe and of life."[52] Delaunay's entry to that Salon, the quasi-figurative *Cardiff Team* (fig. 63), reminiscent of his epic *City of Paris* the year before, again won Apollinaire's warmest praise. He called it "the most modern painting of the Salon," estimable for its "grand popular character"—"one of the greatest praises one can give to a painter today."[53]

In the same room at the Salon, Picabia's highly abstracted *Procession* (fig. 64) received the following comments from Apollinaire:

> Picabia seems to me to have progressed. His canvas *Procession* lacks a veritable subject, all is dead surface . . . his blues torture the eye, his wine-colored squares and a certain curve at the left act with force.
>
> One must regard this as the incomplete effort of a gifted painter, as one regards a machine whose use we do not know but whose movement, whose force astonishes and disquiets us. All this seems too unconscious to confine

50. In December 1912, while living with the Delaunays, Apollinaire published in *Der Sturm* an article entitled "Réalité, peinture pure" (*Chroniques d'art*, 266–70), which was largely a quotation of Delaunay's statement. Essentially the same article appeared that same month in *Les Soirées de Paris*. In January 1913 Apollinaire and Delaunay went to Berlin for the latter's exhibition at Der Sturm (January 27–February 20, 1913). Apollinaire's lecture there served as the basis for an article on "Die Moderne Malerei" (*Der Sturm*, Berlin, February 1913; *Chroniques d'art*, 271–75) which placed Delaunay at the head of Orphism. On the occasion of that exhibition, Delaunay published an album of eleven prints prefaced by Apollinaire's poem, "Les Fenêtres," which had been inspired by Delaunay's paintings.

51. Apollinaire, "La Peinture moderne" (*Der Sturm*, February 1913; *Chroniques d'art*, 274).

52. Apollinaire, "Le Vernissage des 'Indépendants' " (*L'Intransigeant* [Paris], March 25, 1913; *Chroniques d'art*, 295).

53. Apollinaire, "A travers le Salon des Indépendants" (*Montjoie!*, Paris, March 18, 1913; *Chroniques d'art*, 302).

to orphic Cubism. Cerebral, instinctive, let us wait before praising, let us wait before honoring.[54]

A pause would seem to be in order at this point when the principal spokesman for Orphism appears to have attached no particular importance to abstraction as a feature in what he first announced as a movement of "pure painting" and which has long been regarded as France's first movement in abstract art.

And, in fact, if Orphism is to retain any coherence as the name for that movement of abstract art, Apollinaire's comments after early 1913 must be viewed guardedly. This warning is not intended to devaluate his overall quality as an art critic. Apollinaire possessed a superb sense for what was new and vital in art—and he supported it whether or not it ran counter to his innermost personal taste or to other work he was defending. He also had a remarkable eye for quality, and a thoughtful manner for adverse criticism which—even when directed at friends—did not always sacrifice friendships or his own intellectual integrity. Moreover, he had served both Orphism and Picabia well, but he was not inexorably bound to any man or movement—and both Orphism and Picabia posed problems for him. In all likelihood pure painting was not close to Apollinaire's innermost taste—witness the rapid absorption of Orphism into his new interest for simultaneity, his utter neglect of Kupka, his brief commentary on Kandinsky and Mondrian, the conversation with Picabia in Boulogne and, finally, his continuing susceptibility for Delaunay's grand epic paintings like *The City of Paris* and *The Cardiff Team*.[55]

In the instance of Picabia, Apollinaire simply did not see that the work of his friend fulfilled all the standards for Orphism, namely, a simultaneous experience of pure aesthetic pleasure, self-evident structure and sublime meaning. Apollinaire was not insensitive to the force of Picabia's work, but at the Salon des Indépendants he had found too much disquieting force and too little aesthetic pleasure. And in *Les Peintres cubistes* he also remarked on a conflict between formal properties and subject matter in Picabia's painting:

. . . with Picabia the form is still symbolic, while the color should be formal; . . .

. . . Picabia tried to give himself entirely to color, without ever daring, when approaching his subject, to grant it a personal existence. . . .

. . . These pictures are so far from a priori abstraction that the painter can tell you the history of each one of them; *Danses à la source* is simply the expression of a natural plastic emotion experienced near Naples.

54. Apollinaire, *Chroniques d'art*, 302. *Procession* is not fully documented as Picabia's entry to this Salon; however, it is the only known work by that title, it is compatible in style and subject with documented works of late 1912 and it was reproduced in early 1913 ("Picabia, Art Rebel, Here to Teach New Movement," *New York Times*, February 16, 1913, sec. 5, 9).

55. L.C. Breunig has argued persuasively that Apollinaire, long identified as the champion of Cubism, was uncomfortable in that role and shed it as soon as possible ("Apollinaire et le Cubisme," *La Revue des lettres modernes*, nos. 69–70, Paris, spring 1962, 7–24).

The possibilities of aesthetic emotion contained within this art, if it were pure, would be immense.[56]

Apollinaire's criticism was perceptive, not just for those paintings of 1912, but for the entire period of 1909–1912, and later periods as well. A survey of Picabia's work from 1909 to 1912 reveals a disconcerting restlessness as he passed through phases associated with Neo-Impressionism, Fauvism, a superficial synthesis of Fauvism and Cubism, Fauvism again in 1911, Cubism once more, and then Orphism—most phases further complicated by oscillations between relative abstraction and figuration. With the exception of some superbly resolved paintings, primarily in 1912, his work over these years was, in effect, one of search in borrowed visual idioms of others. And in that ceaseless flux one questions if he was ever really a fauvist, cubist or orphist.

Already some critics suggested his fluctuating work was the by-product of a wealthy playboy who was not a serious artist. It was true that Picabia did not depend on art for his living and was rarely known to pass up an adventure in order to work day and night in the studio. Nonetheless, he had been a serious member, an organizer even, of the young groups, and throughout the flux of his styles he had steadfastly pursued a way to express his inner experiences of life. Fortified by an extension of symbolist theories of *correspondance*, he had carried that search to its logical conclusion in abstract art. Yet he found no resolution there either. His overall course remained restless, and his individual paintings frequently harbored inner tensions. The abstract forms in *Abstract Composition* (fig. 65) cannot be satisfactorily accounted for by formal analysis; they refuse to subside into pattern, provoking instead speculation about their origin and meaning. Is, for example, the ribbonlike shape swinging across the left side of the drawing related to similar forms which appear on the left in *La Source* (fig. 60) or the tree trunk in a *Landscape* of 1910 (fig. 42)? Comparable tension between form and subject characterized *Caoutchouc* (fig. 38) as early as 1909. Visually and psychologically, *Abstract Composition* remains provocative, an expression of tension on several levels which becomes so prominent in Picabia's oeuvre after 1909 that it must be considered a basic characteristic of his personality and his vision. Such tensions waxed and waned throughout his career; occasionally they were resolved, sometimes left in conflict, and, in several masterpieces of 1913–1914, made synonymous with the spirit of the painting.

Happily, Apollinaire's reservation about the conflict of form and subject in Picabia's painting did not spoil a remarkable friendship. Picabia had found his way and he knew it. In January 1913 he headed for the Armory Show with exuberance, and if he ever read Apollinaire's criticism, it made not one iota of difference.

56. Apollinaire, *Les Peintres cubistes* (Paris, 1965), 88–90.

4. NEW YORK, THE ARMORY SHOW AND "291"

FROM 1912 through 1914 Picabia's work is of a piece, but his trip to New York for the Armory Show was of such consequence for himself and America that it merits a place apart.

The Armory Show was organized by the Association of American Painters and Sculptors, a secessionist group founded during December 1911 in opposition to the powerful, long-established National Academy of Design. Upon the election of Arthur B. Davies as president, a statement of purpose was read which called for exhibition not only of the works of the members but also of "the best examples procurable of contemporary art, without relation to school, size, medium or nationality."[1]

To that end, they began immediate plans for an exhibition in February or March 1913, and secured use of the cavernous armory of the Sixty-ninth Regiment of the National Guard. Ultimately, a circulating exhibition was arranged which, following the stand in New York (February 17–March 15), was shifted to Chicago and then to Boston. While the exhibition was being organized, the liberal but still rather conventional and America-oriented concepts of the Association expanded enormously after Davies saw a catalogue of contemporary avant-garde art on exhibit in Cologne, the so-called Sonderbund Show.[2] He dispatched Walter Kuhn to Cologne, and Kuhn was stunned by what he saw. Having arrived on the final day of the exhibition (September 30, 1912), he could not arrange anything with the Sonderbund, but he went on to The Hague, Berlin, Munich and Paris, where he put together the bulk of the Armory Show with the assistance of a fellow American painter and writer, Walter Pach. Pach was well acquainted with the contemporary art scene in Paris and a close friend of the Duchamp brothers, particularly Raymond Duchamp-Villon, who had invited him to the gatherings at Puteaux.[3]

1. See Milton W. Brown, *The Story of the Armory Show* (Greenwich, Conn., 1963, 41–42), for this statement and a comprehensive account of the *International Exhibition of Modern Art* popularly known as *The Armory Show*.

2. *Internationale Kunstausstellung des Sonderbundes Westdeutscher Kunstfreunde und Künstler*, Cologne, September 1912.

3. Pach published a study of Duchamp-Villon's work in 1924. The American artists Alfred Maurer and Jo Davidson also helped Kuhn in Paris.

Accordingly, Kuhn, and then Davies, when he arrived in November, met many Section d'Or artists in their rounds of the studios, galleries and bistros of Paris. The enthusiasm of Kuhn and Davies was infectious, and Picabia, disappointed by the surly reception of himself and his friends at the Salon d'Automne, not only agreed to enter four paintings in the show but resolved to attend the exhibition, apparently as a self-ordained cultural missionary with some notion that the proverbial pioneering spirit of Americans would make them more open-minded than the Parisians.

On January 14, 1913, Picabia and his wife sailed for New York on the *Lorraine*, leaving behind the convoluted affairs of Orphism and one painting for the Salon des Indépendants. While that painting, *Procession* (fig. 64), was being "skied" by the hanging committee and kept at arm's length by Apollinaire, Picabia was savoring one of the most delectable moments of his life.[4] It began on board ship where the rehearsals of a fellow passenger, the captivating dancer Napierkowska (illus. 6), provided an unexpected treat;[5] it continued in New York where, as the sole representative of the so-called European "extremists" and creator of two of the most notorious paintings in the exhibition, Picabia became an instant celebrity. He was an obliging subject for a stream of interviews, and charmed a good many of his critics, who accorded his paintings and aesthetic theories voluminous coverage in the press. Two days after the Armory Show closed in New York, Alfred Stieglitz gave him a one-man exhibition at "291" which revived the hubbub over modern art and Picabia's place in it. These events left a mark on American art—and on Picabia himself, who was stimulated not only by those art activities but by the entire vitality of the city and the people he met there, particularly those contributing to the golden age of Greenwich Village and the intellectual/artistic ferment at "291."

The Picabias were awed by the great bridges and skyscrapers of New York, its feverish vehicular traffic, hordes of workers, bright lights and garish signs. But their experience went beyond those impressive, superficial aspects of the city. Their hotel stood in the midst of one of New York's liveliest cultural centers. A short walk to the northeast lay the Sixty-ninth Regiment Armory on Lexington Avenue which housed the Armory Show. Two blocks south was Washington Square and the edge of Greenwich Village—then teeming with aspiring poets, painters, actors, playwrights, journalists, anarchists, socialists, union leaders and all varieties of the "new women," from suffragettes to birth controllers and free-lovers. Insofar as matters of birth control and women's suffrage touched social, economic and political rights, the "new women" sometimes found themselves working side

4. In a letter to Alfred Stieglitz, Edward Steichen wrote that Picabia's painting at the Salon des Indépendants had been "skied," that is, hung at the top of the room (undated letter of April 1913 in the Alfred Stieglitz Archive, Collection of American Literature, Beinecke Rare Book and Manuscript Library, Yale University, hereafter cited as A.S.A., Yale).

5. Stacia Napierkowska was a popular dancer of Polish origin who resided in Paris and had received considerable publicity there during 1912 (see the column "Echos," *Comoedia* [Paris], February 15, 1912, 1, and G. Davin de Champclos, "Désentravons-nous!" *Comoedia* [Paris], March 20, 1912, 2).

by side with such figures as Big Bill Haywood, head of the notorious I.W.W. (Industrial Workers of the World); Max Eastman, editor of a socialist magazine *The Masses*; and Emma Goldman, the grandmotherly-looking leader of an anarchist group which normally expressed itself in street rallies and in the magazine *Mother Earth*, but advocated direct action (murder) if necessary. The militant, confident spirit of those groups also rang out in magazines of the "new women," *The Freewoman* and *The Woman Rebel*, the latter directed by Margaret Sanger, who later faced prison for advocating radical changes in sexual mores and the dissemination of birth-control information. Harriet Rodman excelled in the more typical affronts to parents and society by flaunting conventions in hair, clothing and middle-class customs. Besides working for women's suffrage and explaining sex to her high-school students, Miss Rodman agitated for sane, simple attire, cropped her hair, wore sandals with a loose gown, and received callers in the nude. Young people by the score flocked to the Village as this spirit of revolt and freedom spilled out into the city and beyond.[6]

These individuals provide more than mere background for Picabia's visit in New York because he met many of them in the streets and restaurants of Greenwich Village and still others at Mabel Dodge's weekly soirées just across the street from his hotel.[7] Mabel Dodge, "new woman" *par excellence* at the most sophisticated social level, made front-page news with her parties that mingled editors and anarchists, Negro dancers and "extremist" painters, suffragettes, clergymen, free-lovers, Columbia University professors and Freudian psychologists. She sought to promote an exchange of energy and ideas among leaders of the most vital activities in New York, and to that end a representative from each group assumed the program one evening. At one of the soirées the Picabias attended, Big Bill Haywood described the proletarian society of the future, where art would serve the masses and all men would have time to be artists. Haywood's ideas were hardly compatible with those of Picabia, the arch-individualist, or with his closest friend in New York, Alfred Stieglitz.

Stieglitz (1864–1946) operated "291," aptly described by one critic as a trinity composed of a place, a spirit and a man and his associates. In 1913 the closest associates were Marius de Zayas, a Mexican caricaturist and art theorist, and Paul Haviland, the American representative for the Haviland porcelain factory in Limoges, France. The place was a small three-room gallery on Fifth Avenue where for six years Stieglitz had exhibited some of the best painters and photographers of Europe and America and had published the most important art journal in America, *Camera Work*. The spirit of "291" was a rousing blend of comrade-

6. Van Wyck Brooks, *The Confident Years* (New York, 1952), includes a good survey of this epoch which may be augmented by the publications of the various groups citied in the text and by daily newspapers. See also Delaware Art Museum, Wilmington, *Avant-Garde Painting and Sculpture in America 1910–1925*, April 4–May 18, 1975, edited by William Innes Homer.

7. For Mabel Dodge see Luhan, *Movers and Shakers*, vol. III of her *Intimate Memories* (New York, 1936).

ship and intellectual stimulation through far-ranging explorations into the nature and relationship of art, life and photography.[8]

Picabia never forgot his experiences in New York, and, conversely, American art may still reflect some consequences of his visit. Within a week after his arrival on January 20, two articles appeared with specific comments on Picabia, one of them by Stieglitz.[9] Those were followed on February 16, the eve of the Armory Show, by a full-page article in the *New York Times* which covered the history of Picabia's career, his recent work, aesthetic theories and motive for visiting America:

> France is almost outplayed. It is in America that I believe that the theories of The New Art will hold most tenaciously. I have come here to appeal to the American people to accept the New Movement in Art in the same spirit with which they have accepted political movements to which they at first have felt antagonistic, but which, in their firm love of liberty of expression in speech, in almost any field, they have always dealt with an open mind.[10]

Such articles and the vigorous public relations of the Armory Show notwithstanding, America was unprepared for what it encountered. Excepting a handful of artists and devotees of "291," few Americans had seen modern European art, and the American artists represented at the Armory Show were largely ignored amidst the paroxysms of outrage, laughter and sheer incredulity provoked by the European contributions. Duchamp, Matisse and Picabia, about in that order, sustained the heaviest critical reaction, but everyone more "modern" than the impressionists was designated an "extremist," and a field day at their expense—unparalleled before or after in this country—was enjoyed by press and public alike.

Picabia was represented by four paintings of 1912, *Paris*, *Souvenir de Grimaldi*, *Danses à la source* I and *Procession Seville* (figs. 55, 56; illus. 8; color pl. v), the latter two of which quickly numbered among the most controversial works in the show. *Procession Seville* became a target of the doggerel that flourished:

> Of fair Sevilla's towers
> I gain a faint impression,

8. For a substantial account of Alfred Stieglitz and his important place in American art, see *Camera Work*, 1903–1917; Waldo Frank et al., eds., *America and Alfred Stieglitz* (New York, 1934); William Innes Homer, *Alfred Stieglitz and the American Avant–Garde* (Boston, 1977); and Dorothy Norman, *Alfred Stieglitz* (New York, 1973).

9. Anon., "French Cubist Here," *American Art News*, no. 16 (New York, January 25, 1913), 4; Alfred Stieglitz, "The First Great Clinic to Revitalize Art," *New York American*, January 26, 1913, sec. CE, 5.

10. Anon., "Picabia, Art Rebel, Here to Teach New Movement," *New York Times*, February 16, 1913, sec. 5, 9.

> But still am several hours
> In rear of that "procession."[11]

Danses à la source I (fig. 56) was described as a "chipped block of maple sugar" and was attributed with having powers of vertigo over children.[12] After reading an interview with Picabia, a citizen of Brooklyn decided that Picabia and Duchamp were "sensationalists" who endeavored to give "a pictorial representation of the physical reaction to sense stimuli." He granted them the right to do whatever they pleased, but concluded with the opinion that their work "would be more appropriately placed in the lecture room of a professor of psychology than in an art gallery."[13]

Cartoon parodies abounded, and, ironically, several of them almost prophesied future styles in Picabia's career. A burlesque of *Procession Seville* (see illus. 7) is—excepting two feet at the bottom—as abstract as anything produced by Picabia during 1912–1914, and next to it is a spoof on Braque's *Poster of Kubelick* rendered as a fanciful machine two years in advance of Picabia's droll contraptions. An actual machine of sorts was exhibited on March 22 at the Academy of Misapplied Arts, one of several mock modern art exhibitions spawned by the Armory Show. The "Nonsense Machine" was described by a reporter at the opening:

> Gelett Burgess . . . has contributed four spasms and a Burgess Nonsensator, No. 4, with the Picabia Neurasthenic Transformer. The latter is a nut machine, a thing of spools and wires and interlocking cogs and trembling, sensitive steel fingers. In mechanics it represents Mr. Burgess's emotions after watching a taxi meter steadily for half an hour.
>
> The spasms are attempts to express in color Mr. Burgess's notions of a tea party of gentlemen, of a male and a female, and of mortal mind. Any one of the four might be 5 a.m. in Jack's.[14]

11. Quoted in Brown, *The Story of the Armory Show*, 111.

12. An anonymous journalist for the *Chicago Daily Tribune* (March 31, 1913) wrote:
"A crowd stood before the *Dance at the Spring* by Francis Picabia. A women and her little daughter studied the picture seriously.
" 'How many people can you see in the picture?' asked the mother.
" 'I think I can see one, mother,' the girl replied. 'Is it a puzzle picture?'
" 'No, it is supposed to show the dancer dancing. But where is the figure that you see?' asked the mother.
" 'It's gone. I can't see it now,' answered the girl in astonishment. 'O, mother, take me away. I feel dizzy. My head is swimming.' "

13. Letter to the editor in the column of Edith Cary Hammond, *New York Tribune*, March 11, 1913, 8.

14. Clipping from unidentified New York paper, ca. March 23, 1913 (Mabel Dodge Luhan Archive, Collection of American Literature, Beinecke Rare Book and Manuscript Library, Yale University, hereafter cited as M.D.L.A., Yale). For several months, mock Armory Show exhibitions were very popular. This one, sponsored by the Lighthouse for the Blind, was accorded extensive attention in the press, attracted over 5,000 visitors in two weeks and closed with a successful auction.

Such spoofs of Picabia's work may be related to his curious little watercolor, *Mechanical Expression Seen Through Our Own Mechanical Expression* (fig. 66). Contrary to the opinions of some authors, this manner of machine drawing was not pursued by Picabia until 1915, but it is prophetic of his later machines both in style and abstruse personal content, and it must be counted among the important experiences carried with him back to Paris.[15]

In addition to the humorous and antagonistic reactions to Picabia's work, there was some serious criticism which, to an extent, confirmed his faith in the intelligence and open-mindedness of his audience. Charles Caffin alone perceived more than a dozen Parisian critics combined:

> To all of us Picabia represents a newer problem than Matisse, and, for my own part, I admit that as yet his pictures do not appeal to me as much as the latter's. The one that I seem to have grasped is "La Procession Seville." I was attracted to it first by the grave and refined harmonies of black, rose, gray and ashy white tones. I felt a certain fascination in the forms and combination of forms. I began to enjoy its rhythms both of form and color. Then I gradually discovered that this pattern of color, which seemed to have been composed solely as a rhythmic arrangement of shapes and colors, really involved the suggestion of shrouded figures, carrying candles. Nor was it long before the mere suggestion developed into a strong mental impression, giving me the real sensation—not, it is true, of the actuality of the figures, but what the artist desired to give me—a real sensation of the spiritual impressiveness of the scene.
>
> So now . . . I begin to understand Picabia's method. It is the reverse of Matisse. While the motive of both is abstract expression, the latter's method involves a simplification that strips away as much as possible of the details of objective appearance. Picabia, on the other hand, emulating the musicians as he manipulates the notes of the octave, starts with a few forms, colored according to the key of the impression he wishes to create and combines and recombines these in a variety of relations until he has produced a harmonic composition in which one discovers that the theme of his subject has been built. In a word, he does not proceed from the concrete to the abstraction, but from abstraction to a spiritual impression of the concrete.[16]

15. This watercolor drawing was first exhibited in 1916 (Modern Gallery, New York, *Picabia Exhibition*, January 5–25, 1916, no. 15), but it may have been on hand at "291" during the Armory Show since the 1913 date is supported by internal evidence. The rectangular forms in the drawing are similar to those in works done in New York during 1913, especially *La Ville de New York aperçu à travers le corps* (fig. 77), and Picabia also employed the term "mechanical representation" in reference to art which copies the external appearance of things (see his preface, p. 50). The exact content of the drawing is not apparent despite its simple composition and references to "New York" and "Npierkowska [sic]."

16. Charles Caffin, "The International—Yes—But Matisse and Picabia?" *New York American*, March 3, 1913.

Caffin's statement was remarkable—for its sensitive comprehension, for its pithy description of Picabia's creation by a deductive approach and for its concentration on paintings and the creative process. Most of the serious criticism tended to focus on Picabia's art theories while paintings remained in the background. In fact, thanks to Picabia's vocal presence, most of the earnest attempts to understand any of the "extremist art" in the Armory Show depended to some degree upon his theories.

When confronted by objects which defied their training and education about the good, the true and the beautiful, floundering spectators grasped for any means that could make those objects more understandable or less threatening. Defenders of "extremist art" provided several arguments: they appealed to American respect for individuality; they invoked the popular notion of constant evolution; they even implied that "extremist art" was more "traditional" than what was commonly accepted as traditional because it had returned to the "primitive," emotional sources of art lost by illusionistic painting.[17] However, these arguments only encouraged open-mindedness; they did not offer much in the way of either visual or theoretical understanding for specific, dumbfounding objects. Those needs were largely served by Picabia.

Of the many interviews with him published by New York journalists, Hutchins Hapgood's article on February 20, 1913, is the most informative. Hapgood began by praising Picabia for his French "love . . . of the internal self, of its states, his clear analysis of those states, and his power of expressing them." Hapgood then proceeded to outline the "spirit" of what Picabia had said:

> Nearly all painting, now and always, has attempted in part at least to reproduce objects in nature—a woman, a child, a landscape, other objects or combinations of objects. Aristotle said that art is a copy of life.
>
> But that is just exactly what art is not. Art is a successful attempt to render external an internal state of mind or feeling, to project on to the canvas emotional, temperamental, mental, subjective states. All great art in the past has done that in spite of the fact that it has also had an element of the objective. . . . Great art has always been crystallized feeling which in itself is unseen.
>
> Photography has helped art to realize consciously its own nature, which is not to mirror the external world but to make real, by plastic means, internal mental states. . . .
>
> Art resembles music, he said, in some important respects. To a musician the words are obstacles to musical expression, just as objects are obstacles to pure art expression. . . .
>
> Art deals with deep, brooding fundamental, simple soul states. How do these states arise? They are the result of the artist's experience of life. Suppose the artist, in this case Picabia, has felt the quality of our skyscrapers, of our city and our life, and tries to reproduce it. This experience has affected

17. This subject is discussed more fully in Brown's *The Story of the Armory Show*, 150–59.

his mood. He renders plastic that mood on canvas. But the resulting picture has no skyscraper in it, and no city. It contains only the results of the skyscrapers and the city on his temperament.

But, of course, there must be technical means by which his soul-mood is rendered plastic, by which his soul-mood is expressed. What are these technical means? In Picabia's case they are the arrangement of line and color in such a way as to suggest the equilibrium of static and dynamic qualities, of rest and motion, of mass and balance.[18]

Among numerous Armory Show articles which reflect and/or cite the content of this interview, one by the critic of the *New York Times* stands out. He comprehended Picabia's advocacy of totally abstract art and granted that it was "an entertaining experiment, demanding intellectual activity and balance." However, he then observed: "But it [the theory] is terribly confused by the habit which Picabia and Picasso and all the others share, the habit of trying to explain themselves by titles. If their work is music it is programme music, and the programme plays an important part in their conception. Masterpieces are independent of programme, and we see no chance for the new school until it throws over the literary element and stands alone."[19]

Such criticism was not new to Picabia; it expressed essentially the same reservation voiced by Apollinaire, but Picabia effectively answered that criticism in some of the watercolors which he exhibited at Stieglitz's "291" immediately following the close of the Armory Show.

Soon after his arrival in New York, Picabia had begun a series of watercolors and drawings—partly as a result of exhilarating experiences since leaving Paris and partly in response to requests from an editor of the *New York Tribune*. That editor wanted to stage an exhibition comparing Picabia's reaction to such scenes as the mounted policeman at Fifth Avenue and Thirty-fourth Street with traditional representations of the same subject. Picabia declined the gimmicky proposal, but the *Tribune* published a full-page interview and three of the sixteen works which Picabia chose instead to exhibit at "291."[20]

The exhibition catalogue included sixteen watercolors and drawings (see figs. 67–77) and a preface by the artist which provoked almost as much response as the

18. Hutchins Hapgood, "A Paris Painter," *Globe and Commerical Advertiser* [New York], February 20, 1913, 8. This interview was conducted prior to the Armory Show and reprinted in *Camera Work*, nos. 42–43 (New York, April-July 1913), 49–51. Picabia's views as described by Hapgood have much in common with Apollinaire's almost exactly contemporary article, "Méditations esthétiques" (*La Vie* [Paris], February 8, 1913; see Apollinaire, *Chroniques d'art*, ed. L.C. Breunig, Paris, 1960, 277–82).

19. Anon., "History of Modern Art at the International Exhibition Illustrated by Paintings and Sculpture," *New York Times*, February 23, 1913, sec. 6, 15.

20. For the interview see Francis Picabia, "A Post-Cubist's Impression of New York," *New York Tribune*, March 9, 1913, pt. II, 1. Picabia probably saw John Marin's futurist studies of New York on exhibit at "291" early in February 1913.

drawings themselves.[21] The drawings dealt with three areas of personal experience—New York City, Negro songs heard there and the dancer Napierkowska.

Vestiges of recognizable forms exist in some of the works, for example, two watercolors of *New York* and studies for them (figs. 67–70) which suggest ships, skyscrapers and puffs of smoke. However, the degree of abstraction is considerable, and several other drawings are totally abstract insofar as they harbor no identifiable forms—or at least the search for them seems futile. The expressive content of *New York* (fig. 72) and *Chanson nègre* II (*Negro Song* II, fig. 73) is projected not by identifiable objects but by form, rhythm, color and composition—the soulful purple and brown of *Chanson nègre*, and the dynamic composition and energetic orange-red colors of *New York* which evoke sensations of heat, urban noise and vitality. None of the drawings was abstract, however, in origin or intention, as Picabia stressed by printing titles on the works and repeatedly explaining his aims:

> . . . you should quickly understand the studies which I have made since my arrival in New York. They express the spirit of New York as I feel it, and the crowded streets of your city as I feel them, their surging, their unrest, their commercialism, their atmospheric charm. . . .
>
> . . . I walk from the Battery to Central Park. I mingle with your workers and your Fifth Avenue mondaines. . . .
>
> I hear every language in the world spoken . . . the flags of all countries add their color to that given by your sky, your waters, and your painted craft of every size.
>
> I absorb these impressions. I am in no hurry to put them on canvas. I let them remain in my brain, and then when the spirit of creation is at flood-tide, I improvise my pictures as a musician improvises music.[22]

In contrast to most spectators who saw nothing in the paintings, a few overindulged their quest for forms, claiming to see in *Chanson nègre* I (fig. 74) everything from "large lips and a dancing figure," to "a dressed chicken standing on its head."[23] This drawing may generate such speculation, but hardly gratifies it even though it was based on a specific evening in a restaurant where, as reported in the press, Picabia "for the first time in his life—heard and saw an American Negro sing a 'Coon Song.' "[24] The two *Chanson nègre* drawings differ somewhat in effect,

21. Little Gallery of the Photo-Secession ["291"], New York, *Picabia Exhibition at the Little Gallery of the Photo-Secession,* March 17–April 5, 1913, preface by Francis Picabia and extract from Plato's *Dialogues*.

Contemporary reviews and photographs identify most of the works on exhibit despite the fact that six bore the same title, *New York* and three were called *Study for a Study of New York.*

22. Francis Picabia, "How New York Looks to Me," *New York American*, March 30, 1913, magazine section, 11. This is one of the most informative interviews with Picabia, but it essentially repeats points quoted from previous interviews.

23. The former image was offered by Philip Pearlstein in "The Symbolic Language of Francis Picabia" (*Arts*, XXX, New York, January 1956, 37–43). The latter interpretation came from an anonymous reporter ("Mr. Picabia Paints 'Coon Songs,' " *New York Herald*, March 18, 1913, 12).

24. Anon., "Mr. Picabia Paints 'Coon Songs,' " *New York Herald*, 12.

but both are dominated by purplish hues—which Picabia said sprang to his consciousness when he heard the songs—and both are abstract. Picabia's friend, the sculptor Jo Davidson, put it in his bumptious way:

> Picabia . . . is exhibiting his recent New York pictures. . . . One of his subjects is a "Danse Nègre"—a buck and wing by two coons he saw on the east side. Do you think he shows us the coons? Not he! He shows us a grand shuffle of deep purple and brown curved globs of color—not the cubes this time. He interprets that clog dance in color exactly as Richard Strauss would in music. And any one with half an eye can see what he means.[25]

The third theme represented in the exhibition dealt with a "star dancer," namely, the popular dancer Napierkowska (illus. 6), who had concluded a highly acclaimed stand in Paris and was en route to a tour of American music halls when the Picabias met her on the transatlantic steamer to New York. The New York run of her act was abbreviated after police inspectors found her performance too risqué,[26] but, on board the steamer, she had enjoyed an appreciative audience, including Picabia and—to his lasting amusement—a Dominican priest unable to conceal a keen interest in the rehearsals of Mlle Napierkowska and her troupe. The priest remained a furtive spectator, but Picabia had occasion to establish a closer relationship with Napierkowska during some rough days at sea when they were among the few not suffering from seasickness.[27]

For two years, aspects of that shipboard experience constituted a major theme in Picabia's work, beginning with two handsome watercolors brushed in New York, *Danseuse étoile et son école de danse* (*Star Dancer and Her School of Dance*, fig. 75) and *Danseuse étoile sur un transatlantique* (*Star Dancer on a Transatlantic Liner*, fig. 76).[28] In terms of visual properties alone, these are among the most appealing works produced by Picabia, but, literally speaking, form followed subject. Picabia made certain that no one missed the importance of his subjects by printing titles on the compositions, while form and color served aesthetic concerns as well as the subject. In these watercolors there are some identifiable forms—images of dancing figures in one and smokestack shapes in the other. Even the priest, though unidentifiable, is probably indicated as a "presence" by the color harmony in *Danseuse étoile et son école de danse*, notably a chord of blue, black, gray and buff which recalls *Procession Seville* and *Figure triste* (color pl. v; fig. 58) with their connotations of clericalism and melancholy.

25. Quoted by Harriet Monroe in "Davidson's Sculpture Proves that Artist Has Ideas," *Chicago Sunday Tribune*, March 23, 1913, sec. 8, 5.

26. Mlle Napierkowska was given top billing in a Broadway variety show that opened at the Palace on March 24, 1913 (advertisement in the *New York American*, March 23, 1913, sec. CE, 11). A short time later she was summoned to appear in court by Detective William McCafferty who "complained to the Magistrate Samuel D. Levy against certain features of Napierkowska's dance." McCafferty was supported by an inspector who also observed the dance (unidentified newspaper clipping, M.D.L.A., Yale).

27. Mme Buffet-Picabia in conversations with the author, July 1968.

28. Gabrielle Buffet-Picabia, "Picabia, l'inventeur," *L'Oeil*, no. 18 (Paris, June 1956), 35.

Though in many ways related to such paintings of 1912, the star-dancer drawings introduce the mounting density of content in Picabia's work of 1913–1914. The relatively simple, separate themes of dance and religious procession in 1912 have been combined and enriched by new elements—sexuality, humor and touches of a personal "philosophy"—as Picabia pits celibacy and sensuality, the exotic dancer living by her body and the cleric pledged to a life of the spirit.

La Ville de New York aperçu à travers le corps (*New York Perceived Through the Body*, fig. 77), the most unusual of the watercolors exhibited at "291," requires special attention. One author has suggested that Picabia deliberately signed and entitled the painting upside down in order to secure an inverted image.[29] While that may seem farfetched, the composition is improved when rotated 180 degrees, and there are other roughly contemporary examples of that practice. *Abstract Composition* (fig. 78) is a curiously disjointed composition that works relatively well with either long side as the bottom, but Picabia signed it along all four sides, permitting or inviting rotation at will. It is tempting to imagine that he was responding to critics who professed to be unable to differentiate between top and bottom in his works, but he may also simply have intended to stress the abstractness of the painting.

The critical response to these paintings ran much the same gamut established during the preceding Armory Show, but Picabia's preface for the "291" exhibition catalogue generated a controversy of new dimensions. In it he again defended abstraction as the visual language of the contemporary generation:

> The objective representation of nature through which the painter used to express the mysterious feelings of his ego in front of his subject "motive" no longer suffice [*sic*] for the fullness of his consciousness of nature. . . .
>
> . . . When we look at a tree we are conscious not only of its outside appearance but also some of its properties, its qualities, and its evolution. Our feelings before this tree are the result of this knowledge acquired by experience through analysis; hence the complexity of this feeling cannot be expressed simply by objective and mechanical representation.
>
> The qualitative conception of reality can no longer be expressed in a purely visual or optical manner. . . .
>
> The resulting manifestations of this state of mind which is more and more approaching abstraction, can themselves not be anything but abstraction. . . .
>
> But expression means objectivity otherwise contact between beings would become impossible, language would lose all meaning. This new expression in painting is "The objectivity of a subjectivity." . . .

29. The London Gallery, *The Cubist Spirit in its Time*, March 18–May 3, 1947, 23, catalogue by E.L.T. Mesens. This watercolor is signed and dated "Picabia 1912," but the date must be an error. In Paris during 1912 Picabia had no cause to deal with the subject of New York, and all contemporary accounts—including Picabia's own statements—refer to all the works on exhibit at "291" as studies made since his arrival in New York.

. . . The new form of painting puzzles the public only because it does not find in it the old objectivity and does not yet grasp the new objectivity. The laws of this new convention have as yet been hardly formulated but they will become gradually more defined just as musical laws have become more defined and they will very rapidly become as understandable as were the objective representation [sic] of nature. Therefore, in my paintings the public is not to look for a "photographic" recollection of a visual impression or a sensation, but to look at them as an attempt to express the purest part of the abstract reality of form and color in itself.[30]

Editors of the *World* reprinted the entire preface and offered for the best translation of it in 150 words or less "a prize of one original cubist drawing to be made by a member of the art staff of *The Sunday World* on any subject the winner may select."[31] Harriet Monroe, familiar with this preface and the earlier Hapgood interview, granted that Picabia brought one "to the picture by a process of reasoning as faultless as a multiplication table" but felt that spirit had been displaced by "mathematical formula."[32] Another critic lamented over what might be described as the absence of sufficient formula. Referring specifically to Picabia's description of the modern vision of a tree, this critic raised questions about abstract art that continue to engage its creators and audience alike:

> Very well; but there are a thousand and one ideas, practical, speculative and sentimental, that the sight of a tree might suggest and it might easily arouse different emotions or feelings in the same individual at different times. . . .
>
> . . . what chance would there be that anyone else would ever see the representation who would recognize in it his own feelings or emotions upon looking at a tree? . . . Now certainly no one has succeeded in expressing anything who has not succeeded in making his idea understandable to others.[33]

All of this criticism, whether earnest or humorous, endorsing or exasperated, augmented the widespread influence of Picabia's theories. His preface (or ex-

---

30. Little Gallery of the Photo-Secession ["291"], New York, *Picabia Exhibition*, March 17–April 5, 1913, preface by Francis Picabia. Immediately following this preface was printed an extract from Plato's *Dialogues—Philebus*: "Socrates: What I am saying is not, indeed, directly obvious. I must therefore try to make it clear. For I will endeavor to speak of the beauty of figures, not as the majority of persons understand them such as those of animals, and some paintings to the life; but as reason says, I allude to something straight and round, and the figures formed from them by the turner's lathe, both superficial and solid and those by the plumbline and the angle rule, if you understand me. For these, I say, are not beautiful for a particular purpose, as other things are; but are by nature ever beautiful by themselves, and possess certain peculiar pleasures, not at all similar to those from scratching; and colors possessing this character are beautiful and have similar pleasures."

This passage had been quoted earlier in New York in *Camera Work*, no. 36 (October 1911), 68.

31. *Sunday World* [New York], March 23, 1913.

32. Harriet Monroe, "Record-Breaking Crowds See the Cubist Exhibit," *Chicago Tribune*, April 13, 1913.

33. Unidentified magazine clipping (M.D.L.A., Yale).

cerpts from it) was reprinted from coast to coast. Mme Buffet-Picabia read it to the Civitas Club in Brooklyn, and personal disciples gave Chicago a particularly strong dose of it.[34] Jo Davidson, on hand for the opening of the Armory Show at the Chicago Art Institute, was an ardent spokesman, and Arthur Jerome Eddy relied heavily on Picabia's theories for a lecture there on modern art.[35] Later in the year, the preface was reprinted in Frederick Gregg's *For and Against* and expanded by Maurice Aisen, Oscar Bluemner and Mme Buffet-Picabia in articles for a special issue of *Camera Work*. It was kept before the public by Eddy's book, *Cubists and Post-Impressionism* (1914), and by Christian Brinton's book on the 1915 Panama-Pacific Exposition.[36]

At this point it should be stressed that Picabia was not the first to introduce such theories to America. The American philosopher George Santayana had lectured on similar aesthetic theories at Harvard University during the 1890s, and prior to the Armory Show, a number of American artists were familiar with such ideas, among them Arthur Dove, Max Weber, Alfred Maurer, Arthur Carles, Patrick Bruce, John Marin and Jo Davidson. Many of these artists had worked awhile in Paris between 1905 and 1912, some of them as students of Matisse. Most of them returned to America before the Armory Show and sooner or later became associated with Stieglitz's "291." Also during these years, *Camera Work* was laced with aesthetic theories akin to Picabia's—in exhibition reviews of the work of Max Weber, Picasso and Gelett Burgess; in articles by Sadakichi Hartmann,

34. Scrapbooks in the Stieglitz and Luhan Archives, Yale, have relevant clippings from several New York papers, the *Chicago Tribune*, the *Nashville Democrat*, *Philadelphia Bulletin*, *Milwaukee Sentinel*, *Hartford Times*, *Christian Science Monitor* and others. Mme Buffet-Picabia's appearance before the Civitas Club on April 9 was reported in the *Brooklyn Daily Eagle*, April 10, 1913, 7.

35. Concurrent with the Armory Show in Chicago, Jo Davidson exhibited thirteen of his sculptures ("systematically numbered and dated according to the wise system of musical composers") at the Reinhardt Gallery and talked about Picabia's theories with more fervor than Picabia himself. See Monroe, "Davidson's Sculpture," *Chicago Sunday Tribune*, 5.

In a lecture at the Art Institute of Chicago on March 27, Arthur J. Eddy discussed Picabia and the relation of his work to the theory of *correspondance*. See articles by Joan Candoer (*Chicago Examiner*, March 28, 1913) and Caryl B. Storrs, "Gazing at Weird Work of the Cubists is Rude Shock to One's Nervous System" (unidentified Chicago news clipping, ca. March 1913, M.D.L.A., Yale). Eddy, a Chicago lawyer and audacious individualist, purchased twenty-five works out of the Armory Show, including Picabia's *Danses à la source* I which he acquired on March 2 for $400 (Brown, *The Story of the Armory Show*, 99–101, 275).

36. Full references for the publications cited are: Frederick J. Gregg, ed., *For and Against: Views on the International Exhibition Held in New York and Chicago* (New York, 1913); *Camera Work*, special no. (New York, June 1913): Gabrielle Buffet, "Modern Art and the Public," 10–14, Maurice Aisen, "The Latest Evolution in Art and Picabia," 14–21, Oscar Bluemner, "Audiator et Altera Pars: Some Plain Sense on the Modern Art Movement," 25–38; Arthur Jerome Eddy, *Cubists and Post-Impressionism* (Chicago, 1914), passim, esp. chap. 6; Christian Brinton, *Impressions of the Art at the Panama Pacific Exposition* (New York, 1916), 22–23.

The article by Mme Buffet-Picabia is particularly lucid, and as applicable to modern art today as it was in 1913.

Marius de Zayas and Benjamin de Casseres; in excerpts from Bergson's *Laughter* and Kandinsky's *Concerning the Spiritual in Art*.[37]

It was a far cry, however, from the intellectual awareness of such theories and the inundation of the Armory Show, accompanied by Picabia's earnest arguments and the startling, physical confrontation with abstract art. Picabia's updated version of old symbolist theories swept the country, and even American artists long familiar with such aesthetics spoke as though they represented a new revelation.

Picabia's impact upon the canvases of American artists is more difficult to assess, partly because of the futility of filtering specific influences out of the monolithic wave of the Armory Show; partly, too, because of the sober, personal responses of America's early modern artists. Few if any outright disciples emerged, but within the prominent influence of Cubism and cubist-derived abstraction—for example, Morton Schamberg's abstract compositions of 1913–1914 (see fig. 79)—Picabia contributed as much as Picasso, Braque or Duchamp. Arthur Dove's *Pagan Philosophy* (fig. 80) might also reflect Picabia's presence in New York, although by the spring of 1913 Dove was a mature abstract painter capable of taking in stride both Picabia and the Armory Show.[38] On the other hand, Marius de Zayas's radical shift, during the spring of 1913, from murky symbolist caricatures to abstract caricatures (see fig. 81) suggests the direct impact of Picabia. Some of the geometrical shapes in those caricatures recall forms in Picabia's paintings and were intended by de Zayas to serve as "geometrical equivalents" of the "material self."[39]

37. For George Santayana see his *The Sense of Beauty* (New York, 1896).

An appendix would be required to sketch the history of the relevant aesthetic interests among American artists, but an adequate sampling is available in *Camera Work*: no. 27 (New York, July 1909), review of Alfred Maurer exhibition; no. 36 (New York, October 1911), reviews of Max Weber and Picasso exhibitions; no. 37 (New York, January 1912), review of Burgess exhibition and excerpt from Bergson's *Laughter*; no. 39 (New York, July 1912), extract from Kandinsky's *Concerning the Spiritual in Art*; no. 41 (New York, January 1913), articles by de Zayas.

38. By the beginning of 1912 Dove had developed a personal style of painting, intimate in scale and feeling and highly abstracted from motifs in nature. Along with it went theories like those of Picabia (George Cram Cook's review of a Dove exhibition, *Chicago Evening Post Literary Review*, March 29, 1912). Samuel Swift reported the meeting of these artists at "291" (article from the *New York Sun* quoted in *Camera Work*, nos. 42–43, New York, April–July 1913, 48–49):

". . . Arthur Dove . . . came into the sanctum of Alfred Stieglitz . . . while the new studies by Picabia were being placed upon the walls. . . . They conveyed to him as definite a meaning, in terms of emotion, as any formula might have done that had already been accepted the world over.

"Why? Because Dove himself, working independently . . . and evolving these symbols out of his inner consciousness, utilized similar modes of expression a year ago. If you wish evidence Mr. Stieglitz will produce the actual canvases from under his shelf. . . . And while Mr. Dove was looking at Picabia's cryptograms the Frenchman was confronted without warning with what Dove, of whom it is probable that he had never heard, had done. Recognition followed as quickly as though two persons born with strawberry marks upon their arms had suddenly discovered the fact."

39. De Zayas's caricatures were exhibited at "291" from April 8 to May 20, 1913. In the catalogue preface he wrote that representation was "only a matter of equivalents," and that he

However, within the sphere of "291," the matter of influence is more accurately described as one of mutual stimulation and reinforcement. Nothing in America changed the course of Picabia's aesthetic intent or formal development—that had been established in Paris during 1912. But Picabia did leave New York supercharged with projects and an admiration for everything about "291." Just prior to his departure, the Picabias, Mabel Dodge and others laid plans to open in Paris a gallery and magazine modeled after "291" and *Camera Work* respectively. That project was short-lived, but others, including some of the most important paintings in his career, continued to be nourished by the stimulating personal and intellectual exchanges enjoyed at "291."[40] Picabia's previous esteem of Nietzsche was also rekindled by Benjamin de Casseres, an active associate of "291" and a flamboyant disciple of that philosopher. De Casseres's articles in *Camera Work* exactly express Picabia's ideals of life:

> In poetry, physics, practical life there is nothing . . . that is any longer moored to a certainty, nothing that is forbidden, nothing that cannot be stood on its head and glorified. The indefinite, the uncertain, the paradoxical, is the scarlet paradise of intellectual intoxication.
>
> Anarchy? No. It is the triumph of discrimination, the beatification of paradox, the sanctification of man by man. . . .
>
> Nothing which lasts is of value. . . . That which changes perpetually lives perpetually. Incessant dying and renewing, incessant metamorphosis, incessant contradiction. . . .
>
> . . . I desire as many personalities as I have moods. . . . I desire to be ephemeral, protean. . . .
>
> I find my supremest joy in my estrangements. . . . I desire to become unfamiliar to myself. . . . I cling to nothing, hope for nothing. I am a perpetual minute.[41]

represented "(1) The spirit of man by algebraic formulas; (2) his material self by geometrical equivalents; (3) his intellectual force by trajectories within the rectangle that encloses the plastic expression and represents life."

Similar ideas were "in the air" at "291" as early as 1911–1912. See Paul Haviland's review of the Gelett Burgess exhibition in *Camera Work*, no. 37 (New York, January 1912), 46–47. See also Claude Bragdon, *Man the Square: A Higher Space Parable* (Rochester, N.Y., 1912), 65, which came to my attention while reading the Ph.D. dissertation of Linda Dalrymple Henderson ("The Artist, 'The Fourth Dimension' and Non-Euclidean Geometry. 1900–1930: A Romance of Many Dimensions," Yale University, 1975, fig. 38).

40. The participants in the gallery project were the Picabias, Mabel Dodge, Jo and Yvonne Davidson, Maurice Aisen, Charles Fitzgerald and a Mrs. Blumenthal. It disintegrated quickly (see letter from Aisen to Stieglitz, May 24, 1913, A.S.A., Yale, and Luhan, *Movers and Shakers*, 165–67). Mme Buffet-Picabia revived it later in the year (letter to Stieglitz, November 17, 1913, A.S.A., Yale); that too failed.

41. Benjamin de Casseres, "Modernity and the Decadence," *Camera Work*, no. 37 (New York, January 1912), 17–19. De Casseres (1873–1945) was a newspaperman and writer on the staff of the *New York Herald* during the years of his close association with "291" from about 1909 to 1913. After an unsuccessful campaign for mayor of New York in 1913 he was no longer active at "291" but continued to work as a critic, columnist and author.

Whereas de Casseres articulated Picabia's general view of life, Stieglitz and particularly de Zayas, shared many of Picabia's convictions about art and photography. Stieglitz's photographs were striking evidence that art could be produced with a machine (the camera), although both this master photographer and de Zayas were absorbed in differentiating the nature of photography and art (painting) during the very months of Picabia's sojourn in New York. De Zayas's writings on the subject are murky and laborious, but with careful reading their essence coalesces. Initially, he argues, art was subjective, and still is subjective in the sculpture of the African Negroes who try "to reproduce . . . not form itself, but the expression of the sentiment or the impression represented by a geometrical combination."[42] With the rise of civilization, however, art had become more and more objective until that mode of expression became exhausted. Modern art had broken that tradition and was returning to a subjective expression, not in the manner of the primitive artists but with the assistance of science, anthropology, psychology and mathematics, which in recent generations had proved that what the primitives attributed to supernatural elements were really natural qualities existing within man. Modern art properly deals with emotional and intellectual truth, with metaphysics and psychological analysis; it represents moods and states of mind with abstract equivalents of feeling, in the manner of music. Photography, to the contrary, properly deals with objective, material truth, with concrete forms rather than abstract equivalents.

No subtle analysis is required to recognize the substantial overlaps between Picabia's interests and de Zayas's heady, Hegelian synthesis of "objective" and "subjective" expression. Picabia's comment, for example, about the "new expression in painting" being "the objectivity of a subjectivity" closely parallels de Zayas's conclusion. Questions of precedence among these two men do not seem useful. Present documents record Picabia's earlier departure along this route, but each man developed his views independent of the other and gave them mature expression about the same time. Their relationship was more that of a perfectly timed mutual reinforcement. If influences are sought, it should be noted again that the basic tenets of both men derived from the symbolist generation; in the instance of the very term "objectivity of a subjectivity," Picabia's source was the symbolist writer, Gustave Kahn.[43] It should be stressed, however, that they had developed the older symbolist position to incorporate abstract art and all relevant data from

42. Marius de Zayas, "Photography," *Camera Work*, no. 41 (New York, January 1913), 17–20. The following synthesis of de Zayas's thought is based on a booklet written in collaboration with Paul Haviland, *A Study of the Modern Evolution of Plastic Expression*, the preface to de Zayas's exhibition of caricatures at "291" and five of his articles in *Camera Work*: "Photography" and "The Evolution of Form—Introduction," no. 41 (New York, January 1913); "Photography and Artistic Photography," nos. 42–43 (New York, April–July 1913); "Modern Art—Theories and Representation," no. 44 (New York, October 1913); and "Material, Relative and Abstract Caricatures," no. 45 (New York, January 1914).

43. Gustave Kahn, "Réponse des Symbolistes," *L'Evénement* [Paris], September 28, 1886, quoted in John Rewald, *Post-Impressionism* (New York, 1956), 148.

the social and physical sciences. Stieglitz thought of "291" as a laboratory where experiments were conducted and problems solved. De Zayas was prone to such exaggerated claims as: "We are now in a position for the first time to clear up the complex evolution of Form, if not of Art . . . because we are in possession of the data needed from Anthropology, Psychology, etc., . . ."[44] Picabia himself wrote that the laws of the new expression in painting "will become gradually more defined just as musical laws have become more defined and they will very rapidly become as understandable as were the objective representation [*sic*] of nature" (see p. 51).

Though Picabia never seriously considered formulating "laws," such statements and his activities throughout 1912–1913 attest to serious convictions often dismissed by subsequent critics enamored by the Nietzschean and dada characteristics of the man. This is not to deny those traits. De Casseres rightly praised Picabia as a descendant of Heraclitus, for whom chance, the irrational and constant change were principles of existence. In the near future those principles became increasingly descriptive of Picabia's life, but never to the exclusion of other characteristics of that complex man. And in the experience of Stieglitz, those "other characteristics" were to the fore during the Armory Show visit. The day after the Picabias' departure for France he wrote to the Philadelphia painter Arthur B. Carles:

> Picabia left yesterday [April 10]. All at "291" will miss him. He and his wife were about the cleanest propositions I ever met in my whole career. They were one hundred percent purity. This fact added to their wonderful intelligence made both of them a constant source of pleasure. Picabia came to "291" virtually daily and I know he will miss the little place quite as much as we miss him. It is all very wonderful. He has let us have five of his New York things, so that we can use them as we see fit.[45]

44. De Zayas, "The Evolution of Form—Introduction," *Camera Work*, 44–48. Stieglitz's fondness for characterizing "291" as a laboratory is discussed by William B. McCormick in "Patrons Vote to Decide Fate of Photo-Secession Gallery at No. 291 Fifth Avenue," *New York Press*, October 4, 1914, 6.

45. Letter from Stieglitz to Carles, April 11, 1913 (A.S.A., Yale).

5. CULMINATION OF THE "PSYCHOLOGICAL STUDIES," PARIS, 1913-1914

FRANCIS and Gabrielle returned to a lively Paris in late April 1913. They picked up immediately with old friends Duchamp and Apollinaire, and with a new acquaintance, Gertrude Stein.[1] As predicted by Stieglitz, however, "291" was missed; they extolled its virtues throughout the capital, talked of returning to America and maintained significant contact with their New York friends through an exchange of letters, magazines, photographs and press clippings.[2] Personal contact was also reestablished when Paul Haviland visited Paris in the summer of 1913 and de Zayas worked there for several months during 1914. This continued relationship had substantial consequences for French and American art after the outbreak of World War I. In the meantime, Picabia produced some of the best work in his entire career while modern art in the cultural center of the western world was at the peak of its energy.

Perhaps the most spectacular single event was the première of Stravinsky's *Rite of Spring* (May 30, 1913), but poetry and painting in Paris were incredibly vital. In the visual arts alone the production of 1913–1914 included the evolution of synthetic Cubism with its features of collage and construction; the mature development of abstract art by Kupka, Delaunay, Picabia, Mondrian and others; the proto-dada work of Marcel Duchamp; the proto-surrealist paintings of Giorgio de

1. Alfred Stieglitz and Mabel Dodge had urged the Picabias to meet Gertrude Stein, and Picabia wrote Stieglitz on June 16, 1913 (A.S.A., Yale), that an enjoyable meeting had occurred although they did not agree on every point. Miss Stein later acknowledged that during 1913 she had not liked Picabia's "incessantness" and "delayed adolescence," but during the 1930s she and Picabia established an important friendship (*The Autobiography of Alice B. Toklas*, New York, 1933, 164; and Gertrude Stein, *The Flowers of Friendship*, ed. Donald Gallup, New York, 1953, 74).

2. An anonymous author recorded in *La Vie parisienne*, May 3, 1913, 309, that Picabia had returned to Paris "enchanted with the land of dollars" and talking with enthusiasm about the sale of paintings "brushed in half a day." The Stieglitz-Picabia correspondence (A.S.A., Yale) documents the exchange of material between these friends, Picabia's intent to visit New York on three occasions and Gabrielle's pursuit of the project for a gallery.

Chirico and the influential "primitivizing/classicizing" modes of André Derain. The dynamic conditions in music, art and literature were reflected in important avant-garde journals, among them two founded in 1912—Apollinaire's *Soirées de Paris* and Barzun's *Poème et drame*—and two new magazines that entered the arena during Picabia's sojourn in New York, Canudo's *Montjoie!* and Beauduin's *La Vie des lettres*.[3] Prominent in those publications was a concern for simultaneism in contemporary art and life—and as that property seemed more and more to be the touchstone for the epoch, competition over priority and proprietorship led to simultaneous warfare among the painters and poets. The complex web of issues and participants is outside the focus of this study, but Apollinaire, Delaunay, Umberto Boccioni, Henri-Martin Barzun and Blaise Cendrars were among the principal protagonists. Apollinaire's concepts of simultaneism were nourished by the work of all those about him, but especially by Cendrars's expression of modern life, which was characterized by the simultaneity of events, enormous energy, a taste for popular culture and the impact of the "machine age." It was those qualities of modern life which eclipsed Apollinaire's interest in "pure painting," leading instead to a rapprochement with Boccioni and the futurists, and his embrace of Delaunay's *Cardiff Team* (fig. 63) at the 1913 Salon des Indépendants. Abstraction was no longer an issue in that painting—instead it put simultaneous formal properties of light, color, movement and space to the service of subjects referring to a new age abuilding, popular culture, and machines with contemporary-cosmic parallels.[4]

Picabia was a keen observer of that activity, and his friendship with Apollinaire grew apace, but his own work maintained the independent, intensely personal course in abstract art which had evolved during the latter half of 1912.

3. For *Montjoie!* (Ricciotto Canudo, ed., Paris, 18 numbers from February 10, 1913, to June 1914) see the article by N. Blumenkranz-Onimus, " 'Montjoie!' ou l'héroïque croisade pour une nouvelle culture" (L. Brion-Guerry, ed., *L'Année 1913*, II, Paris, 1973, 1105–1116). For *Les Soirées de Paris* see Galerie Knoedler, Paris, *Les Soirées de Paris*, May 16–June 30, 1958, and also in *L'Année 1913*, II, Blumenkranz-Onimus's article on "Les 'Soirées de Paris' ou le mythe du moderne," 1097–1104. For *La Vie des lettres* see the chapter "Nicolas Beauduin et son 'paroxysme' " in Pär Bergman's *"Modernolatria" et "Simultaneità"* (Stockholm, 1962), 279–90. In the same publication see the chapter on "Henri-Martin Barzun et son 'simultanéisme,' " 291–307.

4. For thoughtful and partly differing studies on the relationship of Cendrars and Apollinaire, see Bergman, *"Modernolatria" et "Simultaneità,"* 308–36, 375–87; Michel Décaudin, *Le Dossier d'alcools* (Geneva, 1960), 30–31, 81–89; *Mercure de France*, Blaise Cendrars number (Paris, May 1962, especially Robert Goffin's contribution), 105–112.

For an introduction to Apollinaire's relationship to Delaunay and Boccioni see Guillaume Apollinaire, *Chroniques d'art*, ed. L.C. Breunig (Paris, 1960), 292, 295, 297, 302, 333–34, 344–46, 348–49, and Bergman, op. cit., 270–71, 354–59.

Apollinaire last wrote about Orphism on the occasion of the *Erster Deutscher Herbstsalon* (Berlin, September 20–December 1, 1913), which he called a "salon" of Orphism (*Chroniques d'art*, 344–46). Picabia was represented there by an unidentified study of New York and *Procession* (fig. 64). Delaunay was extensively represented and praised by Apollinaire, but one of the latter's pro-Boccioni remarks permanently strained the Delaunay-Apollinaire friendship. By the 1914 Salon des Indépendants, Apollinaire eliminated Orphism as one of the two basic movements in modern art. At that time, he held that the two major currents were based on the Cubism of Picasso and the Cubism of André Derain (*Chroniques d'art*, 348–49).

While still in New York, Picabia had indicated his intention to undertake paintings that would synthesize his experiences there, and as early as June he announced to Stieglitz that he had plunged into the project: "I am working at the moment on a very large painting which concentrates several of my studies exhibited at 291—I am thinking moreover of a painting, a purer painting of a dimension having no title, each painting will have a name in rapport with the pictorial expression, [an] appropriate name absolutely created for it. . . . Excuse the brevity of my letter. I am a little fatigued and tormented by my new evolution."[5]

According to Gabrielle, he was indeed so preoccupied with his painting that he worked day and night, hardly pausing to eat, and just two days after the above letter to Stieglitz, forgot a call to his studio announcing the birth of a daughter (Gabrielle, called Jeannine).[6] In August, Gabrielle wrote Stieglitz that her husband was still struggling "without success . . . very neurasthenic and fatigued,"[7] but by the opening of the Salon d'Automne in November, Picabia had completed at least two enormous paintings, *Udnie* and *Edtaonisl* (fig. 82; color pl. VI), which count as "masterpieces," both in the framework of his own career and in the context of modern art.[8]

Udnie and *Edtaonisl* provoked considerable reaction at the Salon, most of it hostile. One critic bemoaned what impressed him as "a gigantic enlargement of trunks ripped open in a train crash"; Gustave Kahn saw as "tragic" the ribbonlike lines and "tango of color" in *Udnie*, and André Salmon fumed over the prominent position given Picabia's paintings in the Salon: "Bah! The place, if not the one of honor, is not bad in that regard. One sees Picabia's canvas six times while making the tour of the galleries and mounting the stairs."[9]

Apollinaire alone praised the paintings: "I find them very important. And the ridicule changes nothing." But he responded more on instinct than understanding and, having proclaimed their importance, lapsed into generalities about "ardent and lyrical paintings from the imagination of the artist in contact with nature."[10] The bewilderment of one earnest reporter led, however, to an informative interview. Admitting that he, like thousands of spectators, was irresistibly attracted to *Udnie* and *Edtaonisl* but unable to advance beyond astonishment, the reporter asked for public enlightenment. Picabia "responded softly, 'The Public! . . . But, always, what concerns art was inaccessible to it!' "

"Then, explain it to the elite," rejoined the reporter, and Picabia replied:

> But the elite understands . . . in part. . . . Follow me. A certain melody by
> Mendelssohn is entitled "The Marriage of the Bees." Let the gods be my wit-

5. Picabia letter to Stieglitz, June 16, 1913 (A.S.A., Yale).

6. Gabrielle Buffet-Picabia, "Picabia, l'inventeur," *L'Oeil*, no. 18 (Paris, June 1956), 35.

7. Letter from Buffet-Picabia to Stieglitz, August 1913 (A.S.A., Yale).

8. Salon d'Automne, Paris, November 15, 1913–January 5, 1914, no. 1675 *Edtaonisl* (*ecclésiastique*) and no. 1676 *Udnie* (*jeune fille américaine*) [danse].

9. For these criticisms see *Le Matin* [Paris], November 16, 1913; Gustave Kahn, "Art. Le Salon d'Automne," *Mercure de France* (Paris, December 1, 1913), 648; and André Salmon, "Le Salon d'Automne," *Montjoie!*, nos. 11–12 (Paris, November–December 1913), 9.

10. Apollinaire, *Chroniques d'art*, 337, 342.

ness, nothing in this admirable music ever brought to mind a hornet. It cannot therefore be a matter of an imitative harmony. . . . However . . . one accepts its title by tradition and without debating it. Then, for a painting, why not accept a sign which does not evoke accepted conventions?

Udnie is no more the portrait of a young girl than *Edtaonisl* is the image of a prelate, such as we commonly conceive them. They are memories of America, evocations from there which, subtly opposed like musical harmonies, become representative of an idea, of a nostalgia, of a fugitive impression.

One needs, it is true, an education and a special training of the eye and the intellect to savor my art in its plenitude. It is not of the popular domain, as I said.[11]

In addition to reasserting aesthetic defenses employed earlier in New York, Picabia's statement provides welcome insight into three aspects of his work at this moment in his career. It confirms the themes of the paintings as "memories of America," and, secondly, it records a turning point in his attitude toward his work and the public. He accepted more fully the fact that his art was a personal, even private, means of expression, and though he always delighted in the few who could savor his work "in its plenitude," he seldom troubled himself about the education or understanding of the public. Finally, the reporter himself gave witness to the continuing tension within Picabia's work and the corresponding reaction generated in its audience. Though gripped by the striking visual properties of the paintings, the reporter was not content to let it go at that. In the face of abstract forms and incomprehensible titles, he still felt compelled to pursue subject matter and meaning. That tension of form, subject and content was not new in the experience of Picabia's work, but rare indeed were the stimulating richness and balance of those properties in *Udnie* and *Edtaonisl*.

These paintings were conceived as a pair; each is nine feet square and, as noted by Picabia, "subtly opposed like musical harmonies" in color, composition and psychological effect. *Udnie*'s composition is extroverted; from a central cluster of forms her rhythms explode in aggressive color planes of blue, white, green and gray which evoke the hard, sharp-edged qualities of finely rolled steel. *Edtaonisl* is an introverted composition; its central cluster of soft gold and cream-colored shapes is embedded in a writhing field of somber blue, black, brown and purple forms most reminiscent of the color harmonies in *Chanson nègre* and *Danseuse étoile et son école de danse* (figs. 73–75).

These formal properties appear to be intimately coordinated with the subject and content of *Udnie* and *Edtaonisl* insofar as they can be determined. The question of content, or meaning has eluded most spectators from the beginning, and, to be sure, no "definitive" interpretation is possible. Nevertheless, for Picabia con-

11. Anon., "Ne riez pas, c'est de la peinture et ça représente une jeune américaine," *Le Matin* [Paris], December 1, 1913, 1. *Udnie* (fig. 82) is reproduced in this review.

tent was primary, and he offered clues beginning with the titles of the paintings and contemporary statements made both in private and in public. Only the primary titles *Udnie* and *Edtaonisl* appear on the canvases, but in the Salon catalogue he entered the full titles, *Udnie (jeune fille américaine; danse)* (*Udnie* [*Young American Girl; Dance*]) and *Edtaonisl (ecclésiastique)* (*Edtaonisl* [*Ecclesiastic*]). His intentions are more easily followed in the latter. As indicated by Philip Pearlstein, the alternate letters of this invented word form two French words

$$\text{E T O I L [E]}$$
$$\text{D A N S [E]}$$

which, in conjunction with the subtitle *ecclésiastique* indicate the familiar subject of the Dominican priest and Napierkowska. This theme has been verified by Mme Buffet-Picabia and Picabia's good friend, Georges Isarlov, who wrote of Picabia's contemplation of the "ocean, a dancer, [and] a clergyman of furtive glance" who were represented "in their eternal human rapport" in a "condensed form" where the "rhythm of the dancer, the beating heart of the clergyman, the bridge of the packetboat . . . [and] the immensity of the ocean strike and entangle each other in metallic forms."[12]

Edtaonisl's companion piece, *Udnie*, has not yielded as far to interpretive efforts. Its color harmony has less precedent in Picabia's career, and the title has not been decoded, although it is another invented, composite word reflecting a contemporary fascination for creative play with language. Apollinaire's "POF" technique and Duchamp's "experiments" with grammar were examples of that interest well known to Picabia.[13] One plausible suggestion holds that *Udnie* is an adaptation of the French word for nudity, *nudité*, but other hypotheses are more intimately related to the painting. An adaptation of Undine seems particularly relevant by combining a seductive water spirit with the subtitle themes of "young American girl" and "dance."[14]

12. Pearlstein, "The Paintings of Francis Picabia" (M.A. thesis, New York University, Institute of Fine Arts, 1955), 109. Georges Isarlov, *Picabia peintre* (Paris, 1929), 12. Mme Buffet-Picabia first mentioned *Udnie* and *Edtaonisl* in a letter to Stieglitz (November 17, 1913, A.S.A., Yale): "I am sending you 2 photographs of the paintings my husband is exhibiting at the Salon d'Automne. I think they may interest you for they are the result of all the impressions of New York and of the studies which he exhibited with you." In a later article, "Picabia, l'inventeur," *L'Oeil*, 35, she identified Napierkowska and a Dominican priest as specific themes in the two paintings.

13. Apollinaire described the "POF" technique in the *Mercure de France* (Paris, November 16, 1917; cited in Marcel Adéma, *Apollinaire*, New York, 1955, 151): "Before the war, among friends, we had invented the game of pof, which consisted in taking a name and making each one of its letters the initial of a word, the words together forming a sentence. The name of the game came from the initials P.O.F., which stood for Parti Ouvrier Français."

Duchamp's notes for *The Green Box* indicate that he subjected language to the same wry, creative assault directed at sex, science, art and machines. He suggested, for example, a new language made of "Prime words (divisible only by themselves and by unity)," whose characteristics would include the use of colors "to differentiate what would correspond in this [literature] to substantive, verb, adverb, declensions, conjugations, etc." See Marcel Duchamp, *Marchand du sel: Ecrits de Marcel Duchamp* (Paris, 1958), 43.

14. Pearlstein, *op. cit.*, 109, first suggested the adaptation of *nudité*. The relevance of

While those themes were primary to Picabia's concerns, they do not dominate our experience of the paintings. Like that early reporter, one is simultaneously stimulated by the abstract, visual properties of *Udnie* and *Edtaonisl*, by an impulse to identify their emphatic forms, and by a desire to know the "meaning" of those forms. More than in previous works, the forms and colors in *Edtaonisl* can stand as a striking example of "pure painting"; yet the colors also set a mood and refer by past association to themes of a priest, a dancer, troubled celibacy and mournful songs. The tangle of forms and tormented space in *Edtaonisl* are likewise one with those themes and moods, just as the brassy forms and extroverted rhythms of *Udnie* may be presented as plastic-psychological equivalents for Picabia's impressions of young American girls, dance and, perhaps, New York and Napierkowska.

This synthesis of time and space, of inner experiences and exterior events, was Picabia's expression of the ubiquitous cultural concern for simultaneity in contemporary art and life. One may still sense in it a background in synthetic Cubism with touches of Duchamp, Léger and Futurism, but that background has been transformed into a potent individual creation—intensely personal in content, grand in scale, abstract in form and addressed to a universal audience.[15]

Picabia's successful struggle over *Udnie* and *Edtaonisl* opened a productive period which was complemented by the activities of his wife. Gabrielle, having passed the early, demanding months with their baby daughter, contributed occasional articles on contemporary music to *Les Soirées de Paris* and revived the project for a gallery modeled after "291." Works by Braque, Picasso, Duchamp and Picabia were assembled, and about January 1914 the gallery opened with Georges Ribemont-Dessaignes and Jean Cocteau as associates, the latter apparently as editor of a magazine.[16] Later in January, the Picabias departed on their customary

---

Undine was stressed by Harriet Anderson in conversations with this author while he was pondering that possibility and an obscure contemporary reference to *la vie unanime*.

During the 1940s, in a discussion about pre–World War I days in Paris, Picabia himself made an intriguing statement—perhaps partly in jest? He told his young friend, Henri Goetz, that all the talk then about the fourth dimension had made him want to do something one-dimensional; *Udnie* was "uni-dimensionel" (interview with Henri Goetz and Christine Boumeester, Paris, June 20, 1968).

15. *Udnie* is related to synthetic Cubism in its creation of an "image" by means of "cutout" color planes, abstract in themselves and assembled together—rather than color planes arrived at by reducing and/or fragmenting existing forms in nature. The abstract conception of *Udnie* is verified by a study (fig. 83) which bears some resemblance to forms in the upper center of *Udnie*, notably the white biomorphic shape, the dark ribbonlike band sprouting from it and several adjacent forms. Some of these forms can be traced back to earlier works, for example, the biomorphic shape which appears (reversed) in *Danseuse étoile sur un transatlantique* (fig. 76) and curvilinear bands which appear in *Chanson nègre* I (fig. 74).

16. For the music criticism, see Gabrielle Buffet, "A propos de vernissage" and "Musique d'aujourd'hui," *Les Soirées de Paris* (December 15, 1913), 5, and (March 15, 1914), 181–83.

Mme Buffet-Picabia announced the revised gallery in a letter to Stieglitz on November 17, 1913 (A.S.A., Yale): "I am organizing a gallery in Paris on the order of the idea we discussed so much in New York last year. . . . Do I need to tell you that the memory of '291' is a great point of

winter jaunt through Switzerland and the Midi,[17] and that absence, plus the specter of war over Europe, reduced the gallery to no more than a lingering dream for Picabia. His painting, however, was little affected by those travels. A score of interesting works were produced, some of them documented in 1913 before his departure to Switzerland and others during 1914. Still more are attributable to 1913–1914 on stylistic grounds.

Catch as Catch Can (fig. 84) continues both the quality of *Udnie* and *Edtaonisl*, and Picabia's custom of basing paintings on events in his personal life. Gabrielle preserved a vivid memory of its origin. One evening while she, her husband and Apollinaire were eating in a restaurant, they became fascinated by a fearsome Chinese wrestler seated nearby. They followed him to the match of catch-as-catch-can, and Picabia commemorated that evening's experience with several figurative drawings and an abstract painting (see figs. 84, 85) bearing the same title, clearly visible at the top of the canvas.[18] Another inscription in the form of a signature at the bottom, "Edtaonisl 1913," suggests, however, a more complex content incorporating somehow the "star dancer" motif. As suggested by Pearlstein,[19] Picabia may have come to associate "Edtaonisl" with any sort of star performer, in which case it could refer to himself as creator of the painting and/or to the Chinese wrestler whose impact on opponents was as devastating in its own way as the performance of Napierkowska. The presence of such themes is raised only by inscriptions on the canvas and, for "insiders," by a knowledge of Picabia and his preceding work; the painting itself is an abstract composition, appropriately chaotic in its shattered color planes.

support for me in this enterprise?" In terms reminiscent of Stieglitz, she described requirements for the success of the gallery as noncommercial aims, moral dedication, courage and patience. A small shop, to be called "L'Ourse," had been purchased at 29, rue d'Astorg. It opened (see *Lanterne* [Paris], January 1, 1914), apparently with plans for a magazine (or literary publications) under the direction of Jean Cocteau, although the announcement for that activity (*Le Gil Blas* [Paris], December 31, 1913) gives a different name and address ("L'Ours," Boulevard Haussmann) for the gallery.

17. On January 13, 1914, Picabia wrote to Gertrude Stein from Gstaad, Switzerland (A.S.A., Yale), and a note in *Paris-Journal* (L'Atelier, "Aquarelles de Picabia," May 29, 1914, 3) records an exhibition in Amsterdam of works made during the spring of 1914 in the Midi.

18. Gabrielle Buffet-Picabia, *Aires abstraites* (Geneva, 1957), 68–69.

In a letter of January 22, 1915, to Mme Buffet-Picabia, Apollinaire wrote that Picabia had given him "des dessins faits d'après souvenir du *Catch as Catch can* qui sont merveilleux" (Dossier Picabia III, 90; published in Michel Sanouillet, *Dada à Paris*, Paris, 1965, 536). Nothing more was known of those sketches until the recent exhibition of four figurative drawings formerly in the collection of Apollinaire (Centre National d'Art et de Culture Georges Pompidou, Musée National d'Art Moderne, *Francis Picabia*, Paris, Grand Palais, January 23–March 29, 1976, no. 40).

The Picabia dossiers, hereafter cited as D.P., are thirteen scrapbooks housed in the Bibliothèque Littéraire Jacques Doucet, Paris, hereafter cited as B.D. In all references to these dossiers in this text, the Roman numeral following the abbreviation "D.P." indicates the scrapbook number; the Arabic numeral refers to the numbered item within that scrapbook. Material drawn from the dossiers will always be acknowledged, followed, whenever it has been published, by the more accessible published source.

19. Pearlstein, "The Paintings of Francis Picabia," 111.

Among Picabia's major abstract works of 1913–1914, *Culture physique* (*Physical Culture*, fig. 86) has attracted less verbal attention, perhaps because it seems so devoid of clues from nature or the artist's private life. As recently noted, however, it may contain reference to a contemporary magazine of the same title edited by Apollinaire. But if that reference exists it cannot be "read" in the forms of this painting; *Culture physique* remains one of Picabia's most successful and demanding paintings "as a painting."[20]

The major characteristics of these paintings of 1913—hard-edged abstraction coupled with curious titles which allude to a veiled symbolism—continued apace through 1914 in what Picabia called "psychological abstractions." Some works maintained established themes, the golden brown *"Little" Udnie* (fig. 88), for example, whose wirelike lines and cut-up ribbon forms look more like documented paintings of 1914 than her earlier counterpart (fig. 82). Other examples, *Animation* and *Embarras* (*Predicament*, figs. 89, 90), do not appear to harbor the complex themes of *Edtaonisl* or *Catch as Catch Can*, although the formal properties of these compositions do evoke psychological responses in accord with their titles.

The contrary is more accurate for many of Picabia's paintings during 1914—*Une Horrible Douleur* (*A Horrible Sadness*); *Moi aussi, j'ai vécu en amérique* (*Me, Too, I Have Lived in America*); *Impétuosité française* (*French Impetuosity*); *Ad Libilum, aux choix; a la volonté* (*Ad Libilum, To the Choice of the Will*); *Force comique* (*Comic Force*); and *Chose admirable à voir* (*Things Admirable to See*, figs. 91–96).[21] In these paintings there is a more provocative gap between the verbal, ideational properties of the title and the visual, material qualities of the painting. This collagelike juxtaposition of seemingly disparate forms of expression had a substantial progeny from Dada onward—and some of Picabia's titles already bear not only the droll, debunking spirit of a proto-dada phase in Paris but, according to the discovery of Jean-Hubert Martin, an origin in the same source claimed to

20. For reference to Apollinaire's magazine, see Centre National d'Art et de Culture Georges Pompidou, Musée National d'Art Moderne, *Francis Picabia*, Paris, Grand Palais, January 23–March 29, 1976, 72–73. A date of 1913 is attributed to *Culture physique* on the basis of stylistic analysis and its exhibition at the 1914 Salon des Indépendants (March 1–April 30). In Apollinaire's review of that Salon, his comments on *Culture physique* generated an interesting public response and reply with an acquaintance of Picabia, Gaston Thiesson. See Apollinaire, *Chroniques d'art*, 349, 365–66, 445–51, 477–78.

21. *Force comique* and *Une Horrible Douleur* (signed and dated 1914) were exhibited in Amsterdam during May–June 1914 (De Onafhankelyken, 3de *Internationale Jury-Vrije Tentoonstelling*, nos. 412, 413), and identified as works done that spring ("Aquarelles de Picabia," *Paris-Journal*, May 29, 1914, 3). *Force comique* apparently belonged to Apollinaire, who inquired about it during the war (Apollinaire letter to Gabrielle Buffet-Picabia, January 22, 1915, D.P. III, 90; Sanouillet, *Dada à Paris*, 536).

The other four paintings named in the text are attributable on stylistic grounds to 1913–1914, and in the opinion of this author 1914 is the more likely date. All four have one or more forms in common with the documented *Une Horrible Douleur*: concentric arcs or bands, wirelike lines, phallic and scalloped forms, a biomorphic bladderlike shape and curious overall compositions.

have provided the very name "Dada," the *Petit Larousse* dictionary.[22] More specifically, Picabia utilized the "red pages" of the *Petit Larousse* with their translations of phrases from foreign languages and Latin, as exemplified in the following extract which bears striking resemblance to the title for *Moi aussi, j'ai vécu en amérique* (fig. 92):

Et in Arcadia ego!	Exclamation touchante qui sert
(*Et moi aussi, j'ai vécu*	d'épigraphe au célèbre tableau
en Arcadie!).	de Poussin: *les Bergers d'Arcadie* (v. *Part.*
	hist.), et qu'on emploie pour rappeler la duré
	éphémère du bonheur et le regret d'un bien
	que l'on a perdu.

In this instance, Picabia's use of the *Petit Larousse* may suggest something about his intentions (the ephemeral quality of happiness) as well as providing insight into his reading and working habits. But the *Larousse* red pages neither account for all of his titles during this period nor necessarily reveal anything about content. The title for *Chose admirable à voir* (fig. 96) seems utterly private and unrelated to the forms of the painting, unless mockery lurks in its application to such an awkward composition.[23]

Une Horrible Douleur (fig. 91) is somewhat more accessible, at least in the experience of its formal properties, although subject and content are so cryptic as to permit only subjective speculation. It is divided into three vertical sections consisting of an ominous, totemic configuration in black, white and gray forms on the left; two large planes of a brooding sea green on the right; and a central area with rainbowlike bands in blue and orangish colors evocative of spatial depth and serenity. In the center foreground is a black postlike form linked by wiry lines to both the greenish planes on the right and the sinister shape on the left, but oriented toward the radiant central space. The implied relationships between the shapes and colors of these three sections simultaneously encourage and frustrate interpretive efforts. However, the major forms of that central space reoccur in contemporary paintings which suggest more clearly a basic theme of Picabia's work throughout 1913–1914.

Of these, the one most accessible to interpretation is *Impétuosité française* (fig. 93), a cool blue, white and gray watercolor which contains concentric arcs, a phallic form and looping, wirelike lines similar to those around the black "post" in *Une Horrible Douleur*. On appearances alone the probability of sexual content cannot be overlooked as the phallic shape thrusts into an opening defined by the looping lines and concentric bands noted above. The title causes some pause by

22. Centre National d'Art et de Culture Georges Pompidou, Musée National d'Art Moderne, *Francis Picabia*, Paris, Grand Palais, January 23–March 29, 1976, 43–44, 47–49.

23. The inscription on this painting, "En souvenir très affectueux à Jeanne Lecomte des Nouÿ," does not contribute much to interpretive efforts and could have been added at a later date.

attributing impetuosity to the female, but that may have been Picabia's intent. In fact, the male part can be seen not as the aggressive element, but as a dumb, defenseless form drawn into a trap bristling with aggressive objects. Whatever Picabia's intent in *Impétuosité française*, this watercolor does appear to be charged with sexual content which had become a major ingredient of his work since early 1913. Then and later those themes revealed a man who sometimes viewed himself as a passive victim of sex, but was more often burdened by an insatiable appetite for woman as mother, muse and mistress. Yet his paintings rarely operated as indulgent autobiographical documents; the conditions of his personal life were transformed into abstract compositions suggestive of more universal longings, frustration and despair. His masterpiece in that genre was probably completed in Paris after returning from the Midi about April 1914.

Once again the Picabias found Paris alive with activity, and they immediately resumed contact with Apollinaire and the circle around *Les Soirées de Paris*, with Duchamp, Cendrars, Gertrude Stein, Max Jacob and dozens of other artists, entertainers and socialites. They had missed the March opening of the Salon des Indépendants, attended by Arthur Cravan's scandalous magazine, *Maintenant*, and a three-cornered conflict over the relationship of Simultaneism, Futurism and Delaunay which had been sparked by Apollinaire's comments.[24] They observed firsthand, however, the climax of that expanded argument during June and July as a score of poets, painters and critics lambasted each other in the pages of as many journals and newspapers. Also prominent in contemporary discussions and publications was the dramatic music of Albert Savinio (brother of Giorgio de Chirico); the Russian Ballet; popular culture heroes ranging from Buffalo Bill to the legendary Fantômas; Apollinaire's new poem-pictures, the *calligrammes* (illus. 11); and varied futurist works and activities, including Marinetti's "Words in Liberty."[25] Apollinaire's union of word and image in his *calligrammes* is noteworthy for the later development of "peinture-poésie" in Dada and Surrealism—and, in fact, during that summer of 1914 he made an intriguing, unexplained reference to the *poèmes peints* ("painted poems") of Picabia.[26] It is not inconceivable that Picabia, who began to write poetry in 1914, considered some of his paintings as visual equivalents of poems. But, under any conditions,

24. Apollinaire's review of the Salon (*L'Intransigeant* [Paris], March 4, 1914; *Chroniques d'art*, 351–52) raised a storm of protest letters which led to his resignation from the staff of *L'Intransigeant* (*Chroniques d'art*, 474–76). In May, Apollinaire's art criticism was published in *Paris-Journal*.

On the steps outside the 1914 Salon des Indépendants, Arthur Cravan (Fabian Lloyd) sold copies of *Maintenant*, which contained a hilarious, scabrous review of the Salon, art, artists and art critics. The proto-dada spirit of Cravan touched Picabia again at a critical point in his career during 1917, when they were both refugees from the war.

25. For an excellent description of the controversy over Simultaneism see Bergman, "*Modernolotria*" et "*Simultaneità*," esp. pp. 299–307. For the variety of other issues cited in the text, see *Les Soirées de Paris*, nos. 23–27 (April–August 1914).

26. Apollinaire, "Simultanisme-Librettisme," *Les Soirées de Paris* (June 15, 1914), 322–25. This article also constitutes Apollinaire's most comprehensive statement on Simultaneism.

Apollinaire's comment suggests the more complex, cerebral content of Picabia's art; painting, like music, had been freed from the imitation of nature, and, like poetry, might also incorporate more "literary" content.

In May 1914, Marius de Zayas stepped into this hive of activity on an important mission for "291." The operation of the gallery had posed constant strain and sacrifice for Stieglitz, and, after the Armory Show and several crucial exhibitions at "291" during 1913, he had come to feel that the gallery had served its purpose. When plans to demolish the building which housed "291" became known, a ready-made occasion for terminating the gallery was at hand.[27] However, the building was not razed immediately, and the younger men around Stieglitz, especially de Zayas, pressed him to support new projects, at least for one more season. As conceived by de Zayas, that season was to consist of a coordinated series of exhibitions representing nothing less than Art itself as it had been defined by contemporary artists armed with the insights of social and physical sciences. The organization of those exhibitions was the mission which took him to Europe, primarily to Paris, where the Picabias provided extraordinary assistance. Francis introduced him to the people and activities centered around *Les Soirées de Paris*, and a spark of mutual esteem led to collaboration which continued on into important projects at "291" during 1915. Issues of *Camera Work* and *Les Soirées de Paris* were exchanged between Stieglitz and Apollinaire; the latter also offered his poems and the letters of Henri Rousseau for publication in *Camera Work* while de Zayas's caricatures were exhibited in Paris and reproduced in a summer issue of *Les Soirées de Paris*. Moreover, when it became clear that de Zayas could not secure many of the works crucial to his mission, Francis and Gabrielle placed their personal collection at his service, from which he selected for exhibit at "291" about twenty works by Braque and Picasso, and a collection of superb African sculpture.[28]

27. Stieglitz expressed this view several times later in his life (letter from John Weichsel to Alfred Stieglitz, July 31, 1917, A.S.A., Yale) and noted the tenuous future of the building and "291" in a letter to Mme Buffet-Picabia (January 15, 1914, A.S.A., Yale). The issue of *Camera Work* devoted to statements from friends on "What 291 Means to Me" (no. 47, New York, July 1914; published January 1915) was in part a poll to aid Stieglitz in his decision about the future of "291" (see William B. McCormick, "Patrons Vote to Decide Fate of Photo-Secession Gallery at No. 291 Fifth Avenue," *New York Press*, October 4, 1914, 6).

Prior to the Armory Show, Stieglitz had led an almost solitary crusade for modern art and photography. Afterwards, important patrons and new galleries began to emerge, including the Charles Daniel Gallery, which (assisted by Stieglitz) opened in December 1913, followed by the Bourgeois and Montross galleries in February 1914.

28. For de Zayas's work in Paris see the de Zayas-Stieglitz correspondence (A.S.A., Yale), especially the letters of May 22, ca. June 1 and June 30, 1914.

De Zayas also collaborated with Apollinaire, Picabia and Albert Savinio on a pantomime by Apollinaire (never produced) entitled "A quelle heure un train partira-t-il pour Paris?" (Centre National d'Art et de Culture Georges Pompidou, Musée National d'Art Moderne, *Francis Picabia*, Paris, Grand Palais, January 23–March 29, 1976, 72), and he may have become a carrier for news of the vorticists and other avant-garde groups in London. During a visit there in June 1914, he met, among others, Roger Fry, George Bernard Shaw and Alfred Coburn, and wrote that he might take a position with a London magazine (de Zayas letter to Stieglitz, June 11, 1914, A.S.A., Yale).

Initially, de Zayas had not intended to include Picabia's work in the exhibitions at "291," but after observing it for several weeks he wrote to Stieglitz:

. . . by what I see in the latest work of Picabia I also feel that you ought to have an exhibition of Picabia's work. My reason is the following: Picasso represents in his work the expression of pure sensibility, the action of matter on the senses . . . while Picabia's work is the expression of pure thought. Picasso could never work without dealing with objectivity while Picabia forgets matter to express only, maybe the memory of something that has happened.[29]

De Zayas further described Picabia's recent paintings as very large—one which he especially liked being two and one-half meters high—and suggested that "it would make quite an impression to have only three big paintings in it ["291"] covering almost the entire three walls from the floor to the ceiling." Stieglitz agreed, and in January 1915 "291" opened "An Exhibition of Recent Paintings—Never Before Exhibited Anywhere—by Francis Picabia," an exhibition further described by de Zayas as one of a "definite series of experiments begun at '291' some years ago" whose "underlying idea . . . was summed up in the exhibitions of Negro Art, Picasso-Braque, closing with Picabia."[30] No catalogue accompanied the exhibition, but contemporary reviews identified the three large oil paintings as *Je revois en souvenir ma chère Udnie* (*I See Again in Memory My Dear Udnie*), *C'est de moi qu'il s'agit* (*It's About Me*) and *Mariage comique* (*Comical Marriage*, fig. 97, and color pl. VII; figs. 98, 99).[31]

Je revois en souvenir ma chère Udnie is one of Picabia's best-known works and a masterpiece on the order of *Udnie* and *Edtaonisl*; until recently, all trace had been lost of the other two. Now rediscovered, *Mariage comique* and *C'est de moi qu'il s'agit* appear too perversely personal and indifferent to aesthetic harmony to run the risk of being hailed as masterpieces. However, they are fascinating paintings and unlike anything produced elsewhere during 1914—excepting, of course, Picabia's own work. The title of *Mariage comique* may sanction temptation to "read" some of the vaguely suggestive forms in that composition, but without a program from the artist how could one know if his comment on marriage was general or biographical, truly comical or quite serious? *C'est de moi qu'il s'agit* is equally obscure, but when Stieglitz identified it as "the last painting from the hand of Mr. Picabia, . . . done just before he started for the front," several reporters indulged in one-upmanship—one interpreting it as "a picture of the wreckage resulting from the collision of an automobile, an aeroplane and a submarine."[32]

29. De Zayas letter to Stieglitz, June 30, 1914 (A.S.A., Yale).

30. *Camera Work*, no. 48 (New York, published October 1916).

31. [Elizabeth Luther Carey], "Art at Home and Abroad: News and Comments," *New York Times*, January 24, 1915, sec. 5, 11. *C'est de moi qu'il s'agit* and *Mariage comique* were among the recently discovered works from the Meyer collection; see n. 39, chap. III.

32. Both quotations appear in an unsigned review, "Here is Picabia's Cubist Portrait on Going to War," *New York Herald*, January 19, 1915, 12. See also Anon., "Cubist Painter Paints

Both then and now, *Je revois en souvenir ma chère Udnie* has discouraged such levity. The title of this enormous, disquieting painting seems to reflect once more Picabia's use of the *Petit Larousse*,[33] but the content refers to his experiences on the 1913 voyage to New York, and in this instance the forms themselves —cream-colored "female" parts and rubbery, probing "male" elements—suggest more clearly the erotic character of those experiences. Far, however, from enshrining a memory of sensuous pleasure, Picabia seems to have registered a sense of futility. The female forms alone are animated by warm colors; the dumb male forms express helpless frustration—qualities effectively conveyed in this composition with its labyrinthine space which compels exploration yet leads nowhere, and its half-visceral, half-animated plant forms that beg to be identified but for the most part remain tantalizingly out of reach. In Picabia's work, these frequently cited traits of tension, ambiguity and mystery sometimes lapsed into simple confusion, but in *Je revois en souvenir ma chère Udnie* they were positive qualities, at one with the content. The disturbing content in this instance does not deny the popular image of Picabia as one of the "characters" of Paris, painter of ties on Apollinaire's shirtfront and avid collector of fast cars and women. That sobering content does, however, provide witness to the complexity of the man and an occasion for comparison with his close friend, Marcel Duchamp.

Since 1911–1912 Duchamp had taken an increasingly cerebral approach in his art, and that art had been dominated by themes of sexuality, movement and separation (or absence of meaningful contact)—often within a sexual context. Crucial works in that development during 1912 included *The King and Queen Surrounded by Swift Nudes* and the series on *The Virgin*, *The Bride* (fig. 62) and *The Passage from the Virgin to the Bride*. By 1913–1914, with an astoundingly expanded sense of irony, Duchamp was pursuing similar themes in "mechanical" drawings for *The Bride Stripped Bare by Her Bachelors, Even* (fig. 114). Picabia was familiar with Duchamp's work and thought and had even been given *The Bride* (fig. 62), whose entire hanging apparatus seems reflected in some membranelike forms and the pendulant biomorphic shape in the upper center section of *Je revois en souvenir ma chère Udnie*. Nonetheless, as in *Udnie* and *Edtaonisl*, Picabia has transformed such influences in accord with his own ends and personality. In contrast to Duchamp, his forms tend to be more emphatic, the space less ambiguous, the sexuality more evident. In terms of theme and content, both men select sex as

Himself in Cubist Style," *New York Herald*, January 18, 1915, 13, and Royal Cortissoz, "Exhibitions and Other Matters of Fine Art," *New York Tribune*, January 17, 1915.

33. Jean-Hubert Martin (Centre National d'Art et de Culture Georges Pompidou, Musée National d'Art Moderne, *Francis Picabia*, Paris, Grand Palais, January 23–March 29, 1976, 47) associates the title of *Je revois en souvenir ma chère Udnie* with the Latin phrase

Dulces moriens reminiscitur Argos   Expression dont Virgile (*Enéide*, X, 782)
. . . . . . *(Mourant, il revoit en souvenir*   se sert pour rendre plus touchante la
sa chère Argos).   douleur d'un jeune guerrier, Antor, qui
    avait suivi Enée en Italie, et meurt loin de
    sa patrie, tué par Mézence.

a vehicle for multiple comments on life, but in Duchamp's temperament sex seems less a personal experience than a preposterous activity, whereas for Picabia sex may sometimes have been frustrating or unable to fulfill greater longings, but never preposterous. Sex was literally simpler, more material and sensuous, less self-conscious, more natural and rooted in personal experience.

Overnight the declaration of war on August 2 shattered this vital period in Picabia's career and the entire scintillating avant-garde scene in Paris. Within a couple of weeks Picabia found himself in uniform and facing the prospect of a German siege on the capital itself. He made some effort to sketch at the front, and apparently sought assignment as a military artist.[34] Finally, however, he was spared from the infantry (or vice versa?) through the efforts of his father-in-law, a former colonel in the calvary, who discovered that an old friend, a General Boissons, needed a chauffeur. That more fitting assignment was secured, and Picabia moved to Bordeaux with the government in exile, while Gabrielle volunteered as a nurse's aid. Later that fall, de Zayas, who managed to get out of France with most of the art works for his exhibition at "291," wrote Stieglitz that he had "left the Picabias in a very bad fix."[35]

34. These efforts are referred to in Apollinaire's letters to Gabrielle Buffet-Picabia on January 22 and March 20, 1915 (D.P. III, 86, 90; Sanouillet, *Dada à Paris*, 536–37), and in de Zayas's letter to Stieglitz of about October 1914 (A.S.A., Yale).
35. De Zayas letter to Stieglitz, ca. October 1914 (A.S.A., Yale).

TEXT ILLUSTRATIONS

1. Francis Picabia and his parents, ca. 1882.
2. Francis Picabia and his father, ca. 1889.
3. Collège Stanislas, certificate for first prize in drawing
to Francis Picabia, 1889.
4. Left to right: Rodo Pissarro, Mme Orliac,
Francis Picabia and Georges (Manzana) Pissarro, ca. 1902?.

Illustrations 1–4

5. Francis Picabia in his studio at 82, rue des Petits-Champs (now 26, rue Danielle Casanova), Paris, 1912.

Illustration 5

6. Stacia Napierkowska, ca. 1912?.

7. Cartoon for *World*, New York, February 17, 1913.

8. Installation photograph (detail) of the Armory Show, Chicago, March–April, 1913.

Illustrations 6–8

Une passion!

†30 HP Delage 1922

La Prakard file, mais on m'arrête!
il a l'air de dire. 1922

Au volant de la Peugeot F. Picabia 1911
+ sa femme (Gabrielle Buffet)

Avec sa Mercer et
gabrielle Buffet
1917

9. Picabia and some of his automobiles, ca. 1911–1922.

Illustration 9

10. Francis Picabia, Gabrielle Buffet and
Guillaume Apollinaire at Magic City, Paris, ca. 1914.

11. Guillaume Apollinaire,
"The Tie and the Watch," *Calligrammes*, Paris, 1918.

12. Marius de Zayas, caricature of
Francis Picabia in military uniform, 1915.

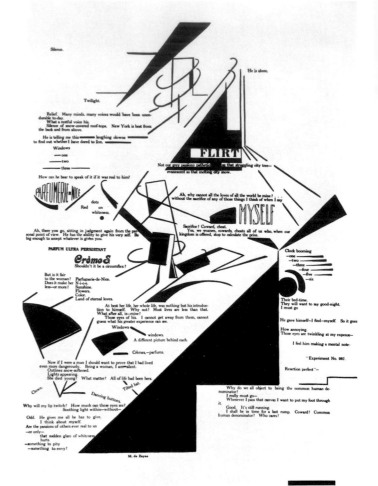

13. Cover for *291*, no. 2, New York, April 1915.

14. Page 3, *291*, no. 2, New York, April 1915.

15. Marius de Zayas and Francis Picabia hand-tinting issues of *291*, New York, 1915.

Illustrations 13–15

16. Beach photograph, Barcelona, ca. 1916.
Seated foreground: Albert and Juliette Gleizes?;
standing left to right: Picabia, unidentified woman,
Otto van Watgen, unidentified woman, Marie Laurencin?,
Gabrielle Buffet-Picabia and Olga Sackaroff.

17. Marcel Duchamp, Francis Picabia and
Beatrice Wood at an amusement park, New York, 1917.

18. Francis and Gabrielle Picabia and
their children, Pancho, Marie and Jeannine, ca. 1918.

391

Au pluriel

"Une définition n'a jamais été qu'un mot pour un autre — et le commun des mortels l'appelle erreur".

De plus en plus, de moins en moins, Trois cent quatre vingt onze est un oiseau à poils, la Vierge satisfaite le tient dans ses bras, la pluie des grands jours, un biceps bien tendre, une ombre à plusieurs, les paupières comme des ongles ou les ongles comme des heures ou.

Petit, petit trois cent quatre vingt onze est une mère en plus ou moins, une liqueurs de desser, de plus en plus, de moins au moins, une lumière derrière un coup de poing, un coup de poing sur une lumière.

Je suis comme les autres, je vais au café. Aussitôt, j'entends : "Garçon un 391 des dimanches". Je suis discret, je ne répète jamais ce que j'écoute dans les water-closets.

Un aimable désordre simili, or n'étant qu'un effet de l'art, j'ai au enjamber deux ou trois fois dans ma vie une belle religieuse aux cornes d'ivoire, une belle, très belle.

Le livre sur lequel j'écris est ouvert à la page 202.

En le lisant, les Cubistes ont bien pleuré.

PAUL ÉLUARD.

TABLEAU DADA par MARCEL DUCHAMP

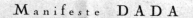

L H O O Q

Manifeste DADA

Les cubistes veulent couvrir Dada de neige ; ça vous étonne mais c'est ainsi, ils veulent vider la neige de leur pipe pour recouvrir Dada.

Tu en es sûr ?

Parfaitement, les faits sont révélés par des bouches grotesques.

Ils pensent que Dada peut les empêcher de pratiquer ce commerce odieux : Vendre de l'art très cher.

L'art vaut plus cher que le saucisson, plus cher que les femmes, plus cher que tout.

L'art est visible comme Dieu ! (voir Saint-Sulpice).

L'art est un produit pharmaceutique pour imbéciles.

Les tables tournent grâce à l'esprit ; les tableaux et autres œuvres d'art sont comme les tables coffres-forts, l'esprit est dedans et devient de plus en plus génial suivant les prix de salles de ventes.

Comédie, comédie, comédie, comédie, comédie, mes chers amis.

Les marchands n'aiment pas la peinture, ils connaissent le mystère de l'esprit..........

Achetez les reproductions des autographes.

Ne soyez donc pas snobs, vous ne serez pas moins intelligents parce que le voisin possèdera une chose semblable à la vôtre.

Plus de chiures de mouches sur les murs.

Il y en aura tout de même, c'est évident, mais un peu moins.

Dada bien certainement va être de plus en plus détesté, son coupe-file lui permettant de couper les processions en chantant " Viens Poupoule ", quel sacrilège !!!

Le cubisme représente la disette des idées.

Ils ont cubé les tableaux des primitifs, cubé les sculptures nègres, cubé les violons, cubé les guitares, cubé les journaux illustrés, cubé la merde et les profils de jeunes filles, maintenant il faut cuber de l'argent !!!

Dada, lui, ne veut rien, rien, rien, il fait quelque chose pour que le public dise : "nous ne comprenons rien, rien, rien". " Les Dadaïstes ne sont rien, rien, rien, bien certainement ils n'arriveront à rien, rien, rien ".

Francis PICABIA

qui ne sait rien, rien, rien.

Illustration 19

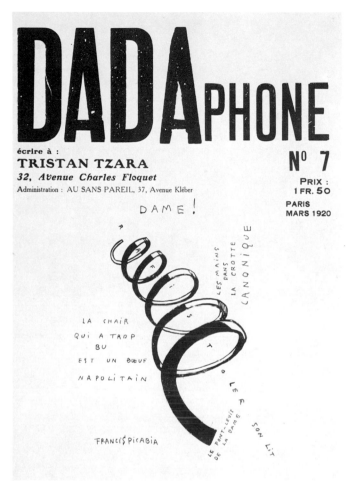

20. Cover for *Dadaphone*, no. 7, Paris, March 1920.

21. Program for "Festival Dada," Salle Gaveau,
Paris, May 26, 1920.

Opposite:
19. Cover for *391*, no. 12, Paris, March 1920.

23. Page 2, *Le Pilhaou-Thibaou*, Paris,
July 10, 1921 (no. 15 of *391*).

22. André Breton in sandwich board
by Picabia at the "Festival Dada,"
Salle Gaveau, Paris, May 26, 1920.

Illustrations 22–23

24. Francis Picabia, "Funny-Guy Handbill,"
ca. October 1921.

25. Francis Picabia and Christian,
cover for *La Pomme de pins*,
St. Raphael, February 25, 1922.

26. Marcel Duchamp, Jacques Doucet and
Francis Picabia, at Picabia's Maison Rose,
Tremblay-sur-Mauldre, ca. 1922–1924.

27. Jean Borlin and Mlle Bonsdorff in *Relâche*
by the Swedish Ballet, Paris, premiere December 4, 1924.
Directed by Rolf de Maré; scenario and decor by Picabia;
music by Érik Satie.

28. *Relâche*, Swedish Ballet,
premiere Paris, December 4, 1924.

29. René Clair (filmmaker) and Francis Picabia
(scenarist), *Entr'acte*, Paris, 1924.

Illustrations 27–29

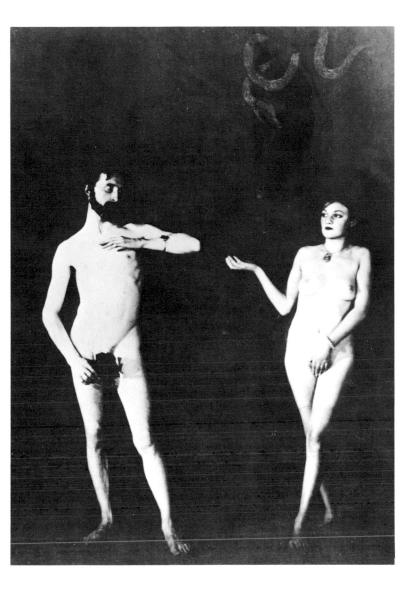

30. Marcel Duchamp and Brogna Perlmutter in *Cinésketch*
by Francis Picabia, Paris, December 31, 1924.

31. Francis Picabia and Germaine Everling,
Château de Mai, Mougins, ca. 1927–1929.

32. Germaine Everling and Lorenzo,
Château de Mai, Mougins, ca. 1925–1929.

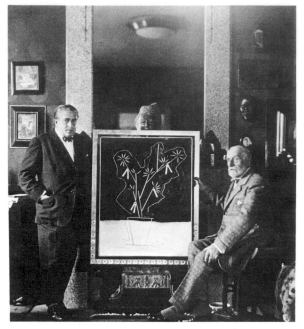

33. Francis Picabia and Jacques Doucet with
Straws and Toothpicks (see fig. 260), ca. 1924–1927.

35. "Fêtes des cannibales," Château de Madrid,
Cannes, ca. September 1930.
Picabia (center left) with "x" on his chest;
Olga (upper left) in elaborate face paint.

34. Installation photograph, Galerie Alexandre III,
Cannes, *Exposition Picabia*, August 1930.

36. Picabia's studio at the Château de Mai, Mougins, summer 1935.

37. Francis and Olga Picabia on the *Yveline*, Golfe-Juan, 1938.

Illustrations 33–37

38. "The Parisian Bath in 1900,"
act at the Bal Tabarin, Paris, ca. 1938.

39. Francis Picabia in his studio,
Paris, 1939.

40. Francis Picabia with his new bike
and Sizou, Golfe-Juan, 1940.

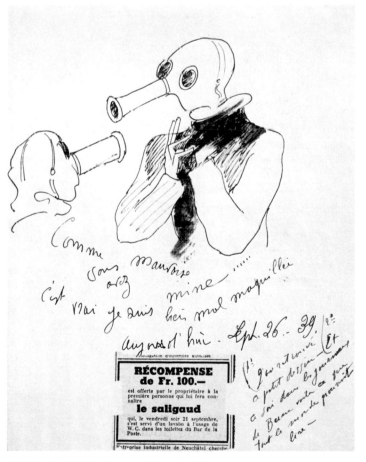

41. Francis Picabia, letter to Christine Boumeester
with drawing, collage and poem (on reverse), Paris, ca. 1946.
Christine Boumeester–Henri Goetz collection, Paris.

42. Francis Picabia, letter-drawing to
Christine Boumeester and Henri Goetz, 1946.
Christine Boumeester–Henri Goetz collection, Paris.

43. Francis Picabia,
"Egoism," page from *Chi-Lo-Sa*,
Alès: PAB, 1950.

44. Jean van Heeckeren
and Francis Picabia at the opening
for *Quelques Oeuvres de Picabia*
(époque Dada 1915–1925),
Galerie Artiste et Artisan,
Paris, November 1951.

6. NEW YORK AND THE MECHANOMORPHIC STYLE, 1915

AROUND November 1914, with the German threat to Paris repulsed and the war already settling into the trenches, the French government—General Boissons and his chauffeur included—returned to the capital. For several months Picabia's lot there was tolerable, thanks to his favorable military assignment, the presence of some good friends and his own incorruptibly civilian temperament. A de Zayas caricature (illus. 12) records the hopelessly nonmilitary demeanor of Picabia, which bedeviled the poor general and doubtless amused the handful of nonuniformed friends who gathered in his apartment, among them Duchamp, Gleizes, Ribemont-Dessaignes, Max Jacob and Jean Crotti.[1] Even in that company, however, there was no escape from the war. Rampant chauvinism and the horrors of the slaughter not only engulfed public life but penetrated every individual refuge. Friends were dispersed and some already killed; avant-garde art and literary activities such as *Les Soirées de Paris* were immediate cultural casualties, and a curfew cut into even the café and entertainment life. In every nation caught up in the war, young men who were exempt from the draft, who evaded it or deserted, found the situation so unbearable that they headed for neutral countries. Switzerland was the most convenient haven, but others turned to Spain and America, among them Duchamp, Gleizes and Crotti, who perhaps responded in part to Picabia's praise of New York.[2] Picabia preceded them unexpectedly during June 1915.

1. For a description of the early wartime gatherings in Picabia's apartment see Georges Ribemont-Dessaignes (*Déjà jadis*, Paris, 1958, 50). Crotti was exempted from service owing to his Swiss nationality; Duchamp had a mild heart condition; Gleizes had been conscripted but was demobilized in 1915 owing primarily to the intervention of the magistrate Granié, who opposed the slaughter of France's artists.

2. Duchamp reached New York in mid-August. His motivation for visiting New York probably included the memory of his own success (commercial, moral and "de scandale") at the Armory Show (see Milton W. Brown, *The Story of the Armory Show*, Greenwich, Conn., 1963, 240). Gleizes arrived in New York during September on a honeymoon with his bride, Juliette Roche,

Threatened with reassignment to the infantry, he searched for alternatives, and, once more, family contacts provided a rescue. During the early months of 1915, arrangements were made for Picabia to travel to the Carribean in order to secure sugar or molasses for the army.[3] When it was learned that his ship would lay over in New York, Gabrielle cabled de Zayas and Haviland on May 27, 1915: "Francis Arrives New York By Transatlantic Spain/Will Be Happy To See You."[4] He reached New York before mid-June, fell in with old friends, new acquaintances and stimulating activities, and simply abandoned his military mission until the fall of 1915, when Gabrielle went to New York and physically escorted him to Panama and Cuba.

Picabia's conduct, which placed him in legal jeopardy throughout the war, was not so much a deliberate antiwar protest as an example of his self-centered behavior, which ranged from unthinking self-indulgence to a resounding defense of individual liberties against restraints of any sort. He was not unpatriotic but apatriotic, unable to comprehend—much less to serve—the demands of any institution, including the French government. He never understood and never forgave Apollinaire for his passion to serve as an officer, although his foreign birth exempted him from conscription.[5] In contrast, Picabia sought to evade the existence of that monstrous holocaust. Even in America that was impossible, for there, too, the war was a primary concern. But compared to Paris, New York offered enormous freedom and intellectual stimulation—such, at least, was the opinion of Picabia, Duchamp, Gleizes and Crotti, who formed a colony of French artists there by the late summer of 1915.[6] Their activities were centered in three locations, Greenwich Village, the salon of Walter and Louise Arensberg and "291," which had entered an important phase in its history. Picabia and Duchamp became central figures for a time in American art, Picabia primarily associated with "291," and Duchamp at the hub of the Arensberg salon.

Some aspects of Greenwich Village had changed little since Picabia's visit in

daughter of the director of *La Republique française* (see Sarah Addington, "Interview with M. and Mme. Gleizes," *New York Tribune*, October 9, 1915, 7). Crotti's reasons for visiting the United States are unknown, but he did have relatives in the Midwest (Anon., "French Artists Spur on an American Art," *New York Tribune*, October 24, 1915, pt. iv, 2).

3. According to family tradition, Cuba was Picabia's destination, and one of Gabrielle's cousins, a M. de Jussieu, who was the French consul in Colon, Panama, helped to arrange the mission (conversation with Mme Buffet-Picabia, October 1962; see also Michel Sanouillet, *Francis Picabia et "391,"* II, Paris, 1966, 34, 39). Correspondence with the present French ambassador to Panama has not led to more useful information (letter to the author, June 1, 1972), and efforts to secure documents from the French army have been unsuccessful.

4. Cable from Gabrielle Buffet-Picabia to Marius de Zayas and Paul Haviland, May 27, 1915 (A.S.A., Yale).

5. In a special edition of *L'Esprit nouveau* devoted to Apollinaire, Picabia began his statement: "I was . . . very amicably connected with Guillaume Apollinaire; if our friendship cooled a little at the very end of his life, it was uniquely a question 'of uniform'!" *L'Esprit nouveau*, no. 26 (Paris, October 1924).

6. See an informative interview with these four artists, de Zayas, and Frederick MacMonnies by an anonymous reporter in the *New York Tribune* ("French Artists Spur on an American Art").

1913. Negro jazz and parties at the Liberal Club were as good as ever; Max Eastman still guided *The Masses*, Margaret Sanger continued her crusade for birth control and Emma Goldman maintained the monotonous siren of anarchism in street rallies and in the pages of *Mother Earth*. The complexion of the Village had changed, however. Like all "Bohemias," it had been "discovered"; it was becoming self-conscious, a point on the itinerary of uptowners and tourists. Nonetheless, it was still a young, vital "Bohemia," and for the first time painters, poets and dramatists seemed more numerous than the unionists, socialists and anarchists. Two important theater groups had been founded, the Washington Square Players and the Provincetown Players. And although New York was not to match the Chicago-based magazines, *Poetry* and *The Little Review*, Boni's Village bookstore displayed the efforts of young Village poets in volumes entitled *Rogue, Glebe* and *Others*.[7]

The Arensberg salon also had its distinctive tone. Walter Arensberg (1878–1954), a wealthy Harvard graduate, and his wife, Louise, had settled in New York in 1915. Gentle, generous, intelligent and seemingly interested in everything, the Arensbergs gradually established an informal open house, where intellectual and artistic interests reigned supreme in contrast to the earlier soirées of Mabel Dodge, which had been semi-organized and atuned to social and political reform. Arensberg's keenest personal interests included poetry, chess, the Shakespeare-Bacon controversy, psychoanalysis and, following the Armory Show, modern art. A comparable range of interests was reflected in the frequent guests at the Arensberg apartment—among them such prominent American artists, poets, authors, editors and entertainers as William Carlos Williams, Margaret Anderson, Amy Lowell, Isadora Duncan, Carl Van Vechten, Katherine Dreier, Charles Demuth, Man Ray, John Covert, Charles Sheeler, Morton Schamberg, Beatrice Wood, Alfred Kreymborg, Ernst Southard, Helen Freeman, Walter Pach, Mina Loy and the Stettheimer sisters. The European guests were equally distinguished—Duchamp and his friend H.P. Roché, Picabia, Jean Crotti, Albert and Juliette Gleizes, the composer Edgar Varèse and the strange baroness Elsa von Freytag-Loringhoven—and most of them have recalled with pleasure the stimulation of those gatherings which formed at will during the late evening hours. But the most stimulating relationship of all was the friendship between Arensberg

7. For general information on Greenwich Village see Van Wyck Brooks, *The Confident Years* (New York, 1952), and Albert Parry, *Garrets and Pretenders* (New York, 1933). Society-page editors discovered the Village in 1915 (see *Sun*, New York, December 5, 1915, and *New York Tribune*, November 14, 1915). Guido Bruno's magazine, *Greenwich Village*, appeared the same year with advertisements (see *The Egoist*, New York, October 1915) frankly promotional for the Village.

For the magazines *Rogue, Glebe* and *Others* see Alfred Kreymborg, *The Troubador* (New York, 1925), 202–34, passim. The important work of Margaret Anderson and Jane Heap with *The Little Review* in New York did not begin until their migration from Chicago in 1917.

For many of the issues, American artists and patrons discussed in this chapter, see the Delaware Art Museum, Wilmington, *Avant-Garde Painting and Sculpture in America 1910–1925*, April 4–May 18, 1975, edited by William Innes Homer.

and Duchamp. Arensberg provided Duchamp a studio in his apartment building—and there Duchamp began to bring together his long preparation for *The Bride Stripped Bare by Her Bachelors, Even* (fig. 114), which, along with other major examples of Duchamp's work, eventually entered Arensberg's superb collection of modern and primitive art. For his part, Duchamp remarked about the same time in 1915 that "the artist should be able to work in one place quite as well as another." "But," he added, "I love an active and interesting life. I have found such a life most abundantly in New York."[8] Picabia went further, claiming to sense a oneness between the spirit of America and the spirit of modern art which would make New York the center of the art world.[9]

To be sure, the relationship between New York and the European artists was not one-sided, and the impact of the latter was reflected in many ways. A back-handed witness was provided in the peevish grumblings of Royal Cortissoz, who bemoaned the cubists, futurists and post-impressionists: "All those freakish incompetents who . . . have for some time been making their way here . . . and, with the usual facility, . . . are creating their public."[10]

A society-page witness was provided by a *Tribune* columnist:

> . . . the artist colony of America, once just New Yorkese, is feeling the invasion of the war—scattered artists from other worlds. Greenwich Village is . . . taking on the tone of original Bohemia, acquiring the polish of European culture and even talking French. You see a new face at Polly's, ask who it is and learn that it is Picabia, the Spanish modernist, who packed his drawings in a suitcase, left Paris and settled his handsome self as a villager.[11]

More significantly, the work and spirit of Duchamp and Picabia touched some of the best young American artists, not only such painters as Man Ray, Morton Schamberg, Charles Demuth, John Covert and Charles Sheeler, but several writers as well. William Carlos Williams claimed that he and his colleagues learned more from European painters than from foreign authors.[12]

The mutual support of American and French resources was most visible in two new projects at "291," a magazine also entitled *291* and a "branch" gallery called the Modern Gallery. Since demolition of the building had again been postponed, Stieglitz had maintained both *Camera Work* and the gallery, but without a full measure of conviction for their need. Increasingly, he withdrew to a position approximating that of an honored sage and advisor, while initiative was taken by his younger associates, Paul Haviland, Marius de Zayas and Agnes Meyer, the

8. Anon., "French Artists Spur on an American Art," *New York Tribune*.

9. Ibid.

10. Royal Cortissoz, "The Old Order and the New in the Art of Painting," *New York Tribune*, December 12, 1915, sec. 3–4, 3.

11. Sarah Addington, "Who's Who in New York's Bohemia," *New York Tribune*, November 14, 1915, sec. 4, 2.

12. Constance Rourke, *Charles Sheeler* (New York, 1938), 47.

energetic young wife of Eugene Meyer, editor of the *Washington Post*. De Zayas was particularly keen to carry on and proposed both the new magazine and the Modern Gallery. Those new "experiments" received Stieglitz's blessings and began in March and October respectively of 1915. Without Stieglitz's approval, they might not have materialized, but he had planned neither of them, and, in a respectful way, they were critical of him—projects of ardent younger men impatient with his sense of a concluded effort and his fixation on a small, elite operation. In the first issue of *291* (March 1915) Haviland went so far as to publish a discussion between a "professor" and "291" (Stieglitz) in which the professor first chided "291" for having been marking time and then presumed to lead "291" into a realization of what it represented and what the future course of action might be.[13] In a later issue, at the peak of a family debate over the proposed Modern Gallery, de Zayas contrasted Stieglitz's approach with success American-style: "America has not the slightest conception of the value of the work accomplished by Stieglitz. Success, and success on a large scale, is the only thing that can make an impression on American mentality. Any effort . . . which does not possess the radiation of advertising remains practically ignored."[14]

Such success eluded de Zayas, but modern art is richer for his efforts. *291*, a handsome oversize magazine of twelve issues (March 1915–February 1916), focused on modern art, satire and criticism, and although it was unlike any American or European predecessors, it combined sources from both sides of the Atlantic in form and content. The contributors were evenly divided between New York and Paris, and a number of the texts appeared in French or in both French and English.[15] The extraordinary quality of the paper, printing and layout was a legacy of *Camera Work*, while experimental typesetting and design reflected de Zayas's contact in 1914 with futurist publications, Apollinaire's *calligrammes* and perhaps the vorticist magazine *Blast*.[16] De Zayas called the typography "psychotype, an art which consists in making the typographical characters participate in the expression of the thoughts and in the painting of the states of the soul, no more as conventional symbols but as signs having significance in themselves."[17] The sec-

13. Paul B. Haviland, untitled entry in *291*, no. 1 (New York, March 1915).

14. Marius de Zayas, untitled entry in *291*, nos. 5–6 (New York, July–August 1915).

15. Most of the foreign contributors to *291*—Apollinaire, Max Jacob, Picasso, Braque, Savinio and Ribemont-Dessaignes—were associates of *Les Soirées de Paris* and/or friends of Picabia whom de Zayas had met while staying with the Picabias during the summer of 1914. However, de Zayas had known Picasso for several years.

16. The vorticist magazine *Blast* consisted of just two issues dated London, June 20, 1914, and July 1915. As yet no published documents indicate that de Zayas and the vorticists had anything more than a meager knowledge of each other's work, but de Zayas was in contact with one of their associates, Alfred Langdon Coburn, and Ezra Pound and Wyndham Lewis knew something of Picabia's work and commented on it (Lewis in *Blast*, no. 2, London, July 1915, 44: "Picabia, . . . reducing things to empty but very clean and precise mathematical blocks, coldly and wittily tinted like a milliner's shop-front, stands apart from the rest").

17. Anon., "*291*—A New Publication," in *Camera Work*, no. 48 (New York, October 1916), 62. *Camera Work* was suspended during publication of *291*.

ond issue of *291* (April 1915; illus. 13, 14) provides both a good example of "psychotype" and the general scope of the magazine: page one bears a reproduction of a 1913 drawing of New York by Picabia and a collection of critical/satirical notes ranging from unwed motherhood to criticism of the Metropolitan Museum of Art and a recent concert of color music; this is followed by an abstract design by Catherine Rhoades; a psychotype poem by Agnes Meyer united with a design by de Zayas; and, on the last page, a portion of a musical score by Albert Savinio. Although Picabia had not been present for the planning of *291*, upon his arrival in June he became a major collaborator and figured prominently in nine of the twelve issues, particularly the July–August issue, which was devoted to his new mechanomorphic style.

Picabia was more central to the founding of the Modern Gallery. Plans for it followed his arrival in New York and were partly indebted to his conviction that America was destined to become the center of modern art. He also provided some financial support and considerable help in obtaining art from Paris.[18]

After exciting conversations throughout August, de Zayas summarized the purpose of the gallery in a letter to Stieglitz:

> . . . our object in opening a new gallery is to do *business* not only to fight against dishonest commercialism but in order to support ourselves and make others be able to support themselves; . . . and make them be able to continue the evolution of modern art. Also to make of New York a center of modern art, commercially and intellectually. . . .
>
> Practically, we are not going to start a new enterprise, we are only going to continue your work with two different methods which complete each other: one purely intellectual at 291 and the other purely commercial at the new gallery.[19]

In October 1915, at a prime location on Fifth Avenue and Forty-second Street, the Modern Gallery opened with the passionate commitment of its director, Marius de Zayas, the blessing of Stieglitz, the money of the Meyers and varied support from Picabia, including a stock of paintings. Within a few months it was clear that the two-sided effort (intellectual at "291" and commercial at the Modern Gallery) would not work, and over the winter of 1915–1916 there was a separation of the two galleries and old friends. Mutual respect eventually restored the personal rifts, but Stieglitz soon terminated "291" and *Camera Work*, while de Zayas

18. As early as August, de Zayas and Picabia planned to stock the Modern Gallery in part with paintings Gabrielle would bring to New York (letter from de Zayas to Stieglitz, August 27, 1915, A.S.A., Yale). Eugene and Agnes Meyer were the primary financial backers of the gallery, but Haviland and Picabia also made commitments (see Haviland's letter to de Zayas, November 29, 1915, in the de Zayas Archive, Paris, hereafter cited as M.de Z.A., copies housed with the A.S.A., Yale, and in Butler Library, Columbia University, through the generosity of Rodrigo de Zayas).

19. De Zayas letter to Stieglitz, August 27, 1915 (A.S.A., Yale).

plunged ahead with exhibitions of primitive and modern art, including the entire first phase of Picabia's mechanomorphic style.[20]

This new style in Picabia's oeuvre was sudden and startling in its appearance, reinforcing the opinion of those who already considered him a frivolous playboy in art. Nonetheless, in the eyes of the public, it has perhaps been the most fascinating period of his career—and probably the most misunderstood. Because those machines were later identified with Dada, many critics fell prey to a dada complex. Assuming that the cryptically inscribed contraptions were intended only to mock and mystify, they suspended critical analysis and attributed dada content and dates (ca. 1913–1922) to everything remotely resembling a machine. Picabia, however, made several statements during 1915 which pinpoint that year as the beginning of the machine paintings and preclude exclusively dadaist interpretations of them. Moreover, those statements provide welcome insight into some unexpected constancy within the seemingly erratic evolution of his work.

The first statement occurred in an interview with a New York reporter during October 1915. Regarding the beginning of the style, Picabia claimed that: "This visit to America . . . has brought about a complete revolution in my methods of work. . . . prior to leaving Europe I was engrossed in presenting psychological studies through the mediumship of forms which I created. Almost immediately upon coming to America it flashed on me that the genius of the modern world is in machinery, and that through machinery art ought to find a most vivid expression." As to the thrust of his paintings Picabia stressed that:

> The machine has become more than a mere adjunct of life. It is really a part of human life—perhaps the very soul. In seeking forms through which to interpret ideas or by which to expose human characteristics I have come at length upon the form which appears most brilliantly plastic and fraught with symbolism. I have enlisted the machinery of the modern world, and introduced it into my studio. . . .
>
> Of course, I have only begun to work out this newest stage of evolution. I don't know what possibilities may be in store. I mean to simply work on and on until I attain the pinnacle of mechanical symbolism.[21]

Although there was no stylistic transition from the "psychological studies" of 1913–1914 to the machines of 1915, this statement—and the paintings themselves—attest to continuities of aim and content. Instead of developing a vocabulary of abstract forms and colors, Picabia now sought machine equivalents or symbols to comment on man and human situations, much as the ancient Greeks

20. For the separation of the Modern Gallery and "291" see the undated 1915 letter of Agnes Meyer to de Zayas (M.de Z.A.), and Stieglitz's letters to Annie W. Brigman, 1915 and 1916, and to John G. Bullock, March 1917 (A.S.A., Yale).

21. Anon., "French Artists Spur on an American Art," *New York Tribune*.

and Romans had developed personifications of gods, virtues, vices, war and peace. The most relevant influences on his mechanical symbolism hardly went back that far, but, contrary to how it may have seemed to Picabia, the concept did not just "flash" upon him. His mechanomorphic style was nourished by a variety of precedents in art, and its very existence depended upon a mental climate so imbued with the wonders of science and technology that the term "machine age" has been employed to characterize the era.

Two authors who have addressed the concept of a machine age, Siegfried Giedion and Reyner Banham, concur that after long maturation it finally arrived during the second decade of the twentieth century and was characterized by a stage of mechanization in which an abundance of machines that altered everyday life came to be owned and operated by the middle classes. Those machines included telephones, typewriters, electrical appliances and, especially, automobiles. A survey of newspapers and illustrated journals supports their views and further indicates that no class was untouched by exhilarating advances in aircraft, automotive design and the cinema, by the impact of industrial exhibits at world's fairs, or by startling developments in science, including the discovery of new atomic theories, X—ray and the emission of rays from radium.[22]

Reaction to such "progress," however, was sometimes ambivalent. Many people were confident that science, industry and technology had carried man to the threshold of a new age in which his needs would be fulfilled with unprecedented efficiency. De Zayas had something of that in him. But others, some just skeptics, some stirred by the fundamental mysteries of life, looked upon the triumvirate of science-technology-machine as a false and pompous trinity.

Prior to the development of his mechanomorphic style, Picabia was exposed to such ambivalent attitudes in the art and literature of his contemporaries. He was familiar with the Italian futurists who glorified the modern, machine-dominated era and strived in their paintings to express the simultaneous experience of its speed, noise and power. He also knew the rayonist-futurist paintings of Goncharova and Larionov, the symbolic locomotives of de Chirico and the robot-like figures in Léger's paintings and in the relief constructions of Archipenko. He knew the ready-mades and curious machine forms created by Duchamp. He saw Villon's collages which incorporated reproductions of real machines clipped out of journals, and he followed the visual-functional analogies between animal and machine in Duchamp-Villon's *Horse* of 1914–1915. He may also have heard of the English vorticists, who attributed to machinery a crucial role in the burgeoning dehumanization of society and developed a machine-inspired aesthetic which rendered man and nature alike in dynamic, semi-abstract compositions of hard,

22. See Reyner Banham, *Theory and Design in the First Machine Age* (New York, 1960), 9–12; Siegfried Giedion, *Mechanization Takes Command* (New York, 1948), 41–44, and *Space, Time and Architecture* (Cambridge, Mass., 1962), 241–88; and K.G. Pontus Hultén, *The Machine* (New York: The Museum of Modern Art, 1968). For contemporary popular information see such trade journals as the *Electrical World* (New York, 1883 to present) and such French newspapers and illustrated magazines as *Le Journal*, *Je sais tout* and *Le Figaro illustré*.

sharp-edged and vaguely machine-made forms.[23] He esteemed the efforts of Cendrars and Apollinaire to express the new era in their poetry. He was also familiar with the similar concerns of Barzun and Beauduin, the latter of whom was fond of such metaphors as metros being the "veins" of Paris.[24] Above all, he was enchanted by the writings of Alfred Jarry and Raymond Roussel, who employed pseudoscientific procedures, mathematics and fantastic machines to mock the follies of man.

Alfred Jarry founded a new science, pataphysics, "the science of the particular." He dedicated pataphysics to the study of "laws which govern exceptions" and employed it in a mathematical proof of God whom he fixed algebraically as "the shortest route from zero to infinity."[25] In *The Supermale*, Jarry presented sexual intercourse in a manner that not only devaluated that intimate human experience but mocked science and technology and portrayed man as a creature devoid of reason and love.[26] Roussel excelled in the depiction of elaborate rituals and demonstrations centered about either humans who perform with mechanical perfection, or about fantastic machines whose operation depends equally on magic and extraordinary scientific-technological knowledge.[27] The impact of war machinery and Picabia's own adoration of automobiles should not be omitted from

23. Picabia probably did not know the writings of T.E. Hulme, a critic-philosopher loosely associated with Vorticism. Hulme's very early, perceptive observations on the machine age merit notation, particularly "Modern Art and Its Philosophy" (lecture delivered on January 22, 1914, and printed in Hulme's *Speculations*, ed. Herbert Read, London, 1954).

24. Beauduin's imagery was popularized by G. de Pawlowski, editor of the primary newspaper on the arts, *Comoedia*. On December 3, 1912, Pawlowski wrote in an article entitled "Voyage au pays de la quatrième dimension/Un Massacre": "From its head, with its eyes, to the black exhaust of its muffler, the automobile behaves like a simple animal . . . with the beating heart of its valves, the vertebral column of its transmission . . . the circulation of water, the circulation of oil, the electrical enervation . . ."

25. Alfred Jarry, *Gestes et opinions du Docteur Faustroll*, vol. I of *Oeuvres complètes* (Lausanne, 1948), 217, 317–20.

26. Alfred Jarry, *Le Surmâle*, vol. III of *Oeuvres complètes*, 197–229.

In the second part of this book, the Supermale dismissed the act of love as a machinelike action which could be repeated indefinitely when fortified with "perpetual motion food," a compound of alcohol and strychnine. An experiment was arranged to verify his claim, and while "science" (represented by a doctor) recorded the data of the experiment, the Supermale proceeded to surpass the world's record for intercourse. Complications arose when his partner, a young American girl, fell in love with the indifferent Supermale. To stimulate a reciprocal carnal desire in the Supermale, the girl's father (determined that his daughter should have her man) appealed to an engineer to make a love-inspiring machine. The machine was hastily constructed and strapped to the Supermale despite warnings by the engineer that it might not do what it was intended to do. "So much the better, this will be an experience," interrupted the girl's father, as he pressed the commentator. In a bizarre turn of events the love-inspiring machine fell in love with the Supermale, overheated, short-circuited and killed him.

27. Among the numerous mechanisms in Roussel's *Impressions d'Afrique* (Paris, 1912) there is a painting machine that satirizes Impressionism (pp. 195–209) and an apparatus that mocks color organs and the concept of synesthesia (pp. 52–61). Michel Carrouges describes some of Roussel's inventions as celibate machines in his important study, *Les Machines célibataires* (Paris, 1954), 61–92. He extends this interpretation to Jarry's *Le Surmâle*, Kafka's *Penal Colony* and Duchamp's *The Bride Stripped Bare by Her Bachelors, Even* (fig. 114).

this survey, but it is fitting that his machinist style began in New York, where in 1913 he had experienced his first overwhelming encounter with a modern, machine-age city, further enriched by the pseudoscientific passions of Marius de Zayas and the conviction of Stieglitz that art (photography) could be produced with a machine, the camera.

Upon his return to New York in 1915, Picabia encountered those experiences anew and, in his own words, suddenly perceived machinery as the "genius of the modern world"—"brilliantly plastic and fraught with symbolism." A contemporary statement by Haviland in *291* records the physical-functional analogies of men and machines which were central to the outlook of the inner circle at "291":

> We are living in the age of the machine.
>
> Man made the machine in his own image. She has limbs which act; lungs which breathe; a heart which beats; a nervous system through which runs electricity. The phonograph is the image of his voice; the camera the image of his eye. The machine is his "daughter born without a mother." That is why he loves her. He has made the machine superior to himself. . . . Having made her superior to himself, he endows the superior beings which he conceives in his poetry and in his plastique with the qualities of machines. After making the machine in his own image, he has made his human ideal machinomorphic. But the machine is yet at a dependent stage. Man gave her every qualification except thought. She submits to his will but he must direct her activities. Without him she remains a wonderful being, but without aim or anatomy. Through their mating they complete one another. She brings forth according to his conceptions.
>
> Photography is one of the fine fruits of this union. The photographic print is one element of this new trinity: man, the creator, with thought and will; the machine, mother-action; and their product, the work accomplished.[28]

Haviland's description of the machine as a "daughter born without a mother" had been used several months earlier by Picabia as the title for his first work associated with the mechanomorphic style, *Fille née sans mère* (*Girl Born without a Mother*, fig. 100). This simple, fetching drawing has withstood considerable debate about its date and its meaning. In the opinion of this author, it is a work of 1915 which suggests what little transition exists between the psychological studies of 1913–1914 and the machinist drawings of 1915. It does resemble somewhat *Je revois en souvenir ma chère Udnie* (fig. 97, and color pl. VII), but a clearer suggestion of rods and springs introduces the machine element which Picabia himself

28. Paul B. Haviland, statement in *291*, nos. 7–8 (New York, September–October 1915). Note that there is some ambiguity in this statement about the identity of machines—at one point referred to as "mother" (partner) of man, and at another point as the "daughter born without a mother," that is, as the product (art) of man and machine.

claimed for 1915, the year in which the existence of *Fille née sans mère* is first documented.[29] Her content is more elusive. This concept of the female creature-machine born without a mother has prompted reference to the feminine gender of the French noun "la machine," to alchemy as a magical means of fertilization and to the birth of Athena from the head of Zeus.[30] The "genealogy" of *Fille née sans mère* is not complete, however, even by the addition of the creation story from Genesis, where God created Eve not from woman but from man and for man's use or companionship. In this framework, the artist—as Picabia frequently implied—was a godlike creator-figure. And while pursuing in his oeuvre this theme of creation without the aid of a mother, one eventually encounters not only numerous offspring but a "unique eunuch," a "merry widow" and a reversal of the creation story so that man creates God in *his* image (figs. 102, 194, 202 and p. 114).

Such at least is the implication of the subtitle for *Fantaisie* (*Fantasy*, fig. 102). The source for this work appears to have been an early nineteenth-century horizontal-beam steam engine (fig. 103) reduced to a highly abstract composition whose precision and geometric simplicity were related to the rising sensitivity for machine aesthetics. Picabia's primary interests resided, however, neither in machine aesthetics nor in antique machines, but with symbolism which becomes apparent as one coordinates the image and its accompanying inscriptions. Contrary

29. For many years this drawing was a cornerstone for authors who specified 1913 as the beginning of Picabia's mechanomorphic style. Generally they relied on unchallenged tradition or on the fact that *Fille née sans mère* is on the reverse of a sheet of stationery from the Brevoort Hotel, reportedly Picabia's residence during the Armory Show. However, there is no sign of the drawing's existence until it was reproduced in *291*, no. 4 (New York, June 1915), with "New York 1915" printed at the lower left of the image. Gabrielle's letter to Apollinaire on October 21, 1915 (Michel Sanouillet, *Dada à Paris*, Paris, 1965, 538), also indicates that the *Fille née sans mère* was a recent, exciting development in Picabia's work.

One forerunner of the mechanomorphic style was indeed produced in 1913, *Mechanical Expression Seen Through Our Own Mechanical Expression* (fig. 66), and some paintings of 1913–1914, *Udnie*, for example (fig. 82), have contributed to the development of machine aesthetics. However, these documented works of 1913–1914 substantiate extensive evidence (including Picabia's own statement) that the mechanomorphic style did not begin until the summer of 1915 in New York. Only one challenge to that date remains known to this author, a previously unpublished drawing, *Machine* (fig. 101), which is signed on the front and signed and dated on the reverse "New York 1913[?]." The last digit, difficult to read, is probably a 3 and the date of both signatures appear to be in Picabia's hand. It is possible that this drawing is another one-of-a-kind work like *Caoutchouc* (fig. 38). But it is totally alien to all known works of 1913; it looks like the documented works of ca. 1916–1919, and, in the opinion of this author, it is far more likely that Picabia misdated the drawing some years later.

30. See Hultén, *The Machine*, 82–83; Philip Pearlstein, "The Symbolic Language of Francis Picabia," *Arts*, XXX (New York, January 1956), 37–43; Bazon Brock, "Immaculée Conception et machines célibataires," in Kunsthalle Bern, *Junggesellenmaschinen. Les Machines célibataires*, July 5–August 17, 1975, 75–82, edited by Harald Szeemann.

Continued use of the *Petit Larousse* red pages is also indicated for this title and about twenty other mechanomorphic works. See Centre National d'Art et de Culture Georges Pompidou, Musée National d'Art Moderne, *Francis Picabia*, Paris, Grand Palais, January 23–March 29, 1976, 47–49.

to most critics who perceived no association between the images and inscriptions in Picabia's mechanomorphic paintings, he claimed they were intimately related: "In my work the subjective expression is the title, the painting is the object. But this object is nevertheless somewhat subjective because it is the pantomime—the appearance of the title; it furnishes to a certain point the means of comprehending the potentiality—the very heart of man."[31]

In *Fantaisie* the subtitle *L'Homme créa dieu à son image* (*Man Creates God in His Image*) implies, in a manner consistent with Picabia's convictions, that God is the "fantasy" because He has been created by man in man's own image. And since Haviland and Picabia also believed that man had created the machine in his own image (see p. 80), the following set of equations can be established according to the theorem that the equals of equals are equal:

$$God = creation \ of \ man \ in \ man's \ image$$
$$Machine = creation \ of \ man \ in \ man's \ image$$
$$God = Machine$$

And if God were a machine, it seems appropriate that His symbol should be the steam engine, king among machines and pathbreaker for the Industrial Revolution.

Immediately after *Fille née sans mère*, Picabia produced symbolic machine portraits (figs. 104–109) of himself and colleagues at "291," which were featured in a summer issue of *291*.[32] In one of *Voilà Haviland* (*Here is Haviland*, fig. 104) the correspondence of man and machine is expressed in terms as simple as those employed by Haviland when he associated the phonograph with man's voice and the camera with his eye (see p. 80). For the object portrait of his friend, Picabia selected an advertisement for a common portable electric lamp (fig. 105), copied it, eliminating unwanted details and inscriptions and added one comment of his own, "La Poésie est comme lui" ("Poetry is like him"). The directness of this process approximates (and possibly reflects) Duchamp's "discovery" of ready-mades, and, like Duchamp, Picabia was highly selective in his appropriation of objects. Although it is possible to perceive the lamp as an upright iconlike figure, Picabia was primarily interested in functional analogies, that is, Haviland and the lamp correspond as sources of light. Even the selection of a portable lamp seems

31. Francis Picabia, statement in *291*, no. 12 (New York, February 1916).

32. *291*, nos. 5–6 (New York, July–August 1915) reproduced Picabia machine object portraits (figs. 104, 106–109) with *Ici, c'est ici Stieglitz* as the cover. In the publication of *291* it was the practice to print deluxe and regular copies, the former distinguished by fine paper and sometimes by hand-tinted reproductions. In apparent reference to the 100 deluxe copies of nos. 5–6, Marie Rapp Boursault, secretary for "291," wrote Stieglitz (August 11, 1915, A.S.A., Yale), "Mr. de Zayas and Mr. Picabia worked all day yesterday painting '291s.' They have mailed sixty, all to France." Accordingly, Picabia's machine portraits were known in France by late August 1915.

A photograph in the album of Mme Olga Picabia (illus. 15) shows Picabia and Marius de Zayas at work on what appear to be papers bearing the *Fille née sans mère* (fig. 100). This photograph, dated many years later as "New York 1913," must show instead the preparation of *291*, no. 4 (June 1915).

deliberate, for Haviland was preparing to leave for Europe and therefore about to become a mobile or "portable" light.[33]

In a later issue of *291* (nos. 10–11, December 1915–January 1916), the poet and foreign correspondent for *291*, Max Jacob, was also symbolized by a modern light source which probably harbors personal comment (fig. 112). Just above his signature Picabia suggests that this flashlight portrait of Jacob was for a laugh ("pour rire"), and indeed this most portable and temporal of all lamps is mounted on a tombstone with inscriptions like "Nec plus ultra," which seem to poke fun at what is a rather humble source of light, or "Tu as péché" ("You have sinned"), which may refer to Jacob's recent conversion to Catholicism.

Such simplicity of form and mocking, multiplicity of content also characterizes the portraits appropriated from automobile parts (figs. 106, 108, 111). An early critic who failed to identify the spark plug in *Portrait d'une jeune fille américaine dans l'état de nudité* (*Portrait of a Young American Girl in the State of Nudity*, fig. 106) wondered if Picabia "intended to show that the young American girl is a hard, unchangeable creature without possibilities." His idea, plausible on visual grounds alone, is completely transformed by focusing on the functional correspondence drawn by Picabia between a nude American girl and a spark plug.[34]

The choice of a camera to symbolize Stieglitz (fig. 107) seems both obvious and appropriate, although Picabia's intentions are clouded by several features, notably the accompanying inscriptions, the fact that the camera appears to be broken and the addition of two foreign objects along the right side of the drawing which have been identified as the gear and brake levers of an automobile. The key to these puzzling elements lies outside the drawing in an adjacent text by de Zayas to the effect that Stieglitz, despite his great talent, "faith and love," had failed to realize his "ideal" of discovering America and helping Americans to discover themselves through art and photography.[35] His aim, de Zayas implied, was too lofty and pursued "by suggestion" behind a "shield of psychology and metaphysics" which was simply uncongenial to the American mind. Picabia's drawing appears then to be a plastic equivalent of the evaluation of Stieglitz by his younger

33. Haviland sailed to Europe soon after a farewell party on July 4, 1915 (see letter from Agnes Meyer to Alfred Stieglitz, July 4, 1915, A.S.A., Yale).

34. Robert J. Cole, review in the *Evening Sun* [New York], October 12, 1915.

Professor William I. Homer, noting that Picabia's other object portraits deal with friends and associates at "291," postulates that this may be the portrait of Agnes Meyer who was, in the colloquial sense of the word, a "spark plug" in the founding of the Modern Gallery ("Picabia's 'Jeune fille américaine dans l'état de nudité' and Her Friends," *The Art Bulletin*, LVII, New York, March 1975, 110–15).

Phrases from the *Petit Larousse* red pages may figure in this drawing and most of Picabia's other object portraits. For references to *Le Saint des saints, De Zayas! De Zayas!, Gabrielle Buffet. Elle corrige les moeurs en riant* and *Portrait Max Jacob* (figs. 108, 109, 111, 112), see Centre National d'Art et de Culture Georges Pompidou, Musée National d'Art Moderne, *Francis Picabia*, Paris, Grand Palais, January 23–March 29, 1976, 47–49.

35. These and the immediately following statements were made by de Zayas in *291*, nos. 5–6 (New York, July–August 1915).

associates, and, more specifically, the basic points of de Zayas's statement, for the bellows of the camera has fallen away from its "Ideal" aim, and the gear lever is depicted in the neutral position.[36]

The portrait of Stieglitz also introduces Picabia's practice of fashioning portraits not only by the simple appropriation of objects, but by combining machine parts and manufactured objects in a manner akin to the technique of collage or to Duchamp's assisted ready-mades like the *Bicycle Wheel*. One of these was a self-portrait, *Le Saint des saints* (*The Saint of Saints*, fig. 108). Like most of the mechanomorphic works of 1915, this object portrait is characterized formally by machine objects that are frontal, rigid, basically symmetrical, highly simplified and silhouetted against a lighter field. Moreover, like the other object portraits, this emphatic image is pitted against puzzling inscriptions, particularly the title which may involve at least a double play on French sounds.[37] Interpretation of this self-portrait is handicapped by that possibility and the fact that only one of the two machine parts has been securely identified, namely, the Klaxon horn which overlies (or thrusts into) what may be the cylinder of a gasoline engine. Nonetheless, a contemporary advertisement for the popular Klaxon horn may suggest something of Picabia's intentions: "The note of the Klaxon is a true warning note. It is not pleasant to hear, but it at once expresses—and is instinctively understood as meaning danger."[38]

The composite machine portrait of de Zayas is still more complex (fig. 109). It is chiefly derived from schematic diagrams of electrical systems (fig. 110), but Picabia devised his own system incorporating heterogeneous items which (moving clockwise from the upper left) can be partly identified as an empty corset joined by a line from the region of the heart to what appears to be a gigantic spark plug, a hand crank, and two automobile headlights (lower left and right) with a female plug between them that eventually connects (as does the hand crank) at the point of sex on the corset. On the basis of preceding portraits and what can be identified here, the presence of a deliberate comment must be entertained, but until all of the machine parts can be identified and properly associated with each other and with the cryptic inscriptions, the privacy of Picabia's portrait of de Zayas will not be violated.[39]

A less enigmatic example of Picabia's composite machines in the summer of

36. Identification of the automobile gear shift and brake lever was first made by Paul Schweizer and published by Homer in "Picabia's 'Jeune fille américaine . . .' and Her Friends," *The Art Bulletin*, 111.

37. With a little license, the French pronunciation of *Le Saint des saints* could also register as "The Saint of Breasts" (Le Saint des seins) or "The Healthy Drawing" (Le Sain Dessin).

38. *Hardware Dealer's Magazine*, XLIII, no. 254 (New York, February 1915), 357–58.

39. The inscriptions read, "I have seen / and it is you that this concerns" (upper right) and "De Zayas! De Zayas! / I have come to the shore of Pont-Euxin" (lower left). William I. Homer ("Picabia's 'Jeune fille américaine . . .' and Her Friends," *The Art Bulletin*, 111) has taken the latter inscription, with its reference to the Black Sea (Pontus Euxinus in Latin), as an analogy between Picabia, who was dispatched on a mission to the Caribbean, and Ovid, who was banished to Tomi on the Black Sea. The phrase was taken from Ovid's *Tristia* V.4.1.

1915 is *Voilà elle* (*Here She Is*, fig. 113), which was presented alongside de Zayas's psychotype poem, "Woman." A contemporary critic reported that "according to the artist's sworn word" these works were portraits of the same woman made at different times and in different places "without collusion."[40] At first glance there appears to be a compositional relationship between the printed portrait and the drawn portrait. Closer examination does not sustain that compositional correspondence but does reveal similarities in content. De Zayas's poem is a scathing denunciation of the unidentified woman as a creature without intelligence and consumed by carnal desires. Picabia's message is less evident but susceptible to a similar "reading." The prominent forms in this machine consist of a mount supporting a pistol that is connected by mechanical linkage to a target. The pistol and target, forms repeatedly employed by Picabia as male and female sexual symbols, are aligned with the clear implication that a target hit would cause the pistol to be recocked and discharged again in a repetitive, mechanical action. *Voilà elle* constitutes, therefore, an automatic love machine akin in theme and spirit to Duchamp's *Bride Stripped Bare by Her Bachelors, Even* (fig. 114)—and at this point further comparison of the work of these lifelong friends is in order.

Like Picabia, Duchamp was an "intellectual" artist for whom form followed content—and from 1912 onward machinery and products of machines offered most poignantly the form and content he wished to express. To some extent his machinist style was nourished by a dadalike desanctification of art and artist. He often aired his disgust for artists of small minds but great conviction in their "genius" for manipulating paint. In contrast, by employing mechanical drawing instruments and the modern materials of glass and metal, Duchamp created forms which appear amenable to (if not the result of) mass production. In choosing ready-mades he went further, totally eliminating the hand of the facile artist, yet invariably discovering-selecting objects which reflect his personality in their cool, spare, precise and incredibly suggestive forms. Duchamp's work was far more, however, than a slap at prevailing concepts of art and artists. Again, like Picabia, it dealt primarily with man, not machines. Jarry and Roussel had revealed machinery as the vehicle for Duchamp's intellectual-emotional preoccupations with movement, sexuality, a sense of isolation (or absence of meaningful contacts) and the absurdities of life. Those themes, already noted in the paintings of 1912 (pp. 30, 69), had continued in the curious machines and the ready-mades of 1913–1914, culminating in *The Bride Stripped Bare by Her Bachelors, Even*, or as it is known by the short title, *The Large Glass*.

Work on the final piece began in New York during 1915 and continued intermittently, with excruciating craftsmanship, until abandoned, unfinished, in 1923. This inexhaustibly provocative work lies beyond explanation but may be described broadly as an intricate philosophical object-statement about life expressed through the theme of sexual love. This view is not only supported by Duchamp's notes but is dependent upon them since the forms of *The Large Glass*

40. Anon., *Arts and Decoration* (New York, November 1915), 35.

are not explicit in themselves. The notes have, in fact, come to be viewed as an equal partner in the piece, and along with preceding works they identify the upper and lower divisions of *The Large Glass* as realms reserved respectively for "the Bride" and her "Bachelors." The bachelors are associated with:

1) a chocolate grinder (lower center). "The bachelor," wrote Duchamp, "grinds his chocolate himself"
2) a glider which in moving to and fro cites litanies "Slow life. Vicious circle. Onanism. Horizontal. Buffer of life. . . ."
3) nine malic moulds representing uniformed figures (gendarme, priest, busboy, etc.), all different in shape but filled with the same substance (illuminating gas) and united at their plane of sex
4) sieves through which flows illuminating gas from the malic moulds, exiting as a drop that is shot past oculist witnesses into the realm of the
5) bride who is "basically a motor" with a reservoir of "love gasoline" at her base and a "desire magneto" which, with sparks from the electrical stripping by the bachelors, "should supply explosions in the motor with quite feeble cylinders."[41]

Although a more detailed exploration of *The Large Glass* is not possible here, correlation of the notes and the object indicate that Duchamp stripped the sexual act of all love, intimacy and delight by making its procedure preposterous and by frustrating its consummation. And this devaluation of love, devastating as it is, is only a piercing means to the larger comment that man is not a creature so distinguished by powers of reason and love. Outwardly, man, as represented by the malic molds, is determined by (and often judged by) his uniform or mold; inwardly he is activated by biological drives which function with the relentless rhythm of a machine, and taunted from above by woman, an erotic motor whose parts and their relationships are incommensurable. Duchamp perceived in machines not the beauty of logic and economy that thrilled Léger and the purists, nor the speed and power glorified by the futurists; he dealt with animated mechanisms that operated

41. Marcel Duchamp, *The Bride Stripped Bare by Her Bachelors, Even*, trans. George Heard Hamilton, typographic version Richard Hamilton (London, 1960). For the numerous serious studies of *The Large Glass* see John Golding, *Marcel Duchamp: The Bride Stripped Bare by Her Bachelors, Even* (London, 1973) and his bibliographical note, pp. 107–108, which cites major interpretive works and/or translations by André Breton, Robert Lebel, Arturo Schwarz, Lawrence D. Steefel, Jr., Michel Carrouges, George H. Hamilton, Octavio Paz, Nicolas Calas and Richard Hamilton. An interpretation was also offered by Marcel Jean (*Histoire de la peinture surréaliste*, Paris, 1959, chap. iv), and Duchamp's notes for *The Large Glass* were reunited by Michel Sanouillet, ed., in *Marchand du sel* (Paris, 1958), 30–95. Still other serious considerations of *The Large Glass* were included in two recent exhibitions, *Marcel Duchamp* presented by the Museum of Modern Art, New York, and the Philadelphia Museum of Art, 1973 (see especially Richard Hamilton's "The Large Glass," 57–67, and Arturo Schwarz's "The Alchemist Stripped Bare in the Bachelor, Even," 81–98); and *Marcel Duchamp* presented by the Centre National d'Art et de Culture Georges Pompidou, Musée National d'Art Moderne, Paris, 1977 (see especially Jean Clair's "Marcel Duchamp et la tradition des Perspecteurs," III, 124–59).

largely without will, intelligence or passion—mechanisms fraught with visual, functional and psychological analogies to his view of life as a folly-ridden affair where biological drives, social conventions and notions of reason and morality constantly subvert the freedom and intelligence of man.

While it may seem unfair to compare Duchamp's masterpiece with a small drawing, *Voilà elle* (fig. 113), which holds no comparable importance within Picabia's oeuvre, some interesting, essentially valid points may be made. In contrast to Duchamp's work, Picabia's machine images tend to be simpler in both form and content, less marked by painstaking craftsmanship and less dependent on external documents, although such documents are usually necessary as a guide to his intentions. Moreover, Picabia's machines are frequently based on specific persons and events in his private life while Duchamp seems never to have admitted personal mementos into the metaphysical realms of his machines—a phenomenon wholly in accord with their respective personalities. Both ridiculed man's undue attachment to any ideal or institution, whether it be reason, love, morality, church, state, art, or whatever. But Duchamp did so to free himself from the follies demanded by false gods while Picabia was less concerned about the falsity of those gods than by their power to check the fulfillment of his every impulse. Duchamp possessed uncanny discipline and objectivity; Picabia was an utter hedonist. And in that light it is interesting to note that Duchamp left *The Large Glass* unfinished, abandoning the concerned parties in a state of suspended frustration, while *Voilà elle* appears to be in good working order.

In January 1916, de Zayas presented at the Modern Gallery an exhibition of Picabia's work which was dominated by his mechanomorphic style in all its variety. The simple, appropriated object portraits such as *Voilà Haviland* (fig. 104) were augmented by larger paintings and collages of composite-imaginative machines and by yet another mode of painting related more to optical art than to machinist art.[42]

Voilà la femme (*Here is Woman*, fig. 115), one of the imaginative inventions on exhibit, continues the general theme of *Voilà elle* and reintroduces Picabia's practice of attaching associative or symbolic attributes to color. "Woman" is presented as an upright apparatus attractively tinted in red, green, blue, brown and black and set afloat in a brownish fog which enhances her presence as an icon-machine or machine goddess. Although her nature and function are not explicit, sexual analogies are suggested by the center shaft, the two receptacles and a color scheme which reserves the hot reds for what is literally portrayed at the bottom center of the machine as a "door" to "woman."

42. Modern Gallery, New York, *Picabia Exhibition*, January 5–25, 1916. Picabia's paintings associated with "optical" art are not accurately described by that term since responses to them are more of a psychological-philosophical order than a retinal one. Nonetheless, certain paintings in Picabia's mechanomorphic period have pronounced "optical" properties akin to a variety of more recent perceptual paintings provisionally designated "optical" by William C. Seitz, *The Responsive Eye* (New York: The Museum of Modern Art, 1965), 18f. His terms will be used in this study.

The thrust of *Révérence* (fig. 116) appears to be quite different, although the search for its visual source and content is not yet resolved. Precise geometrical forms rendered in glittering metallic paint make this painting an impressive representative of the machine age, and one author views it as derived from a machine already established in the proto-dada iconography of Duchamp, the chocolate grinder. This author, struck by the ultimate visual ambiguity of *Révérence*, has suggested a possible source in charts dealing with optics or the psychology of perception.[43] And pursuing that direction, efforts to correlate the striking image and baffling inscriptions suggest that he may have simultaneously celebrated the formal properties sacred to classical art and subverted them into an anticlassic system. On one level, order, balance, clarity and stability prevail in "pure" square and circular forms covered with gold and silver metallic paint. But an initial impression of compositional balance and stability is undermined by the off-center alignment of the diagonal shaft, the displacement of the smaller circles along that shaft and the interior modeling of the two trapezoids which create thoroughly ambiguous illusions of space, light, weight and shape. As Picabia wrote along the bottom of the large circle, this painting is an object "that does not praise times past" but merits "reverence" for placing the cherished values of classicizing art at the service of a new antirational system.

The striking machine aesthetics of *Révérence* also dominate one's initial experience of *Très rare tableau sur la terre* (*Very Rare Painting on Earth*) and *Cette Chose est faite pour perpétuer mon souvenir* (*This Thing is Made to Perpetuate My Memory*, figs. 119, 120). Like other works of 1915, they are rigid, frontal, basically symmetrical and composed of precise machine forms brushed in metallic paint and silhouetted against a field of contrasting color. *Très rare tableau sur la terre* is distinguished, however, as the first known example of collage in Picabia's career—in this instance two wooden half cylinders coated in gold metallic paint which deceived a contemporary critic into thinking they were actually metal.[44] *Cette Chose est faite pour perpétuer mon souvenir* has no collage elements, and in fact its black, brown, reddish and silver forms against a metallic gold background

43. For these two viewpoints see Jean-Hubert Martin, "Ses Tableaux sont peints pour raconter non pour prouver" (Centre National d'Art et de Culture Georges Pompidou, Musée National d'Art Moderne, *Francis Picabia*, Paris, Grand Palais, January 23–March 29, 1976, 45, 48) and William A. Camfield "The Machinist Style of Francis Picabia" (*The Art Bulletin*, XLVIII, New York, September–December 1966, 316). Martin also notes a *Petit Larousse* source for the inscription, "Objet qui ne fait pas l'éloge du temps passé."

Discrepancies about the title are resolved by contemporary reviews which establish that *Révérence* was exhibited by that title at the Modern Gallery during January 1916 (Anon., "Picabia's Puzzles," *Christian Science Monitor* [Boston], January 29, 1916). After World War II, *Révérence* was referred to as *Dédée d'Amérique*, and it has also been confused with another painting entitled *Révérences* (fig. 87) of ca. 1913.

44. Anon., "Picabia's Puzzles," *Christian Science Monitor*. No machine source for this collage has yet been discovered. Ulf Linde speculates that Picabia has created an alchemical turbine; see Centre National d'Art et de Culture Georges Pompidou, Musée National d'Art Moderne, *Francis Picabia*, Paris, Grand Palais, January 23–March 29, 1976, 24.

are so flat in appearance that a critic associated it with Japanese wood-block prints.[45] Only after savoring awhile the formal properties of this bold, harmonious composition does one begin to focus on some inscriptions along the pipelike forms. A command, printed above the uppermost pipe, directs the spectator to "Lis—C'est clair comme le jour" ("Read—it is as clear as day"), while a comment along the bottommost pipe states: "Ils tournent—vous avez des oreilles et vous n'entendrez pas" ("They turn—you have ears and you do not hear"). This statement and the four black circles suggest that the discs represent gramophone records, but the privacy of Picabia's intention on this occasion rebuffs interpretive efforts except to note that he has combined within one frame image, word and reference to sound.

Even more provocative and baffling is Picabia's intention in *Petite Solitude au milieu des soleils* (*A Little Solitude in the Midst of Suns*, fig. 121), a composite machine composed of a separator (fig. 122) and an unidentified mechanical object with five numbered circles identified in a key at the lower right as "1. Ecclesiastical Sun; 2. Lycée Student Sun; 3. Hotel Manager Sun; 4. Superior Officer Sun; and 5. Artist Officer Sun." Several interpretations of the title have been offered, but, as previously indicated, any interpretation not based on full identification of the parts and their correlation with accompanying inscriptions is bound to miss the mark.[46] That assumes, of course, that Picabia's aim was not merely to mock and mystify, that he was preoccupied with man-machine correspondence or symbolism in which title and image were related. Previous analyses suggest that such is the case, that intelligible content exists in the mechanomorphic paintings, that Picabia's machines in effect do "work." Inclinations to view his mechanisms as antimachine rest on the neglect of the visual sources of his paintings and the nature of his mechanical symbolism.

When the visual properties of Picabia's machines are compared with the real machines and diagrams on which they were based, it becomes evident that the operation of his contraptions is no less convincing than that of real machines.

45. Anon., "Current News of Art and the Exhibitions," *Sun* [New York], January 16, 1916, sec. 3, 7.

46. Hultén related the title of this painting to the female sex organ (*The Machine*, 85); Mme Buffet-Picabia claimed that it was derived from a poem of Jules Laforgue (conversation with the author, July 1965), and Jean-Hubert Martin offers phrases from the *Petit Larousse* red pages (Centre National d'Art et de Culture Georges Pompidou, Musée National d'Art Moderne, *Francis Picabia*, Paris, Grand Palais, January 23–March 29, 1976, 48). Marc Le Bot imposes a social interpretation ("Le Mythe de la machine," in Kunsthalle Bern, *Junggesellenmaschinen. Les Machines célibataires*, July 5–August 17, 1975, 172–79, edited by Harald Szeemann).

The whereabouts of the original painting of *Petite Solitude au milieu des soleils* is unknown. Two or more versions are extant, all different in size, media and details. Some of them were probably painted in 1920 when Marie de La Hire published a booklet (*Francis Picabia*, Paris: Galerie La Cible, 1920) with a deluxe edition bearing tipped-in prints possibly hand-tinted by Picabia. The version published by this author (*Francis Picabia*, New York: The Solomon R. Guggenheim Museum, 1970, 94) turned out upon arrival at the museum to be a serigraph from a publication by *Art d'aujourd'hui* (sixteen serigraphs of works by modern artists, Boulogne, Seine, July 1953, 300 numbered copies).

Even when confronted with a relatively common machine (fig. 123), one may be unable to determine either its purpose or manner of operation.[47] Removal of exterior plates to reveal the engine, and reference to cross-sectional diagrams of that engine are more confusing than clarifying for those spectators without special training. The designing engineers themselves, in order to clarify the operation of their machines, constructed models and reduced complex electrical, chemical and mechanical actions to simple symbols in renderings which rely heavily on number and color codes, labels and directional arrows. Yet the ability of an automobile electrical system to function (fig. 110) is not likely to be questioned, whereas *De Zayas! De Zayas!* or *Voilà la femme* are susceptible to immediate classification as nonsense contraptions.

These observations are not intended to convince the reader that Picabia's mechanical contrivances are conceived to function as conventional machines. They do not function in an ordinary manner because their contacts are psychological, not mechanical; he was interested in man, and with few exceptions Picabia commented on man or human conditions and only indirectly on machines, science and technology. When viewed in this context, Picabia's machines do work.

47. When Henry Adams compared the Virgin to huge dynamos observed at the Paris World's Fair in 1900 (*The Education of Henry Adams*, Boston and New York, 1918, chap. xxv), he remarked that there was something miraculous about machines that produced astounding noise, motion and end products or effects without a visible source of power.

7. BARCELONA, NEW YORK, 391 AND THE STIRRINGS OF DADA

THE FIRST phase of Picabia's mechanomorphic period was concluded in the fall of 1915 when Gabrielle went to New York to escort her husband on his military mission to the Caribbean. She found him in an agitated state, euphoric over his own work and the vital activities of his friends, but also subject to renewed crises of neurasthenia, complicated by excessive drinking, the use of drugs, depression over the war and his embroiled personal affairs. Within a few weeks, however, he was ready to travel, and by late November they reached Panama, where one of Gabrielle's relatives in the French diplomatic service assisted them in their mission. After that port of call they sojourned in Cuba; then early in 1916 Francis apparently returned to New York while Gabrielle made a quick round trip to Europe in order to look after their children, who had been left in the care of a nurse in Switzerland.[1]

During those months of incessant travel and illness, Picabia was unable to paint much but he did begin his first serious, sustained efforts at writing poetry.

1. Events in Picabia's life from the fall of 1915 to the spring of 1916 are not well documented. His letter to Max Jacob on October 21, 1915 (B.D., A-IV-5, 7. 198–88; Michel Sanouillet, *Francis Picabia et "391,"* II, Paris, 1966, 55), documents Gabrielle's presence in New York by that date. Their arrival in Panama is verified by a postcard from Picabia to de Zayas (A.S.A., Yale) postmarked simply "November 22." The year must be 1915 since Picabia's whereabouts are known for November in all relevant years.

In letters and conversations with this author, Mme Buffet-Picabia has recalled that Cuba was their next stop ca. December 1915 or January 1916. Sanouillet (loc. cit.) cites a letter to Max Jacob from Picabia in New York which indicates that Gabrielle was in Paris on March 14, 1916. Picabia was hardly mentioned in New York during the early months of 1916. However, one letter from Stieglitz to de Zayas (April 25, 1916, A.S.A., Yale) suggests he might have been there recovering from an illness, and Edgar Varèse later attributed Picabia's first attack of tachycardia to early 1916 (1963 interview with Sanouillet, op. cit., 40). The Picabias sailed together for Spain ca. June or July 1916 and are recorded in Barcelona during August (letter from Marie Laurencin to H.P. Roché, August 20, 1916, The Carlton Lake Collection in the Humanities Research Center, The University of Texas at Austin).

Picabia was not an utter novice as a poet. He claimed 1914 as the date of some of his first published poems, and Gabrielle recalls that he already possessed an interest in poetry and a flair for Nietzschean aphorisms when they met in 1908.[2] Those earlier writings are no longer extant, or cannot be identified. But from 1916 onward, work as a poet, polemicist, editor and scenarist was an integral part of Picabia's life; from 1916 through 1924 it vied in importance with his painting, and it will figure prominently in the next chapters.

More is known of Picabia's life after the summer of 1916 when he and Gabrielle left New York for Spain. They settled in Barcelona in August after landing in Algeciras on the coast below Seville and journeying by a circuitous route to the Catalonian capital. For Picabia, whose military status was too irregular to risk a return to France, Barcelona offered several advantages. It was a pleasant city in a neutral country and relatively near both France and his children, whom he hoped to see in Switzerland. It also possessed the Mediterranean climate he adored, and a small colony of friends from Paris.

Albert and Juliette Gleizes had preceded the Picabias to Barcelona and may have contributed to their decision to settle there. More to Picabia's taste was the notorious Arthur Cravan, whose disastrous boxing match with the former world heavyweight champion, Jack Johnson, likewise preceded his arrival but continued to provide amusement for the group. Also on hand were Marie Laurencin and her German husband, Otto van Watgen, who had fled France to avoid imprisonment owing to van Watgen's German citizenship; Max Goth (Maximilien Gautier), a poet and former art critic for *Les Hommes du jour*; Otho St. Clair Lloyd and Olga Sackaroff, Cravan's brother and sister-in-law respectively; Nicole Groult, sister of the couturier Paul Poiret; and Valentine de Saint Point, an outspoken woman of varied talents who had been prominent in the cultural affairs of Paris before the war. One new friend discovered there, the young Spanish art dealer, José Dalmau, had already committed himself to avant-garde art and was to aid Picabia in many ways during their long friendship. Joan Miró, a timid young Catalonian artist, also supported by Dalmau, savored the activities concocted by those foreigners in the back rooms of Dalmau's gallery.[3]

Although Picabia never intended to tarry long in Barcelona, the interlude there became longer and far more important than could have been anticipated. Moreover, until his inherent restlessness set in again, it was a pleasant sojourn. Photographs (see illus. 16), letters and memoirs attest to good health and good

2. For comments on Picabia's early literary efforts see P.A. Benoit, *A propos des "Poèmes de la fille née sans mère"* (Alès, 1958); Marc Le Bot, *Francis Picabia* (Paris, 1968), 138; Sanouillet, *Francis Picabia et "391,"* II, 49–50.

3. For additional information on this group of people see Sanouillet, *Francis Picabia et "391,"* II, 41–44. Prior to the war Valentine de Saint Point had painted, contributed critical articles to *Montjoie!*, founded Le Théâtre de la Femme and advocated a "pure" dance form, "La Métachoire," liberated from words and music. Dalmau's *Exposicio d'art cubiste* (Barcelona, April 20–May 10, 1912) was one of the earliest exhibitions of cubist art organized outside Paris and the occasion for the first exhibit of Duchamp's *Nude Descending the Staircase*.

times, with many hours passed in the movies indulging his taste for American westerns and comedies, or along the Ramblas—drinking, talking, watching the girls and playing chess. Other days were spent sailing, swimming and clowning on the beach—and, under such conditions, Picabia began to work again. In a letter to de Zayas he noted not only that he was well but that he had "worked a lot."[4] Some of his efforts went to fulfill commitments to the Modern Gallery as a contact for European paintings, but he really was referring to his own work, which then included poetry, a revival of the ubiquitous Spanish subjects (see fig. 124), a distinct second phase of the mechanomorphic style and, beginning in January 1917, the publication of a magazine entitled *391*.[5]

That magazine, which became one of the most piquant representatives of Dada, was born of boredom in Barcelona. Despite an initial enthusiasm for the life there, Picabia's moments of happiness were mercurial, dogged by a profound restlessness and melancholy which drove him from one temporary haven to another. From late December 1916 through January 1917 repeated plans were made to leave for Cuba or for New York, where he longed to rejoin the Modern Gallery and launch a magazine to succeed the expired *291*.[6] As those trips were frustrated and the boredom mounted, Picabia began his own magazine with the collaboration of his expatriot friends and the good services of Dalmau. Just three days prior to the first issue on January 25, 1917, Picabia wrote Stieglitz: "You will receive a magazine '391' which is a duplicate of your magazine '291.' It is the *Gallerie Dalmau* [sic] which has just published it[;] it is not as well done but it is better than nothing, for truly here there is nothing, nothing, nothing."[7]

391 continued through nineteen issues, which appeared at erratic intervals until 1924. The format was seldom repeated, but during 1917 it generally consisted of either four or eight pages with a cover designed by Picabia, followed by several pages of poems, articles and illustrations, concluding with a page of news and gossip where Picabia indulged his caustic humor. Some of the deluxe editions are striking, but, as Picabia acknowledged to Stieglitz, it was not as well made as *291*. Instead, the importance of *391* resided in its role as a carrier of a dadaist spirit in Barcelona, New York and Paris before that spirit had a name in those

4. Picabia letter to de Zayas, December 20, 1916 (M. de Z.A.; Sanouillet, *Francis Picabia et "391,"* II, 253).

5. Professor Sanouillet's two-volume publication of *391*, I, a reedition (Paris, 1960), and *Francis Picabia et "391,"* II, with extensive critical comments (Paris, 1966), is an invaluable study of that magazine.

6. In Picabia's letters to de Zayas from Barcelona (M. de Z.A.; Sanouillet, *Francis Picabia et "391,"* II, 252–53), see especially the December 20 letter: "Not a day passes that one does not talk of the Modern Gallery. . . . A magazine must be made, think about it." Mme Gleizes ("Memoires," unpublished manuscript written 1959–1963, collection Mme Albert Gleizes, Paris) recalls that she, her husband and the Picabias sailed for Cuba about December 16, but a storm forced them into Lisbon. The Picabias returned to Barcelona while the Gleizes went on to Cuba, then to Bermuda and finally to New York.

7. Picabia letter to Stieglitz, January 22, 1916 (A.S.A., Yale; Sanouillet, *Francis Picabia et "391,"* II, 46).

cities.[8] The pages of *391* became almost an anthology of Dada in Paris and provide invaluable insight into the persons, events and spirit associated with the entire movement. But, above all, *391* was Picabia's personal forum, a place to vent his enthusiasms and his disgust, his humor and his anguish; a place to attack his enemies and to celebrate the activities of himself and his friends. Regular issues were totally alien to such a personalized publication; *391* appeared when the exigencies of Picabia's private or public life made it necessary.

With few exceptions, the four numbers published in Barcelona were wholly the work of Picabia and his band of expatriot friends—poems and critical articles by Max Goth, poems and drawings by Marie Laurencin, drawings by Lloyd and Olga Sackaroff, Gabrielle's article on the cinema and Picabia's own contribution of drawings, poems and the gossip page. Second to Picabia, Max Goth provided the most interesting material, including an article on art in which he divided the world into two spiritual families composed of the children of Adam and Abraham:

> The artists of the family of Adam can pass a lifetime turning around a compotier filled with three apples. . . .
>
> The artists of the family of Abraham consider secondary the knowledge of an object "in itself. . . ."
>
> The world of ideas and forms appears to them [spiritual children of Abraham] as a sympathetic cosmos, all in correspondences, rapports and resemblances. He perceives what there can be in common . . . between a flower and a combustible engine, between a line and an idea, a color and a memory, a love and a chemical phenomenon, a Biblical person and a doctrine of art, a piano and a comb, the sea and a tramway. What one may take in him as comic affectation is only the effect of a pure ingenuity, of a firm and sincere desire to express all that is human by the most direct means. His sole objective is to entrust, to project into matter, the realities of his inner being. Thus each work of art becomes the representation of a special world, recreated in the image of a man.[9]

Although Picabia is not mentioned by name, the article clearly deals with him, and Picabia's drawings for *391* bear witness to the human-machine correspondence reaffirmed by Goth. The very first cover of *391* (fig. 125) is a provocative juxtaposition of crisp machine forms and palsied inscriptions which include the title *Novia au premier occupant* (*Sweetheart of the First Occupant*) and the sig-

8. Like other avant-garde magazines of the war years, *391* found its way to interested people everywhere. Max Jacob (letter to Jacques Doucet, March 7, 1917, in Max Jacob, *Correspondance*, I, Paris, 1953, 144) and Pierre Albert-Birot (*SIC*, no. 15, Paris, March 17, 1917, 8) record the presence of *391* in Paris soon after its publication. In turn, *391* (no. 5, New York, June 1917) referred to the leading avant-garde magazines in Paris, *L'Elan*, *SIC* and *Nord-Sud*, and to the editor of *Dada*, Tristan Tzara.

9. M[aximilien] G[autier] [Max Goth], "D'un certain esprit . . . ," *391*, no. 2 (Barcelona, February 10, 1917).

nature, "The Saint of Saints / Picabia." Despite the visual clash of sharp machine image and clumsily printed words, Picabia's principal interest resided in correspondence—here the correspondence between a sweetheart machine made by Picabia, the "Saint of Saints," and Eve (sweetheart of the first occupant, Adam), who was also made by her Creator without the aid of a mother. The cover of *391*, no. 3, *Flamenca* (fig. 126), associates the clatter of a flamenca dancer with the exhaust valve of a gasoline engine, and the cover of no. 4 (fig. 127) associates the round forms and the action of automobile brakes with the form and operation of a roulette wheel. Among other illustrations of a similar nature, there is one interesting exception, the portrait of *Max Goth* (fig. 128), on the final page of *391*, no. 1. It is a simple line drawing except for the head, which was a photograph of Goth, cut out and pasted on the drawing in derision of a recent turn in Picasso's work reported in an adjacent text by Picabia:

> Picasso repentant:—At the moment when the nations of France, Spain and Italy simultaneously lay claim to the honor of counting him as one of theirs—he is in effect Spanish by his father, Italian by his mother and French by education—Pablo Picasso . . . has decided to return to the Ecole des Beaux-Arts (studio Luc Olivier Merson).
>
> *L'Elan* has published his first studies "after the model." Picasso is henceforth the chief of a new school to which our collaborator Francis Picabia, not hesitating a minute, gives his adhesion. The kodak published above is the solemn sign of it.[10]

On the gossip pages of *391*, Picabia's budding dada spirit grew apace. Some of the news was pure fabrication, but for the most part he took potshots at any pompous target which happened to come his way. He continued to poke fun at Picasso, culminating with an announcement of his election as mayor of "half-breed City"; he ribbed Edgar Varèse about his ever-promised never-produced "Dance of the Cold Water Faucet"; he needled Delaunay for his elephantine projects and Gleizes and Metzinger for assuming roles as censors within Cubism. Apollinaire got a turn for his militarism and literary posturing: "Scarcely returned from recent literary and war triumphs, will we see Guillaume Apollinaire here? Some desire it. But the God of the Armies, will he yield his lieutenant? Saint Max Jacob, pray for us."[11]

Such a statement about Apollinaire—wounded warrior and impresario of the avant-garde—would have been inconceivable in the pages of the "daring" art and literary journals of wartime France, *L'Elan*, *SIC* and *Nord-Sud*. Since recovering

10. Pharamousse [Picabia], "Odeurs de partout," *391*, no. 1 (Barcelona, January 25, 1917). For several years Picabia sometimes used the pseudonym "Pharamousse," which has been attributed to a child's deformation of "frimousse" ("little face"; see Sanouillet, *Francis Picabia et "391,"* II, 53). It also seems plausible that Picabia constructed a name playing on the multiple possibilities of "phare" (beacon or headlight) and "mousse" (whipped cream, moss, or foam).

11. [Picabia], "De nos envoyés spéciaux," *391*, no. 3 (Barcelona, March 1, 1917).

from a serious head wound sustained at the front, he had been surrounded by old friends and young poets like André Breton, Philippe Soupault, Louis Aragon and Pierre Reverdy, who regarded him as the great *modern* poet of France and a guide to some vague new spirit arising from the war. In contrast to the deference accorded Apollinaire in Paris, Picabia took a swipe at him, joshing Max Jacob in the process over his religious conversion.

This burgeoning irreverence and sarcasm of Picabia, his private noncommercial, anti-anything-established attitude, suggest the proto-dada qualities of *391* and set it apart from other contemporary magazines—even the somewhat more serious review entitled *Dada*, which appeared in Zurich in July 1917. The humorous, dadaist aspect of Picabia's painting and writing has always had an appreciative audience; however, his first published poems in *391* present a difficult, tortured aspect of his nature—and their audience has been minuscule.[12] A selection of those poems reveals—sometimes incisively, often obscurely—an autobiographical content imbued with melancholy, pessimistic moralizing and brutal disruptions of any sense of wholeness or logical relations. That content, in his poetry as in his painting, was patently more important for Picabia than form. At times the form seems as unconsidered and improvisational as the scruffiest machine drawing. Finally, however, form and content are inseparable. Ambiguous words and shocking, disrupted thoughts are paralleled by formal shocks and ambiguities—ambiguities of punctuation and division into slashing, irregular lines, rude juxtapositions, bewildering sequences of ideas and inconsistent rhyme, rhythm and alliteration. Ideally such poetry should be reproduced in facsimile. Approximating that costly standard, Picabia's poetry is presented here in the original French, retaining its composition of lines, its punctuation and capitalization—followed by English translations which, as all translations, suffer in comparison with the original, but have been deemed useful for the English-speaking reader.[13]

In "Revolver" (*391*, no. 1) the general intellectual cohesion and measured visual descent of the lines is ripped asunder by a coarse final line, "Virgins do not cure syphilis." That intellectual disruption is akin to, but more jarring than, the formal-intellectual conflict of handsome machine forms and halting inscriptions in *Novia au premier occupant* (fig. 125) on the cover of the same issue of *391*.

12. No full-scale study of Picabia's poetry and other writings has been undertaken, but an excellent collection of his writings up to 1920 has been published (Picabia, *Ecrits 1913–1920*, ed. Olivier Revault d'Allonnes, Paris, 1975), and some helpful consideration of Picabia's literary work occurs in P.A. Benoit, *A propos des "Poèmes de la fille née sans mère"*; Pierre de Massot, *Francis Picabia* (Paris, 1966); Sanouillet, *Francis Picabia et "391,"* II, esp. 49–50, 51–58, passim; and Le Bot, *Francis Picabia*, 135–57. Mme Buffet-Picabia has written briefly about Picabia's poetry and also helped him write it—at least to the extent of completing and editing occasional poems (conversations with this author; Le Bot, op. cit., 141). Her hand has not detracted from the sensation of a single author.

13. This author's translations have been substantially refined and corrected by Ms. Karen Coffey. Editorial decisions regarding the poetry include retaining, without comment, Picabia's "errors" in spelling and grammar, and, for the translations, the primacy of literal content over style.

REVOLVER

Chercher à contraindre moins qu'à plaire
 Odieuses caresses
  Femmes ou hommes litières
   Homicide égoïste et malheureuses victimes
   Et ils prétendent aimer
   Besoin Sexuel
   Eglises
    Ecoles de petites filles
    Promenades publiques
     Les vierges ne guérissent pas la syphilis.

REVOLVER

Seek to constrain less than to please / Odious caresses / Discarded women or men / Egoistic homicide and unfortunate victims / And they pretend to love / Sexual need / Churches / Schools for young girls / Public promenades / Virgins do not cure syphilis.

"Singulier Idéal" (*391*, no. 3) is more perplexing, with its vaguely related and rather sluggish succession of unpunctuated sentences. However, as noted by Sanouillet,[14] it exhibits techniques which, in a perfected form, characterized the later poetry of Tzara, Eluard and Picabia himself; for example, its coupled substantives like "Butin souplesse de la couleur locale" ("Booty suppleness of local color"), and its "sliding" words which fit just as well with the preceding phrase, the following phrase, or with both.

SINGULIER IDÉAL

*Un flair plus subtil peut glisser sur une forme humaine
victorieuse bravoure liberté cruauté plus douce mais ils perdent
pied immédiatement par divination—Butin souplesse
de la couleur locale pour combien de temps déchaîné et radicalement
fou mais formes attractives c'est exactement la même chose.—
Des créateurs un mensonge des destructeurs un mensonge
trônes fous grimpeurs aux longues oreilles tout est volé—
Avons-nous appris quelque chose critique tentatives courageuses
très difficile à comprendre du moins pas pour nous—
Miroir universellement déprimant qui tyrannise des esclaves
arrivés à dominer l'existence d'hypersentimentalité—
Opinions d'idiots non-valeurs de pantins la victoire moraliste—
Il faut être beaucoup de choses—*

PECULIAR IDEAL

A more subtle scent can glide by a human form / victorious bravery liberty sweeter

14. Sanouillet, *Francis Picabia et "391,"* II, 58.

cruelty but they lose / foot immediately by divination—Booty suppleness / of local color how many times unchained and radically / mad but attractive forms it is exactly the same thing.— / From creators a lie from destructors a lie / thrones insane long-eared climbers everything is stolen— / Have we learned something critical courageous attempts / very difficult to understand at least not for us— / Universally flattening mirror that tyrannizes slaves / arrived to dominate the existence of hypersentimentality— / Opinions of idiots non-values of puppets the moralist victory— / One must be many things—

"Bossus" (Hunchbacks, *391*, no. 4) is also composed of unpunctuated and seemingly unrelated phrases and sentences which could stand alone or in other combinations. Here they are gathered in a prose form whose placid, blockish composition on the page rests in maddening contrast to the totally illogical, proto-surrealist "content" of the first sentences:

BOSSUS

Il se perd beaucoup de fruits si la fatuité garde son trésor de vieux rats mais d'une façon d'ordre contraire à Napoléon unique synthèse des occasions. Car le salut toujours prêt des déboires d'honnêtes gens inféodés à la papauté fruit dégénéré et abâtardi fait la guerre aux révolutionnaires au plus haut degré de civilisation. . . .

HUNCHBACKS

Many fruits are lost if the self-conceit guards its treasure of old rats but in a fashion of order contrary to Napoleon unique synthesis of circumstances. For the greeting always ready from the disappointments of honest men beholden to the papacy degenerate and spoiled fruit makes war for revolutionaries in the highest degree of civilization. . . .

Of all the poems in the first issues of *391*, "Magic City" (*391*, no. 4) reveals most clearly the formal structure and autobiographical content of his work:

MAGIC CITY
Un vent dangereux et tentateur de sublime nihilisme
nous poursuivait avec une allégresse prodigieuse.

Idéal inattendu.
Rupture d'equilibre.
Enervement croissant.
Emancipations.

Partout hommes et femmes avec une musique qui me plaît
publiquement ou en secret
déchaînent leurs passions stériles.

Opium.
Whisky.
Tango.

Spectateurs et acteurs
de plus en plus subtils
surmontent les satisfactions grossières.
Femmes moins fortes
plus belles et plus inconscientes.
Les hommes avec une silencieuse arrière-pensée
regardent leur plaisir.
Années de génie et de soleil oriental.
1914–1915

MAGIC CITY

A dangerous and tempting wind of sublime nihilism / pursues us with a prodigious cheerfulness. / Unexpected ideal. / Rupture of equilibrium. / Growing exasperation. / Emancipations. / Everywhere men and women with a music which pleases me / publicly or in secret / unleashed their sterile passions. / Opium. / Whiskey. / Tango. / Spectators and actors / more and more subtle / surmount gross satisfactions. / Women less strong / more beautiful and more unaware. / Men with a silent ulterior motive / regard their pleasure. / Years of genius and oriental sun. / 1914–1915

This nascent dada spirit in Picabia's contributions to *391* is also perceptible in the second phase of his mechanomorphic style dating from ca. 1916 to 1919. The distinctive features of this new phase are most readily perceived in formal properties; changes in subject matter and content are more sublte, but also significant in assessing emerging dada qualities. Within the considerable variety of this phase, three recognizable modes may be suggested. Some works retain the hard, clean machine aesthetics of the earlier paintings (figs. 133, 134; color pl. VIII); others are rendered in a sketchy, painterly manner (figs. 135–137), while many are droll, gangling and improvisational in form (figs. 129, 131, 132). Regardless of their mode, almost all of the new works, unlike those of 1915, are asymmetrical in composition.[15]

Comparison of *Portrait de Marie Laurencin, Four in Hand* (fig. 129) with the object portraits and larger paintings of 1915 offers a telling introduction to the new phase. The images of 1915 were basically simple, symmetrical, rigid, frontal and firmly drawn. Some of them were quite handsome; few had a high level of dadaist content in the sense of deliberate mockery and protest. In contrast, the *Portrait de Marie Laurencin* presents not only an implausible machine with baffling inscriptions, but a junky machine, seemingly haphazard in composition and so casual in technique that one is sorely tempted to regard it as a dadaist (or proto-dadaist) insult to art and technology. In her memoirs of that epoch, Juliette Gleizes,

15. Many of Picabia's works from 1916 to 1920 are neither dated nor documented by exhibitions. A general evolution has been proposed, using stylistic analysis within a framework based on the few dated works, reliable witness accounts and reproductions or identifiable references in newspapers, journals and exhibition catalogues.

another subject of Picabia's machine portraits, recalled that she had been struck by Picabia's ardent fixation on spontaneous expression and his hatred of painting, evidently painting taken too seriously.[16] However, at the same time, she noted that Picabia assured her that the portraits were "good likenesses" and "did not hide that there was an entire philosophy behind those objects . . ."—even though he refused all explanations, putting her off with the response: "But it is you who must explain it to me. God doesn't explain to you by creation. It is we who say to Him: 'This is a dog.' 'This is a tree.' He knows nothing about that."[17] Reconsidered in that light, *Portrait de Marie Laurencin* seems to have less to do with dadaist comments on aesthetics and machines than with Picabia's established preoccupation for symbolism, in this instance symbolic reference to Marie Laurencin and the condition of her life in Barcelona. The inscriptions—partially adapted from the *Petit Larousse* red pages—identify her as the subject and refer to Barcelona, to her dog Coco and to a "boche" (slang for "German"), namely, her husband whose nationality had cast a "shadow" ("ombre") over their life in war-struck Europe. The machine forms, though improvised and not very comprehensible in themselves, also represent a deliberate selection. Mme Buffet-Picabia recalled that Picabia associated the freshness of Marie Laurencin with the effect of a ventilator (the major form in the drawing), and that the subtitle *Four in Hand* might have referred to the men in her life.[18]

Those observations notwithstanding, there is an offhandedness to the style of the *Portrait de Marie Laurencin* which contrasts sharply with the crisp machine aesthetics prevalent in another mode of Picabia's work represented in *Machine tournez vite* (*Machine Turn Quickly*, color pl. VIII). One is instantly struck by the bold, hard-edge forms of this painting, arranged asymmetrically in light blue and gold against a dark, fluidly painted ground. Only with longer study is it apparent that a code in the lower left corner establishes a sexual theme for the painting—"woman" is the smaller gear which must "turn quickly" to operate the larger male wheel above.

Picabia's "painterly" machines provide still further variety. *Etude pour novia* (*Study for Sweetheart*, fig. 135) lacks the mass-production personality, streamlines, precision and efficiency that would endear her to a Léger; she is instead a soft, beguiling, irresistibly helpless female gadget—a veritable sweetheart. While her status as a "study" could account for her sketchy, painterly qualities, *Etude pour novia* is satisfying on her own merits, and similar drawings (figs. 136, 137) appear to be totally independent of more finished works.

16. Gleizes, "Memoires." No trace has been found of Picabia's 1916 portrait of Mme Gleizes as a manometer.

17. Ibid.

18. Mme Buffet-Picabia, conversations with the author, June 1968. Marie Laurencin did not discuss this portrait in her contemporary correspondence with H.P. Roché, but Picabia was one of the men in her life and, in her typically frank manner, she wrote of moments of both intimacy and outrage with him (The Carlton Lake Collection in the Humanities Research Center, The University of Texas at Austin).

Other paintings are attributable to ca. 1916–1918 on the basis of their resemblance to various themes and formal properties in the works above. *Novia* (*Sweetheart*, fig. 138), for example, does not fit any of the three modes gracefully, but in form and subject it is related to *Etude pour novia* (fig. 135) and *Novia au premier occupant* (fig. 125). Moreover, its forms are also contrasted against a darker, painterly ground similar to that in *Machine tournez vite* (color pl. VIII). *La Musique est comme la peinture* (*Music is like Painting*, fig. 139) is another of the singular paintings in Picabia's career, and, like the others, it is difficult to date. Given its "abstraction" and a title which refers to the concept of *correspondance*, a date of ca. 1913–1914 should not be excluded. However, a date of ca. 1916–1917, just prior to its exhibition in New York during the spring of 1917, seems more likely, given its striking visual effects of brightly colored bands against a dark, painterly ground, and Picabia's use of a physics diagram showing the effect of a magnetic field on alpha, beta and gamma particles (fig. 140).[19]

Toward the end of March 1917, the Picabias embarked again for America, arriving on April 4, shortly after the United States had entered the war. Though discouraged by that unshakable war, Picabia was once more revitalized by New York, his friends there and their lively activities—for awhile at least. He immediately renewed contact with Stieglitz, de Zayas and the circle around Duchamp and Arensberg, which by then included Henri Pierre Roché, Beatrice Wood and Edgar Varèse.[20] Arthur Cravan had preceded the Picabias to New York and was to star in some of the more scandalous occasions. Albert and Juliette Gleizes, who reached New York soon after the Picabias, contributed a complementary element of sobriety. Both the Gleizes and the Picabias took apartments in the large home of Louise Norton—former coeditor of *Rogue*, who left her husband to marry Edgar Varèse—and, as noted by Mme Gleizes, the rhythm of the entire household was immediately transformed: "Picabia could not live without being surrounded morn-

19. *La Musique est comme la peinture* was first exhibited at the Grand Central Palace, New York, First Annual Exhibition of the Society of Independent Artists, April 10–May 6, 1917, no. 77.

Multiple versions of the painting are known, all identical in composition, but varied in color, media and size. Three are either studies for the original or hand-tinted prints by Picabia for various deluxe editions of Marie de La Hire's booklet, *Francis Picabia* (Paris: Galerie La Cible, 1920). The original painting is probably the version in the Manoukian collection reproduced here.

20. Edgar Varèse was a young French composer known to the Picabias before the war. He went to New York in 1916 and became an American citizen in 1926, two years after the completion of his famous *Ionisations*. Henri Pierre Roché was a young writer, painter and collector who had passed some time in a diplomatic post in Washington before settling in New York, where he became one of Duchamp's closest friends (Sanouillet, *Francis Picabia et "391,"* II, 77). Beatrice Wood was a young woman who came by chance into contact with the Arensberg-Duchamp circle after her bourgeois parents had frustrated a stage career. She became a fascinated participant, tried her hand at art and later accompanied the Arensbergs to California (Beatrice Wood, "Marcel Duchamp and the Arensbergs in New York," unpublished manuscript presented to this author, June 1962, collection William A. Camfield, Houston). See Francis Naumann, "I Shock Myself: Excerpts from the Autobiography of Beatrice Wood," *Arts Magazine*, LI, no. 9 (New York, May 1977), 134–39.

ing and night by a troop of uprooted, floating, bizarre people whom he supported more or less. The whole artistic Bohemia of New York plus several derelicts of the war. . . . Noise at any time or knocks on the door, 'We are having a party. Come down.' "[21]

Most of the parties and projects during Picabia's third sojourn in New York were associated with members of the Duchamp-Arensberg constellation. His relationship with Stieglitz continued to be excellent, but Stieglitz was at last really closing "291," *Camera Work* and, in effect, a whole phase of his public and private life. Also, the situation at the Modern Gallery, which haunted Picabia's thoughts in Barcelona, never materialized.[22] Instead, the exciting exhibition of the day was the first American Independents' Exhibition (April 10–May 6), and the magazines Picabia had anticipated were directed not by de Zayas but by Duchamp, Roché and Beatrice Wood on the occasion of that Independents' show.

The Society of Independent Artists sprang from much the same anti-National Academy reform movement which had produced the Armory Show, although certain features of its organization were modeled after the French Société des Artistes Indépendants. Like its French predecessor, anyone could join and exhibit two works merely by paying a fee of six dollars. Picabia's two entries, *Culture physique* (fig. 86) and *La Musique est comme la peinture* (fig. 139), produced no hullabaloo, but Duchamp's ready-made urinal (fig. 141), placed on its back, signed "R. Mutt" and entitled *Fountain*, generated a heated controversy. Duchamp protested vigorously when the hanging committee refused to display *Fountain*, and when the committee ruling was sustained, he resigned. The hour was too late to expose the Society's censorship in the magazine *The Blind Man*, which Duchamp and Roché

21. Gleizes, "Memoires."
In addition to her memoirs, Mme Gleizes has written a veiled, partly fictionalized story about Marcel Duchamp, *La Minéralisation de Dudley Craving MacAdam* (Paris, 1924), which suggests a great deal about his associates and the conditions of their life in New York. The names of the characters are disguised, but most of them can be identified, including Picabia, who is described (p. 12) as "un gros philosophe."
22. On May 17, 1917, Stieglitz wrote to de Zayas that he had instructed George Of to return works by Picabia, de Zayas and Derain to the Modern Gallery, "as radical changes are being made in my life" (A.S.A., Yale). In that same month, "291" closed permanently with an exhibition of the work of Georgia O'Keeffe, a young artist who later became Mrs. Stieglitz. In June 1917 the last issue of *Camera Work* was published. Stieglitz maintained his career as a photographer and opened the Intimate Gallery in 1928, where Picabia was again accorded a one-man exhibition (see p. 227). The correspondence between these two men reveals an abiding mutual respect, particularly on the part of Picabia. One Stieglitz letter to Marie Rapp Boursault (A.S.A., Yale) on July 23, 1917, merits notation for it describes an interesting evening at the Picabia's apartment in the company of Duchamp, the Arensbergs, the Gleizes and an unidentified Russian.
Picabia and de Zayas also maintained contact for several years, but barely collaborated during 1917 for unknown reasons—possibly inadequate finances, de Zayas's preoccupation with the gallery proper, or disagreements over policy. Picabia criticized severely an exhibition at the Modern Gallery of the work of Robert Frost. De Zayas continued the gallery until 1921, the last years under his own name.

had prepared for the occasion of the Independents' Exhibition. However, Arensberg caused a scene by demanding that *Fountain* be produced so that he might buy it, the committee was pelted with letters of protest and for the next issue of *The Blind Man*, the affair was aired with a superb Stieglitz photograph of the offending object and a classic editorial.[23]

Event tumbled upon event in the wake of the Independents' exhibition and *The Blind Man*. Roché organized the *Blind Man*'s masquerade ball; a psychiatrist friend of Arensberg gave a public lecture on modern art and psychopathic art; and Arthur Cravan was scheduled to lecture on Oscar Wilde—although Picabia and Duchamp sabotaged that lecture by plying him with liquor beforehand, hoping to liberate his outrageous sense of humor. They overshot their mark as the inebriated Cravan, angered by audience protest over his foul language, unleashed his insults upon the elegant gathering, began to disrobe and, finally, had to be forceably removed by the New York police.[24] Other events were more innocent—picnics, parties, outings to Coney Island and drunken celebrations atop Washington Square Arch in honor of the Republic of Greenwich Village (see illus. 17).[25] These and other activities are recorded in memoirs, in the pixie genre paintings of Florine Stettheimer and in the pages of still more magazines.

Around June, Duchamp, Roché and Beatrice Wood edited the single issue of another magazine, *Rongwrong*, which—among some rather dull efforts at humor and literature—contained interesting works by John Covert and Clifford Williams and several entertaining contributions by and about Picabia.[26] One of those con-

23. [Duchamp, Roché and Wood], editorial, *The Blind Man*, no. 2 (New York, May 1917). The most extensive account of this incident is provided by Arturo Schwarz, *The Complete Works of Marcel Duchamp*, 2nd rev. ed. (New York, 1970), 466–67.

The two numbers of *The Blind Man* were edited by Duchamp, Henri Pierre Roché and Beatrice Wood. Roché's recollection of that epoch in New York ("Souvenirs of Marcel Duchamp" in Robert Lebel's *Sur Marcel Duchamp*, Paris, 1959) is complemented by several unpublished letters and statements by Beatrice Wood (see Schwarz, op. cit., 466, and her statement, "Marcel Duchamp and the Arensbergs in New York").

24. For more extensive accounts of these events, see Gabrielle Buffet-Picabia, "Arthur Cravan and American Dada" (Robert Motherwell, ed., *The Dada Painters and Poets*, New York, 1951, 13–17); Sanouillet, *Francis Picabia et "391,"* II, 68; and Städtische Galerie im Lenbachhaus, Munich, *New York Dada*, December 15, 1973–January 27, 1974, catalogue by Arturo Schwarz.

25. For the celebration of the Republic of Greenwich Village, see Albert Parry, *Garrets and Pretenders* (New York, 1933), 275–76.

26. Arturo Schwarz (*Marcel Duchamp: 66 Creative Years*, Milan: Galleria Schwarz, 1972, 35) cites a letter from Duchamp to Mrs. Arensberg, dated August 1917, which indicates that *Rongwrong* was recently published, perhaps in July. However, some material was gathered as early as May, including a letter to Duchamp from an engineer named Marcel Douxami who could not bear the work of Picabia. Duchamp considered the letter and Douxami's name worthy of publication in *Rongwrong*.

John Covert (1882–1960) was an art student and cousin of Arensberg who, stimulated by the work of Duchamp and Picabia, quickly developed into one of the most interesting artists in America from ca. 1915/16 to 1920. Edith Clifford Williams (1885–1971), daughter of a prominent

tributions consisted solely of the record of a chess game between Picabia and Roché, who represented respectively *391* and *The Blind Man*. At stake were their magazines.[27] Picabia won; *The Blind Man* and *Rongwrong* ceased publication and, through the summer of 1917, three issues of *391* dominated the proto-dada publications of New York.

The first New York issue of *391* (no. 5, June 1917) was a rousing one in the tradition established in Barcelona but with a new cast of associates. Edgar Varèse contributed statements and a poem, de Zayas a verbal caricature, Gleizes a serious article on "Modern Painting," Arensberg two remarkable poems and Max Jacob up-to-date news of Paris, including Reverdy's magazine *Nord-Sud*, Picasso's collaboration with the Ballets Russe, and comments on various artists, art dealers, Apollinaire and a new poet, Tristan Tzara. Picabia contributed poems, aphorisms, a news and gossip page of biting humor and several drawings.

For the cover of all three New York issues of *391* (figs. 142–144), he produced handmade ready-mades perhaps reflecting renewed contact with Duchamp, given their more literal reference to actual objects. *Ballet mécanique* (*Mechanical Ballet*, fig. 144) offers a straightforward visual correspondence between the automobile part from which it was copied and a circle of dancing figures.[28] In *Américaine* (*American* [female], fig. 143), a retouched photograph of an electric light bulb, the analogy is probably functional rather than visual, that is, the inscriptions "Flirt / Divorce" suggest the "on / off" action of a light bulb as well as respresenting two aspects of American women which had impressed Picabia. *Ane* (*Ass*, or *Donkey*, fig. 142) is richer in both visual and intellectual possibilities and probably constitutes an unprintable bilingual play on the form, function and location of the ship's screw from which it was copied.

Picabia's New York gossip page was less subtle and more caustic. He wrote bitterly on the quality of life in Barcelona, spewed contempt on an exhibition of Robert Frost at de Zayas's Modern Gallery and insulted Isadora Duncan who "has certainly aged as much as the drawings [of her] of Rodin and Segonzac."[29] Other items were less corrosive; he even alluded good-humoredly to his own marital strife, but there was a tendency to drift from delicious humor into malevolent remarks. That tendency was one facet of the escalating inner torment of a hyperindividualist who, perceiving God as an indifferent and rather doltish creator, was

---

geology professor at Yale and Cornell, participated in the "magnetic fields" around Stieglitz and Arensberg for several years, producing a handful of interesting works, including sculpture designed to be experienced by touch rather than by sight.

27. Reported by Sanouillet, *Francis Picabia et "391,"* II, 67.

28. Sanouillet (*Francis Picabia et "391,"* II, 81) identifies the object as a metal cushion used to support the axle in early automobiles. The concept of mechanical ballets took various forms in modern art, the best known being Léger's 1924 film entitled *Ballet mécanique*.

29. Picabia's harsh remarks (*391*, no. 5, New York, June 1917, 8) hardly ended his relationship with Isadora Duncan (see pp. 105, 169), but his comments on Frost could have alienated both de Zayas and Cravan, the latter a close companion of Frost.

daily driven to answer his own enormous sensuous and spiritual needs. Those needs were frustrated on every hand—constantly thwarted by the exigences of wife, war and social customs, and only fleetingly relieved by flights into madcap activities, art, sex, drugs and travel. According to one witness he was subject to delirium tremens, suffered attacks of tachycardia and exhibited a fear of death.[30] Strains multiplied in his friendships and in his marriage. He worked on the last New York issues of *391* almost without collaborators, publishing poems which echo his condition:

1093

Il me faut l'amulette de dégel

Pour mon Etat idéal

Avant que la nuit

Se mette autour de mon cou

Epouvantable obéissance

Inintelligences qui ordonnent

Frontières de folies

Méchancetés

Envies

Je veux mon existence pour moi.

1093

I need a thawing amulet / For my ideal Condition / Before the night / Places around my neck / Frightening submission / Unintelligences which order / Frontiers of follies / Wickednesses / Envies / I want my existence for myself.[31]

Around this time Picabia entered the care of a neurologist, Dr. Collins, the first of several physicians who attended him over an eighteen-month period of repeated crises. In mid-September 1917, Gabrielle returned to their children in Switzerland, leaving Stieglitz a note[32] which speaks of her own exhaustion with touching reserve, considering that she was still burdened with efforts to save their marriage, to keep her husband out of a military court-martial, to care for their three young children and to preserve something of the social life which had been both craving and custom for a woman of her intelligence. She had hardly departed before Picabia was composing tender, private poems on their relationship—and simultaneously seeking refuge in the embrace of Isadora Duncan.[33]

30. Edgar Varèse in a 1963 interview with Sanouillet (cited in *Francis Picabia et "391,"* II, 40).

31. Picabia, *391*, no. 6 (New York, July 1917).

32. Buffet-Picabia letter to Stieglitz, September 15, 1917 (A.S.A., Yale).

33. Isadora Duncan retained an open affection for Picabia and advised his next wife, Germaine Everling, that she would gladly claim him if he was ever released (Germaine Everling, *L'Anneau de Saturne*, Paris, 1970, 140). Picabia's poem, "Départ," dated September 16, 1917, clearly refers to Gabrielle; "Gstaad," written about October on his way to Europe, is open to vari-

Parade amoureuse (*Amorous Parade*) and *Prostitution universelle* (*Universal Prostitution*) are close in date to those events and thoroughly imbued with the spirit of Picabia's poetry and life in Barcelona and New York during 1917. *Parade amoureuse* (fig. 132) is a brightly colored, preposterous machine that prompts speculation about its gangling construction and droll possibilities for noise and action. Its prominent title suggests that Picabia intended it to be just that, namely, a "parade" of love, perhaps a spoof on the noisy, thrashing spectacle of love. But he provides only a "show" of love, and not necessarily an altogether comical one at that, for the forms are sexually ambiguous and, if activated as a love machine, helpless to accomplish that function, flail and clang as they might. No humor at all mingles with the harsh message of *Prostitution universelle* (fig. 131). The forms of this bleak composition and a related drawing (fig. 130) identify male and female machines in an act of love which has been stripped of all that is intimate, sacred, or fulfilling. Sexual love appears, literally, as an unthinking mechanical action, particularly for the male machine with the dotted line to his center contact, suggesting—in Picabia's metamechanics—a heavenly source for his energy or function. His drab partner is more independent but equally impersonal, poised with her "sac de voyage" like a mechanical cricket ready to snap her connections in a moment and spring to the next unconnected male.

In 1917 Picabia left New York never to return, but he savored fond memories of America throughout his life and left something for the Americans as well. By and large, efforts to distinguish Picabia's specific influence on American artists at that time invite frustration for two reasons: first, the difficulty of separating reaction to Duchamp and to Picabia; and, secondly, the mature, personal response of the relevant American artists. Duchamp and Picabia offered emancipation, not servitude, and a handful of Americans were able and eager to take advantage of that. Nonetheless, some discussion of influence is in order, for a survey of the careers of six important American artists—Joseph Stella, Man Ray, John Covert, Morton Schamberg, Charles Demuth and Charles Sheeler—reveals that the development of each man shifted and / or accelerated substantially sometime between 1915 and 1919 after personal contact with Duchamp and Picabia.

Duchamp tended to be more important for them. In addition to the stimulation of his work and personality, he spoke English, was gentle and considerate and was present for three uninterrupted years; Picabia, on the other hand, was crisscrossing the Atlantic Ocean, spoke no English and was unpredictable in his relationships. However, both Frenchmen opened the eyes of those artists to machine-age America in a manner which offered two distinct experiences—the clean, spare, hard forms of machine aesthetics, and a dada or proto-dada sensation in terms of content, materials and techniques. The two experiences were not

---

ous interpretations but refers to Gabrielle on one level (Francis Picabia, *Cinquante-deux Miroirs*, Barcelona, 1917, 20, 25).

necessarily incompatible—witness Duchamp's *Fountain* and *The Large Glass* (figs. 141, 114), or Picabia's *Cette Chose est faite pour perpétuer mon souvenir* (fig. 120). Charles Demuth was able to fuse those seemingly disparate approaches in his immaculate images of American industrial forms imbued with a wry, debunking content—in this instance, *Business* (fig. 145), the association of factory windows with a calendar and the monotonous repetition of time and tasks for those who work at that business. Though avowedly influenced by his good friend Duchamp, Demuth's union of machine aesthetics and dadaist content was finally his own personal solution—as well as an important element in the so-called precisionist movement in American art, and part of an ongoing American tradition which became relevant to diverse artists of the 1960s.[34]

Morton Schamberg was less inclined to fuse dada qualities and machine aesthetics, but prior to his untimely death in 1918 he produced remarkable work in both veins. He was able to relax with the extravagant baroness Elsa von Freytag-Loringhoven over a dadaist construction of plumbing pipe and mitre box entitled *God* (ca. 1918, Philadelphia Museum of Art). But his primary sensitivity resided in delicate machine aesthetics, as exemplified in *Machine* (fig. 146), which harbors neither symbolism nor dada buffoonery, but does exhibit a perception of beauty and order in machinery which preceded similar purist tendencies in Europe.[35]

Charles Sheeler and, for a briefer time, Joseph Stella, also responded to the Duchamp and Picabia-ignited concern for machine aesthetics and the machine-age environment of America, although their backgrounds, sources of influence, and future developments do not permit a simple assessment. Sheeler owed a great deal to photography, to Shaker furniture and some architectural traditions of eastern Pennsylvania. Stella, on the other hand, had sketched Pittsburgh's industrial scenes in 1908 and had painted in a futurist-inspired idiom since 1913, although machine aesthetics and such objects as bridges, ships and airplanes became prominent in his work only after his friendship with Duchamp in 1915. John

34. For the acknowledged influence of Duchamp on Demuth see Forbes Watson, "Charles Demuth," *The Arts*, III, no. 1 (Brooklyn, January 1923), 78.

While Duchamp and Picabia were crucial catalysts for the precisionist movement, other sources were equally important, most notably Cubism and earlier traditions of American realism, which prompted Milton Brown to refer to the movement as "Cubist-Realism" (*American Painting from the Armory Show to the Depression*, Princeton, 1955, 113–14).

Regarding Demuth's reconsideration in the 1960s, the obvious reference is Robert Indiana's homage to his *I Saw the Figure 5 in Gold*. However, Demuth and his precisionist colleagues are also imbedded in the background of some abstract art, Pop Art and photo-realism.

35. Schamberg was particularly prepared to accept Duchamp's and Picabia's interest in machines for he had begun to depict modern mechanical appliances before their arrival in June 1915 (see his *Telephone* exhibited at the Montross Gallery, New York, March–April 1915).

The baroness Elsa von Freytag-Loringhoven (active in New York after Picabia's departure) was a bizarre creature whose uninhibited conduct and outlandish dress (and undress) endeared her to members of the Duchamp-Arensberg group.

Covert responded not to machines but to unorthodox materials and collage techniques which he handled with tasteful craftsmanship—augmented by inscriptions and titles that impart unexpected associations. In one of his simplest collages, *Brass Band* (ca. 1919, Yale University Art Gallery), the forms and cords recall Duchamp's *Chocolate Grinder No. 2*, while a Picabia influence may lurk in its "abstraction" and its exhibition of the concept of correspondence between sounds and visual forms.[36]

Although the humor, intellectual content and unorthodoxy of Covert's work exhibit a creative response to Duchamp and Picabia, he stood apart from the more irreverent, dadaist qualities of his French friends. Those qualities were still more alien to the temperament of other American artists, and, as stressed by Arturo Schwarz, the so-called phenomenon of "New York Dada" was largely a European transplant.[37] This is not to deny that Duchamp and Picabia exerted a considerable, healthy influence, but their dada progeny was sparse and short-lived. Of all the Americans around 1915–1920, only Man Ray was instinctively one with their dadaist spirit—or, strictly speaking, proto-dadaist spirit inasmuch as there was no conscious identity for Dada in New York until 1920. The forms of *The Impossibility*, or *Danger-Dancer* (fig. 147) indicate that Man Ray was not impervious to the burgeoning interest in machine aesthetics, but the deliberate ambiguity achieved by partially obscuring the letter "g" (or "c") reveals that the entire thrust of his work—materials, technique and content—plunged into the realm of Dada.[38] Man Ray had a particular genius for constructions using found objects from the products of American industry, and he also developed great skill in creating art with two machines—the camera and an airbrush gun. *My First Born* (fig. 148), reminiscent of Picabia's "daughter born without a mother" theme, was a spray-gun painting of the air compressor which operated his spray gun. Given his affinity for the dada activities which emerged in Paris just as the possibilities in New York were dwindling, it is no wonder that Man Ray left to join his friends Duchamp and Picabia in 1921.

Equally important in the subsequent history of Dada in Paris was Jean Crotti, a Swiss artist known to Picabia and Duchamp before the war, who also made his way to New York in 1915 and soon fell under the sway of their work. His *Mechanical Forces of Love in Movement* (fig. 149) looked enough like Picabia's paint-

36. For John Covert see George Heard Hamilton, "John Covert: Early American Modern," *College Art Journal*, XII, no. 1 (New York, fall 1952), 37–42, and Michael Klein, "John Covert's 'Time': Cubism, Duchamp, Einstein—A Quasi-Scientific Fantasy," *Art Journal*, XXXIII, no. 4 (New York, summer 1974), 314–20.

37. For Man Ray and New York Dada, see the Städtische Galerie im Lenbachhaus, Munich, *New York Dada*, December 15, 1973–January 27, 1974, 36–40, 79–100, catalogue by Arturo Schwarz.

38. *The Impossibility* is inscribed on the reverse "L'Impossibilité," but its title, date and original form are all open to other possibilities. It has been identified in some publications as *Danger-Dancer*, and it was incorporated in a larger assemblage entitled *The Impossibility*, exhibited in 1921 as a work of 1917–1920 (Librarie Six, Paris, *Exposition Man Ray*, December 3–31, 1921).

ings to deceive one critic,[39] but its use of glass was derived from his future brother-in-law, Marcel Duchamp, and the influence of both Picabia and Duchamp was rapidly transformed to personal ends by Crotti.

When Picabia returned to Europe in the fall of 1917, there remained then a small but important group of artists who had been stimulated by his work and that of Marcel Duchamp. Within a year, that situation changed radically—Duchamp departed for Argentina, Schamberg died and the end of the war prompted an exodus of most of the Europeans. Duchamp and Man Ray briefly rallied the dadaist energies of New York once more during 1920, but Paris saw the heyday of Dada—and the reunion of Picabia, Duchamp, Man Ray and Crotti.

39. André Warnod, "Le Salon des Indépendants," *L'Avenir* [Paris], January 28, 1920, 2.

8. POETRY, SWITZERLAND, AND DADA IN ZURICH, 1918-1919

WITHIN a month after Gabrielle's departure for Europe, Picabia followed, landing once more in Barcelona, owing to his unresolved military status. Reminiscent of the voyage to Spain in the preceding year, he occupied himself by writing, and in Barcelona during October 1917 his first volume of poetry was published under the apt title *Cinquante-deux Miroirs* (Fifty-two Mirrors).[1] These poems mirror Picabia's response to the conditions of his life—sometimes clearly but in other instances so darkly that even the most sympathetic reader cannot penetrate their veiled, perverse reflections. "Cuvette" (Washbasin), for example, offers an almost surrealist experience in its juxtaposition of provocative, illogical thoughts and images: "Animals meet the solitude of screws at the arabesque hour in keys." But "Terre" (Earth) bares anguish and bitterness over the war and concludes with an undisguised lament over his neurasthenic condition.

"Escalier" (Stair) bears witness to Picabia's scorn for any sort of religious promise to life, while his wholly egocentric moral code is flaunted in "Mie" (Crumb).

ESCALIER

Tout ce qui est sur la terre
bien loin de la vérité
est un ouragan de routes divines
comme la lumière du paradis.

1. *Cinquante-deux Miroirs: 1914–1917* (Barcelona, October 1917). Although the full title indicates the poems in this volume date from 1914 to 1917, the great majority must have been written in 1916–1917. One-third of them had been published previously in *391*, and several others are dated as late as August and September 1917. P.A. Benoit (*A propos des "Poèmes de la fille née sans mère,"* Alès, 1958) and Michel Sanouillet (*Francis Picabia et "391,"* II, Paris, 1966, 50, 84) attribute "Idéal doré par l'or," the only prose work in the volume, to 1910. However, it is compatible in spirit with the poems of 1916–1917, whereas several other poems are clearly distinctive, among them "Une Agrafe," in which Picabia writes of being thirty-five years old, his age in 1914.

Pour celles qui nient la vie future
il y a une place auprès de moi.
Je suis le guide vertueux
dans la ville de cristal.

STAIR

Everything which is on the earth / far from the truth / is a hurricane of divine routes / like the light of paradise.

For those women who deny future life / there is a place beside me. / I am the virtuous guide / in the crystal city.

MIE

Malentendu qui surpasse la raison
Création du vice à un degré supérieur
En somme je n'entre pas en ligne de compte
Elle pense que je suis un monstre
Je l'ai choisie sans me laisser distraire
Un seul jour avait allumé en moi
Ce lien merveilleux et immortel.

CRUMB

Misunderstanding which surpasses reason / Creation of a vice of a superior degree / In sum I do not enter into accountability / She thinks that I am a monster / I chose her without allowing myself to be distracted / A single day had kindled in me / This marvelous and immortal bond.

Numerous poems reveal the primacy of eroticism—passionate in "Petit Main" (Little Hand), serene in "Modeste" (Modest) and exclamatory in "Guichet" (Counter—with a grilled window, like those typically found in railroad stations and post offices).

GUICHET

Je suis sans récréation depuis des années
Le désir d'être tranquille en amour
Est un véritable crime sexuel
La chasteté dans la vie
M'est funeste
Car le génie de mon coeur
Que j'appelle idéal courageux
N'est pas un bric-à-brac
Destinée formidable
N'irai-je pas jusqu'au fond
De la distance
Pour une seule heure agréable
De passion vertigineuse.

COUNTER (WITH GRILLED WINDOW)

I have been without recreation for years / The desire to be tranquil in love / Is a veritable sexual crime / Chastity in life / Is deadly for me / For the genius of my heart / Which I call courageous ideal / Is not bric-a-brac / Formidable destiny / Will I not go to the depth / Of the distance / For one enjoyable hour / Of vertiginous passion.

Picabia did not tarry long in Barcelona. Fewer friends and distractions were available, and when Gabrielle finally secured a passport which permitted him to reenter France safely, they went immediately to Paris.

Wartime conditions there were much the same as they had been when Picabia left in 1915, but the art scene had changed substantially. He had missed by a few months the two most exciting events of the year, the premiere of Apollinaire's *Les Mammelles de Terésias* and the Stravinsky-Picasso-Satie-Cocteau collaboration on *La Parade* for the Ballets Russe.[2] Those performances still figured prominently, however, in conversations and in the pages of the two avant-garde journals of the day, Pierre Albert-Birot's *SIC* and Pierre Reverdy's *Nord-Sud*. Those journals were complemented by the work of two ambitious gallery directors, Paul Guillaume and Léonce Rosenberg, who had emerged during the war as the most eminent dealers of contemporary art. Through café gatherings and special events sponsored by the directors of those various galleries and magazines, Picabia renewed old friendships.[3] But there was nothing which ignited his interest like the situation in New York, and he languished. Moreover, his marriage grew more troubled. Gabrielle left again to tend to the children in Switzerland, and little time elapsed before Picabia found solace in the companionship of Mme Corlin (Germaine Everling), a charming younger woman introduced to him by Georges and Dodo de Zayas, the brother and sister-in-law respectively of Marius de Zayas. Picabia was immediately smitten, and simply swept Germaine out of the dejected mood which had engulfed her during her own pending divorce. Thinking Francis was permanently spearated from his wife, she soon yielded to his enchantment, and a serious liaison was established which, after two tumultuous years, settled into a common-law marriage that lasted for over a decade.[4]

The initial memoirs of Picabia's enraptured companion provide a convincing description of him at that time—his appearance and surroundings; his eccentric

2. *La Parade* opened May 20 at the Théâtre du Châtelet. In a program note, Apollinaire referred to that ballet as "sur-réaliste." His own *Les Mammelles de Tirésias*, subtitled *Drame surréaliste*, was presented at the Théâtre Maubel on June 24 in a manifestation organized by *SIC*.

3. Picabia attended Apollinaire's lecture at Paul Guillaume's gallery on November 13 (Germaine Everling, *L'Anneau de Saturne*, Paris, 1970, 17), but it is not known if he was present at the Théâtre du Vieux-Colombier on November 26 when Apollinaire spoke on "L'Esprit nouveau et les poètes."

4. This author is deeply indebted to Mme Germaine Everling for her unreserved support. Her memoirs, *L'Anneau de Saturne*, also provide a priceless witness to Picabia, particularly from late 1917 until the early 1930s.

behavior and incredible self-centeredness. He appeared to her to be of no identifiable nationality; physically he was small and stocky, his skin fine and dark, like an "exotic fruit," his eyes piercing, his voice wonderfully nuanced, his gestures and expressions lively. He was an impeccable dresser, down to his fascination for expensive jewelry. He was ardent, impulsive, unpredictable, prone to dumbfounding extravagance in the midst of bleak wartime economics—and his apartment reflected it all:

> Opposite the entrance, a painting bearing in black letters on a cream ground, . . . "Bonjour, Picabia!" . . . The junk room began at the threshold: books, newspapers, magazines and letters scattered at random on a dusty rug. In the corners, golf clubs, pell-mell with broken skis . . . some beautiful furniture and large leather-covered divans . . . a grand piano . . . a model sailboat . . . Negro [African] sculpture . . . a magnificent racing bicycle. . . .
>
> . . . I had lived among artists, but their studios presented a purely professional disorder. At Picabia's, this disorder seemed to be an integral part of life. Papers, cigarette butts littered the floor of the studio, forming a carpet comparable to the piling up of autumn leaves.[5]

In late November the sale of a painting enabled Germaine and Picabia to leave chilly Paris for a "honeymoon" in his old haunt at Martigues. There he began work on a second volume of poetry, *Poèmes et dessins de la fille née sans mère* (Poems and Drawings of the Girl Born Without a Mother), but his writing and the "honeymoon" were interrupted in December by a letter from Gabrielle announcing her return to Paris.[6]

A tense relationship developed there as Picabia lodged first with his mistress and then with his wife. His neurasthenic condition was seriously aggravated, and in February 1918 it was decided that he required the care of Dr. Brunnschweiller, a neurologist and family friend residing in Lausanne. The Picabias settled in nearby Gstaad, followed—as prearranged—by Germaine, who took up residence around mid-March in a Lausanne hotel. According to his custom, Picabia divided his time during that early spring between his wife and children in Gstaad and Germaine Everling in Lausanne. His nervous condition, of course, did not improve; he remained in Dr. Brunnschweiller's care and painted very little save for a spritely watercolor, *Esprit de jeune fille* (*Spirit of a Young Girl*, fig. 150), dedicated to the doctor who had ordered total rest including a ban on painting. *Abstract Lausanne* (fig. 151) may also have been produced about this time. Though signed, dated and long ascribed to ca. 1918 by family tradition, this buoyantly naive composition is difficult to relate to his contemporary production. It is another unique work in his career, suggestive of both Miró's abstract paintings eight years later and Picabia's own abstract paintings of the 1940s.

During that spring of 1918, writing remained a more important means of

5. Ibid., 20.   6. Ibid., 37.

self-expression than painting. By April he had largely completed *Poèmes et dessins de la fille née sans mère* begun in Martigues.[7] The fifty-one poems and eighteen drawings in this volume—dedicated to his neurologists—continue the style and spirit of *Cinquante-deux Miroirs*. Delicate, private memories of the honeymoon in Martigues ("Oiseau réséda") are exceptions among pervasively brooding, pessimistic poems in which Picabia lashes out at reason ("Bonheur") and the war ("Télégraphie sans fils") or hints darkly of suicide and destruction and seeks refuge in sexual love.

OISEAU RÉSÉDA

Un soir, ses longs cheveux en arrière
la petite danseuse bizarre se faisait une ceinture.
avec la fièvre des marais souvenir de promenade
Animée elle pressait sur ma bouche un buisson.

Gâteaux de sucre rouge renflement en chignon
où l'église vieille boîte à musique
parée avec un collier de perles de petit chien
entra dans ma chambre magnifique.

La nuit mes bras tournoient sur l'herbe
son sourire scintillait par derrière immobile
dans la pièce particulièrement silencieuse
et toujours droite elle s'endormit.

RÉSÉDA BIRD[8]

One evening, her long hair in back / the bizarre little dancer made herself a girdle. / with the swamp fever memory of promenade / Animated she pressed a thicket to my mouth.

Red sugar cookies swelling in chignon / when the church old music box / adorned with a little dog's pearl necklace / entered my magnificent chamber.

7. *Poèmes et dessins de la fille née sans mère* (Lausanne, 1918) is signed and dated Gstaad, April 5, 1918, although Picabia was still recasting it in May and did not publish the volume until late in the year. See Benoit, *A propos des "Poèmes de la fille née sans mère,"* and Picabia's letter to Tzara on September 3, 1918 (Collection Tzara, 2970; published in Michel Sanouillet, *Dada à Paris*, Paris, 1965, 467). In this and in all subsequent references to the Collection Tzara, hereafter cited as C.T., the numbers following the abbreviation refer to numbered items in that collection. Sanouillet's excellent study of Dada includes an appendix of 230 letters, many of which will be cited in this book with references both to that useful publication and to the actual location of the letters—some of which have been accessioned and/or recatalogued at libraries subsequent to the publication of Sanouillet's book.

Benoit mentions changes made by Picabia in the number of poems and drawings, and the elimination of the main title, *Décapuchonné*, in favor of the subtitle. As noted by Sanouillet (*Francis Picabia et "391,"* II, 90) several drawings later published in *391* may represent illustrations eliminated from the final version of *Poèmes et dessins de la fille née sans mère*.

8. The word "réséda" has not been translated. It is used to designate a delicate, yellow-green color, but it is also a fragrant plant with calming, medicinal properties.

At night my arms turn in the grass / her smile scintillated from behind immobile / in the room particularly silent / and always straight she falls asleep.

BONHEUR

Je veux que l'objet
Comme l'alcool païen
Gribouille l'estomac de la raison
Et que le chant du coq
Maudisse le soleil
Passe-temps du diable
Lubies quel bonheur
Je me porte bien
Au hasard.

HAPPINESS

I wish that the object / Like pagan alcohol / Would scramble the stomach of reason / And that the cock's crow / Would curse the sun / Pastime of the devil / Whims what happiness / I am well / By chance.

TÉLÉGRAPHIE SANS FILS

Ma maladie écoute mon cœur
Bouton clos des joies perdues
Je veux en espiègle m'assombrir dans les bras
De ma jolie maman
Souvenir du ciel bleu
Où j'aurais pu me blottir
Il faut tâcher de tout oublier
L'agonie du monde en vertige
De héros qui tournoient
les valses hideuses de la guerre
Dans l'atmosphère énigmatique
Et masquée.

WIRELESS (RADIO)

My malady listens to my heart / Closed button of lost joys / I wish impishly to grow gloomy in the arms / Of my pretty mother / Memory of blue sky / Where I could have snuggled up / One must try to forget everything / The agony of the world in vertigo / Heroes who spin / the hideous waltzes of the war / In the atmosphere enigmatic / And masked.

The spare machine drawings interspersed among the verse are independent in the sense that they are interesting in themselves and do not illustrate the poems. Nevertheless, they deal with the same themes: a number are sexual in content (see fig. 152); *Narcotique* (*Narcotic*, fig. 153) makes sarcastic comment on "error," "truth," "Christian," and "Jew"; *Egoïste* (*Egoist*) is biographical with inscriptions referring to a "convalescent Narcissus," a doctor, Americans, landscapes, women, and a pneumatic clock in the desert (Switzerland) (fig. 154).

These drawings are representative of Picabia's style around April when he began to work with Carlos Gregorio, a young amateur artist who lived with her husband in the same Lausanne hotel occupied by Germaine Everling. Painting with Carlos was a tonic for Picabia; his health improved, and, according to Germaine, a distinct phase of his machinist style emerged at that time, exemplified by *Muscles brillants* (*Brilliant Muscles*, fig. 155). Volumetric forms and greater three-dimensional space do distinguish this painting from Picabia's earlier mechanomorphic compositions. Moreover, a reproduction of it in February 1919 with the title *Vagin brillant* (*Brilliant Vagina*) further substantiates a date of ca. 1918 and identifies the muscles involved.[9] Only a few paintings of this genre are known (see fig. 156). Their rarity apparently stems from a premature, violent termination in early June, when Costico Gregorio discovered an affair between Picabia and his wife and fired two shots at Picabia.[10]

Picabia's neurasthenic condition flared up again and he urgently recalled Mme Everling from Paris, where she had gone to finalize her divorce. Owing to an epidemic of Spanish grip, Dr. Brunnschweiller recommended that Picabia retire from Lausanne to greater safety and complete rest at the spa of Bex. Picabia refused to budge unless accompanied by the entire troop of wife, mistress and children—and a few days later he was installed there in the center of a network of connecting rooms.[11]

It was in Bex on August 21 that Picabia received a letter from Tristan Tzara inviting his collaboration with Dada in Zurich. By early September they were exchanging enthusiastic pledges of collaboration and copies of *Dada*, *391*,

9. *Muscles brillants* was reproduced in *391*, no. 8 (Zurich, February 1919). Its present location is unknown, but the following inscriptions are visible in old reproductions: "Muscles," "Brillants," "Petit male," "Frottement," "Buche à bouche," "Mécanique de la region sacreé [*sic*]."

10. Mme Everling described the episode with Carlos and Costico Gregorio (pseudonyms employed to conceal the identity of a Rumanian and his French wife) in *L'Anneau de Saturne*, 53–66. According to her, the assault occurred in the Hôtel de Beau-Séjour, and that event may be the subject of a drawing, *Colonel* (fig. 158), which has an inscription about "two revolvers." A prose-poem, "L'Ilôt de beau-séjour dans le canton de nudité" (The Island of Beau-Séjour in the Canton of Nudity), also appears to be linked to events at that moment in Picabia's life, including the affair with Carlos. That prose-poem, dated Lausanne, June 23, 1918 (about twelve days after the crisis), is dedicated to a "Princess Victoria Malcolm" who has been identified as an Iranian resident of "l'hôtel Beauséjour" whose charm and knowledge of art made her a stimulating companion for Francis and Gabrielle (Picabia, *Ecrits 1913–1920*, ed. Olivier Revault d'Allonnes, Paris, 1975, 271). The cryptic text does not encourage interpretation, but both it and the title seem biographical—the Hôtel de Beau-Séjour as an island of beau-séjour in the canton of nudity, that is to say, in Switzerland, which Picabia habitually described as a "desert" or as "naked" because for him it was spiritually barren.

11. Everling, *L'Anneau de Saturne*, 65–67.

Cinquante-deux Miroirs and *Poèmes et dessins de la fille née sans mère*.[12] Although plans to meet in Zurich did not materialize immediately, their contact remained close. Picabia commemorated Apollinaire's death (November 9, only days before the Armistice) with a machine portrait (fig. 159) and a statement, the latter dispatched with a provocative poem and drawing for *Dada 3*, the first issue of that review characterized by the exciting format and aggressive tone associated with dada publications.[13] He also mailed copies of his most recent works in prose and poetry—*L'Athlète des pompes funèbres* (Funeral Parlor Athlete) and *Râteliers platoniques* (Platonic False Teeth), which were produced during a period of intense work in Bégnins during October–December 1918.[14] Tzara published a perceptive review of these two volumes in the next issue of *Dada* (the *Anthologie Dada 4–5*):

> These poems have no end, this prose never begins. He writes without "working," presents his personality, does not control his sensations. Pushes into the flesh of organisms. Neither the stability nor the music of the word predominates as I glide along these phrases of subterranean harmony. Picabia illuminates the rotation of realities and of misery and reduces important matters or pretensions to the relative equality of cosmic formation—kills the declamation, the hysterical pathos along little paths which one still finds everywhere.[15]

12. For the Tzara-Picabia correspondence, see Sanouillet, *Dada à Paris*, 466–502. Tzara and Picabia had known of each other perhaps as early as 1916, when Marius de Zayas was corresponding with Tzara (M.de Z.A. and C.T. 4257; Sanouillet, op. cit., 569, 572) and certainly by 1917 (*391*, no. 5, New York, June 1917, 5). However, they had no effective knowledge or interest in each other until this contact in Switzerland in August 1918.

13. Tzara published only a portion of Picabia's statement on Apollinaire in *Dada 3* (Zurich, December 1918); the entire text first appeared in *Temps mêlés*, nos. 31–33, (Verviers, March 1958), 67–68. Machine models for the symbolic portrait of Apollinaire have not been identified, but inscriptions on it have been traced to phrases from the writings of Horace translated in the *Petit Larousse* red pages (Centre National d'Art et de Culture Georges Pompidou, Musée National d'Art Moderne, *Francis Picabia*, Paris, Grand Palais, January 23–March 29, 1976, 49).

The new boldness of *Dada 3* reflects Picabia's influence, but other factors were important. A crucial article in the issue, Tzara's rousing "Manifeste Dada 1918," dates from July 1918, before personal contact with Picabia. Moreover, futurist publications, *291* and *SIC*—all known to Tzara as well as *391*—offered handy models for iconoclasm and unconventional typography. Indeed, in a recent issue of *SIC* (no. 25, Paris, January 1918), Albert-Birot had criticized the "conservative" design of *Dada 2*.

14. *L'Athelète des pompes funèbres* is a long poem in five parts, signed and dated Bégnins, November 24, 1918, and dedicated to Walter Conrad Arensberg. *Râteliers platoniques* is a prose-poem signed and dated Lausanne, 1918, and dedicated to the memory of Guillaume Apollinaire.

No trace remains of *Le Mâcheur de pétards*, a volume of twenty-five poems and drawings to be published with a preface by Jean Cocteau in Paris at the end of 1918. Picabia considered it his most important work up to that time (see his letters to Tzara on November 19 and 26, 1918, C.T. 2.976, 2.977; Sanouillet, *Dada à Paris*, 471–73).

15. Tzara, "Livres notes revues diversités divertissantes," *Anthologie Dada 4–5* (Zurich, May 15, 1919).

While Tzara was particularly stimulated by Picabia's writings, all the Zurich dadaists were fascinated by Picabia's machine paintings, which he submitted in September 1918 for the Salon d'Art Wolfsberg in Zurich. Prophetic of the coming years in Paris, the director of the Salon decided he could not exhibit such things and returned them (collect) to Picabia—but not before Tzara, Hans Arp, Marcel Janco, Hans Richter and others had seen and admired the paintings.[16] Those dadaists immediately sought Picabia's participation in the exhibition of "Das Neue Leben," which opened in Basel in November and moved to Zurich during January 1919.[17]

As Picabia's contacts with the Zurich dadaists were multiplying, an unexpected spark of life in Paris also caught his attention. De Zayas was trying to organize a new Modern Gallery there and Picabia instructed Germaine, who had returned to Paris in November, to help de Zayas until his arrival.[18] Francis and Gabrielle were on the verge of returning to Paris when the receipt of *Dada 3* and new letters from Tzara finally prompted the trip to Zurich. Their three-week visit (January 22–February 8, 1919) was an unforgettable experience for everyone involved. A mutual rejuvenation of spirit pulsates in their subsequent letters and memoirs, in new issues of *391* and *Dada* and, most importantly, in the eventual attraction of Tzara to Paris for the climactic eruption and disintegration of Dada.

391 had lain dormant since Picabia's departure from New York, but in Zurich he, his wife and Tzara collaborated on what is one of the most spirited issues of that magazine combining particularly provocative texts and poems with an entertaining gossip page, the customary machine drawings, reproductions of work by two Zurich artists, Hans Arp and Alice Bailly, and two untitled writings by Tzara and Picabia which have been cited as important precedents for the "automatic" (or dictation-of-the-unconscious) texts by Breton and Soupault.[19] Considerable progress was also made on Tzara's *Anthologie Dada 4–5*, the largest and most luxurious of the *Dada* numbers.[20] Like *391*, it radiates vitality; the bold layout and typography used in *Dada 3* were expanded, and the content was simultaneously

16. For an account of the affair at the Salon d'Art Wolfsberg, see the Picabia-Tzara correspondence for September 18, 26 and 29, 1918 (C.T. 2.972, 2.973; D.P. I, 237; Sanouillet, *Dada à Paris*, 468–70). These letters also indicate Arp's desire to purchase one of Picabia's paintings.

17. Many of the artists associated with Dada in Zurich—Arp, Sophie Taeuber, Janco, Oskar Lüthy—were members of "Das Neue Leben" and participated in this exhibition. Janco contributed a statement to the catalogue of the Zurich show (Kunsthaus, January 12–February 5, 1919) and both Janco and Tzara lectured there. Picabia was represented by eight works, simply listed as Compositions I–IV and a–d, which have not been securely identified.

18. Everling, *L'Anneau de Saturne*, 78.

19. Sanouillet notes (*Francis Picabia et "391,"* II, 90) that this issue of *391*, no. 8 (Zurich, February 1919), was known in Paris just as Breton and Soupault undertook *Les Champs magnétiques*, a text later claimed by Breton as the first surrealist work owing to its systematic application of automatic writing. For an informative consideration of this subject, see Sanouillet, *Dada à Paris*, 121–30.

20. After repeated delays, *Anthologie Dada 4–5* was published in Zurich on May 15, 1919. Picabia was prominently represented by two poems and three full-page reproductions of machine drawings.

stripped of the once prominent futurist element and imbued with the new spirit of personalities who would later form the core of Dada in Paris. Picabia had secured the collaboration of Georges Ribemont-Dessaignes, but Tzara, gifted organizer and promoter, was responsible for most of the contributors—including the melange of warring avant-garde figures from Paris, André Breton, Louis Aragon, Philippe Soupault, Jean Cocteau and Pierre Albert-Birot.

The obvious rejuvenation of dada publications was not matched by comparable repercussions in Picabia's art or in that of the Zurich dadaists. For the most part, Picabia's drawings reproduced in the new issues of *Dada* and *391* simply continued the style, content and quality of his earlier work. Nonetheless, two drawings, *Construction moléculaire (Molecular Construction)* and *Mouvement Dada* (figs. 160, 161), are interesting documents, and *Réveil matin (Alarm Clock,* fig. 162) represents a fitting addition to Picabia's machine style, namely, painting with the physical aid of machine parts. Arp described the creation of one of these drawings on the day he and Tzara went to meet Picabia at his hotel:

> We found him very busy pulling a clock to pieces. . . . He attacked his alarm clock ruthlessly till [*sic*] he got to the spring which he pulled out triumphantly. He stopped working to greet us, then taking the wheels, the spring, the hands, and other secret parts of the clock, he immediately impressed them on paper. He connected these imprints together by lines and added to the drawing sentences full of wit.[21]

Thanks to the circulation of *391* and *Dada 4–5*, several German dadaists, particularly Max Ernst (see fig. 163), looked to machine forms as an important element in their art, but the Zurich artists were not diverted into experiments with a machine idiom. They were intrigued by Picabia's work, but his paintings were simply too alien to the variously abstract, cubist and expressionist manners that characterized the work of Arp, Sophie Taeuber, Marcel Janco, Hans Richter, Viking Eggling, Augusto Giacometti, Otto van Rees, Oskar Lüthy, Walter Helbig, Arthur Segal and others.[22]

Inasmuch as the essential character of Dada in Zurich had been established during 1916–1918, it should hardly be expected that Picabia would substantially alter the art of the dadaists there—or, for that matter, their literary, social and philosophical values. By the time of his visit in 1919, Dada had existed for three lively years—a full life-span for such a movement in the twentieth century. Indeed clear divisions had already emerged among the dadaists in Zurich: Hugo Ball and Tzara parted ways in June 1917; Richard Huelsenbeck returned to Ger-

21. Rose Fried Gallery, New York, *Picabia*, February 15–March 31, 1950, preface by Jean Arp. Another version of *Réveil matin*, surely contemporary in date, exists in the Schwarz collection, Milan, and an entirely hand-drawn clock composition, erroneously dated "Zurich 1918," exists in D.P. IV, 20.

22. Oskar Lüthy worked in a cubist idiom, Walter Helbig painted in a manner derived from expressionism and Arthur Segal showed abstract woodcuts and paintings reminiscent of Paul Klee. The other artists produced abstract art in a variety of styles and media.

many that same year, also with some bitterness toward Tzara; and other quarrels during 1918–1919 resurfaced in Paris during 1920–1921.[23] With the conclusion of the war in November 1918, the most important cohesive element in their life was eliminated, and not even the stimulation of Picabia's visit could stem the demise of Dada in Zurich. Tzara strived to maintain the movement, marshaling in April 1919 the largest assembly of dadaists ever witnessed there for a climactic demonstration that set the pattern for Dada in Paris.[24] But after that performance at the Salle Kaufleuten, Dada rapidly declined in Zurich: some dadaists left; a new magazine, *Der Zeltweg*, failed to arouse any interest; and Tzara's letters to Picabia reveal a flagging, irresolute spirit. Only then, long after Picabia had left, did Tzara yield to his friend's persistent pleas to visit Paris. Undoubtedly the most important result of the meeting of Tzara and Picabia was the subsequent installation of Tzara in Paris. Picabia may have fueled the last flame of Dada in Zurich, but Dada in Paris might never have flourished without Tzara's presence.

Before moving to Paris, Tzara was aware that the city offered essential ingredients for Dada, namely, gifted collaborators and a fresh audience. But the primary factor for his transfer was his uncommon rapport with Picabia. Those two men shared remarkably similar aesthetic and philosophical values, and, given the central roles of Picabia and Tzara in Dada, those values merit consideration.

Tzara spoke with two voices on art: one attributed to it lofty ideals; the other devaluated it mercilessly. Underneath that apparent dichotomy lay some consistent ground. The familiar Tzara is the strident, nihilistic voice in "Manifeste Dada 1918" and "Proclamation sans prétention" (Proclamation Without Pretension):

ART NEEDS AN OPERATION.
ART is a PRETENSION warmed by the
TIMIDITY of the urinary basin, the *hysteria* born
in THE STUDIO.[25]

. . . art is not as important as we, mercenaries of the spirit, have been proclaiming for centuries.

All pictorial or plastic work is useless: let it then be a monstrosity that

23. For an early account of quarrels among the dadaists in Zurich see Richard Huelsenbeck, *En avant Dada. Eine Geschichte des Dadaismus* (Hanover, 1920), trans. in Robert Motherwell, ed., *The Dada Painters and Poets* (New York, 1951), 21–47. The rekindling of old quarrels will be considered in chap. XI.

24. The eighth Dada soirée was held on the evening of April 9 in the Salle Kaufleuten. About 1,000 people appeared for the three-part program that contained lectures, manifestos, music, poetry and dancing, with sets and costumes by the dadaists. At the end of the first section of the soirée, Tzara's simultaneous poem, read by twenty people, provoked vociferous audience protest. Later, during the proclamation of Walter Serner's manifesto "Letzte Lockerung," the performance was temporarily interrupted when members of the audience stormed the stage. For accounts of this soirée see Tzara's "Livres notes revues diversités divertissantes" in *Anthologie Dada* 4–5 and Hans Richter, *Dada: Art and Anti-Art* (New York, 1965), 77–80.

25. Tristan Tzara, "Proclamation sans prétention," *Die Schammade* (Cologne, February 1920), trans. in Motherwell, ed., *The Dada Painters and Poets*, 82.

frightens servile minds, and not sweetening to decorate the refectories of animals in human costume.[26]

The unfamiliar Tzara is a man capable of exalting art. On several occasions in 1917 and 1918 he wrote that the artist "makes man better" and described art as a direct expression of an interior reality that was intimately related to a cosmic order necessary "to the life of every organism."[27] Most often, he emphasized the intensely personal nature of art: "There is a literature that does not reach the voracious mass. It is the work of creators, issued from a real necessity in the author, produced for himself. It expresses the knowledge of a supreme egoism, in which laws wither away."[28]

In effect, Tzara's positive and negative attitudes toward art were inseparable—as is manifest in his compact, lucid statement at the Weimar Congress in 1922:

> We have had enough of the intelligent movements that have stretched beyond measure our credulity in the benefits of science. What we now want is spontaneity. Not because it is better or more beautiful than anything else. [But] because everything that issues freely from ourselves, without the intervention of speculative ideas, represents us. . . . Art has not the celestial and general value that people like to attribute to it. Life is far more interesting. Dada knows the correct measure that should be given to art. . . . The Beautiful and the True in art do not exist; what interests me is the intensity of a personality transposed directly, clearly into his work; the man and his vitality.[29]

Those ideas are so like Picabia's that they could have been written by or about him. For both Tzara and Picabia, art answered first to the needs of the life of the individual, not to the demands of art. Art was a transposition of a vital personality into some form or material, and every obstacle to that unadulterated transposition was assaulted—tradition, reason, desire for financial success, service to the state, moral, social and religious restraints, or pompous notions about beauty and the sanctity of art, its subject matter, media and the creative act.

Those ideas were not altogether new and did not prescribe a "style" for dadaist art. Dada was indebted to Cubism, Futurism, Expressionism and abstract art—and what has passed for dadaist art has been extraordinarily varied, much less yielding than Cubism or Impressionism to a general description or to some single, representative image. Picabia's own dadaist oeuvre is an example.

26. Tristan Tzara, "Manifeste Dada 1918," *Dada 3* (Zurich, December 1918), trans. in Motherwell, ed., *The Dada Painters and Poets*, 76–82.

27. Tzara, "Note 2 sur l'art. H. Arp," and "Notes," *Dada 2* (Zurich, December 1917).

28. Tzara, "Manifeste Dada 1918," *Dada 3*, trans. in Motherwell, ed., *The Dada Painters and Poets*, 78.

29. Tzara, "Conférence sur Dada" presented at Dada Kongress in Weimar, 1922, published in *Merz*, II, no. 7 (Hanover, January 1924), 68–70, trans. in Motherwell, ed., *The Dada Painters and Poets*, 246–51.

By placing a premium on the unfettered expression of a potent individual, the ideas of Tzara and Picabia were generally compatible with various strains of Expressionism and later developments from Surrealism to Abstract Expressionism of the 1940s and 1950s. But that embraced multiple possibilities, and, in the final analysis, the element of deliberate protest seems to be the crucial ingredient for separating their notion of vital (dada) art from avant-garde art in general. Lippard adroitly described the dada attitude as "a broad idealist anarchy with an immense intolerance for pomposity of all forms."[30]

And of all the pompous targets taken on by the dadaists, art itself was the toughest. Finally, most of the artists associated with Dada took themselves and their work too seriously to produce antiart. In Zurich, not a single artist was really sympathetic to antiart. Marcel Janco did produce at least one object, *Construction 3*, which appears to be antiart in form and in intent, but even it was attributed lofty intentions by Tzara, and for the most part Janco made abstract woodcuts and polychromal reliefs in a mode derived from Cubism.[31] Arp was intrigued with accident and automatism in art as a means of escaping man's exaggerated notions of reason, order and eternity, but he seemed incapable of actually making something which was not the product of a refined aesthetic sensibility. As Hamilton remarked, "however much Arp in his poetry and memoirs cherished his Dada past," his work belongs "to the larger movement of abstract art in Europe."[32]

Picabia, on the other hand, upon his return to Paris in the spring of 1919, was equipped by temperament, talent and the times to operate at the core of dadaist art. Strains of Dada or proto-Dada had been perceptible in his work perhaps as far back as 1913; by 1917 those strains had become prominent characteristics, but it was not until Paris in 1919 that Picabia's work was most fully and consistently dadaist—dadaist as tested not in a limited or superficial manner, but in the wholeness of subject, style *and* content.

30. Lucy R. Lippard, *Pop Art* (New York, 1966), 22, contributions by Lawrence Alloway, Nicolas Calas and Nancy Marmer.

31. See the reproduction of *Construction 3* in *Dada*, no. 1 (Zurich, July 1917), and Tzara's accompanying statement, "Marcel Janco."

32. George Heard Hamilton, *Painting and Sculpture in Europe, 1880–1940* (Baltimore, 1967), 242.

9. THE RETURN TO PARIS AND PREPARATION FOR DADA, 1919

ABOUT one month elapsed between Picabia's departure from Zurich and his return to France. As indicated in his correspondence with Tzara, those weeks in Gstaad and Lausanne were occupied with the final assembly and mailing of the Zurich issue of *391* and completion of yet another volume of poetry, *Poésie Ron-ron*.[1] Despite such work, Picabia found Switzerland unbearably enervating and urged Tzara to visit him, concluding March 8 with an outright plea while in the grips of a severe neurasthenic crisis: "I have more and more horror of life. . . . I can no longer support life. . . . Can you come here for several days?"[2]

Before Tzara could reply, Picabia suddenly decided to return to Paris. There his nervous condition gradually improved despite continued complications in his private life and his disenchantment over both the arts and the general postwar atmosphere in the city. Initially, he resided in his avenue Charles Floquet apartment with Gabrielle, who was pregnant with their fourth child. But as soon as he recovered, Picabia resumed his relationship with Germaine Everling and reacquainted himself with life in Paris. He was hardly enthusiastic about the conditions he encountered. The experience of the war still permeated everything. Calls for reparation and a new world order had replaced battlefield reports, but superpatriotism had hardly abated, and Picabia did not miss the barbed curiosity of those who asked, "And what did you do during the war?" "I got bored as hell" was his response to one individual, and in a series of three articles he publicly ridiculed everything from military morality to grandiose—but unfunded—plans to rebuild France.[3] He was equally scornful of the prominent personalities and events

1. *Poésie Ron-ron* was a small edition of 100 copies, signed and dated Lausanne, February 24, 1919, and printed by the first week of March. See Picabia's letters to Tzara (C.T. 2.987; Michel Sanouillet, *Dada à Paris*, Paris, 1965, 482). Duchamp's single-issue magazine, *Rongwrong* (New York, 1917), perhaps inspired the title of *Poésie Ron-ron*, although the style and content are consistent with Picabia's previous poetry.

2. Picabia letter to Tzara (C.T. 2.988; Sanouillet, *Dada à Paris*, 482–83).

3. For Picabia's response, "I got bored as hell," see Picabia, "Billets de faveur," *Littérature*, II, no. 5 (Paris, October 1, 1922), 11. His articles, signed "Pharamousse," appeared under the

in art and literature—snorting over the "arrivisme" of Picasso and scoffing at the "perfumed collections of Jacques Doucet," the courturier and art collector who had stirred widespread attention by selling his collection of Renaissance art in order to patronize contemporary art and literature. Picabia likewise belittled the cultural efforts of the art dealers Paul Guillaume and Léonce Rosenberg, who varied their offerings of modern art with soirées on the work of Jean Cocteau, Erik Satie, Max Jacob and Blaise Cendrars. "Little assemblies," Picabia called them, "teas 'vain' and compromising as a member of the Institute"—although later in his life both Doucet and Rosenberg were to become friends and patrons of his work.[4] Finally, Picabia lamented the timidity of the "so-called modern" magazines, probably meaning (but not naming) *SIC*, *Littérature* and *La Nouvelle Revue française*. *SIC* was the only avant-garde journal of art and literature in Paris which survived the war, and it soon waned. But *La Nouvelle Revue française*, suspended during the war, reappeared as the forum of generally established, distinguished authors such as Paul Valéry, André Gide and its editor Jacques Rivière. *Littérature*, founded in March 1919 by André Breton, Louis Aragon and Philippe Soupault, bridged the older and younger generations, while serving primarily as a forum for younger, searching writers who would figure later in Dada and, especially, nascent Surrealism.[5]

Military assignments and literary aspirations had brought those three young men together; thereafter, many shared interests cemented their friendships. As a premedical student and military intern, Breton was profoundly influenced by the study of psychiatry and the irrational life and suicide of Jacques Vaché. Both experiences fixed his fascination on an unconscious reality more significant than the reality of conscious, "rational," everyday life.[6] Breton abandoned medicine to pursue that interest via literature. While supporting himself by doing editing for *La Nouvelle Revue française*, he steeped himself in the writings of Rimbaud, Lautréamont, Reverdy and Apollinaire. Like others, Breton seems to have felt that he was on the track of that "l'esprit nouveau" and "sur-réalisme" enunciated by Apollinaire but never clarified by him. By early 1919, the work of Tzara also nourished Breton's cravings. Tzara initiated the contact in January 1919 after encountering the writings of Breton and his friends, Aragon and Soupault, in *SIC*. All three contributed to the next issue of *Dada* (no. 4–5, April 1919), although

title "Carnet d'un sédentaire" in *La Forge* (Paris, April, May and June 1919). Reprinted in Picabia, *Ecrits 1913–1920*, ed. Olivier Revault d'Allonnes (Paris, 1975), 151–53, 155–57.

4. For Picabia's comments on Picasso, Doucet and Rosenberg, see his letters to Tzara on March 28 and June 4, 1919 (C.T. 2.991, 2.996; Sanouillet, *Dada à Paris*, 485, 487–88). Picasso's financial success had continued to mount, and, following his 1918 marriage to the Russian ballerina, Olga Koklova, a new level of elegant social activity characterized his life.

5. For an account of this review and its founders see Sanouillet, *Dada à Paris*, 75–110. Two series of *Littérature* were published: I, nos. 1–20 (March 1919–August 1921), and II, nos. 1–13 (March 1922–June 1924).

6. Breton (*Entretiens 1913–1952*, 10th ed., Paris, 1952, 29) attributes decisive influence on his thought to Dr. Raoul Leroy of the psychiatric center of the Second Army at St.-Dizier. For Breton's comments on Vaché, see his preface to Jacques Vaché, *Lettres de guerre* (Paris, 1919).

they disliked the participation of other French avant-gardists, notably Cocteau, Paul Dermée and Albert-Birot—and they said as much to Tzara. Tzara's writings, however, impressed them, especially Breton, who was haunted by Tzara's "Manifeste Dada 1918." Its nihilistic, antiart thrust simultaneously repelled and fascinated him, and throughout 1919 he was as persistent as Picabia in urging Tzara to transfer to Paris.[7] Tzara repeatedly vacillated, but did strive to unite Breton and Picabia. He failed in that effort, for someone in Paris had warned Breton to steer clear of Picabia, and Breton did just that for almost a year.[8] Picabia's corresponding neglect of Breton was a matter of following his own taste. Excepting the poems of Tzara, *Littérature* offered little of interest to him. It was a "serious" magazine, conservative in design and carefully balanced in contributors who represented the entire spectrum of Breton's interests. Works by the three editors and Tzara were interspersed with those of Apollinaire and Reverdy, Rimbaud and Mallarmé, and even contributions by the associates of *La Nouvelle Revue française* whom Breton continued to cultivate. Tzara likewise viewed the contributors to *Littérature* with some reservation, observing to Breton that "It seems to me you wish to accentuate in your magazine the passage between the old and the new literature, which is (very) necessary, but . . . more a work of criticism and history."[9]

For Picabia, the only people who counted in Paris were Georges Ribemont-Dessaignes, Marius de Zayas (still seeking support for a Paris gallery) and, later in the year, Marcel Duchamp.[10] Instead of collaborating with any French group or magazine, Picabia occupied himself with his own work and a few friends, looked after a lively demand for copies of *Dada* and *391* and produced another volume of poetry, *Pensées sans langage* (Thoughts Without Language).[11] Picabia's advice to "read my little book after having made love" comes too late in the text (p. 89) to be of practical use for most readers, and, accordingly, many concluded the title was merited. For over 100 pages this poem runs an erratic course unmarked by titles, uppercase letters, or punctuation. In most instances, each page or pair of facing pages constitutes a unified poem, but there are exceptions where a page concludes with a line that may just as well terminate that page or bind it to the following one.

7. For the Breton-Tzara correspondence during 1919 see Sanouillet, *Dada à Paris*, 440–53. Breton's distaste for Cocteau, Dermée and Albert-Birot is expressed in several letters, for example, one of April 4 (C.T. 552; Sanouillet, op. cit., 443).

8. On February 18, 1919, Breton wrote Tzara (C.T. 550; Sanouillet, *Dada à Paris*, 441) that the exclusion of Picabia from plans for *Littérature* was no elision. He later confessed to Picabia, in a letter on January 4, 1920, that he had been advised not to meet him (D.P. V, 213; Sanouillet, op. cit., 504).

9. Tzara letter to Breton, March 1 or 5, 1919 (Sanouillet, *Dada à Paris*, 441–42).

10. See Picabia's letters to Tzara on March 12, May 21 and June 4 (C.T. 2.990, 2.995, 2.996; Sanouillet, *Dada à Paris*, 483–84, 487–88). De Zayas's plans for a gallery in Paris did not materialize, but he did include four works by Picabia in the exhibition he organized for the Arden Gallery, New York, *The Evolution of French Art*, April 29–May 24, 1919.

11. *Pensées sans langage*, preface by Udnie (Paris, 1919), was signed and dated April 28, 1919. Picabia wrote Tzara on August 3 that it would be printed within a few days (C.T. 2.998; Sanouillet, *Dada à Paris*, 490). Sanouillet (op. cit., 111) claims it as the first work connected to Dada to appear under that title in Paris.

This defiant ambiguity also exists in the sequence of lines on the same page, intensifying the already baffling content of poems veiled by private, cryptic analogies.

Nevertheless, many passages express poignantly enough specific events in Picabia's life or his sentiments on love, war, God and morality:

> l'homme cerveau introduisit dans la vie
> ce que Dieu n'a pu faire
> l'intelligence
> Dieu inventa les maladies
> l'homme les médecins
> Dieu inventa la reproduction
> l'homme l'amour
> le ciel est froid
> sur le bûcher public

brain man introduces into life / what God has not been able to do / intelligence / God invented illnesses / man doctors / God invented reproduction / man love / the sky is cold / on the public pyre

> j'ai trouvé la poule malade
> laisse-moi t'embrasser
> câliner en massages le secret de la vertu
> joie naïve de bonheur
> regardant la fidélité
> qui aime les vœux de chasteté
> en fils de madone bordel de soir usé

I found the streetwalker sick / let me caress you / coaxing, massaging the secret of virtue / naive joy of happiness / pondering fidelity / who loves vows of chastity / as a madonna's son brothel of worn night[12]

Around the time that *Pensées sans langage* was published during the late summer of 1919, the tempo of Picabia's private and public life accelerated. For a while painting again became an important means of expression, and he sought to organize an exhibition of his work at the Bernheim Jeune Gallery. He also considered a new issue of *391* for the occasion of the Salon d'Automne and collaborated with Gleizes, Archipenko and others on plans for a new Section d'Or.[13] All of this transpired under new living conditions. Early in August, just six weeks before the birth of his child by Gabrielle, Picabia moved into the apartment of Germaine

12. Picabia, *Pensées sans langage*, 30, 12.
13. Picabia asked Tzara on August 3 (C.T. 2.998; Sanouillet, *Dada à Paris*, 490) to write a preface for the proposed exhibition. The exhibition was never arranged; the location of Tzara's preface is unknown. Plans for new issues of *391* and a revived Section d'Or are mentioned in letters between November 10 and December 30, 1919 (C.T. 2.999, 3.004; Sanouillet, op. cit., 492–96).

Everling, who was also carrying a child by him.[14] Cordial relations were retained with Gabrielle, including collaboration on several dada projects. But the separation was permanent, and Germaine's unlikely bourgeois apartment at 14, rue Emile-Augier was to become a major gathering point for Dada in Paris.

Marcel Duchamp, recently returned to Paris after a four-year absence, became one of their first guests, and Picabia then wrote Tzara that there were three who counted, "You are, with R. Dessaignes and Marcel Duchamp, the only intelligent beings who exist for the moment."[15] Almost by definition Duchamp's presence on the eve of Dada in Paris would seem to be important, but it is difficult to assess his role, since his activities and our records of them are limited. Only three works by Duchamp are documented during his six months in Paris: *Paris Air*, *L.H.O.O.Q.* and the *Tzanck Check* (see figs. 164, 165), the latter an oversized, handmade check given in payment to his dentist. Moreover, he did not participate in the controversies which swirled around *391* and the Salon d'Automne during November–December 1919, and he returned to New York in January 1920 just before Dada broke loose in Paris.

Despite his public distance from those activities, Duchamp's presence was—as always for Picabia—an occasion of grand camaraderie, intellectual stimulation and vital moral support. Duchamp's cessation of painting in 1918 had set at that time the extreme measure of antiart, but he had not ceased creative discovery and production and probably exerted a direct impact on Picabia's work. *Tzanck Check* is a noteworthy predecessor to Picabia's *L'Oeil cacodylate (The Cacodylic Eye*, color pl. XI) with its implication that art—instead of being merely a lofty spiritual expression—is also money and has a lot to do with the signature. Duchamp had also brought from Buenos Aires a glass and metal construction, *To Be Looked At (From the Other Side of the Glass) with One Eye, Close to, for Almost an Hour* (fig. 166), which may have contributed to Picabia's more rigorous geometrical compositions during 1919–1922, some of them related to optical phenomena. The relationship of Duchamp's *L.H.O.O.Q.* (fig. 164) and Picabia's *Le Double Monde (Double World*, fig. 167) is more speculative, for these two works are contemporary in date and both men have been attributed authorship of the indecent pun which reads in French, "She has a hot arse" ("Elle a chaud au cul").[16] Duchamp, however, was more inclined toward such punning, and this one seems more integral to the image and content of his moustachioed Mona Lisa than to Picabia's *Le Double Monde*. Sexual ambiguity, a major theme in Duchamp's work during the epoch of Dada, is central to *L.H.O.O.Q.* as the mous-

14. Laurente Vincente was born to Gabrielle and Francis on September 15, 1919, and officially recorded before the mayor of the arrondissement by Germaine and Francis. Lorenzo Salvador was born to Francis and Germaine on January 4, 1920.

15. Picabia letter to Tzara, November 10, 1919 (C.T. 2.999; Sanouillet, *Dada à Paris*, 492).

16. Most authors have considered Duchamp as the primary creator in this matter, but Sanouillet has discussed the absence of irrefutable proof (*Dada à Paris*, 146) and claimed paternity for Picabia (*Francis Picabia et "391,"* II, Paris, 1966, 113).

tache and beard are disturbingly effective in transforming or confusing the sex of Leonardo's La Giaconda, while the inscription (title) reasserts a female identity. Questions of precedent aside, both *L.H.O.O.Q.* and *Le Double Monde* are major dada works which attest to the sparks generated by Duchamp and Picabia on the eve of Dada in Paris.

Along with Duchamp, Ribemont-Dessaignes provided the intellectual stimulation and humor required to nourish Picabia's happiness. Many members of the avant-garde in Paris were interested in Dada; some had also collaborated with Tzara, but none was able to participate with the gusto of this old friend from the Section d'Or days. Following a moral crisis in 1913, Ribemont-Dessaignes had abandoned painting, but after induction into the army in 1915 he began to compose music and poetry, and, in 1916, he wrote *L'Empereur de Chine*, which has been considered the first dada play.[17] Throughout the war years Picabia maintained contact, seeking Ribemont-Dessaignes's collaboration on *391* and recommending him to Tzara for *Dada*. Picabia's regard for Ribemont-Dessaignes is understandable, for his writings are similar in style and spirit to Picabia's own work, though perhaps even more biting. And in 1919 Ribemont-Dessaignes resumed painting, working in a mechanomorphic manner inspired by Picabia (see fig. 168).

These two men, with their paintings and polemics in the fall of 1919, scandalized all of Paris. Technically speaking, the scandal was not part of Dada in Paris for no conscious dada group existed there; no activities were waged under its banner or viewed as such by the small, imperfectly informed audience then available. But spiritually speaking, the action of Picabia and Ribemont-Dessaignes was Dada to the core and crucial for a rapid concentration of the men and means who made Dada in Paris. It began on November 1 at the Salon d'Automne.

Inasmuch as the large national Salons had been suspended during the war, the reopening of the Salon d'Automne in 1919 assumed uncommon importance. As the first salon to reopen, it constituted an unofficial presentation of the status of art in France after a great national struggle for survival. The organizers of the Salon were sensitive to their opportunities and responsibilities; they attended to their publicity and secured use of the government's Grand Palais to accommodate the anticipated surge of visitors and state dignitaries. The reception of Picabia and Ribemont-Dessaignes is more comprehensible under those conditions and within the overwhelmingly conservative context of the other works on exhibit. Two of Picabia's paintings at the Salon are extant, *L'Enfant carburateur* (*Child Carburetor*) and *Serpentins* (*Streamers*, fig. 169, and color pl. IX; fig. 171), and one of Ribemont-Dessaignes's can be identified, *Young Woman* (fig. 168).[18] Such abstract and mechanomorphic paintings had never been exhibited in Paris, and

17. Sanouillet, *Dada à Paris*, 116.
18. Another version of *Serpentins* exists which is larger (32 x 21¼ in.) and more sketchily brushed, but identical in color, composition and inscription to the version reproduced here. It has not been determined which painting was exhibited at the 1919 Salon d'Automne.

most of the mortified members of the Salon committee could only view them as tasteless jokes or calculated insults. To their chagrin, they could not refuse the work of associates, but they did hang the paintings in a dark alcove underneath the grand stairway. That solution backfired when Picabia and Ribemont-Dessaignes protested vociferously and the paintings themselves proved to be so provocative that every critic sought them out and published some derogatory comment. One critic who studied the inscriptions on *L'Enfant carburateur* remarked: "A painter, named Picabia, exhibits the portrait of a machine 'to kill the future'; he should look next time for a machine 'to kill the past' and try it out on himself."[19]

Genuinely disgusted by the narrow-minded reception of his paintings and perhaps delighted by the shock they generated, Picabia resolved to exploit the situation by means of an open letter of protest and a new issue of *391*.[20] That issue of *391* was dominated by Ribemont-Dessaignes's review of the Salon—a vicious review that asked for trouble by insulting Marshal Foch, France and a score of well-known artists:

> There [the Salon], everything is dead for the Country, although all may not be dead on the field of honor. Confusion of genres. The skeleton of Marshal Foch prowls in the dark when the doors of the Palace [Grand Palais] are closed and calls the muster. The teeth of the artists, which are almost as filthy as the nails of the sculptors, chatter with fright.—Am I enough of a corpse? Do I smell bad enough? Marshal! Marshal! I assure you, I have at least been to the censor!—[21]

Ribemont-Dessaignes also smeared in passing "the old grimaces of Matisse," Frantz Jourdain as "an ersatz Alexandre Duval" and the "sadistic still lifes of Maurice Denis, who wallows in his own humility, mixing masochism and onanism."

Though many were seared, none screamed so loudly as that painter of simpering religious scenes, Maurice Denis, who proclaimed to the committee of the Salon d'Automne that either he or his vile insulter should resign. Ribemont-Dessaignes, summoned before the committee, further incensed them, refused to

19. Anon., *Le Matin* [Paris], November 1, 1919.

20. Picabia addressed his open letter ("Protestation," *Le Journal du peuple* [Paris], November 2, 1919, 2) to Frantz Jourdain, president of the Salon. After noting the half-hidden location of his paintings, Picabia asked about "the aim of the Salon d'Automne":

"Does it exist uniquely to sustain the dealers and painters whose place should be at the Artistes Français or at the Société Nationale des Beaux-Arts [the conservative salons in Paris]? I know the great difficulties which you have had in order to obtain the Grand Palais; is that a reason to sacrifice the truly modern artists in order to please the imbeciles?

". . . The Salon d'Automne must above all be modern; if that is impossible, it must disappear, having no longer any reason to exist."

21. Georges Ribemont-Dessaignes, "Salon d'Automne," *391*, no. 9 (Paris, November 1919), 2–3.

resign and inserted in the next issue of *391* (no. 10, December 1919) a blistering reaffirmation of his position. That in turn so infuriated the art critic Louis Vauxcelles, a member of the committee, that he demanded a retraction by Ribemont-Dessaignes or satisfaction by arms. The letter was not withdrawn, and Ribemont-Dessaignes sent word by his seconds, Picabia and Gleizes, that fighting was against his principles.[22]

That chain of events now seems disproportionate to the paintings which spawned it. *Serpentins* and *L'Enfant carburateur* are handsome, technically proficient paintings. Indeed, the latter is a masterpiece of Picabia's mechanomorphic oeuvre. Though it contributes no innovations to the mechanical symbolism and machine aesthetics developed by him since 1915, *L'Enfant carburateur* does present an especially effective balance of visual and intellectual properties. An immediate visual harmony is projected by the balance of the irregular patterns in the stained plywood ground and the bold machine forms silhouetted against it in black, white and gold metallic paint. The title, long thought to be mere dada nonsense, actually identifies those machine forms, for they are based on an automobile carburetor, that is, the part of a gasoline engine which controls the mixture of gasoline and air to secure maximum firing of the cylinders (see fig. 170). In fact, the actual model may have been a Claudel racing carburetor in one of the luxurious autos purchased by Picabia in 1919, and, given his adoration of cars, one should not exclude the possibility that a private comment on automobiles has been made in *L'Enfant carburateur*.[23] Germaine Everling tells us that Picabia spent hours at the end of that year with a newly arrived American Mercer, in rapture over every detail, patting it and proclaiming with conviction, "It's the most beautiful car you can see."[24] At the same time, suggestively male and female parts to the carburetor bear witness to an even keener preoccupation of Picabia's, and still more dimensions are revealed by the discovery of puzzling inscriptions—"Crocodile Method," "Dissolution of Prolongation," "Flux and Reflux of Resolutions," "Sphere of the Migraine," "To Destroy the Future" and "Waltz in Jacket." Initially, such inscriptions might strike one as ranging somewhere between mockery and a curiously fragmented poem independent of the painted forms. But those inscriptions are explicitly associated with forms in the painting, implying that Picabia has again linked forms and inscriptions with the mechanomorphic symbolism long established in his work and in the career of Duchamp, most notably in this instance the bride in Duchamp's *Large Glass* (fig. 114), which he had described as a kind of motor operated by "love gasoline." Considering that background alongside the current conditions of Picabia's life—torn between wife and mistress, each carrying a child by him—such inscriptions

22. For contemporary accounts of this episode see *391*, no. 10 (Paris, December 1919), and Louis Vauxcelles, "Carnet des ateliers," *Carnet de la semaine* (Paris, December 28, 1919).

23. For this carburetor source and an excellent discussion of *L'Enfant carburateur* see Angelica Zander Rudenstine (*The Guggenheim Museum Collection: Paintings 1880–1945*, II, New York, 1976, 591–95).

24. Germaine Everling, *L'Anneau de Saturne* (Paris, 1970), 95.

as "child carburetor" and "flux and reflux of resolutions" refer in all likelihood to conditions in his private life. More precise interpretive efforts are discouraged, however, by the multileveled possibilities of *L'Enfant carburateur* and by Picabia's silence.

Since *L'Enfant carburateur* can be attributed to 1919 with reasonable assurance,[25] it also serves the practical purpose of indicating dates for similar paintings that are not so well documented, notably *L'Oeil* (*Eye*), *Balance* (*Scale*) and *Souvenir du rien* (*Memory of Nothing*, figs. 172–174). These paintings are generally related to *L'Enfant carburateur* by their spare compositions and restrained color harmonies. More specifically, they share the distinctive metal rods, springs and, excepting *Souvenir du rien*, the feature of an arc embracing a circle which appeared in earlier works of 1919, for example, *Mouvement Dada* (fig. 161). The prominent use of circles and concentric circles in these paintings is also basically similar although the forms vary, especially in *Balance*, where the circular form in the upper right has a magnifying property which may reflect the contemporary optical interests of Duchamp.

C'est clair (*It is Clear*, fig. 175) combines the rods and circles of these paintings with the palette and curvilinear forms of *Serpentins* (fig. 171). *Prenez garde à la peinture* (*Watch out for the Painting*, fig. 176) does not appear closely related to this group of paintings, but Germaine Everling attributed it to 1919,[26] and two features support her memory—a dadaist quality about the inscriptions and the use of taut and slack lines similar to those found in *Balance*, *L'Oeil* and *Souvenir du rien*.

Le Double Monde (fig. 167), a signed and dated painting of 1919, reaffirms the variety of Picabia's work during any phase of his career and, more importantly, represents one of the first of a handful of works which constitute his purest dada creations in the visual arts. It is a balance of biting inscriptions and an abstract interlace whose convoluted loopings seem compatible with the world it describes—"fragile," peopled by "the sick God has never cured," "haut" (top) near the bottom and "bas" (bottom) upside down near the top. Plastered down the center are the huge letters "LHOOQ," an indecent pun related to the previously discussed painting of the same title by Duchamp.

M'amenez-y (*Bring Me There*, color pl. x) partakes of the same spirit although the bright colors and sensuously brushed pigment of this painting provide a striking contrast to the restrained palette and brushwork of *Le Double Monde*. Visual and verbal contrasts, in fact, abound within the painting itself. Hard-edged machine forms are pitted against sensuous pigment, and the entire visual experience

25. Although not dated, *L'Enfant carburateur* is compatible in style and content with what is known of Picabia's life and his mechanomorphic works of 1919—the year in which the painting was first documented by the witness of Germaine Everling (*L'Anneau de Saturne*, 90) and exhibited at the Salon d'Automne. Mme Everling's witness is indirectly supported by Picabia's letter to Alfred Stieglitz on September 11, 1919 (A.S.A., Yale), in which he writes of having done two paintings which will appear in the Salon d'Automne.

26. Everling, *L'Anneau de Saturne*, 91.

is challenged by the literary-audio effect of inscriptions which insinuate provocative meanings. In the lower left, "Pont l'Evêque" (a strong, creamy cheese) may be linked by association to nearby creamy colors or to the inscription across the top, "Portrait à l'huile de Ricin!" ("Portrait of Castor Oil!"). "Râtelier d'Artiste" ("Artist's False Teeth") suggests a play on "atelier d'artiste" ("artist's studio") but, in this context, certainly refers to the neighboring inscription "peinture crocodile" ("crocodile painting") which, in turn, raises an association with crocodile tears. The prominent title, *M'amenez-y*, is equally open to interpretive efforts but, under the circumstances, appears to be an irrational, joking request.[27]

The Salon d'Automne had barely closed its doors when Picabia became the center of another controversy. The director of the Cirque d'Hiver, a M. Sandberg, invited him to participate in an exhibition of modern art in the foyer of the circus during December. But Sandberg took offense at the inscriptions on Picabia's entries, *Parade amoureuse* and *Muscles brillants* (figs. 132, 155), and asked him to suppress them. Picabia refused, but offered to remove the paintings. When other participants—Gleizes, Villon, Ribemont-Dessaignes, etc.—threatened to remove their paintings if Picabia left, Sandberg relented and the issue appeared to be settled. At the last minute, however, Sandberg found a twentieth-century equivalent for Pope Paul IV's censorship of the nudes in Michelangelo's *Last Judgment*: whereas Daniele da Volterra painted panties for the pontiff, Sandberg employed collage, pasting paper over the offending inscriptions, and Picabia aired the entire affair in the press.[28]

Toward the end of 1919 a portentous response was building to the spirit and scandal generated by Picabia in the Salon d'Automne, the Cirque d'Hiver, issues of *391* and *Pensées sans langage*. In November, after stalling for eight months, Breton sought to meet Picabia, writing: "You are one of the three or four men whose attitude I entirely approve, and I would be happy to count myself among your friends. For months, I have read nothing with such emotion as your *Pensées sans langage*."[29] Another young poet, Paul Eluard, also sought out Picabia after having read *Pensées sans langage*. "I read *Pensées sans langage*," he wrote Tzara, "and it is for me as though the divine Marquis de Sade had become a poet whom I

27. *M'amenez-y* is another undated, unique work in Picabia's career which cannot be attributed a date on grounds of obvious stylistic relationships with documented paintings. Nonetheless, it is compatible in form, inscriptions and spirit with Picabia's dadaist oeuvre of ca. 1919–1920, and the phrase, "M'amenez-y," was current at that time. It appears on *Le Double Monde* (fig. 167) and was chosen as the title for a dadaist magazine projected by Céline Arnauld during 1920 (see chap. X, n. 15). Marcel Jean (*The History of Surrealist Painting*, trans. Simon Watson Taylor, London: Weidenfeld and Nicolson, 1960, 86) and William Rubin (*Dada, Surrealism and Their Heritage*, New York: The Museum of Modern Art, 1968, 27, 189) have suggested that "M'amenez-y" is a substitution for "Amenez-y-moi" and involves a play on the word "amnésie."

28. For this affair see Picabia's open letter to the editor in *Comoedia* [Paris], December 22, 1919, and "Une Protestation de Picabia" in *Le Journal du peuple* [Paris], December 19, 1919, 2.

29. Breton letter to Picabia, December 11, 1919 (D.P. I, 264; Sanouillet, *Dada à Paris*, 503).

love."[30] For his part, Tzara allowed that he had been sleeping, but had been awakened by *391*.[31] He may also have been attracted by the publication of Breton's and Soupault's first "automatic writing," *Les Champs magnétiques*, and he had been informed of plans for a new Section d'Or, Eluard's forthcoming magazine *Proverbe* and Dermée's *L'Esprit nouveau*.[32] And Tzara, too, after months of vacillation, resolved to be in Paris by January. That union of Tzara, Picabia and Breton assured Dada a future in Paris.

30. Eluard letter to Tzara, November 28, 1919 (C.T. 1300).

31. Tzara letter to Picabia, undated [end of 1919] (D.P. III, 16; Sanouillet, *Dada à Paris*, 493).

32. See Breton's letter to Tzara on December 26, 1919, and Paul Dermée's letter to Tzara, undated [December 1919] (B.D., C.T. 563; Sanouillet, *Dada à Paris*, 453–54, 545). Extracts from *Les Champs magnétiques* were published in *Littérature*, I, nos. 8, 9 and 10 (Paris, October, November and December 1919). Soupault has stressed that he and Breton were influenced by Pierre Janet's *L'Automatisme psychologique* (Paris: F. Alcan, 1889) just before collaborating on *Les Champs magnétiques* (interview with the author, June 10, 1974).

10. THE FIRST DADA SEASON IN PARIS

THE THREE principal figures of Dada in Paris, Tzara, Breton and Picabia (see figs. 177–179), were finally united during January 1920. After an exchange of letters in December, Breton and Picabia met in the latter's apartment on the evening of January 4; Tzara joined them two weeks later.[1] Each man brought with him a variety of collaborators, contacts and experiences—all of which contributed to a prolific, turbulent, multifaceted form of Dada, and a short-lived one.

Breton and Picabia began with a salutory confrontation of the obstacles between them, Breton even writing the next day to reassure Picbia that, "It would be very distressing for me if you took as an act of any ambition the orientation given to *Littérature*. We only use Gide, Valéry and several others to compromise them and to augment the confusion as much as possible."[2] With that problem aired, their first meeting—by all accounts—turned into a memorable evening. According to Germaine Everling, the Picabia-Breton discussion of contemporary French art and literature, Tzara and Dada, Nietzsche, Rimbaud and Lautréamont became so animated that neither perceived the signals of anxiety coming from her adjacent room. Finally, Georges and Dodo de Zayas, who were attending Germaine that evening, had to rout Breton and Picabia while she gave birth to François Lorenzo Salvador.[3] His arrival interrupted Picabia and Breton only a few days. The latter soon wrote Tzara that "I hardly see anyone but him [Picabia] in Paris, in both senses. . . . He is perhaps with you the only man with whom I can speak without concealed thoughts. I pass at least two evenings with him each week and it is without doubt the best of my time."[4] For his part, Picabia vowed to Breton that "you are truly the man one must meet once or twice in his life in order to have the courage to continue to live."[5]

1. Breton first wrote Picabia on December 11, 1919, and his letters on January 4 and 5, 1920, document their first meeting (D.P. I, 264, D.P. V, 41, 213; Michel Sanouillet, *Dada à Paris*, Paris, 1965, 503–505). Tzara's arrival on January 17 is documented by his identification card issued by the Paris police (Sanouillet, op. cit., 140). His arrival and installation at Picabia's apartment is described by Germaine Everling, *L'Anneau de Saturne* (Paris, 1970), 98–99.

2. Breton letter to Picabia, January 5, 1920 (D.P. V, 41; Sanouillet, *Dada à Paris*, 505). Breton's later actions did not wholly substantiate that claim.

3. Everling, *L'Anneau de Saturne*, 95–96.

4. Breton letter to Tzara, January 14, 1920 (C.T. 563; Sanouillet, *Dada à Paris*, 455).

5. Picabia letter to Breton, January 10, 1920 (collection A. Breton, Paris; Sanouillet, *Dada à Paris*, 505).

When Tzara arrived on the seventeenth, Breton and his coeditors of *Littéra-ture* were less enthusiastic, initially, it seems, because Tzara failed to fulfill their mental image of the long-awaited personification of Dada from the East. In contrast to Breton's magistral bearing and exquisite, measured French, Tzara was small, myopic, somewhat jerky in his gestures and spoke imperfect French with a gutteral Slavic accent. More substantial objections developed later, but for the time being Tzara provided the missing rallying point and sense of mission to ignite the explosive energies recently gathered around Breton and Picabia. Within hours of his installation in the Picabias' apartment, their salon looked like dada campaign headquarters. And in short order scandalous festivals, exhibitions, manifestations and publications erupted at a dizzying pace which understandably appeared to the bewildered, antagonized citizens of Paris as a coordinated assault on French culture.

Even during that heyday of Dada in Paris, Picabia was too much of an individualist to be wholly absorbed by it. Nevertheless, the history of his career and Dada in Paris are so inseparably interwoven that it is both practical and necessary to follow him through the framework of dada events, pausing occasionally to focus separately on his work.

What became the first dada program in Paris, the "Matinee of *Littérature*" on January 23, was planned before Tzara's arrival by the coeditors of *Littérature*, Aragon, Breton and Soupault. In accord with the traditions of their magazine, they conceived the program as moving from a base in the poetry of such established men as Apollinaire, Jacob, Reverdy and Cendrars to recitations of poems by themselves, Tzara, Picabia and others. Separating those blocks of readings were interludes devoted to the music of Satie, Milhaud, Auric, Poulenc and Cliquet, and a presentation of the paintings of Gris, Léger, de Chirico, Lipchitz, Ribemont-Dessaignes and Picabia. After Tzara's arrival, it was decided to keep his presence a secret until he could be introduced at the critical point in that fundamentally serious, structured program.

The "Matinee of *Littérature*" was indeed a tasteful, avant-garde affair followed by an intelligent and appreciative audience until Breton presented two works by Picabia, *Le Double Monde* (fig. 167) and *Riz au nez*. *Le Double Monde*, exhibited for the first time, exceeded in impertinence anything seen before in Paris—including Picabia's recent controversial paintings at the Salon d'Automne. And once the indecent pun of its major inscription registered on the audience, the howls began. Breton quickly shifted to another work wheeled on stage, a chalk drawing bearing cryptic inscriptions and the not-so-cryptic title, *Riz au nez*, which may be translated as *Laugh in Your Face*. The audience protest intensified and Breton, as preplanned by Picabia, erased the offending art work and called for music. The audience was mollified briefly but then challenged again by the surprise introduction of Tzara, who read the latest discourse of the firebrand deputy, Léon Daudet, while Aragon and Breton rang bells offstage.[6] The remainder of the

6. Léon Daudet, controversial neo-royalist writer and politician, had been elected to the Chamber of Deputies in 1919. For contemporary accounts of the "Matinee," see Marius Boisson,

program was presented to an almost empty house and within twenty-four hours the editors of *Littérature* were besieged by angry acquaintances.

Tzara and Picabia, experienced troopers in the public arena, took it in stride. Breton the beginner was rattled, but recovered quickly.[7] The die had been cast and there was another matinee to be prepared—the first under the banner of Dada—at the Salon des Indépendants on February 5. Plans were worked out in what became the habitual gathering places of the dadaists—Picabia's apartment and the Café Certà, a Basque bar-restaurant in the Passage de l'Opéra which the editors of *Littérature* had recently adopted. Tzara quickly exerted his gifts for leadership and promotion, assembling a new issue of *Dada* (no. 6, the *Bulletin Dada*) and releasing false news items which created considerable publicity for the movement. One press release claimed that Gabriele d'Annunzio, Henri Bergson, the Prince of Monaco and Charlie Chaplin had converted to Dada, and that the beloved American comedian might appear at the matinee.[8]

Even greater interest in the forthcoming matinee was generated by the paintings of Picabia and his colleagues at the Salon des Indépendants which opened on January 28 at the Grand Palais. Picabia submitted six large, striking examples of his mechanomorphic style although all of them were older works, mostly dating from 1915: *Révérence, Machine sans nom (Machine Without Name), Très rare tableau sur la terre, Cette Chose est faite pour perpétuer mon souvenir, Petite Solitude au milieu des soleils* and *Cannibalisme* (figs. 116, 117, 119, 120, 121, 156).[9] He was joined by Georges Ribemont-Dessaignes, Jean Crotti and Suzanne Duchamp-Crotti, Duchamp's sister who had married Crotti in April 1919. They, too, submitted interesting works in a mechanomorphic mode (figs. 149, 181),[10] and from that point onward such machine paintings were identified with Dada. Despite the quality of his colleagues' entries to the Salon, Picabia was viewed as the chief dadaist and his paintings became the sole focus of the critics. They uniformly rejected his paintings as works of art and made no effort to provide the public with intelligent criticism or even information save for one writer who did secure a straightforward statement from Picabia:

"Le Premier Vendredi de 'Littérature,' " *Comoedia* [Paris], January 24, 1920, 3, and Félix, "La Potinière," *Fantasio*, no. 315 (Paris, March 1920), 433, where Picabia's puns and paintings are discussed. See also Sanouillet, *Dada à Paris*, 142–48.

7. See the Breton letter to Picabia of January 24, 1920 (D.P. III, 63; Sanouillet, *Dada à Paris*, 507).

8. Emile Decharme, "Charlie Chaplin et le mouvement Dada," *Le Journal du peuple* [Paris], February 2, 1920, 2.

9. Salon des Indépendants, Paris, January 28–February 29, 1920, nos. 3550–55. Since Picabia's mechanomorphic style was barely known in Paris, he had no reason to exhibit only recent work, but his choice of older paintings is puzzling. For the proposed Galerie Bernheim exhibition in 1919, he had called in all his paintings left in Zurich and New York, and, presumably, he had many works at his disposal ranging in date from 1915 to 1919.

10. The works reproduced here were among those exhibited at the Salon des Indépendants by Ribemont-Dessaignes (nos. 3835–38), Crotti (nos. 4870–72) and Suzanne Duchamp-Crotti (nos. 4891–93).

We paint without preoccupying ourselves with the representation of objects, and we write without looking out for the sense of words. We seek only the pleasure of expressing ourselves, but while doing so, giving to the diagrams we draw, to the words we align, a symbolic sense, a value of expression not only outside of all current convention, but by an unstable convention . . . which lasts only for the very instant we use it. Also, the work finished, that convention lost from sight, it is unintelligible to me and besides no longer interests me. It is of the past.[11]

One week after the opening of the Indépendants, the dadaists had reserved for their "Movement Dada" one of the twelve matinees scheduled to coincide with the Salon. Owing to mounting publicity since the "Matinee of *Littérature*," the hall at the Grand Palais was packed with an audience ready to respond to the anticipated provocations of the organizers. Tzara's *Bulletin Dada*, which doubled as a program distributed at the door, graphically displayed the rapid assertion of his spirit over the movement in Paris. In contrast to the prim format of *Littérature*, the *Bulletin Dada* was big, splashy and artfully casual in layout with an insouciant melange of puns, aphorisms and Picabia drawings, a list of "391" presidents of Dada and advertisements for their varied publications. The program, as listed on the cover, had no lectures, no poetry, no references to Apollinaire, Reverdy, Cendrars, or Jacob—only aggressive manifestos by the dadaists which provoked ever more audience participation and publicity.[12]

Picabia missed the "Matinee of the Movement Dada" and the next two matinees as well, one at the Club du Faubourg on February 7 and another at the Université Populaire du Faubourg St.-Antoine on the nineteenth. He and Germaine had left Paris around February 2 for a three-week vacation in balmy Martigues, site of their honeymoon in 1917.[13] Under these vacation conditions, Picabia completed an unexpectedly lyrical, melancholic "manifesto," his "Dada Philosophe," which was read at the dada matinee at the Université Populaire.[14] That particular matinee was a rather dispirited near-repetition of the earlier outings, but as the ranks of Dada swelled and the range of semi-independent ac-

11. M.B. [Marcel Boulanger?], "Le Dadaisme n'est qu'une farce inconsistante," *L'Action française* [Paris], February 14, 1920, 2. Following Picabia's statement, the journalist noted that, "The title for him [Picabia] has in effect no forced bond with the work for, he says, 'a man can be named Brown and be blond.' " See also Picabia's statement "L'Art," *Littérature*, I, no. 13 (Paris, May 1920), 12–13; reprinted in Picabia, *Ecrits 1913–1920*, ed. Olivier Revault d'Allonnes (Paris, 1975), 227.

12. See Sanouillet, *Dada à Paris*, 152–56. The manifestos read at the "Matinee of the Movement Dada" were printed in *Littérature*, I, no. 13 (Paris, May 1920). Picabia's, listed first on the program as "Manifesto read by 10 persons," appears in *Littérature* as "L'Art" (pp. 12–13).

13. See the Picabia-Tzara and Picabia-Breton correspondence (C.T. 3.006; D.P. V, 32, 35; Sanouillet, *Dada à Paris*, 496–97, 507–508).

14. Picabia's "Dada Philosophe" is discussed in the Picabia-Tzara and Picabia-Breton correspondence (C.T. 3.006; D.P. V, 32, 35) and was published in *Littérature*, I, no. 13 (Paris, May 1920), 5–6.

tivities became more numerous, the dadaists rode waves of self-generating scandals into the doldrums of the summer months.

Two new dada periodicals, Eluard's *Proverbe* and Dermée's *Z*, appeared in February to augment the basic journals, *Dada* and *391*.[15] In that same month at Au Sans Pareil (recently established as the publishing agent for *Littérature*), René Hilsum opened a "Collection Dada" devoted to the publication of more specifically dadaist writings and, a short time later, staged one-man exhibitions of the art of Picabia and Ribemont-Dessaignes. One of the first dada publications at Au Sans Pareil was Picabia's *Unique Eunuque* (Unique Eunuch), a rambling, hermetic poem in which he played with disrupted sound, sense and rhythm by writing random passages backwards.[16] The droll title, also used on a painting during 1920 (fig. 194), has no obvious relation to the poem, but the notion of a "unique eunuch" does not seem farfetched in the context of Picabia's concept of the artist as a godlike creator producing "daughters born without a mother."

The variously antagonizing, mystifying writings of the dadaists invited parodies from the beginning. The first appeared in Marseille under the name "Fada," followed by "Toutou" and "Gaga."[17] And as early as mid-February so many readers of *Comoedia* (Paris' leading newspaper on the arts) had requested an explanation of Dada that the principal art critic of the paper, conservative portraitist Jacques-Emile Blanche, announced a survey of the dada movement. Within a week numerous replies were received, many signed by such well-known figures as Pierre Reverdy, Roger Allard and Louis Vauxcelles. But some replies were identified as forgeries, and Blanche cancelled the survey.[18] The dadaists themselves were not exempt from such games. False Picabia poems were published,[19] and he

15. *Proverbe*, nos. 1–6 (Paris, February 1920–July 1921), editor Paul Eluard; *Z*, nos. 1–2 (Paris, February and March 1920), director Paul Dermée. Two other magazines, Céline Arnauld's *M'amenez-y* and Ribemont-Dessaignes's *D₆ O⁴ H²*, were announced and carried on the letterhead of the "Movement Dada," but never appeared. *Littérature*, though listed with the magazines embraced by the "Movement Dada," never looked like a dada magazine and contained only one issue (no. 13, May 1920) completely dominated by the dadaists.

16. Francis Picabia, *Unique Eunuque* (Paris, February 20, 1920), prefaces by Tristan Tzara and "Pascal." For the scrambled word order, see p. 34:

Allemands les déteste je

Guerre la pendant que cela pour est 'c

Possible loin plus le reste suis je

Picabia dated *Unique Eunuque* January 6, but apparently worked on it several days longer. He claimed to have started the poem more than four months earlier and was indebted to Breton for its publication at Au Sans Pareil (see Picabia correspondence to Breton, January 10 and 17, 1920, collection A. Breton; Sanouillet, *Dada à Paris*, 505–506).

17. See Onésime Dougue, "Mouvement Fada à Marseille," *Le Merle blanc* [Paris], January 14, 1920, 3; Zy, ". . . Da . . . DA . . . ," *La Tribune de Genève*, January 23, 1920, 5; and "Le Mouvement Toutou (1920)" in *Le Crapouillot* [Paris], May 15, 1920, 8–9.

18. A response falsely signed "Pierre Reverdy" was published by Blanche on February 26. On March 3, Blanche noted the forgery and the termination of his survey (see his column, "La Semaine artistique," *Comoedia* [Paris], March 3, 1920, 2).

19. See Paul Gsell's column, "Nos Echos" in *La Democratie nouvelle* [Paris], February 13, 1920, 2, and February 18, 1920, 2. Gsell notes that his colleague, Valmy-Baysse, had received a poem signed "Picabia" and published it. Picabia protested that it was a false poem. Gsell ac-

and Tzara received an offensive poem-letter signed "Paul Eluard," which was not from Eluard. At least his persuasive denial of authorship prompted a search for the "real" author. Eventually most of the dadaists, their enemies, and even Tzara and Picabia themselves were suspected until attention centered on Reverdy, whom Picabia accused publicly and unjustly.[20] Amends were made, and finally the foolish, destructive quest was abandoned, but Dada—dedicated to casting doubt on the values, systems and institutions of the world—was itself rift by doubt. For awhile longer, however, the abundance of common targets prevented irreparable internal dissension.

One of the first targets was the group of cubists who revived the Section d'Or. In November 1919 Gleizes, Archipenko and Survage laid plans for a new Section d'Or which, like its predecessor in 1912, was to be a liberal forum for diverse contemporary movements in art, music and literature. On those grounds, Picabia became an enthusiastic collaborator, and a complete dada program of antiart, antimusic and antiliterature was announced for March 2. However, leaders of the dominant cubist faction changed their minds about Dada after observing the series of dada matinees. Antagonism mounted and, on February 25 at a general meeting in the Closerie des Lilas, the dadaists were informed that they were not free to hold their own program. A tumult erupted with cubists and dadaists paired off in heated debate, while Gleizes sought vainly to mollify the dadaists. Picabia, recently returned from the Midi, proclaimed that the dadaists were resigning and taking with them use of the Galerie La Boétie and the name "Section d'Or." Survages countered by mounting a chair and shouting, "Expulsed. You are expulsed." With a potential riot on his hands, the proprietor turned off the lights, and the furor adjourned to the street and the studios of the combatants. As it turned out, the cubists retained the disputed name and gallery, but the dadaists garnered extensive publicity and a heightened esprit de corps which nourished their activities in the weeks ahead.[21]

It was too late for Picabia to retaliate against the Section d'Or cubists in the February issue of 391, a relatively mild number printed just three days after the meeting at the Closerie des Lilas.[22] However, in the March issue (391, no. 12; see

knowledged the protest, but defended his colleague by observing that it was difficult to tell the difference between a hoax and a masterpiece of dadaist poetry (February 13). That prompted another letter of protest, also signed "Picabia," which Gsell published (February 18) along with the observation that it, too, might be false.

20. The principal letters in this affair (D.P. V, 123, 131, 222) are published and discussed by Michel Sanouillet, *Francis Picabia et "391,"* II (Paris, 1966), 111–13.

21. See Paul Dermée's letter to Tzara, ca. December 1919 (C.T.1185; Sanouillet, *Dada à Paris*, 545–46), and his "Premier et Dernier Rapport du secrétaire de la Section d'Or. Excommuniés," *391*, no. 12 (Paris, March 1920), 6. The exhibition of "La Section d'Or" was held in the Galerie La Boétie, Paris, March 3–16, 1920, but the announced rebel exhibition of the dadaists (*391*, no. 12, 2) was never organized.

22. *391*, no. 11 (Paris, February 1920), is distinguished by a more restrained design, Breton's first contribution, a major article by Ribemont-Dessaignes and the amusing "Carnet du Docteur Serner" (written by Picabia). The Picabia drawing on p. 1 was first reproduced in his *Poèmes et dessins de la fille née sans mère* (Lausanne, 1918).

illus. 19) Paul Dermée contributed a devastating chronicle of the entire affair, and Picabia and Ribemont-Dessaignes subjected the Section d'Or cubists to merciless ridicule beginning with Picabia's front page "Dada Manifesto":

The cubists want to cover Dada with snow; . . .

They think that Dada can prevent them from practicing this odious trade: selling art very expensively. . . .

Buy reproductions of autographs.

Don't be snobs, you will not be any less intelligent because your neighbor will possess something similar to yours. . . .

Cubism represents the dearth of ideas.

They have cubed primitive paintings, cubed Negro sculpture, cubed violins, cubed guitars, cubed illustrated newspapers, cubed shit and the profiles of young girls, now they must cube money!!!

Dada, it wants nothing, nothing, nothing, it does something in order for the public to say: "We understand nothing, nothing, nothing."

"The Dadaists are nothing, nothing, nothing, certainly they will come to nothing, nothing, nothing."

Francis Picabia
who knows nothing, nothing, nothing.

The occasion even prompted one of Picabia's rare favorable comments regarding Picasso, "Pablo Picasso, Juan Gris, your cubist colleagues claim that you have taken everything from them: that is indeed the impression they give me! Francis Picabia the Joker."[23]

Despite such attacks, that issue of *391* was not merely an anti-Section d'Or number. Indeed, along with the contemporary *Dadaphone* (*Dada*, no. 7), it constitutes one of the outstanding examples of dada publications in Paris (see illus. 19, 20). Both are characterized by a gifted disregard for layout and by a stimulating variety of authors, typefaces, printed and pictorial material, poems, statements, manifestos, advertisements and aphorisms abounding with the bile and buffoonery of Dada. Different temperaments are discernible, but Aragon, Breton, Soupault, Eluard and Dermée all seem to have been more infected than usual by the irreverent style of Tzara, Picabia and Ribemont-Dessaignes.

Picabia's "Dada Cannibalistic Manifesto" in *Dadaphone* (no. 7, March 1920) was one of the most cynical, nihilistic statements of the movement:

You are all accused; stand up. The orator will speak to you only if you are standing.

Standing as for the Marseillaise,

standing as for the Russian hymn,

standing as for God save the king,

standing as before the flag.

23. *391*, no. 12 (Paris, March 1920).

Finally standing before DADA, which represents life and accuses you of loving everything out of snobism from the moment that it becomes expensive. Are you completely settled? So much the better, that way you are going to listen to me with greater attention.

What are you doing here, parked like serious oysters—for you are serious, right?

Serious, serious, serious to death.

Death is a serious thing, huh?

One dies as a hero, or as an idiot, which is the same thing. The only word which is not ephemeral is the word death. You love death for others.

To death, death, death.

Only money which doesn't die, it just leaves on trips.

It is God, one respects it, the serious person—money respect of families.

Honor, honor to money; the man who has money is an honorable man.

Honor is bought and sold like ass. Ass, ass represents life like fried potatoes, and all of you who are serious, you will smell worse than cow shit.

DADA doesn't smell anything, it is nothing, nothing, nothing.

It is like your hopes: nothing.

like your paradise: nothing

like your idols: nothing

like your political men: nothing

like your heroes: nothing

like your artists: nothing

like your religions: nothing

Whistle, cry, smash my mouth and then, and then? I will tell you again that you are all pears. In three months we, my friends and I, are going to sell you our paintings for several francs.

Picabia's scruffy, sexually suggestive drawing on the cover of *Dadaphone* (illus. 20) continued traditions established in previous issues of *391*, but in that March issue of *391* Picabia reproduced two nonmechanomorphic art works which reside within the core of dada creations in Paris, the authorized remake of Duchamp's *L.H.O.O.Q.* (illus. 19) and his own ink splotch drawing blasphemously titled *La Sainte Vièrge* (*The Blessed Virgin*, fig. 182).[24] Appropriately for the Blessed Virgin, she appears to be a pure splash, unmodified by aesthetic considerations subsequent to the act of creation. Such speculation is based on iden-

24. Duchamp had returned to New York in January, taking *L.H.O.O.Q.* with him. When he could not return it quickly enough for reproduction in *391*, Picabia produced a remake but forgot that Duchamp had provided the Mona Lisa with a beard as well as a moustache. Picabia's remake was completed some years later when Arp showed the remake to Duchamp, who added the missing beard and dutifully inscribed the work, "Moustaches by Picabia, beard by Duchamp." See Arturo Schwarz, *The Complete Works of Marcel Duchamp*, 2nd rev. ed. (New York, 1970), 476.

A second version of *La Sainte Vièrge* exists in the Bibliothèque Littéraire Jacques Doucet, Paris, and is reproduced in Sanouillet's reedition of Picabia's *391* (Paris, 1960), 134.

tification of the ink splashes as the Blessed Virgin; if instead Picabia conceived her as the white sheet of paper, the nature of his blasphemy becomes graver still.

That use of chance duly impressed some colleagues of Picabia who, as founders of Surrealism a few years later, sought and developed the psychic dimensions of the technique. Picabia, as so often in his career, displayed no strong inclination to exploit an interesting concept and technique, although for about three years isolated experiments with chance occasionally surfaced alongside his mechanomorphic studies. On one occasion he produced a wet ink drawing of his name (fig. 183) which in a dumbfoundingly simple gesture affirms, parodies and expands the proposition raised by Duchamp in *Tzanck Check* (fig. 165) that it is the signature or "handwriting" of the artist which counts.[25] On another occasion Breton recorded a project by Picabia with parallels to the currents of conceptual and ephemeral art during the 1960s: "to gather about twenty balls in the corner of a billiard table, then push them forward in a single movement . . . , photograph the result obtained and sign it."[26]

The March 1920 issue of *391* with Picabia's *La Sainte Vièrge* was distributed at the "Manifestation Dada" held in Lugné-Poe's Maison de l'Oeuvre (Salle Berlioz) on the evening of March 27. Six weeks of escalating publicity had transpired since the last outing of the dadaists, and an expectant audience overflowed the hall. The dadaists were ready with a far more varied and provocative program than had been presented during the February matinees, and the results disappointed no one: "It was a beautiful uproar," reported one critic:

> No "artistic" endeavor, not even the most audacious, could ever have released such a tumult. Neither *Ubu Roi*, nor the *Roi Bombance* . . . were so magnificently "hooted." . . . The public booed, whistled, scoffed at the Dadas, who greeted their insults with bright faces. One would have thought he was among madmen, and the wind of folly blew as well on the stage as on the hall. The Dadas exasperated their spectators and I think that is all they desired, exactly.[27]

The extravagant program was distinguished by the first public presentation of dada music, Ribemont-Dessaignes's "Dance of Curled Chicory," and by four dada plays: Dermée's "Untuned Ventriloquist," Ribemont-Dessaignes's "Dumb Ca-

25. Ulf Linde emphasizes the role of the artist's name or signature for Duchamp and Picabia and presents other ideas for *La Sainte Vièrge* (Centre National d'Art et de Culture Georges Pompidou, Musée National d'Art Moderne, *Francis Picabia*, Paris, Grand Palais, January 23–March 29, 1976, 21–23).

A series of Rorschach-like ink blots (D.P. IX, 16, 18, 19, 21–25), dedicated to Picabia and slightly amended to include his name, further reveal a preoccupation with the artist's name and with chance which flourished in the Duchamp-Picabia circle of late 1919. These ink blots, all dated simply "December 1," are adjacent to documents in the Dossiers Picabia which suggest dates of 1919 or 1922.

26. André Breton, "Idées d'un peintre" in *Les Pas perdus* (Paris, 1924), 109.

27. G[eorges] C[harensol], "Manifestation Dada," *Comoedia* [Paris], March 29, 1920, 2.

nary," Tzara's "First Celestial Adventure of Mr. Antipyrine" and Breton's and Soupault's "Please." Picabia did not take part on the stage, but he was in the audience and well represented throughout the production. His vitriolic "Dada Cannibalistic Manifesto" (accompanied by music) was read by Breton with great effect in a darkened hall. As the booing reached a crescendo, and coins, handkerchiefs, umbrellas and assorted objects pelted around Breton, an ecstatic Tzara congratulated Picabia offstage, "Listen to them . . . Dada lives! It's magnificent!"[28] Picabia also contributed two drawings for the program which was distributed at the door and designed both the costumes and stage decor. The latter consisted of a bicycle wheel suspended over the center of the stage, cords stretched in front of the performers, and signs bearing such inscriptions as "If you stretch out your arms your friends will cut them off" and "Paralysis is the beginning of wisdom."[29] Picabia's final contribution to the manifestation was the presentation of a painting. Advance press releases described it as a "live painting," and Picabia reportedly intended to exhibit a live monkey.[30] When that did not work out, he settled for a toy monkey (fig. 184) mounted on a board with its tail pulled between its legs aimed at the spectator. Around the monkey, in a superior example of his graffitilike penmanship, Picabia inscribed "Portrait of Cézanne," "Portrait of Renoir," "Portrait of Rembrandt" and "Still Lifes" ("natures mortes," literally translated, "dead lifes"). This wrenching assault of revered artists, their spectators and art itself embodies such a unity of subject, style and content that it is, ironically, a masterpiece—a masterpiece of antiart which completed a Picabia trilogy of antiart, antisociety (Le Double Monde, fig. 167) and antireligion (La Sainte Vièrge, fig. 182).

The lively publicity accorded Dada before the "Manifestation Dada" in March was nothing compared to the deluge which followed it. That contemporary criticism of Dada merits consideration at this point for it is an interesting aspect of the history of Dada, and it had a role in shaping the subsequent moves of the dadaists.

Most of the early criticism was derogatory, and much within that could be described as inane and/or nationalistic. Jacques-Emile Blanche, already burned by his survey of Dada, attempted an earnest article inflated with silly, stuffy re-

28. Everling, L'Anneau de Saturne, 122.
29. For a description of the scenery and costumes see C[harensol], "Manifestation Dada," Comoedia, 2, and Gustave Geffroy, "Le Mouvement Dada," France libre [Paris], April 3, 1920 (attrib.). For Tzara's "First Celestial Adventure of Mr. Antipyrine," Picabia clothed the performers in immense paper sacks of different colors with placards bearing their names, "M. Bleubleu," "M. Pipi," etc. All clustered about Tzara, whose name was scrawled across his chest.

The cords stretched in front of the performers probably derived from Picabia's easel-sized construction in cord mentioned in Breton's letter to him of February 15, 1920 (D.P. V, 35; Sanouillet, Dada à Paris, 507). That construction has not been identified but it may have been the Danse de Saint-Guy (fig. 204) exhibited two years later.

30. A press release on "Movement Dada" letterhead dated March 23, 1920 (Menil Foundation, Houston), announces the presentation of an "animate painting" by Picabia at the forthcoming "Manifestation Dada."

marks which earned him a dada portrait by Picabia (fig. 185) and assorted comments in dada journals. The nationalistic attack was more popular given the freshness of wartime sentiments and a vague awareness that somewhere in the background of Dada there were unsavory political ties with Zurich and Berlin.[31] Representative of such critics was Marcel Boulanger, who wrote two articles, one totally frivolous and the second a surly, chauvinistic piece which sought to discredit the dadaists by associating them with Germany, bolshevism and just about anything radical, foreign or un-French.[32] Mme Rachilde, a celebrated woman of letters and wife of the founder of the *Mercure de France*, also attacked the dadaists in an unbecomingly nationalistic tone and recommended that they be met with "the silent smile." Her counsel may have led to an almost total news boycott of a Picabia exhibition at Au Sans Pareil during April. She paid heavily for that, however, in a devastating exchange of open letters with Breton and Picabia.[33]

Such critics aside, there were others whose observations were perceptive and, at times, prophetic. Renée Dunan attributed a surrealist flavor to Dada before Surrealism had a name. She dwelt on a new philosophy evolving from the work of Freud and others preoccupied with the unconscious and its fundamental control over life. She concluded: "A new psychology will correspond to a renewed aesthetic. The dada group searches in extravagance the mysterious law which will become the next aesthetic. . . . Dada is not a mystification: it is the entire human mystery."[34] H.R. Lenormand also pursued a Freudian interpretation of Dada, noting the profound human tendency for returning to childhood in search of regeneration. As such, he allowed that Dada was justified, although he lamented that in modern times the spiritual quality and material results of regression to childhood were so inferior to ancient examples, especially in Dada, which he implied was

31. One of the first articles on Dada ever published in Paris ([Jacques Rivière], "Mouvement Dada," *La Nouvelle Revue française*, no. 72, Paris, September 1, 1919, 636–37) set the tone for many which followed. Rivière noted that it was foreign born (Zurich and Berlin), politically active in Berlin and ridiculous. When Tzara's response to Rivière was not published by the editors of *La Nouvelle Revue française*, Breton, who was on good terms with both parties, published it in *Littérature* ("Lettre ouverte à Jacques Rivière," no. 10, Paris, December 1919).

32. Marcel Boulanger, "De l'utilisation du mouvement Dada," *Comoedia* [Paris], March 28, 1920, 1, and "Herr Dada," *Le Gaulois* [Paris], April 26, 1920, 1.

33. For this exchange in the pages of *Comoedia* see: Rachilde, "Le Sourire silencieux," April 1, 1920, 1; Picabia's response (in a style indicative of a collaborative effort or another author), "Origines du mouvement Dada," April 3, 1920, 2; Rachilde's and Breton's letters under "A propos du mouvement Dada," April 4, 1920; Rachilde's "Encore un mot sur D.A.D.A.," April 14, 1920, 1; and finally Picabia's coup de grace, "A Madame Rachilde," *Cannibale*, no. 1 (Paris, April 25, 1920), 4.

Picabia's exhibition at Au Sans Pareil (Paris, April 16–30, 1920) consisted of twenty-two works from the years 1915 to 1920, including some of the best examples of his mechanomorphic style. The exhibition was barely mentioned in the press, and Ribemont-Dessaignes wrote: "A delicate silence surrounds the exhibit of Francis Picabia at Sans Pareil. It is the silence full of the charms of vengeance" ("François Picabia," *L'Esprit nouveau*, no. 1, Paris, October 1920, 108–110).

34. Renée Dunan, "Gazette littéraire."/"Dada?" *Le Journal du peuple* [Paris], March 6, 1920, 3.

akin to precocious dementia.[35] To refute that implication, Picabia wrote a thoughtful reply, stressing the dadaists' exercise of will—"negative at the moment when the association of ideas is formed, it becomes positive then from the 'choice' which follows"—and their goal of disintoxication: "Our ideal is 'the disintoxication,' we want . . . to become an antidote for all the Immunized from our fallen art. We tend toward the White considered as a psychic entity or, in order to concretize this tendency thanks to immutable rapports of color and music, we tend toward the 'la' pure = 435 vibrations."[36]

For unknown reasons Picabia's friend and editor of *Comoedia*, Georges Casella, did not publish that statement, but another journalist printed an interview with Germaine Everling which reflects Picabia's contemporary opinions:

> The "dada" movement is not a pleasantry. . . . Our goal, in separating recently from the cubists, has been the manifestation of our distaste for chapels and little schools. . . . We want to liberate art. . . . Art is not a dogma and a religion, . . . art is a joy. And since we think that art is a joy liberated from dogmas, you realize that it is perfectly indifferent to us to excite laughter. We are very satisfied, on the contrary, for laughter is a liberation.[37]

Of all the serious criticism, that which most directly affected the dada movement in Paris stressed the presence of two basic factions which had indeed existed from the beginning. Georges Charensol, a longtime acquaintance of Picabia, singled out Tzara and Picabia as the "two Dadas worthy of the name" and described Aragon, Breton, Soupault, Eluard and Ribemont-Dessaignes as young men who "have adhered to this farce passingly and whom we will rediscover seated not long from now in some solemn magazine."[38] André Gide, writing in the prestigious *Nouvelle Revue française*, also perceived two groups within Dada, but judged them differently. Dada itself he dispatched quickly: "The day the word Dada was found, there remained nothing more to do. These two syllables had attained the goal of 'sonorous inanity.' "[39] The foreigners in the movement, especially the "inventor of Dada," were subjected to chilling, condescending criticism, but Gide left a door open for the new literary forms of the youth, implying that some would comprise the "legitimate heirs" of French culture. He gave no names and had no need to do

35. H.R. [Henri-René] Lenormand, "Dadaïsme et psychologie," *Comoedia* [Paris], March 23, 1920, 1.

36. Picabia's "Lettre ouverte à Monsieur H.R. Lenormand" (D.P. V, 240) has been published in Picabia, *Ecrits 1913–1920*, 215–17, and in the Centre National d'Art et de Culture Georges Pompidou, Musée National d'Art Moderne, *Francis Picabia*, Paris, Grand Palais, January 23–March 29, 1976, 87–88.

37. Germaine Everling, quoted by Jean-Gabriel Lemoine in "Le Mouvement Dada," *Le Gaulois* [Paris], March 20, 1920, literary supplement, 2. Though unidentified by Lemoine, Mme Everling identified herself as the subject in *L'Anneau de Saturne*, 107.

38. C[harensol], "Manifestation Dada," *Comoedia*, 2. The inclusion of Ribemont-Dessaignes with editors of *Littérature* is surprising.

39. André Gide, "Dada," *La Nouvelle Revue française*, no. 79 (Paris, April 1, 1920), 447–81.

so. Tzara had been extensively publicized as the inventor of Dada, and it was common knowledge that the editors of *Littérature* had maintained good standing with the writers of *La Nouvelle Revue française*. In all likelihood, such criticism reflected mounting strains among the dadaists which were reported in the press and duly denied.[40]

Albert Gleizes entered the fray in April with a long, serious article, "The Dada Affair," based largely on his thorough acquaintance with Picabia.[41] Gleizes chastised the mindless critics who dismissed the dadas as fakers and idiots. Instead he avowed that they were mature, intelligent men, their work "always full of taste" and their texts so "impenetrable that nothing would justify indignation." Comprehension of Dada, he claimed, was possible only when considered "in relation to the epoch," "a great turning point in the history of mankind" where "the hierarchy of bourgeois capitalism, is crumbling." "It is by juxtaposing the rot of the material plane with the rot of the spiritual plane that one will understand exactly the Dada movement." The dadaist, Gleizes writes, is characterized by a wealthy bourgeois background, by a driving "need to be first" and by sensuous excesses which lead to artificial stimulation, a nervous system lashed with liquor and drugs and "the illusion of being liberated from the physical laws which govern us."

> The Dada domain opened at this moment. The impossibility of constructing, of organizing anything whatsoever, not having even the foggiest notion of it, led [the dadaist] to decree that nothing existed and that he could do anything under the guise of instinct. . . .
>
> What they call instinct is anything which passes through their heads [and] from time to time something very good passes through them. . . .
>
> But very soon we become aware of . . . the "leitmotivs" which recur in their paintings and literary works. And the pathological case becomes brutally evident. Their minds are forever haunted by a sexual delirium and a scatalogical frenzy. . . . Their frolics abandon themselves freely around the genital apparatuses of either sex. . . . Moreover, by lingering in these realms, they have found . . . another source of instinctive inspiration. They have discovered the anus and the intestinal by-products. . . . They confuse excrement with products of the mind. They use the same word to designate two different things.
>
> It is indeed confusion which most characterizes the leveling movement called Dada. . . . The thinkers of the group have acquired solid certainties. Nothing exists. All is appearance and convention. There is no difference be-

40. An unsigned notice in *Carnet de la semaine* ("Une Grave Scission chez les Dada-istes," Paris, April 18, 1920, 9) signaled a quarrel between Breton and Picabia which the latter denied in *Cannibale*, no. 1 (Paris, April 25, 1920), 7: "André Breton and I have never been angry; the noises which circulate are imbecilic inventions dictated by idiots."

41. Albert Gleizes, "L'Affaire Dada" (*Action*, no. 3, Paris, April 1920, 26–32), trans. Ralph Manheim in Robert Motherwell, ed., *The Dada Painters and Poets* (New York, 1951), 298–303.

tween a beautiful work and an ugly work. Nothing is bad and nothing is good.
. . . But it is impossible to dwell on discussions on this point, since the
Dadaists affirm that to affirm is a heresy, and that there is nothing, nothing,
nothing.

Nevertheless, it is delightful to follow them in the field of propaganda.
Never has a group disposed of so much capital for the purpose of saying nothing, never has a group gone to such extents to reach the public and offer it
nothing. . . . For these men who say nothing, nothing, nothing, are terrified
of silence. They cannot live alone. They seek the crowd.

Gleizes's criticism was a stinging attack—disfigured by a pent-up anger toward Picabia, but too close to home to leave unanswered. Picabia's reply was artful and malicious:

It does not astonish us that he has written "The Dada Affair." Everything is
affairs for this man! During the war, being in Spain, he wanted to be natu-
ralized a German. . . . Today, a bread crumb socialist, he disavows his family, petite bourgeoisie of Courbevoie, but finds it convenient enough to have
married the Grand Bourgeoisie Dada, with whom he is not even capable of
making children! His sexual apparatus, as he so elegantly names it, of what
can it serve him? No doubt to construct aquatic cubism.[42]

Picabia answered Gleizes in *Cannibale*, a new magazine under his direction
which temporarily replaced *391*.[43] Relative to the best issues of *Dada* and *391*,
the two numbers of *Cannibale* offered less visual material and more restrained design. But thanks partly to the substantial collaboration of Tzara, the literary content of *Cannibale* was the most impressive of all the ephemeral dada magazines.
The first issue contained just three reproductions, Duchamp's *Tzanck Check* (fig.
165) and the *Portrait de Cézanne . . .* and *Portrait de Tristan Tzara* (figs. 184,
186) by Picabia. Picabia's numerous literary contributions included a poem, the
"Coeur de Jésus" (Heart of Jesus), which surpassed his previous attacks upon the
French language; a dementing "refrain"; and an impenetrable prose piece entitled
"Avoir le mal de mer sur un transport de joie" (To Be Seasick on a Transport of
Joy). Those writings were rounded out by some of his better aphorisms, a searing
open letter to Mme Rachilde and a personal letter from Jean Cocteau describing
his disapproval of Dada. Picabia did not provide any new visual material for the
second issue of *Cannibale*, but once more his literary contributions were substantial, including a major poem, "Je suis des Javanais" (I Am of the Javanese) and

42. Francis Picabia, "L'Affaire Dada," *Cannibale*, no. 2 (Paris, May 25, 1920), 4.

43. *Cannibale* lasted for only two issues, April 25 and May 25, 1920, each consisting of
eighteen pages. In the next issue of *391* (no. 13, July 1920) Picabia announced, "Truly it is impossible for me to bring out 'Cannibale' regularly, it is too idiotic. I hope you will accept for this
time '391.' "

For extensive comment and a reedition of *Cannibale* see Sanouillet, *Francis Picabia et
"391,"* II, 99–100, 181–220.

the "Festival-Manifeste-Presbyte" (Farsighted-Festival-Manifesto), which were read at the last dada program of the season, the "Festival Dada" in the Salle Gaveau on May 26.[44]

Since the "Manifestation Dada" in March, two months of constant publicity had created an ever larger, hungrier audience for the dadaists. The May issue of *Littérature*, devoted to dada manifestos, contributed to that publicity, but the irresistible touch was an announcement (false, of course) that all of the dadaists would have their heads shaved onstage. The prestigious Salle Gaveau overflowed with the friends and enemies of Dada, chic Paris and a horde of reporters. Many came prepared to take full advantage of the audience participation invited by the dadaists, and, thanks to numerous reviews and witness accounts, the result is well documented.

Early arrivals could peruse an extensive program overlaid with a Picabia drawing (illus. 21), or ponder the curious stage decor—also by Picabia—which consisted of mysterious packages bearing names of the dadaists, and stepped panels of imitation grass flanking a large black-and-yellow-striped pole that was topped by an open umbrella inscribed "Francis le Loustic" ("Francis the Joker").[45] The opening number, listed as "The Sex of Dada," featured an enormous phallic form constructed in white paper and supported at its base by balloons. To Tzara's dismay, the sex of Dada quickly deflated, but the program continued with vigor. Tension in the hall was liberated during an early number in which Soupault in blackface released from a trunk some buoyant, brightly colored balloons, introducing them one by one as "Clemenceau," "Wilson," "Rachilde" and "Cocteau." When "Cocteau" sagged back to the floor, Soupault struck it viciously with a knife and the uproar was on. Catcalls and small missiles rained on the stage, countered by frenetic applause from dada sympathizers. From time to time relative order was restored only to be triggered by some new irritation such as Ribemont-Dessaignes's musical composition, the "Unauthorized Belly Button," which prompted a switch in the audience from boos to animal calls and efforts to imitate the "music." Picabia, as usual, did not participate onstage. Instead, he observed from a box in the company of Germaine and the popular singer, Marthe Chenal. But he was well represented on the program, and many journalists referred to him as the chief of the dadaists in Paris. The press did not comment on his first venture in music, "The American Nurse" (subtitled "Sodomist Music"), but a lively response greeted his other two numbers, "Je suis des Javanais" and "Festival-Manifeste-Presbyte." The latter was read by Breton wearing a Picabia-designed sandwich board/shield bearing a target and an inscription calling the

44. The pictorial material in *Cannibale*, no. 2, consisted of a photograph of Tzara and Picabia in the latter's 85 hp Mercer, a Picabia drawing of ca. 1918 previously reproduced in *391*, no. 7 (February 1919), and what appears to be an untouched ticket stub signed by Tzara.

45. For Picabia's stage decor see H.S., "Dada ou les croquemorts facétieux," *Carnet de la semaine* (Paris, June 6, 1920), 15, and Jacques Patin, "Un Festival Dada," *Le Figaro* [Paris], May 27, 1920, 1 (attrib.).

audience a "heap of idiots" (illus. 22). Audience response seems to have peaked, however, during Ribemont-Dessaignes's "Baccaret Manifesto." A torrent of coins, paper, fruit, vegetables, eggs and even a beefsteak cascaded on the stage; one stray tomato hit Mme Gaveau; a cane-wielding man dared Picabia to meet him outside, and the final numbers played out before a spent audience.[46]

From the standpoint of most of the audience, Dada must have seemed as virulent as ever, but almost without exception the witness of the dadaists themselves indicated the contrary. Some of them found Tzara so absorbed by the movement that his well-being had to be fed by constant activities, and, under such conditions, the once-rousing meetings at Picabia's were becoming strained. "Everytime a dada manifestation was anticipated—naturally by Tzara," wrote Breton, "Picabia invited us to his salon and we, one after the other, were to have ideas for this manifestation. Finally, the harvest is not very abundant. The pièce de résistance will be inevitably constituted by the first, or the second . . . or the ninth 'Adventure of Mr. Antipyrine.' "[47] Given the temperaments of Tzara and Picabia, Breton soon discovered, too, that he had to assume responsibility for all the practical matters—arranging for the hall, paying bills and assuring a program of at least some interest. He was also vexed by Picabia's friendships with people totally outside of Dada, or, as with Jean Cocteau, someone actually scorned by most of the dadaists. For his part, Picabia began to miss the gaiety and spontaneity of the "good old days," and later grumbled about the "seriousness" of those around him.[48] Finally, Ribemont-Dessaignes noted the vague uneasiness experienced by most of them about the end of Dada. Dada was on the verge of becoming a noisy but artful form of entertainment, a "success" which "as far as liberation and disorganization were concerned, [was] merely organizing and chaining itself."[49]

46. For accounts of the "Festival Dada" see H.S., "Dada ou les croquemorts facétieux," *Carnet de la semaine*, 15, and Patin, "Un Festival Dada," *Le Figaro*, 1; P[aul] S[ouday], "Le Coq et Dada," *Le Temps* [Paris], May 28, 1920, 1 (attrib.); T. Trilby, "Lettre parisienne," *L'Alger* [Algeria], June 9, 1920 (attrib.); Everling, *L'Anneau de Saturne*, 124–25; and Sanouillet, *Dada à Paris*, 173–78. Present in the audience among others were: Gide, Valéry, Jacques Rivière, Jules Romains, Mme Rachilde, Jacques Barzun, Gleizes, Léger, Metzinger, Brancusi, Alexandre Mercereau, Paul Poiret, Roger Allard, René Blum and Georges Duhamel.

47. André Breton, *Entretiens 1913–1952*, 10th ed. (Paris, 1952), 58.

48. Francis Picabia, "Francis Picabia et Dada," *L'Esprit nouveau*, no. 9 (Paris, June 1921), 1059–60.

49. Georges Ribemont-Dessaignes, "Histoire de Dada" (*La Nouvelle Revue française*, no. 213, Paris, June 1931, 867–79, and no. 214, Paris, July 1931, 39–52), trans. Ralph Manheim in Robert Motherwell, ed., *The Dada Painters and Poets*, 101–120.

11. EARLY DISSENSION, THE SECOND DADA SEASON AND THE DEFECTION OF PICABIA

DADA'S spectacular *succès de scandale* made it a topic of public interest long after most of the dadaists had dispersed for the summer. Both popular and specialized journals abounded with articles, augmented by news of dada activities in foreign countries, especially in Italy and Germany.[1] New converts also continued to appear. In addition to Pierre de Massot and Benjamin Péret, who had already declared themselves, Picabia was contacted by Serge Charchoune, Enrico Prampolini and Clément Pansaers.[2] At that time, however, there was no organized activity for them to join. As a group, the dadaists had quietly disbanded after the "Festival Dada," and when all of them finally returned to Paris in the fall of 1920, a schism between Picabia and Breton precluded any unified activity until an uneasy reconciliation was established during January 1921. Belated plans were then made for a second dada season scheduled for April, May and June, but the exuberant spirit of the first manifestations was never regained.

1. Reported activities in Germany included the *Erste Internationale Dada-Messe*, Kunsthandlung Dr. Otto Burchard, Berlin, June 5–August 25, 1920, in which Picabia was represented. Gino Cantarelli and Giulio Evola devoted substantial attention to Dada in their magazine *Bleu*, founded in Mantua during July 1920. For a concise account of Dada in Italy, see Galleria Schwarz, Milan, *Cinquant'anni a Dada-Dada in Italia 1916–1966*, June 24–September 30, 1966, essay by Daniela Palazzoli, "Dada in Italia," 103–110.

2. Pierre de Massot, who wrote Picabia in February 1920 (D.P. V, 41), became one of his most loyal associates and a lifelong friend. Max Jacob introduced Benjamin Peret to Picabia by letter on March 9, 1920 (D.P. V, 152; Michel Sanouillet, *Dada à Paris*, Paris, 1965, 557). Theo van Doesburg, founder of De Stijl in Holland, was not a dadaist, but a sympathetic observer and occasional collaborator who praised Picabia's paintings at the 1920 Salon des Indépendants and requested a meeting in June or July (D.P. V, 237).

Serge Charchoune, a young Russian artist in Paris, declared himself an "admirer and student" of Picabia in a letter of May 30, 1920 (D.P. II, 193). Enrico Prampolini, an early collaborator with Dada in Zurich, had been neglected for over a year. He wrote from Rome in June (D.P. VI, 144) urging Picabia and Tzara to pay attention to them because they were young revolutionaries with a magazine and a gallery. Clément Pansaers of Brussels met frequently with Picabia

Picabia was the only dada of authority who remained in Paris throughout the summer of 1920, and it was a productive one which saw the completion of two major paintings for the Salon d'Automne, publication of another issue of *391* (no. 13, July) and completion of a "philosophical treatise" entitled *Jésus-Christ Rastaquouère*. Tzara, apparently with the financial aid of Picabia, left Paris in June for an extensive trip through eastern and central Europe where he reestablished many contacts, particularly with Arp in Zurich.[3] Breton did not leave Paris until late July, but in a painfully self-conscious letter of mid-June, he acknowledged to Picabia that he had been in a state of anxiety, was uneasy in Picabia's presence and sought to be alone.[4] Picabia was also troubled about their relationship, and a few weeks later he unleashed his vexation in a letter to Tzara: "I write you . . . after much reflection and introspection—*Littérature* screws us, 'Sans Pareil' hides our books and magazines, finally I am in the presence of facts—Breton is an accomplished comedian and his two little friends think like him that it is possible to change a man as one changes boots."[5] There was a brief rapprochement of Breton and Picabia during late July–early August, but then a sharp break ended all communication between them for several months. Plans for a second dada season had to be suspended, and Pansaer's projects for dada manifestations in Brussels were almost ruined.[6]

Breton accepted responsibility for the schism. Since the Festival Dada in May, he had been tormented by self-doubt regarding his attitude toward Dada. While in that state of mind, he committed several acts which Picabia viewed as treacherous—censorship of an article by Ribemont-Dessaignes, refusal to write the preface promised for *Jésus-Christ Rastaquouère* and publication of a curiously disengaged article about Dada in *La Nouvelle Revue française*.[7]

Breton's article, "For Dada," appeared in the August issue, accompanied by Jacques Rivière's "Recognition of Dada," an important statement openly keyed on

during August 1920. He envisioned a publishing house for Dada in Brussels, a Société Anonyme and a dada festival in November or December with the participation of the major dadaists in Paris.

3. See Tzara's letters to Picabia (D.P. VI, 60, 243, 393, 394, 399, 431; Sanouillet, *Dada à Paris*, 499–502), which trace his movement from Paris to Zurich, Bucharest, Athens, Constantinople, Naples, Milan, Venice, Zurich again, and finally Paris around mid-October 1920.

4. Breton letter to Picabia, June 19, 1920 (D.P. II, 316; Sanouillet, *Dada à Paris*, 508).

5. Picabia letter to Tzara, July 3, 1920 (C.T. 3.010; Sanouillet, *Dada à Paris*, 498).

6. Evidently with some encouragement from Picabia and other dadaists in Paris, Pansaers had gone ahead with plans for a dada festival in Brussels around December. When the quarreling Parisians failed to collaborate, he turned to such men as Cocteau, Albert-Birot, Reverdy and Jacob—and was chastised by Picabia for it (Sanouillet, *Dada à Paris*, 226–27).

7. Censorship of the article by Ribemont-Dessaignes (referred to as "Geo") is mentioned in Picabia's letter to Tzara on July 13, 1920 (C.T. 3.011; Sanouillet, *Dada à Paris*, 500). Breton described his refusal to write the preface for *Jésus-Christ Rastaquouère* in a letter to Simone Kahn on July 31, 1920 (Marguerite Bonnet, *André Breton*, Paris, 1975, 235). He wrote to Tzara on October 14, 1920 (C.T. 565; Sanouillet, *Dada à Paris*, 456–57), "Everything that he [Picabia] has told you of me is unfortunately true; I have conducted myself with him in such a bizarre manner that he must be angry. If you judge it proper, tell him, my dear friends, that I regret it with all my heart."

a thorough acquaintance with Breton's thought.[8] Breton's article was brilliantly cautious, seemingly constructed to offend no friend of substance. Essentially he disputed critics who had offered some "explanation" of Dada, but never himself attempted to describe Dada. Nonetheless, Breton expressed —and exposed— himself. Despite his previous talk about "compromising" Gide, Valéry and *La Nouvelle Revue française*, there he was—in closer collaboration than ever with Rivière—contributing a "reasonable" article for that prestigious magazine, and, in that article, citing Gide and Valéry favorably along with the more predictable cast of Vaché, Rimbaud, Lautréamont, Apollinaire and his own dadaist colleagues. Breton also suggested the demise of Dada and the existence of something beyond: "It is most of all our differences that bind us together. Our common exception to the artistic or moral rule gives us only an ephemeral satisfaction. We are well aware that over and above this, an irrepressible personal imagination, more 'dada' than the movement, will have free reign. J.-E. Blanche made this clear when he wrote: 'Dada will survive only by ceasing to be.' "

Breton's reference to something beyond Dada and his continued ties with *La Nouvelle Revue française* were not basically double-dealing with the dadaists. Hindsight permits us to see in those acts the embryonic notions of Surrealism and Breton's ongoing esteem for each person who had helped him discover his way— even when, as with Gide, Valéry and Rivière, that respect compromised him in the eyes of some of the dadaists. And in this instance, Rivière's accompanying article did magnify the vague suspicions generated by Breton's more cautious, elusive phrasing. Rivière's intelligent and pro-dada statement contained a single identifiable slur directed at the "bewildering litanies" of Tzara and Picabia. In contrast, there were repeated respectful references to Breton and intriguing reverberations/extensions of Breton's article. Rivière placed Dada in a historical evolution, implied a future for it once a critical creative spirit displaced its reigning nihilism and discussed the movement in proto-surrealist terms more compatible with Breton than with any other member of Dada. Rivière even used the word "surrealism"—as had Breton—in reference to an undefined idea of Apollinaire's which continued to intrigue a number of his admirers.[9] During a moment of reconciliation, Picabia noted in a postscript to Breton that the articles were "good pub-

8. André Breton, "Pour Dada," *La Nouvelle Revue française*, no. 83 (Paris, August 1, 1920), 208–15; Jacques Rivière, "Reconnaissance à Dada," 216–17. Breton's article was reprinted in *Les Pas perdus* (Paris, 1924; 8th ed., Paris, 1949, 85–94) and translated by Ralph Manheim in Robert Motherwell, ed., *The Dada Painters and Poets* (New York, 1951), 199–203.

9. Rivière's "proto-surrealist" tone is suggested in several passages:

"To seize the being before it has ceded to compatibility; to attain it in its incoherence, or better in its primitive coherence, before the idea of contradiction has appeared . . . to substitute for its logical unity, inevitably acquired, its absurd unity . . . such is the goal pursued by all the Dadas in writing" (p. 218).

"Language for the Dadas is no longer a means: it is a being. Skepticism in the matter of syntax doubles here as a sort of mysticism. Even when they do not dare to avow it frankly, the Dadas continue to tend toward that *surrealism* which was the ambition of Apollinaire" (p. 221).

licity for the 'Movement' "[10]—but within a few weeks their tense relationship exploded over *Jésus-Christ Rastaquouère*.[11]

The blasphemous title of *Jésus-Christ Rastaquouère*, awkwardly translatable as "Jesus Christ, flashy (foreign) adventurer," was more a symbol of Picabia's scorn for a vast array of gods than a specific assault on Christianity. Nevertheless, that title was too much for potential publishers, most distressing of all for Hilsum at Au Sans Pareil who, as Picabia raged to Breton, "has declared to me that if I would like to be published at S.P.—at my expense, mind you!—it would be necessary to change several passages and the title of this book and this in order to observe prudence toward a rich and churchy sponsor of these ladies!"[12] Breton did intervene on Picabia's behalf and *Jésus-Christ Rastaquouère* was published without censorship. But when he refused to write the preface promised for it, Picabia broke off all communication and turned to Gabrielle Buffet for a preface to the text which he described as a "philosophical treatise," dedicated to "all young girls." The treatise is imbued with Picabia's style and spirit, that is to say, a sampling of excerpts reveals a typically unstructured, uneven collection of tales, homilies and aphorisms whose audacious irreverence, eroticism, humor and megalomania envelop the reader in a pervasive moral atmosphere:

> The thoughts of the heart, the thoughts of the soul, the thoughts of the brain are the same as automatic chemical reactions; the current which makes them move comes from you yourself, from the sun or from the Great Bear. . . . Your reflections, dear readers, though they be antireason or antitruth, are but so many conventions on an absolute which itself is only a convention (p. 17).

> There is nothing to understand, live for your pleasure, there [is] nothing, nothing, nothing but the value you yourself give to everything (p. 18).

> . . . there are no obstacles, the only obstacle is the goal, march without goal. Analyze the blood of a hero and that of a coward, you will see that they are exactly alike, your objectivity makes you love heroes more only because you are snobs, the courage to be cowardly is in my opinion infinitely more attractive (p. 58).

10. Picabia letter to Breton, August 6, 1920 (collection A. Breton, Paris; Sanouillet, *Dada à Paris*, 510–11). Picabia also scorned (see his "Zona," *La Vie des lettres*, Paris, July 1921) the *Nouvelle Revue française* publication of Aragon's novel *Anicet* (February 1921; chaps. 1 and 2 first published in *La Nouvelle Revue française*, no. 84, Paris, September 1, 1920, 346–82).

11. Francis Picabia, *Jésus-Christ Rastaquouère* (Paris, 1920), introduction by Gabrielle Buffet, drawings by Georges Ribemont-Dessaignes. It is dated "Paris, July 10, 1920," although Picabia worked on it after that date. The first portion of this text was translated in *The Little Review* (New York, autumn–winter 1924–1925), 51–58. The entire text was reprinted in Picabia, *Ecrits 1913–1920*, ed. Olivier Revault d'Allonnes (Paris, 1975), 237–58.

12. Picabia letter to Breton, August 6, 1920 (collection A. Breton; Sanouillet, *Dada à Paris*, 510–11).

Picabia also spoke to Bernard Grasset about publishing *Jésus-Christ Rastaquouère*, but Grasset had reservations similar to Hilsum's and declined the project on July 27 (D.P. VI, 183).

God was jewish. He was duped by the catholics (p. 46).

Me, I am disguised as a man in order to be nothing (p. 46).

There is a species of bird of great rarity and very difficult to know; for these birds never set; the female lays its eggs in the air at a great altitude and the hatching of the little ones takes place before they have had time to reach the earth; flying ceaselessly, ignorant of repose, the beating of their wings is like the beatings of our heart; stopping signifies death (p. 33).

Picabia launched his own publicity for *Jésus-Christ Rastaquouère* in a summer issue of *391* (no. 13, July). Though only a modest four-page number, that issue of *391* also included prime examples of dada manifestos by Tzara and Ribemont-Dessaignes, and three interesting reproductions, Man Ray's *Lampshade*, Duchamp's *To Be Looked At (From the Other Side of the Glass) with One Eye, Close to, for Almost an Hour* (fig. 166) and Picabia's own *Far-niente beau parti* (*Beautiful Party of Blissful Ease*, fig. 187). This undated drawing was probably a work done that summer. It is related stylistically to the *Portrait de Jacques-Emile Blanche* (fig. 185) in the manner in which circles are combined with lines of a distinctive quality; note especially the prominent line in *Far-niente beau parti* labeled "La couleur/de la lune" where Picabia seems to work deliberately with elements that are straight and curved, thick and thin. Similar features occur in a few more documented works of 1920—a year characterized by a production limited in number but extraordinarily varied in kind including paintings, collages, wire constructions, inkblots, ready-mades and drawings which ranged from naturalistic portraits to abstract machines.

La Danseuse Jasmine (*The Dancer Jasmine*, fig. 188) was a small, intimate sketch, a private memento of a summer evening at the Olympia Theater where his friend, the dancer Jasmine, starred in a performance of "L'Antre des gnomes."[13] *Adam et Eve* and *Le Rastaquouère* (fig. 190) were enormous paintings destined for the public at the 1920 Salon d'Automne. With those two paintings and an outstanding issue of *391* (no. 14, November 1920), Picabia reengaged the public that fall with the same two-pronged offensive he had employed in 1919.

Unfortunately, neither of those Salon paintings is extant, but the available sources of information—contemporary reviews, Picabia's letters and one poor reproduction of *Le Rastaquouère*—attest to the importance of the two works. With obvious pleasure Picabia first mentioned *Adam et Eve* (by its initial title, *Fougère*

13. During July 1920 the dramatization of a fantastic legend, "L'Antre des gnomes," was staged at the Olympic Theater by Georges Casella and Robert Quinalt with Mlle Jasmine in the principal role and music by Claude Debussy. See Louis Laloy, "L'Antre des gnomes," *Comoedia* [Paris], July 4, 1920, 1. Inscriptions on this drawing—"Olympia," "Gnome" and "La Danseuse Jasmine" indicate Picabia attended the production of his good friends, Jasmine and her husband, Georges Casella. The inscriptions also provide a date for the drawing and affirm Picabia's private, symbolic approach to his art, but the precise content of the drawing remains untouched—even with what appears to be a study for it (fig. 189), initialed upside down to the orientation of the more complete drawing.

royale, "Royal Fern") in a letter to Breton: "*Fougère royale* is a very big painting. Three meters by two and one-half meters. It is made of 261 black rings on a field of crushed strawberry, in a corner of the painting is an enormous cup-and-ball toy in gold; as for inscriptions, I prefer to leave it for your surprise."[14] Most of the inscriptions for both paintings were recorded by a baffled critic from Bordeaux who marveled that there were "thirty persons before each of the paintings" although *Le Rastaquouère* was "a bizarre assemblage of triangles and the arcs of circles in which the common eye could distinguish nothing."[15] He consoled himself that the public was "more amused than moved," but other critics frankly conceded that the paintings were good. One called Picabia a "sage" whose works were "charged with humor" and "skepticism";[16] another, seldom friendly toward Picabia or his work, observed: "It is strange that Picabia, who denies wanting to make a work of art, nevertheless comes, by his natural gifts, to compose a harmony of colors whose rapports are an enchantment. The most terrible adventure which could come to Henri Matisse would be to be placed side by side with one of these paintings, extravagant but of charming color."[17]

A few weeks after his spectacular showing at the Salon d'Automne, Picabia published one of the most stimulating issues of *391* (no. 14, November 1920), and he was fixed more firmly than ever in the eyes of the public as the chief dadaist in Paris. His preeminence seemed all the greater in the absence of competing activities. Owing to the quarrel with Breton, no public manifestations were produced. Moreover, Picabia's paintings at the Salon were, in effect, the only representatives of Dada, and of all the dada magazines which had sprouted in the spring, *391* was the sole survivor.[18] One important new magazine, *L'Esprit nouveau*, was founded that fall (October 1920) by the erstwhile dadaist Paul Dermée, with the collaboration and, later, the leadership of Amédée Ozenfant and Charles Edouard Jeanneret (Le Corbusier). But from the beginning those editors were preoccupied with an indwelling order to all of life, and—regarding art—with a classicistic bias for universal laws and the relevance of tradition. In brief, *L'Es-*

14. Picabia letters to Breton, August 6 and 11, 1920 (collection A. Breton; Sanouillet, *Dada à Paris*, 510–12).

15. Anon., "Laglane du jour," *La France* [Bordeaux], October 26, 1920 (attrib.; D.P. VI, 224). He gave the inscriptions on *Adam et Eve* as, "Adam and Eve, what is their name?," "Invisible bas-relief" and "Royal Fern." Regarding *Le Rastaquouère* he wrote: "From the point of a triangle where there appears the 'zone of obscure stars' descends a dotted line which forks at the bottom of the painting; on one side is 'the male egg,' on the other 'the female egg' separated by an 'armpit circumflex.' . . . A red spot is the 'fan louse' . . . . All along the frame on the right runs this phrase: 'There is nothing more.' It is true that, along the frame, on the left, one can read 'It's here that everything is.' "

16. Lucien Aressy, "Le Salon d'Automne," *Le Journal du peuple* [Paris], October 20, 1920.

17. André Warnod, "Le Salon d'Automne," *L'Avenir* [Paris], October 16, 1920, 3.

18. Ribemont-Dessaignes exhibited one painting alongside Picabia at the Salon d'Automne, but it was barely mentioned by the critics. As for dada magazines, publication of *Z* and *Cannibale* ceased with the issues of May 1920; *Dadaphone* (March 1920) became the last issue of *Dada*, excepting *Dada au grand air* (October 1921), which is sometimes considered the last number. After *Proverbe*, no. 5 (May 1920), Eluard published only one more number in May 1921.

prit nouveau was anti-Dada, opposing rational, constructive forces against what its editors deemed to be the destructive individualism of Dada.[19] That attitude was a crucial ingredient in the direction of art during the 1920s, and even Breton—in his own way—possessed something of that spirit. That aspect of Breton was to become more evident later; meanwhile, through the intermediary of Tzara, he was earnestly striving to repair the rifts among the dadaists. He was ignored, however, by Picabia, and excluded from the provocative issue of *391* published in November.

A superb balance of visual and literary material was achieved in that issue. Picabia reproduced works by Crotti, Man Ray, Charchoune and Tzara as well as four of his own. The cover page (fig. 191), designed by Picabia, contained two ready-mades. One was a reproduction of Ingres's letter to his parents seeking permission to marry a young Italian woman. Picabia transformed it into a rectified ready-made simply by adding "Francis" before the signature "Ingres." On the same page a pari-mutuel horse race ticket was reproduced without any alteration except the printing of "Dada Drawing" above it and Picabia's name below it. On page six appeared a collaborative work—a photograph of Picabia attributed to Man Ray on which Picabia inscribed "Vive Papa / Francis / Le Raté" ("Long live papa Francis, the Washout"). A short time later, still more inscriptions and collage additions transformed it into a Christmas greeting entitled *Tableau rastadada* (*Rastadada Painting*, fig. 193).[20]

These reproductions are thoroughly integrated with the composition of each page, and that layout in turn reflects its author and the current state of affairs in the dada movement. Picabia's cover page is more stable and symmetrical in structure; Tzara's "A Night of Fat Chess" (fig. 192) is more dynamic, aggressive and seemingly chaotic. Picabia's cover incorporates his friends outside of Dada—Cocteau, Satie and Varèse; Tzara's page reflects his renewed contacts with the Swiss, German and Italian dadaists, and the total exclusion of the *Littérature* group including Hilsum, whose services at Au Sans Pareil were replaced by a new publisher, Jacques Povolozky. Though Breton, Aragon and Soupault were excluded from *391*, they were not attacked, except in a passing, private manner accessible only to the dadaists and a few friends.[21] The primary targets were once again the Salon d'Automne itself and Cubism—above all, Albert Gleizes. Gleizes had recently published a book entitled *Du Cubisme et des moyens de la comprendre*

19. In addition to *L'Esprit nouveau* itself (nos. 1–28, Paris, October 1920–January 1925), see the Tate Gallery, London, *Léger and Purist Paris*, November 18, 1970–January 24, 1971, texts by John Golding and Christopher Green.

20. Attribution of this photograph to Man Ray must be viewed with some skepticism since he did not settle in Paris until the following year, and no other documents regarding the photograph are known.

21. In Picabia's "Notre-Dame-de-la-peinture" (*391*, no. 14, Paris, November 1920), the reference to "la rue Madame" is directed at *La Nouvelle Revue française*, situated on that street, and reference to his "boots" is linked to expressions used in their quarrels (see Picabia's letter to Tzara on July 3, 1920, quoted here, p. 151).

and also had secured special permission from the Salon d'Automne to hang a huge "demonstration" painting in a position dominating the grand stairway.[22] While most critics praised Gleizes's book and paintings, *391* offered Ribemont-Dessaignes's outrageous review of the Salon and Tzara's fake interview with Gleizes's former friend and coauthor, Jean Metzinger:

Tz.[ara]	what do you think of Gleizes's book *Cubism and the Ways to Understand It*?
M.[etzinger]	absolutely idiotic
Tz.	what aim did he pursue in writing this book?
M.	to explain cubism to himself because he still has not understood it! . . .
Tz.	Who is the founder of cubism?
M.	Raphael.[23]

One of the non-dada contributors to this issue of *391*, Marie de La Hire, was a writer, former art student and friend of Picabia's not seen by him since their student days with Fernand Cormon. Attracted by the publicity attending Dada, she reestablished contact with Picabia in May, proposing to write an article about him. That article turned into a superficial booklet, and for awhile during the summer of 1920 she and Picabia together sought a publisher for their books. Her booklet was finally published by Jacques Povolozky, an interesting minor figure in the history of modern art who operated a Russian bookstore and the Galerie La Cible.[24] Povolozky also took over distribution of the dada publications abandoned by Hilsum at Au Sans Pareil and gave Picabia a one-man exhibition in December 1920 which became the dada event of the winter season.[25]

Few of the critics had much to say about the exhibition itself, except to note their astonishment upon discovering that most of the works were unexpectedly competent impressionist landscapes and naturalistic drawings of nudes, portraits, entertainers and Spanish figures. The selection may have been partly La Hire's

22. Albert Gleizes's *Du Cubisme et des moyens de la comprendre* (Paris, 1920) was published about September. Regarding Gleizes at the Salon d'Automne, André Warnod wrote (*L'Avenir*, 3): "Gleize [*sic*], in a gigantic panel, juxtaposes and orders magnificent colors chosen according to firm principles. Gleize [*sic*] asked that his painting be hung there, and he had reason. The visitors who mount the stairs meet an invigorating and happy impression, and this . . . is a victory whose importance Gleizes understands. On the ground floor, in the obscurity of the periphery, are the large paintings of Picabia and Ribemont-Dessaignes."

23. Tristan Tzara, "Interview de Jean Metzinger sur le cubisme," *391*, no. 14 (Paris, November 1920), 8.

24. Marie de La Hire, *Francis Picabia* (Paris: Galerie La Cible, 1920). Out of an edition of 1,100, ten of these booklets were for private use and fifty were on a type of paper with linen content. The various small-scale versions of such works as *Petite Solitude au milieu des soleils* (fig. 121) may represent hand-tinted prints by Picabia for the tipped-in reproductions in those deluxe editions.

25. Galerie Povolozky, Paris, *Exposition Picabia*, December 10–25, 1920. Marie de La Hire's booklet on Picabia, printed on December 9, contained a catalogue of the exhibition.

responsibility for she preferred his figurative and impressionist work, but it also reflected Picabia's insouciant independence from any code or convention—including notions about a proper image, conduct or associates for a dadaist. For the most part, the critics reveled in the gala opening that continued until 2 a.m. All of Paris—artists, writers, entertainers, socialites, reporters, family friends and enemies—packed the street and gallery across from the Ecole des Beaux-Arts.[26] Since it was impossible to look at the paintings, few were distracted from the main event—the opening with its whiskey, Mistinguett dancing to "The Vamp," Tzara's manifesto on "Weak and Bitter Love" and Cocteau's "infernal jazz band." The latter consisted of Cocteau, Georges Auric and Francis Poulenc performing "New York Fox-trott" and "Tango of Le Boeuf sur le Toit" on piano, drums, cymbals, castanets, reed pipes, Klaxon horn and glasses. Cocteau, wrote one critic, had a grave air about him "worthy of the conductor at the Opera. He makes a signal and suddenly a deafening racket fills the hall. . . . He raises his hand, the music stops, and in the midst of a profound silence, this great straight-faced wag [Tzara] begins to deliver, with the incoherent terms of a madman, a talk on 'Weak Love and Bitter Love,' a lecture so untranslatable that only one phrase rests in my memory . . . 'Dadaism works to make people idiots!' "[27]

Breton, Aragon and Soupault were among the guests at the opening, but it was not to their taste and relations remained exceedingly chilly between them and the counterpart threesome of Picabia, Tzara and Ribemont-Dessaignes. Up to that point in December 1920, the latter group had provided all the renewed dada activity in Paris, and they planned to continue unilaterally with publication of Tzara's ambitious *Dadaglobe* and a manifestation at the forthcoming Salon des Indépendants. The initiative changed hands rather quickly, however, during January 1921. Picabia, Tzara and Ribemont-Dessaignes abandoned plans for a manifestation at the Salon des Indépendants because the wary committee specified unacceptable conditions.[28] And Tzara's *Dadaglobe*, an anthology of the international dada movement, bogged down when some of the German dadaists, notably Walter Serner, Christian Schad and Richard Huelsenbeck, inexplicably withdrew their support for that publication.[29] About the same time, Breton finally succeeded in

26. Guests included Picabia's uncle Maurice Davanne, Aragon, Breton, Soupault, Cocteau, Max Jacob, Albert-Birot, Picasso, Brancusi, Léger, Dunoyer de Segonzac, Derain, Erik Satie, Georges Auric, Francis Poulenc, Mistinguett, Hania Routchine, Marthe Chenal, Princess Lucienne Murat, the Minister of Cuba, Alexandre Mercereau, Paul Poiret, Georges Casella, Ribemont-Dessaignes, Tzara, Valmy-Baysse, Marcelle Meyer, Marcelle Evrard, Dr. Serner and many more.

27. A. d'Esparbès, "Autour du Dadaïsme, le vernissage Francis Picabia," *Comoedia* [Paris], December 12, 1920, 1–2. The invitation for the evening first listed a talk by Ribemont-Dessaignes on "What Is Not Permitted to Be Said About Art." Other invitations were stamped to announce Tzara's manifesto which, for unknown reasons, replaced the talk by Ribemont-Dessaignes.

28. Letter from Carlos Reymond of the Salon des Indépendants to Picabia, December 14, 1920 (D.P. VI, 595; Sanouillet, *Dada à Paris*, 234–35).

29. Schad letter to Picabia, December 20, 1920 (D.P.II, 321) and Serner letter to Picabia, January 31, 1921 (D.P.IV, 223; Sanouillet, *Dada à Paris*, 568). Picabia also reported in a letter

arranging a reconciliation with Picabia, and, in the renewed gatherings of the dadaists during January–February 1921, it was the faction from *Littérature* that dominated.

The reunion of the dadaists was celebrated by a brief flurry of activity; first, a joint assault on Marinetti's latest passion (an art form called "Tactilism"), then Picabia's entries to the Salon des Indépendants, and the distribution of leaflets announcing the new dada season.[30]

Picabia, sole representative of Dada at the Salon, submitted two paintings, *Le Double Monde* (fig. 167) and *Le Lierre unique eunuque* (*The Unique Eunuch Ivy*, fig. 194).[31] The latter is another unusual work in his career. The forms in it resemble cells rather than machine parts, although a metallic quality is imparted by silvery gray colors and schematic drawing. In all likelihood, the general content of the painting reflects Picabia's suggestive association of god, man, art, sex and machines in his established mechanomorphic framework of creator-creative act-creation (or product). Nonetheless, the specific content is obscure and private, while the contrary is true of *Le Double Monde*, which attracted most of the critical comment. One called it the "folly of a millionaire who jokes";[32] another considered it offensive enough to caption his article, "We Demand that Picabia Be Led Back to the Spanish Border."[33]

While the controversy of those paintings was still fresh, the dadaists announced the "Great Dada Season." Handbills distributed during early February projected a Salon Dada, a Congress, plebiscites, commemorations, operas, visits, acquisitions, trials and an exhibition of the work of Max Ernst. Even in its reduced final form, the season seemed more varied and imaginative than the relatively homogeneous manifestations of the preceding year. Often, however, both the planning sessions and the execution of the events were disappointing. Picabia participated only in the initial meetings and without enthusiasm. He nursed a lingering resentment toward Breton and could not tolerate the meetings at the Café

to Schad (December 23, 1920, collection C. Schad, Spessart im Krahennest, Germany) that Huelsenbeck had refused to participate.

30. At the Théâtre de l'Oeuvre on January 14, 1921, Marinetti lectured on "Tactilism," a form of collage intended to be experienced by the sense of touch rather than by sight (see F.T. Marinetti, "Le Tactilisme," *Comoedia* [Paris], January 16, 1921, 1). The dadaists distributed there a provocative tract, "Dada soulève tout," and disrupted the lecture with hoots and whistles (see André Rigaud, "M. Marinetti nous révèle le 'Tactilisme,' " *Comoedia* [Paris], January 15, 1921, 1). Picabia, present but not an active demonstrator, accused Marinetti of plagiarizing the concept of Tactilism from an obscure member of the Stieglitz-Arensberg circles in New York, Edith Clifford Williams (see Francis Picabia, "Selon M. Picabia, le 'Tactilisme' aurait été inventé par Miss Clifford-Williams en 1916," *Comoedia* [Paris], January 18, 1921, 1).

31. Salon des Indépendants, Paris, January 23–February 28, 1921, nos. 2764a and 2764b. Charchoune also contributed two paintings to the Salon, but they were not noted and at least one of them (*Cubisme ornamentale*) was not dadaist.

32. Armand Altmann, "32e Salon des Indépendants," *Arts et lettres* [Geneva], January 25, 1921 (attrib.; D.P. IV, 215).

33. A.D., "Nous demandons qu'on reconduise Picabia à la frontière espagnole," *Le Merle blanc* [Paris], January 29, 1921, 1.

Certà which, for his taste, had become more like seminars than the convivial gatherings of the past. The meetings were indeed more serious and disciplined for, in the eyes of Breton, Aragon and Soupault, Dada was not mere farcical entertainment; it was viewed as a serious manifestation of contemporary culture, a revolution active in the world, with roots in the past and a future—even if its direction was unknown.[34] Tzara was less alienated than Picabia by Breton and the new dada program, but he was acutely conscious that his own directing role of the preceding year had now been assumed by Breton. Only the operas and the Salon Dada had been central to Tzara's interests; every other aspect of the program had derived from Breton and his associates.

The late opening of the dada season contributed to an uneventful early spring. Picabia's own career was marked only by a quiet exhibition in Limoges[35] and by invitations to collaborate with two magazines, *La Vie des lettres* and *The Little Review*.[36] Ezra Pound's contact on behalf of the latter was significant, leading to considerable attention to Dada in *The Little Review*, including articles by and about Picabia and a special feature devoted to his work in the spring issue of 1922. In the meantime, a painful eye disease and continued disenchantment over some of his colleagues prompted Picabia to withdraw from all meetings and public activity.[37]

In April the dadaists opened their season with an amusing leaflet announcing "Dada Excursions and Visits": "The dadaists passing through Paris, wanting to remedy the incompetence of suspect guides and cicerones, have decided to undertake a series of visits to selected spots, in particular those which truly have no reason to exist."[38]

The first site chosen was the church of St. Julien-le-Pauvre on the left bank across from Notre Dame. Despite a heavy rain on the appointed day, April 14, a crowd of dadaists gathered in the church garden. The audience, however, was

34. For this shift in the dada movement, see André Breton, *Entretiens 1913–1952*, 10th ed. (Paris, 1952), 66–67, and Sanouillet, *Dada à Paris*, 239. Breton cited their polls as one of the first signs of a shift. Several were conducted on a great variety of qualities, concepts and people, including the dadaists themselves; one was published in *Littérature* (no. 18, Paris, March 1921) in which men listed alphabetically from Alcibiades to Zola were graded on a scale from +25 to −25 with the midpoint 0 representing complete indifference.

35. Galerie Dalpayrat, Limoges, *Exposition Picabia*, February 1–15, 1921. Most of the works were figurative studies, many of them apparently from Picabia's December exhibition at Povolozky's gallery.

36. Nicolas Beauduin, editor of *La Vie des lettres*, secured Picabia's collaboration in January 1921 (see Beauduin's letter of January 3, D.P. IV, 124). Picabia contributed two poems, one of which, "Zona" (July 1921), was dictated under the influence of drugs prescribed for an eye malady (see Germaine Everling, *L'Anneau de Saturne*, Paris, 1970, 141–43).

Ezra Pound asked Picabia on April 12, 1921 (D.P. IV, 406), to serve as a foreign editor for *The Little Review*.

37. Germaine Everling attributed Picabia's condition to an ophthalmic malady and severe reaction to the drugs used to treat it (see n. 36 above).

38. Handbill for "Excursions et Visites Dada," reproduced in Robert Motherwell, ed., *The Dada Painters and Poets* (New York, 1951), 114.

small, and the dadaists themselves were so disappointed with the program that other announced visits were abandoned.[39] Although Picabia's name had been included on the initial announcement, he was not present at the church and in an interview published on the day of the visit he disclaimed any part in it, adding: "All that I hope is that it will not present any political, clerical, or nonclerical character, for I will always abstain from participation in a manifestation of that kind, considering *Dada* as a personage having nothing to do with beliefs—whatever they may be."[40]

A short time later, two events—a letter from Christian Schad and the incident of the waiter's pocketbook—transformed Picabia from a disillusioned dadaist into one who disowned the movement.

At the weekly dinner gathering of the dadaists in the Café Certà on April 25, a waiter left his bulging wallet on their table. It was confiscated by one of the dadaists, and at a nearby café a heated argument developed over the proper course of action. Some wished to return the wallet; others suggested they drink it up or apply it to a new issue of a magazine; still others urged that stealing from the poor and giving to the rich was the proper dada gesture. Unable to reach agreement that evening, they decided to place the wallet in Eluard's custody. It was returned anonymously to the owner, touching off rebukes from several colleagues, including Breton in particular. Picabia was not present at the dinner, but it was described to him by Clément Pansaers, who was disgusted by the incident and had resolved that very night to break with Dada.[41]

On the same day the Swiss-German dadaist Christian Schad wrote Picabia a shocking letter. Schad and Dr. Serner had been impressive guests at Picabia's salon during their visit to Paris in late 1920, but they had departed abruptly without explanation. Picabia's curiosity mounted as they repeatedly wrote to demand the return of material left for Tzara's *Dadaglobe*. Other German dadaists also failed to cooperate with that project, and finally Picabia urged Schad to tell him what was going on. The reply was clear:

> The word Dada was found by Mr. Hülsenbeck and Mr. Ball. There is a lot of evidence that Mr. Tzara was far from that discovery. . . . It was only with the manifesto of Dr. Serner which appeared in "the German edition" of dada 4/5 that the great boom of dada began in Germany. Although the 1918 dada manifesto of Mr. Tzara was known in Germany, all the German dadaists refer to

39. See Asté d'Esparbès, "Les Disciples de 'Dada' à l'église Saint-Julien-le-Pauvre," *Comoedia* [Paris], April 15, 1921, 2, and Sanouillet, *Dada à Paris*, 246–48.

40. A[sté] d'E[sparbès], "Les 'Dadas' visitent Paris," *Comoedia* [Paris], April 14, 1921, 2.

41. For information on this incident see Clément Pansaers, "Une Bombe déconfiture" (*Le Pilhaou-Thibaou*, Paris, July 10, 1921, 8; no. 15 of *391*) and "Dada et moi" (*Ça ira*, no. 16, Antwerp, November 1921, 111–15); Ribemont-Dessaignes, "Histoire de Dada" (*La Nouvelle Revue française*, no. 214, Paris, July 1931, 39–52, trans. Ralph Manheim in Robert Motherwell, ed., *The Dada Painters and Poets*, 114–15); Sanouillet, *Dada à Paris*, 272–73, and *Francis Picabia et "391,"* II (Paris, 1966), 138.

the manifesto of Dr. Serner. . . . Dr. Serner had developed his ideas orally before many people in Zurich long before he wrote them. That is why one knows very well how Mr. Tzara found the most important ideas of his manifesto. Now you understand why Mr. Tzara was so afraid when Dr. Serner arrived in Paris that he did not open his mouth.[42]

Picabia's reaction to Schad's letter is not preserved in any known contemporary document, but subsequent events indicate that the accusations against Tzara, on top of everything else, completed Picabia's disgust for what had become of Dada.

Now both currents within Dada seemed contaminated, and during the next two weeks Picabia withdrew even further while most of his colleagues were absorbed in two major events—the Max Ernst exhibition which opened on May 2 and the mock trial of Maurice Barrès, set for May 13. The opening of the Ernst exhibition was a dada event *par excellence* with Jacques Rigaut at the door shouting out the number of arriving automobiles and counting the pearls in necklaces on the women visitors, while, inside, other dadaists played hide-and-seek, continually lit matches and shook hands, or made noises and wry comments from hidden positions behind a trap door and a closet.[43] The works of Ernst managed to compete with that spectacle, and, befitting that point of crisis for Dada, they appear in hindsight to have been closer in spirit to Surrealism than to Dada. Ernst's earlier, Picabia-inspired machine drawings (see fig. 163) had given way to a variety of personal developments, among them collage landscapes clipped from scientific journals on botany and human anatomy, and then transformed with hallucinatory effect into ominous dream worlds inhabited by dangerous plant animals (see fig. 195). Within a year, Ernst was producing such paintings as *Oedipus Rex* (fig. 196), characterized by a seemingly literal transcription of dream images; by vast, silent spaces on unknown planets; disturbing, irrational juxtapositions of scale and objects; and haunting themes of imprisonment, penetration, sexuality and mystery. One may still note the influence of de Chirico and the cubist collage technique—along with fainter strains of Picabia and Duchamp—but Ernst's work was unlike anything produced by the dadaists, and, in effect, was surrealist art *avant la lettre*.[44]

42. Letter from Schad to Picabia, April 25, 1921 (D.P. VII, 65; Sanouillet, *Dada à Paris*, 566–68). Other letters were posted to Picabia by Schad on December 20, 1920 (D.P. II, 321) and February 1, 1921 (D.P. IV, 146). Picabia wrote to Schad on December 23, 1920, and April 15 and May 19, 1921 (collection C. Schad). Serner wrote Picabia on December 25, 1920 (D.P. VI, 569), and January 31, 1921 (D.P. IV, 223; Sanouillet, *Dada à Paris*, 568).

For Tzara's unpublished project *Dadaglobe*, see Sanouillet, "Le Dossier de 'Dadaglobe,'" *Cahiers de l'Association Internationale pour l'Etude de Dada et du Surréalisme*, no. 1 (Paris, 1966), 111–43.

43. Au Sans Pareil, Paris, *Exposition Dada: Max Ernst*, May 3–June 3, 1921, preface by André Breton. For contemporary accounts see Asté d'Esparbès, "Un Vernissage mouvementé" (*Comoedia* [Paris], May 7, 1921, 2); Georges Oudard, "Une Soirée chez Dada" (*Le Gaulois* [Paris], May 4, 1921, attrib.); and Sanouillet, *Dada à Paris*, 248–53.

44. See Lucy R. Lippard, "Dada into Surrealism. Notes on Max Ernst as Proto-Surrealist," *Artforum*, V, no. 1 (Los Angeles, September 1966), 10–15.

Picabia's reaction to the Ernst exhibition is not known, but the next event of the dada season, the trial of Maurice Barrès, confirmed his decision about Dada. A mock trial of that author and patriot was held on May 13 before a dada tribunal with Breton presiding. Ribemont-Dessaignes was the public prosecutor, Aragon and Soupault served as defense attorneys and Tzara headed a cast of more than a dozen witnesses.[45] With the exception of Tzara, who disregarded the script to testify in a refreshingly outrageous manner, the trial was essentially serious and, to those who came for a spectacle, definitely boring. For Picabia the very concept of a "dada tribunal" was evidence of Dada's death. He took no part in the trial—except to exit dramatically in the midst of it. Two days earlier he had exited with equal drama from Dada itself, renouncing the movement in a prominent article in *Comoedia*.[46] And, on the day of the Barrès trial itself, Picabia wrote a more explicit renunciation:

> The spirit of Dada really existed only during three or four years; it was expressed by "Marcel Duchamp and me" at the end of 1912; Huelsenbeck, Tzara or Ball found the "nom-écrin" Dada in 1916. With this word, the movement touched its culminating point, but it continued to evolve, each of us bringing to it as much life as possible.
>
> We were treated as crazy men, as practical jokers, as queer fellows, etc., etc.; finally it was a grand success! This success . . . attracted in 1918 several persons who were Dada only in name. Then everything changed around me, I had the impression that like Cubism, Dada would have disciples who "understood" and I had only one idea, to flee as far as possible. . . .
>
> Now Dada has a court, lawyers, soon probably police. . . .
>
> I do not like illustriousness, and the directors of "Littérature" are nothing but illustrious men. I prefer to walk at random, the name of the streets matters little, each day resembles the other if we do not create subjectively the illusion of something new, and Dada is no longer new.[47]

The dada movement in Paris was indeed dying, but appropriately enough this defection of one of its leaders spurred the dada activities of both the dada loyalists and Picabia the anti-dada dadaist—and the protagonists were worthy of each other.

The last event of the dada season was the "Salon Dada" set for June 6–30 in the Galerie Montaigne, a hall on the top floor of the Studio des Champs-Elysées in

45. The most extensive account of the trial of Barrès is provided by Sanouillet, *Dada à Paris*, 254–66. *Littérature*, no. 20 (Paris, August 1921), was devoted to texts of the trial. For contemporary reviews see Asté d'Esparbès, "Les Dadas ont dépassé la mesure" (*Comoedia* [Paris], May 15, 1921, 1); Anon., "Encore des Dadas" (*Carnet de la semaine*, Paris, May 22, 1921, 9); and Mme Rachilde, "Les qu'est-ce que nous faisons ce soir?" (*Comoedia* [Paris], July 29, 1921, attrib.).

46. Francis Picabia, "M. Picabia se sépare des Dadas," *Comoedia* [Paris], May 11, 1921, 2.

47. Francis Picabia, "Francis Picabia et Dada," *L'Esprit nouveau*, no. 9 (Paris, June 1921), 1059–60, dated May 13, 1921. In response to inquiries, Picabia wrote a third statement about his defection from Dada which appeared as an open letter in *Comoedia* [Paris], May 17, 1921, 1.

which dada manifestations were also to be held on June 10, 18 and 30. Early in the year Picabia had been interested in this Salon, but as he withdrew Tzara took charge and made it the most entertaining event of the season. The absence of Duchamp, Picabia, the Crottis and most of the German dadaists cut deeply into his aim for an international exhibition of dada painters and writers.[48] Breton, in a gloomy mood over Picabia's denunciations of Dada, also held back, but Tzara still managed to put together an intriguing catalogue and a collection of eighty-one objects by Arp, Aragon, Johannes Baargeld, Gino Cantarelli, Charchoune, Paul and Gala Eluard, Ernst, Giulio Evola, Aldo Fiozzi, Théodore Fraenkel, Walter Mehring, Péret, Man Ray, Ribemont-Dessaignes, Rigaut, Soupault, Joseph Stella, Tzara and Vaché. There were also two unidentified pieces and three works done in collaboration by Breton and Fraenkel, Tzara and Ribemont-Dessaignes, and Eluard and his wife Gala. Many of these works have disappeared, but contemporary reviews and the droll titles of such entries as Tzara's *Mon*, *Cher* and *Ami* indicate the humorous, inventive nature of the exhibition.[49]

The first manifestation at the "Salon Dada," a soirée on June 10, was also a success, but the matinees scheduled for June 18 and 30 never opened.[50] During the month of June, Jacques Hébertot, director of the Théâtre des Champs-Elysées, had scheduled several performances in the theater, two of them by *bêtes noires* of the dadaists—a concert of bruitist music by the Italian futurists on June 17 and Jean Cocteau's *Mariés de la Tour Eiffel* on the eighteenth. Such an opportunity could not be neglected, and Russolo's presentation of bruitist music was disrupted by a howling band of dadaists with Tzara at the forefront. Hébertot, mindful of the dadaists' reception of Marinetti in January, had anticipated trouble, and when Tzara did not accept Hébertot's invitation to leave the hall, a gendarme was stationed beside him and he was informed that the "Salon Dada" was closed as of that moment.[51] When the dadaists reached the theater on the following afternoon to present their matinee, the doors were indeed locked. Having nothing more to lose, they returned that very evening and disrupted Cocteau's *Mariés de la Tour*

48. The absence of the Crottis was probably a result of their close friendship with Picabia, although they had recently concluded a major exhibition of their works in the same gallery. Crotti assisted Tzara as an intermediary, eliciting Duchamp's famous response: "PODE BAL" (Duchamp telegram to Crotti, June 1, 1921, C.T. 1249). Of all the German dadaists, only those in Cologne—Arp, Ernst and Baargeld—were on friendly terms with Tzara and Breton and contributed to the Salon.

49. Contemporary description of the exhibition was provided by Asté d'Esparbès ("Le Vernissage de l'exposition Dada," *Comoedia* [Paris], June 7, 1921, 2).

50. Within the varied program of the soirée, the most successful numbers were Soupault's impersonation of the President of Liberia visiting the Salon, Tzara's "Coeur à gaz" and the singing of M. Jolibois, a genuine itinerant mender of china who advertised his trade by chanting in the streets. See Jean Jacquemont, "Chronique parisienne," *Le Petit Havre*, June 14, 1921 (attrib.; D.P. VII, 209), and Sanouillet, *Dada à Paris*, 280–83. Breton did not take part, and in his *Entretiens 1913–1952*, 70, called it a fiasco, although most of the dadaists disagreed with that assessment.

51. Pierre Scize, "Après le concert des bruiteurs," *Bonsoir* [Paris], June 20, 1921, 3.

Eiffel. Throughout the performance dadaists stationed at various points in the theater continually stood up and sat down, shouting "Vive Dada."[52] However, at a post-performance party those dadaists were chagrined to find themselves mixed with scores of artists, poets, philosophers, musicians, socialites and critics they deemed insufferable, including members of the troop of the *Mariés*, Marinetti and the futurists.[53]

The dadaists were more than chagrined when Picabia celebrated his recent independence with a special issue of *391* (no. 15, July 1921) in which they were subjected to intolerable insults (see illus. 23). That issue, entitled *Le Pilhaou-Thibaou*, included no visual material but some of the most entertaining texts in the history of *391*. Picabia, writing under the pseudonym "Funny-Guy," was joined by Cocteau, Dermée, Ezra Pound, Clément Pansaers, Pierre de Massot, Satie, Crotti, Serner, Duchamp, Auric, Arnauld and others—in brief, a large cast of dissident dadaists who had also left the movement, or friends, like Cocteau and Pound, who had never been part of it. The content of many of the texts is correspondingly anti-Dada, but in Picabia's freewheeling style he opposed a statement needling Ribemont-Dessaignes with an anti-Picabia statement by Ribemont-Dessaignes, and simultaneously praised Cocteau as a person while ridiculing his *Mariés de la Tour Eiffel*. As Picabia noted in an open letter to Cocteau: "My metamorphoses, my dear Jean, irritate those who surround me and my 'screw myself' scandalizes those who are not with me."[54]

Le Pilhaou-Thibaou would not go unanswered, but for several reasons the dadaists did not counterattack immediately. To begin with, Picabia—who was usually brazen about his printed attacks—did not distribute *Le Pilhaou-Thibaou* promptly, and even then sent a copy only to Soupault.[55] By that time Tzara had left Paris for a visit to Czechoslovakia and, later, a vacation with Arp and Ernst in the Tyrolean Alps. Breton, though furious with Picabia, was preoccupied with his impending marriage and again despondent over the directionlessness of his activities; indeed, instead of using *Littérature* to attack Picabia, Breton suspended publication of the journal with the August issue. The battle would not be engaged until the fall.

52. See the *New York Herald* ("Sidelights of Paris, 'Mariés de la Tour Eiffel' " [Paris], June 22, 1921, 2); Jean Cocteau ("Les Mariés de la Tour Eiffel," *L'Esprit nouveau*, no. 10, Paris, July 1921); Sanouillet (*Dada à Paris*, 284–85).

53. Pierre de Massot, "Post-scriptum aux Mariés de la Tour Eiffel," *Le Pilhaou-Thibaou* (Paris, July 10, 1921, 14; no. 15 of *391*).

54. Francis Picabia, "Chef-d'oeuvre," *Le Pilhaou-Thibaou* (Paris, July 10, 1921, 5; no. 15 of *391*). Picabia subtitled this issue "Illustrated Supplement of *391*," apparently because it had no illustrations. The significance of the title remains undiscovered. The pseudonym "Funny-Guy," used frequently for awhile after this date, was a nickname given Picabia by Gleizes while they were in New York.

55. Soupault letter to Tzara, July 28, 1921 (C.T. 3822; Sanouillet, *Dada à Paris*, 289, as July 25, 1921).

12. PICABIA THE ANTI-DADA DADAIST; NEW CONFLICTS AND PROJECTS, 1921-1922

AS the second dada season closed in June 1921 amidst a flurry of activities and defections, the direction of Dada in Paris was an unknown of rather dubious prospects. As a movement, Dada was essentially finished there, but that was not yet fully apparent. Moreover, the spirit of Dada flourished as keenly as ever in certain individuals, Man Ray's arrival in July injected some new life and Picabia's irritating *Pilhaou-Thibaou* assured that the confusing array of dadaists, anti-dadaists and former dadaists would reengage each other after the summer recess.

In the meantime, a rejuvenating summer was enjoyed by all. In July, Tzara, Arp, Ernst, their wives and girl friends gathered for a vacation in the Tyrolean Alps. André and Simone Breton joined them following their marriage in mid-September, and the Eluards arrived a short time later.[1] As for Picabia, he began writing articles for *Comoedia*, and basked in the light of some eulogistic articles, especially one by Ezra Pound who called him a "sort of Socratic or anti-Socratic vacuum cleaner" whose "mental sensitivity" was comparable to that of Dante.[2] Francis and Germaine also spent an idyllic vacation with Marthe Chenal at her estate in Villers-sur-Mer, dining frequently with Baron Henri de Rothschild on his yacht in Honfleur harbor as they planned a neo-dada musical for the fall. Enthusiastic plans for the musical, "Les Yeux chauds" (Hot Eyes), subsided without explanation, but the title "Les Yeux chauds" and Picabia's interest in popular entertainment would reappear in new forms.[3]

1. Tzara left Paris about July 20 to visit Maya Chrusecz in Czechoslovakia. Toward the end of August they went to Tarrenz (near Innsbruck), where they were soon joined by Arp and Ernst. André and Simone Breton reached Tarrenz ca. September 20; Paul and Gala Eluard arrived ca. October 1. See Michel Sanouillet, *Dada à Paris* (Paris, 1965), 287–88.

2. Ezra Pound, "Literature Abroad," *The Literary Review* [London], August 13, 1921, 7.
Picabia wrote two articles for *Comoedia* during the summer, and beginning in November 1921 he contributed monthly articles until the death of his friend and editor of *Comoedia*, Georges Casella, in May 1922.

3. Marthe Chenal announced the production of "Les Yeux chauds" in *Comoedia* [Paris], August 17, 1921, and in *La Vie parisienne* (Anon. "Air nouveau," September 3, 1921, 751). In an

Arp, Ernst and Tzara were more successful with their summer project, the unique issue of *Dada au grand air*, which served in part as the celebration of their summer together and in part as a means for Tzara to repay Picabia for comments published in *Comoedia* and *Le Pilhaou-Thibaou*.[4] In response to Picabia's claim that he and Duchamp had invented Dada, Tzara wrote: "A friend from New York tells us that he knows a literary pickpocket; his name is Funiguy [*sic*], celebrated moralist . . . Funiguy [*sic*] invented dadaism in 1899, cubism in 1870, futurism in 1867 and impressionism in 1856. In 1867 he met Nietzsche, in 1902, he remarked that it was only the pseudonym of Confucius."[5]

Arp joined the attack with his droll and frequently cited statement on the origin of the word "dada":

> I declare that Tristan Tzara found the word DADA on February 8, 1916, at 6 in the evening; I was present with my 12 children when Tzara pronounced for the first time this word which has aroused in us such legitimate enthusiasm. This took place at the Café Terrasse in Zurich and I wore a brioche in my left nostril. I am convinced that this word has no significance, and that only imbeciles and Spanish professors can be interested in dates. What interests us is the Dada spirit and we were all Dada before the existence of Dada. The first Holy Virgins I painted date from 1886 when I was a few months old and amused myself by pissing graphic impressions. The morality of idiots and their belief in geniuses make me shit.[6]

Breton and his bride reached Tarrenz just before the departure of Arp, Ernst and Tzara, but too late to contribute to *Dada au grand air*, which Tzara carried back to Paris in manuscript form at the end of September. When the Eluards arrived later still, only the Bretons remained. The two young couples vacationed there for most of October, but, at Breton's suggestion, they visited Vienna in order for him to meet Freud, and, at Eluard's suggestion, they returned to Paris via Cologne to meet Max Ernst.[7] When Breton and Eluard finally reached Paris in

undated letter of about August 1921, Igor Stravinsky's secretary wrote Picabia that Stravinsky was interested in the project (D.P. VII, 343). About this time Gabrielle Buffet was living in the home of Mme Stravinsky. Picabia and Chenal also sought to buy a theater with some assistance from Cocteau (letter from Cocteau to Picabia, August 18, 1921, D.P. VII, 362), and apparently some financial backing from Baron Rothschild, but the projects collapsed (letter from Ribemont-Dessaignes to Tzara, September 17, 1921, C.T. 3268).

4. *Dada au grand air* (subtitled *Der Sängerkrieg in Tirol*) was dated September 16, 1921, and printed in Paris during October. It is sometimes considered the last issue (no. 8) of *Dada*.

5. Tristan Tzara, "Net," *Dada au grand air* (Paris, September 16, 1921, 1; no. 8 of *Dada*).

6. Hans Arp, "Déclaration," *Dada au grand air* (Paris, September 16, 1921, 3; no. 8 of *Dada*).

7. The Bretons and Eluards were in Vienna ca. October 6–10, 1921. From then until early November they were again in Imst (near Tarrenz). The week of November 4–10 was spent in Cologne, and ca. November 12 they were in Paris (chronology based on Eluard's letters to Tzara) from September 22 to November 13, 1921 (C.T. 1339–46; Sanouillet, *Dada à Paris*, 289). Breton's disappointing interview with Freud was presented in the first issue of the second series of *Littérature* (Paris, March 1922, 19).

November, Tzara had already distributed *Dada au grand air*, and Picabia had struck back with his "Funny-Guy Handbill" (illus. 24) passed out by the thousands on the steps of the 1921 Salon d'Automne. That scintillating example of Picabia's "I screw myself" technique disarmed the invectives of Arp and Tzara, but it was essentially aimed at a small group, whereas his paintings at the Salon d'Automne, *Les Yeux chauds (Hot Eyes)* and *L'Oeil cacodylate* (fig. 197; color pl. XI), agitated a vast audience.

Frantz Jourdain, president of the Salon d'Automne, had worked to eliminate the discriminatory treatment and raucous publicity which had accompanied the dadaists at the Salons of 1919 and 1920. To the astonishment of everyone, Picabia was elected a member of the Salon committee for 1921, all dadaist paintings were moved from under the stairway into a major room visible from the entrance of the Grand Palais and Jourdain talked to reporters about the Salon's motto of "Evolve or perish."[8] Those generous gestures cost him dearly, for unpredictable events worked against accommodation, and Picabia's entries became notorious even before the opening of the Salon. It began when, according to one journalist, "The rumor went around that M. Picabia would send to the Salon an explosive painting. Immediately anxiety was at its peak. M. Picabia . . . would he adopt direct action and brutally suppress all the philistines of the earth? One feared it."[9] In fact, so many people took the rumor literally that Jourdain finally had to reassure the public that there was no danger. After conducting an investigation, he wrote a major newspaper, *L'Intransigeant*, "I would be grateful if you will let the public know that there is nothing to fear from the explosive painting of Picabia. All the paintings have been carefully inspected and none appeared suspicious. Visitors may therefore proceed to the vernissage of our Salon in total security."[10]

That publicity multiplied when the former fauve painter Kees Van Dongen picked a public quarrel with Picabia and the Salon. The fashionable Van Dongen had insisted on exhibiting three portraits, but the hanging committee, faced with numerous entries and limited space, refused him more than the two items normally permitted for associates of the Salon. He thereupon denounced the committee as a bunch of "art bolsheviks" who had submitted to the "hypnotic influence" of Picabia.[11] Picabia denied such influence, but aggravated the situation by calling Van Dongen's rejected portrait of beautiful Maria Ricotti "a monstrosity. . . . a libel of a lovely woman [that] ought to be destroyed," and an American correspondent described the aftermath as the "greatest art war of the century" with "hundreds of prominent artists" threatening "to withdraw their paintings."[12]

8. Anon., "Paris Autumn Salon," *Morning Post* [London], October 31, 1921 (attrib.). The location of the dadaist paintings is commented on by Ch. Gir., in "La Foire aux croûtes," *Paris-Journal*, ca. November 1921 (attrib.; D.P. VII, 492–93). Picabia's membership on the Salon committee is cited in a press release by C.F. Bertelli, "Portrait Rejected for Salon, Bitter Art War Stirs Paris," dispatch (?) for *New York American*, October 28, 1921 (D.P. VII, old p. 254).

9. Anon., "L'Oeil cacodylate," *Le Rappel* [Paris], October 30, 1921, 3.

10. Frantz Jourdain, open letter in "Les Arts au Salon d'Automne," *L'Intransigeant* [Paris], October 13, 1921, 2.

11. Bertelli, "Portrait Rejected for Salon," *New York American*.   12. Ibid.

Les Yeux chauds (fig. 197), boldly inscribed "Thanks to the Salon d'Automne" and "Homage to Frantz Jourdain," was devoted to the new openness of the Salon toward Dada. Nevertheless, a suspicious audience and some mystifying forms and phrases precluded easy acceptance of that homage—apparently for good reason. Upon discovering that *Les Yeux chauds* was copied from a diagram for the governor of an airplane turbine (fig. 198), a contemporary journalist published the painting alongside its model with belittling remarks.[13] Picabia responded sarcastically, "I congratulate the newspaper *Le Matin* not only for having discovered the secrets, but for understanding them."[14] "To copy apples, that is comprehensible to everyone, to copy a turbine, that's idiotic."[15] Despite that journalist's discovery, several interpretive efforts came nowhere near Picabia's probable symbolism. Wanting statements from the artist, speculation is necessary, but in the context of Picabia's mechanomorphic work, the identification of Frantz Jourdain with the governor of a flying machine does not seem accidental, and the inscription, "The Onion Makes for Strength," is likely a simple reference to the attention accorded something (someone) with a strong odor.[16]

The companion piece of *Les Yeux chauds*, *L'Oeil cacodylate* (color pl. XI) was a large painting/collage done in collaboration with about fifty friends (and a few enemies) as they dropped by the apartment. Each was invited to take his turn at the canvas, which was eventually covered with a scattering of collage elements, signatures, puns, doodles, aphorisms and greetings by a veritable who's who among the artists, writers, musicians and entertainers in Paris during 1921—Tristan Tzara, Marcel Duchamp, Jean Cocteau, Darius Milhaud, Gabrielle Buffet, Isadora Duncan, Francis Poulenc, Fatty, Marthe Chenal, the Fratelli clowns, Jean Metzinger, Jean Crotti, Georges Auric, Paul Poiret, Georges Casella and others.[17] One critic called Picabia a "realist" who exhibited the "interior of a pissoir," on which one opening-night guest did not hesitate to add some "uncivil judgments" regarding some of "our more respectable senators."[18] Frivolous criticism and uninvited graffiti notwithstanding, *L'Oeil cacodylate* survived to reign over the chic bar of Paris, Le Boeuf sur le Toit, and Picabia published under the same title, "L'Oeil cacodylate," one of his most direct, revealing statements:

13. Anon., "La Turbine et le Dada," *Le Matin* [Paris], November 9, 1921, 1.

14. Francis Picabia, open letter, *Le Matin* [Paris], November 10, 1921, 1.

15. Francis Picabia, "L'Oeil cacodylate," *Comoedia* [Paris], November 23, 1921, 2.

16. A facetious theory involving a play on "onion" and "union" was offered by Etienne Bricon, "Salon d'Automne," *Le Gaulois* [Paris], November 5, 1921, 4.

17. The prominent eye in the lower right quadrant, the title, Picabia's signature, date and perhaps the photograph of his head are by Picabia's hand. Presumably everything else is by Picabia's friends. A few additions were made to *L'Oeil cacodylate* after it was reproduced in November 1921 (see Picabia, "L'Oeil cacodylate," *Comoedia*, 2), namely, three small collage heads in the upper center, and the inscription by Fatty in the upper right quadrant.

Cacodylate (used for Picabia's eye trouble in the spring of 1921) is an acid salt, a combination of methyl and arsenic giving off noxious fumes, used as a medicine in the treatment of tuberculosis, malaria and skin diseases.

18. Jean Varé, "Visite au Salon d'Automne," *Le Canard enchaîné* [Paris], November 9, 1921, 2.

The painter makes a choice, then imitates his choice so that the deformation constitutes *the Art*; the choice, why not simply sign it, in place of making like a monkey before it? There are certainly enough accumulated paintings, and the sanctioning signature of artists, uniquely sanctioners, would give a new value to art works destined for modern mercantilism. . . . This canvas was finished when there was no longer space on it, and I find this painting very beautiful . . . it is perhaps that all of my friends are artists just a bit![19]

In another passage in this article, Picabia made clearer still his rejection of Grand Art in favor of an art wholly responsive to life: "Me, I would like to found a 'paternal' school to discourage young people from what our good snobs call Art with a capital 'A.' Art is everywhere, except with the dealers of Art, in the temples of Art, like God is everywhere, except in the churches. . . . Look, boredom is the worst of maladies and my great despair would be precisely to be taken seriously, to become a great man, a master."[20]

Picabia had no worries on those counts. It is true that since 1919 he had been considered the chief of a small group of dada artists in Paris, but by the end of 1921, that group no longer existed. Ribemont-Dessaignes had almost abandoned painting, choosing instead (partly for financial reasons) to write quietly in the suburbs; Charchoune was developing a personal style based on Cubism, and the Crottis, who exhibited alongside Picabia at the 1921 Salon d'Automne, introduced on that occasion a two-man movement called "Tabu-Dada."[21] Their paintings, *Chainless Mystery* and *Masterpiece: Accordion* (figs. 199, 200) were unfortunately overwhelmed by their scandalous neighbors, and some authors have tended to view Tabu as merely a facetious offshoot of Dada. Picabia, however, was proud to claim it as a child of Dada, and Crotti acknowledged that parentage while stressing that Tabu was a new movement and a serious one. Indeed, he called it "a philosophical religion. . . . Up to this time the arts have all been sensual, as have religions. We no longer wish to produce an art for the body but for the mind. We wish through forms, through colors, through it matters not what means, to express the mystery, the divinity of the universe, including all mysteries."[22]

Chainless Mystery (fig. 199), called the first attempt at plastic Tabu, characterizes much of Crotti's work through 1922: delicate geometrical abstractions suggestive of views of the cosmos, of planets, orbits, particles and trajectories. His statements, poems and drawings suggest a vague symbolism of form and color, particularly in ubiquitous circles variously associated with eyes, the human head, radio-wave diagrams and other phenomena. This practice is commensurate with our knowledge of Crotti's preceding work under the influence of Duchamp and

19. Picabia, "L'Oeil cacodylate," *Comoedia*, 2.   20. Ibid.

21. The Crottis had used the word "Tabu" on the cover of their exhibition at the Galerie Montaigne in April 1921. Jean Crotti had also used it in a poem, "Sous-entendu," in *Le Pilhaou-Thibaou* (Paris, July 10, 1921, 3; no. 15 of *391*), but the "official" presentation of Tabu, complete with handbill, occurred at the 1921 Salon d'Automne.

22. Jean Crotti, "Tabu," *The Little Review*, VIII, no. 2 (New York, spring 1922), 45.

Picabia, but it is possible that in 1921–1922 Crotti reversed the roles, suggesting the spare astronomical diagrams and wave patterns which figure prominently in Picabia's work of 1922.[23]

While the Crottis, Ribemont-Dessaignes and Charchoune were moving away from dadaist art, one of its finest representatives, the American Man Ray, settled in Paris. He arrived on July 14, 1921, an inauspicious time with the dadaists divided, demoralized and about to disperse for the summer. However, Duchamp introduced him to the crowd at the Certà, and the dada loyalists were so impressed by Man Ray's work that plans began for an exhibition in December. They may have seen him as another challenger to Picabia's continued domination of dadaist art in Paris, but Man Ray also maintained cordial relations with Picabia who, along with Gabrielle Buffet, helped to start him off as an artist and photographer in Paris.[24]

Man Ray's exhibition, the first dada event of the winter, was well publicized, equipped with an interesting catalogue and topped off with an entertaining vernissage.[25] The preparation was justified by a fascinating exhibit of paintings, drawings, collages and constructions (see fig. 201) which was well-attended, including a visit from Picabia, who toured the opening with Man Ray while studiously ignoring all his former dadaist colleagues. But critical attention and sales were pitifully slight, and from that point onward Man Ray found it necessary to rely primarily on photography to earn a living. The results for photography were happy ones since he brought to it the talent and inventiveness evident in his dada assemblages.

While the dada loyalists were cavorting at the Man Ray exhibition, Picabia and Marthe Chenal were planning a New Year's Eve celebration called the "Réveillon cacodylate." With the aim of mingling their personal friends from the diverse fields of French officialdom, arts, letters and entertainment, Chenal and Picabia assembled a guest list that included such contemporaries as M. and Mme Picasso, Léonce Rosenberg, Deputy Henry Pathé, Senator Lederlin, Prince Rospigliosi, Baronness Jeanne Double, Jean Cocteau, Ezra Pound, Georges Auric, Ambroise Vollard, Brancusi and Paul Poiret. Picabia reveled in such freewheeling parties, taking mischievous delight in the amusing encounters—some of which he set up by misidentifying his friends to co-host Marthe Chenal.[26]

Such merrymaking preceded one of the most productive years for Picabia as painter, writer, polemicist and celebrity. Although poetry declined sharply in his

23. Crotti's symbolic use of forms and colors is most clearly expressed in the poems and drawings of his *Courants d'air sur le chemin de ma vie, 1916–1921* (Paris, 1941), engravings after Crotti by Jacques Villon. The poem "Tabu-Dada" in this volume indicates Crotti had the inspiration for Tabu in Vienna during February 1921.

24. See Man Ray, *Self Portrait* (Boston, 1963), 107–112.

25. Librairie Six, Paris, *Exposition Man Ray*, December 3–31, 1921, with statements by Aragon, Arp, Eluard, Ernst, Ribemont-Dessaignes, Soupault, Tzara and Man Ray. It was a retrospective exhibition of thirty-five works from 1914 to 1921.

26. See L.H., "Le Réveillon cacodylate," *Comoedia* [Paris], January 2, 1922, 3, and Germaine Everling, *L'Anneau de Saturne* (Paris, 1970), 138–40.

interests during 1921–1922, he wrote numerous articles for newspapers and journals and exercised his polemical gifts in the spectacular quarrels over Breton's Congress of Paris. At the same time, painting once more became a major activity for him, and during 1922 tumultuous controversies swirled around some of the outstanding works of his career exhibited at the Salon des Indépendants, the Salon d'Automne and a one-man show in November at the Barcelona gallery of his old friend José Dalmau.

The uproar over Picabia's entries to the 1922 Salon des Indépendants, *La Veuve joyeuse (The Merry Widow)*, *Chapeau de paille? (Straw Hat?)* and *Danse de Saint-Guy* (figs. 202–204) may have exceeded that at the Armory Show. In each of these works, Picabia's inimitable penmanship and impertinence attained a level that characterizes the best of his dada art. *La Veuve joyeuse* is an unprimed canvas bearing two simple forms. Above, glued to the canvas, is a signed and dated Man Ray photograph of Picabia at the wheel of his handsome Mercer. It is studiously labeled "Photograph." Below is Picabia's drawing after the photograph clearly labeled "Drawing." The whole was completed by the addition of the title in the upper left and Picabia's signature and date in the lower right corner. The visual-intellectual pitting of "art" and photography is a wordless delight, augmented by a title which, as usual, poses teasing questions of intent. Who or what is the "merry widow"—painting (*la* peinture)? photography (*la* photographie)? the machine (*la* machine)? The possibilities are as delightful as the liberating, antiart qualities of the work itself.[27]

Like *La Veuve joyeuse*, *Chapeau de paille?* (fig. 203) is a collection of curious inscriptions and collage elements on an unprimed canvas. The pasted parts consist of an invitation to the "Réveillon cacodylate," linked by a clumsily arranged cord to one of Picabia's calling cards cut in a heart shape. The composition was completed by the addition of the title and an inscription scrawled diagonally across the canvas, "M . . . . . . for he who looks at it!" As will be seen later, the uncompleted word invited spectator participation which contributed several theories relevant (or irrelevant?) to the content.

The original form of *Danse de Saint-Guy*, possibly a construction of about 1919–1921, is documented by a contemporary photograph (fig. 204) and reviews which identify the inscriptions as "Tobacco," "I am going to bed" and "What beautiful sun."[28] *Danse de Saint-Guy* may have been conceived initially as part of

27. Speculation should also include Franz Lehar's operetta, *The Merry Widow*, written in 1905, performed in Paris and surely known to Picabia, who counted numerous musicians and composers among his friends since his marriage to Gabrielle Buffet in 1909.

28. The inscriptions were recorded by Ellen Prevot, in "Au Salon des Indépendants, Loufoqueries," *Le Midi* [Toulouse], February 19, 1922, 1.

Danse de Saint-Guy could have been made as early as 1919–1920, for in a letter to Picabia on February 15, 1920 (D.P. V, 35; Sanouillet, *Dada à Paris*, 507), Breton apologized about laughing at a "tableau en cordes." Picabia's stage design for the "Manifestation Dada" on March 27, 1920, also seems related to such wire-and-cardboard constructions. Sometime before its exhibition at the Galerie René Drouin in Paris (*491, 50 ans de plaisir*) in 1949, *Danse de Saint-Guy* acquired a new title, *Tabac-Rat*, and a new composition (fig. 205) when Picabia rearranged the old, loose cords

a larger assemblage announced in advance by Picabia: "At the Indépendants, I count on exhibiting white mice, living sculpture; a guard will be next to them to sell bread to the public in order to assure the life of these little animals indispensable to my work."[29] An anonymous critic elaborated on the work: "A frame— gilded? one still does not know—but grilled like a cage. Behind the trellis will be fastened on the wall a sheet-iron wheel of a thickness suitable for white mice to activate in the manner of squirrels. Very proud of his painting (?), Mr. Picabia has already informed the Committee that he will post, at his expense, a guard— braided?—charged with receiving gifts of bread crumbs from the public."[30]

Since no such construction was submitted, Picabia may have intended only to harass the Salon. If so, he wasted his time, for the Salon committee itself went out of its way to provoke a public controversy. On January 17 Picabia received a letter from the Société des Artistes Indépendants signed by the president, Paul Signac, and the secretary general:

> Monsieur,
>
> I have the honor to inform you that the work you present to the Société des Artistes Indépendants under the title *Chapeau de paille* as well as the one containing a photograph, not coming within the categories of works admitted to the Exhibition, have made the Committee decide not to authorize the hanging of these two works.[31]

Picabia immediately posted open letters to several papers. He informed them of the rejection of his work, described the works and asked that the papers register his protest against the unprecedented action of the committee in refusing— at a jury-free salon—two works that were in no way pornographic.[32] Reporters sought out Signac, who showed them the rejected entries and made the following statement:

> We have not judged . . . if that is painting or not. We are content to apply the rule. Article 12 declares that photographs cannot be accepted, and article 13, that the committee reserves rights in the matter of works which pose a question of publicity or of impropriety: "La Veuve joyeuse" is simply the portrait of M. Picabia, and "Chapeau de paille" carries this inscription: "M . . . . for he who looks at it." M. Picabia pretends that M . . . . means

---

(conversation with Mme Olga Picabia, July 1968). Despite these changes in its form, Picabia insisted that *Tabac-Rat* be suspended away from the wall in order for movement and transparency to become elements of the work (see Georges Charbonnier, *Le Monologue du peintre*, Paris, 1959, 136).

29. Picabia, "L'Oeil cacodylate," *Comoedia*, 2.

30. Anon., "Ce que l'on dit," *Echo de Paris*, December 17, 1921, 2.

31. Paul Signac letter to Picabia, January 17, 1922 (D.P. VIII, 110; Y. Poupard-Lieussou and M. Sanouillet, eds., *Documents Dada*, Paris, 1974, 76).

32. See Picabia's open letters in *Comoedia* [Paris], January 19, 1922, 3, and in the *New York Herald* [Paris], January 19, 1922, 3. In each letter he claimed that "M . . . . for he who looks at it" should read "Merci for he . . . "

"merci." For us, that resembles a . . . mural in the hall of a military barracks. . . . We do not want the government to refuse us the Grand Palais next year. Already, last year M. Picabia caused us an interpellation at the Chamber [of Deputies]. We do not care to repeat the experience. . . . we are hardly disposed to tolerate excesses which can only discredit or dishonor our Salon.

Isn't it something scandalous to see more than three hundred francs of canvas wasted like that, when so many artists have unheard of difficulties to live?

. . . M. Picabia can do whatever he wants against us, we do not fear it.[33]

Signac stood firm; only *Danse de Saint-Guy* was exhibited at the Salon, and the battle raged on. Picabia responded to Signac's statement with one of his better one-liners, "A novelty, which lasts only five minutes, is better than an immortal work that bores everyone,"[34] and with a biting open letter in *Comoedia*:

Dear Monsieur Signac,

I always have with me a little frame, in gilded wood, through which I contemplate sunsets; today it serves me to look at you, you and the Société des Indépendants . . .

The publicity which is going around me, it seems to me that it's you who create it. I had no desire to be refused at the Indépendants . . . yes I make paintings so that people may talk about them and also to sell them; you, you make them so that no one talks about them and without doubt only with museums in view.

As for the reproach people make about my being too rich, understand that I am enough of a profiteer to propose that you exchange your revenues against mine, but look out, it would be a bad affair for you and you would be quickly obliged to live solely by the product of your works. . . .

Francis Picabia
Cord Master[35]

Picabia hit harder still in a popular magazine[36] and in a stinging handbill distributed at the doors of the Salon. On one side of the handbill was a reproduc-

33. Interview with Paul Signac quoted by R. Cogniat, "Pourquoi M. Signac a refusé 2 toiles à M. Picabia," *Comoedia* [Paris], January 21, 1922, 2.

34. G. Ch., "M. Paul Signac, M. Francis Picabia et Dada," *Le Figaro* [Paris], January 20, 1922, 3.

35. Francis Picabia, open letter to Paul Signac, *Comoedia* [Paris], January 23, 1922, 3.

36. Francis Picabia, "Sur les bords de la scène," *Les Potins de Paris*, February 3, 1922, 1:

"Messieurs the independent artists, you are a pompous bunch [*tas de pompiers*], . . . and the only way to get rid of your independent works would be to call the nightmen! . . .

"Everything is art: Love is art; to offer a cup of tea is art, . . . Lhote, natural son of Maurice Denis and Picasso, makes art, but I prefer the paintings of Boechlin; . . . Léger makes art, but I prefer the cider of Normandy."

tion of Signac's letter rejecting the two works; on the other side was the following statement:

> The Salon des Indépendants is no longer independent!!! It has refused two paintings by Francis Picabia!
>
> The Salon des Indépendants has for its president a man who had himself decorated with the Legion of Honor with the title artist-painter!
>
> Well, the motto of the Independents is "neither jury, nor awards!" The Salon des Indépendants becomes very "Salon d'Automne." The Salon d'Automne has become "the National." The National has become the "Salon des Artistes Français." The Salon des Artistes Français has become shit!!! One must found a new Salon which will become . . . ??? The two rejected paintings are exhibited at the bar Moysès, 28, rue Boissy-d'Anglas, for the duration of the exhibition of the Independents.

Few newspapers or magazines with a column on the arts refrained from entering the fray. A handful of critics sided with Picabia, generally defending the principle of his right to exhibit at the Salon rather than the artistic merit of the rejected works.[37] However, hostile critics and cartoonists were far more numerous. One observed simply, "Life has reserved two joys for me this week . . . The first has been to learn that they refused the canvases of M. Picabia at the Salon des Indépendants."[38] But most critics were concerned about the inscription "M . . . . for he who looks at it!" and several of them—extending insinuations by Signac— suggested that the inscription should not read (as Picabia claimed) "Merci for he who looks at it!" but " 'Merde' for he who looks at it!"[39] Soon, of course, that speculation was reported as physical fact,[40] and the scandal rumbled on, covering in its dust some important dada works by Man Ray and the Tabu-Dada entries of the Crottis. A mere glance at their contributions to the Salon verifies the committee's vendetta against Picabia, for Crotti's *Explicative* (fig. 206) and Man Ray's *Boardwalk* (fig. 207) seem as vulnerable as Picabia's work to any purge based on "impropriety" and "noisy publicity." Picabia was one of the few to recommend their work at the Salon, thereby extending his importance to that of a critic as well as artist and prophet challenging the Salon to uphold its purpose. His earnestness in the latter capacity should not be belittled. Long after the heated exchanges of January, Picabia wrote an article on the Salon des Indépendants which, though still critical of the society, emphasized that it operated the only Salon in Paris which might remain truly independent—free of bonds that constricted the other respectability-conscious Salons. He urged the Indépendants to adhere to their

37. Jean Kols, "La Liberté dans l'art," *La Presse* [Paris], January 20, 1922, 1.

38. Odette Dulac, "Deux Joies," *Le Petit Bleu* [Paris], January 27, 1922, 1.

39. A. Gybal, "Le 'Truc' de M. Picabia," *Le Journal du peuple* [Paris], January 21, 1922, 2.

40. G. Maillot-Duparc, "Le Bon Truc . . . ," *Tribune* [Paris] (?), January 31, 1922 (attrib.; D.P. VIII, 225).

original ideals and called upon all independent artists not to forsake the Salon to the imbeciles.[41]

Eight months elapsed before Picabia again presented his work to the French public. In the meantime, he hardly dropped out of sight, given his role in the famous Congress of Paris and the numerous articles by or about him that appeared in French newspapers and periodicals.

On January 3, 1922, André Breton announced an "International Congress for the Determination of the Directions and the Defense of the Modern Spirit," the "Congress of Paris" by its short title.[42] It was to be organized for March 30, by seven presumably equal partners of the organization committee, Georges Auric, André Breton, Robert Delaunay, Fernand Léger, Amédée Ozenfant, Jean Paulhan and Roger Vitrac—but it was Breton's creation and everything about it suggested an utterly serious undertaking determined to bring together representatives of different arts and viewpoints in a quest for nothing less than the "modern spirit." In his announcement Breton stressed the openness of the Congress. Everyone was invited to participate who "attempts today, in the domain of art, science or life a new and disinterested effort," and he underscored that the "members of the Organization Committee . . . profess such diverse ideas that no one can suspect them of conspiring to limit the modern spirit to the profit of anyone." Breton concluded that with the collaboration of all interested parties "we may proceed to the confrontation of new values, we may render for the first time an exact account of present forces and we may be able at least to specify the nature of their result." When some complained that the aims and format of the Congress seemed too vague, a second press release was issued: "In order to fix the ideas here are two of the numerous questions which the Congress will examine: Has the modern spirit always existed? Among so-called modern objects, is a top hat more or less modern than a locomotive?"[43]

Breton's sponsorship of such a project must have surprised many of his contemporaries; even today it is difficult to comprehend his action without knowledge of his career from about 1916 through 1922. In that regard, Breton's statements during and soon after the Congress of Paris are exceptionally useful, not so much for the naively conceived and quickly aborted Congress itself, but for a better understanding of Breton and his uneasy relationship to Dada. In a later article penned as the proposed Congress was beginning to crash in upon him, Breton wrote that he (and Eluard and Soupault) had never regarded Dada as anything but

41. Francis Picabia, "Le Salon des Indépendants," *L'Ere nouvelle* [Paris], September 20, 1922, 1–2.

42. [André Breton], "Avant le Congrès de Paris," *Comoedia* [Paris], January 3, 1922, 2. The most complete documentation for this enterprise is the "Dossier of the Congress of Paris" (Manuscript Room, Bibliothèque Nationale, Paris), a large scrapbook of letters, manuscripts and articles collected by Breton himself. Sanouillet (*Dada à Paris*, 319–47) presents a sound history of the Congress of Paris based on that indispensable dossier and also publishes several interesting documents in the appendix, pp. 572–75.

43. G. de la Fouchardière, "Hors d'oeuvre," *Oeuvre* [Paris], January 17, 1922 (attrib.).

"the rough image of a state of spirit that it by no means helped to create."[44] He added that the funeral of Dada had occurred "about May 1921" and that he had abstained from demonstrations organized at the Galerie Montaigne because he saw in such activities "a means of attaining my twenty-sixth, my thirtieth birthday without striking a blow. . . . It seems to me that the ratification of a series of utterly futile 'dada' acts is in the process of gravely compromising attempts at liberation to which I remain deeply attached."

Later in the year Breton spoke simply of what led him to propose the Congress: "I thought I had distinguished a minimum of common affirmation, and I burned to free from it a law of tendency for myself. . . . to consider successively cubism, futurism and Dada is to follow the flight of an idea which is now at a certain height and awaits only a new impulse to continue to describe the curve assigned to it."[45]

Such statements go far in clarifying the ambivalence that had dogged Breton's relationship to Dada. Before, during and after Dada, Breton had, in effect, searched for something that was too personal to be satisfied by Dada and too important to be sacrificed to its destructive energies.

Breton seems to have been driven by the desire to discover and liberate not only the essence of his being, but to determine the essence/direction of modern art and life, and, finally, to relate himself to those directing forces of contemporary life. Dada had been vitally important, but it was neither a permanent nor a desirable spirit for Breton. Like Lautréamont, Rimbaud, Vaché and Apollinaire, like Symbolism and Cubism, Dada had become part of the selected, honored past which had contributed to Breton's search for a liberated self in a comprehensible life. Pursuit of that shadowy, haunting goal had already caused him inner anguish and awkward relations with his dadaist friends; its extension into the Congress of Paris demolished what was left of the dada movement in Paris.

Immediately after announcement of the Congress, letters began to flow into Breton's office from both well-known and totally unknown figures scattered about western Europe.[46] Most of the dadaists also associated themselves with Breton, but hardly with enthusiasm for a project which on the face of it was a near parody of their previous aims and activities.

44. André Breton, "Après Dada," *Comoedia* [Paris], March 2, 1922, 2. Reprinted in Breton's *Les Pas perdus* (Paris, 1924; 8th ed., Paris, 1949, 123–27); trans. Ralph Manheim in Robert Motherwell, ed., *The Dada Painters and Poets* (New York, 1951), 204–206.

45. André Breton, "Caractères de l'évolution moderne et ce qui en participe," lecture at the Ateneo, Barcelona, November 17, 1922, on the occasion of Picabia's exhibition at the Galeries Dalmau, Barcelona, November 18–December 8, 1922. Printed in Breton's *Les Pas perdus*, 8th ed., 181–212 (quotes 187 and 192).

46. On January 6, a letter was received from Paul Dermée, Florent Fels, Georges Gabory, André Malraux and Robert Mortier—all of the magazine *Action*—expressing interest in the Congress. Roger Vitrac, editor of *Aventure* and a member of the organization committee of the Congress, automatically brought in some adherents, as did Jean Paulhan of *La Nouvelle Revue française*. Other letters were received from such men as Franz Hellens, director of *Signaux* in Brussels, Marinetti and Theo van Doesburg (see the "Dossier of the Congress of Paris," 14, 44, 49).

Not everyone joined, of course. Gide refused to have anything to do with the Congress, and Picabia, in his monthly article for *Comoedia*, denounced the organizers as "these Jesuits of 1922 . . . [who] have no ideas." "I have a horror of these organizations where the herd wants to lead the shepherd." He did note one condition under which the Congress would be interesting: "Undoubtedly this Congress of Paris would not displease me if my friend André Breton succeeded in throwing into the crucible all our 'celebrated modernists' . . . Unfortunately, Breton himself is not 'rough' ['*brut*'], also I fear that he will not succeed in his enterprise and that he will only come to aggravate the ugliness of some delicate scars."[47]

Within a few weeks, Picabia's fears were fulfilled, for the Congress became a disaster covered with the gore of warring dadaists, ex-dadaists and anti-dadaists. But as the battle lines were drawn, Picabia sided with Breton and the Congress party. That maneuver, stunning on its face, is comprehensible only after examination of the circumstances and the nature of Picabia's "subversive support" for Breton.

After Picabia's potentially damaging anti-Congress article appeared in *Comoedia*, Breton began to court him assiduously. He evidently secured at least a tenuous commitment of participation, for it was the prospect of Picabia's participation that sparked Tzara's opposition.[48] During a discussion of the Congress on February 1 (among Breton, Aragon, Eluard, Fraenkel, Rigaut, Vitrac, Soupault and Tzara), Tzara proclaimed that Picabia was wholly undesirable and expressed for the first time reservations about his own participation. On the following day Breton met with four members of the organization committee (Auric and Paulhan were absent) and secured approval for Tzara's addition to the committee—presumably in an effort to insure his commitment. This action was presented to Tzara on February 3, but later that same day he notified Breton by mail that he would not participate in the Congress. Tzara's letter was a model of courtesy and candor,[49] but Breton's account of Tzara's other activities on February 3 and 4 portray him as a malicious conspirator.[50] Furious with Tzara and fearful for his fragile project, Breton persuaded the members of the organization committee (all present but Paulhan) to release to the press an attack on Tzara coupled with a reaffirmation of the openness of the Congress to all movements:

47. Francis Picabia, "Trompettes de Jéricho," *Comoedia* [Paris], January 19, 1922, 1.

48. Breton asked to see Picabia on January 21 and was invited to come to the Picabias' apartment on January 27 (see Breton-Picabia correspondence in Sanouillet, *Dada à Paris*, 513).

As presented in this study, subsequent events relevant to the Congress up to February 10 are based on Breton's detailed account ("Dossier of the Congress of Paris," 36–38) published by Sanouillet (*Dada à Paris*, 331–32).

49. Tzara letter to Breton, February 3, 1922 ("Dossier of the Congress of Paris," 21; quoted in Sanouillet, *Dada à Paris*, 328–29).

50. According to Breton's account, Tzara sought during the evening of February 3 to enlist Picabia's help in demolishing the Congress. Picabia refused and revealed Tzara's overtures to Vitrac, Rigaut and Morise that same night. The next day, Tzara sought to persuade Vitrac and Delaunay that plans to attack the Congress had come from Picabia. That claim was undone the same day by a confrontation of Tzara and Picabia in the presence of Breton, Delaunay, Eluard, Vitrac and Pierre de Massot (see Breton's account in the "Dossier of the Congress of Paris," 36–38; Sanouillet, *Dada à Paris*, 331–32; Breton's statement is initialed in the margins by most of the witnesses to the events described).

. . . the undersigned, members of the organizing committee, hold their opinion in guard against the machinations of a personnage known as the promoter of a "movement" from Zurich, . . . which no longer responds today to any reality.

The committee takes this opportunity to guarantee again to each one, contrary to certain malevolent insinuations, complete liberty of action in the Congress. . . . What will not be permitted is only that the destiny of the enterprise be subject to the calculations of an impostor voracious for publicity.[51]

That intemperate condemnation provoked on the following day an unruffled reply from Tzara, "I did not think for a second that a refusal might be taken for a crime. . . . A few days ago, I was not yet an impostor voracious for publicity, since I was worthy of sitting in that noble conclave."[52] From that date onward Tzara worked openly against the Congress, and about a week later in another letter to the press he struck the note which rallied the majority to his side, "An 'international' congress which reproaches someone for being a foreigner no longer has a reason to exist."[53] That same day Eluard, Ribemont-Dessaignes, Satie and Tzara mailed letters (which later appeared in several newspapers) demanding a public hearing of the entire affair at the Closerie des Lilas on February 17.[54] Tzara had already asked that a hearing be conducted by Ozenfant, who had accepted the commission and requested in turn that both Tzara and Breton prepare statements about the incident.

At the Closerie des Lilas on February 17, Breton was censured as "the sole instigator of the communication in question." A resolution was also passed that condemned the organization committee for having exceeded its authority, and the meeting concluded with a declaration of no confidence signed by over forty men including Cocteau, Eluard, Satie, Ribemont-Dessaignes, Man Ray, Dermée, Brancusi and Metzinger.[55] After the publication of this resolution on February 18, a steady defection of supporters sapped what little life existed in the Congress of Paris.[56]

As usual, Picabia missed the major battles, having traveled to St. Raphael

51. Auric, Breton, Delaunay, Léger, Ozenfant and Vitrac, open letter, *Comoedia* [Paris], February 7, 1922, 1. The same letter was published several days later in other papers. It concluded with the announcement: "We learn that Francis Picabia has just given his adhesion to the Congress of Paris."

52. Tristan Tzara, "A propos du Congrès de Paris," *Comoedia* [Paris], February 8, 1922, 3.

53. Tristan Tzara, note dated February 10, 1922, quoted in "La Ville et les arts," *Paris-Midi*, February 14, 1922, 2.

54. Eluard, Ribemont-Dessaignes, Satie and Tzara, open letter dated February 14, 1922, published in *Comoedia* [Paris], February 20, 1922, 2.

55. These resolutions began to appear in Paris newspapers on February 18, 1922 (see the notice in *Le Journal du peuple* [Paris], February 22, 1922), and are published in Sanouillet (*Dada à Paris*, 334–35).

56. A severe blow fell on February 27, 1922, when Jacques Rivière wrote Breton ("Dossier of the Congress of Paris," 52; Sanouillet, *Dada à Paris*, 335–36) that personnel of *La Nouvelle Revue française* would no longer participate in the Congress.

around February 5 for a visit with an old friend, Christian (Georges Herbiet), that lasted about six weeks.[57] The efficacy of his support was accordingly reduced, and, moreover, it is impossible to overlook the fact that he served very personal and subversive ends, perhaps tolerated by Breton in lieu of any other support during a discouraging episode in his life.

Although Picabia seems to have made some commitment to Breton before February 1, he made no public statement until after the explosion between Breton and Tzara over February 3–5, and his statement at that time was probably made out of animosity toward Tzara rather than approval of the Congress. Indeed, only a towering disgust for Dada and all who strived to perpetuate it can account for Picabia's willingness to take part in anything so alien to his convictions as the Congress of Paris. Breton, at any rate, did not take Picabia's support for granted. His letters to Picabia in St. Raphael contain passages of almost obsequious praise: "You give me pleasure as I recall that I love you very much, that your example sustains me in life, and that in large measure I am at your disposal."[58]

To such adulation Picabia replied: "I am happy that we may be friends . . . we are several [Christian, Jean Crotti and Suzanne Duchamp-Crotti] whose regards are turned toward you, toward this 'Congress of Paris' which can become what we want . . . (we can say to all those people that we have united them in order to show them how useless it was to unite them!) and other things too."[59]

After the undisguised mockery of that opening paragraph, Picabia proceeded to rekindle Breton's spirit. He recommended new adherents to the Congress, viciously criticized its opponents and announced publication of a tract, *La Pomme de pins* (The Pine Cone), in support of the Congress. This tract (illus. 25), assembled in St. Raphael during February and distributed in Paris around March 5, is one of Picabia's most delightful "dadaist" publications.[60] It contained no articles, poems or reproductions, but a lively potpourri of puns, epithets, aphorisms, personal greetings and advertisements in some of the most whimsical layout and typography of the dada epoch. It is pro-Congress of Paris insofar as ridicule of its

57. Pierre de Massot was writing to Picabia in St. Raphael by February 9, 1922 (D.P. VIII, 251, mistakenly dated "1921" by de Massot); Breton's letters to Picabia on March 13 and 26, 1922, indicate he returned to Paris during those dates (D.P. VIII, 278, 546; Sanouillet, *Dada à Paris*, 517–18).

The Crottis, Roland Dorgeles, his wife Hania Routchine and Christian were together with Picabia in St. Raphael. Christian (Georges Herbiet, 1895–1969) was a writer, literary critic and painter who was one of Picabia's closer friends from 1919 to about 1928. From 1920 to 1923 he operated a bookstore, Au Bel Exemplaire, in St. Raphael (see Y. Poupard-Lieussou, "Christian 'Le Pélégrin dans l'ombre,'" *Cahiers Dada Surréalisme*, no. 3, Paris, 1969, 20–21).

58. Breton letter to Picabia, February 10, 1922 (D.P. VIII, 255; Sanouillet, *Dada à Paris*, 514). In this letter Breton asked Picabia to help him get an article published in *Comoedia*. The article, "Après Dada," which was published there on March 2, was pro-Picabia in thrust.

59. Picabia letter to Breton, February 17, 1922 ("Dossier of the Congress of Paris," 45; Sanouillet, *Dada à Paris*, 516–17).

60. Francis Picabia, ed., *La Pomme de pins* (St. Raphael, February 25, 1922). Reprinted by Sanouillet in *Francis Picabia et "391,"* II (Paris, 1966), 221–24.

The origin of the title was explained by Christian in a letter to Sanouillet, November 5, 1965

enemies (principally Tzara) establishes a theme against which the phrase "Congress of Paris" flashes like a blinking light. At the same time Picabia and his collaborators served themselves generously. Crotti's "Tabu-Dada" figures prominently on three of the four pages; Christian advertised his bookstore, Au Bel Exemplaire, and Picabia exercised all his whims and whipping posts. On page one a tiny greeting, "Bonjour Pound," is tucked under an appropriate aphorism, "Our head is round to permit our thought to change direction"; page two is dominated by an "end of the season sale of ideas at unprecedented prices"; God fares poorly on page three; and on the final page Cubism is called a "cathedral of shit" just above the statement "The Congress of Paris is fucked, Francis Picabia takes part in it."

Despite Picabia's subordination of the Congress to his own ends, Breton was somewhat encouraged and continued to fight for it in the cafés and in the pages of the new series of *Littérature* which reopened in March.[61] Opponents of the Congress, especially Tzara and Ribemont-Dessaignes, responded with important statements of their own, and Picabia's *La Pomme de pins* was answered tit for tat in *Le Coeur à barbe* (The Bearded Heart), published by Tzara and his friends in April.[62]

By that time the opening date of the Congress had passed without action. No major figure had ever shared Breton's commitment to the project, and as it evolved from a Congress on the "Directions and the Defense of the Modern Spirit" into a catharsis for Dada, the potential participants either withdrew or chose sides between the Breton and Tzara camps. During March, as Breton himself became despondent, neglected correspondence and failed to appear at meetings of the or-

---

(Sanouillet, op. cit., 257), and in an article (Christian, "Annales du pélican," *Cahiers Dada Surréalisme*, no. 2, Paris, 1968, 185–97, esp. 194–95). On the central table of Christian's bookstore was a pine cone, with head and feet (like Picabia's drawing on p. 1 of *La Pomme de pins*) and delicately balanced on a spring so that it bobbed at any disturbance. Christian and his friends amused themselves by consulting it about daily matters, and chose it for the brochure to manifest both the nonsense of the movement and the fact that Picabia, like the little creature in his drawing, had his feet on the ground.

61. *Littérature*, II, nos. 1–13 (Paris, March 1922–June 1924), directors André Breton and Philippe Soupault. Breton's "Lâchez tout," *Littérature*, II, no. 2 (Paris, April 1, 1922), 8–10, was a farewell to the turmoil of Dada and the Congress of Paris.

62. *Le Coeur à barbe*, no. 1 (Paris, April 1922), director Tzara, editor Ribemont-Dessaignes.

For Tzara see "Les Dessous de Dada," *Comoedia* [Paris], March 7, 1922. For Ribemont-Dessaignes see "La Cravate de Dada," *Le Journal du peuple* [Paris], February 10, 1922, 1; and "Les Greniers du Vatican," *Les Ecrits nouveaux* [Paris], February 1922 (attrib.; D.P. VIII, 364–68). In the former article, Ribemont-Dessaignes expressed political interests which had begun to be a concern for some dadaists during 1921. That condition was reflected in Picabia's article, "Bonheur moral et bonheur physique" (*Ça ira*, no. 16, Antwerp, November 1921, 98–101), where he belittled communism:

"I am against communism, against that idiot Lenin who makes of a general a soldier and of a soldier a general, which will come out exactly the same. . . .

"The only thing that interested me for an instant with the Russians was the Revolution, but that only lasted a few weeks and now they have the same 'bourgeoise family' spirit as here."

ganization committee, the Congress expired without lamentation.[63] As a group or movement in Paris, Dada died with it—strangled, appropriately enough, in doubt, bitterness and the incredible confusion of shifting values and alliances.

Dada, however, had exerted an enormous impact and left a limitless legacy. For two turbulent years it had captured the allegiance of a group of the most vital authors and artists of the epoch; it had attracted talented younger men and commanded influence and accommodation in the culture around it. Thereafter efforts to revive group action were few, strained and unsuccessful, but Dada as a spirit and a view of life was immortal. The major participants were haunted by it throughout their lives; in numerous publications from 1922 onward they seem compelled to address the movement and the spirit of Dada—not merely in defense of themselves or in opposition to a former colleague, but to assess for themselves the nature of their experience.

Some rejected and some savored that spirit as they understood it; for Picabia it was intrinsic to his life and art regardless of their surface appearances, and that spirit has continued to nourish an endless variety of kindred spirits from the generation of Rauschenberg, Johns, Ives Klein and Tinguely in the 1950s, through happenings, Pop and Minimal Art in the 1960s, into the currents of conceptual and ephemeral art of the early 1970s.

63. See Ozenfant's sad letter to Breton on April 5, 1922 ("Dossier of the Congress of Paris," 63; Sanouillet, *Dada à Paris*, 345–46):
"My dear friend,
I again waited for you in vain Monday. . . .
I believe . . . that the Congress no longer has any great attraction for you. . . . The Cabals have been more efficacious than we have wanted to admit."

13. A NEW HOME, NEW PROJECTS AND RENEWED PAINTING: FIGURATIVE ART AND THE LATE DADA-MACHINIST STYLE

THE DISINTEGRATION of the dada movement marked a watershed in Picabia's own life and career. The state of Dada alone hardly accounted for the changes which occurred; the causes were more complex and may best be suggested while examining the abundant evidence of change in Picabia's prodigious production as artist and author during 1922.

To some extent the patchwork of enmities and alliances established during the breakup of Dada continued to shape the events. Breton sought on several occasions to reunite the warring factions for new causes, but his efforts were futile, and for some time there remained a handful of former dadaists associated with Tzara, others in the orbit of Breton and Picabia, and a few who were independent or, like Ernst and Eluard, able to associate with both camps. Tzara seemed little disposed to any group activity;[1] Breton and Picabia, despite basic differences of temperament, strengthened their fragile rapprochement and embarked on new ventures.

They first had to resolve differences, apparently over a course of action in the aftermath of the Congress of Paris. For Picabia, the Congress had never been more than a handy vehicle for agitation, and he wanted to press the attack against Tzara and Ribemont-Dessaignes. Breton, however, had sustained a serious setback; he was depressed and disinclined to pursue any purely combative activity. "Let go of

---

1. Tzara did propose a second summer in the Tyrol which attracted the Eluards, the Ernsts, the Josephsons, Arp and Sophie Taeuber. From there, Arp and Tzara went to the Constructivist Congress in Weimar (September 1922) where Tzara, in addition to provoking a dadaist uproar, presented an important "Lecture on Dada" (published in *Merz*, II, no. 7, Hanover, January 1924, 68–70; trans. Ralph Manheim in Robert Motherwell, ed., *The Dada Painters and Poets*, New York, 1951, 246–51).

everything" was his response. "Let go of Dada . . . Let go of your hopes and fears . . . Let go of the need for an easy life . . . Set off on the routes."[2]

Another two years passed before Surrealism came into focus as Breton's goal along those routes, but within two months his spirit was revived by the persistent flickering of those shadowy goals and his imperious need for action. In mid-May the future course of *Littérature*, recently surrendered to his sole direction, became a cause for invigorating conversations.[3] He opened the magazine to Picabia without reservations and also introduced him to Jacques Doucet, who became a friend and important collector of Picabia's work.[4] That same month, when the death of Georges Casella eliminated their access to *Comoedia*, Picabia and Breton planned to found a newspaper.[5] Later in the year they labored to open a new Salon and traveled together to Barcelona, where Breton lectured on the occasion of an important exhibition of Picabia's new work at Dalmau's gallery.[6]

Throughout the year they visited frequently in each other's homes, and during the fall Picabia was a participant in Breton's experiments with spiritualism—another non-dada, proto-surrealist effort to probe or liberate the individual. René Crevel introduced spiritualism to the circle around Breton in September 1922, and Breton quickly recognized it as another important means—along with dreams and automatic writing—to bypass moral, rational and aesthetic barriers. Tzara and Soupault declined overtures for a rapprochement at that time, but Crevel, Robert Desnos, Péret, Max Morise and Eluard were keenly interested in the experiments. No participant in those seances has recalled that Picabia actually en-

2. André Breton, "Lâchez tout," *Littérature*, II, no. 2 (Paris, April 1, 1922), 8–10.

Breton's letter to Picabia on April 27, 1922 (D.P. VIII, 476; Sanouillet, *Dada à Paris*, Paris, 1965, 518–19), mentions their disagreements. In his own writings Picabia continued to lambast Tzara, Ribemont-Dessaignes and Philippe Soupault (see, for example, his article "Condoléances," *Littérature*, II, no. 6, Paris, November 1, 1922, 19), while Breton took a more conciliatory approach.

3. Despite disagreement over the Congress of Paris, Breton and Soupault had maintained relations sufficiently to work as coeditors for the second series of *Littérature* (March 1922–June 1924). However, Soupault could not tolerate Picabia, and, when Breton persisted in linking Picabia to *Littérature*, he resigned (interview with the author, June 10, 1974, and Breton letter to Picabia, undated [early May 1922], D.P. VIII, 622; Sanouillet, *Dada à Paris*, 520–21).

4. Breton had counseled Doucet on the purchase of modern art and literature since 1919, but there is no evidence that he introduced Doucet and Picabia before 1922 (see Breton's letter to Picabia in early May, D.P. VIII, 622; Sanouillet, *Dada à Paris*, 520–21). From then until 1927, Doucet and Picabia exchanged infrequent but friendly, informative letters now housed in the Bibliothèque Littéraire Jacques Doucet.

5. Picabia announced in an interview (see Jack Pencil, "Vacances d'artistes," *Le Figaro* [Paris], August 20, 1922, 2) that he and Breton planned to publish a newspaper entitled *La Vie*.

6. During a visit to Barcelona in late April–early May 1922, Francis and Germaine arranged the *Exposition Francis Picabia* held at the Galeries Dalmau from November 18 to December 8, 1922. Breton wrote the preface for the catalogue, and on November 17 also lectured at the Ateneo, Barcelona, on "Caractères de l'évolution moderne et ce qui en participe" (see Breton's *Les Pas perdus*, Paris, 1924; 8th ed., Paris, 1949, 181–212). In the lecture he traced the evolution of modern art up to 1922, including serious reflection on Dada and the abortive Congress of Paris, but revealed no conception of Surrealism despite the existence of its basic ingredients.

tered trances during which he might have produced drawings or writings, but ink blots occur in some of his works of 1922, and it is possible that the Rorschach-like drawings cited earlier (p. 142) were done on December 1, 1922, in response to ideas stimulated by the experiments in Breton's apartment. That possibility is supported by one of Picabia's letters to Breton: "I think one could go very far with spiritualism, certainly not on the side of death, but in the other direction, beginning with the material, one must insist on rejecting the seances and employing perhaps several methods."[7]

During those months of close collaboration with Breton, Picabia maintained a vigorous independent activity, and in the midst of all his painting, writing and short-lived projects, he and Germaine moved from their Paris apartment to a rustic suburban home. They had begun to think of moving from Paris in the early fall of 1921 when, during a period of reconciliation with Ribemont-Dessaignes, they had passed several enjoyable weekends at his country home in Montfort-l'Amaury. An auxiliary pleasure had been the discovery of a good automobile mechanic in the neighboring village of Tremblay-sur-Mauldre, and when one day in the spring of 1922 that mechanic announced he was leaving Tremblay, Picabia bought his house-garage on the spot.[8]

It was small and ill-equipped for their household needs, but Germaine recognized that Picabia had a great "thirst for events . . . little matter to him under what form they presented themselves: women, houses, automobiles, pets . . ." and the house at Tremblay, christened "La Maison Rose," was "pretext for a new activity."[9] For weeks he amused himself by making plans, studying estimates, supervising the work and chatting with workmen. Finally the dwelling was transformed and filled with the contents of their apartment in Paris—French and Spanish furniture of the sixteenth to the eighteenth centuries, mechanomorphic paintings, collections of crystal paperweights, old dada publications, sailing ships in bottles and a new menagerie of cats, dogs, pet birds and chickens. Before long their neighbors included Blaise Cendrars, Ambroise Vollard and the comedian Marcel Lévesque, but by then the novelty of La Maison Rose had faded, and as Germaine noted, "Picabia had only one idea, to return to Paris!"[10] For the next

7. Picabia letter to Breton, October 1922 (collection A. Breton, Paris; Sanouillet, *Dada à Paris*, 524–25). For comments on the seances and Picabia see Germaine Everling, *L'Anneau de Saturne* (Paris, 1970), 150–52; Marguerite Bonnet, *André Breton* (Paris, 1975), 262–67; and Breton, "Entrée des médiums," *Littérature*, II, no. 6 (Paris, November 1, 1922), 1–16, reprinted in Breton, *Les Pas perdus*, 8th ed., 147–58. Picabia's own account written in 1923–1924 and published in 1974 (*Caravansérail*, Paris, 1974, 83–99) is partly fiction and parody, but revealing nonetheless.

8. The story of the new home in Tremblay is related by Everling in *L'Anneau de Saturne*, 145–46. See also Gaston-Ch. Richard, "Dada aux champs," *Le Petit Parisien*, October 27, 1922 (attrib.).

9. Everling, *L'Anneau de Saturne*, 146.

10. Ibid., 146–48.
The friendship with Marcel Lévesque extended to his son and daughter-in-law, Jacques-Henri and Angelica Lévesque. Jacques-Henri Lévesque wrote some sensitive articles on Picabia and became a collector of his work.

two and one-half years they did in fact divide their time between La Maison Rose and inexpensive Montparnasse hotels, and the two faces of those living conditions were reflected in Picabia's career. In both his writing and his painting Picabia seems to have had one foot in the vital, dada-tinged activities of the capital and the other foot in the new rhythms and projects of a country retreat.

His outpouring of articles, aphorisms, poems and dadaist fables appeared in a number of publications. Upon the death of Casella, Picabia's connection with *Comoedia* was severed, but for the remainder of the summer he contributed monthly articles to *L'Ere nouvelle*. Then from September 1922 through the spring of 1923 *Littérature* became his principal forum, although he also submitted major articles to *La Vie moderne* and was well represented in *The Little Review*, including one issue which featured his work.[11] Throughout those writings there was an unmistakable dada spirit as Picabia lambasted schools, snobs, hypocrites and just about anyone who restrained newness and vitality in art or life. Cubism, Dada, the Salons, Lenin and *L'Esprit nouveau* were frequent targets. At the same time some changes were also apparent. Prose had displaced poetry and polemics as the favored form, and his articles were generally more serious in tone—not to mention occasional statements unthinkable during the heyday of Dada, for example, his kind words for Gide, Jesus, Renoir and Cézanne.[12]

Picabia's ideals for art and life were ably expressed in two articles for *L'Ere nouvelle* during the summer of 1922. In the articles entitled "La Bonne Peinture" (Good Painting), he began by lamenting that so many painters had taken to imitating the primitives and remarked:

> Good painting is not what sells. . . . good painting does not exist; what exists is the man who has something to say and who uses the medium of painting . . . to externalize his personality. Henri Matisse . . . does the contrary. . . . after having astonished and charmed us with a little attractive audacity, he is content to be a good artist-painter . . . he paints little pictures from morning to night . . . "very pretty, very expensive," with the promise

11. In the spring 1922 issue of *The Little Review* (London) there were nineteen reproductions of Picabia's work, one poem and a representative article entitled "Anticoq." In later issues there appeared the first English translations of his work, the article "Good Painting" (autumn 1922, 61–62, n. 12 this chapter) and a partial translation of *Jésus-Christ Rastaquouère* (autumn–winter 1924–1925, 51–58).

12. For Picabia's comments on the Salons see his two articles on "Le Salon des Indépendants" (*L'Ere nouvelle* [Paris], September 20, 1922, 1–2, and *La Vie moderne*, Paris, February 11, 1923). His derogatory observations on Communism in "Souvenirs sur Lénine. Le Communisme jugé par un peintre cubiste" (*L'Eclair* [Paris], August 23, 1922, 1) went against the grain of several colleagues. *L'Esprit nouveau* was the primary target in "Le Génie et le fox-terrier" (*Comoedia* [Paris], May 16, 1922, 1), while Dada was lambasted in a summer interview with Jack Pencil, "Vacances d'artistes" (*Le Figaro*, 2). Picabia's most revealing personal statements on art and life at this period appear in the articles "Ondulations cérébrales" (*L'Ere nouvelle* [Paris], July 12, 1922, 1–2; trans. Lucy R. Lippard in *Surrealists on Art*, Englewood Cliffs, N. J., 1970, 184–86); "La Bonne Peinture" (*L'Ere nouvelle* [Paris], August 20, 1922, 1–2; trans. in *The Little Review*, London, autumn 1922, 61–62); and "Francis merci" (*Littérature*, II, no. 8, Paris, January 1, 1923, 16–17; trans. Lucy R. Lippard in *Dadas on Art*, Englewood Cliffs, N. J., 1971, 171–72).

that one will be able to resell the merchandise for still more than he will have paid for it. . . .

The personality [Paul Signac] which springs from a system can no more interest us than that of a maniac who could only write with orange ink. . . .

Ah! Certainly I prefer the cubism of Picasso and Braque in 1913 . . . the pity is that many people do not yet see how much creative spirit there was in the cubism of those two men; they often confound them with the group of idiots cast in their wake . . .

Delacroix, Ingres, Corot, Cézanne, Sisley, Pissarro, Seurat, Gustav Moreau, Picasso, Marcel Duchamp, these are men who have laid bare life, their life: their pictures have real pollen and their names can only be asserted under the nose of those who think that an epoch is great because it lasts a long time and those who participate in it are numerous. Such is the idea of the small school of the beaux-arts-cubists founded by *L'Esprit nouveau*; they know the why of everything, they have their laws, they know good and evil, they imitate God driving Adam and Eve out of paradise, God not being able to endure sin! Sin, the serpent, that is Dadaism! . . .

L'Esprit nouveau will only be new when it is dead, at least then it will have evolved!

In several weeks "the Salon of good painting," the Salon d'Automne, will open. In finishing, may I offer a word of advice to the members of the jury: to refuse pitilessly all that they like and accept only what horrifies them; in this way we might perhaps have an exhibition less stupid and less monotonous and some innovators would run the risk of having the great luck to exhibit in a palace consecrated to the glory of French art and decreed a public utility.[13]

In another article for *L'Ere nouvelle* that summer, he described the artist he would like to see:

. . . A man who would not be influenced by anyone, who would not be preoccupied with modernism or cubism or dadaism; who would not be socialist or communist or the contrary; a man who would simply be himself . . . A man who would succeed in communicating to us the desire for a life of openness and full activity, . . . A man, finally, who would lead us toward the new world to discover: the world of love which the mediocre have no desire to enter and which frightens the "intellectuals" for fear of ridicule.

Jesus Christ invented that manner of life long ago; I would prefer it to the present dilution.[14]

13. Picabia, "La Bonne Peinture," *L'Ere nouvelle*, August 20, 1922, 1–2.
14. Picabia, "Ondulations cérébrales," *L'Ere nouvelle*, July 12, 1922, 1–2. The unexpected closing statement about Jesus may reflect the work of the friendly priest in Tremblay who became, to the astonishment of his parishioners, an habitué at La Maison Rose. Once when he complained that no one attended vespers, Picabia counseled "Suppress them. . . . That truly serves nothing! You'll come and take tea with us, in place of vespers—and everyone will be happy!" (Everling, *L'Anneau de Saturne*, 147).

Picabia's contemporary painting offers a comparable mixture of new forms and content within the familiar framework of his implacably individualist and dadaist temperament. Correspondence with Breton and Pierre de Massot records two revolutionary paintings, *La Feuille de vigne* (*Fig Leaf*, fig. 209), completed around May or June, and *La Nuit espagnole* (*Spanish Night*, fig. 210), finished by early August.[15] Like the first mechanomorphic works of 1915, these large figurative paintings were startling, unexpected creations in Picabia's oeuvre, arriving like Athena, full-blown from the head of Zeus. It is true that Picabia had never wholly abandoned figurative art, but for ten years it had been an almost negligible element among his abstract, mechanomorphic and dadaist works. And nothing since his academic student drawings with Cormon approached the classicistic form of these figures. Unlike the beginning of the mechanomorphic style, Picabia provided no statement about his intentions, but *La Feuille de vigne* may have been undertaken as a comment on the preoccupation with classicism and tradition so prominent in some contemporary art, including the work of Picasso (fig. 208), Léger and a number of authors and artists associated with *L'Esprit nouveau*.

So frequent, in fact, was Picabia's work an apparent response or reaction to the art of others that this phenomenon looms as a basic element in his creative process. That process of response or reaction never included copying; it was a complex process which might be keyed to a specific work (Duchamp's *Tzanck Check* and Picabia's *L'Oeil cacodylate*, fig. 165; color pl. XI) or stimulated by the major trend of Neo-Classicism in French art of the 1920s. At times Picabia's response reflected respect for the source—as in the visual dialogue between the work of Duchamp and himself since 1911–1912; on other occasions, his reaction smacked of sarcasm and contempt—as in *La Feuille de vigne* (fig. 209), where firm drawing and an idealized nude refer to an academic, classicizing tradition, but in an exaggerated manner which seems to parody that tradition.[16] Moreover, curious inscriptions, the deformed nose and an unduly prominent fig leaf mock that tradition outright with special emphasis on two characteristics of the Salons which disgusted Picabia, namely, prudery (censorship) and nationalism. Attribu-

15. In a letter to Picabia during early May 1922, Breton asked permission to reproduce *La Feuille de vigne* in *Littérature* (D.P. VIII, 622; Sanouillet, *Dada à Paris*, 520–21). On August 13, 1922, Breton wrote Picabia that he was eager to see the "definitive state of 'L'Amour espagnole' " ('Spanish Love'; D.P. VIII, 716; Sanouillet, op. cit., 521). Pierre de Massot, in a letter to Picabia on August 14, 1922 (D.P. VIII, 719), referred to *La Nuit espagnole* as a "miracle of humor and philosophy" and a direct, logical work from *La Feuille de vigne*. Ribemont-Dessaignes referred to *La Nuit espagnole* as *Nuit d'amour* (*Night of Love*; letter to Tzara, August 17, 1922, C.T. 3299; Sanouillet, op. cit., 370).

16. Diverse examples of this process of response/reaction appear in subsequent chapters. One of the first authors to articulate this phenomenon in Picabia's work associates it with "evolution by successive reactions" which has characterized the development of avant-garde art in recent years (Jean-Hubert Martin, "Ses Tableaux sont peints pour raconter non pour prouver" in Centre National d'Art et de Culture Georges Pompidou, Musée National d'Art Moderne, *Francis Picabia*, Paris, Grand Palais, January 23–March 29, 1976, 41, 45).

For a major portion of the neo-classicist current in French art of the 1920s see the Tate Gallery, London, *Léger and Purist Paris*, November 18, 1970–January 24, 1971, texts by John Golding and Christopher Green.

tion of such mockery to *La Feuille de vigne* is speculative, but the act of painting it did involve one dadaist gesture rarely matched by any of his colleagues: Picabia painted *La Feuille de vigne* over *Les Yeux chauds* (fig. 197), completely effacing that notorious work from the 1921 Salon d'Automne and asserting again the primacy of "life now" over attachments to the past. The painting over of earlier compositions became, in fact, a commonplace in Picabia's career from this date onward and can be observed in another roughly contemporary painting, the striking and highly abstracted *Le Jardin* (*Garden*, fig. 211).[17]

Visually speaking, *La Nuit espagnole* (fig. 210) is particularly interesting given the interplay of its formal and thematic elements—forms which are white and black, positive and negative, abstract and figurative, and, at the same time, inseparable from the oppositions of male and female, clothed and nude, active and passive. Finally, however, subject and content are the overriding concerns for most spectators—and for Picabia, too, one suspects. The titles first considered by him, "Spanish Love" and "Night of Love," reinforce a general impression that the content deals with the sexual relationship of the aggressive male dancer and the demure female nude. Her passive form is animated by two glowing pink and yellowish concentric circles which, by being placed over one breast and the vulva, "read" as erotic targets splattered with bullet holes. Indeed, when *La Nuit espagnole* was exhibited at the 1922 Salon d'Automne, Pierre de Massot referred to it as a "revolver trap," a description which both verifies the erotic target interpretation and recalls a work of 1915, *Voilà elle* (fig. 113).[18] Having linked the basic themes of these two works, it is easier to see that despite obvious differences of date and style, they also share formal properties which stress lines, planes, frontality and value contrasts.

Similar contacts bind Picabia's figurative paintings of 1922 to the other major current in his oeuvre that year. The paintings in this second current are almost too varied to support a single title, but for the sake of simplicity and want of a better term, they will be referred to as the "late dada-machinist style."[19] All of them

17. The images under *La Feuille de vigne* and *Le Jardin* are not visible in photographs, but are discernible in the presence of the paintings themselves, and an X-ray photograph has been published which reveals *Les Yeux chauds* (fig. 197) under *La Feuille de vigne* (Centre National d'Art et de Culture Georges Pompidou, Musée National d'Art Moderne, *Francis Picabia*, Paris, Grand Palais, January 23–March 29, 1976, 97). The date of *Le Jardin* is problematical. It was exhibited in 1926 as a work of 1921–1922 (Hôtel Drouot, Paris, *Tableaux, aquarelles et dessins par Francis Picabia appartenant à M. Marcel Duchamp*, March 8, 1926, no. 37). However, there are errors in the catalogue, and the closest visual parallel to *Le Jardin* exists in some pages for the program of Picabia's ballet *Relâche* in 1924. Pending further documentation, a date of ca. 1921–1924 will be carried here. The use of ripolin for *Le Jardin* also becomes more prominent in Picabia's work from 1922 onward.

18. This description occurs in a handbill by Pierre de Massot which was distributed at the door of the Salon d'Automne: "Spanish Love is a revolver trap!"

For additional discussion of targets and symbolism, see Robert Pincus-Witten, "On Target: Symbolist Roots of American Abstraction," *Arts Magazine*, L, no. 8 (New York, April 1976), 84–91.

19. These paintings are not dated on the works themselves but may be attributed to 1922 or 1922–1923 with confidence. None of them has been documented before 1922; many of them ap-

share formal properties derived from the earlier mechanomorphic paintings, but they are generally distinguished from those earlier works by sparer compositions, fewer inscriptions and more severe machine aesthetics. Moreover, few of them are mechanomorphic; an important group consists of abstract compositions; others are evidently based on astronomical charts, optics and diagrams of wave patterns. At a glance, all of these paintings seem to be alien to *La Feuille de vigne* and *La Nuit espagnole* (figs. 209, 210), but the superimposition of idealized torsos on some of them (figs. 227, 229, 233, 236) stresses that the figurative and late dada-machinist currents not only flowed side by side, but occasionally came together and always shared the use of flat, hard-edged forms, an emphasis on line and value contrasts and a touch of dadaist subversion in the relationship of image and title.

Sphinx, Hache-paille (Chaff-cutter) and *Totalisateur (Totalizer*, figs. 212–214), all exhibited at the Dalmau Gallery in 1922, are representative of the late dada-machinist mode as a whole and the works within it that actually suggest machines. They are asymmetrical compositions of simple geometrical forms, flat, frontal, static and usually rendered in arid color harmonies in gouache and water-color over pencil guidelines. Inscriptions are limited to Picabia's signature and titles which may establish a provocative relationship to the image. The title of *Sphinx*, for example, flaunts the mocking or secret, personal aim of that fanciful contraption. However, the title of *Hache-paille* reaffirms the suggestion of gears and belts in that drawing, and the title of *Totalisateur*, a calculating machine used to register pari-mutuel horse race bets, is relatable to its composition of electrical wires, a magnetic field (upper right) and a motor (lower left) connected to a dry-cell battery in the lower right.

The forms of *Décaveuse (Digger*, fig. 215) suggest a paddle-wheel action at least remotely related to the title, but intellectual concerns give way here to the intrinsic interest of this composition and its handsome frame. Rows of nails (upper right and lower left corners), driven through the wood frame from the back so that their points are directed at the spectator, accentuate the brittle rods in the composition and create shifting sensations of form, light, shadow and texture as the spectator changes position. This is one of the first of at least twenty or thirty unique frames commissioned by Picabia during the 1920s from such decorative artists as Pierre Legrain.[20]

The date of *Novia (Sweetheart*, fig. 216) is not documented, but this drawing

---

peared for the first time at Picabia's exhibition in Barcelona that fall (Galeries Dalmau, Barcelona, *Exposition Francis Picabia*, November 18–December 8, 1922) where Breton wrote in the preface that the oldest of them had been done only a few months earlier. Letters between Picabia, Breton and Jacques Doucet verify these dates for several works (Breton letter to Picabia, undated [ca. September–October 1922], D.P. VIII, 688; Sanouillet, *Dada à Paris*, 526–27; Doucet letter to Picabia, October 11, 1922, D.P. VIII, 706).

20. *Décaveuse* was exhibited at Picabia's Dalmau Gallery exhibition in Barcelona during November 1922 (no. 14). According to Mme Simone Collinet (conversation with the author, March 18, 1974), its frame was made by M. Faucheux rather than Pierre Legrain.

shares all of the features described above, plus the value contrasts and dark-light background division of *La Nuit espagnole*. It seems that Picabia recast some themes of the earlier mechanomorphic style (fig. 138) in his new mode—much as he had done with certain sites during the evolution of his impressionist paintings (figs. 11, 25). *Tickets* and *Tickets annulés* (*Cancelled Tickets*, figs. 217, 218) exhibit another work method, namely, the variation and combination of motifs which was to be employed extensively in the later period of the "transparencies."

The late dada-machinist style also incorporated what might be called a number of nonobjective paintings (figs. 219–221, 223). All of them are exceptionally spare compositions of simple, two-dimensional geometrical forms—circles, squares, triangles, bars and rectangles—which, excluding for a moment their titles, seem to be wholly devoid of reference to anything outside of themselves, and are capable of standing on formal properties alone. *Fixe* (fig. 219) is the most severe of all, four black geometrical shapes hovering on a white field in a dynamic equilibrium which seems to be in deliberate contrast to the title. *Radio Concerts*, *Presse hydraulique* (*Hydraulic Press*) and *Volucelle* I (figs. 220, 221, 223) are equally abstract and almost as spare save for *Radio Concerts*, which is distinguished by a symmetrical composition and lively colors.

Excepting their titles, these paintings by Picabia are not dissimilar to other nonobjective compositions by contemporary Russian and northern and eastern European artists whose work was vigorously supported as early as 1921–1922 by Theo van Doesburg in Holland, Herwarth Walden in Berlin and Walter Gropius at the Bauhaus.[21] Presently, Picabia's direct contact with that art is not firmly documented, but he knew of it, at least through acquaintances or magazines, and, moreover, his own essays in nonobjective painting were probably stimulated by it.[22] At the same time, precedents exist in his own work to some degree (fig. 189),

21. In 1921 the western nations' suspension of their economic blockade against the Soviet Union fostered cultural contacts largely interrupted since 1914. Germany became the meeting ground for international currents in nonobjective and constructivist art. The Hungarian Moholy-Nagy had worked in Berlin since 1920, and in 1921 the Russian Jean Pougny exhibited his constructivist drawings at Walden's Der Sturm Gallery before settling in Paris in 1923. An important exhibition of modern Russian art was shown in Berlin (Van Diemen Gallery, ca. November 1922) and Amsterdam, and El Lissitzky, who accompanied that exhibition, also published with Ilya Ehrenburg a constructivist periodical (*Vesch-Objet-Gegenstand*, Berlin, March 1922–April 1923) which represented such artists from Paris as Léger, Gleizes and Lipchitz alongside Russian constructivists. A Constructivist Congress was organized at the Bauhaus in September 1922 which, at the insistence of van Doesburg, included Arp and Tzara as well as Lissitzky, Moholy-Nagy and others. The work of the De Stijl group in Holland was also known in Paris, and the foremost artist of the group, Piet Mondrian, was living in Paris.

22. The publications which might have been available to Picabia include catalogues of the exhibitions cited in n. 21, Laszlo Moholy-Nagy's and Ludwig Kassak's *Buch Neuer Künstler* (Vienna: MA, 1922) and various periodicals. All of the artists from Paris represented in those exhibitions and publications were known to Picabia. Moreover, Gropius had tried to contact him as early as January 1922 (letter from Gropius to Picabia, December 16, 1923, D.P. X, 182), and van Doesburg had been in touch with Picabia since 1920 (letter from van Doesburg to Picabia, March 29, 1920, D.P. V, 237). Picabia was also familiar with a group of Russian intellectuals ("L'Uni-

and, finally, it is the differences between Picabia and those northern and eastern artists, Malevich, for example, which are most instructive.

Compared to "nonobjective" paintings by Picabia, the composition of Malevich's *Supremus No. 50* (fig. 222) is more tense and complex, its suggestion of space and size more ambiguous. The forms of *Fixe* or *Presse hydraulique* (figs. 219, 221) are isolated in space, relatively more stable and restricted in number and shape; the overall composition is also simpler in structure and psychological effect, and sensations of tension and ambiguity are generated less by formal properties than by the charged gap between the depicted forms and their title. Not even the artist's signature—much less the other inscriptions—are permitted in the rarefied space of Malevich's painting; Picabia prints his title boldly above the forms, inviting or forcing the spectator to contend with that baffling juxtaposition of form and title.

These bare abstract paintings hardly encourage efforts to bridge the gap. Nevertheless, some interpretive effort seems in order given the tradition of symbolism in Picabia's work, and the contemporary thought of two of his closest friends, namely, the abstract symbolism of Crotti's Tabu-Dada considered in the previous chapter (p. 170; fig. 206) and a frequently quoted statement by Duchamp which seems fitting at this point, "I came to feel an artist might use anything—a dot, a line, the most conventional or unconventional symbol—to say what he wanted to say."[23] Picabia made a similar statement in 1923, just as he was abandoning his abstract and late machinist style: "I thought that I had done everything there was to do in abstract art, in the art of suggestions. To trace a line on a canvas, to name it 'Pierre de Massot,' or to make the portrait of Nicole Groult with a gear, that was to go as far as possible in abstraction."[24]

While Picabia's statement confirms his use of symbolism in the late dada-machinist style, it also underscores the near futility of interpretation since a dot or line could mean almost anything. Dots and circles, prominent in his work since 1912, became so ubiquitous during 1922 that he must have attached special significance to them. But inasmuch as they had already been used to represent wheels, gears, gramophone records, targets and erotic zones, how is one—without statements by Picabia or reliable witnesses—to correlate the title "volucelle" (fig. 223) with four black and two blue dots on a white field? Within the context of

versité du 41 degré") around Ilia Zdanévitch, a friend of Picabia's former dadaist colleague, Charchoune. Charchoune had moved to Berlin in May 1922 and assumed an active role in avant-garde art and literature there including the publication of articles and a periodical on Dada (see Musée National d'Art Moderne, Paris, *Charchoune*, May 7–June 21, 1971, 67).

23. Marcel Duchamp, interview with James Johnson Sweeney, "Eleven Europeans in America," *The Museum of Modern Art Bulletin*, XIII, nos. 4–5 (New York, 1946), 20. Duchamp did not specify the date of that concept, but implied that it was relevant to *The Large Glass* (1915–1923).

24. Francis Picabia, "Manifeste du bon goût," unpublished manuscript intended as a preface for an exhibition in May 1923 (Exposition chez Danthon, Paris, *Francis Picabia*, May 1923). A preface by Germaine Everling was used instead; Picabia's text was published by Michel Sanouillet, *Francis Picabia et "391,"* II (Paris, 1966), 149.

Picabia's career during 1922, one speculation will be ventured, namely, that the configuration of dots in *Volucelle* is not unlike charts of constellations (see fig. 224). Clear astronomical references occur in the work of contemporary artists who may have influenced Picabia and are documented in such drawings by Picabia himself as *Mercure* (*Mercury*) and *Astrolabe* (fig. 225), exhibited at Dalmau's gallery in November 1922. The arcs and circles of the latter suggest planets, orbits and trajectories which are plausibly related to an astrolabe—an ancient instrument used for problems of astronomy and navigation—and to diagrams of seventeenth-century world systems (see fig. 226).

Astronomical references and symbolic possibilities become still more tantalizing in a third group of late dada-machinist paintings based on a variety of wave patterns (figs. 227–229, 231, 233, 234, 236). Two basic patterns are evident, one comprised of concentric circles and another of vertical bands. All of them possess interesting optical effects, and Duchamp documented Picabia's concern for optical illusions in one of them, *Optophone* I (fig. 227).[25] However, neither optics nor machine aesthetics seem as important as Picabia's taste for human-mechanical analogies—or, in this instance, human-electrical analogies. The circular patterns here resemble a diagram of a static magnetic field around a current-bearing conductor, and by placing the female nude with her point of sex at the center of the field, Picabia identifies her as a "charged body" or as the "conductor of the charge." The significance of the reddish "shadow" on the nude remains a mystery, but the title, *Optophone*, reinforces the interpretation offered above since an optophone is an instrument which converts energy from one form into another, notably light variations into sound variations. Picabia seems to have in mind an optophone which converts electrical energy into sexual energy.

Both *Lampe cristal* (*Crystal Lamp*) and *Optophone* II (figs. 228, 229) employ the concentric ring pattern with variations. The optical properties of *Lampe cristal* are muted by several meandering lines, by the truncated form of the circle and by the use of colored bands rather than the alternating black and white rings in *Optophone* I. It also seems totally abstract, whereas *Optophone* II reasserts the erotic themes of *Optophone* I. In this instance an eye is identified with the center of a field of expanding rings possibly based on several phenomena—diagrams of magnetic fields, diffracted or interrupted light waves, or a simple longitudinal wave spreading out in ever broader rings like ripples on a pond (fig. 230).[26] Float-

25. Marcel Duchamp, notes for the Hôtel Drouot sales catalogue, *Tableaux, aquarelles et dessins par Francis Picabia appartenant à M. Marcel Duchamp*, Paris, March 8, 1926. *Optophone* I was entitled by Picabia simply *Optophone*; this author has added Roman numerals "I" and "II" to distinguish works by the same title (figs. 227, 229) and to indicate that *Optophone* I was probably painted first.

26. Diagrams of these phenomena are available in standard books on physics and optics, for example, Michel Cagnet et al., *Optischer Erscheinungen* (Berlin: Springer Verlag, 1962).

Diffraction is the spreading of a wave behind an obstacle, e.g., a light wave passing through a tiny aperture in an opaque screen. Light interference is a pattern that appears when light waves from a single source are perceived after they have traveled different paths, e.g., light waves reflected from the surface and the bottom of a thin film of oil. Newton explored this phenomenon

ing in that field is a variety of amorphous shapes, checkerboard patterns and three female nudes who seem to be the focus of attention for the eye in the center. Reference to Duchamp is in order at this point, for he had previously exposed Picabia to his interest in optics with the *Rotary Glass Plate* (1920), the *Oculist Witnesses* (1920) and *To Be Looked At (From the Other Side of the Glass) with One Eye, Close to, for Almost an Hour* (1918, fig. 166), the latter two of which specifically associate eyes and voyeurism with the center of concentric rings.

Still another variety of the circular wave or field pattern occurs in an untitled, abstract composition (fig. 231) which presents an intriguing array of formal contrasts. Rigidly controlled geometric shapes are set against amorphous ink runs on rectangular patches of absorbent paper glued to the drawing. Further contrasts exist within the geometrical elements themselves as straight vertical lines are pitted against curved bands whose own entity or unity is challenged by sections of different colors. The ink spots in this composition reassert Picabia's intermittent cultivation of chance in forms which ranged from the dadaist gesture in *La Sainte Vièrge* (fig. 182) to a curious watercolor of about 1922, *Un Bouton* (*A Button*, fig. 232), which combines the full repertory of his modes during that year—traditional figurative art, late machinist forms and ink stains.

The vertical bands in *Abstract Composition* (fig. 231) are related to the second group of wave or field paintings (figs. 233, 234, 236). Like the preceding circular patterns, these are probably based on scientific diagrams (see fig. 235) and vary from bands of fixed width (*Chariot*, fig. 233) to bands of progressively increasing (or decreasing) width in *Volucelle* II and *Conversation* I (fig. 234; fig. 236, and color pl. XII)—with or without an overlay of academic nudes.[27] *Volucelle* II is by far the largest known painting among the late dada-machinist phase, and crucial to the symbolism of a cluster of works. At first glance it seems to be a very simple, wholly abstract composition of stripes and circles—more precisely, eight colored circles containing small black rings and hovering on a field of vertical black-and-white bands. With longer exposure, this painting appears far more complex in form and content. Most of the visual complexity derives from the black-and-white field with its optical tension, its ambiguous positive-negative space relationships and the diminishing width of the black bands which might be viewed as a literal, physical diminution, or as a recession in space or as movement in time. The circles hovering on that field are not charged with such visual ambiguities, but one wonders about Picabia's choice of colors: two circles in black; three in the primaries, red, yellow and blue; and three in their complementaries,

---

using flat and spherical surfaces, and the pattern of light and dark bands resulting from his experiments are referred to as Newton's rings (fig. 230). Concentric circle patterns are most frequently reproduced in texts, but the surfaces involved determine the pattern.

27. These striped patterns may be formed by diffraction as described above in n. 26 except that slits or straight edges form the obstacle. Line spectrum are less convincing visual models, but merit notation. As in the case of *Optophone* I and II, this author has employed Roman numerals to distinguish between two works entitled *Volucelle* and to indicate that *Volucelle* I was probably painted first.

green, violet and orange. Curious, too, are the smaller black rings distributed among the circles in units of one through seven, except for the black circle at the lower right which bears only the signature "Francis Picabia." When consideration of these formal elements is expanded to include their relationship to the title, *Volucelle*, and to other paintings, the complexities are multiplied.

"Volucelle" is a scientific term for two-winged insects, and Picabia probably used it knowingly, since later in the 1920s he frequently employed the scientific names of birds, butterflies, etc., as titles for his paintings. Presently, however, the identification of that title does not seem as helpful as two related paintings, *Volucelle* I (fig. 223), which shares with *Volucelle* II its title and the use of colored circles, and *Conversation* I (color pl. XII), which suggests fascinating links to both of the *Volucelle* paintings as well as a touch of dada irony in the choice of "conversation" as a title for a painting of headless, limbless figures. Given the almost identical fields of *Conversation* I and *Volucelle* II, there is an implied association of circles and nude bodies which is bolstered by the same number of circles and torsos (six) in *Volucelle* I and *Conversation* I, and by the seemingly deliberate role of color. Each torso in *Conversation* I is overlaid with a transparent, colored "shadow" (two in blue, two in green and one each in red and yellow) which in most instances suggests another female body in an exaggerated or distorted form. The possible relationship between nude bodies and circles becomes more explicit upon reintroducing star charts as possible sources. Among the variety of star charts produced, the most relevant ones are the simple star-cluster diagrams already associated with *Volucelle* I (figs. 223, 224) and elaborate seventeenth-century maps with classically proportioned figures—Hercules, Orion, etc.—superimposed on the stars of their constellations (fig. 237) in a topsy-turvy fashion akin to the gravity-free nudes in *Conversation* I. There is also a contemporary collage by Max Ernst, *Les Pléiades* (1921, private collection), which seems relevant insofar as it depicts a female nude, with her head and one arm partially defaced, floating on a blue field in a weightless manner like the torsos in Picabia's *Conversation* I. In classical mythology the Pleiades were the seven daughters of Atlas, placed in the sky as stars to save them from the pursuit of Orion. According to ancient Roman accounts, all seven stars were visible, but, subsequently, one became invisible to the eye, leaving six major stars now charted for the Pleiades and one "hidden" star. Although the colors and compositions of *Conversation* I and *Volucelle* I do not exactly correspond to each other or to diagrams of the Pleiades known to this author, the common thread of six stars (dots or circles) and six female figures makes it worthwhile to note the possibility of some correlation between Picabia's paintings, the constellation of the Pleiades, the classical myth and the general relevance of the unexplored theme of astronomy for art during the 1920s.

With these new paintings and several aggressive articles, Picabia once more challenged the increasingly stodgy "liberal" Salons of Paris over the winter of 1922–1923. *La Nuit espagnole* and *La Feuille de vigne* (figs. 209, 210) were exhibited at the 1922 Salon d'Automne, while three examples of the late dada-machinist style appeared at the 1923 Salon des Indépendants, among them *Volucelle* II and one of the *Optophones* (fig. 234; and either fig. 227 or fig. 229). A letter to Jacques Doucet reveals that Picabia took his role at the Salons seriously:

> I am working now on a very large painting [probably *Volucelle* II] that I plan to exhibit at the Indépendents, an exhibition which formerly caused scandals but which unfortunately has let be imposed upon it, by the grandeur and folly of a palace, bad taste for the commonplace. Being placed always under the stairway or in the buffet, I consider that I have reason to exhibit there again and that the little scandal which results, may save this salon, like that of the [Salon d'] Automne, from the banality so dear to provincial people.[28]

Members of the Salon d'Automne committee, mindful of Picabia's abuse of their generosity the preceding year, did pay tribute to *La Nuit espagnole* and *La Feuille de vigne* by hanging them in what one observer described as the highest, dirtiest, most obscure vault of the hallway.[29] But such measures were no longer necessary. Pierre de Massot's stinging dadaist leaflet distributed at the door of the Salon passed without duels and special hearings,[30] and most of the critics who bothered to consider Picabia's paintings wrote not in outrage but with the unruffled disdain of Marcel Hiver, who described Crotti and Picabia as "old clowns" who "no longer amuse anyone."[31] Response to Picabia's striking paintings at the 1923 Salon des Indépendants was even more negligible.

Those two "liberal" Salons had passed through their period of service to such revolutionary movements as Fauvism, Cubism and Dada—and Picabia's exhortation for them to return to the principle of courageous service was futile. Those Salons had not merely aged or drifted; the revolutionary movements had passed, and art in Paris had become dominated by conservative adaptation of those more radical movements in modern art to traditional forms.

Serious efforts by Breton and Picabia to found a new Salon disintegrated about this time, and that failure, along with other disappointments, was taken by Breton as a personal defeat which brought on another spell of morose self-analysis. In an interview during April 1923, he declared that he no longer intended to write and was going to terminate the publication of *Littérature*.[32] Picabia

28. Letter from Picabia to Jacques Doucet, January 5, 1923 (B.D., A. III. 4-1149-25; Sanouillet, *Francis Picabia et "391,"* II, 253–54).

29. Maurice Raynal, "Au Salon d'Automne," *L'Intransigeant* [Paris], October 31, 1922, 1–2.

30. De Massot's manifesto is quoted in Sanouillet, *Dada à Paris*, 370.

31. Marcel Hiver, "La Peinture," *Montparnasse* (Paris, November 1, 1922), 3.

32. Roger Vitrac, "André Breton n'écrira plus," *Le Journal du peuple* [Paris], April 7, 1923, 3.

Breton expressed his discouragement over efforts to found a new Salon and the results of a "promenade" at the 1923 Salon des Indépendants in letters to Picabia (December 20, 1922, D.P. IX, 87; February 9, 1923, D.P. IX, 152; and an undated letter of early 1923, D.P. IX, 153; Sanouillet, *Dada à Paris*, 526–29). Duchamp registered opposition to the project in a telegram

suffered no such anxiety; he maintained his pace as an author and artist ever open to new diversions—which soon included ballet, film and further development of a figurative art that reflected the conservative trends of the twenties in a personal manner that retained a dadaist flavor.

and letter to Picabia (December 18, 1922, D.P. X, 113, and January 20, 1923, D.P. IX, 89; Sanouillet, *Dada à Paris*, 552–53). Breton may have been influenced by the example of Duchamp who, upon resettling in Paris during February 1923, had virtually abandoned art.

14. FIGURATIVE ART; SURREALISM; RELÂCHE AND ENTR'ACTE

PICABIA'S full-fledged return to figurative art was celebrated by still another return—an exhibition at M. Danthon's Galerie Haussmann, site of his debut as an impressionist in 1905. For old times' sake, a few drawings and canvases from his impressionist period were included among more than 100 recent drawings of toreadors, Spanish belles, friends and entertainers (figs. 238–241), many of whom joined a crowd of celebrities on opening night.[1] Picabia urged his former dadaist friends to attend also, claiming it "can amuse you for a few days."[2]

These drawings, particularly the Spanish subjects, recall Picabia's early career, but also reflect his general style of 1922–1923 by virtue of their simpler, bolder forms and strong value contrasts. Most contemporary critics were too surprised and suspicious to perceive such connections, but, once recovered, several of them wrote their first favorable reviews of Picabia's work, praising his direct, refreshing vision and the pure, simple quality of his forms. "After all, perhaps Dadaism never existed," wrote one.[3] Such approval was not universal, however. Breton, for one, viewed the work with misgiving, and most subsequent critics have been outspoken in their disregard or distaste for the various figurative styles that dominated Picabia's work from then through the mid-1940s.[4] Those styles never stirred the interest which swirled about Picabia from 1912 to 1922/1924, and never resided solidly in the mainstreams of modern art. For many critics and collectors, that shift in Picabia's work registered as a drastic, total change charac-

1. Exposition chez Danthon, Paris, *Francis Picabia*, May 1923, preface by Germaine Everling. Picabia's "Manifeste du bon goût" (Michel Sanouillet, *Francis Picabia et "391,"* II, Paris, 1966, 149) was initially intended as the preface for this catalogue. Few of the drawings of ca. 1922–1923 have been positively identified among extant works, but the *Espagnole* and *Portrait of Simone Breton* (figs. 238, 241) are documented works of 1922 exhibited at chez Danthon.

2. Picabia letter to Breton, undated [May 1923] (collection A. Breton, Paris; Michel Sanouillet, *Dada à Paris*, Paris, 1965, 529).

3. Anon., *Comoedia* [Paris], May 24, 1923, 3.

4. Breton denied that he was distressed by Picabia's exhibition at Danthon (undated letter to Picabia in June 1923, D.P. X, 112; Sanouillet, *Dada à Paris*, 531–32), but Picabia knew better (see his statement, "L'Exposition Francis Picabia," unidentified newspaper [Paris], ca. June 1923, attrib.; D.P. X, 105).

terized by an inexplicable loss of quality or, at best, by a lamentable reflection of the conservative spirit of the 1920s and a relaxation of creative intensity, accompanied in the instance of Picabia by physical retreats to suburban Tremblay in 1922 and to the Midi in 1925.

Such opinions—largely based on superficial elements of style and subjective judgments of quality—not only deterred sensitive consideration of Picabia's "unloved" figurative art, but actually fostered distorted views of the esteemed dadaist oeuvre. Closer, comprehensive examination of Picabia's figurative art—subject, style and content—is in order, not with the aim of promoting or demoting any period of his work, but of enhancing one's experience of the whole of it.

Picabia's shift from the late dada-machinist style to figurative art was, indeed, a major change accomplished over a relatively brief span of time—but that was hardly unusual in his career, and not as sudden or as thoroughgoing as his development of the mechanomorphic style in 1915. Figurative art and a love of paint were rooted in Picabia's early career, and his dada temperament was a permanent, irrepressible trait in his life, in his paintings, regardless of their surface appearance, and in his publications, regardless of their date. Picabia's contemporary statements about the new direction of his work offer a representative mixture of "straight" comments with a familiar dadaist humor and disregard for approbation:

> . . . The paintings that I make are very much in rapport with my life. They change according to the people that I see, the countries that I traverse.[5]

> The reason [for the change in style] is just that I thought I had done everything there was to be done in abstract art, in the art of suggestions. . . .
> . . . Now I consider that painting must evolve toward the reproduction of life, without attaching to that the servile imitation of photography.[6]

> . . . There are people who do not like machines: I propose Spanish women for them. If they do not like Spanish women, I'll make them French women.[7]

> . . . I find these women beautiful, and not having any "speciality" as a painter . . . I do not fear compromising myself with them vis-à-vis the elite . . . [8]

> To make love is not modern; however, that is still what I like best.[9]

Picabia maintained the spirit of such comments in numerous publications through 1924 and was frequently invited to collaborate with still more magazines

5. Roger Vitrac, "Francis Picabia, évêque," *Le Journal du peuple* [Paris], June 9, 1923, 3.
6. Picabia, "Manifeste du bon goût" (Sanouillet, *Francis Picabia et "391,"* II, 149).
7. Roger Vitrac, "Exposition René [*sic*] Picabia," *Les Hommes du jour* (Paris, May 19, 1923), 10.
8. Picabia, "L'Exposition Francis Picabia," unidentified newspaper (D.P. X, 105).
9. Picabia, "Jésus dit à ces juifs," *La Vie moderne* (Paris, February 25, 1923), 1.

and newspapers, Salons, benefits and group exhibitions.[10] He was not interested in pursuing all of them and also chose not to participate in the "Soirée of the Bearded Heart," the last event generally considered as part of the historical movement of Dada in Paris. That soirée (Théâtre Michel, July 6 and 7, 1923) of avant-garde music, poetry and drama was only partially dadaist in its participants and program, but Tzara's prominent role in it invited a brouhaha. Breton, Aragon, Eluard, Desnos, Péret and Morise repeatedly disrupted the program, twice intervened violently on the stage itself and were ejected when Tzara called in the police.[11] Desnos's letter to Picabia that same evening implies that the latter was still identified with the anti-dada and anti-Tzara group but had not attended the soirée.[12]

Picabia also missed a lighthearted mock trial of himself and *Jésus-Christ Rastaquouère* organized for July 21 by Léo Poldès.[13] By that date, he and Germaine were vacationing in Pornichet, where on August 4 he was notified of the death of his uncle, Maurice Davanne. Several of Picabia's letters and a poem express touching affection for that uncle who had been so important for his youth and who now left a large estate which enabled Picabia to move in 1925 to a rambling château in the hills above Cannes.[14]

Other propitious events also had their beginning during the summer in Pornichet and the following autumn in Paris. Sometime during August Picabia received a proposal to collaboate with Erik Satie, the filmmaker Marcel L'Herbier and the actress Georgette Leblanc on a film to be produced by Jacques Héber-

10. In March 1923, Jacques Hébertot reorganized *Paris-Journal* and Picabia was invited to contribute to it. On July 2, 1923, Dermée asked Picabia to contribute regularly to his magazine *Interventions* (letter, D.P. X, 79). Nicolas Beauduin sought his collaboration for *L'Etat présent des lettres et des arts* (letter, November 23, 1923, D.P. X, 313), and various requests were received from the editors of *L'Esprit nouveau*, from Walter Gropius of the Bauhaus (letter, December 16, 1923, D.P. X, 182) and from A. de Ridder for *Selections* in Antwerp (letter, June 2, 1924, D.P. X, 178).

11. Sanouillet (*Dada à Paris*, 380) attributed initiative for the soirée to Tzara but the overall program was organized by a group of Russians in Paris associated with Ilia Zdanévitch's "41°." The program included (along with the participation of some obscure Russians) the presentation of Tzara's "Le Coeur à gaz"; poems by Apollinaire, Soupault, Eluard and Cocteau; works by Auric, Milhaud, Satie and Stravinsky, and films by Charles Sheeler, Hans Richter and Man Ray. A manifesto by Pierre de Massot incited Breton, Desnos and Péret to accost him on stage, during which Breton broke de Massot's arm with a blow from his cane. Later Eluard, furious that his poems had been included in the program without permission, leaped on stage to attack Tzara. The latter's call for the police and subsequent damage suit against Eluard were bitter memories for those in Breton's circle.

12. Desnos letter to Picabia, undated [July 6, 1923] (D.P. X, 119; Sanouillet, *Dada à Paris*, 547–48).

13. This mock trial was held in the Théâtre du Chateau-d'Eau with Pierre de Massot serving as defender of the accused. Contemporary press accounts and Poldès's letter to Picabia on June 4, 1923 (D.P. X, 36) provide little additional information.

14. See Picabia's letter to Breton and poem "Mon Oncle est mort" on August 8, 1923 (collection A. Breton; Sanouillet, *Dada à Paris*, 532).

tot.[15] Enthusiastic discussion continued until December 1923 whereupon the project collapsed for unknown reasons. Picabia's interest in collaborating on a film had been activated, however, and it was to be satisfied during 1924 within the framework of a ballet—still another project which began in 1923 when his friend and neighbor, Blaise Cendrars, asked Picabia to help on the Swedish Ballet production of *La Création du monde*.[16] Picabia's hand in that ballet is undocumented and presumably amounted to little more than neighborly advice. Nonetheless, it established contact with Rolf de Maré who, since founding the company in 1920, had challenged the prestigious Russian Ballet with a repertoire drawn from Swedish folklore and avant-garde productions done in collaboration with contemporary (and occasionally controversial) artists and composers.

Before the film and ballet projects were reborn in 1924, Picabia renewed collaboration with Breton and participated for the last time in the Salon d'Automne and the Salon des Indépendants. For the October issue of *Littérature*, Picabia submitted three poems[17] and an interesting cover (fig. 243) composed of male and female nudes suspended in space among a starlike sprinkling of small "X" marks and the letters of *Littérature*. These highly simplified contour figures are divided into black-and-white forms which may be perceived together or as independent shapes—a characteristic which establishes stylistic connections between such seemingly disparate works of the 1920s as *Conversation* I of ca. 1922 (fig. 236 and color pl. XII), the *Matchwoman* II collage of ca. 1923–1924 (color pl. XIII) and *L'Ombre* (*Shadow*) of ca. 1928 (fig. 306).

Picabia's *Dresseur d'animaux* (*Animal Trainer*, fig. 244) at the 1923 Salon d'Automne likewise combines multiple references to past and future aspects of his work.[18] The silhouette form of the male nude, classicistic in proportion excepting his deformed nose, resembles *La Feuille de vigne* (fig. 209), but also predicts Picabia's subversive use of classical models during the periods of the "monsters" and the "transparencies." A dadaist touch lingers, too, in the prominent false date, "July 5, 1937," and Picabia's parting shot at the Salon d'Automne as a trained dog act.

15. Duchamp seems to have been the coordinator between Georgette Leblanc and Picabia (Duchamp telegram to Picabia, August or September 7, 1923, D.P. X, 228). During a tour to North America, Mme Leblanc was reported as scheduled to do a film with L'Herbier and Picabia in Paris during the spring of 1924 ("Mme. Georgette Leblanc," *Presse* [Montreal], December 15, 1923, attrib.; D.P. X, 207).

16. The Swedish Ballet production of *La Création du monde* opened October 25, 1923, at Hébertot's Théâtre des Champs-Elysées with scenario by Cendrars, music by Milhaud and decor by Picasso.

17. Picabia, "Bonheur nouveau," "Colin-Maillard" and "Irréceptif," *Littérature*, II, nos. 11–12 (Paris, October 15, 1923), 21–23.

18. Salon d'Automne, Paris, November 1–December 16, 1923. *Dresseur d'animaux* is securely documented by contemporary reproductions (*Arlequin*, Paris?, December 1, 1923, attrib.; D.P. X, 210), and reviews (Whip, "Au Salon d'Automne," *Le Canard enchaîné* [Paris], November 7, 1923, 4). The landscape which Picabia exhibited at the Salon has not been identified.

Prior to leaving Paris for a visit to Cannes during January–February 1924, Picabia also arranged to pay his last respects to the Salon des Indépendants with an interesting drawing-construction and another accusative article.[19] In the latter he scored Signac's attempt to "refuse the foreign painters permission to exhibit in the same rooms with the good little French. Why not a Salon for women alone?" he jibed, "And another for smokers?" Picabia's drawing-construction at the Salon, *Lampe* (fig. 245)—and a related work or study for it, *Echynomie livide* (fig. 246)—continues the mixture of abstract and figurative elements common during 1922. Like *Décaveuse* (fig. 215) it also has an unusual frame (attributed to Pierre Legrain) which is composed of wood covered with aluminum paper and black cloth (painted) and fitted across the top and bottom with three glass tubes filled with colored liquids that bubbled whenever the work was moved. With the demise of the once scandalous dada manifestations, several critics paused before Picabia's entry with a touch of nostalgia. "No follies, as I have remarked with a shade of regret," wrote one critic, "Nevertheless there is Picabia, the likeable and touching Picabia . . . I amused myself for a good quarter of an hour with this inoffensive toy."[20] Picabia's intentions in *Lampe* are unknown, but it is unlikely that he meant it merely as a toy. In his oeuvre, the symbolic correspondence of lamps and human beings had a long history (see figs. 104, 112, 143), and by this date in 1924, that simple symbolism had been enriched by the multiple associations attached to circles—associations which in *Lampe* alone included the human face or head, eyes, light bulbs and perhaps the sun or other points of energy.

Picabia, meanwhile, was in Cannes, savoring the direct energy of the sun, losing at the baccarat tables and laboring over a book entitled *Caravansérail* (Caravanserai), which he planned to submit to *La Nouvelle Revue française*, where Gaston Gallimard was then publishing several books by Breton and his friends. That rambling, part-factual, part-fictional autobiographical writing was a disappointment to Picabia himself; nevertheless its rejection by Gallimard angered him and strained the ever-fragile relationship with Breton.[21]

At the same time, another project undertaken in Cannes during January 1924 became a source of delight. On January 22, Pierre de Massot wrote: "I am charged by Erik Satie to ask your collaboration on a ballet for the Swedes [Swedish Ballet]: 'entire liberty' will be granted you. 'Everything waits on you.' Hébertot

19. Salon des Indépendants, Paris, February 9–March 12, 1924. Picabia's article, "A Note on the Salons," appeared in *The Arts*, V, no. 4 (New York, April 1924), 191.

20. Pierre Varenne, "Le Salon des Indépendants," *Bonsoir* [Paris], February 9, 1924, 2. The frame for *Lampe*, attributed to Legrain by Charensol ("Au Salon des Indépendants, Découvertes," *Paris-Journal*, February 15, 1924, 4), has been preserved although it is difficult to photograph and no longer has colored liquids in the glass tubes.

21. *Caravansérail* was finished in late January 1924 and was to have included a preface by Aragon (see Picabia's letters to Breton on January 21 and February 1, 1924, collection A. Breton; Sanouillet, *Dada à Paris*, 534–35). Aragon did not write the preface, and the text itself was eventually misplaced and presumed lost until recently found and published in Francis Picabia, *Caravansérail*, ed. Luc-Henri Mercié (Paris, 1974). It is revealing of Picabia that he counted on Breton's support in the publication of a book laced with passages offensive to Breton.

and de Maré are enchanted."[22] The claim of total liberty was exaggerated inasmuch as the ballet, scheduled for the fall of 1924, had a scenario by Cendrars entitled *Après dîner* (After Dinner). Picabia was to provide only stage decor and costumes. Nevertheless, when Cendrars did not return promptly from a trip to South America, his anxious collaborators began to tinker with the sketchy scenario, and around late April or early May Picabia was given responsibility for it. Within a month he and Satie had transformed the ballet under a new title, *Relâche* (No Performance), and a talented young filmmaker, René Clair, was retained to direct a film which would serve as the intermission.[23]

While that work was going on, Picabia continued his journalistic activity with caustic articles on art, literary prizes and André Derain.[24] He also maintained an active social life at the Jockey Club, Le Boeuf sur le Toit and various salons in the city. But, above all, Picabia's work throughout 1924 was dominated by *Relâche* and his role in the emergence of a major movement in the art and literature of the twentieth century—the movement of Surrealism.

Picabia and Breton broke sharply over Surrealism in May 1924. If a specific event triggered their conflict, it has not been documented, but a combination of contemporary statements and past histories provides the framework for that saga in the extraordinary relationship of those two grand friends and adversaries. Despite the amicable relations that had prevailed between them since early 1922, both Breton and Picabia were acutely conscious of their opposed temperaments

22. Pierre de Massot letter to Picabia, January 22, 1924 (D.P. X, 331; Sanouillet, *Francis Picabia et "391,"* II, 168).

23. Cendrars stated in his poem "Baggage" that the scenario was written on board ship "between Le Havre and la Pallice from where I sent it to Satie" (Louis Parrot, *Blaise Cendrars*, Paris, 1948, 139). Cendrars's manuscript (D.P. X, 479) has been published by Sanouillet (*Francis Picabia et "391,"* II, 255–56).

Letters from Rolf de Maré to Picabia on April 14 and 30, 1924 (D.P. X, 262, 408), indicate that substantial coordination began at that time. The evolution from Cendrars's scenario to *Relâche* is indicated in a typed manuscript (D.P. X, 479; Sanouillet, *Francis Picabia et "391,"* II, 256 57) originally entitled *Après dîner* but crossed out and retitled *Relâche*, "d'Erik Satie, Jean Borlin et Picabia." The use of a filmed intermission appears in this intermediate scenario, but considerable changes were later made in the scenarios for both the ballet and the intermission.

24. Picabia's criticism of Derain ("André Derain," *Paris-Journal*, April 11, 1924, 6) was also an oblique attack on Breton, who esteemed Derain and had recently published an article on him ("Idées d'un peintre," *Les Pas perdus*, Paris, 1924; 8th ed., Paris, 1949, 105–110). In "Prix littéraires et Dada" (*Paris-Journal*, March 21, 1924, 1) Picabia goaded editors who "fabricate geniuses like the merchants of the rue Saint Sulpice fabricate Virgins, Saints and Gods in painted plaster!" His article, "Ils n'en mourraient pas tous . . ." (*Paris-Journal*, May 23, 1924, 4), discussed art in the format of an imaginary interview:

"You don't believe in the Holy Virgin?
"I believed in her only on the day I lost my virginity!
"You do not believe in art?
"For me, art is dead like religion. . . .
". . . If you are so clairvoyant, why do you paint, why do you draw, why do you write?
"Because I am the only one who, after the death of Art, has inherited none of it; all the artists who follow its procession . . . figure in its testament; me, it disinherited me, but it thus left me free to say everything that passes through my head and to do what pleases me."

and of past quarrels and suspicions. Many of the suspicions had arisen from Breton's periodic efforts to organize group activities designed to discover or liberate the individual psyche (dreams, spiritualism and automatic writing) or to assess modern culture (the Congress of Paris) with the ultimate aim of reconciling the creative individual in the modern world. Viewed in retrospect, his course was courageous, for his eventual discovery, Surrealism, was an unknown, unnamed domain taken on faith by Breton as he floundered from occasional exhilarating promises of land through the storms of Dada and the trough of the Congress of Paris. Picabia's derring-do on the open sea had given vital confidence to Breton, but their companionship was ever tenuous. Picabia had no tolerance for organized voyages and was less concerned about conquering new worlds than avoiding comfortable ports of any kind—and he perceived such ports on every hand.

When Breton at last began to distinguish the substance of Surrealism during the spring of 1924, Picabia grossly (though understandably) misjudged it as another all-too-familiar and forced or artificial experiment. In an interview shortly before their break, Picabia made several statements seemingly aimed at Breton's promotion of Surrealism and its cast of honored forerunners beginning with Rimbaud and Lautréamont:

> Is there a new movement coming on?
>
> Certainly! There is always a movement, but it is impossible for me to specify it for you. What I can tell you is that it will be beyond those who seek to fabricate it. Artificial eggs don't make chickens. . . .
>
> Don't you like Lautréamont . . . ?
>
> I read Lautréamont when I was 19 and it bores me to talk again of a man whom my friends have discovered twenty-six years later.[25]

Even before that interview was published, Picabia had declared open war on Surrealism. He engaged Pierre de Massot as the manager for a new series of *391* and announced the reappearance of his journal in a press release on May 3, 1924, calculated to evoke the wrath of Breton:

> The famous review *391*, which astonished the world at the time of the dada movement, will reappear monthly under the unique direction of its former director, Francis Picabia, with the collaboration of MM. Erik Satie, Man Ray, Marcel Duchamp, Rrose Sélavy, Pierre de Massot, Robert Desnos, Stieglitz, Cassanyés, Huelsenbeck, Serner, Jacques Rigaut, Lila Robertson, Igor Stravinsky, Marthe Chenal, F.T. Marinetti, etc. etc.
>
> MM. André Breton, Louis Aragon, Roger Vitrac, Max Morise, Marcell Noll, etc. are cordially invited by the master of the house.
>
> It will be consecrated to Surrealism . . .[26]

25. R.J., "Chez Francis Picabia," *Paris-Journal*, May 9, 1924, 5. Some friendly remarks about Breton indicate that this interview took place before May, but overall there is a Breton-baiting tone to it, much like Picabia's contemporary article on Derain (see n. 24).

26. Notice in "Petites Nouvelles," *Le Journal du peuple* [Paris], May 3, 1924, 3. Variants of this notice appeared in several Paris newspapers. A total of four issues of *391* were published in

That insulting invitation provoked an instant reply from Breton, who first rejected collaboration with a movement deemed to be of his own creation, and then enumerated his quarrels with Picabia: "You know what reservations I have about your recent activity, about the sense even of that activity (Montparnasse, the Swedish Ballet, a very boring novel [*Caravansérail*], *Paris-Journal*, etc.)."[27] Picabia printed Breton's entire letter in the next issue of *391*, followed by his blunt response: "When I have smoked cigarettes, it is not my habit to keep the butts." Elsewhere in the new issues of *391*, he ridiculed Surrealism in several drawings and in parodies of the automatic writings produced by members of Breton's circle.[28] The most explicit drawing (fig. 247) depicts Breton as a cloudlike form with the pinched features, spectacles and wig of a Daumier-caricatured judge who simultaneously supports and fondles an entranced female subject before the cup of Rimbaud. An undated drawing possibly contemporary in date (fig. 248) depicts Breton and Aragon at the foot of the cross of "391" on which is a crucified figure labeled "Surréalistes" across its face and "Communistes" across the loincloth.

Breton did not respond in kind to the shower of barbed comments from Picabia; he even published one of them—a drawing of cooked ducks—as the cover of the final issue of *Littérature* (no. 13, June 1924). But he did lead a manifestation against Erik Satie, Picabia's closest associate of the day for both *391* and *Relâche*. Ever since the Congress of Paris, Breton and Satie had regarded each other as absolutely insufferable. At this date in 1924, Satie was also in conflict with some members of "Les Six," particularly Georges Auric, who was active in the circle around Breton—and the lot of them, Breton, Aragon, Auric and others, chose to settle several scores with a manifestation at the June 15 performance of the ballet *Mercure* (music by Satie, decor by Picasso and choreography by Massine). Shouts of "Bravo Picasso!" and "Down with Satie!" provoked countercries, police intervention and repercussions in the press for several weeks. Picabia, who had missed the manifestation while vacationing in Luchon, contributed to the exchange in the press with a laudatory article on Satie and more mischief in *391*.[29]

May, June, July and October 1924. Picabia had made no effort to contact everyone listed as a collaborator, and several names, Marinetti's, for example, should be taken facetiously. However, at this time Picabia was contacted by A. de Ridder and E.L.T. Mesens from Antwerp and Brussels regarding exchanges between their projected magazine *Période* and *391* (see their letters to Picabia of June 2, September, and October 6, 1924, D.P. X, 178, 496, 498). Picabia published poems and aphorisms by Mesens and René Magritte in *391*, no. 19 (Paris, October 1924), and Mesens published some of Picabia's simple figurative drawings. The latter may have been of modest influence on Magritte at this point prior to the mature development of his style.

27. Letter from Breton to Picabia, May 3, 1924, published by Picabia under the heading "Une Lettre de mon grand-père," *391*, no. 17 (Paris, June 1924), 4.

28. Picabia's new mumbo-jumbo pseudonym, Cattawi-Menasse, and his parodies, "Hyperpoésie trophique," "Hypertrophie poétique" and "Tabac" are probably aimed at such writings as Roger Vitrac's "Peau-Asie" (*Littérature*, II, no. 9, Paris, February–March 1923, 18), and Robert Desnos's "L'Aumonyme" (*Littérature*, II, no. 10, Paris, May 1923, 24).

29. Satie's droll jibes at Georges Auric can be followed in his contributions to *Les Feuilles*

A relative lull during the middle of the summer gave way at the end of August to a bitter three-cornered fight over Surrealism between Breton's group, Paul Dermée and a young poet, Ivan Goll. Ever since 1917, when Apollinaire first coined the word "surrealism" in reference to the ballet *Parade* and to his *Mamelles de Tirésias*, it had been used in a variety of ways by a number of writers, most of whom felt that *they* were the true heirs of whatever it was Apollinaire had meant by "surrealism."[30] When word came out in August that Breton planned to launch a movement under that banner, complete with manifesto, books and a magazine entitled *La Révolution surréaliste*, other pretenders to Surrealism were furious, notably Goll and Dermée. At that very moment, Goll was assembling the first issue of a magazine entitled *Le Surréalisme*, and as early as January 1924 Dermée had captioned his magazine *Interventions surréalistes, Organe officiel du Surréalisme international*.[31] In open letters, placed side by side in *Le Journal littéraire* on August 30, Dermée and Goll attacked Breton's claim to Surrealism.[32] They were answered by Breton himself in an article on September 6,[33] but the

---

libres and *391* ("Cahiers d'un mammifère," nos. 17 and 18, Paris, June and July 1924).

The premiere of *Mercure* on June 14 was an unmarred success, but the second performance was disrupted by the manifestation described above. (See de Massot's letter to Picabia, June 16, 1924, D.P. X, 460; Sanouillet, *Francis Picabia et "391,"* II, 164.) Aragon denied any intention other than a spontaneous demonstration for Picasso ("Pour arrêter les bavardages," *Le Journal littéraire*, no. 9, Paris, June 21, 1924, 10).

Picabia extolled Satie and attacked Aragon and Breton in an article, "Erik Satie," *Paris-Journal*, June 27, 1924, 1. In *391*, no. 18 (Paris, July 1924), he published without permission a private letter to him from Gabrielle Buffet, who made uncomplimentary remarks about "the Breton band" and attributed a clear Picabia and Duchamp influence on Picasso's decor for *Mercure*.

30. Reconsideration of Apollinaire was lively at this time. Scores of authors and artists had been asked to contribute statements to a special Apollinaire issue of *L'Esprit nouveau*, or to donate works for a sale whose proceeds would go toward his tomb. Picabia, who contributed to both projects, was the only one who offered a word of criticism, noting that the "perspective of a possible Legion of Honor haunted him [Apollinaire]" and that a slight reserve in their friendship at the end was uniquely "a question 'of uniform' [military]." See Picabia, "Guillaume Apollinaire," *L'Esprit nouveau*, no. 26 (Paris, October 1924).

31. Ivan Goll's single issue of *Le Surréalisme* (Paris, October 1924) revived to some extent the tone of Pierre Albert-Birot's *SIC*. Birot, who had considered himself an heir to the literary spirit of Apollinaire, collaborated with Goll.

Dermée had also considered himself the heir of Apollinaire's "esprit nouveau" and chose that phrase for the title of his earlier magazine. His new journal, *Interventions*, had been founded in December 1923 with the subtitle *Gazette internationale des lettres et des arts modernes*. In the second issue (January 1924) that subtitle was changed to *Organe officiel du Surréalisme international*, but no further issues were published until November 1924, when it reappeared with yet another title, *Le Mouvement accéléré*. Although other issues of *Le Mouvement accéléré* were announced, none was published.

A humorous survey of the various pretenders to Surrealism was published by Fernand Divoire, "Un Nouveau Surréalisme," *Le Journal littéraire*, no. 26 (Paris, October 18, 1924), 5.

32. Paul Dermée and Ivan Goll, open letter under the heading "Autour du Surréalisme," *Le Journal littéraire*, no. 19 (Paris, August 30, 1924), 4. Goll had also submitted an earlier article, "Une Réhabilitation du Surréalisme," *Le Journal littéraire*, no. 17 (Paris, August 16, 1924), 8.

33. Breton, "La Querelle du Surréalisme," *Le Journal littéraire*, no. 20 (Paris, September 6, 1924), 10. For the complete exchange see Ivan Goll's article in *Le Journal littéraire* on August 16 and the surrealists' response on August 23.

major event in this exchange was the publication of Breton's *Poisson soluble*, prefaced by the "Manifesto of Surrealism" with its now famous statements on "pure psychic automatism," "the omnipotence of dream," "the disinterested play of thought" and the love of the marvelous.[34] Breton had found his way. His manner was stamped with self-confidence and his statements—in contrast to the dull, carping comments of Goll and Dermée—were personal, fascinating and pregnant with possibilities.

Picabia's collaboration was solicited by all three groups, though his only point of contact with Breton was Robert Desnos, who esteemed both Picabia and Breton and earnestly sought to reconcile them.[35] Picabia responded to both Desnos and Dermée, but the latter received a far milder, more independent statement than he had requested,[36] and Desnos's reconciling efforts were demolished when Picabia resumed harsh criticism of Breton and Surrealism in two old forums, *L'Ere nouvelle* and the final issue of *391* (no. 19, October 1924).[37] As in the spring, Picabia continued to view Surrealism as a misappropriation of Dada by a band of pedants who knew little of Dada or life:

> The only men who created the Dada movement are Marcel Duchamp, Tristan Tzara, Huelsenbeck and Francis Picabia. . . .[38]

> The works of Messieurs Breton and, how do you say it? Philippe Coupeaux, I think, are a poor imitation of Dada and their Surrealism is exactly of the same order.[39]

34. André Breton, *Manifeste du Surréalisme. Poisson soluble* (Paris, October 1924). Contrary to the claims of some authors, the editors of *La Revue europénne* did not devote an issue to Surrealism. In a review of contemporary poetry, Soupault (an editor of that magazine) did discuss Surrealism briefly and announced the forthcoming publication of *Poisson soluble* ("La Poésie," *La Revue europénne*, no. 20, Paris, October 1, 1924, 77–78).

35. Desnos wrote Picabia early in September to announce the publication of *La Révolution surréaliste* and to request a poem for it (undated letter, D.P. X, 372; Sanouillet, *Dada à Paris*, 549). Goll wrote Picabia on September 29 (D.P. X, 490) and Dermée wrote on October 3: "Breton's book with his preface on Surrealism will appear this week. . . . Send me immediately a very violent, very categorical article on Surrealism" (D.P. X, 497; Sanouillet, *Francis Picabia et "391,"* II, 167).

36. Picabia, "Première Heure" *Le Mouvement accéléré* (Paris, ca. November 20, 1924), 1. Though critical of Breton in this article, Picabia remarked that he had sent one of his best poems to Desnos for *La Révolution surréaliste* and was convinced of the futility of pursuing any movement save the perpetual movement of life. Sanouillet (*Francis Picabia et "391,"* II, 166) states that *Le Mouvement accéléré* appeared on November 4, but a letter from Dermée to Picabia on November 19 indicates that it was to be delivered by the printer the next day (D.P. XIII, 45; Sanouillet, *Dada à Paris*, 546).

37. For the plight of Desnos see his letters to Picabia (D.P. X, 443, 446, 449; Sanouillet, *Dada à Paris*, 550–51).

38. Picabia, "Poissons volants," *L'Ere nouvelle* [Paris], November 24, 1924, 3. The title of this article probably represents a comment on Breton's *Poisson soluble* (Paris, October 1924).

39. Picabia, "Opinions et portraits," *391*, no. 19 (Paris, October 1924), 2. Picabia keyed his statement on an article by Maurice Martin du Gard ("Le Surréalisme? André Breton," *Les Nouvelles littéraires*, Paris, October 10, 1924) which was largely based on Breton's concept of Surrealism, though not entirely to Breton's liking.

André Breton is not a revolutionary . . . he is an arriviste . . . he has nothing to say; having no sensitivity, never having lived, this artist is the type of petit bourgeois who loves little collections of paintings; he hates traveling, he only likes his café. . . .

. . . Art is not fabricated, *it is*, simply, but rare. You are too numerous, Messrs. the surrealists, for there to be a rare man among you.[40]

In contemporary statements, Tzara and Ribemont-Dessaignes expressed milder but essentially comparable assessments of Dada and Surrealism, reconfirming, in a way, two streams observed in Dada by Gide and Charensol in 1920, namely, the "dadaist" current of Tzara, Picabia and Ribemont-Dessaignes, and the "proto-surrealist" current of Breton, Aragon and Soupault.[41] The latter group had become the core of Surrealism; members of the dadaist branch remained dadaists—but independently, outside of any group activity and at odds with each other. Picabia did provide some droll, deliberately modest drawings (figs. 249, 250) for Tzara's *Sept Manifestes Dada* (1924), but the old friendship was not pursued.[42] Picabia persisted in saying: "I believe there is truly only one thing that can seduce us, it is the perpetual evolution of life. . . . In order to have something to say, one must begin by living. . . . I hold to being and remaining outside of every chapel."[43]

Those convictions about the perpetual evolution of life and the priority of life over art sound very much like the dadaist Picabia of yore, and they characterize his antidote to Surrealism, a one-man "movement" entitled Instantanism. Indeed, Picabia equated Dada and Instantanism on the cover of the final issue of *391*, and on the last page of that issue he announced the primary manifestations of Instantanism, the ballet *Relâche* and the film *Entr'acte* (Intermission). The production of that ballet and film dominated Picabia's life during November–December 1924, subsuming his role in the wranglings over Surrealism.

Relâche and *Entr'acte* were largely completed during the summer, and beginning in July tantalizing announcements were released to the press.[44] Opening

40. Picabia, "Poissons volants," *L'Ere nouvelle*, 3.

41. See René Crevel's interview "Voici . . . Tristan Tzara," *Les Nouvelles littéraires* (Paris, October 25, 1924, attrib.); Ribemont-Dessaignes's "A propos du Surréalisme," *Le Mouvement accéléré* (Paris, November 1924), 2; and the letter from Ribemont-Dessaignes to Tzara on October 9, 1924 (C.T. 3306; Sanouillet, *Dada à Paris*, 427).

42. Tristan Tzara, *Sept Manifestes Dada* (Paris, 1924). The drawing in fig. 249 was reproduced four times, each time oriented in a different direction in playful rejection of fixed notions of top and bottom, right and left. In the drawing of dada mathematics, fig. 250, columns of figures are added, subtracted and otherwise manipulated at will, outside any established logical system. The latter drawing appeared in a modern edition of *Sept Manifestes Dada* (Paris: Jean-Jacques Pauvert, 1963). Both drawings were originally in the Tzara collection.

43. Picabia, "Première Heure," *Le Mouvement accéléré*, 1.

44. De Maré announced the film and ballet in an interview with René Bruyez, "La Prochaine Saison des Ballets Suédois," *Comoedia* [Paris], July 10, 1924, 2.
De Massot wrote Picabia on June 16 that René Clair had filmed *Entr'acte* Wednesday (June

night was set for 9 p.m. November 27 in Hébertot's Théâtre des Champs-Elysées. *Relâche* shared the program with two works previously produced by the Swedish Ballet, *La Création du monde* and *Skating Rink*, a collaboration with Canudo, Léger and Honnegar. As the only new ballet being offered by a company noted for its avant-garde work, *Relâche* was placed as the climactic closing number, and an accelerating publicity campaign concluded on the eve of the premiere with long articles by Rolf de Maré and Picabia in major newspapers.[45] The machine portraits accompanying some of Picabia's articles (see fig. 251) underscore the persistent dada temperament in his comments about *Relâche*: "It is perpetual movement, life, it is the minute of happiness we all seek; it is light, richness, luxury, love far from prudish conventions; without morality for fools, without artistic research for the snobs."[46] Members of the audience were advised to bring dark glasses and earplugs, and ex-dadaists among them were invited to shout, "Down with Satie!" "Down with Picabia!" "Long live *La Nouvelle Revue française!*"[47]

Uneasy curiosity about the titles, *Relâche* and *Entr'acte*, prompted Picabia to assure his readers that *Relâche* was not "relâche" but *Relâche*.[48] Nevertheless, conditions beyond his control made the title *Relâche* more appropriate than could have been imagined or intended. On opening night *Relâche* was "relâche," and although it did open on the next scheduled date (December 4), the ballet closed in Paris after only twelve performances, and the Swedish Ballet company disbanded after the winter season of 1924–1925. The failure to open on November 27 was caused by the sudden illness of the principal dancer-choreographer, Jean Borlin, but few among the 3,000 at the door resisted rumors that Picabia had played his greatest hoax.[49] Still they took it in good humor; many milled about in the celebrity-studded crowd for hours and returned to join a packed house for the eventual opening on December 4. *Skating Rink* and *La Création du monde* were virtually neglected in reviews of the performance. The critics, at least, had come for *Relâche*, and on hand to introduce them to the new ballet was an intriguing

11) in Luna Park (D.P. X, 460), and on July 1 Clair invited Picabia to preview the film on July 3 (D.P. X, 468).

Satie wrote Germaine Everling on August 27 that the ballet was "entirely composed" and that Borlin must have finished the choreography for the first part (D.P. X, 377; Sanouillet, *Francis Picabia et "391,"* II, 169). On October 19, the ballet was presented for Picabia (Sanouillet, loc. cit.). Minor adjustments continued through November, during which time Francis and Germaine led a carefree life in the Hotel Istria (Germaine Everling, *L'Anneau de Saturne*, Paris, 1970, 155–56).

45. Rolf de Maré, "A propos de 'Relâche,' ballet instantanéiste," *Comoedia* [Paris], November 27, 1924, 2; and Picabia, "Pourquoi j'ai écrit 'Relâche,' " *Le Siècle* [Paris], November 27, 1924, 4.

46. Picabia, "Pourquoi j'ai écrit 'Relâche,' " *Le Siècle*, 4.

47. Advertisement in *391*, no. 19 (Paris, October 1924), 4.

48. Picabia, "Pourquoi j'ai écrit 'Relâche,' " *Le Siècle*, 4.

49. One reviewer (P.M., "Relâche," *Paris-Journal*, December 5, 1924, 1) estimated the waiting crowd at 3,000, including such celebrities as Tzara, Picasso, Duchamp, Brancusi, Jacques Doucet, Marthe Chenal, Napierkowska, Milhaud, Léger, the Crottis, Man Ray, Kiki, Roland Dorgelès and others. See also Everling, *L'Anneau de Saturne*, 156.

program in which comments by the collaborators and drawings by Picabia were integrated with dadaist aplomb (figs. 252, 253). Picabia's own statement abounds with an outlook indistinguishable from his attitudes during the heyday of Dada:

> *Relâche* is life, life as I love it; life without tomorrow, the life of today, everything for today, nothing for yesterday, nothing for tomorrow. . . . *Relâche* promenades in life with a great burst of laughter. ERIK SATIE, BORLIN, ROLF DE MARE, RENE CLAIR, PRIEUR and I created *Relâche* a little like God created life. . . . *Relâche* is the happiness of instants without reflection; why reflect, why have a convention of beauty or of joy? . . . *Relâche* advises you to be livers, for life will always be longer in the school of pleasure than in the school of morality, in the school of art, in the religious school, in the school of worldly conventions.[50]

A brief, filmed prologue by René Clair showed Satie and Picabia descending from Heaven and firing a cannon shot from the roof of the Théâtre des Champs-Elysées into the city of Paris. That shot, as filmed by Clair, literally turned the world upside down.[51] The curtain then opened to a bare stage with a backdrop composed of 370 large metal reflecting discs (illus. 28), each bearing an automobile-sized headlight which was dimmed and brightened according to the movement of the music, at times blinding the audience. The dancers consisted of a troop of men attired in dinner jackets and top hats, and a single ballerina, Mlle Bonsdorff, who danced when the music ceased and stopped dancing whenever the music began. Jean Borlin entered in a self-propelled paralytics cart (illus. 27), but was "healed" by the allure of Mlle Bonsdorff. At another point, a stagehand putted across the stage in a small automobile trailing balloons, and throughout the performance a chain-smoking fireman decorated with the Legion of Honor studiously emptied water from one bucket into another. Satie's correspondingly simple, insouciant music included passages based on indecent student and army songs which, according to one critic, elicited humming "by those who have done their military service."[52]

Following the filmed intermission *Entr'acte*, Act II opened to a slightly modified setting. The reflecting discs and lights remained, but enormous signs had been suspended from the discs, and spectators were now blinded by light reflected from mirrors. One sign read, "If you are not content, whistles are on sale at the box office for two coins," and de Maré had 1,000 whistles on hand, though no one

50. Picabia statement in the program for *Relâche*, printed in *La Danse* (Paris, November–December 1924), number consecrated to the Swedish Ballet.

51. This filmed episode is often shown as the beginning of Clair's film *Entr'acte*, run during the intermission of *Relâche*. Clair has corrected that misunderstanding, but the prologue does link gracefully with *Entr'acte* (René Clair, *Cinema Yesterday and Today*, trans. Stanley Appelbaum, New York, 1972, 11).

52. Louis Schneider, "Music in Paris," *New York Herald* [Paris], December 8, 1924 (attrib.; D.P. XIII, 91).

went out to purchase them.[53] While the fireman continued to empty and refill his buckets, two hospital attendants carried Mlle Bonsdorff on stage on a stretcher. When she arose, the languishing male dancers began to remove their dinner clothes, emerging finally in their top hats and leotard bathing suits or clown costumes. All proceeded to dance, at first joyfully about the ballerina, but then with disdain around a Tanagra statuette brought in to replace Mlle Bonsdorff. At the close of the performance, a female dancer followed a beam of light into the audience and placed a wreath of orange blossoms on Marthe Chenal, seated in the central box of the auditorium. At curtain call Picabia and Satie, clad in furs and jewels, drove onstage in a midget 5 hp Citroën to an ovation that astounded most of the critics.

For some critics, *Relâche* was absolute nonsense, but, as reconstructed here from contemporary accounts, the ballet abounds with the spirit and basic themes of Picabia's art: his audience-provoking inversion of the expected, as in the blinding of the spectators and the injection of music-hall slapstick within the realm of "serious" ballet; the fireman as a symbol of the academy, namely, a uniformed, decorated hypocrite devoid of imagination; a disarming "I screw myself" attitude in the signs and whistles; the power of sexual attraction; and, finally, disdain for the past and/or art as represented by the Tanagra statuette.

Judging from the lively audience reaction, Picabia's aims were fulfilled. Some critics, many friends and even a few enemies were delighted. Léger exclaimed that *Relâche* was "a lot of kicks in a lot of behinds, sacred or not," with a music that was "luminous, electric, cinematic . . . incredibly light . . . perfectly regulated, without the air of it. . . . Bravo *Relâche*, Satie-Picabia, René Clair, the Electrician . . . I tip my hat to you."[54] But two out of three critics vied with each other in damning the scenario and the music—hollow, sad, atelier farce, music beneath criticism, willful poverty and on and on.[55] To their surprise, however, most of the critics discovered they liked the film. Some attributed that experience to the independent talent of René Clair, but the situation was more thoughtfully

53. Paul Achard, "Soirs de Paris," *Le Siècle* [Paris], December 6, 1924, 4. The account of *Relâche* offered here is based on this article and others cited below, principally one by Maurice Bouisson ("La Musique. Relâche-Entr'acte de Picabia et Erik Satie," *L'Evénement* [Paris], December 4, 1924, 2).

54. Fernand Léger, "Vive 'Relâche,' " *Paris-Midi*, December 17, 1924, 4. Léger's praise seems all the more genuine inasmuch as Picabia had recently criticized him and the film (*Ballet mécanique*) Léger had made with Dudley Murphy ("L'Art moderne," *L'Ere nouvelle* [Paris], August 5, 1924, 2).

55. These adjectives were employed by Georges Auric ("*Relâche*, les ballets suédois," *Les Nouvelles littéraires*, Paris, December 13, 1924, 7); Eugène Marson et al. ("Relâche," unidentified newspaper [*Le Siècle*?], December 6, 1924, attrib.; D.P. XI, 96); and Louis Schneider ("Music in Paris," *New York Herald*; D.P. XIII, 91). In a more recent evaluation, Roger Shattuck describes Satie's music as simple and formless when played separately, but excellent film music—unassertive, timed to fit the action of the film and parallel to film techniques in its use of abrupt transitions (*The Banquet Years*, rev. ed., Garden City, N. Y. 1968, 170–72).

described by one critic as "the film of Picabia, understood, married by René Clair in such a manner that one asks himself who is the one who conceived it and who is the one who made it."[56]

Analysis of the film reveals that *Entr'acte*, like *Relâche*, abounds with the spirit of Picabia, and contemporary statements by Clair and Picabia attest to a rare union in their collaboration. As far as Picabia was concerned, he gave Clair "a little scenario of nothing at all; he made it a masterpiece." And Clair avowed that *Entr'acte* "belonged to Picabia. . . . My task is limited to realizing technically the aims of Francis Picabia."[57] Both men were unduly modest; Clair was far more than a technician and Picabia brought to *Entr'acte* not just a sketchy scenario but a conception of what film could be:

> The cinema must give us vertigo, be a sort of artificial paradise, a promoter of intense sensations, surpassing "looping the loop" in an airplane and the pleasure of opium; for that it must orient itself toward spontaneity of invention. . . .
>
> . . . The cinema must not be an imitation but an evocative invention as rapid as the thought of our brain.[58]

Clair's film prologue with the cannon shot that turned the world upside down was picked up smartly in *Entr'acte* proper by Picabia's ubiquitous dots and circles that appear in rapid succession as lights, boxing gloves, heads, balls and balloons, reasserting in a congenial new media his taste for simultaneity, perpetual movement and the ceaseless association of images and symbols. By employing a glass-floored stage, he indulged a desire to observe a ballerina from below, but the effect is that of an abstract visual experience rather than an erotic one, and any remaining potential for sexual stimulation is shattered when one finally sees the ballerina from a normal viewpoint only to discover that "she" is a bearded and bespectacled "he." A frustrated marksman played by Jean Borlin becomes the victim instead of the hunter, and an incredible funeral follows (see illus. 29). The hearse, drawn by a camel, breaks loose and with the droll mourners in hot pursuit rolls at dizzying speed through town, countryside and the roller coaster of an amusement park. Finally the casket tumbles off in a field, and as the panting mourners gather round, the "deceased" springs up triumphantly. Rejoicing turns to incredulity as he causes each mourner and then himself to disappear with the touch of a wand. A blank screen labeled "The End" is broken from behind when the "deceased" and another man jump through the screen with one parting gesture.

56. J.L. Croze, "Entr'acte," *Comoedia* [Paris], December 5, 1924, 4.

57. Statements by Picabia and Clair in the program for *Relâche*, printed in *La Danse* (Paris, November–December 1924). Picabia's statement continues: "The intermission of *Relâche* is a film that interprets our dreams and the unrealized events that take place in our brain; why describe the things everyone sees, or can see every day? *Entr'acte* is a real entr'acte, an intermission in the monotonous boredom of life and conventions full of ridiculous, hypocritical respect."

58. Picabia, "Instantanéisme," *Comoedia* [Paris], November 21, 1924, 4.

Neither the scenario nor the film techniques were wholly new,[59] but ever since its premiere *Entr'acte* has enjoyed both popular success and critical recognition as an important work by a filmmaker of extraordinary potential. Fulfillment of that promise has tended to obscure the role of Picabia, who never again collaborated on a film; however, he did publish another scenario, and, more importantly, incorporated his experience with film into other aspects of his work beginning immediately after *Entr'acte* in a New Year's Eve spectacular entitled *Cinésketch*.[60] For that festive show, Picabia again had the collaboration of René Clair, the Théâtre des Champs-Elysées, the best jazz band in Paris and the help of a score of friends from the stage, screen, ballet and music halls of Paris. His scenario dealt with a bourgeois woman, asleep and dreaming of terrestrial paradise until awakened by a robber who in turn was followed by the woman's lover, his wife, the woman's husband, a policeman, a maid and Jean Börlin as a ballerina. The course of this farce was revealed in sketches technically realized on a stage divided into three compartments—bedroom, hallway and kitchen—which were illuminated and darkened separately in a rapid rhythm akin to frames in a film. Indeed, Picabia stated: "Until the present, the cinema has been inspired by the theater. I have tried to do the contrary in bringing to the stage the method and lively rhythms of the cinema."[61]

The principal roles were filled by Mlle Bonsdorff as the dreaming bourgeoise and Marcel Lévesque as the robber, while Marcel Duchamp and "Francine Picabia" (Brogna Perlmutter) appeared for a second as Adam and Eve (illus. 30), completely nude save for some jewels in emulation of the painting by Lucas Cranach which Picabia chose as the model for that particular sketch.[62] Numerous

59. J.L. Croze remarked that most of the techniques employed by Clair were not new, and films had been used in theatrical productions prior to *Relâche*, but "this variety in sensation and pleasure has never seemed to me so new, so brutal . . ." ("Entr'acte," *Comoedia*, 4).

Professor Stan Lawder has also brought to the attention of this author the similarity between *Entr'acte* and Mack Sennett's comedy, *Heinze's Resurrection* (1913), particularly in the funeral, grand chase and final scene. Picabia, who loved American westerns and comedies, may have drawn some ideas from Sennett; likewise, Clair himself, who cited in the program for *Relâche* "certain American comedies" as among the few works worthy of the cinema. A contemporary critic also perceived the spirit of a Mack Sennett comedy in *Entr'acte* (Léon Moussinac, "Entr'acte, par René Clair," *Le Crapouillot* [Paris], January 1, 1925, 19).

60. For Picabia's other film scenario, *La Loi d'accommodation chez les borgnes "Sursum corda" (Film en 3 parties)* (Paris, 1928), see p. 230.

A scenario for *Cinésketch* has been published in the Centre National d'Art et de Culture Georges Pompidou, Musée National d'Art Moderne, *Francis Picabia*, Paris, Grand Palais, January 23–March 29, 1976, 133. Some discrepancies exist between the scenario, the program for *Cinésketch* and contemporary reviews.

61. Paul Achard, "Picabia m'a dit . . . avant 'Cinésketch' au Théâtre des Champs-Elysées," *Le Siècle* [Paris], January 1, 1925, 4.

62. Ibid. This scene has long been attributed to *Relâche* but it is mentioned in several reviews of *Cinésketch*, including this interview with Paul Achard where Picabia states: "I reconstitute a painting by Cranach, the only painter I find supportable now: one will see rise up in a kitchen this evocation of Adam and Eve. I prefer to tell you immediately that the persons will be completely nude so that there might be no misunderstanding. Marcel Duchamp and Francine Picabia, one of my psychic children, will revive this charming painting."

other friends, principally such popular entertainers as Maria Ricotti, Mlle Jasmine, Mlle Cariathys and Pierrette Madd also lent their talent to this witty, sexy production. As such, *Cinésketch* retained some of the spirit of Dada, but it was neither as serious nor as insulting as a dada production; it assumed a congenial audience; it was relaxed and fun-loving, and, in hindsight, already indicative of the Picabias' imminent life in the Midi.

15. COLLAGES, ESPAGNOLES AND "MONSTERS" IN THE MIDI, 1924-1928

THE PERFORMANCE of *Cinésketch* had hardly concluded before Francis and Germaine set off to establish a new home in the Midi. Within a month they decided on property in Mougins and began construction of a rambling villa named the "Château de Mai." The site was a terraced hill overlooking Cannes on the south, with a view toward the French Alps in the northeast. Among terraces of rosebushes, orange and olive trees, Picabia had constructed to his design an extravagant Mediterranean residence—sprawling, informal and cheerful with its ochre and vermilion walls, red tile roof, and numerous gardens and porches (see illus. 31, 32). Large windows introduced the light of the south into ample interior rooms, cluttered, as was Picabia's custom, with a melange of silver, ceramics and model sailing ships, with collections of art, mounted butterflies, and French and Spanish furniture of the sixteenth, seventeenth and eighteenth centuries. Both the château and its contents grew apace; every day Picabia appeared with a new object for the house or exotic plants for the gardens. One day, eleven thirty-foot palm trees were ordered "just for the pleasure of watching the caravan of trucks which delivered them."[1] A swimming pool was added; then two towers, and finally an enormous studio. Several servants were hired to care for the house and its inhabitants, and in December 1925 a young Swiss girl, Olga Mohler, was employed as a governess for Lorenzo.[2]

1. Germaine Everling, *L'Anneau de Saturne* (Paris, 1970), 163. Descriptions of the Château de Mai are also provided by Paul Gordeaux, "Hôtes d'été. Francis Picabia," *L'Eclaireur de Nice*, September 6, 1925, 3, and Nantille, "Portraits d'interieurs, le Château de Mai," *La Saison de Cannes*, January 8, 1927 (attrib.; D.P. XII, 321).

2. From this date onward many of the essential documents regarding Picabia's life and career are in the possession of Mme Olga Picabia, Paris, namely, her unpublished manuscript, "Un Quart de Siècle avec Picabia," and her album of photographs, statements, catalogues and press clippings. Henceforth these two sources will be referred to as the Olga Picabia manuscript and the Olga Picabia album, the latter recently published in partial facsimile as Olga Mohler Picabia, *Francis Picabia* (Turin, 1975), essay by Maurizio Fagiolo. I am deeply indebted to Mme Picabia for her indispensable support of this study.

For several years, Francis and Germaine savored an idyllic life. Their letters abound with a joy for "the beauty of this place," and, while Picabia welcomed reports on activities in Paris, he tended to belittle the affairs there. He ignored Breton's respectful desire to number him among the surrealists and rejected invitations to collaborate on new magazines.[3] The activities that had previously occupied him—controversial exhibitions, caustic articles, internecine squabbles, etc.—gave way with few exceptions to the pleasures of the beach, the casino, jaunts along the Riviera and a revived interest in painting. "This country which seems . . . to make some lazy, stimulates me to work," he wrote to Jacques Doucet, "I have more and more pleasure in the resumption of painting."[4] Spells of assiduous work in the studio seem, however, to have been effortlessly integrated into the easy rhythm of their life and a stream of old friends. Jean and Suzanne Crotti built their summer home across the road; other friends settled nearby, and visitors at the Château de Mai ranged from Picabia's father, stepmother and half sister to his first mistress, Mme Orliac, his first wife Gabrielle Buffet and his children by her; Marcel Duchamp, Man Ray, Jacques Doucet, Picasso, René Clair, Rolf de Maré, Marthe Chenal, Paul Eluard, Robert Desnos, Cocteau, Brancusi, Léger, Gerald Murphy and scores of others.

While Picabia was quite content without Paris, he was not forgotten in the capital. A comedy team based a routine on his work, and a chef attempting to overthrow traditions in French cuisine was dubbed the "Picabia of cookery."[5] He was solicited in polls of artists, and one critic mused over the vital role he once fulfilled at the now solemn Salon des Indépendants.[6]

A similar sense of nostalgia marked the reception of the only major showing of Picabia's work in Paris between 1923 and the fall of 1927, the so-called

3. Breton wrote in 1928: "I will continue in spite of everything to count on Francis Picabia. . . . Only his perfect incomprehension of Surrealism and his refusal, very likely, to accept some ideas which I express here prevent me from considering carefully, *as I would like to do*, what he has done and what he can still do and to try to place him as a painter, according to my criteria" (*Le Surréalisme et la peinture*, Paris, 1928; 2nd ed., New York, 1945, 48–49).

Although nothing came of it, Picabia did agree to collaborate on one new magazine entitled *392* when Tzara wrote seeking his participation and authorization for use of that title (Picabia letter to Tzara, 1926, C.T. 3017; Michel Sanouillet, *Francis Picabia et "391,"* II, Paris, 1966, 172): "Naturally take *392*. There is *much to do*. The life of the art world is congealed, transformed into gelatin, there are only grand men, just men, men who know . . .

. . . "I certainly wish to collaborate with your paper, but *392* above all must be unjust, commercial and egotist."

4. Picabia letter to Jacques Doucet, February 27, 1926 (B.D. 7204-166).

5. See Pierre Veber's review of Rip's and Briguet's "Où allons-nous?" ("Première Représentation," *Petit Journal* [Paris], January 29, 1925, attrib.; D.P. XII, old p. 7), and an anonymous article " 'Modernist' Chef in Paris Cooks Strange Recipes," *Herald Tribune* [Paris], May 29, 1927 (attrib.; D.P. XII, 459).

6. Picabia responded to a poll regarding the creation of a Museum of Modern French Art (*L'Art vivant*, no. 16, Paris, August 15, 1925, 37). His absence from the Salons was noted by Michel Georges-Michel, "Journal d'un boulevardier," *Le Siècle* [Paris], February 26, 1926, 1–2.

Duchamp sale at the Hôtel Drouot on March 8, 1926.[7] Duchamp assembled for auction a collection of eighty works ranging from impressionist paintings of ca. 1905 to the recent work in Mougins. It was the most important, comprehensive collection of Picabia's oeuvre to date, and attracted considerable attention. Several critics sought to assess his career; Desnos, in particular, wrote a perceptive résumé. Others dwelt on memories of the dada epoch or multiplied tales of his eccentric life-style.[8] Picabia himself wrote his first article in over a year and granted Christian an interview permeated with a dadaist spirit:

> . . . Painting, for me, resides in the pleasure of invention. What would give me the most pleasure would be to be able to invent without painting.
>
> Is it indiscreet to ask if you renounce your earlier painting?
>
> I don't remember it.
>
> But can't you name for me the best painting you have made?
>
> All of them, even those I have destroyed, for each gave me for a second the impression that it was the best.
>
> Why are you always amused to destroy the artistic movements that you have created?
>
> For love of my next one.
>
> . . . will you please tell me the reason you sold all your paintings to M. Marcel Duchamp?
>
> Because he was the only man who proposed it to me.[9]

At the auction itself, a crowd of illustrious friends (and former friends) vied for some of Picabia's most important works. Breton went away with *Procession Seville* and *Catch as Catch Can* (color pl. v; fig. 84); Léger purchased *Optophone* I (fig. 227); Tzara got *Flirt* (fig. 258); and Doucet made several purchases, including the recent *Les Rochers à St.-Honorat* (*Rocks at St.-Honorat*, fig. 255).[10]

Duchamp's sale and the serious catalogue accompanying it are particularly

7. Hôtel Drouot, Paris, *Tableaux, aquarelles et dessins par Francis Picabia appartenant à M. Marcel Duchamp*, March 8, 1926. Duchamp was also responsible for the important catalogue of the sale and claimed in conversations with Arturo Schwarz that the sale was organized to enable him to earn some money.

8. R[obert] D[esnos], "Picabia," *Paris-Soir*, March 5, 1926 (attrib.; D.P. XII, 162).

Michel Georges-Michel first published the grossly embroidered account of Picabia and a wedding party in the Midi. As the story goes, he and Picabia stopped to dine at a hotel in Valence, but found it taken over by a wedding party. Picabia promptly joined the celebration, toasted the newlyweds, opened dancing with the bride and took her for a spin in his automobile which continued all the way to the Italian border. (Georges-Michel, "Journal d'un boulevardier," *Le Siècle*, 1–2.) Other versions of this tale were developed later.

9. Francis Picabia, "Interview," *Volonté* [Paris], March 4, 1926, 3. This interview by Christian was reprinted in *This Quarter*, I, no. 3 (Monte Carlo, 1927), 297–300. For Picabia's article see "Soleil," *Paris-Soir*, March 5, 1926, 1.

10. For an account of the audience and prices see Maurice Monda, " 'Prenez garde à la peinture,' Quatre-vingts Picabias," unidentified newspaper [Paris], ca. March 7, 1926 (D.P. XII, 136).

useful as an introduction to Picabia's new work in Cannes, indicating at the outset the three major currents which occupied him during ca. 1924–1927: the ubiquitous Spanish subjects, the so-called "monsters" and "dadaist" collages long misattributed to 1918–1920.

Several examples of the "monster" style figured in the auction (figs. 255–257). Their variety precludes simple description although they deal with popular or traditional subjects—landscapes, embracing couples, women with parasols and the like—deliberately distorted in form and often rendered with ripolin paint in jolting color combinations. Those paintings were accompanied in the catalogue by two works, *Flirt* and *La Lecture* (*Reading*, figs. 258, 259), which, except for their added collage elements, belong to the "monsters" in subject and style and were attributed to "Cannes 1924–1925." In fact, it is impossible to determine if Picabia initially conceived *Flirt* and *La Lecture* in their present forms or reworked what had once been "finished" paintings in the monster style. Whatever the circumstances, they possess a sense of wholeness and furnish direct evidence of Picabia's simultaneous production of collages and monsters. Other documents suggest that some of the collages may have appeared first, probably in 1923, although no reliable documents are presently known before 1924.[11] Excluding the distinctive dada examples of ca. 1919–1921 (figs. 184, 202–204), the first of Picabia's collages now documented is *Pailles et cure-dents* (*Straws and Toothpicks*, fig. 260), loaned by Jacques Doucet to the "Tri-National Exhibition" which opened in Paris in May 1925.[12] It is a striking image of potted flowers constructed out of wooden straws, cord and quill toothpicks on a succulent ripolin ground— the whole enclosed by Pierre Legrain in a wood frame painted aluminum and studded with buttons. Despite the imaginative, unorthodox frame and collage elements, there is nothing essentially dadaist about the subject or the content of

11. A serious challenge to the chronology proposed here is presented by the only collage in the group dated on the canvas itself, *Matchwoman* I (fig. 261), signed and dated 1920. However, that date is not supported by any other document, and stylistically *Matchwoman* I belongs not with the dada collages of 1920–1921 (figs. 184, 202–204) but with the collages documented from 1924 to 1928 (figs. 258–60, 262–69, and esp. color pl. XIII). Pending additional information, it seems prudent to consider the possibility that the 1920 date on *Matchwoman* I is a later, erroneous addition.

12. In the catalogue of the tri-national exhibition (Paris, London, New York) organized by Marius de Zayas, this collage was listed as *Pailles et cure-dents* (Galeries Durand-Ruel, Paris, *Exposition tri-nationale*, May–June 1925). Contemporary reviews and correspondence provide secure identification: "These straws and real toothpicks represent ideally a bouquet in a pot" (Louis de Meurville, "Une Exposition tri-nationale," *Le Gaulois* [Paris], May 31, 1925, 2); "Picabia has composed a picture with an elaborate arrangement of toothpicks and buttons on a black enameled background" (Anonymous notice in *The Arts*, VIII, no. 2, New York, August 1925, 109).

A date of ca. 1924 is indicated for *Pailles et cure-dents* on the basis of circumstantial evidence and stylistic compatibility with *Flirt* and *La Lecture*. Breton, who had followed Picabia's work closely, was unaware of this collage prior to its exhibition at the Galeries Durand-Ruel (Pierre de Massot letter to Picabia, June 19, 1925, D.P. XII, 82), and Picabia mentioned the work to be exhibited in a letter to the owner in January 1925 (Picabia letter to Jacques Doucet, January 7, 1925, B.D. 7204-159).

this work; its thrust is not witty, mocking or antiart; instead, its appeal is direct, sensuous and very effective. When Doucet balked at permitting *Pailles et cure-dents* to travel with the exhibition to London and New York, Picabia negotiated the loan of a replacement—probably *Matchwoman* II (color pl. XIII), one of the most subtle and beautiful of his collages.[13] It may also be slightly earlier in date, for two formal properties recall features in works of 1923. The curvilinear color planes forming the head have—like the floating figures on the cover of *Littérature* (fig. 243)—that curious property of existing equally well as separate planes or as a unified head. The thick, rippling lines of the hair also appear in other works attributed to ca. 1923–1924/1925, *Landscape* (fig. 254) and *Femme à l'ombrelle* (*Woman with Parasol*, fig. 257), while the matches recall a scene in *Entr'acte* where burning matches were superimposed on a head of hair.

A relatively early date is also recommended for *Plumes* (fig. 262) given the presence of similar color planes, thick lines and a painted, doweled frame reminiscent of *Lampe* (fig. 245). The macaroni-and-feather palm trees of *Plumes* appear in another collage, *Midi* (fig. 263), distinctive for its more literal scene, receding perspective space and an extravagant double-flanged frame covered with snakeskin.[14] Although *Midi* has not been securely identified in early documents, it appears to reside within the framework of the remaining documented collages— *Retour des barques* (*Return of the Boats*, fig. 264), exhibited in 1927 as a recent work; *Portrait* (fig. 266), exhibited in 1926; and *Vase of Flowers* (fig. 265), reproduced in 1927 as a work of ca. 1925.[15] *Pot of Flowers* (fig. 268) has not yet been identified in those early exhibitions, but it is compatible in subject and style with *Pailles et cure-dents* (fig. 260) and presents a witty comment on art made with the tools of art—paintbrushes, paint-can lids, pen points and stretcher wedges. *Cen-*

13. Picabia wrote Doucet (June 26, 1925, B.D. 7204-160) that a friend was leaving for Paris the next day with a replacement for *Pailles et cure-dents* before the exhibition was sent to London. On July 16, 1925 (B.D. 7204-162), he wrote that his "blue painting with matches . . . must be in London" and not to worry about its being fragile. When this exhibition reached the Wildenstein Galleries in New York, Picabia was represented by a *Portrait*.

14. *Plumes* was also in the collection of Jacques Doucet, while *Midi* was given by Picabia to the Société Anonyme, Yale University, in 1937. It may have been in the hands of the Société Anonyme earlier, for the files at Yale include a biographical statement on Picabia, dated "Venice, May 22, 1926," which mentions a *Promenade des anglais* with a frame by Pierre Legrain that was sent with the "third shipment." Mme Olga Picabia has confirmed the use of this title for *Midi* (conversations with the author, June 1968).

15. According to Picabia's close friend and collector Jean van Heeckeren ("Picabia, l'imprévisible," unpublished manuscript, 1939, 14, collection Olga Picabia, Paris), *Retour des barques*, made of shoe soles on ripolin, was first exhibited in 1927 with that title at the Galerie Van Leer, Paris, *Exposition Picabia*, October 24–November 5, 1927, no. 2.

Portrait was first exhibited at the *Internationale Kunstausstellung*, Dresden (not in catalogue), organized by El Lissitzky in 1926, and appears in an installation photograph published in El Lissitzky and Mary Whitehall, *El Lissitzky* (Greenwich, Conn., 1968), 187. It is referred to there as a *Portrait of* [*Raymond?*] *Poincaré* (Lissitzky and Whitehall, op. cit., 76).

Vase of Flowers is first documented by a photograph of Picabia in his studio, labeled "Almost black after 7 months in Cannes" (*This Quarter*, I, no. 3, Monte Carlo, 1927).

timeters (fig. 269) also lacks early documents—and probably a Pierre Legrain frame that once went with it; nonetheless, it remains one of the most engaging of Picabia's collages. Rich colors and varied forms and textures strike an immediate sensuous appeal that may be savored with or without the intellectual possibilities suggested first of all by the broken meter tape—a symbol of rationality and order which brings to mind Duchamp's *Three Standard Stoppages*. The tape is arranged so that, in conjunction with the loosely brushed paint and matches (sticks which make fire), it suggests a "tree" or "fiery eruption." But any simple perception of ground plane and sky is confounded by small, radiating "suns" etched into the field of white paint at the "bottom" of the composition.

An eleven-centimeter fragment, missing from the tape in *Centimeters*, was used for the nose in *Portrait* (fig. 266). Combs, cord, curtain rings, toothpicks, erasers, pen points and ripolin paint complete that portrait, which was then framed by Pierre Legrain in corrugated cardboard and sandpaper. A moderate dadaist spirit may be experienced in Picabia's imaginative use of these materials, especially in the definition of the hair by combs and unruly cords, but, as in most of the collages, there is nothing essentially dadaist about the subject, content or aesthetic quality of this delightful, well-crafted portrait. The dadaism in *Portrait* occurred five or ten years later (fig. 267) when Picabia, in a dumbfounding act of self-liberation, transformed the collage with new combs and the superimposition of a rather crudely brushed head and hand in the style of his "transparencies." With the subsequent acquisition of a new title as well, *Le Beau Charcutier* (*The Beautiful Pork Butcher*), all links to the original *Portrait* were forgotten for many years.[16]

Following the Duchamp sale in March 1926, Picabia did not have a one-man exhibition in Paris until the fall of 1927. During that time, however, he drew and painted prodigiously. Owing to the variety of his work, infrequent exhibitions and the absence of dated canvases, a precise evolution cannot be reconstructed.[17]

16. *Portrait* was reproduced in its original form, including frame, in an article on the occasion of its exhibition at the Galerie Van Leer, *Exposition Picabia* (see M.F. "Picabia," *Artwork*, III, no. 12, London, January–March 1928, 248). In the Galerie Van Leer catalogue it is probably no. 1, "Peignes, aiguilles, gommes et plumes." It was next reproduced without frame in the catalogue for the Galerie Goemans, Paris, *Exposition de collages*, March 1930, but did not figure in the list of works exhibited. The revised version with new combs and overlaid forms is first documented in a 1935 photograph of Picabia's studio (illus. 36), at which time the original frame was still intact. *Portrait* was again reproduced in 1938 (Gabrielle Buffet-Picabia, "Matières plastiques," *XXe Siècle*, I–II, no. 2, Paris, May 1, 1938, 34), this time in its original form but minus frame and attributed to 1915. It finally appeared after the war in its present form, bearing a new date and title, *Le Beau Charcutier*, 1920 (Galerie René Drouin, Paris, *491, 50 ans de plaisir*, March 4–26, 1949, no. 20), which was not questioned until 1970 (William Camfield, *Francis Picabia*, New York: The Solomon R. Guggenheim Museum, 1970, 36–38). Imprints of the original collage elements on *Portrait* are visible front and back on *Le Beau Charcutier*.

17. Picabia was represented by one to three works in a half dozen exhibitions from early 1926 to the spring of 1927 (see the list of exhibitions, p. 337), but few of those paintings can be securely identified. Several, however, were described as collages, sometimes with frames by Pierre Legrain. A work by Picabia at the Galerie Bernheim Jeune's *Exposition multinationale*

Nonetheless, the general course of his career is documented by occasional minor projects, such as illustrated programs for children's bathing-beauty contests or galas at favorite nightclubs (fig. 270), and his major work is documented by two events of early 1927, an exhibition in Cannes and an issue of *This Quarter* dedicated to Picabia's recent work.

The exhibition at the Cercle Nautique was dominated by watercolors of Spanish figures (see fig. 271), complemented by a few beach scenes, portraits, landscapes and compositions described by contemporary critics as "dream fantasies" (see fig. 272).[18] The opening attracted the itinerant royalty of Cannes and a throng of friends and reporters, who were astounded by those recent drawings. "Dada is dead, Picabia remains," began one critic, "Francis Picabia himself, yes. He who was the hero of dada. The author of Jésus-Christ Rastaquouère. . . . the miracle is there: you have never seen drawing so pure, so stripped to its essentials. I say: Ingres. But no!"[19] That audience was further gratified by Picabia's statement in the catalogue, "Lumière froide" (Cold Light), and by a contemporary article published in *Comoedia* under the title "Picabia contre Dada ou le retour à la raison":

> Never having been a believer, I was forced to fabricate a soul for myself because I love to love. My soul believes in me and . . . what I want! . . .
>
> Everything may or may not be a joke, right? Things only have the value which one accords them. Nonetheless, one must not confound force with fashion; force elevates itself, fashion remains little and mediocre, mediocre like the imbecility of communism. Mussolini may be a dangerous, disturbing madman, but he will always seem more sympathetic to me than the effigy of a Lenin, sculpted in such a manner that men share it like the little bits of sugar one gives to dogs! . . .
>
> Poor revolutionaries, made in series, carrying their labels like a flag; their niches are too narrow for my soul of a wolf.[20]
>
> Socialism was invented only for mediocre people and imbeciles. Do you see socialism, communism, in love, in art? . . .
>
> Be assured that my intention is by no means to talk politics, that is a thing

<hr>

(Paris, January 1927) was described as a composition of "hair curlers, matches and pins" (Léon Werth, "Les Arts et la vie," *Impartial français* [Paris], January 25, 1927, attrib.; D.P. XII, 333).

18. Cercle Nautique, Cannes, *Exposition Francis Picabia*, January 28–February 7, 1927, with a statement by Picabia, "Lumière froide," signed and dated "Mougins December 11, 1926." Figs. 271 and 272 were reproduced in the catalogue with the titles employed here. This gallery, directed by Emile Fabre, was sometimes referred to as Chez Fabre.

19. F. Jean-Desthieux, "Dada est mort; Picabia reste," *L'Homme libre* [Paris], January 27, 1927, 1–2. Guests at the opening included Grand Duke Michael Mikhaylovich, Baron J. de Mayronnet de Saint-Marc, Comte Arthur de Gabriac and Princess Hohenloe (Anon., "Second Day of Racing at Cannes Attracts Large Crowd to Course," *New York Herald* [Paris], February 1, 1927).

20. Picabia, "Lumière froide," in Cercle Nautique, Cannes, *Exposition Francis Picabia*, January 28–February 7, 1927.

of which I am profoundly horrified, but our life is at this comical point where everything is mixed up together and the arts do not escape this lot.

I invented dadaism as a man who sets a fire around himself, in the midst of a raging inferno, in order not to be burned, and there were several of us who gave the best of ourselves in the center of that infernal circle; now we touch the end of that drama and here are certain ones who were only belated spectators, having understood nothing, foolishly trying to imitate those who risked everything in order to save themselves from the democratic perils of vulgarization . . .

Art cannot be democratic, do you believe that the worker . . . wants a democratic phiz to decorate his bedroom? But no, he dreams of beautiful women, of Versailles, of honor and decency.[21]

In fact, neither article was anti-Dada. Both of them were comparable in style and content to the articles of 1921–1924, but, in the context of the time, Picabia's opposition to democracy, socialism and communism in art was appreciated by many in his audience. Notable exceptions included the surrealists, who were the target of some indirect comments, and the editors of the socialist newspaper *L'Humanité*, who published a venomous critique of both Picabia's exhibition and his statement at the Cercle Nautique.[22]

While simple, delicate drawings of Spanish subjects had dominated that exhibition, extravagant monster paintings were featured in the Picabia issue of *This Quarter* (see fig. 273, and color pl. xv).[23] All of them develop the basic characteristics established in the early examples of 1924–1925 (figs. 254–257). With few exceptions the subject matter is prosaic and figurative, but imbued with "monstrous" distortions of form, jarring color combinations and the use of numerous shorthand motifs. The earlier *Femme à l'ombrelle* (fig. 257) is a useful introductory work, for her pointed nose and multiple eyes (including one targetlike eye) still bear faint resemblance to their forerunners in *Optophone* II (fig. 229) and *Dresseur d'animaux* (fig. 244). There are also thick, rippling lines in the hair reminiscent of *Matchwoman* II (color pl. xiii), but in other respects, line included, *Femme à l'ombrelle* provides a rude, lush contrast. Lines associated with her parasol reinforce the form in some instances, but elsewhere suggest its move-

21. Francis Picabia, "Picabia contre Dada ou le retour à la raison," *Comoedia* [Paris], March 14, 1927, 1. A partial translation of this article appeared in *The Art Digest*, no. 13 (New York, May 1, 1927). The title of the article was probably provided by the editors of *Comoedia*.

22. Parijanine, "Une Belle 'Profession de foi,' " *L'Humanité* [Paris], February 26, 1927, 4. Picabia responded with an open letter which was not published but, instead, subjected to criticism itself (see Parijanine, "Petite Marché des lettres et des arts. Portrait du peintre par lui-même," *L'Humanité* [Paris], March 14, 1927, 2).

23. "Francis Picabia in his Latest Moods," *This Quarter*, I, no. 3 (Monte Carlo, 1927), 296–304. Picabia wrote Doucet as early as March 22, 1926 (B.D. 7204-167) that the director of *This Quarter* was going to publish an important selection of his recent paintings. As finally published, the issue included a variety of poems, statements and photographs; Picabia's portrait of Ernest Walsh (director of *This Quarter*); and full-page reproductions of fourteen of the monsters.

ment and extension into space. Thick lines or brushstrokes also define the woman's chest, arms and entire fingers, but at the same time they suggest patterns in her dress and dematerialize form to such an extent that they become surface patterns independent of either form or apparel. Finally, it may be misleading to speak of line, for opulent color is the basis of the painting. Color is identical with line, form, texture and pattern; color suggests space and movement, sets the mood of the painting and, in the passage of luxurious pink pigment in the lower left (cloth?), exists as an autonomous area of paint per se.

Les Trois Grâces (*The Three Graces*, fig. 273, and color pl. XV) exhibits another basic characteristic of the monster period—Picabia's frequent reference to art of the past, in this instance, the ancient subject of the Three Graces (fig. 274) as depicted by Rubens.[24] *Les Trois Grâces* is also distinguished by a veritable inventory of linear shorthand motifs common to the monster period, and a lighter blue, cream and pink color harmony befitting the subject. Three standard shorthand motifs occur within the figures themselves—multiple eyes, pointed noses and curious flamelike "shadows"—while the space about them is replete with dots, cross-hatchings and contrasting lines that are variously straight, rippling, undulating and zigzagged. An emanation of power is suggested by the lines around the nude figures, the fairest of whom is indicated by a lighter body tone, the greatest number of eyes and the more active zigzag lines.

The most common subject among the monsters was that of amorous couples, a direct reflection of Picabia's preoccupations and, often, his occupations. Within this category of subject matter the form and expression varied considerably. *Les Amoureux* (*The Lovers*, fig. 256) possesses a dark demonic quality which attracted André Breton, while *Le Baiser* (*The Kiss*, color pl. XIV) is distinguished for its superb painterly qualities.[25] *Idyll* (fig. 275), a sentimental postcard composition of young lovers, plays with symbolism and the notion of transparency which would characterize Picabia's next major period. Here the technique of partial transparency is employed in a way that associates woman with the sea and man with mountains and towers.

Content also looms as an interesting question in other paintings of ca. 1925–1927, many of them based on works by sixteenth-century Italian masters. *Four-footed Sibyl* (fig. 276), a gouache in subdued terra-cotta and gray colors, is representative of several muscular nudes derived from Michelangelo (fig. 277). Two paintings of *Venus and Adonis*, based on compositions by Titian and Paolo Veronese in the Prado (figs. 278, 280), are typical of another group of paintings characterized by exaggeratedly long, pointed noses and chins, by an enormous

24. The Prado was one of Picabia's basic sources for models in art of the Renaissance-Baroque epoch. See also fig. 278.

25. *Les Amoureux* was purchased by Breton at the Duchamp sale in 1926. It was reproduced in his *Le Surréalisme et la peinture* (Paris, 1928) and has remained in his collection to the present.

Baiser was exhibited in Picabia's exhibition at the Galerie Van Leer (Paris, October 24–November 5, 1927) under that title. After World War II it was referred to as *Carnaval*, indicative of the shifting titles which make positive identification difficult for many paintings of this period.

lozenge eye, curly hair and the use of parallel lines, cross-hatching and concentric arcs to model the human figure.[26] Picabia's intentions in these direct references to old masters is unknown, but it is unlikely that the paintings were undertaken with an attitude of reverence. To the contrary, he seems to be commenting pungently on both the hallowed Renaissance tradition and the classicizing, tradition-conscious trend of much Western art during the 1920s. The ideal human form of Michelangelo's sibyl was rudely distorted and dematerialized in the filmy, transparent passages of the legs and stomach; distortion of Titian's figures was carried further still, and their modeling in hash marks and concentric arcs mocks Renaissance methods for suggesting the mass and motion of three-dimensional forms in space.

Picabia's paintings of the monster period also suggest contact with the work of contemporary artists, above all Picasso, who was on cordial relations with Picabia during his summer sojourns of 1925–1926 in neighboring Golfe-Juan.[27] Already in his neo-classical period, Picasso had referred to the forms and subjects of ancient Greco-Roman art, and from ca. 1922 to 1926 he produced many works relevant to Picabia's interest in grotesque figures, shorthand symbols, rich textures and patterns (see fig. 284).[28] No such clear examples of surrealist influence are apparent in Picabia's paintings, but the framework within which he operated, and all kinds of monstrous, nightmarish images during the 1920s, depended in part on Surrealism. In a more direct way, there are some paintings, Picabia's *Blue Phantoms* (fig. 285), for example, whose shadowy forms and looping lines seem related to Max Ernst's series of paintings in 1927 called "The Hordes." Surrealism was nourished in turn by Picabia. Breton included him in his 1928 book, *Le Surréalisme et la peinture*, and personally owned several of Picabia's monsters. Others were exhibited at the Galerie Surréaliste, and his collages were a respected source at hand when the surrealists developed a lively interest in collage and as-

26. The paintings considered here, figs. 276, 278, 280–83, have not been positively identified in early exhibitions, but dates of ca. 1924–1927 can be attributed on grounds of stylistic and circumstantial evidence. Similar images appear underneath superimposed forms of Romanesque inspiration in paintings which are documented in late 1927 and early 1928 (fig. 287).

For many years *Venus and Adonis* went by the title *Faun*. This author suggested a source in Michelangelo's sibyls and ignudi from the Sistine Chapel (Camfield, *Francis Picabia*, 129). The source in Titian was pointed out by Professor Richard Spear and Mr. John M. Moore. The Paolo Veronese source for the *Venus and Adonis* in fig. 280 was published by Maurizio Fagiolo Dell'Arco in Galleria Civica d'Arte Moderna, Turin, *Francis Picabia*, November 28, 1974–February 2, 1975, 123.

27. The Picassos, the Picabias and their sons, who were the same age, were together occasionally in each other's homes and at the beach. See Everling, *L'Anneau de Saturne*, 165–66.

28. Other likely models for Picabia's use of specific motifs include Catalan Romanesque frescoes, astrological symbols and paintings by Léger, Miró, Klee and others. For such motifs as undulating lines with dots, cross-hatching, chevrons and symbols for natural forms see *St. Peter's Boat* (twelfth-century fresco from San Pedro de Sopre, Museo de Bellas Artes de Cataluña, Barcelona), Léger's *Big Tugboat* (1923, Musée National Fernand Léger, Biot) and Miró's *Vegetable Garden with a Donkey* (1918, reproduced in Jacques Dupin, *Joan Miró: Life and Work*, New York, 1962).

semblage in the late 1920s.[29] Joan Miró's *Spanish Dancer* collages of 1928 reflect his long esteem for Picabia's work, though not so much the collages of the mid-1920s as the dadaist examples of 1920–1921 (figs. 193, 202–204; color pl. XI). Likewise in his "magnetic field" paintings of 1925–1927 and his droll *Smile of My Blonde* (1924, private collection, Paris), Miró seems to have savored and then transformed Picabia's dadaist work—its wit and eroticism, its exploitation of "chance" in blot and splash techniques, its use of words and poetry within painting.[30]

Following a vacation in Barcelona during the summer of 1927, Picabia was impressed by the art of still another past culture, Catalan Romanesque fresco painting, and it contributed substantially to the evolution of his monster period. For an approaching exhibition in Paris, Picabia decided it was imperative to do some "research" with Spanish subjects, and on July 30 he announced to José Dalmau and the poet Cassanyés his imminent arrival by boat from Marseille.[31] Shortly afterward, Picabia, accompanied by Olga Mohler and Lorenzo, established his work schedule in Spain—beach in the mornings, visits to churches and museums in the afternoon and research into the midnight hours with Olga, Dalmau and Cassanyés in the cabarets of Barcelona.[32] Germaine Everling joined them later, and after they had returned to Mougins, results of the Barcelona research emerged in paintings exhibited in Paris and Cannes over the winter of 1927–1928.

The most striking examples of new elements in Picabia's work appeared at the Galerie Briant-Robert in Paris in November 1927.[33] Securely identified works in that exhibition include *Phébus* (*Phoebus*, or *Apollo*), *Lazarus and the Lamb*, *Machaon* and *Hôtel ancien* (*Old Hotel*, figs. 286, 287, 295, 300). Excepting *Phébus*, each of these paintings serves to indicate dates for similar but presently undocumented paintings. *Phébus* appears to have been a rather solitary work at that time, but one prophetic of Picabia's later preference for classical themes and figures and for the feature of transparency, limited here to the head overlaid with an abstracted sun symbol.[34]

29. Pierre de Massot wrote Picabia in 1925 that Breton and the surrealists greatly admired *Pailles et cure-dents* (fig. 260; June 19, 1925, D.P. XII, 82). Picabia's *Femme à l'ombrelle* (fig. 257) appears in the window of the Galerie Surréaliste in a photograph reproduced in Marcel Jean, *The History of Surrealist Painting*, trans. Simon Watson Taylor (London: Weidenfeld and Nicolson, 1960), 142.

30. For consideration of these issues in the work of Miró, see Rosalind Krauss and Margit Rowell, *Joan Miró: Magnetic Fields* (New York: The Solomon R. Guggenheim Museum, 1972).

31. Picabia letter to José Dalmau, July 30, 1927, cited courtesy of Señor Santos Torroella, Barcelona.

32. This trip is described in the Olga Picabia manuscript, 13–14.

33. Galerie Briant-Robert, Paris, *Francis Picabia*, November 11–30, 1927. See also Galerie Van Leer, Paris, *Exposition Picabia*, October 24–November 5, 1927, and Chez Fabre, Cannes, *Exposition Francis Picabia*, February 20–25, 1928.

34. There is a faint inscription in the upper right center which reads "Punition de Core," but this panel was first exhibited by the title *Phébus* at the Galerie Briant-Robert, November 11–30,

The direct impact of Catalan Romanesque frescoes is evident in *Lazarus and the Lamb* (fig. 287). In a manner reminiscent of his methods for composite machine portraits in 1915 (fig. 109), Picabia combined parts of two separate panels from the twelfth-century frescoes at San Clemente de Tahull (figs. 288, 289), modifying them somewhat and eliminating Lazarus's dog to form a new composition.[35] Any temptation to speculate about Picabia's aesthetic or intellectual considerations is complicated by the fact that these images are painted over an earlier work which is faintly visible through the forms of Lazarus and clearly contributes to one's experience of the painting. That earlier composition can be identified as male and female nudes in the style of *Venus and Adonis* (fig. 278), but in this instance based on Michelangelo's *Temptation of Adam and Eve* in the Sistine Chapel.

The missing dog of Lazarus appears in other paintings, among them *Barcelona* (fig. 290), which also includes the wings of seraphim, the Lamb, three of the four living beasts of the Apocalypse, and, under that tangle of forms, two human figures, one of which appears to be a modified image of an Espagnole.[36] The painting is signed and dated "Barcelone 1924," but inasmuch as such use of Catalan Romanesque forms is not otherwise documented in Picabia's oeuvre before 1927, this painting, like *Lazarus and the Lamb*, may be the result of two separate campaigns, one in 1924, and another in 1927.

It is clear from contemporary reviews and extant works (figs. 293, 294) that Picabia continued to paint and exhibit Spanish subjects which were not subjected to the superimposition of Romanesque figures.[37] Nevertheless, the impact of the

1927, no. 61, and also by that title in the *Bulletin de l'Effort Moderne*, no. 38 (Paris, October 1927), 8–9.

35. This painting was reproduced in the catalogue of the Galerie Briant-Robert exhibition, but cannot be identified in the list of works. The story of Lazarus and the rich man occurs in the Bible, Luke 16: 19–31, especially verses 20 and 21. The Lamb of the Apocalypse is described in Revelation 5: 6: "Then I saw standing in the very middle of the throne, inside the circle of living creatures and the circle of elders, a Lamb with the marks of slaughter upon him. He had seven horns and seven eyes, the eyes which are the seven spirits of God sent out over all the world." All quotes are from *The New English Bible* (New York: Oxford University Press, Cambridge University Press, 1970).

Georges Isarlov was the first to point out Catalan Romanesque frescoes as a source for these paintings (*Picabia peintre*, Paris, 1929, 14).

36. Varied representations of seraphim in Catalan Romanesque frescoes reflect the confusion of seraphim and the four living creatures in the Bible. Isaiah (6:1–3) attributes six wings to seraphim but says nothing about eyes. See also Ezekiel 1:5–28 and Revelation 4:6–8, where St. John combines imagery of seraphim and the four living creatures: "In the center, round the throne itself, were four living creatures, covered with eyes, in front and behind. The first creature was like a lion, the second like an ox, the third had a human face, the fourth was like an eagle in flight. . . . each of them with six wings, had eyes all over, inside and out."

37. *Totó* (fig. 293) was exhibited at Chez Fabre, Cannes, *Exposition Francis Picabia*, February 20–25, 1928, no. 4. *Bullfight* (fig. 294) has not been positively identified but corresponds to entries in the same catalogue and is identical in style with a bullfight scene reproduced in the catalogue. Several critics noted the social success of that exhibition and praised Picabia's sensuous Espagnoles and charming drawings of animals (see P.B., "Le Vernissage de l'exposition Picabia, à Cannes," *L'Eclaireur de Nice et du Sud-Est*, February 22, 1928, 6).

latter was extensive, and as time passed transparency became an increasingly willed and controlled feature in his work. In some of these paintings, Picabia seems to have overlaid earlier compositions with transparent Romanesque forms (see fig. 292), but others, like *Toreador* (fig. 291), appear to be the result of a single campaign. *Toreador* is still an awkward work, lacking visual unity, but content may have been foremost in Picabia's mind. *Toreador* embodies a personal memento of his experience of Spain—beautiful women (pious and otherwise), the Church, toreadors and bullfighting. The interrelationship of these subjects is underscored by the horned beast—simultaneously associated with the toreador and with the Church as one of the four living beasts, the ox symbol of St. Luke. Picabia's concerns suggest that *Toreador* may also be viewed in terms of such broader themes as man and woman, man and beast, Christianity and paganism, life and death.

Machaon (fig. 295), exhibited at the Galerie Briant-Robert in November 1927, represents another contemporary current in Picabia's work linked to the "fantasy" watercolors of ca. 1926 (see fig. 272).[38] Like the works above with transparent overlays of Romanesque forms, *Machaon* juxtaposes disparate forms and scales, but the subject matter is different, the images are seldom transparent and are enclosed by an irregular, biomorphic shape. This distinctive feature of an enclosing biomorphic form occurs in numerous examples as diverse as the striking drawing of two heads (fig. 297) and the delicate, complex composition (fig. 298) whose passages of transparency may indicate a slightly later date.[39] The sensation of a private reverie about these works was initially even more intimate in *Machaon* before the accidental destruction of mounted butterflies in its deep, glass-covered frame. The original effect of that frame may be judged in another example (fig. 296).[40]

38. *Machaon*, no. 53 in the catalogue, is entitled after a type of butterfly. The face in this watercolor appears to be a portrait, but has not been identified. The nude couple on the left is adapted from Picabia's earlier drawing, *Thermometer Rimbaud*, published in *391*, no. 16 (Paris, May 1924), 4. The childlike stick figures occur in a number of contemporary works by Picabia. Both couples and the butterfly suggest a general theme of sexual attraction, but otherwise the content remains private.

39. Neither of these works has been securely identified in contemporary catalogues, but the title *Harp of George*, which appears in the Galerie Briant-Robert exhibition (no. 17), is tentatively offered for fig. 298. It contains a harp just to the right of the principal figure, and a date before 1927 is unlikely given several features common to the first stage of the "transparencies" during 1927–1928, notably the quattrocento quality of that visage, the vine motif and passages of transparency.

40. As in so many instances, this work is also unidentified in contemporary catalogues, although it or kindred compositions are referred to in reviews of the exhibitions. Marcel Duchamp promoted an exhibition of Picabia's work at Alfred Stieglitz's new gallery (The Intimate Gallery, New York, *Picabia Exhibition*, April 19–May 11, 1928) which included works described by one critic as "strange pictures set in frames so deep as to accommodate real butterflies pinned here and there" (Elizabeth L. Carey, "Pictures by Chase, Some Energetic Rebels, and Others," *New York Times*, April 29, 1928, sec. 10, 18). This exhibition, advertised as "the most recent work of Francis Picabia," was made up of works from the Galerie Van Leer and Galerie Briant-Robert exhibitions held in Paris the preceding fall. According to Duchamp, all eleven paintings sent to Stieglitz were framed by Pierre Legrain (letter to Stieglitz, January 15, 1928, A.S.A., Yale), and Stieglitz

The combination of such seemingly unrelated forms, sometimes accompanied by cryptic titles, invites consideration of content and the relationship to two preoccupations of the surrealists—dream images and the technique of "juxtaposition of disparate objects." On all counts Picabia remains essentially independent. This is not meant to imply that he did not work at least marginally within the surrealist movement. The very production of irrational spaces and monstrous figures suggests a response to the climate that fostered Surrealism. And, after 1926, as the work of more surrealists approached maturity, the juxtaposition of disparate objects was not only much more important in Picabia's work but different in quality. Earlier in his career, for example *Optophone* I (fig. 227), or the machine portrait of *De Zayas! De Zayas!* (fig. 109), his combination of objects had been provocative in effect; after 1926 the spirit of his compositions was more evocative than provocative. Nonetheless, Picabia was not a surrealist, never wished to be one of them and could not really have been a surrealist under any conditions. He was fifteen to twenty years older than most of the surrealists; and his career and lasting convictions were established before the first stirrings of that movement. By temperament and aesthetic convictions he was an uncompromising individualist for whom it was natural that the combination of disparate forms was practiced in a manner which—ostensibly unlike Surrealism—served conscious gratification of his whims, reveries and opinions, not the transcription of dreams. Or, in contrast to the pervasive "seriousness" of most surrealist art, Picabia's art frequently served his personal amusement.

Machaon and especially *Butterflies* have a playful quality which he indulged to the full in other works. In *Bucolic* (fig. 299), Picabia seems more preoccupied with the relationship of beefy human and horse posteriors than with painting for posterity. That horse and an assortment of cheeky nudes in his oeuvre of ca. 1927–1928 are based on "ideal" female nudes by the Northern Renaissance master, Albrecht Dürer (fig. 302), and Picabia's intentions appear insolent on the surface.[41] In *Chiromis* (fig. 301), the superimposition of Dürer's Nemesis figure over a seraphim might suggest more serious possibilities, but the design of her body stocking, her attributes and title all suggest further irreverence.[42]

This spirit was never wholly absent in Picabia's career, but it was less pronounced during the period of the transparencies, which began to emerge during 1928.

---

kept three of them: "Yes, I think it was wonderful of you to have kept 3 of the paintings. Picabia is one of the few today who are not 'a sure investment' " (Duchamp letter to Stieglitz, July 2, 1928, A.S.A., Yale). Those three paintings, though not securely identified, probably coincide with three works Stieglitz gave to New York's Metropolitan Museum, *Portrait*, *No. 1 Bird and Turtle* and *No. 2 Global*, the latter referred to in this study as *Hôtel ancien* (fig. 300) in accord with its first known exhibition at the Galerie Briant-Robert, no. 44.

41. The horse in fig. 299 is based on Dürer's engraving, *The Large Horse* (1505); the reclining figure in *Hôtel ancien* is adapted from his engraving of *The Sea Monster* (ca. 1498).

42. *Chiromis* was reproduced in color in the catalogue Chez Fabre, Cannes, *Exposition Francis Picabia*, February 20–25, 1928, but does not appear by that title in the list of paintings there. The title is probably based on the scientific name "chiromys" for a small lemur native to Madagascar.

16. THE TRANSPARENCIES, 1928-1932

PICABIA'S interest in the concept and techniques of transparency was not a sudden development. Ultimately it derived from preoccupations with simultaneity during the epoch of Cubism and Orphism; more recently he had experimented with simultaneity/transparency in the film *Entr'acte* and in a number of the monster paintings of ca. 1927. But in 1928 his work evolved into the early mature paintings of a type which became known as "the transparencies"—a style so named for its multiple layers of transparent images, although it was also characterized by pervasive moods of wistfulness and melancholy, and by extensive reference to art of the past.

While the style and spirit of the transparencies are readily perceived, the motivations behind them are dimly understood. Many of Picabia's visual sources in past art were also quiet and wistful in mood, but he selected those models so that, finally, he was not responding simply to them but to larger forces within his art and life and the art and life about him. No answers are at hand, but a few observations may be offered, beginning with the fact that the transparencies evolved during a period of personal turmoil. As usual, the source of the trouble was Picabia's bittersweet love affairs.

At least as early as the 1927 voyage to Barcelona, Picabia had begun to think of Olga Mohler as more than the governess of Lorenzo and an efficient manager of the château. She was not impervious to his charm, and toward the end of December 1927 they finally expressed their feelings for each other.[1] In January 1928, Picabia took Lorenzo and Olga for a brief winter vacation in Switzerland, leaving Germaine in Mougins. Soon afterward, he began to join Olga and Lorenzo on their evening jaunts to the movies, and then there were late movies without Lorenzo. This conventional triangle was short-lived; it expanded into a rectangle in the spring of 1928 when Benjamin Guiness installed his family in Cannes. His vivacious young daughter, Méraud, had fallen in love with Picabia's paintings on exhibit at the Cercle Nautique, and, not long after becoming his "pupil," she fell in love with the artist as well.[2]

1. Olga Picabia manuscript, 16–18 (collection Olga Picabia, Paris).
2. This episode is reported in the Olga Picabia manuscript, 21–22, and, more extensively, in Germaine Everling's *L'Anneau de Saturne* (Paris, 1970), 183–87, where Miss Guiness is identified as "Stephen." Picabia contributed a preface and portrait drawing of Méraud Guiness for the catalogue of her first exhibition at the Galerie Van Leer, Paris, December 2–15, 1928.

For several months the potential for a major crisis was dissipated as spells of assiduous work in the studio alternated with a rollicking summer-camp atmosphere in a Château de Mai then brimming with young people. Olga and Michel Corlin, Germaine's son by her first husband, lived in the château; Méraud had rented the neighboring cottage of a friend and a young couple by the name of Sarrazin lived across the road. During the summer months those lively youths were frequently joined by Marcel Duchamp and a friend, Roland Toutain, who was notorious for his outlandish behavior. But at the center of it all, "tu-toied" by Méraud and Olga, was "Uncle Francis," originating incessant pranks and excursions, helping to toss breakfast-time sleepyheads into the pool and flipping food at dinner guests. When reprimanded for the example he set Lorenzo, Picabia replied, "If I do all that, it is to show you how bad it is!"[3]

Despite such antics and a couple of minor crises of the heart, Picabia also painted a great deal and resumed writing on a somewhat more regular basis. By early summer he had written his first article for *Orbes*, a new magazine edited by his friends Jacques-Henri Lévesque and Jean van Heeckeren, and had composed a film scenario, *La Loi d'accommodation chez les borgnes "Sursum corda"* (The Law of Accommodation Among the Disreputable "Sursum corda").[4] The latter is delightfully dadaist in its exposé of life's sundry absurdities and injustices—and in the spirit of Picabia's preface, where he advised that his film scenario was not to be filmed, except by the readers on their own "magic screen, incomparably superior to the poor white and black calico of cinemas. . . . all the seats are the same price and one may smoke without bothering his neighbor."[5]

The concept of that interior "magic screen" seems relevant to the transparencies, which were begun simultaneously in a new studio completed that spring of 1928. All members of the family have preserved vivid memories of the fervor with which Picabia worked. On some mornings he went to the studio at 5 a.m. and would not emerge until the noon or evening meal, all the while barring entrance to the studio and insisting that food be left at the door. Olga helped him raid older paintings for frames and stretchers and labored daily to keep a steady supply of paint and clean brushes.

3. Everling, *L'Anneau de Saturne*, 169. Most of the information regarding the summer of 1928 occurs in the Olga Picabia manuscript, 21–24.

4. Francis Picabia, "Jours creux," *Orbes*, no. 1 (Paris, spring–summer 1928), 29–33; and *La Loi d'accommodations chez les borgnes "Sursum corda"* (Paris, May 15, 1928).

5. The characters in the scenario include a professor of theology who sells filthy postcards; an inept detective preoccupied with modern art; a painter wholly absorbed by detective work; and a beautiful manicurist who is revealed as a common, dirty woman, when, at home, she discards her wig, uniform and manners. Nevertheless, she is idolized by most of the male characters, including a priest (whose statues of St. Sulpice take on her appearance when he regards them) and a rich American who gives a ball in her honor. During the party, the lowest character, a legless cripple, kills and robs the American. But by virtue of damning notes he has kept on the weaknesses of his "superiors," the cripple implicates them in the murder and frees himself. He is last seen as rich and married to the manicurist whose coquetry with the inspector convinced him of her innocence.

By late September Picabia had completed work for his forthcoming exhibition at the Galerie Théophile Briant, and most of the inhabitants of the Château de Mai transferred to a friend's residence on the Quai Conti in Paris.[6] Toward the end of that visit the inevitable explosion occurred in Picabia's complex personal affairs, but, prior to that, festivities reigned about the successful exhibition and reunions with such old friends as Pierre and Robbie de Massot, Jacques-Henri and Angelica Lévesque, Marcel Duchamp, Jean van Heeckeren and the scholar Georges Isarlov, who published an important study on Picabia the next year.[7]

Transparencies of ca. 1927–1928 dominated the exhibition, and presently documented works reveal various stages or experiments in Picabia's course toward the fully developed examples of 1929. *Jeune Fille au paradis (Young Girl in Paradise,* fig. 303) resembles a work of late 1927–early 1928 given its clear-cut superimposition of Catalan Romanesque forms over what is probably an earlier *Espagnole.*[8] The result is a jarring but deliberate contrast of human and heavenly beings, the one sensuous and naturalistic in form, the others rigid, stern and abstracted. *Pilar* (fig. 304) is closer in style to the mature transparencies.[9] Although Picabia also combined in it an *Espagnole* with figures from a distant culture, the result is completely different. Not only are the figures classical rather than Romanesque, but the composition seems to have been conceived and executed in a single operation, with the effect of a harmonious, delicately sketched and tinted whole.

Head with Cellophane and *L'Ombre* (figs. 305, 306) represent early essays in transparency achieved by use of cellophane.[10] *L'Ombre* is particularly interesting for its apparent play on the "fear of one's own shadow," and its reference back to the simplified figurative forms of ca. 1922–1924 with their manipulation of light and dark, positive and negative (see figs. 236, 243).

Jésus et le dauphin (Jesus and the Dolphin, fig. 307) is representative of the fully developed transparencies at their earliest stage. Typical of its kind, it is a complex figurative painting, derived in large part from ideal forms in the classical tradition of art history (fig. 308), but re-created by Picabia in multiple layers of

6. Galerie Th. Briant, Paris, *Francis Picabia,* October 26–November 15, 1928. The visit in Paris is described in the Olga Picabia manuscript, 23–24, and in Everling, *L'Anneau de Saturne,* 188–92.

7. Georges Isarlov, *Picabia peintre* (Paris, 1929). For reviews of the exhibition see Charensol, "Les Expositions," *L'Art vivant* (Paris, November 15, 1928), 899–900; and G.-J. Gros, "La Semaine artistique," *Paris-Midi,* October 27, 1928, 2.

8. The catalogue of the exhibition at the Galerie Th. Briant lists a "Jeune fille au paradis" (no. 2), and this painting, inscribed in the lower left, "Barcelone. Jeune fille au paradis," has a Galerie Th. Briant label on the reverse.

9. *Pilar* has not yet been identified with an early exhibition. The title appears on the reverse in an unknown hand.

10. *L'Ombre* is reproduced in the Galerie Th. Briant catalogue (no. 3). The forms of the shadow and the butterfly are made with cellophane. *Head with Cellophane* has not been identified in that exhibition, but it is compatible in style with Picabia's work of ca. 1928, and four entries to the exhibition are listed as "Cellophane" (nos. 21–24).

transparent images that are disparate in subject and scale and fraught with ambiguities of form and space.[11] One's visual, mental and emotional reactions are constantly shifting as initially perceived forms fuse with others or give way to images overlooked at the first encounter. The mere combination of such incongruous forms kindles a curiosity about content, and in this instance the possibility of meaningful relationships is further implied by formal properties, notably by a muted, unifying color harmony, and an ordered composition which flows clockwise from the legs and torso (upper right) that fuse with the dolphin, around to the dog and up the vine and arm of Christ. It is conceivable that Picabia had in mind some comparison of Dionysus and Christ—whose histories share themes of fish, the vine, life and rebirth—but that speculation leaves much unexplained, and, without a program from the artist, it seems impossible to ascertain what he was about with any assurance.

In other works of ca. 1928–1929, *Lunaris*, for example (fig. 311), the fine-grained plywood ground and pervasive blue tonality, the melancholic faces and poetic title all evoke such a delicate reverie that intellectual considerations about content seldom intrude on the experience of the spectator.[12]

To a casual observer, the mood of such paintings would hardly have seemed compatible with the life of the artist after he returned to Mougins toward the end of 1928. Outwardly, there was the appearance of a perpetual holiday as Picabia provided the programs and decor for galas at stylish nightclubs, and ran through a succession of cars and boats. With automobiles already in the garage, he bought a Ford, then a Citroën; swapped one car for a motorboat, the *Cocolo*, and traded that in on the purchase of his first yacht, the *Henriquetta I*. Within this carefree lifestyle, however, there were renewed periods of intensive painting, serious writing and deep personal tensions as Picabia continued to reign over a triangle in which Olga steadily displaced Germaine as mistress of the Château de Mai.[13]

Picabia's writings during 1929 numbered a typical article for *Orbes*, a somewhat huffy, out-of-character contribution to *Bifur* and five short poems for *La Révolution surréaliste*, a once-only collaboration with that magazine, thanks probably to Paul Eluard, who was a guest on Picabia's yacht during the summer of 1929.

> Don't accuse me of cowardice in objecting that God cannot answer me in the next issue, he answers me every day in the form of judges, country, family; under the form of daily nuisances, under the form of everything which deforms life.

11. *Jésus et le dauphin* is listed as no. 7 in the Galerie Th. Briant catalogue. The Annibale Carracci *Pietà* and the image of Christ in Picabia's painting do not correspond in every detail, but they are very close, and the National Museum in Naples provided many models for his transparencies.

12. *Lunaris* has not been identified in early exhibitions, but it appears in Olga Picabia's album as a work of 1928 from the collection of Léonce Rosenberg. The spiraling, tendril-like forms in it are most common in works of ca. 1927–1928 (figs. 281, 286, 298, 309) but also appear in 1929 (fig. 314) along with the Botticelli-inspired faces.

13. The tenor of this life and the transactions for cars and boats is described in the Olga Picabia manuscript, 25–26. During 1929, Méraud Guiness married Alvaro Guevara.

Life, for an artist, must be to work for himself without preoccupation for the results of his work regarding dealers, critics, amateurs, but only in the joy that work can give him: marvelous curiosity of himself, luminous introspection, never completely satisfied, each day renewed.[14]

This story seems to me to express modern life: desire to acquire quickly, without control, something facile, something . . . of poor quality which sparkles!

Fear of continued work, with the ideal of perfecting what must be obtained by pain, fear of the almost austere life which must be that of the man desiring to work hard, far from influences which never contribute to anything but a hybrid inviable result.[15]

Picabia's recent drawings and paintings were presented at an exhibition in Cannes during the spring of 1929 and at the Galerie Théophile Briant, Paris.[16] By and large the critical response was negative, but two exceptions, by an art dealer and a film critic, merit attention. Léonce Rosenberg, reviled and ridiculed during Dada, so esteemed the transparencies that he offered Picabia an arrangement with his gallery, commissioned a group of paintings for his wife's room and soon transformed their past antagonism into a warm friendship. The film critic, Gaston Ravel, was mightily impressed by the quality of the paintings and their relationship to the cinema: "The multiple impressions which we have used, and abused, in our films . . . are here . . . immobilized by a magic brush! . . . At first glance, some confusion perhaps; but, little by little, everything comes clear, slowly. . . . It is a miracle! it is an enchantment. . . . an homage, involuntary perhaps, rendered to the cinema."[17]

As exemplified by two major examples, *Dispar* and *Hera* (fig. 312, and color pl. XVI; fig. 314), these paintings of ca. 1929 are simultaneously more complex than those of 1928 and curiously serene: serene in their cool, delicate color harmonies and pensive, classicizing figures; complex in their more numerous layers of transparent images with correspondingly greater ambiguities of form and space and richer evocations of mood and content. Even the titles affixed to these paintings seem to expand suggestions of private symbolism rather than identify subject matter.

Picabia described the transparencies as spaces where he might express for himself "the resemblance of my interior desires," as paintings "where all my in-

14. Francis Picabia, "La Fosse des anges," *Orbes*, no. 2 (Paris, spring 1929), 81–83.

15. Francis Picabia, "Avenue Moche," *Bifur*, no. 2 (Paris, July 25, 1929), 24–29.

16. Galerie Théophile Briant, Paris, *Exposition Picabia*, November 12–December 7, 1929. For Picabia's earlier exhibition at Chez Fabre (Cannes, *Exposition Francis Picabia*, April 11–27, 1929), no catalogue has been found and meager reference exists in the press.

17. Gaston Ravel, "Exposition de peinture," *La Critique cinématographique* (Paris, October 29, 1929, attrib.). Léonce Rosenberg's support of Picabia as a dealer fluctuated during the 1930s as a result of financial crises, but their correspondence is a touching and informative witness to a meaningful friendship. The author is indebted to Mme Olga Picabia and Mlle Odette Rosenberg for the privilege of quoting from those letters.

stincts may have a free course."[18] But insofar as is known, he shared not one word of more specific explanation about his intentions, visual sources or titles with anyone, not even close friends and family. Accordingly, never was he more successful in painting for himself than in these works—transparent perhaps in form but veiled in content. Yet, typical of Picabia, the images and titles of the transparencies project the primacy of content and provoke a corresponding desire on the part of the spectator to explore questions of meaning. Both the titles and the images do yield somewhat to analysis which, however limited, tentative and frustrating, also provides useful chronological data, occasional glimpses of content and unexpected information about his method of work.

At the simplest level of identification, most titles among the transparencies pose few problems. Many are based on the protagonists of Greek and Roman mythology—Hera, Medea, Artemis and Ino—while some refer to historical sites and figures, Nicaea and Rasputin, or to scientific names for birds, plants and insects, Statices and Manucode. Still other titles, *Dispar* and *Atrata*, for example, have not been identified or represent invented words, perhaps anagrammatic constructions on the order of *Edtaonisl*.[19] The more difficult question regarding these titles, namely, their relationship to the images in the paintings, will be postponed until the images themselves have been explored.

Picabia's imagery, impenetrably personal and inventive at first glance, was in fact extensively dependent on models in past art which can be identified because he worked in 1929 much as he had done in 1915 with machine portraits (figs. 104, 105, 109, 110). That is to say, he appropriated existing images, modified them slightly and then combined those eclectic sources in a novel, personal manner. With little exaggeration it might be said that Picabia did not "create" any of the images in the transparencies; instead his creation was comparable to that of a collagist who recognizes the material (images) which answers his needs and then combines it in a way which—if successful—transforms the material and becomes more than the mere sum of its parts. As always in Picabia's career, his work was uneven and, accordingly, there are transparencies in which heavy-handed borrowing from past art and/or disdain for technical finesse distract from the unity of the painting. But in the best of them Picabia achieved a fusion of suggestive symbolism and poignant visual experiences that transform his sources into an utterly personal creation.

Some contemporary drawings are veritable mini-catalogues for Picabia's models. *Trifolii* (fig. 310) is doubly useful on that count, verifying Picabia's identification of dots with erogenous zones, while recording models that range from

18. Francis Picabia, statement for Chez Léonce Rosenberg, Paris, *Exposition Francis Picabia*, December 9–31, 1930.

19. Mme Olga Picabia has confirmed (conversation with the author, June 24, 1968) that Picabia did construct some titles by combining syllables from the names of butterflies and flowers. Her impression at the time was that he had only phonetic or poetic aims for such invented titles.

Greco-Roman art to seventeenth-century Italian painting.[20] The horse and rider in *Trifolii* were derived from the equestrian statue of Marcus Aurelius (2nd century A.D., Campidoglio, Rome); they also appear (reversed) in *La Harpe de Georges* (*Harp of* [*St.*] *George*, fig. 298). The kneeling nude behind the horse appears in another early transparency (fig. 309), and the fallen nude below it is a sketch after Bartolommeo Schedoni's *St. Sebastian Cured by the Pious Women* (ca. 1615, fig. 333), which reappears in a painting entitled *Artemis* (fig. 332). The variety of those models notwithstanding, the dominant sources for Picabia's transparencies of 1929 are to be found in Greco-Roman art and the paintings of Botticelli. During 1930 the latter was displaced by Piero della Francesca.

Catax (fig. 315) is representative of numerous transparencies in 1929 which are evocative of Botticelli—for example, his *Birth of Venus* (fig. 316)—in both the pensive mood of some of the faces and in the expressive use of hands and cascading flowers. The sensation of a gentle reverie is further enhanced by thin washes of cool blues, greens and creamy flesh tones which harmonize delicately with the fine-grained plywood surface.[21]

Other transparencies of 1929 exhibit a combination of images from Botticelli and ancient art. *Briseis* (fig. 317) is a less successful example in which the direct appropriation of a famous work from antiquity (fig. 318) dominates any other experience of the painting.[22] *Atrata* (fig. 326) and *Ino* (fig. 322) are not so encumbered by their sources.[23] The primary figure of the latter is derived from the representation of Andromeda in a Pompeiian fresco (fig. 323), but she is given a Botticellian face and proportions and a heavy chain likely inspired by his drawings for Dante's *Inferno*. Heads in the lower portion of *Ino* also exhibit general traits of Botticelli, and, thanks to a preparatory drawing, the head in the lower left corner may be traced to St. John the Baptist in the Louvre's *Madonna and Child with St. John* (see figs. 324, 325). Except for the downcast eyes of the Madonna, her head is also very similar (in reverse) to the adjacent head in *Ino*, and at this point it is

20. *Trifolii* can be attributed a date of ca. 1928–1929 on the basis of style and its reproduction in *Variétés*, special unnumbered issue on "Le Surréalisme en 1929" (Brussels, June 1929), between pp. 14 and 15.

21. *Catax* was exhibited in 1929 at the Galerie Théophile Briant, no. 7. The significance of the title is as yet undetermined. There are also specific quotations from Botticelli, for example, the clasped hands in the lower right which are copied (and rotated 90 degrees) from the hands of two angels directly below God in Botticelli's *Coronation of the Virgin* (Uffizi, Florence).

22. *Briseis* was first exhibited at Chez Léonce Rosenberg, Paris, *Exposition Francis Picabia*, December 9–31, 1930, no. 48, as a work of 1929. The title refers to Briseis, daughter of the King of Lyrnessus in Homeric mythology. The large head and hand in the painting are derived from Botticelli. See his *Portrait of a Young Man* (National Gallery, Washington, D.C.) for the model for the hand.

23. *Atrata* was first exhibited at the Kunstsalon Wolfsberg, Zurich, *Produktion Paris 1930*, October 8–November 15, 1930, no. 65. The significance of the title is unknown. *Ino* was first exhibited at Chez Léonce Rosenberg, Paris, *Exposition Francis Picabia*, December 9–31, 1930, no. 59, as a work of 1930. The title from Greek mythology refers to Ino, second wife of Athamas.

convenient to observe that the sex of Picabia's Botticelli-inspired faces is frequently difficult to specify.

In *Atrata* (fig. 326) Picabia has likewise appropriated, modified and recombined diverse models. The prominent head in the upper center and the hands below it, with thumbs touching near the center of the painting, are adapted from Botticelli's *Portrait of a Man with a Medal* (fig. 328). Layers of forms beneath those images include a Roman statue of Atlas (fig. 327), but the large hands around the globe of Atlas are again Botticelli in origin—as is the hand with grapes at the lower left.[24]

Occasional Italian Baroque models enriched Picabia's repertory of classical and Renaissance forms, for example, Guido Reni's *Nessus and Dejanira* in *Villica-Caja* (figs. 329, 330), or more precisely, his Nessus since a Pompeiian Venus displaced Dejanira (fig. 331).[25]

Many other models could be presented, but having introduced a sampling of them and Picabia's methods of composition, additional examples will be considered only when they are relevant to questions of form and content.

The prevalence of titles and visual sources from classical antiquity suggests further research in that direction as one attempts to cope with possible relationships between images and titles. To date, most of the transparencies have resisted efforts to intrude on their privacy, but a few have yielded moderately to such probing, and both "positive" and "negative" results may be useful.

No obvious rapport stands out, for example, between Picabia's painting *Briseis* (fig. 317) and the myth of Briseis, the beautiful daughter of the King of Lyrnessus, who became the favorite slave of Achilles. Interpretive efforts seem more hopeless still before the enigmatic title and complex forms of *Dispar* (fig. 312, and color pl. XVI). This does not mean that no rapport exists between the forms and titles in *Dispar* and *Briseis*, but, for the time being at least, the content of such works is too personal or esoteric and simply beyond our interpretive means.

In other instances some tentative observations may be recorded. The stand-

24. For the sources of these last hands see the attending angel in Botticelli's *Madonna of the Pomegranate* (Uffizi, Florence) and the hand of an angel in his *Virgin of the Eucharist* (Gardner Museum, Boston).

25. *Villica-Caja* is documented by a photograph of Picabia in his studio, *Variétés*, no. 2 (Brussels, June 15, 1929), between pp. 94 and 95.

The specific source for the figure of Nessus was probably an engraving after Guido Reni's painting of *Nessus and Dejanira* which was (and still is) in the possession of Germaine Everling. The prevalence of models from Botticelli and Greco-Roman art suggests that Picabia had prints or books on those subjects, and perhaps guide books for Naples and environs and the Prado, given the high incidence of borrowings from those collections (see figs. 274, 279, 308, 320, 323, 327, 331, 333, 351).

Neither Germaine Everling nor Olga Picabia ever observed Picabia using such books, although one of his closest friends during the 1940s, Christine Boumeester, did see him with a picture book on Italian Renaissance art (interview with Christine Boumeester and Henri Goetz, Paris, June 20, 1968).

ing figure and four faces in *Ino* (fig. 322) suggest a simple correspondence with the story of Ino, second wife of Athamas, ruler of Boeotia. She bore him two sons, but her schemes to eliminate Athamas's two older sons by his first wife led to a series of disasters in which Athamas was struck mad and Ino and all four of the sons lost their lives. The chain and gesture of the large single hand might also be accommodated, but neither a knowledge of that myth nor of Picabia's models in Botticellian and Pompeiian frescoes seems essential to the experience of this painting.

Hera (fig. 314) appears even more independent of its visual and literary sources. The initial effect of this painting is primarily a delicate visual experience of hands and serene classical faces, apparently female, suspended among flowing tendrils, leaves and flowers in a sea of light blue. Further search reveals a nude, viewed from behind in a curious, dejected pose, and one begins to muse about identities, relationships and the title. Pursuit of such musings may lead to an association with Hera Anthea (flowery),[26] but there is no way to verify that facet of Hera for this painting, and, finally, the indeterminate condition of such queries seems in accord with Picabia's work. While references to classical mythology may suggest an intriguing additional dimension to *Hera*, the quiet visual appeal of this painting keeps reasserting itself, transforming visual models from Botticelli, and putting the mythology of the ancients in the service of Picabia's private reveries.

Although *Artemis* (fig. 332) is a complex composition which discourages analysis, it seems to present another example of Picabia's frequent play on Christian and pagan subjects. Across the lower half of the canvas is the faintly visible nude image of St. Sebastian (fig. 333), a Christian victim of Roman archers who here occupies a large portion of a painting named after the pagan Greek goddess of the hunt.[27]

Medea (fig. 334) is one of the few transparencies in which the relationship between images and title may be of substantial significance. The ram's head, dragon, wings, standing masked figure and large faces suggest the episode in the life of Medea and Jason which deals with the death of Pelias. During Jason's quest for the golden fleece, Pelias usurped his throne and killed his parents and infant brother. Medea, disguised as an old crone, set out to avenge her husband. She appeared before Pelias to announce that Artemis, just arrived in a chariot drawn by winged serpents, wished to acknowledge Pelias's piety by rejuvenating him so that he might begat filial heirs. To allay the suspicions of Pelias, Medea first restored her own youth, a feat accomplished in the theater by changing masks. Next she dissected and boiled an old ram which she pretended to rejuvenate by restoring it as a frisky lamb—produced surreptitiously from a concealed compartment in an image of Artemis. The thoroughly deceived Pelias was then charmed to

26. Before the temple of Hera Anthea at Argos was a common grave of the women who went to aid Dionysus in a war against the Argives. Every year at that temple a flower festival in honor of Hera Anthea was celebrated by the women of the Peloponnesus.

27. *Artemis* was purchased in the summer of 1929 from Picabia's studio by the son of the present owner. It has never been exhibited.

sleep, whereupon Medea persuaded two of his daughters to dissect and boil him as she had done with the ram.

Many remaining forms in the painting may be accounted for by later incidents in the life of Medea. Her violent resistance to Jason's desertion aroused the admiration and love of Zeus, but his sad-faced eagle symbol may reflect her stout defense against his advances. Shortly after this episode and the sacrifice of her children, Medea was carried away from Corinth by her grandfather, the sun god Helios, in his chariot drawn by winged serpents. And, finally, after her banishment from Athens, it is recorded that Medea sailed to Italy, where she taught the art of snake charming to the Marrubians.

The correspondence of so many images in *Medea* with her myth is unlikely to be coincidental. Nonetheless, Picabia was not merely illustrating the myth. The episodes and images have been selected and superimposed in a manner so personal that there is no absolute certainty about the relationship of the painting to the myth. For the egocentric Picabia, it is possible that this painting deals as much with his personal life as with the myth of Medea. The mythmaking possibilities of his own life gave away little to either Jason or Zeus, and the lot of Picabia's wives and children, though hardly as tragic as that of Medea, was never an easy one. In the final analysis, *Medea* remains an enigma. Numerous considerations may be relevant for a richer comprehension of it—visual and literary sources, Picabia's life and reflections of classical art and mythology in the work of other contemporary artists.[28] But, like most of the transparencies, *Medea* is a private reverie, deliberately constructed with images which evoke poignant visual experiences, convey moods and invite speculation, but never explain a thing. In that respect Picabia might be compared to the Belgian surrealist René Magritte, who, during the same years, was juxtaposing disparate objects and pitting those images against evocative titles—with the aim, he said, "not to reduce the world to the variety of its material aspects," but "to reveal poetry," poetry which "does not forget the mystery of the world."[29] Despite such general correspondence of the means and ends to their paintings, the work of Magritte and Picabia was vastly different in appearance and effect, and Picabia seems even more independent from the work of other surrealist artists.

Throughout 1930–1932, the course of Picabia's life continued without major change. Some writing and a great deal of painting remained an integral part of that life, but never interfered with other pleasures—new pets, automobiles and yachts; excursions at a moment's notice; a succession of guests and galas. Despite gradual intensification of the Great Depression, his excursions were undertaken in in-

28. The Neo-Classicism of the 1920s had continued in various forms in all the arts— Picasso's prints, Cocteau's dramas (*Orphée*, 1926, and *La Machine infernale*, 1934), Stravinsky's oratorios (*Oedipus Rex*, 1927, and *Persephone*, 1934) and the surrealists' preoccupation with mythologies, including a revision of ancient Greek mythology in terms of modern psychic experience.

29. Arkansas Art Center, Little Rock, *Magritte*, May 15–June 30, 1964, organized by the Art Department, University of St. Thomas, Houston, preface by André Breton.

creasingly elegant vehicles: a Rolls Royce was added to Picabia's fleet of automobiles in 1931, and early in 1930 the *Henriquetta* was replaced by *L'Horizon I*, a sleek seventy-foot motor yacht. For a time this yacht—handily docked just opposite Cannes' municipal casino—became Picabia's primary residence, and Olga Mohler the mistress of it. Picabia, by then a fixture in the society of Cannes, was called upon more and more frequently to provide themes and decors for celebrations at the Château de Madrid, and the Club Ambassadeurs at the casino (see illus. 35). Moreover, his own exhibitions had become significant social events. In August 1930, Emile Fabre chose to inaugurate his Galerie Alexandre III with an exhibition of Picabia's recent work, and the opening was hailed as a social record of sorts, comparable to major events at the peak winter season.[30] Unfortunately, little else about the exhibition was recorded, and it is thanks to a single installation photograph (illus. 34) that the next phase of Picabia's transparencies can be documented as early as the summer of 1930.[31]

The new paintings were well documented, however, in December of that year in Picabia's first exhibition at the gallery of Léonce Rosenberg.[32] It was a major retrospective show, weighed in favor of the transparencies and prefaced by Picabia himself:

> "Picabia has made too many jokes with his painting!" there is . . . what certain people find at the bottom of their sack of acrimony . . .
>
> And me, I say: too many jokes have been made with Picabia's painting! . . .
>
> I worked for months and years making use of nature, copying it, transposing it. Now, it is *my* nature that I copy, that I try to express. I was once feverish over calculated inventions, now it is my instinct that guides me. . . .
>
> This third dimension, not made of light and shadow, these transparencies with their corner of oubliettes permit me to express for myself the resemblance of my interior desires. . . . I want a painting where all my instincts may have a free course. . . .
>
> Those who have said . . . that "I do not enter the line of account" are right. I take part in no addition and recount my life to myself alone.

Documented works from this exhibition and the Galerie Alexandre III indicate that Picabia had not wholly abandoned models from Botticelli, but they had become uncommon, and, as exemplified by the enormous face in *Salome* (fig. 337), Botticellian sources were more exaggerated than emulated (see fig. 338). In

30. Galerie Alexandre III, Cannes, *Exposition Picabia*, August 1930. For the social dimension see the review of an anonymous journalist, "L'Exposition Francis Picabia à Cannes," *L'Eclaireur de Nice et du Sud-Est*, August 22, 1930, 3.

31. The first painting on the left in this installation photograph is *Salome* (fig. 337); the third painting is *Taiti* (private collection, Paris); the fourth is *Chloris* (private collection, Paris); the largest painting on the back wall is *Aello* (fig. 340, and color pl. XVII).

32. Chez Léonce Rosenberg, Paris, *Exposition Francis Picabia*, December 9–31, 1930, with statements by Picabia and Léonce Rosenberg.

other examples, *Oo* (fig. 339), a double-headed Botticellian motif frequently employed in 1929 (fig. 314) is secondary to a large head from Picabia's primary model during 1930, Piero della Francesca.[33] In recognition of that dominant new source, this phase of the transparencies may be referred to as the "Piero phase," although it is further distinguished in many instances by less complex compositions, darker colors and simplified, heavier lines.

All the new formal properties are present in two documented paintings of 1930, *Aello* and *Noctuelles* (fig. 340, and color pl. XVII; fig. 342), but especially in the former, where the delicate light blue, cream, brown and green hues of the earlier transparencies have given way to a darker palette, and the composition is reduced to the superimposition of two transparent heads over a landscape.[34] Those heads themselves are simplified modifications of the two angels in Piero's *Baptism of Christ* (fig. 341), but he has entitled the painting *Aello* after one of the harpies—filthy, ravenous bird-women who carried away the souls of the dead. As usual, Picabia's intentions have not been documented by himself, family or friends, but his play on the reversal of Christian and pagan forms and content occurs too frequently to be wholly coincidental.

Documented paintings like *Aello* and *Noctuelles* enable dates of ca. 1930 to be attributed to such works as *Heads and Landscape* (fig. 344), which have not been identified in documents of that period, but do possess all the features of the Piero phase, including a source in the work of that Renaissance master (fig. 345). Moreover, in comparing that source with the model for *Noctuelles* (fig. 343), it is evident that Picabia found in Piero not only a melancholic mood and images to his taste, but Renaissance precedent for his compositional devices of repetition, inversion and variation. Isolation and repetition of the face at the right in *Heads and Landscape* (fig. 344) served him for another painting of ca. 1930 which now goes by the title *Genie of the Lake* (fig. 346). Although that title is the choice of a later owner of the painting rather than of Picabia himself, it is in harmony with the effect of the painting. The combination of a solid Mediterranean landscape behind the transparent head evokes sensations of contrast between the enduring land and the lives of those who have inhabited it—ephemeral in body but permanent perhaps in their spiritual presence. Whatever Picabia's intentions, *Genie of the Lake* deals with mood, not an intellectual program, and in all probability the source in Piero della Francesca was prompted by the poignant introspective quality of his images and not by the specific identity of its Christian subject.

During the period of Picabia's transparencies—as at other times in his career—there were paintings somewhat outside the major current of his work. *Judith* (fig. 336) is a striking example from ca. 1929; *Setina* (fig. 348) is one from

33. *Oo* was exhibited at Chez Léonce Rosenberg, December 9–31, 1930, no. 61, as a work of 1930.

34. *Aello* was exhibited at the Galerie Alexandre III in August 1930. *Noctuelles* was exhibited at Chez Léonce Rosenberg, December 9–31, 1930, no. 60, as a work of 1930. The significance of its title, based on a type of nocturnal moth, is unclear.

ca. 1930.[35] Neither, however, is very distant from Picabia's mainstream, and modified images from both of them reappear in Picabia's illustrations for André Maurois's science-fiction tale *Le Peseur d'âmes* (The Weigher of Souls).[36] Maurois's story concerns an English physician, Dr. James, who discovered that at a fixed interval of time after death all beings suddenly emit a vital fluid or vapor which could be captured and preserved in airtight glass containers. Further experiments revealed that when the containers were exposed to ultraviolet rays in a darkened room, the vital fluid was visible as a vapor within the glass vessel. When vapors of compatible couples were mingled, an extraordinary movement and radiance were observed; when the fluids of incompatible people were mixed, a sluggish gray vapor was obtained. Realizing that the frailty of his beloved wife Edith precluded more than a few years of life together, Dr. James pursued his experiments for urgent personal ends.

Picabia's transparencies were well suited for the task of illustrating Maurois's sentimental science-fiction story. Of his nine lithographs for the book, one entitled *L'Infinité de Dieu* (*The Infinity of God*, fig. 347) perhaps best combines his dual responsibilities as artist and illustrator. Its blond tonality and delicate linear qualities are reminiscent of the best transparencies of 1929, while the theme of the book is suggested by layers of transparent figural and floral images that include laboratory apparatus, a portrait of Dr. James, the face of his wife within a glass container and a male nude in rapt observation of his dancing female companion.

The theme of Maurois's book may have held special interest for Picabia at that moment, for during an otherwise festive summer, Olga became dangerously ill. She retired to her family home in Switzerland for a long convalescence, and during that period Picabia and Germaine were almost reconciled.[37] But, contrary to Germaine's expectations, Picabia brought Olga back to the Château de Mai and that act removed any lingering doubt about the resolution of the triangle. Germaine presided over the château, but the yacht once more became the primary residence of Francis and Olga, and an open house for numerous friends. During the late summer and fall of 1931, the habitués of *L'Horizon* included Guy Schwob, Sir Francis Rose, Michel Georges-Michel and Count Magnani-Manetti, but, as usual, Picabia also managed to prepare for his next exhibition in Paris.

35. *Judith* was exhibited at Chez Léonce Rosenberg, December 9–31, 1930, no. 41, as a work of 1929. The central hand of *Setina* is copied from the hand of the Madonna in Botticelli's *Madonna of the Magnificat* (Uffizi, Florence).

36. André Maurois, *Le Peseur d'âmes* (Paris, 1931). Maurois's publisher, Antoine Roche, invited Picabia to illustrate the book. Picabia did not meet Maurois and did not read the book. Instead, a friend read passages to him (conversation with Mme Olga Picabia, June 30, 1974). Picabia did nine lithographs in color for the book. Those with figures from *Judith* and *Setina* (figs. 336, 348) are not reproduced here.

37. A severe general infection kept Olga in bed for six weeks. During her convalescence Picabia did the illustrations for Maurois's *Le Peseur d'âmes* and would have gone to decorate the palace of a maharaja except that the latter had also fallen ill (Olga Picabia manuscript, 36–37, 39). See also Everling, *L'Anneau de Saturne*, 195–96.

Picabia, Olga and Germaine drove to Paris that fall in a new Hispano-Suiza and took up temporary residence with Méraud and Alvaro Guevara. Robert Desnos again provided a preface for Picabia in an exhibition held that year in the Galerie Georges Bernheim rather than the gallery of Léonce Rosenberg, who had been forced by the Depression to suspend temporarily all but a marginal gallery operation. Rosenberg did, however, sponsor a lecture by a well-known occultist, Vivian Du Mas, who spoke on "Occultism in the Art of Francis Picabia." After describing the existence of a world beyond this world of appearances, Du Mas commented: "I recognize in the paintings of Picabia the translation in aesthetic language of a part of that other world. I can vow that the representation of it is exact. I affirm that these paintings are not a simple fantasy, but a representation of the astral world."[38]

The Rosenberg-Picabia correspondence indicates that philosophy and occultism were topics of conversation, but Rosenberg politely implied that Du Mas had little to offer.[39] Picabia may have been more interested inasmuch as he did not discourage the lecture and attended others by Du Mas. His paintings, however, continued the established trend toward darker, heavier forms and simpler compositions—and, in terms of sources and compositional techniques, they had about as much to do with "representation of the astral world" as William Blake's Michelangelo-infested drawings a century earlier had to do with the direct transcription of the dictates of messengers from Heaven.[40]

The large, somber-toned canvas *Mélibée* (fig. 349) combines only two layers of forms which are linked to their pagan and Christian sources, namely, one of the shepherds of Virgil ("Mélibée"), and the prayerful figure adapted from Piero's *Virgin and Child with Sts. and Federigo da Montefeltro. Adam and Eve* (fig. 350) is also large, dark, reduced to two layers of forms and keyed to an exchange of Christian and pagan identity. In this instance, however, the title is Christian and the basic image pagan in origin (fig. 351).[41]

Alongside such typical compositions of 1931, Picabia produced other transparencies which were more complex visually and thematically (fig. 352). Neither the forms nor the content of *Olyras* have been fully explored, but two of its major images—the enormous head of a Madonna and a reclining figure visible through

38. The lecture of Vivian Du Mas at this time is recorded by Germaine Everling, *L'Anneau de Saturne*, 175–76. An article by Du Mas, "L'Occultisme dans l'art de Francis Picabia," was published in *Orbes*, no. 3 (Paris, spring 1932), 113–28.

39. Rosenberg wrote Picabia regarding the lecture of Vivian Du Mas, "Certainly, one must praise without reserve the sincerity, the courage and the knowledge of Vivian du Mas, but between us, I find him a little too much of a specialist" (letter, December 23, 1931, Bibliothèque Doucet). In an undated letter of the same period, Rosenberg talks of Max Stirner and Nietzsche and his intention to discuss their writings with Picabia.

40. Sir Anthony Blunt demonstrated (*The Art of William Blake*, New York, 1959, 22–42) that Blake did not restrict himself to slavish copy of visions and observed that although Blake "was by far the most original English artist of his time, [he] borrowed more extensively . . . from the works of other artists than did any of his contemporaries" (op. cit., 32).

41. The legend of Orestes and Electra is so complex and controversial in itself that efforts to correlate it and Picabia's painting of *Adam and Eve* seem futile.

that head—derive from the work of Ambrogio Lorenzetti (fig. 353) six or seven years in advance of the major influence of Italian primitives on Picabia's art (fig. 376).[42]

After three or four weeks in Paris, Picabia returned to Cannes, where he had commitments for the winter social season, beginning that December with the decor for a gala, "A Robinson" at the Ambassadeurs. That was followed in March 1932 by collaboration on the casino's "Night in Singapore" for which caged lions and panthers were rented to inhabit a potted-plant jungle.[43] About May, Picabia and Olga made another quick trip to Paris in order to rent a small apartment for use in their increasingly frequent trips between Cannes and the capital. After taking an apartment on the avenue du Bois de Boulogne, they returned to the Château de Mai and replaced *L'Horizon I* with a new, smaller yacht, *L'Horizon II*, which served for a secondary residence and social gatherings. Among the usual stream of guests during 1932, three old friends were most welcomed—Pierre de Massot, Gertrude Stein and Alice Toklas.

After virtually no association for seventeen years, Picabia and Gertrude Stein renewed contact in 1931, and from then until her death they maintained a lively correspondence and a warm friendship which embraced Olga as well.[44] Miss Stein's keen mind and interest in Picabia's work was a double joy for him, and he promptly invited her to preface his exhibition of drawings at Léonce Rosenberg's gallery in December 1932.[45]

Relatively few drawings from that exhibition have been documented, but by combining those with works from a preceding exhibition in Cannes and other signed and dated drawings of 1932, the major course of his career remains clear (see figs. 354, 355).[46] *Volupté* (fig. 355)—which suggests a direct correlation of forms and title—is a typical work. Lingering models in Botticelli and Piero seem more distant; ink, pencil, conté crayon and charcoal are the dominant materials, and the images range from relatively simple two-layer transparencies to some single opaque figures which foreshadow the simplified naturalistic images and superimpositions that constitute the major currents in Picabia's work from about 1933 to 1939.

42. *Olyras* was exhibited at the Galerie Georges Bernheim, Paris, *Exposition Francis Picabia*, November 10–25, 1931, no. 3.

43. Olga Picabia manuscript, 40.

44. The letters of Francis and Olga Picabia to Gertrude Stein are housed in the Gertrude Stein Archive, Collection of American Literature, Beinecke Rare Book and Manuscript Library, Yale University, hereafter cited as G.S.A., Yale. The first letter of renewed correspondence is dated March 14, 1931; the last letters date from 1946. The letters of Miss Stein to Picabia were recently transferred by Mme Olga Picabia to the Bibliothèque Littéraire Jacques Doucet, Paris.

45. Chez Léonce Rosenberg, Paris, *Exposition de dessins par Francis Picabia*, December 1–24, 1932, poem and preface by Gertrude Stein, translated by Marcel Duchamp.

46. The drawings exhibited at Chez Léonce Rosenberg, December 1–24, 1932, had distinctive titles, but few of them were printed on the drawings themselves, and in multiple changes of ownership most of those titles have been lost.

The catalogue of the preceding exhibition in Cannes was headed *104 dessins par Francis Picabia, présentées par Evelyn Wyld et Eyre de Lanux*, preface by Germaine Everling dated August 19, 1932. No works were listed by title.

17. TRANSPARENCIES, SOLIDS AND SUPERIMPOSITIONS, 1933-1940

FROM the mid-thirties to the outbreak of World War II, the course of Picabia's life was more stable than it had been for some time; his painting, to the contrary, was never more erratic. Excepting a distinct group of abstract compositions (figs. 377, 385), his entire production was figurative, but the variety of shifting, simultaneous modes of realism, transparency and superimposition almost defy categorization, and the scarcity of documents precludes precise dating in numerous instances. Quality is also an issue. In the eyes of many critics, Picabia's work from ca. 1933 to 1945 has seemed generally inferior to that of other periods in his career. And, for the first time in his life, Picabia himself suffered spells of profound doubt and pessimism. Such spells were brief, however, and, along with Olga, his chief aesthetic-moral support came from Gertrude Stein and Léonce Rosenberg.

Rosenberg numbered Picabia among the handful of artists "who counted," and, as the Depression made conditions increasingly dismal for artists and dealers alike, he multiplied assurances to himself and his artists that their art would remain in history while "commercial painting" would only last "like roses, the span of a morning."[1] Picabia's portion of that correspondence has been lost, but his letters to Gertrude Stein remain, and they abound with gratitude for her support: "Those few days passed with you did me enormous good. . . . Our conversations on painting have again affirmed in me the certitude that my researches are becoming coordinated and will be, soon now I hope, an expression in exact accord with myself."[2] Miss Stein's support, in fact, went far beyond the stimulating conversations cherished by Picabia. During the winter of 1932–1933, while Francis and Olga were in Paris for the exhibition of his drawings at Rosenberg's gallery, Miss Stein introduced them to Mme Marie Cuttoli, an influential woman in the artistic and political life of France and director of the Galerie Vignon in Paris. Arrangements were begun then for an exhibition of Picabia's work in her gallery that fall,

1. See the Léonce Rosenberg letters to Picabia, November 29 and December 11, 1934 (Bibliothèque Doucet, Paris).
2. Picabia letter to Gertrude Stein, July 20, 1933 (G.S.A., Yale).

and, unknown to Picabia, action was also initiated regarding his nomination for the Legion of Honor.

Soon after returning to Cannes in December 1932, Picabia plunged into work for his forthcoming exhibition. Mornings were spent in the studio at the Château de Mai, then occupied solely by Germaine Everling, Lorenzo and Michel Corlin. Afternoons, Picabia normally returned to the vagabond life of his yacht. There were exchange visits with Mme Cuttoli in her villa at Cap d'Antibes, and idyllic hours with passing friends and neighboring boat owners, at that time principally Max and Eva Bauer and Jullien du Breuil with whom Picabia enjoyed talking about art, playing chess and devising ways to break the bank at the casino.[3] Occasional trips varied that pace of life. In early June Francis and Olga drove to Bilignin in order to present Gertrude Stein with a chihuahua pup in replacement for a pet recently lost.[4] A month later they passed through Bilignin again, this time on the way to Paris for a July 14 presentation of the Legion of Honor. Picabia's sponsor, Mme Cuttoli, had prudently inquired in advance if he would accept the invitation. Genuinely touched by her action, Picabia accepted and later defended the propriety of such an act by an ex-dadaist by opining that the only thing better than rejecting a deserved honor was to accept an undeserved honor.[5]

No fanfare accompanied the award. Instead Picabia resumed work in Cannes, and at the end of September, when he was satisfied with his work for the Galerie Vignon exhibition, he and Olga again drove to Paris.[6] An illness precluded much work in the weeks prior to the vernissage, although he did do a nude portrait of a friend, the popular entertainer Suzy Solidor (fig. 357).[7] To the already diverse portrait gallery of his entertainer friends—Mistinguett, Napierkowska and

3. Throughout this chapter, most of the references to the people and events in Picabia's personal life are based on the Olga Picabia manuscript (collection Olga Picabia, Paris). Max and Eva Bauer were from Hamburg but passed a major portion of each year on their yacht next to the Picabias. Jullien du Breuil later contributed prefaces for Picabia's exhibitions. The active social life of the Picabias precludes reference to all save their closer friends.

4. Picabia letter to Gertrude Stein, undated [ca. May 1933] (G.S.A., Yale).

Love of pets was an additional bond between Gertrude Stein and the Picabias. The latter usually had a menagerie of birds and small dogs about them, focused in the thirties on a chihuahua couple named "Monsieur" and "Madame." Gertrude Stein received two of their pups, one named "Byron" who, when he died, was replaced by "Pépé," named after Picabia. See Gertrude Stein, *Everybody's Autobiography* (New York, 1937), 48–49.

5. Michel Sanouillet, *Picabia* (Paris, 1964), 52.

Picabia wrote Gertrude Stein on June 27, 1933 (G.S.A., Yale), that he had received a letter from a minister of the government about "la croix," and that he and Olga would leave for Bilignin on July 12. The event is described by Olga Picabia in her manuscript, 54. Picabia's election as Chevalier on July 13, 1933, has been verified by personnel of the Grand Chancellerie de la Légion d'Honneur (letter to the author, July 9, 1974).

6. Letters of Francis and Olga Picabia to Gertrude Stein (July 20, August 10 and 22, September 9 and 15, 1933, G.S.A., Yale) indicate the progress of Picabia's work, his collaboration with Miss Stein on an unidentified project involving Georges Maratier and an intention to visit Miss Stein in Bilignin around October 5. For unknown reasons, Picabia left abruptly for Paris, bypassing Bilignin, and wrote Gertrude Stein from there on September 29, 1933 (G.S.A., Yale).

7. Picabia had earlier painted another portrait of Suzy Solidor (present location unknown). Olga Picabia recorded in her manuscript, 57, that during their visit in Paris, she was impressed by

the dancer Jasmine (figs. 29, 75, 76, 188)—Picabia added an absolutely new image, aggressively direct and simple, with a seductive face and lots of heavily painted flesh within easy arm reach of the spectator.

The few paintings (figs. 356, 358) and documents presently identified with the Galerie Vignon exhibition indicate that it consisted of similar works, except that many of them were overlaid with a single layer of transparent forms.[8] The latter paintings, distinctive in style and subject from the transparencies of ca. 1928–1932, have been designated "superimpositions." The *Portrait of Olga Mohler* (fig. 358) is representative of Picabia's work around 1933 with its simple superimposition of a transparent plant form over the essentially naturalistic image of Olga. Gertrude Stein was perhaps the first to be depicted in that "naturalistic" manner (fig. 356), although her portrait was neither conceived nor executed as merely naturalistic.[9] Her image was simplified, heavily outlined, loosely brushed in muted colors and invested with concerns described in the *Autobiography of Alice B. Toklas*:

> Picabia has conceived and is struggling with the problem that a line should have the vibration of a musical sound and that this vibration should be the result of conceiving the human form and the human face in so tenuous a fashion that it would induce such vibration in the line forming it. It is his way of achieving the disembodied. . . .
>
> All his life Picabia has struggled to dominate and achieve this conception. Gertrude Stein thinks that perhaps he is now approaching the solution of his problem.[10]

In the context of this seemingly simple, solid, earthen-hued image of Gertrude Stein, such theoretical baggage is unexpected, but it verifies the seriousness of his intentions and his constant concern for the expression of interior states inadequately served by mere naturalism.

Francis and Olga returned to Cannes in time to organize the casino's Christmas party around the theme of "La Fête au village," and for five or six months afterward Picabia played more than he painted. In the preceding fall, he had transferred his yacht from Cannes around the point to Golfe-Juan, where it was kept until 1939. There were new friends to be made in Golfe-Juan and frequent

---

Henry Daniel-Rops's *Mort, où est ta victoire* (Paris, 1934), while Picabia was enveloped by *L'Homme à la guitare* and *Les Deux Clowns* (author unidentified).

8. Galerie Vignon, Paris, *Exposition des oeuvres de Francis Picabia*, November 9–23, 1933, preface by Léonce Rosenberg. In a letter stamped with disillusionment about various conditions in Paris, Picabia wrote Germaine Everling that "Léonce . . . is going to be obliged to close and to let go of everything" (undated letter of November 1933 on the reverse of Rosenberg's preface for the Galerie Vignon catalogue; collection Germaine Everling, Cannes).

9. Picabia wrote Miss Stein from Paris that he would like to exhibit her portrait at the Galerie Vignon, and the arrival of the painting was acknowledged in an undated note on the reverse of an invitation to the exhibition (G.S.A., Yale).

10. Gertrude Stein, *The Autobiography of Alice B. Toklas* (New York, 1933), 258.

visits from older friends, especially the Bauers, Jullien du Breuil and Mme Cuttoli. Some of them dined so often at one restaurant that they practically dictated the menu—which suffered from the eating habits of Picabia, who rejected all green vegetables as "cow food" and insisted for weeks at a time on sole and pears or whatever happened to be his pleasure. Excursions by land and sea were common also, highlighted that year by a pleasure cruise to Corsica.

During that leisurely period, Picabia wrote Miss Stein that he had worked very little during the past months, but by July he was so busy preparing for two exhibitions in the fall that he cancelled a trip to Bilignin.[11] Mme Cuttoli was responsible for both exhibitions, the first of which was held at her Galerie Vignon in October 1934, while the second opened on November 5 at the Valentine Gallery in New York.[12] Neither exhibition is well documented. A few older paintings were included in the New York show (see fig. 352), but only scattered references exist for the recent works. Picabia himself said they were "in the spirit of the Gertrude Stein portrait"; a critic described them as heavily varnished "surimpressions" of rather neo-academic heads and figures over landscapes.[13] Some drawings in a large auction at the Galerie Alexandre III during August 1934 may have been studies for paintings at the Galerie Vignon (see fig. 359), but meager documentation does not permit secure identification.[14] For the time being, only a few attributions might be suggested; *Idea* (fig. 360), for example, which is one of several undated paintings that resemble the style of the portrait of Olga (fig. 358).

Francis and Olga remained in Paris through mid-December 1934—painting, calling on old friends, revisiting favorite nightclubs and art galleries—but he was discouraged by much of what he saw. "Here . . . life is more and more difficult," he wrote Miss Stein, "people are increasingly sad and old, art is going third rate;

11. Picabia wrote Gertrude Stein on May 30, 1934 (G.S.A., Yale), "I work little, I am waiting and this has lasted several months." But on July 29 (G.S.A., Yale) he wrote that he was working a great deal and had no chance to visit her as intended.

12. Galerie Vignon, Paris, *Francis Picabia, ses oeuvres récentes*, October 25–November 6, 1934, preface by André Jullien du Breuil. Valentine Gallery, New York, *Recent Paintings by Francis Picabia*, November 5–24, 1934, preface by Gertrude Stein. Mme Cuttoli did not organize Picabia's exhibition at the Valentine Gallery but she seems to have been the contact between Picabia and the gallery. Picabia wrote Gertrude Stein on July 29, 1934 (G.S.A., Yale), "Madame Cuttoli . . . has asked me for the preface for the exhibition in New York, Chicago for the person occupied with the exhibition is going [to set out again? ms. unclear] to America and would like to have it before."

13. Picabia letter to Gertrude Stein, July 9, 1934 (G.S.A., Yale). He also wrote on July 29, "I am working a great deal [;] it does not go badly, you will see, it seems to me that my painting is stronger, simpler, more harmonious; those several months when I was obliged to do nothing may have been a good thing" (G.S.A., Yale).

For critics' comments see C.D., "Les Expositions," *Beaux-Arts*, no. 96 (Paris, November 2, 1934), 6; and Maximilien Gautier, "Les Expositions," *L'Art vivant*, no. 191 (Paris, December 1934–January 1935), 514–15.

14. Galerie Alexandre III, Cannes, *Catalogue des aquarelles et dessins composant l'atelier de Francis Picabia*, August 18, 1934, preface by Maurice Mignon. Of eighty-five drawings in this sales catalogue, about twenty were dated 1932, one 1931, and one 1934; the rest were undated.

in spite of that I work a lot as always, that makes me forget the world and I always hope to make new discoveries."[15]

By the Christmas holidays, they were back in Golfe-Juan, celebrating the New Year with a new luxury car, a Graham Paige, and working on scenery for the casino's gala, "Beasts of the Apocalypse." That theme invoked the imagery of Picabia's monster period, and, according to Olga, they worked with gusto, "Francis enjoying himself like a child, drawing all sorts of horned beasts with triple and quadruple eyes."[16]

In his studio at the Château de Mai, Picabia also completed a distinct group of figurative paintings (illus. 36; figs. 361–363, 365, 366) which are securely documented thanks to his correspondence, the records of Olga Picabia and an exhibition arranged by Gertrude Stein at the Arts Club of Chicago.[17] As additional paintings in that exhibition are identified, greater variety may be discovered, but to date every documented work is characterized by deliberately simplified, heavily outlined and solid images in which transparency is wholly eliminated. In some instances the forms are summarily modeled in light and dark, but for the most part those boldly contoured figures are filled in with bright, flat colors (figs. 362, 363) or washed over with a dark, monochromatic blue-green tone (fig. 361). The subject matter was exceptionally varied—portraits, landscapes, genre scenes, religious and mythological subjects, etc.—but, as before in his career, Picabia turned to models in art of the past (compare figs. 363 and 364) and restudied old themes in his own work (compare figs. 362 and 247).

The inescapably rude simplicity of these images was unnerving for the critics. One of them first asserted that Picabia meant to burlesque the current vogue for naturalism, and then suggested in a proto-Pop Art vein that his aim was to take "naive" sources, for example, "primitive German woodcuts . . . the color 'subtleties' of the Barnum and Bailey circus bills, the classic insipidities (Cupids, Venuses, wrestlers) of his friend Chirico, sweet girls from fashion magazine covers, sweeter girls from candy-box lids" and proceed to "organize them with exquisite taste, and flash them forth to the world."[18] Later in his career Picabia sometimes did employ such popular sources for his paintings, and there are also examples of burlesque intentions in his work. However, the latter element has been susceptible to gross exaggeration owing to the "dada syndrome" in Picabia criticism. His taste for protest and parody is undeniable—but such interests did not provide his basic motivation, certainly not for an entire group of paintings.

15. Picabia letter to Gertrude Stein, December 7, 1934 (G.S.A., Yale).
16. Olga Picabia manuscript, 62.
17. The Arts Club of Chicago, *Paintings by Francis Picabia*, January 3–25, 1936.
Picabia wrote Gertrude Stein on August 7, 1935: "I have just received your letter on the subject of the exhibition. I thank you and accept with pleasure to do the exhibition in Chicago" (G.S.A., Yale). This exhibition is discussed by Olga Picabia (manuscript, 63) and recorded by a number of photographs in her album (illus. 36; figs. 361, 365, 366).
18. C.J. Bulliet, exhibition review, *Chicago Daily News*, January 11, 1936; and *The Significant Moderns* (New York, 1936), 105.

Regardless of the period of his career, Picabia painted essentially for himself; he painted what he wanted to paint, enjoyed doing it and took it seriously. While Picabia's precise intentions are not known for these particular works of 1935, his correspondence with Gertrude Stein and the witness of Olga Picabia make it clear that he considered them significant paintings, not jokes or burlesques of contemporary naturalistic art. His esteem of those paintings was, however, short-lived. Upon receipt of them from Chicago during 1936, Picabia was in another period of dissatisfaction over his work, and some of the paintings were destroyed—in one documented example by the superimposition of new forms which completely transformed the original painting (figs. 366, 367).[19] Picabia continually reworked older paintings during the 1930s and 1940s. One of the more complex examples (fig. 378) is dominated by an African-type mask in an ovoid frame, obviously painted over an earlier image of a male head which in turn appears to have been added to the dark blue, barely visible form of a woman peering into a mirror. These layers of images, though separate in date, suggest a coordinated theme, namely, a frame or mirror with a man's head behind a mask and filled with the image of a woman who contemplates herself.

The paintings exhibited in Chicago were the last ones done at the Château de Mai. Picabia sold the château abruptly in August 1935. He worked thereafter in a studio near the port in Golfe-Juan, while Germaine, Lorenzo and Michel Corlin moved to an apartment in Cannes. Germaine composed at that time a thoughtful farewell statement:

> . . . his life is his painting! Crazy are those men or women who imagine they count beside that exacting deity.
>
> From everything that he has been able to touch, to feel, to understand, Picabia has made painting . . . the events of life, whether they had been from the material, moral or sentimental domain, have only been for him means to serve it [painting], he has mercilessly rejected whatever would have been able to hinder him from doing it. . . .
>
> . . . His life is to live and consequently to evolve. He has no memories, he "forgets in order to be reborn." Superficially his art can be recounted by stages, but if only one might be gifted with sensitivity in feeling how the whole is "linked."[20]

In accord with the tradition established with his previous wife and mistress, Picabia retained cordial relations with Germaine, including occasional outings to-

19. This *Portrait* appears on the mantel in the 1935 photo of Picabia's atelier (illus. 36). According to Picabia's daughter, Jeannine, this painting was offered to her, but when she indicated she did not like it, Picabia said to return in a few days. Upon returning, she was presented *Portrait* in its present form (conversation with the author, September 1962). *At the Theater* (fig. 368), though signed and dated 1935, is distinct from all known works then and may have been repainted in the 1940s. Another layer of paint can be seen through cracks in the surface.

20. Germaine Everling, "Francis Picabia vu d'en haut," unpublished statement in the Olga Picabia manuscript, 102–103.

gether and a touching correspondence. It was simply another aspect of his nature to which his wives had to adjust. At this time in the summer of 1935 Picabia also traded *Horizon II* for a less elegant but more comfortable craft christened *Horizon III*. Once it was reappointed to their taste, Francis and Olga received the usual flock of friends, about fifteen of whom assembled for her maiden voyage to St.-Tropez. Later that fall, Francis, Olga and one of their summer guests, Marthe Pignon, made their customary trek to Paris.

On that occasion, the Picabias remained in the capital through March 1936, visiting galleries, savoring Picabia's favorite girlie shows at Chez Eve or Le Bal Tabarin (illus. 38), and having a grand time with the Guevaras, the Lévesques, the Jullien du Breuils, Jean van Heeckeren and others. Picabia also did some painting and exhibited his most recent work at the Galerie Jeanne Bucher in February.[21] Like so many of his exhibitions during the 1930s, it is almost undocumented. Either no catalogue was published or no copies have been preserved, and contemporary witnesses indicate nothing more than the presence of transparencies or superimpositions of some kind with pronounced blue tonalities. *Dream* (fig. 370) and *Clowns* (fig. 369), a signed and dated painting of 1935, answer to that general description, both possessing the superimposition of double-contoured figures, heavy varnish and blue tonality characteristic of some of Picabia's work during the mid-1930s. *Hercules and His Coursers* (fig. 371) is light in tonality but also exhibits a straightforward superimposition of simplified, heavily outlined forms generally compatible with known works of ca. 1934–1936.[22]

Just before Easter Picabia's work was set aside as he and Olga left Paris in a new Rolls Royce to organize another gala for the casino in Cannes. He was also busily occupied through that summer of 1936 with his painting and an unsuccessful search for a producer of Miss Stein's play *Listen to Me*.[23] More than the customary number of guests passed by as well, though none tarried long and many, like Picasso, were preoccupied with the Spanish Civil War and questions of fascism and communism.[24] For Picabia such matters continued to represent one of the major imbecilities of man which interfered with life. He sought conversation elsewhere and retreated more into painting, grumbling to Gertrude Stein, "What a life! Here we are in the midst of communism . . . the poor idiots want the moon. . . . I work all the day, the workers ought to do like me."[25] But, above all, Picabia

21. Galerie Jeanne Bucher, Paris, *Exposition Picabia*, February 1936 (attrib.).

22. The original title of this painting is unknown, but recent reference to it as *Apollo and His Coursers* is amended to *Hercules and His Coursers* in accord with Picabia's model for the figure and landscape, namely, Annibale Carracci's *Choice of Hercules* (ca. 1596, Pinacoteca Nazionale, Naples). Picabia's models are unknown for the horses' heads which replace Carracci's allegorical figures of "Virtue" and "Pleasure."

23. Picabia's letters to Gertrude Stein on April 27, May 14, June 10 and July 1, 1936 (G.S.A., Yale), indicate futile efforts to find a producer.

24. Guests during the summer of 1936 included Man Ray, the journalist Michel Georges-Michel, the American painter Hilaire Hiler, Roland Toutain, Paul Poiret, Picasso and Dora Maar. Picasso dropped by one morning at 6 a.m. and they talked about the situation in Spain; "painting doesn't seem to interest him," Picabia wrote to Gertrude Stein (September 8, 1936, G.S.A., Yale).

25. Picabia letter to Gertrude Stein, July 1, 1936 (G.S.A., Yale).

looked forward to a September visit in Bilignin where he and Gertrude might renew their conversations before his recent canvases.

A delightful week was spent with Gertrude and Alice during the latter half of September, but Gertrude's praise may have been less enthusiastic on that occasion. At any rate, shortly afterward Picabia was writing both Gertrude and Germaine from Paris that his summer's work did not hold up alongside the paintings left there from the winter of 1935–1936.[26] His letter to Germaine was especially low in spirits, "Everything which touches me goes bad . . . I find my canvases as bad as possible; but I do not want to let myself give in to it, I am going to do everything to rise out of this dreadful current which leads me to nothing."[27] Apparently the offending paintings were similar to a signed and dated work of 1936 (fig. 373) now known solely through a reproduction in Mme Picabia's album and labeled "painting 1936—destroyed."

It is also possible that Picabia's recent paintings had been challenged by contact with work of his distant cubist and dada periods. During 1936 he had been represented in the great retrospective exhibitions of Cubism and Dada-Surrealism at New York's Museum of Modern Art.[28] And over the winter of 1936–1937, action was initiated for two items that appeared in the 1937 summer issue of *Plastique*, Picabia's collaboration on the manifesto of "Dimensionism" and the first of several articles by Gabrielle Buffet.[29]

Back in Golfe-Juan during the first months of 1937, Picabia worked out of his depression. His confidence was boosted when the State purchased three of his paintings (see fig. 361), and he had a financially successful exhibition at the Galerie d'Art Duverney in Cannes.[30] As an extra, he even succeeded at last in finding a producer for Gertrude's play.[31] But, above all, Picabia was pleased again with his work, and on several occasions he wrote Gertrude Stein that he was

26. Picabia letter to Gertrude Stein, September 25, 1936 (G.S.A., Yale), and letter to Germaine Everling, September 25, 1936 (collection Mme Everling, Cannes).

27. Ibid.

28. The Museum of Modern Art, New York, *Cubism and Abstract Art*, March 2–April 19, 1936, and *Fantastic Art, Dada and Surrealism*, December 7, 1936–January 17, 1937, edited by Alfred H. Barr, Jr.

Picabia had also figured prominently in Georges Hugnet's "L'Esprit Dada dans la peinture," *Cahiers d'art*, VII, no. 1–2 (Paris, 1932), 57–65; no. 6–7 (Paris, 1932), 281–85; no. 8–10 (Paris, 1932), 358–64; IX, no. 1–4 (Paris, 1934), 109–114; XI, no. 8 (Paris, 1936), 267–72.

29. Although Picabia joined Arp, Duchamp, Delaunay, Kandinsky and others in signing the "Manifesto of Dimensionism" (published in *Plastique*, no. 2, Paris, summer 1937, 25–28), it was probably of little genuine interest to him. No mention of it has yet been found in his correspondence or in the documents kept by Mme Olga Picabia, but renewed contact with abstract art and artists likely contributed to compositions he began in 1937.

30. Galerie d'Art Duverney, Cannes, *Exposition Picabia*, February 1937. Evidently no catalogue for this exhibition was published. According to Olga Picabia (manuscript, 72), it consisted of about thirty drawings and the three paintings purchased by the State. Picabia wrote Gertrude Stein on March 4, 1937 (G.S.A., Yale), that at Cannes "I sold 14 drawings and a painting" and "I have 3 paintings which were just bought by the State."

31. Picabia began his letter of March 4 (G.S.A., Yale), "Good news: [Claude] *Renoir agrees to stage our play; he has everything he needs for that*." Later, Renoir's support fell through.

working from dawn to dusk, happy with his solitude after observing the "lamentable" work in Paris, and eager to show her his canvases.[32]

The first of the new works, again poorly documented, appeared in April 1937 at the Galerie Serguy in Cannes.[33] Evidently most of them were superimpositions of North African subjects coated with a ship varnish which contributed to the harsh blue-green color and curdled surfaces common to these paintings (see fig. 374). Later in the year, Picabia concentrated on landscapes and figures in landscapes, most of them dark blue in tonality but distinguished by the influence of fourteenth-century Italian "primitives" (figs. 375, 376). It was the latter paintings which Picabia carried proudly to Gertrude Stein about October 1 on the way to Paris, where her friend Georges Maratier had scheduled a retrospective exhibition of Picabia's work in the Galerie de Beaune.[34]

The exhibition ranged from his early impressionist paintings to the recent landscapes, but was focused on the latter works and dada paintings which brought out such former friends as André Breton. Otherwise the exhibition attracted only moderate interest, and Picabia was soon longing for the sun and ease of their life in the Midi.

According to their custom, Olga and Francis returned to Golfe-Juan in a new car in time for the Christmas and New Year's Eve parties, accompanied this year by Maratier and his partner, E. Livengood. Early in the spring a brief trip was made to Paris in order to transfer from their small apartment there to a larger studio apartment atop the family building still owned by Picabia at 82, rue des Petit-Champs (now 26, rue Danielle Casanova). Otherwise Picabia maintained his idyllic routine of intensive painting campaigns relieved by leisurely games of chess, new pets, old friends, good restaurants and nightclubs, and occasional voyages, including yet another trip to St.-Tropez to test a new boat, the *Yveline* (illus. 37). A friend recorded a contemporary impression of that life:

> . . . a light motored yacht, sparkling and clean, on which a young woman occupied herself, smiling and silently as a prestidigitator, to render the things of a radiant life. The cabins were aired, everything had its fixed ineluctable place. God himself would have changed nothing.
>
> A man . . . was playing chess on the bridge with a friend. . . . He seemed to live with complete insouciance, with a profile turned toward every wind, thick hair, tanned skin and bright look of intelligence.[35]

32. Picabia letters to Gertrude Stein, May 30, June 26 and July 26, 1937 (G.S.A., Yale).
Beginning about this time in 1937, one of Picabia's best friends and art confidants was the neighboring boat owner, Dr. Raulot-Lapointe. His Botticelli-looking girl friend, Celli, was the subject of one of Picabia's heavily varnished, realistic portraits.
33. La Galerie Serguy, Cannes, *Exposition Picabia*, April 1937. No catalogue has been found for this exhibition. According to Mme Olga Picabia (manuscript, 72), eight paintings were exhibited at the gallery.
34. Galerie de Beaune, Paris, *Francis Picabia, peintures Dada, paysages récents*, November 19–December 2, 1937.
35. Albert Flament, "Picabia vient d'épouser la nature," statement in Galerie de Beaune, Paris, *Exposition Picabia*, November 4–17, 1938.

In September, Picabia packed the paintings of that insouciant summer and drove with Olga to Bilignin for the long-anticipated visit with Gertrude Stein before going on to Paris for his next exhibition at the Galerie de Beaune.

That exhibition was dominated by landscapes of the Midi (see fig. 380). A few of them may have been summarily sketched but most were unequivocally naturalistic and brushed with an obvious love for color and succulent pigment that caught the gallery visitors completely off guard.[36] "What will you become tomorrow," wrote one critic, you "who know how to shock us as much by your painting as by your Rolls, your yachts and your harem."[37] Another described them as "39 thickly painted canvases depicting sections of expensive real estate in the south of France." He went on to quote the observations of both Picabia and his audience: "Explained tanned, bright-eyed, wise-cracking artist Picabia, with an air of deep subtlety: 'I painted them because I wanted to.' Picabia enthusiasts spoke in awed tones of the master's daring in risking banality by a return to nature. But a growing number of critics called it reversion to type, dismissed Picabia's middle period as the intellectual shenanigans of a brilliant amateur."[38]

Fortunately for the equilibrium of those critics, they were not exposed to other work Picabia had undertaken at that very moment. According to Mme Picabia, the distinctive superimpositions represented by *Asoa* (fig. 383) were begun in December 1938.[39] Those were paralleled by yet another distinctive handful of paintings (see fig. 384) that combine hard-edge, abstract color planes with preoccupations of an older vintage, namely, transparency, superimposition and sultry female visages. Still greater variety was presented by totally abstract compositions (fig. 385) also begun over the winter of 1938–1939—preceded evidently by a few essays in that manner during 1937 (fig. 377), perhaps on the occasion of his association with the abstract artists who participated in "Dimensionism."[40]

These brightly colored, abstract interlace paintings were hardly novel in French art of the 1930s, but they are a refreshing contrast among Picabia's heavy figurative paintings of the mid-thirties. As usual, he became obsessed by the new work, labored day and night on them and could no longer bear the landscapes of the preceding year. Before long, however, he tried his hand at landscapes again, and, on the evidence of a studio photograph from early 1939 (illus. 39), figure painting continued to give him pleasure.

36. Many owners, deceived by the intense colors and thick pigment of these paintings (rarely dated on the canvas), have considered them to be works from the impressionist or fauve epochs of Picabia's career, ca. 1905–1909.

According to Mr. Livengood, codirector of the Galerie de Beaune, *Landscape of the Midi* (fig. 380) was exhibited there in 1938 (conversation with the author, June 1974). No documents exist for the sketchier sunset scene (fig. 382), but it is typical of a number of similar canvases from ca. 1938–1940. The handsome, abstracted *Landscape with Palm Trees* (fig. 381) is another of the unusual, solitary works in Picabia's career.

37. "Les Montparnos," *Le Cri de Paris*, November 18, 1938 (attrib.; in the Olga Picabia album).

38. Anon. critic, *Time* (New York, November 21, 1938), 37–38.

39. Olga Picabia album.   40. See n. 29.

Such images of Picabia notwithstanding, the threat of war by that date in 1939 was sufficient to alarm even him. He decided to sell the *Yveline*, and for the summer in Cannes, he and Olga joined their former neighbors, Raulot-Lapointe and Celli, on their boat. In late July, after the four of them made what was to be their last voyage to St.-Tropez, Picabia and Olga loaded his recent abstract paintings in the car and drove to Bilignin for a visit with Gertrude and Alice.[41] Subsequently they planned to visit Olga's family near Bern, return to Bilignin to pick up the paintings left at a hotel in nearby Belley, and then proceed to Paris for the fall exhibition of those paintings at Léonce Rosenberg's gallery. However, the declaration of war caught them in Switzerland, and owing to Olga's Swiss-German passport and the shortage of gasoline, it was impossible to return immediately to France. When two months later they were able to enter France, they went directly to Cannes, bypassing Gertrude Stein and the paintings left in the hotel in Belley. The exhibition at Rosenberg's gallery was canceled, and most of the paintings left in Belley were lost.[42]

41. The preceding information is based on the Olga Picabia manuscript, 87–88. Picabia wrote Gertrude Stein on May 23, 1939 (G.S.A., Yale), "I finished today a group of paintings I plan to place on exhibition at Rosenberg's. . . . Olga and I will leave for Switzerland from the 5th to the 10th of August and if that does not inconvenience you we will be happy to go to Bilignin to see you."

42. This sequence of events is based on the Olga Picabia manuscript, 88–90, and Picabia's letters to Gertrude Stein. On October 30, 1939 (G.S.A., Yale), he wrote: "For several days we have been in Golfe-Juan . . . It was impossible for us to go to Bilignin . . . I hope this horrible war will not last long . . . I had a group of paintings for the exhibition chez Rosenberg, very important but that may be for later."

18. "REALISM" AND THE WAR YEARS, 1939-1945

WARTIME conditions and Picabia's declining financial situation soon trimmed his life-style. He and Olga resided in a small studio apartment overlooking the port of Golfe-Juan and had to rely on the sale of paintings to defray some of their expenses. Because the scarcity of gasoline eliminated their customary trips, the big Nash was exchanged for a more economical Opel which in turn was replaced by bicycles (illus. 40). Throughout most of the war, however, their life was not unpleasant. Initially, the war was distant and somewhat unreal for inhabitants of the Midi. Cannes was not occupied, the casino remained open and some tourists returned as usual for the winter season of 1939–1940. Picabia, though upset and saddened by the conflict, never comprehended it until perhaps toward the end. It was not his affair, and he repeatedly did and said things without regard for their potential offense to either the French or the Germans. During the winter of 1939–1940, he became the sponsor of a French regiment of Alpine troops based in Golfe-Juan, yet he was oblivious to the impropriety of purchasing a German-made Opel. Later, he and Olga mingled socially with German officers, but Picabia also exhibited with a Jewish artist and wrote a mildly pro-French article.[1] For the most part he sought—as during the war of 1914–1918—to continue his life as best he could without accommodation to such disruptive forces as a world war. He still had a number of old friends and a new pet, a little Pincher named Sizou, that he spoiled beyond measure. Above all, Picabia had his painting. Over the winter of 1939–1940 he worked a great deal and even considered an exhibition in the spring for which Gertrude Stein was asked to send another preface.[2] Those paintings have not been securely identified although Olga Picabia

1. Francis Picabia, "Jeunesse," *L'Opinion* [Cannes], March 1, 1941 (attrib.); and The Lounge Library, Cannes, *Exposition Francis Picabia et Michel Sima*, July 15–31, 1942, preface by Germaine Everling.

2. Picabia requested the preface in a letter of February 2, 1940 (G.S.A., Yale), and acknowledged receipt of it in a letter on February 20 (G.S.A., Yale). He added that although working was difficult, "Each day is a new painting and it has been like that for weeks."

If the exhibition was organized, no trace of it has been found. Picabia did have an exhibition the following year for which there was a preface by Gertrude Stein, La Galerie Serguy, Cannes, *Exposition Francis Picabia*, April 1941.

and friends of the artist recall his production of landscapes similar to *Spring Landscape* (fig. 386).[3]

His work was first interrupted in May 1940, when rumors of an invasion from Italy prompted Picabia to leave Cannes. He and Olga, soon followed by his dealer Serguy and two more friends, drove inland to Calamanne-sur-Lot, near Cahors. The trip was a trying one, for Olga's Swiss passport bore German names and print, and French authorities put the Picabias through long inspections at every checkpoint. Prompted in part by that situation, Picabia and Olga were married in Calamanne on June 14, 1940—the day Paris was occupied by the Germans.

When the Italian threat to the Midi did not materialize, the Picabias returned to Golfe-Juan, where the remainder of the year was distinguished by some new acquaintances and a new mode of figurative painting. One of their new acquaintances, Myron Bibline, wrote a eulogistic pamphlet about Picabia entitled *Sur le chemin de calvaire*.[4] Another, Mme Haguet, interpreted Picabia's handwriting and inkblots, the latter similar to those in his work of ca. 1920–1922.[5] More typical for Picabia was his acquaintance with the pretty young wife of Max Romain, Suzanne, who was soon linked more intimately to the life of the Picabias, opening another bittersweet episode in the personal affairs of Francis.

The new paintings which Picabia began in Golfe-Juan during 1940 have the appearance of "popular" realism, that is, a mode of realism seemingly derived in subject and style from picture postcards, nightclub advertisements, garish reproductions in "girlie" magazines and the like. His subject matter was quite varied, embracing the sentimental postcard view of a *Flower Girl* (fig. 387), the popular subject of *The Corrida* (fig. 388), a great many nudes, (figs. 389, 390), some portraits (figs. 392, 395) and a solitary exception to such pleasant subjects—the frightening *Adoration of the Calf* (color pl. XIX).[6] In the context of the early 1940s, *Adoration of the Calf* looms as a comment on the war, although its nonpartisan nature permits it to operate as a more universal symbol of man and war—and a profoundly disturbing one which Picabia found no need to repeat. Paintings of nudes were more to his taste, and the numerous examples exhibit variety in subject, source and apparent content. Some are generalized while others have distinct portraitlike qualities, either because friends posed for them or because Picabia referred to reproductions of burlesque queens.[7] Content ranges from unmistaka-

3. A date of 1939–1941 has been attributed to this specific painting by Olga Picabia and the owner, a friend of Picabia's during the early 1940s.

4. Myron Bibline, *Sur le chemin du calvaire* (Golfe-Juan, 1941).

5. In Mme Olga Picabia's album, 209, 211 (collection Olga Picabia, Paris), there is a letter from Picabia to Mme Haguet dated November 11, 1940, an inkblot signed "F. Martinez" and two manuscripts regarding the analysis of Picabia's handwriting.

6. Many of these paintings are dated 1941 in Mme Olga Picabia's album. That date is confirmed by reference to some of them in the booklet of Myron Bibline, *Sur le chemin du calvaire*, 15.

7. Mme Romain and a beautiful mulatress named Alpha are two identified models. One of Picabia's letters to Christine Boumeester and Henri Goetz is on a photograph of a stripper which suggests another source of visual material. Mme Olga Picabia has no specific recollection of

ble erotic connotations to light amusement, for example, *Women and Bulldog* (fig. 389), with its droll parody-contrast of sporting ladies and the dog, a time-honored symbol of fidelity in the context of lounging ladies.

These realistic works of 1940–1944 are distinguished from similar figurative paintings in 1935 by their models in contemporary popular imagery, by richer colors, fuller modeling in light and dark and a more painterly application of pigment. However, they shared one feature with those predecessors of 1935, namely, the bewilderment they generated in the vast majority of their audience, friends and foes alike. Almost without exception these paintings of the early 1940s have been described as "ugly," "horrible," or the like; but, after that basic agreement, sharp divisions appear in the critical reaction. In the eyes of some spectators, the paintings simply remain ugly, beneath serious consideration and beyond comprehension as to why Picabia ever did them. Other critics do consider the paintings, but feel it necessary to "excuse" them on the basis that they were potboilers intended for quick commercial profit—and many were sent to Algeria for exhibit in a comercially-oriented gallery.[8] A few critics actually like these paintings and generally defend them on two grounds. A popular view, the "post-dada defense," attributes to them a continuing antiart, dadaist quality. A second approach, which may be categorized as the "proto-Pop Art defense," hails them as precursors in subject, style and content to the phenomenon of Pop Art during the 1960s.[9] To an extent each of these justifications is true, but finally they say more about the critics employing them than about Picabia—whose intentions were never explored.

In the midst of this work, Picabia himself wrote Gertrude Stein: "I work from morning to night—they are my only good moments but, curious thing, for the first time that has fatigued me and I am obliged to rest. I have made many paintings;

Picabia working from photographs or advertisements but thinks that he did. Mr. Livengood, codirector of the Galerie de Beaune, says Picabia was using postcards for some of his compositions in the late 1930s (conversation with the author, May 15, 1974).

8. Galerie Pasteur, Algiers; directed by M. Romanet. Picabia mentioned the exhibition of his paintings in Algeria in a letter to Gertrude Stein on December 27, 1941 (G.S.A., Yale).

9. Among numerous passing criticisms of that sort, Lawrence Alloway stands out for his thoughtful observations about Picabia's figurative art of the 1920s, 1930s and 1940s. Alloway, one of the first critics sensitive to the qualities of popular culture and art nourished by it during the 1950s–1960s, reflects that era of Neo-Dada and Pop Art when he writes (approvingly) of "the odd compound of imitation and parody, of accepting influences and caricaturing them, which characterizes his Neo-Romanticism [Picabia's transparencies]. As so often in Picabia, it is hard to decide whether we are looking at a botched imitation, a brutal parody, or a subtle imagination which operates in a personal territory between loyal copying and ironic parody" ("London Letter," *Art International*, III, no. 9, Zurich, 1959, 24). The element of caricature was still important for Alloway a decade later ("Art," *The Nation*, New York, October 5, 1970, 314–15).

Some artists associated with Neo-Dada and Pop Art likewise esteem Picabia's figurative art, especially the realist canvases of the 1940s. Two such artists, William Copley and Enrico Baj, also formed important personal collections of Picabia's art. Robert Rauschenberg has expressed interest in Picabia's transparencies; Jim Dine has been more interested in Picabia's dada work, and his own art reveals a spiritual affinity with Picabia.

they are in Algeria. My painting is more and more the image of my life and of life, but a life which cannot and does not wish to regard the world."[10]

Close witnesses confirmed Picabia's statements—Bibline, who wrote of Picabia's need for "an exactitude with himself" as the enduring theme of his work,[11] and Olga, who wrote with particular reference to those years: He "is not a revolutionary, much less a madman, and contrary to the legend, he does not mock the public. Each of his works is sincere with his intentions and his originality."[12]

Such statements are discounted only at the sacrifice of the subject. Picabia had always painted his life, painted for himself, painted because he liked to paint—and there is no reason to think that he changed radically around 1940. An element of mockery is not thereby excluded from these works of "popular realism." Repeatedly from the dada period onward, there are inklings that what began as a few mocking, critical essays soon revealed interesting possibilities which Picabia pursued through a long and essentially "serious" body of work. *La Feuille de vigne* (fig. 209), a jibe at Neo-Classicism in art and neo-academicism at the Salon d'Automne, may have been seminal to the entire sweep of his figurative styles during the 1920s. The ineffable mingling of homage and mockery in some of the "monsters" (figs. 273, 274, 301, 302) seems to be of the same order as that which emanates from some of the realist pictures of the 1940s. They are, finally, as much a part of Picabia as the transparencies, monsters, and dadaist machines, and, like his paintings from any period, they are very uneven in quality. Many are ugly and heavily sentimental; some are indifferently brushed. But they are also potent, assertive works which do not settle comfortably in the parlor, and which deserve to stand or fall without the aid of theories.

Within the dominant current of his realistic paintings, Picabia also produced a variety of drawings and some miniature paintings in a more abstracted manner. The latter (fig. 393)—"pocket paintings" Picabia called them—were exhibited in July 1942 in a joint exhibition with the artist Michel Sima.[13] Germaine Everling, who wrote the preface for that exhibition, was depicted in one of Picabia's numerous facile drawings of those years (fig. 395). Her portrait is tightly drawn, delicate and documentary; other contemporary drawings varied from sketchy impressions to the supple, sensuous and more generalized forms of the unidentified *Portrait* (fig. 394). One hundred drawings from various periods in Picabia's career were exhibited in Cannes in September 1943, followed by a reduced exhibition the next month in Monaco.[14]

That outpouring of work by Picabia from 1940 to 1943 had continued despite

10. Picabia letter to Gertrude Stein, December 27, 1941 (G.S.A., Yale).

11. Bibline, *Sur le chemin du calvaire*, 7.

12. Olga Picabia manuscript, 95.

13. The Lounge Library, Cannes, *Exposition Francis Picabia et Michel Sima*, July 15–31, 1942, preface by Germaine Everling.

14. Galerie Art et Artisan, Cannes, *100 dessins et 5 portraits par F. Picabia*, September 7–30, 1943, and Office de Tourisme, Monaco, *50 dessins de F. Picabia*, October 4–20, 1943, preface by Germaine Everling.

wartime conditions, embroiled personal affairs and several changes of residence. Three major moves were made prior to 1943—twice to Tourette-sur-Loup above Cagnes, and once to Felletin in the Creuse.[15] Moreover, the relationship between Picabia and Suzanne Romain persisted throughout those moves and the competition of still another young woman fascinated by Francis. In May 1943, the Picabias finally settled in Golfe-Juan for the duration of the war, taking up residence in a modest dwelling called the "Villa des Orangers." Life was relatively pleasant, surrounded by their little garden, their pets, Picabia's work and a circle of friends. Something about Picabia's nature attracted youth, and their friends soon included a young man, Michel Perrin, and a young couple, Henri Goetz and Christine Boumeester, who numbered among Picabia's best friends for the rest of his life.[16] The Goetzes were deeply committed painters who came often to visit and talk of art. Olga turned to them for help when one splendid spring morning she awoke to discover Francis joyfully painting daisies on every canvas in the studio (fig. 379; color pl. XVIII). He refused to stop for Olga or Henri Goetz, insisting that he was bursting with good spirits and felt like painting flowers on everything. Goetz decided Picabia was right and got what he considered to be the best one for himself and Christine.[17] The flowers now seem so integral to those paintings that it is difficult to conceive of them in any other way.

Such days ended rudely toward the end of the war. Picabia, largely as a result of his incomprehension and indifference regarding the war, was in trouble, first with the Germans and then with the French. Had he not suffered a stroke at that time, he would probably have been arrested for suspected collaboration. As it was, he was confined to the hospital, and by the time of his release, about four or five months later, the charges had been dropped. Francis and Olga lost no time in leaving behind that sad episode in their life; on February 28, 1945, they took up permanent residence in the studio apartment atop the old family building at 26, rue Danielle Casanova in Paris.

15. The Picabias moved into the Auberge Camassade in Tourette-sur-Loup during 1941, but returned to Golfe-Juan after about six weeks. In 1942, they spent three weeks in Haute Savoie and then made what was meant to be a permanent move to Felletin in the Creuse. That, too, lasted only a month or two before they were back in Golfe-Juan, and, from December 1942 to April 1943, again in Tourette-sur-Loup.

16. Both the Goetzes and Michel Perrin have written perceptively about Picabia's work and formed small, personal collections. The correspondence between Picabia and the Goetzes is a rich source of unpublished drawings, poems and insight into Picabia's thought during the last years of his life.

17. Story related to the author by Henri Goetz, Christine Boumeester and Mme Olga Picabia. The original painting under *Figure and Flowers* (fig. 379) is one of the heavily varnished, blue figurative subjects of the mid to late 1930s. The date of 1938 long attributed to *Le Printemps* (*Spring*, color pl. XVIII) is probably correct, except for the flowers which, in the opinion of this author, were added ca. 1943.

19. PICABIA'S RETURN TO PARIS; THE FINAL SYNTHESIS

ONE might debate whether Picabia's reinstallation in Paris during February 1945 was a "return" or a "departure." In accord with liberated Paris, Picabia soon abounded with vitality and the sense of a beginning after the long, dismal years of German occupation. There was a new rhythm to his life, new friends and another radical shift in his style of painting. But within all that was new in the art and life of Picabia, there was also a remarkable sense of a final synthesis which embraced old friends, familiar places and the style and spirit of his work from the past.

He and Olga made their home in an apartment fashioned out of what had once been Picabia's old studio atop the family-owned building at 26, rue Danielle Casanova (see illus. 5). That modest but comfortable, well-lit apartment was handily located for popular nightclubs, cinemas, the Louvre and right-bank art galleries. It soon served, too, as a gathering place for old friends—Gertrude Stein, Léonce Rosenberg, Pierre and Robbie de Massot, Mme Cuttoli, Jean van Heeckeren, Henri Goetz and Christine Boumeester, Michel Perrin, Angelica and Jacques-Henri Lévesque, M. and Mme Saint-Maurice, Roger Grosjean, Dr. Huguenin, Suzy Solidor and many others. As in times past, Picabia drank, smoked, flirted and philosophized; he haunted favorite nightclubs, grumbled about the state of art in the galleries and mused nostalgically over the impressionist paintings at the Jeu de Paume. But through those old friends he also made new contacts among such younger artists as Jean Atlan, Raoul Ubac, Hans Hartung, Pierre Soulages, Francis Bott and Camille Bryen. For awhile Picabia hosted almost daily reunions of assorted friends and young artists attracted by his personality, his "philosophy" of art and his moral support of their work. Goetz, Boumeester and Soulages have retained particularly fond memories of Picabia from those years.[1] He, in turn, was nourished by the youth about him; he main-

1. Soulages recalls with fervor that Picabia, even when old and ailing, attended his exhibitions, introduced him to artists and critics and gave him the moral courage to continue painting when almost no one liked his work (conversations with the author, April 21, 1966).

For public evidence of the affection between Picabia and Henri Goetz and his wife, Christine

tained an extraordinary correspondence with Goetz and Boumeester, wrote touching prefaces for their exhibitions and joined his young friends at the Salon des Surindépendants and the Salon des Réalités Nouvelles.[2]

His new work—like theirs—was predominantly abstract, and, in that respect, Picabia participated in the major movement of avant-garde art after the war in both Europe and America. However, within that phenomenal surge of abstract art, Picabia held an unshakably personal position, essentially independent of such currents of abstract art in France as Fautrier's emphasis on material or the gestural approach of Hartung, Soulages and Mathieu. Picabia's abstract paintings of 1945 to 1951—though obviously different from anything he had done before—reflect his previous career in countless ways: they emerged suddenly, almost without transition from the immediately preceding figurative style; they were uneven in quality, intensely personal in reference and, in a strict sense, seldom wholly abstract. Instead, like *Caoutchouc* (fig. 38) and *Udnie* (fig. 82), they were charged with evocative forms and titles which recall not only his abstract paintings of 1913–1914, but aspects of Dada, the monsters, the transparencies, the superimpositions and the abstract compositions of the late 1930s. That extraordinary synthesis in Picabia's painting was also accompanied by a serious resumption of poetry reminiscent of the dada epoch, although both the poetry and the painting reveal a new dimension of quasi-spiritual concerns. Such concerns had appeared at other points in Picabia's career, but in his old age there seems to have been a pronounced need to look back, to evaluate, to reaffirm and to speak of life and death. With rare exceptions, critics and collectors have ignored or denigrated these works of Picabia's old age.[3] That condition is subject to change for these

Boumeester (1904–1971), see their statements for Picabia's exhibitions at the Galerie Colette Allendy, Paris, 1946; the Galerie René Drouin, Paris, 1949; the Galerie Marbach, Bern, 1952; and Goetz's illustrations for Picabia's poem *Explorations* (Paris, 1947). The unpublished records of their love for Picabia include their unfailing generosity to every student of Picabia, and their invaluable collection of letters, poems and drawings from Picabia over the years 1945 to 1950/1951. M. Goetz and Maria-Lluisa Borràs are preparing a publication of the Goetz-Boumeester collection. Señora Borràs has also presented a paper which indicates that Picabia drew directly from some of Nietzsche's publications for occasional passages in his poems and his letters to Henri Goetz and Christine Boumeester ("Les Derniers Collages de Francis Picabia, 1945–1951," Colloque Francis Picabia, Paris, Grand Palais, February 28, 1976; organized by the Musée National d'Art Moderne).

2. Picabia provided a preface for the Galerie L'Esquisse, Paris, *Quelques Oeuvres de Henry Goetz et de Christine Boumeester*, March 27–April 27, 1945, and a statement for *Christine Boumeester* (Paris, 1951), texts by multiple authors. He also exhibited with them at the Galerie Marbach, Bern, March 26–April 23, 1952.

Picabia had exhibited at the Salon des Surindépendants in 1930 (data courtesy Josué Seckel), but resumed in 1945. The first Salon des Réalités Nouvelles opened in July 1946.

3. In general, only the closest friends of Francis and Olga Picabia during that postwar period have been at ease with his late abstract paintings. More typical is the assessment of them at the Guggenheim exhibition in 1970 as "perhaps the least sincere" of his works (J. Patrice Marandel, "Lettre de New York," *Art International*, XIV, no. 9, Lugano, November 1970, 66), and "an unsupported group of Abstract paintings of the 1940s which really are inconsequential" (Lawrence Alloway, "Art," *The Nation*, New York, October 5, 1970, 314).

poorly known, very uneven paintings and poems express in some instances a character and gravity which transcend his work in any period.

Some of Picabia's first abstract paintings of 1945 were keyed to earlier compositions and perhaps painted over them. *Asoa*, for example (fig. 397), retains reference to a bird and the outline of a human head that existed in a 1938 painting by the same title (fig. 383); *Le Soleil dans la peinture* (*The Sun in Painting*, fig. 396) was either suggested by his curvilinear abstract compositions of 1937–1939 (figs. 377, 385) or actually composed of one of those paintings transformed by the superimposition of a sunspot and a resonant film of color.[4] Early on, however, there were new works unrelated to the past except for Picabia's habitual cultivation of the gray zone between total abstraction and vaguely anthropomorphic forms that refer to his private life. *Suzanne* (fig. 398) is a strong painting, abounding in formal and psychological contrasts which comment cryptically on a liaison which had continued to be a significant element in Picabia's life. *Viens avec moi là-bas* (*Come with Me There*, fig. 399) strikes an entirely different mood with its soaring, winged form and pensive blue tonality.[5]

Picabia did not wholly abandon figurative art; it was continued in some portrait drawings and in illustrations for his letters and poetry (illus. 41, 42).[6] But those drawings were a minor part within the mainstream of his work, and in an important interview during the fall of 1945 Picabia discussed the conditions which had prompted his return to abstract art. Speaking of several colleagues as well as himself, Picabia remarked:

> After a violent storm, the water of a lake is . . . agitated, . . . [but] I know that certain painters are working, isolated and without noise. . . . They have this desire to remain momentarily excluded from public life in order to fight better against the inflation and the commercialism of values which are reaching an alarming degree . . . for the future of the spiritual civilization. . . . We only want a painting that may be a means of exchange of our sensibilities in the purest state, that may be the expression of what is the truest of our interior being. That is why there can be nothing figurative in this painting, because it is no longer an exploration of an external world but a more and more

4. The present location of *Asoa* (fig. 397) is unknown; accordingly, it has not been determined if it was actually brushed over the earlier painting. Olga Picabia thinks not, but Henri Goetz has verified that Picabia did paint over some of the abstract, curvilinear composition of 1937–1939 (conversation with the author, June 20, 1968). *Le Soleil dans la peinture* (fig. 396) appears to be the small painting visible at the lower right in a 1945 photograph of Picabia's studio published in Colline, "Un Entretien avec Francis Picabia," *Journal des arts*, no. 3 (Zurich, November 1945), 51.

5. *Suzanne* was reproduced in a review of Picabia's exhibition at the Kunsthalle Basel in January 1946 (see Michel Fardoulis-Lagrange, "Exposition Francis Picabia," *Journal des arts*, nos. 5–6, Zurich, January–February 1946, 20–21), but did not figure in the catalogue. *Viens avec moi là-bas* appeared as no. 272 in that exhibition at Basel.

6. Two exhibitions in La Rochelle during 1947 were dominated by recent portraits and figurative drawings. See Galerie Lhote, La Rochelle, *Exposition Francis Picabia*, January 10–20, 1947, and, again, Galerie Lhote, *Francis Picabia*, October 11–22, 1947.

profound contact with an interior universe. . . . for myself personally I experience the imperious need for a dematerialization of the milieu in which we live, of this world of machines and formulas.[7]

In the course of the interview Picabia also addressed popular notions that abstract art could not "communicate" with its spectators and that "everyone can make such a painting." "But no," replied Picabia:

One must think painting, feel painting, that is, feel "colors," love "lines," live "forms," . . . and all this is the result of a long past. It is the result of my continuous research supported by this work of the artisan which is also that of the painter that brings me to the point from which a new "craft," a new "style" will flow.

But what can one see in your canvases now?

Each sees there a different thing and even something else every day according to the state of his spirit. . . . each painting is for me a drama, passing through all the stages of my preceding production, forms, transparencies, superimpositions, in order to carry further and to touch at the end this fleeting but ecstatic instant where I know that I hold the unseizable which is reality.[8]

The tenor of the entire interview reaffirmed the Picabia of yore; so, too, did the contemporary publication of *Thalassa dans le désert*, his first volume of poetry in over twenty years.[9] Some of the poems may have dated from the 1930s, but most of them were recent works and representative of the outpouring of writing in the last years of his life. Their content ranged from the defiant egotism of "Baccara" to the contemplation of life and death in "De l'autre côté" (From the Other Side), the latter a new note which was sounded even in such love poems as "Poème sentimental":

BACCARA

Je suis un beau monstre
qui partage ses secrets avec le vent.
Ce que j'aime le plus chez les autres,
c'est moi.

Je suis un beau monstre;
j'ai comme suspensoir le péché de la vertu.
Mon pollen tache les roses
de New-York à Paris.

7. Colline, "Un Entretien avec Francis Picabia," *Journal des arts*, 50–51.

8. Ibid. Picabia's correspondence with Goetz and Boumeester includes another statement on abstract art; Goetz has also claimed (conversation with the author, June 20, 1968) that Picabia was occasionally annoyed by some abstract art and set out to mock it in his work, but invariably found something which was developed into an unexpected series of serious paintings.

9. Francis Picabia, *Thalassa dans le désert* (Paris, September 3, 1945).

Je suis un beau monstre
dont le visage cache la figure.
Mes sens n'ont qu'une pensée:
un cadre sans
tableau!

Je suis un beau monstre
dont le lit est un vélodrome;
les cartes transparentes
peuplent mes rêves.

Je suis un beau monstre
qui couche avec lui-même.
Il n'y en a que sept au monde
et je veux être le plus grand.

BACCARAT

I am a beautiful monster / who shares his secrets with the wind. / What I like most among others, / is myself. / I am a beautiful monster; / I have as a bandage the sin of virtue. / My pollen stains roses / from New York to Paris. / I am a beautiful monster / whose countenance hides his face. / My senses have only one thought: / a frame without a painting! / I am a beautiful monster / whose bed is a racetrack; / transparent maps / people my dreams. / I am a beautiful monster / who sleeps with himself. / There are only seven in the world / and I want to be the greatest.

DE L'AUTRE CÔTÉ

Assis à l'ombre de l'eau
l'idée mélancolique m'emporte
vers les époques de la main-gauche.
Les oiseaux n'arrêtent que pour pleurer!
L'épouvante est que vous mourrez en petits
    morceaux
dans le mauvais lieu de la vie,
la tête dans les mains, sans but.
Prenez un verre de couleur,
jetez-y trois gouttes de froid,
vous aurez le parfum d'après.
N'ayez de reconnaissance pour personne;
ceux qui survivent sont les assassins.
La mort est le prolongement horizontal
d'un rêve factice,
la vie n'étant pas vérifiable.

FROM THE OTHER SIDE

Seated in the shade of the water / the melancholic thought carries me away / toward the epochs of the left hand. / Birds stop only to weep! / The terror is that you die in little pieces / in the wretched place of life, / one's head in his hands, without aim. / Take a colored glass, / throw in it three drops of cold, / you will have the perfume afterwards. / Be grateful to no one; / those who survive are the assassins. / Death is the horizontal extension / of an imitation dream, / life not being verifiable.

POÈME SENTIMENTAL

L'azur ruisselait sur nos bouches,
comme l'amour parfumé des boutons pourpres.

Les étoiles sont les pétales de nos pensées
au coucher du soleil.

Ce soir, fermant les yeux, debout près de toi,
mes hymnes mûriront, arrosés par la lune.

Si tu voulais, tout nu, je vieillirais
avec ton sourire, les mains sur tes seins.

Surtout ne me jette pas dans le vide!

SENTIMENTAL POEM

The azure was streaming down our mouths, / like the perfumed love of purple buttons / The stars are the petals of our thoughts / at sunset. / Tonight, closing my eyes, standing before you, / my hymns will ripen, watered by the moon. / If you wish, completely nude, I will grow old / with your smile, my hands on your breasts. / Above all do not throw me into the void!

Those themes continued to characterize Picabia's poetry and painting for several years, but beginning in 1946 he could no longer count himself among those artists working quietly outside the public view. He once again became the subject of articles and interviews, and his work—both past and present—was kept before the public by numerous publications and exhibitions. In 1945 an Italian company had published a study of *Entr'acte*, and in May 1946 Jean van Heeckeren and Roger Grosjean collaborated on a handsome publication of drawings from the period of the transparencies.[10] That book coincided with Picabia's first major postwar exhibition which, after opening in the Kunsthalle Basel, was presented in a modified form in Paris under the heading "sur-irréalist" paintings of Picabia.[11] All of those paintings which have been identified were recent abstractions, many

10. Glauco Viazzi, *Entr'acte* (Milan, 1945). Roger Grosjean was a close friend of Picabia and the publisher of Jean van Heeckeren's *Francis Picabia. Seize dessins, 1930* (Paris, 1946).

11. Kunsthalle Basel, *Francis Picabia; Sammlung Nell Walden*, January 12–February 3, 1946. The Nell Walden collection and Picabia's paintings were combined in a single catalogue

of which bore such humorous titles as *J'aime les jolies filles* (*I Like Pretty Girls*), *Veux-tu rire?* (*Do You Want to Laugh?*) and *Tu ne le vendras jamais* (*You'll Never Sell It*). Many of the critics were pleasantly surprised. The most effusive praise came from F. Delanglade, who extolled Picabia's "plastic humor," his manipulation of the elements of painting to satisfy "mysterious orders of a soul state" and, above all, the "poetic" quality of his work:

"Little matter to us that the titles of his painting may be made to baffle the spectator . . .

"They are poetic to a point that one may, without changing the order of them in the catalogue, combine them in a poem. . . .

"In fact, Picabia paints like a poet, . . .

"The work of Picabia . . . seems this time crystallized in its definitive form."[12]

Picabia confirmed that poetry was essential to his painting, that it was "always a poetic emotion which pushes man to express himself"[13]—and during the summer of 1946 there was poetic stimulation aplenty. As was his custom until the very end of his life, Picabia spent about six weeks during August–September with Olga and her family in Rubigen, near Bern. There he learned of the death of two old and profoundly respected friends, Gertrude Stein and Alfred Stieglitz.[14] Despite grief over their deaths, he worked apace and completed a long poem entitled "Ennazus" whose passages of tender memories and moral chastisement bear witness to both a crisis in his relationship with Suzanne Romain and a reassertion of his unique "moral code":[15]

---

which included a statement about Picabia and a list of fifty-three works, nos. 246–98.

Thirty-five paintings, almost all of them exhibited in Basel, figured in the catalogue of the Galerie Denise René, Paris, *Francis Picabia—Peintures sur-irréalistes*, April 26–May 20, 1946.

12. F. Delanglade, "Le Cas Francis Picabia," *France au combat* [Paris], May 9, 1946, 6.

13. Georges Charbonnier, *Le Monologue du peintre* (Paris, 1959), 132, from an interview with Picabia ca. December 1949.

14. Picabia referred to the deaths of Gertrude Stein and Alfred Stieglitz in an undated letter of August 1946 to Christine Boumeester (Goetz-Boumeester collection, Paris).

15. Francis Picabia, "Ennazus," unpublished typewritten manuscript, signed and dated Rubigen, September 13, 1946 (Goetz-Boumeester collection, Paris). "Ennazus" was subtitled "Cerf-Volant" and prefaced by J. Caspar Schmidt. The title of this thirty-page poem, "Suzanne" spelled backwards, indicates the underlying theme although no specific names appear and the poem is effective without such associations. The manuscript of "Ennazus" in the Goetz-Boumeester collection may not have been the final version or the only version. In a letter from Rubigen ca. August 1946 (undated, Goetz-Boumeester collection, Paris), Picabia passed on a different form for much of what exists on p. 4 of the Goetz-Boumeester manuscript. "Ennazus" was presented at that time in blocks of unbroken prose, separated by the repeated verse:

> At the end of the garden
> an open gate
> butterfly tracks
> without leaving tracks
> mount toward the sky

ENNAZUS

Ne plus avoir de sens
est la dernière parte
qu'il me sera possible de faire
grossière frivolité, n'est ce pas.
pour ceux qui, innocents, comme Dieu,
croient aux moeurs immorales.
L'impuissance est une liberté
de l'individualité
créant l'abnégation
de tout le monde
qui rêve la vie radieuse
je l'espère ainsi.   [excerpt p. 1]

Celle qui vit pour un grand amour,
pour une mission sublime,
ne doit se laisser effleurer
par aucune médiocrité,
Elle doit se dépouiller
de tout l'intérêt matériel;
ceci mène au bonheur,
à l'idéal absolu
de la femme dont la vie est de vivre
exclusivement pour l'amour.
En la regardant cette femme idéale,
tu sentiras combien:
Famille, Patrie, Sciences,
ne sont que mêmes mots
dans une langue différente
Et ce mot ne veut rien dire   [excerpt p. 3]

ENNAZUS

To no longer have senses / is the final loss / which will be possible for me to make / gross frivolity, is it not. / for those who, innocents, like God, / believe in immoral customs. / Helplessness is a liberty / from individuality / creating the abnegation / of everyone / who dreams life radiant / I hope it to be like that.

She who lives for a great love, / for a sublime mission, / must not let herself be touched / by any mediocrity, / She must strip herself / of all material interest; / this leads to happiness, / to the absolute ideal / of the woman for whom life is to live / exclusively for love. / In regarding this ideal woman / you will feel how much: / Family, Country, Sciences, / are only the same words / in a different language / And this word means nothing

Later that fall, Picabia's paintings at the Salon des Surindépendants seem to reflect those events of the summer. *Niam* (fig. 400), a figurative painting akin in manner to some second-generation surrealist work then on view in Paris, may have referred cryptically to the relationship with Mme Romain.[16] *Kalinga* (color pl. xx) is more abstract, yet also a more palpable, gripping presence whose ominous form, prickly texture and somber colors of an indescribable Iberian dryness seem to evoke death itself. As in so many of Picabia's "abstract" paintings, the sinister form dominating *Kalinga* simultaneously incites and defies efforts to identify it. The title by which the painting was first exhibited *La Boeuf* (*Beef*),[17] may suggest such works as Rembrandt's *Slaughtered Ox* with its parallels to the crucified Christ, but the image in *Kalinga* also recalls the horned-beef motif and bears traces of both an African mask and mysterious underlying oval forms. In the final analysis, *Kalinga* is unidentifiable, but not abstract; intensely personal but not closed. Rather it is open to the sensuous-spiritual response of any sensitive viewer. Other contemporary paintings maintained that mood, for example, *La Paloma de la paz* (*The Dove of Peace*, fig. 401) in whose interlocking, somber-hued forms Picabia imbedded a white shape simultaneously evocative of a winged form and the Lamb of the Apocalypse.

Direct comparison with Picabia's past work was a simple matter at that moment for, contemporary with the 1946 Salon des Surindépendants, Mme Colette Allendy organized an exhibition of his work of ca. 1907–1924.[18] That was followed in the spring of 1947 with an exhibition of transparencies which stimulated significant articles, reviews and interviews.[19] Henri Parisot performed a similar service for Picabia the poet by publishing an anthology of some of his finest poems.[20] Picabia was touched by that publication in which he encountered work so long forgotten that at first he hardly thought of himself as the author. "I have just read my little book," he wrote Christine Boumeester: "What discreet words, it is a song. Thoughts which come with the stride of a wolf into a universe of unconsciousness and politeness; it is also a terrible abyss in which many people have

16. *Niam* was reproduced in an anonymous review ("Cherchez la femme," *L'Aurore* [Paris], October 9, 1946) of the Salon des Surindépendants. The title "Niam" spelled backwards may be a coincidental reference to "hand" (la main), or a reference to the final syllable in the name of Mme Romain. A partially overpainted inscription "Niam-Niam" ("Yum-Yum") appears in the upper left corner of *Bonheur de l'aveuglement* (*Happiness of Blindness*, fig. 402).

17. In a review of the Salon des Surindépendants, Denys Chevalier reproduced *Kalinga* under the title *Le Boeuf* ("Le XIIIe Salon des Surindépendants," *Arts*, no. 89, Paris, October 18, 1946, 8).

18. Galerie Colette Allendy, Paris, *Francis Picabia*, October 18–November 16, 1946, statement by Henri Goetz.

19. Galerie Colette Allendy, Paris, *Exposition Picabia*, May 30–June 23, 1947, preface by Picabia. A contemporary interview by Paul Guth ("Francis Picabia," *La Gazette des lettres*, no. 39, Paris, June 28, 1947, 1–2) contains interesting information but also helped to establish some of the common biographical errors which have dogged publications on Picabia.

20. Francis Picabia, *Choix de poèmes de Francis Picabia*, ed. Henri Parisot (Paris, July 1947).

fallen for having to understand what they will never understand . . . I am far from the human race. The best proof is that morality is a decadence, but the desire of life can pass for morality in itself."[21]

Picabia's insistent need to reassert those tenets of faith precluded any prolonged savoring of his past; indeed, just a few weeks later in Switzerland, he completed another major poem, "Fleur montée" (Mounted Flower), at one in spirit and quality with his writings of the past.[22] Although Picabia could not resist poking fun at Switzerland and its people, his summer visits to Rubigen tended nonetheless to be pleasant and productive. His letters from there to Goetz and Boumeester during the summer of 1947 are particularly illuminating for his moods and projects—and the letters themselves are fascinating documents, replete with poems, drawings and numerous examples of his humor, philosophy and opinions on art.

In an undated letter attributable to August 1947, Picabia wrote, "Christine, . . . Truly I have nothing much to tell you. Here the simple facts, eat, drink and, for me, try to sleep, but it is a veritable enchantment to do nothing, to think of nothing, to no longer know even if one exists, where the impression that life leaves me sweetly disappointed, the heart and the body, the body and the heart, what double mystery."[23]

Another letter, designed partly as a poem, represents Picabia's frequent lamentation/exaltation over art:

> In other days, artists feared "the chic,"
> today they have unlearned that fear
> today they are sensualists without senses
> in a dangerous and meridional isle
> it is sad
> for their paintings mount to the sun
> Painting is the music of life
> but the painters are without heart and hardly musicians
> their painting is a sort of vampirism
> Painting must be enigmatic
> and a little disquieting[24]

21. Picabia letter to Christine Boumeester, undated [ca. July 1947] (Goetz-Boumeester collection, Paris).

In a similar vein, Henri Goetz once showed Picabia a page of unidentified aphorisms which included several by Picabia himself. Picabia consistently preferred his own aphorisms, but did not recognize them and guessed that they must have been written by Nietzsche (interview with Henri Goetz and Christine Boumeester, Paris, August 20, 1962).

22. Francis Picabia, *Fleur montée* (Alès, November 1952), dated Cousserans, September 3, 1947.

23. Picabia letter to Christine Boumeester, undated [ca. August 1947] (Goetz-Boumeester collection, Paris).

24. Francis and Olga Picabia letter to Christine Boumeester, undated [ca. August 1947] (Goetz-Boumeester collection, Paris).

In still another letter of that summer he jibed at "our friend Picasso" who paints "for impoverished Jews or enriched greengrocers" and insisted that "every painting must be completely absurd and useless, above all vis-à-vis the magic evolution of art." He also spoke of the recently rediscovered paintings of *Udnie* and *Edtaonisl* (fig. 82; color pl. VI): "At last on September 5 or 6 we are going to find again our poor friend *Edtaonisl*, who is always so sad—terrible skin disease. It is not a new painting, but rather a new chaos which one must render clear, sharp and cruel, perhaps full of a subtle magic."[25]

Earlier in 1947 both Duchamp and Breton had inquired about *Udnie* and *Edtaonisl*. Those two paintings had not been seen for years, and Picabia began a search which discovered *Udnie* in the hands of a dealer while *Edtaonisl* was found rolled up in a corner of his own studio. They were transferred to Gabrielle Buffet's high-ceilinged apartment where Picabia and Christine Boumeester had space enough to work on their restoration.[26] Even before that task was finished, friends and prospective buyers streamed through the apartment, and in May 1948 the newly restored canvases were displayed in the hall of honor at the Musée National d'Art Moderne. Meanwhile, Bernard Dorival and Jean Cassou labored to preserve those two grand paintings for France, praising them in articles as masterpieces of nonfigurative art equal, if not superior, in historical and aesthetic importance to the work of Kandinsky and Delaunay.[27] The State did purchase *Udnie* in 1949, although *Edtaonisl* was secured by an American collector and subsequently entered the Art Institute of Chicago.

Picabia seldom lingered over his work in the past, once advising a journalist curious about the history of Dada to see his friend Jean van Heeckeren "who knows all that about me."[28] Nonetheless, Picabia's renewed contact with his work of 1913 may have affected some of his paintings of 1947–1948. In one of the best of them, *Elle danse* (*She Dances*, fig. 404), there are subtle but perceptible reflections in theme and form of such works as *Udnie* and *Je revois en souvenir ma chère Udnie* (figs. 82, 97).[29] Another new champion of his work, Michel Seuphor, perceived those links and wrote in a preface to an exhibition of Picabia's work in 1948, "The cycle is complete. Picabia has refound the sap of the dada epoch, the

25. Picabia letter to Christine Boumeester, undated [ca. August 1947] (Goetz-Boumeester collection, Paris).

26. In conversations with this author (Paris, August 20, 1962) Boumeester stressed that the restoration of *Udnie* and *Edtaonisl* was done with great care to preserve the composition, color and texture of the originals. At a later date some discoloring appeared on *Udnie* and restoration was conducted by the staff of the Musée National d'Art Moderne during 1966 and 1967.

27. Jean Cassou, "Le Musée d'Art Moderne va exposer deux toiles anciennes de Picabia," *Arts*, no. 165 (Paris, May 7, 1948), 5. Bernard Dorival, "Les Nouvelles artistiques," *Les Nouvelles littéraires* (Paris, May 20, 1948 attrib.). Dorival moderated his praise of Picabia the following year ("Les Nouvelles artistiques. De Vallotton à Picabia," *Les Nouvelles littéraires*, no. 1129, Paris, April 21, 1949, 6).

28. Guth, "Francis Picabia," *La Gazette des lettres*, 1–2.

29. *Elle danse* is painted over an earlier composition which is only faintly visible and not yet identified.

same disengagement, the same anti-painting painting. . . . In the ascending generations it is he again who shows the road of complete liberty."[30]

The past, however, was neither nest nor snare for Picabia. *Bal nègre* (fig. 403), a contemporary work similar in theme to *Elle danse*, is not a nostalgic look backwards, but a celebration of the present. Almost every Saturday evening from 10 p.m. until the first subway around 5 or 6 a.m. Sunday morning, Picabia and his closest friends gathered at that popular nightclub to enjoy the extraordinary Negro dancers and Martinique music, to drink, talk, and observe all of Paris in attendance. It was the memory of those evenings which he sought to re-create in the abstract forms, thrashing rhythms, bold colors and sensuous pigments of *Bal nègre*. Different experiences called for correspondingly different forms. *Troisième sexe* (*Third Sex*, fig. 405) is disarmingly droll in form and title; *Je vous attends* (*I Am Waiting for You*, fig. 406) is a sinister presence—somber in color, rough in texture and evocative of a death's head which suggests a simple correlation with the title. Interpretation of content rests largely, however, with each spectator. Picabia, as usual, gave no explanations. "One must not hope to place in light what is in shadow," he wrote Christine Boumeester. "My painting is impudent, diverting for me and little serious . . . my pride would not be happy if I wanted to make myself a grand painter."[31]

That same attitude determined the spirit of Picabia's next major exhibition, a large, retrospective showing in March 1949 at one of the most important avant-garde galleries in Paris, the Galerie René Drouin.[32] Befitting the occasion, a substantial catalogue was projected, but Picabia insisted that everything be the way he liked it, namely, spirited and unconventional. The catalogue was thereupon transformed into a newspaper format with a dadaist layout and reference to *391* in its title, *491, 50 ans de plaisir* (*491, 50 Years of Pleasure*). The prominent art critic Michel Tapié edited it, but there was hardly a preface per se. Instead the poems, drawings and aphorisms of Picabia were interspersed topsy-turvy among personal witnesses, homages and texts by André Breton, Jean Cocteau, Olga Picabia, Pierre de Massot, Gabrielle Buffet, Michel Perrin, Robert Desnos and a dozen other friends. Their contributions as a whole are among the most engaging and perceptive in the Picabia bibliography, and he enjoyed them all—with perhaps a preference for such pithy contributions as his wife Olga's concluding remarks: "He has had 7 yachts, 127 automobiles; that is little compared to his women. And what is rather curious is that he remains a friend with all of them except, as he tells me, 'those who are too tart.' "

30. Galerie des Deux Iles, Paris, *Francis Picabia, oeuvres de 1948*, November 15–December 4, 1948, statement by Michel Seuphor.

31. Picabia letter to Christine Boumeester, undated [attributed to 1948] (Goetz-Boumeester collection, Paris).

32. Galerie René Drouin, Paris, *491, 50 ans de plaisir*, March 4–26, 1949, texts by numerous authors. The Galerie René Drouin, located in the Place Vendome, just around the corner from Picabia's apartment, had exhibited the work of such notorious representatives of the postwar avant-garde as Jean Dubuffet.

The exhibition itself was equally impressive—uneven and unbalanced perhaps in its selection, but comprehensive (136 works), representative and a critical triumph. However, that festive occasion was spoiled for Picabia by a devastating theft of jewelry from his apartment just three days before the vernissage. Picabia, seventy years old and no longer wealthy, had counted on the jewelry as a source of revenue in his old age, and for weeks Olga and various friends labored to rekindle his utterly dejected spirits. Michel Tapié and Robert Assumçao de Aranjo helped by persuading him to do a set of lithographs for a volume of poetry by Murilo Mendès.[33] Picabia had not made lithographs for almost twenty years, but was soon working happily, absorbed by the process and his camaraderie with the technicians while producing six prints that reflect a variety of his figurative and abstract styles. Michel Seuphor also encouraged him to pursue some recent paintings in which dots figured prominently, and a new friend, Pierre André Benoit, took up the publication of his poems with a heartening measure of personal devotion and editorial quality. *Chi-Lo-Sa*, one of the best of those publications, appeared in 1950 with a collection of poems and aphorisms from 1949 which embraced Picabia's full range of philosophy, dadaist humor, private reflections and aggressive egoism (illus. 43):[34]

TOUT HONNEUR DE LA FEMME EST MIS DANS SON CUL

Pourquoi croire à ce qui est bien
surtout à ce qui est bien dit
moi je n'aime pas les gens de goût
ils me font penser au gibier
trop faisandé.

ALL OF WOMAN'S HONOR IS PLACED IN HER ASS

Why believe in what is good / above all in what is well said / me, I do not like men of taste / they make me think of game / hung too long.

INTERPRÉTATION

Partout où je rencontre la morale
je cherche l'instinct.

INTERPRETATION

Wherever I meet morality / I look for instinct.

33. Murilo Mendès, *Janela do Caos* (Paris, 1949), six lithographs by Francis Picabia.
34. Francis Picabia, *Chi-Lo-Sa* (Alès, 1950), dated Rubigen, August 1949, introduction by Jean van Heeckeren.
The publications by Pierre André Benoit (PAB) were exquisitely produced in small editions, normally limited to somewhere between twelve and one hundred numbered copies. Some were no more than two inches square; others were oversize. All were distinguished by tasteful, imaginative layout, by fine paper, and, often, by collage elements, prints and drawings.

LE LIT

Cette nuit
j'avais encore
en peu bu
suffisamment
pour raconter
des histoires
elle mit sa tête
dans ses mains
et pleura.

THE BED

That night / I had again / drunk a little / sufficiently / to tell / stories / she put her head / in her hands / and cried.

After Francis and Olga returned from their customary vacation in Rubigen, Picabia concentrated on his paintings of dots, which were exhibited in December 1949 at the Galerie des Deux Iles.[35] Most of them consisted of a few dots or small circles scattered about a field of contrasting color (fig. 407); occasional examples contained other forms as well (fig. 408), but with few exceptions they were simple compositions, rather crudely brushed and provided with titles which struck most spectators as yet another example of Picabia's mystification and mockery of the public—*Bien et mal sont les préjugés des critiques* (*Good and Bad Are the Prejudices of Critics*), *Sa Pensée est l'ombre du soleil* (*Her Thought is the Shadow of the Sun*) and *Tableau sans avenir* (*Painting Without a Future*) to cite some. Judgment of quality was also an issue, for few of them possessed much formal interest in the relationship of the dots to each other or to the color field. Even Michel Seuphor, who initially encouraged the paintings, seems to have written about them with tongue in cheek,[36] and an American critic described them as paintings of "wobbly-ringed dots on thick monochrome backgrounds . . . [which] had all the monotony and none of the scientific interest of a series of astronomical photographs."[37] In a contemporary interview Picabia did little to defuse suspicion:

> How do you choose your titles?
> After having made the paintings. . . .
> Do you establish a rapport between the canvas and the title?
> Not at all. Some people named "Brown" are blond.

35. Galerie des Deux Iles, Paris, *Picabia Point*, December 12–31, 1949, statement "La Fin de tout" by Michel Seuphor.

36. Ibid.

37. Anon., "Old Trickster," *Time* (New York, April 10, 1950), 66. That comment appeared in a review of Picabia's exhibition at the Rose Fried Gallery, The Pinacotheca, New York, *Picabia*, February 15–March 31, 1950, preface by Jean Arp.

You have written: "My paintings are not serious works." Do you amuse yourself then in painting them?

I am amused as a child has pleasure in making piles of sand beside the sea. He makes them as carefully as possible. He also has pleasure in destroying them. But he made them.[38]

As always in Picabia's career, the dot paintings were imbued with his character, and the best of them hold their own with paintings of other periods—justly composed and, through their colors, evocative of poignant experiences ranging from abstract expressions of joy and despair to suggestions of mysterious night skies. Picabia said nothing about his aims, but figuratively speaking, the "sky was the limit." Since 1913 no form in his career had been more ubiquitous and charged with symbolism than dots and circles—stars, eyes, heads, erotic zones, points of energy, pearls, globes and lights, to recall only some of the references—and Picabia alone possessed the secrets of that private tradition. Many of the dot compositions were, in fact, brushed over earlier paintings whose outlines remain as faint, haunting tracks under or beyond new fields and firmaments from the interior worlds of the artist.

During 1950 the quantity and quality of Picabia's painting fell off somewhat, but his year was active in other ways. He took in stride his promotion to an Officer of the Legion of Honor on March 30, 1950,[39] and was pleased by the renewed exhibition of his work in New York thanks to the efforts of Rose Fried, who served as the primary dealer for Duchamp and Picabia in America for over a decade.[40] In particular, Picabia's writing continued to flourish, and, as was his custom, a major work was completed in Rubigen, *Ne sommes-nous pas trahis par l'importance* (Are We Not Betrayed by Importance), in which sentiments of fatigue and the anticipation of death are more prevalent than usual alongside typical love poems and insouciant comments:[41]

J'AI SAISI CETTE PENSÉE EN PASSANT

> agenouille-toi
> sans parler
> pendant des longues heures
> respire doucement
> comme une petite fille

38. Charbonnier, *Le Monologue du peintre* 139–40, from an interview with Picabia ca. December 1949.

39. Date and title of the promotion of Picabia's rank were verified by personnel of the Grand Chancellerie de la Légion d'Honneur in a letter to the author, July 9, 1974.

40. Rose Fried followed the Picabia exhibition of 1950 (see n. 37) with a joint Duchamp-Picabia exhibition in 1953 (Rose Fried Gallery, New York, *Marcel Duchamp and Francis Picabia*, December 7, 1953–January 8, 1954).

41. Francis Picabia, *Ne sommes-nous pas trahis par l'importance* (Alès, March 1953), dated Rubigen, August 19, 1950, published in an edition of thirty-three copies.

pour que ma bouche
puisse joindre la tienne
et être heureux

I SEIZED THIS THOUGHT IN PASSING

kneel / without speaking / for long hours / breathe gently / like a little girl / so that
my mouth / may join yours / and be happy

NE PAS SAVOIR

je veux choisir
dans toute la forêt
un arbre
à qui
je confierai
un secret

NOT TO KNOW

I want to choose / in all the forest / one tree / to which / I will confide / a secret

NE PENSEZ PLUS AUTANT

on peut tout demander
à une femme
quand elle est nue
et quand elle pense
à sa lointaine destinée

DON'T THINK SO MUCH

one can ask everything / of a woman / when she is nude / and when she thinks / of
her far-off destiny

J'EN AI ASSEZ DE MA SOCIÉTÉ

c'est le cinquième été
que j'ai vu mourir
sur ces montagnes
les feuilles vont tomber
doucement comme la neige
il est temps que je disparaisse
chargé d'années
car elles me fatiguent

I HAVE HAD ENOUGH OF MY SOCIETY

it is the fifth summer / that I have seen die / on these mountains / the leaves will
fall / gently like the snow / it is time that I disappear / burdened with years / for
they fatigue me

Such writings, most of them published by P. A. Benoit, continued to flow—*Le Moindre Effort* (The Slightest Effort), *Le Saint masqué* (The Masked Saint), *Demain dimanche* (Tomorrow Sunday):[42]

DEMAIN DIMANCHE

Demain dimanche à Rubigen
il n'y aura ni journaux
ni lettres
demain je relirai mes journaux
et mes lettres
pour lire entre les lignes

Demain dimanche
les esprits les plus vieux
mettent des habits neufs
en Suisse
comme ailleurs

Une femme embrasse un lapin
je lui demande pourquoi
elle me dit
demain dimanche je vais le tuer

Demain dimanche
nous mangerons du poulet
mesure des choses

TOMORROW SUNDAY

Tomorrow Sunday in Rubigen / there will be neither newspapers / nor letters / tomorrow I will reread my newspapers / and my letters / to read between the lines / Tomorrow Sunday / the oldest minds / will put on new clothes / in Switzerland / as elsewhere / A woman kisses a rabbit / I ask her why / she tells me / tomorrow Sunday I am going to kill it / Tomorrow Sunday / we will eat chicken / measure of things

LE SAINT MASQUÉ [excerpts]

Ma vie est passée
Je cherche et n'ai pas trouvé
Elle fut douleur et erreur

La raison de ma recherche
C'est ce que je cherche
Mais je ne trouve pas

42. Francis Picabia, *Le Moindre Effort* (Alès, December 1950); *Le Saint masqué* (Alès, September 1951); *Demain dimanche* (Alès, March 1954), collages by PAB.

A partir d'aujourd'hui

Je suspends à mon cou

Tout ce que le temps n'a jamais proclamé

Je dois manger mon pain

A la sueur de mon front

Mais j'ai toujours froid

Tout bonheur sur terre

Me plait

Mais il vient trop tôt

Ou trop tard

Que m'importe ce que dit le monde

Je viens pour toujours

THE MASKED SAINT

My life has passed / I seek and I have not found / It was sadness and error / The reason for my search / Is that which I seek / But do not find / Starting tomorrow / I will hang around my neck / Everything which time has never proclaimed / I must eat my bread / By the sweat of my brow / But I am always cold / Every joy on earth / Gives me pleasure / But it comes too soon / Or too late / No matter what the world says / I am here always

In the early summer of 1951 Picabia suffered a stroke, and suddenly the flow of work was almost terminated.[43] Later in the year he did brush a few small canvases, but the damage was shocking; he never recovered, and prior to his death two years later Picabia left the apartment only once for an excellent retrospective exhibition of his work organized by Mme Simone Collinet at the Galerie Artiste et Artisan (illus. 44).[44] Mme Collinet, the first wife of André Breton, went on to become the principal dealer of Picabia's work for about fifteen years, and for a comparable length of time, P.A. Benoit continued his superb publications of poems from every epoch in Picabia's career. Picabia, to the contrary, incapacitated and denied all the activities which had made his life meaningful, faced the end he had once described: "Death doesn't exist, there is only dissolution." While publications and exhibitions of his work went apace, Picabia steadily declined, his last years becoming as grim as the brooding image of *Kalinga* (color pl. XX); death came finally on November 30, 1953.

43. Mme Olga Picabia wrote Goetz and Boumeester on an unspecified date in June 1951 that Picabia had hemorrhaged and had been in the hospital for ten days under the care of Dr. Huguenin (letter in the Goetz-Boumeester collection, Paris).

44. Galerie Artiste et Artisan, Paris, *Quelques Oeuvres de Picabia*, November 20–December 4, 1951, statement by Jacques-Henri Lévesque.

LIST OF REPRODUCTIONS

ORIGINAL titles (followed by English translations) are given in the form and language originally used by Picabia whenever known through inscriptions on the painting or through letters, contemporary exhibition catalogues and the like. When this policy displaces a current popular title, comment is made in the text. When original titles are unknown, an established or descriptive English title is employed. Occasionally titles either require no translation or cannot be translated.

Most dimensions have been taken by the author from the reverse of each work; some dimensions have been supplied by owners of the paintings. Measurements marked "sight" were taken from the frame window. In all instances, height precedes width.

Collections have been identified in accordance with requests by the owners rather than by a standard form. When the collection is unknown, or when the work has been lost or destroyed, the source of the reproduction is acknowledged. Standard photo credits appear following the plates.

Illustrations

1. Francis Picabia and his parents, ca. 1882.
2. Francis Picabia and his father, ca. 1889.
3. Collège Stanislas, certificate for first prize in drawing to Francis Picabia, 1889.
4. Left to right: Rodo Pissarro, Mme Orliac, Francis Picabia and Georges (Manzana) Pissarro, ca. 1902?.
5. Francis Picabia in his studio at 82, rue des Petits-Champs (now 26, rue Danielle Casanova), Paris, 1912.
6. Stacia Napierkowska, ca. 1912?.
7. Cartoon for *World*, New York, February 17, 1913.
8. Installation photograph (detail) of the Armory Show, Chicago, March–April, 1913.
9. Picabia and some of his automobiles, ca. 1911–1922.
10. Francis Picabia, Gabrielle Buffet and Guillaume Apollinaire at Magic City, Paris, ca. 1914.
11. Guillaume Apollinaire, "The Tie and the Watch," *Calligrammes*, Paris, 1918.
12. Marius de Zayas, caricature of Francis Picabia in military uniform, 1915.
13. Cover for *291*, no. 2, New York, April 1915.
14. Page 3, *291*, no. 2, New York, April 1915.
15. Marius de Zayas and Francis Picabia hand-tinting issues of *291*, New York, 1915.
16. Beach photograph, Barcelona, ca. 1916. Seated foreground: Al-

bert and Juliette Gleizes?; standing left to right: Picabia, unidentified woman, Otto van Watgen, unidentified woman, Marie Laurencin?, Gabrielle Buffet-Picabia and Olga Sackaroff.

17. Marcel Duchamp, Francis Picabia and Beatrice Wood at an amusement park, New York, 1917.

18. Francis and Gabrielle Picabia and their children, Pancho, Marie and Jeannine, ca. 1918.

19. Cover for *391*, no. 12, Paris, March 1920.

20. Cover for *Dadaphone*, no. 7, Paris, March, 1920.

21. Program for "Festival Dada," Salle Gaveau, Paris, May 26, 1920.

22. André Breton in sandwich board by Picabia at the "Festival Dada," Salle Gaveau, Paris, May 26, 1920.

23. Page 2, *Le Pilhaou-Thibaou*, Paris, July 10, 1921 (no. 15 of *391*).

24. Francis Picabia, "Funny-Guy Handbill," ca. October 1921.

25. Francis Picabia and Christian, cover for *La Pomme de pins*, St. Raphael, February 25, 1922.

26. Marcel Duchamp, Jacques Doucet and Francis Picabia, at Picabia's Maison Rose, Tremblay-sur-Mauldre, ca. 1922–1924.

27. Jean Borlin and Mlle Bonsdorff in *Relâche* by the Swedish Ballet, Paris, premiere December 4, 1924. Directed by Rolf de Maré; scenario and decor by Picabia; music by Erik Satie.

28. *Relâche*, Swedish Ballet, premiere Paris, December 4, 1924.

29. René Clair (film maker) and Francis Picabia (scenarist), *Entr'acte*, Paris, 1924.

30. Marcel Duchamp and Brogna Perlmutter in *Cinésketch* by Francis

Picabia, Paris, December 31, 1924.

31. Francis Picabia and Germaine Everling, Château de Mai, Mougins, ca. 1927–1929.

32. Germaine Everling and Lorenzo, Château de Mai, Mougins, ca. 1925–1929.

33. Francis Picabia and Jacques Doucet with *Straws and Toothpicks* (see fig. 260), ca. 1924–1927.

34. Installation photograph, Galerie Alexandre III, Cannes, *Exposition Picabia*, August 1930.

35. "Fêtes des cannibales," Château de Madrid, Cannes, ca. September 1930. Picabia (center left) with "X" on his chest; Olga (upper left) in elaborate face paint.

36. Picabia's studio at the Château de Mai, Mougins, summer 1935.

37. Francis and Olga Picabia on the *Yveline*, Golfe-Juan, 1938.

38. "The Parisian Bath in 1900," act at the Bal Tabarin, Paris, ca. 1938.

39. Francis Picabia in his studio, Paris, 1939.

40. Francis Picabia with his new bike and Sizou, Golfe-Juan, 1940.

41. Francis Picabia, letter to Christine Boumeester with drawing, collage and poem (on reverse), Paris, ca. 1946. Christine Boumeester–Henri Goetz collection, Paris.

42. Francis Picabia, letter-drawing to Christine Boumeester and Henri Goetz, 1946. Christine Boumeester–Henri Goetz collection, Paris.

43. Francis Picabia, "Egoism," page from *Chi-Lo-Sa*, Alès: PAB, 1950.

44. Jean van Heeckeren and Francis Picabia at the opening for *Quelques Oeuvres de Picabia (époque Dada 1915–1925)*, Galerie Artiste et Artisan, Paris, November 1951.

Color Plates

I. *Le Pont du chemin de fer, Moret* (*Railroad Bridge, Moret*), 1905, M. René Cavalero collection, Marseille.

II. *Landscape*, 1909, Musée National d'Art Moderne, Paris.

III. *Dolls*, ca. 1911, A.A. Saltzman collection.

IV. *Hen Roost*, 1912, Arturo Schwarz collection, Milan.

V. *Procession Seville*, 1912, private collection, New York.

VI. *Edtaonisl (ecclésiastique)* (*Edtaonisl* [*Ecclesiastic*]), 1913, The Art Institute of Chicago, Gift of Mr. and Mrs. Armand Phillip Bartos.

VII. *Je revois en souvenir ma chère Udnie* (*I See Again in Memory My Dear Udnie*), ca. 1914, The Museum of Modern Art, New York, Hillman Periodicals Fund, 1954.

VIII. *Machine tournez vite* (*Machine Turn Quickly*), ca. 1916–1918, private collection, New York.

IX. *L'Enfant carburateur* (*Child Carburetor*), ca. 1919, The Solomon R. Guggenheim Museum Collection, New York.

X. *M'amenez-y* (*Bring Me There*), ca. 1918–1920, Collection The Museum of Modern Art, New York, Helena Rubinstein Fund.

XI. *L'Oeil cacodylate* (*The Cacodylic Eye*), 1921, Musée National d'Art Moderne, Paris.

XII. *Conversation* I, ca. 1922, The Tate Gallery, London.

XIII. *Matchwoman* II, ca. 1923–1924, private collection, Paris.

XIV. *Le Baiser* (*The Kiss*), ca. 1924–1927, private collection, Paris.

XV. *Les Trois Grâces* (*The Three Graces*), ca. 1924–1927, private collection, Turin.

XVI. *Dispar*, ca. 1929, Georges Marci collection.

XVII. *Aello*, ca. 1930, Robert Lebel collection, Paris.

XVIII. *Le Printemps* (*Spring*), ca. 1938 and ca. 1943?, D. and J. de Menil collection, Houston.

XIX. *Adoration of the Calf*, ca. 1941–1942, formerly Acoris Gallery, London.

XX. *Kalinga*, ca. 1946, Succession Picabia, Paris.

Figures

1. *Landscape*, ca. 1893?–1902, M. and Mme Lionel Cavalero collection.

2. *Landscape*, 1898, Enrico and Roberta Baj collection, Milan.

3. *Sunset at St.-Tropez*, ca. 1897–1900, Poupard-Lieussou collection.

4. *The Roofs of Paris*, 1900, private collection, Paris.

5. *The Banks of the Loing*, 1902, formerly Tooth and Sons, Ltd., London.

6. *Landscape in the Midi*, 1902, Mr. and Mrs. Jack C. Massey collection.

7. *Study of a Nude*, ca. 1901, collection unknown. Photo: Olga Picabia scrapbook, Paris.

8. *Espagnole*, 1902, watercolor, private collection, Buffalo, N. Y.

9. *View of St.-Tropez*, 1903, private collection, Paris.

10. *Les Saules, effet de soleil d'automne* (*Willows, Effect of Autumn Sun*), 1904, collection unknown. Photo: *Le Figaro illustré*, Paris, February 1905.

11. *Le Soleil d'avril* (*April Sun*), ca. 1904, collection unknown. Photo: *L'Art décoratif*, Paris, February 1907.

12. *Banks of the Loing and Mill-houses, Moret*, 1905, Hilde Gerst collection, Miami.

13. Alfred Sisley. *The Bridge and Mills at Moret, Effect of Snow*, 1890, formerly Marlborough Ltd., London.

14. *Landscape*, 1905, The Honorable David Montagu collection, London.

15. *Les Pins, effet de soleil à St.-Honorat, Cannes* (*Pine Trees, Effect of Sunlight at St.-Honorat, Cannes*), ca. 1905–1906, private collection, Paris.

16. *Port de mer dans le Midi, effet de soleil* (*Seaport in the Midi, Effect of Sunlight*), ca. 1906–1907, collection unknown. Photo: Galeries Georges Petit, Paris, *Exposition de tableaux par F. Picabia*, March 1909.

17. *Le Pont du chemin de fer, Moret* (*Railroad Bridge, Moret*), 1905, collection unknown. Photo: Galerie Haussmann, Paris, *Picabia*, February 1907.

18, and color pl. I. *Le Pont du chemin de fer, Moret* (*Railroad Bridge, Moret*), 1905, M. René Cavalero collection, Marseille.

19. *The Port in Martiques*, 1907, Mme H. Saint-Maurice collection, Paris.

20. *Port in the Midi*, 1905, private collection, New York.

21. *Le Pont de Villeneuve, effet de neige* (*Bridge at Villeneuve, Snow Effect*), 1906, Office of the Mayor, Lisieux, France.

22. *Le Pont de Villeneuve-sur-Yonne, effet de soleil* (*Bridge at Villeneuve-sur-Yonne, Sunlight Effect*), 1906, Mr. Richard Smart collection, Kamuela, Hawaii.

23. *Lever du soleil dans la brume, Montigny* I (*Sunrise in the Mist, Montigny* I), 1905, M. René Cavalero collection, Marseille.

24. *Lever du soleil dans la brume, Montigny* II (*Sunrise in the Mist, Montigny* II), 1906, Eva Fischer collection, Rome.

25. *Bords du Loing, effet de soleil* (*Banks of the Loing, Sunlight Effect*), ca. 1908, Mr. and Mrs. Taner collection.

26. *View of St.-Tropez from the Citadel*, 1909, Mme Lucienne Radisse collection.

27. *Tree*, ca. 1904?, private collection.

28. *Abstract Drawing*, ca. 1908?, Succession Picabia, Paris.

29. *Portrait of Mistinguett*, ca. 1907–1911, The Solomon R. Guggenheim Museum Collection, New York.

30. *Port of St.-Tropez*, 1909, private collection.

31. *La Femme aux mimosas* (*Woman with Mimosas*), 1908, Mr. and Mrs. Jack S. Josey collection, Houston.

32. *Sierra Morena*, 1909, private collection.

33. *Houses*, 1909, formerly Gertrude Stein Gallery, New York.

34. *Paysage* à Cassis (*Landscape at Cassis*), ca. 1909–1910, Mr. and Mrs. Neil Reisner collection.

35. *Landscape*, 1909, Musée National d'Art Moderne, Paris.

36. *Lane*, 1909, A. Napier collection, Neuilly-sur-Seine.

37. *Abstract Landscape*, 1909, Musée National d'Art Moderne, Paris.

38. *Caoutchouc*, ca. 1909, Musée National d'Art Moderne, Paris.

39. *Still Life with Pitcher and Peppers*, 1909, private collection.

40. *Still Life*, ca. 1909?, private collection, New York.

41. *Still Life*, ca. 1947, private collection, New York.

42. *Landscape*, 1910, Galerie A.F. Petit, Paris.

43. *Landscape*, 1910, Galerie des 4 Mouvements, Paris.

44. *Landscape in Jura*, 1910, formerly Galerie Furstenberg, Paris.

45. *Le Torrent (The Torrent)*, ca. 1909–1911, private collection, Paris.

46. *Regattas*, 1911, formerly Galerie Jacques Tronche, Paris.

47. *Adam and Eve*, 1911, private collection, Paris.

48. *Landscape*, ca. 1911, collection unknown. Photo: Hôtel Drouot catalogue, Paris.

49. *Les Chevaux (Horses)*, ca. 1911, Musée de Libourne.

50. Picasso. *The Bullfight Fan*, 1912, Oeffentliche Kunstsammlung, Kunstmuseum, Basel.

51. *Tarentelle*, 1912, Mrs. William Sisler collection, Palm Beach.

52. *Port de Naples*, 1912, private collection.

53. *The Red Tree (Grimaldi After the Rain?)*, ca. 1912, private collection, Paris.

54. *Landscape, La Creuse*, ca. 1912, The Lydia and Harry Lewis Winston Collection (Dr. and Mrs. Barnett Malbin, New York).

55. *Paris*, 1912, Count Boël collection, Brussels.

56. *Danses à la source I (Dances at the Spring I)*, 1912, Philadelphia Museum of Art, The Louise and Walter Arensberg Collection, '50-134-155.

57. *Danses à la source II (Dances at the Spring II)*, 1912, The Museum of Modern Art, New York, Gift from the children of Eugene and Agnes E. Meyer: Elizabeth Lorentz, Eugene Meyer III, Katharine Graham and Ruth M. Epstein.

58. *Figure triste (Sad Figure)*, 1912, Albright-Knox Art Gallery, Buffalo, N.Y., Gift of the Seymour H. Knox Foundation, Inc.

59. *Musique de procession (Procession Music)*, 1912, collection unknown.

Photo: *Excelsior*, Paris, October 8, 1912.

60. *La Source (The Spring)*, 1912, The Museum of Modern Art, New York, Gift from the children of Eugene and Agnes E. Meyer: Elizabeth Lorentz, Eugene Meyer III, Katharine Graham and Ruth M. Epstein.

61. Unknown cartoonist's parody of Picabia's *The Spring*. Reproduction attributed to a Kansas City newspaper, February 24, 1913.

62. Marcel Duchamp. *The Bride*, 1912, Philadelphia Museum of Art, The Louise and Walter Arensberg Collection, '50-134-65.

63. Robert Delaunay. *The Cardiff Team, Third Representation*, 1913, Musée d'Art Moderne de la Ville de Paris.

64. *Procession*, 1912, collection unknown. Photo: Der Sturm Galerie, Berlin, *Erster Deutscher Herbstsalon*, September–December 1913.

65. *Abstract Composition*, 1912, private collection, Brussels.

66. *Mechanical Expression Seen Through Our Own Mechanical Expression*, 1913, The Lydia and Harry Lewis Winston Collection (Dr. and Mrs. Barnett Malbin, New York).

67. *New York*, 1913, The Art Institute of Chicago, Alfred Stieglitz Collection.

68. *New York (Study for a Study of New York?)*, 1913, Alfred Stieglitz Archive, Collection of American Literature, Beinecke Rare Book and Manuscript Library, Yale University, New Haven, Conn.

69. *New York*, 1913, private collection.

70. *New York (Study for a Study of New York?)*, 1913, collection unknown. Photo: *291*, no. 2, New York, April 1915.

71. *New York*, 1913, Musée National d'Art Moderne, Paris.

72. *New York*, 1913, The Art Institute of Chicago, Alfred Stieglitz Collection.

73. *Chanson nègre* II (*Negro Song* II), 1913, private collection, New York.

74. *Chanson nègre* I (*Negro Song* I), 1913, The Metropolitan Museum of Art, New York, The Alfred Stieglitz Collection, 1949.

75. *Danseuse étoile et son école de danse* (*Star Dancer and Her School of Dance*), 1913, The Metropolitan Museum of Art, New York, The Alfred Stieglitz Collection, 1949.

76. *Danseuse étoile sur un trans-atlantique* (*Star Dancer on a Trans-atlantic Liner*), 1913, private collection, Paris.

77. *La Ville de New York aperçu à travers le corps* (*New York Perceived Through the Body*), 1913, Galerie Jan Krugier, Geneva.

78. *Abstract Composition*, ca. 1913–1914, private collection, Philadelphia.

79. Morton Schamberg. *Geometrical Patterns*, 1914, private collection, Jenkintown, Pa.

80. Arthur Dove. *Pagan Philosophy*, 1913, The Metropolitan Museum of Art, New York, The Alfred Stieglitz Collection, 1949.

81. Marius de Zayas. *Theodore Roosevelt*, 1913, collection unknown. Photo: *Camera Work*, no. 46, New York, April 1914.

82. *Udnie (jeune fille américaine; danse)* (*Udnie* [*Young American Girl; Dance*]), 1913, Musée National d'Art Moderne, Paris.

83. Study for *Udnie*, ca. 1913, private collection, Turin.

84. *Catch as Catch Can*, 1913, Philadelphia Museum of Art, The Louise and Walter Arensberg Collection, '50-134-155.

85. *Souvenir des Luttes, Catch as Catch Can* (*Memory of Wrestling,*

Catch as Catch Can), 1913, formerly Guillaume Apollinaire collection, Paris.

86. *Culture physique* (*Physical Culture*), 1913, Philadelphia Museum of Art, The Louise and Walter Arensberg Collection, '50-134-157.

87. *Révérences*, ca. 1913, private collection, Paris.

88. *"Little" Udnie*, ca. 1913–1914, M. and Mme Lionel Cavalero collection.

89. *Animation*, 1914, Tarica, Ltd., Paris.

90. *Embarras* (*Predicament*), 1914, Mrs. M. Victor Leventritt collection.

91. *Une Horrible Douleur* (*A Horrible Sadness*), 1914, private collection, New York.

92. *Moi aussi, j'ai vécu en amérique* (*Me, Too, I Have Lived in America*), ca. 1914, collection unknown. Photo: *Art d'aujourd'hui*, IV, Paris, 1953.

93. *Impétuosité française* (*French Impetuosity*), ca. 1913–1914, Luciano Pistoi collection, Milan.

94. *Ad Libilum, au choix; à la volonté* (*Ad Libilum, To the Choice of the Will*), ca. 1913–1914, formerly Rose Fried collection.

95. *Force comique* (*Comic Force*), ca. 1914, Collection The Berkshire Museum, Pittsfield, Mass.

96. *Chose admirable à voir* (*Thing Admirable to See*), ca. 1913–1914, formerly Robert Elkon Gallery, New York.

97, and color pl. VII. *Je revois en souvenir ma chère Udnie* (*I See Again in Memory My Dear Udnie*), ca. 1914, The Museum of Modern Art, New York, Hillman Periodicals Fund, 1954.

98. *C'est de moi qu'il s'agit* (*It's About Me*), ca. 1914, The Museum of Modern Art, New York, Gift from

the children of Eugene and Agnes E. Meyer: Elizabeth Lorentz, Eugene Meyer III, Katharine Graham and Ruth M. Epstein.

99. *Mariage comique (Comical Marriage)*, 1914, The Museum of Modern Art, New York, Gift from the children of Eugene and Agnes E. Meyer: Elizabeth Lorentz, Eugene Meyer III, Katharine Graham and Ruth M. Epstein.

100. *Fille née sans mère (Girl Born Without a Mother)*, ca. 1915, The Metropolitan Museum of Art, New York, The Alfred Stieglitz Collection, 1949.

101. *Machine*, ca. 1915–1919, private collection, Chicago.

102. *Fantaisie (Fantasy)*, 1915, collection unknown. Photo: *291*, no. 10–11, New York, December 1915–January 1916.

103. Illustration of a beam steam engine, mid 19th century. Photo: John Macquorn Rankine, *A Manual of the Steam Engine and Other Prime Movers*, London, 1873.

104. *Voilà Haviland (Here is Haviland)*, 1915, collection unknown. Photo: *291*, no. 5–6, New York, July–August, 1915.

105. Advertisement for the Wallace portable electric lamp (detail), 1915. Photo: *Hardware Dealer's Magazine*, New York, April 1915.

106. *Portrait d'une jeune fille américaine dans l'état de nudité (Portrait of a Young American Girl in the State of Nudity)*, 1915, collection unknown. Photo: *291*, no. 5–6, New York, July–August 1915.

107. *Ici, c'est ici Stieglitz (Here, This Is Stieglitz)*, 1915, The Metropolitan Museum of Art, New York, The Alfred Stieglitz Collection, 1949.

108. *Le Saint des saints (The Saint of Saints)*, 1915, collection unknown. Photo: *291*, no. 5–6, New York, July–August 1915.

109. *De Zayas! De Zayas!*, 1915, collection unknown. Photo: *291*, no. 5–6, New York, July–August 1915.

110. Diagram of Delco starting and lighting system, ca. 1915. Photo: George Williams Hobbs and Ben G. Elliot, *The Gasoline Automobile*, © 1915 by the McGraw-Hill Book Co., Inc., New York. Used by permission.

111. *Gabrielle Buffet. Elle corrige les moeurs en riant (Gabrielle Buffet. She Corrects Manners Laughingly)*, 1915, Tarica, Ltd., Paris.

112. *Portrait Max Jacob*, 1915, collection unknown. Photo: *291*, no. 10–11, New York, December 1915–January 1916.

113. *Femme! (Woman!)*, psychotype poem by Marius de Zayas, 1915, and Picabia's *Voilà elle (Here She Is)*, 1915, collection unknown. Photo: *291*, no. 9, New York, November 1915.

114. Marcel Duchamp. *The Bride Stripped Bare by Her Bachelors, Even (The Large Glass)*, 1915–1923, Philadelphia Museum of Art, Bequest of Katherine S. Dreier, '52-98-1.

115. *Voilà la femme (Here is Woman)*, 1915, Robert Lebel collection, Paris.

116. *Révérence*, 1915, The Baltimore Museum of Art, Sadie A. May Collection.

117. *Machine sans nom (Machine Without Name)*, 1915, Museum of Art, Carnegie Institute, Pittsburgh, Pa.

118. *Paroxyme de la douleur (Paroxysm of Sadness)*, 1915, private collection, Paris.

119. *Très rare tableau sur la terre (Very Rare Painting on Earth)*, 1915, Peggy Guggenheim Foundation, Venice.

120. *Cette Chose est faite pour per-*

pétuer mon souvenir (*This Thing is Made to Perpetuate My Memory*), 1915, The Arts Club of Chicago.

121. *Petite Solitude au milieu des soleils* (*A Little Solitude in the Midst of Suns*), 1915, collection unknown. Photo: *Arts and Decoration*, New York, April 1916.

122. Illustration for a Deere separator, ca. 1927. Photo: Louise Flader, ed., *Achievement in Photo-Engraving and Letter-Press Printing*, Chicago, 1927.

123. Illustration of a Herschell-Spillman tractor engine, exterior and cutaway views, ca. 1920. Photo: *Automotive Industries*, 42, no. 15, New York, April 8, 1920.

124. *Spanish Woman with Rose*, 1916, Mme Suzanne Romain collection, Paris.

125. *Novia au premier occupant* (*Sweetheart of the First Occupant*), 1917, as cover for *391*, no. 1, Barcelona, January 25, 1917. Location of original drawing unknown.

126. *Flamenca*, 1917, as cover for *391*, no. 3, Barcelona, March 1, 1917. Location of original drawing unknown.

127. *Roulette*, 1917, as cover for *391*, no. 4, Barcelona, March 25, 1917. Location of original drawing unknown.

128. *Max Goth*, 1917, collection unknown. Photo: *391*, no. 1, Barcelona, January 25, 1917.

129. *Portrait de Marie Laurencin, Four in Hand*, ca. 1916–1917, The Lydia and Harry Lewis Winston Collection (Dr. and Mrs. Barnett Malbin, New York).

130. *Les Iles Marquises* (*The Marquesas Islands*), ca. 1916–1917, Paride Accetti collection, Milan.

131. *Prostitution universelle* (*Universal Prostitution*), ca. 1916–1917, Yale University Art Gallery, New Haven, Conn., Gift of Collection Société Anonyme.

132. *Parade amoureuse* (*Amorous Parade*), 1917, Mr. and Mrs. Morton G. Neumann collection, Chicago.

133. *Fille née sans mère* (*Girl Born Without a Mother*), ca. 1916–1918, B.C. Holland, Inc., Chicago.

134. *Le Fiancé*, ca. 1916–1918, Musée d'Art et d'Industrie, St.-Etienne.

135. *Etude pour novia* (*Study for Sweetheart*), ca. 1916–1917, Robert Motherwell collection.

136. *Mécanique* (*Mechanical*), ca. 1916–1918, Galerie Denise René, Paris.

137. *Volant qui régularise le mouvement de la machine* (*Wheel Which Regulates the Movement of the Machine*), ca. 1916–1918, private collection, Paris.

138. *Novia* (*Sweetheart*), ca. 1916–1917, private collection.

139. *La Musique est comme la peinture* (*Music is like Painting*), ca. 1913–1917, N. Manoukian collection, Paris.

140. Illustration of the effect of a magnetic field on alpha, beta and gamma particles, ca. 1905. Photo: W. Watson, *A Text-Book of Physics*, London, 1905.

141. Marcel Duchamp. *Fountain*, 1917, original lost from the collection of Louise and Walter Arensberg. Photo by Alfred Stieglitz.

142. *Ane* (*Ass*, or *Donkey*), 1917 (sheet pasted on cover for *391*, no. 5, New York, June 1917), dimensions and location of original drawing unknown.

143. *Américaine* (*American* [female]), 1917, as cover for *391*, no. 6, New York, July 1917. Location of original drawing unknown.

144. *Ballet mécanique* (*Mechanical Ballet*), 1917, as cover for *391*, no. 7, New York, August 1917. Location of original drawing unknown.

145. Charles Demuth. *Business*, 1921, The Art Institute of Chicago, Alfred Stieglitz Collection.

146. Morton Schamberg. *Machine*, 1916, Yale University Art Gallery, New Haven, Conn., Collection of the Société Anonyme.

147. Man Ray. *The Impossibility*, or *Danger-Dancer*, ca. 1917–1920, private collection, Paris.

148. Man Ray. *My First Born*, 1919, location unknown. Photo: *TNT*, New York, 1919.

149. Jean Crotti. *The Mechanical Forces of Love in Movement*, 1916, Tarica, Ltd., Paris.

150. *Esprit de jeune fille (Spirit of a Young Girl)*, 1918, collection unknown.

151. *Abstract Lausanne*, ca. 1918, private collection, Paris.

152. *Cantharides (Cantharis)*, 1918, collection unknown. Photo: Picabia, *Poèmes et dessins de la fille née sans mère*, Lausanne, 1918.

153. *Narcotique (Narcotic)*, 1918, collection unknown. Photo: Picabia, *Poèmes et dessins de la fille née sans mère*, Lausanne, 1918.

154. *Egoïste (Egoist)*, 1918, collection unknown. Photo: Picabia, *Poèmes et dessins de la fille née sans mère*, Lausanne, 1918.

155. *Muscles brillants (Brilliant Muscles)*, ca. 1918, collection unknown. Photo: *Cahiers d'art*, no. 1–2, Paris, 1932.

156. *Cannibalisme*, ca. 1918, collection unknown. Photo: Hugnet, *L'Aventure Dada*, Paris, 1957.

157. *Voilà la fille née sans mère (Here is the Girl Born Without a Mother)*, ca. 1916–1918, Pierre André Benoit collection, Alès.

158. *Colonel*, ca. 1918, private collection, New York.

159. *Portrait de Guillaume Apollinaire*, ca. 1918, William N. Copley collection.

160. *Construction moléculaire (Molecular Construction)*, ca. 1919, as cover for *391*, no. 8, Zurich, February 1919. Location of original drawing unknown.

161. *Mouvement Dada*, 1919, Collection The Museum of Modern Art, New York, Purchase.

162. *Réveil matin (Alarm Clock)*, 1919, The Lydia and Harry Lewis Winston Collection (Dr. and Mrs. Barnett Malbin, New York).

163. Max Ernst. *The Roaring of Ferocious Soldiers*, 1919, Arturo Schwarz collection, Milan.

164. Marcel Duchamp. *L.H.O.O.Q.*, 1919, Tarica, Ltd., Paris.

165. Marcel Duchamp. *Tzanck Check*, 1919, Arturo Schwarz collection, Milan.

166. Marcel Duchamp. *To Be Looked At (From the Other Side of the Glass) with One Eye, Close to, for Almost an Hour*, 1918, Collection The Museum of Modern Art, New York, Katherine S. Dreier Bequest.

167. *Le Double Monde (Double World)*, 1919, private collection, Paris.

168. Georges Ribemont-Dessaignes. *Young Woman*, ca. 1919, Yale University Art Gallery, New Haven, Conn., Gift of Collection Société Anonyme.

169. and color pl. IX. *L'Enfant carburateur (Child Carburetor)*, ca. 1919, The Solomon R. Guggenheim Museum Collection, New York.

170. Diagram of a Claudel carburetor and its nozzle assembly, ca. 1920. Photo: *Automotive Industries*, 42, no. 23, New York, June 3, 1920.

171. *Serpentins (Streamers)*, ca. 1919–1922, private collection, Hubertus Wald, Hamburg.

172. *L'Oeil (Eye)*, ca. 1919, formerly Tarica, Ltd., Paris.

173. *Balance (Scale)*, ca. 1919, private collection.

174. *Souvenir du rien (Memory of*

Nothing), ca. 1919, private collection, U.S.A.

175. *C'est clair* (*It is Clear*), ca. 1919, private collection, Turin.

176. *Prenez garde à la peinture* (*Watch out for the Painting*), ca. 1919, Moderna Museet, Stockholm.

177. *Portrait of Tristan Tzara*, ca. 1920, private collection.

178. *Francis*, 1920, collection unknown. Photo: De La Hire, *Francis Picabia*, Paris, 1920.

179. *Portrait of André Breton*, 1920, collection unknown. Photo: Breton and Soupault, *Les Champs magnétiques*, Paris, 1920.

180. *Ribemont–Dessaignes*, 1920, collection unknown. Photo: *Comoedia*, Paris, March 29, 1920.

181. Suzanne Duchamp-Crotti. *One and One Menaced*, 1916, collection unknown.

182. *La Sainte Vièrge* (*The Blessed Virgin*), 1920, collection unknown. Photo: *391*, no. 12, Paris, March 1920.

183. *Francis Picabia*, ca. 1920–1922, Galerie Jean Chauvelin, Paris.

184. *Portrait de Cézanne, Portrait de Rembrandt, Portrait de Renoir, Natures mortes*, 1920, collection unknown. Photo: *Cannibale*, no. 1, Paris, April 25, 1920.

185. *Portrait de Jacques-Emile Blanche*, 1920, collection unknown. Photo: *Comoedia*, Paris, April 1, 1920.

186. *Portrait de Tristan Tzara*, ca. 1920, collection unknown. Photo: *Cannibale*, no. 1, Paris, April 25, 1920.

187. *Far-niente beau parti* (*Beautiful Party of Blissful Ease*), 1920, as cover for *391*, no. 13, Paris, July 1920. Location of original drawing unknown.

188. *La Danseuse Jasmine* (*The Dancer Jasmine*), 1920, Galleria Schwarz, Milan.

189. Study for *La Danseuse Jasmine*, 1920, formerly Galleria Schwarz, Milan.

190. *Le Rastaquouère*, ca. 1920, collection unknown. Photo: *Les Hommes du jour*, no. 6, Paris, October–November 1920.

191. Cover, *391*, no. 14, Paris, November 1920, with two ready-mades: *Copy of an Ingres Letter by Francis Picabia* and *Dada Drawing*.

192. Tristan Tzara, "A Night of Fat Chess," p. 4, *391*, no. 14, Paris, November 1920.

193. *Tableau rastadada* (*Rastadada Painting*), 1920, private collection.

194. *Le Lierre unique eunuque* (*The Unique Eunuch Ivy*), ca. 1920, private collection, Basel.

195. Max Ernst. *Stratified Rocks, nature's gift of gneiss lava iceland moss 2 kinds of lungwort 2 kinds of ruptures of the prerineam growths of the heart (b) the same thing in a well-polished box somewhat more expensive*, 1920, Collection The Museum of Modern Art, New York, Purchase.

196. Max Ernst. *Oedipus Rex*, 1922, private collection.

197. *Les Yeux chauds* (*Hot Eyes*), 1921, Mme H. Saint-Maurice collection, Paris (under *La Feuille de vigne*, fig. 209).

198. Diagram for the governor of an airplane turbine, ca. 1921. Photo: *Le Matin*, Paris, November 9, 1921.

199. Jean Crotti. *Chainless Mystery*, 1921, Musée d'Art Moderne de la Ville de Paris.

200. Suzanne Duchamp–Crotti. *Masterpiece: Accordion*, 1921, Yale University Art Gallery, New Haven, Conn., Gift of the Artist.

201. Man Ray. *Transatlantic*, ca.

1921, collection unknown. Photo: Städtische Galerie im Lenbachhaus, Munich, *New York Dada*, December 1973–January 1974.

202. *La Veuve joyeuse* (*The Merry Widow*), 1921, private collection, Paris.

203. *Chapeau de paille?* (*Straw Hat?*), 1921, Musée National d'Art Moderne, Paris.

204. *Danse de Saint-Guy*, ca. 1919–1921. Photo: Collection Bibliothèque Jacques Doucet, Paris.

205. *Tabac-Rat* (*Rat Tobacco*), ca. 1919–1921 and ca. 1948–1949, Succession Picabia, Paris.

206. Jean Crotti. *Explicative*, 1921, Musée d'Art Moderne de la Ville de Paris.

207. Man Ray. *Boardwalk*, 1917, private collection, Paris.

208. Pablo Picasso. *Mother and Child*, 1921, The Art Institute of Chicago.

209. *La Feuille de vigne* (*Fig Leaf*), 1922, Mme H. Saint-Maurice collection, Paris.

210. *La Nuit espagnole* (*Spanish Night*), 1922, William N. Copley collection.

211. *Le Jardin* (*Garden*), ca. 1921–1924, private collection, Paris.

212. *Sphinx*, ca. 1922, D. and J. de Menil collection, Houston.

213. *Hache-paille* (*Chaff-cutter*), ca. 1922, formerly Rose Fried Gallery, New York.

214. *Totalisateur* (*Totalizer*), ca. 1922, Mme Cochrane collection, Turin.

215. *Décaveuse* (*Digger*), ca. 1922, private collection, Turin.

216. *Novia* (*Sweetheart*), ca. 1919–1922, Messrs. Sesia collection, Maggi, Turin.

217. *Tickets*, ca. 1922, Galleria Schwarz, Milan.

218. *Tickets annulés* (*Cancelled Tickets*), ca. 1922, private collection.

219. *Fixe*, ca. 1922, private collection, Turin.

220. *Radio Concerts*, ca. 1922, Bruno Piero collection, Milan.

221. *Presse hydraulique* (*Hydraulic Press*), ca. 1922, Robert Lebel collection, Paris.

222. Kasimir Malevich. *Supremus No. 50*, 1915, Stedelijk Museum, Amsterdam.

223. *Volucelle* I, ca. 1922, Galleria Notizie, Turin.

224. Diagram of the Pleiades of Hevelius, 1660. Photo: Camille Flammarion, *Les Etoiles*, Paris, 1882.

225. *Astrolabe*, ca. 1922, private collection, Turin.

226. *Uranus Weighing the World System* (detail), 1651. Photo: Camille Flammarion, *Astronomie populaire*, Paris, 1880.

227. *Optophone* I, ca. 1922, private collection, Paris.

228. *Lampe cristal* (*Crystal Lamp*), ca. 1922, Mr. and Mrs. Harris K. Weston collection, Cincinnati.

229. *Optophone* II, ca. 1922–1923, Musée d'Art Moderne de la Ville de Paris.

230. Newton's rings. Photo: Michel Cagnet et al., *Optischer Erscheinungen*, Berlin, 1962.

231. *Abstract Composition with Optical Patterns and Ink Spots*, ca. 1922, private collection.

232. *Un Bouton* (*A Button*), ca. 1922, Steingrim Lauursen collection, Copenhagen.

233. *Chariot*, ca. 1922, private collection.

234. *Volucelle* II, ca. 1922, private collection.

235. Diffraction fringes from a straight edge. Photo: Michel Cagnet et al. *Optischer Erscheinungen*, Berlin, 1962.

236, and color pl. XII. *Conversation* I, ca. 1922, The Tate Gallery, London.

237. *The Hercules of Hevelius*, 1660. Photo: Camille Flammarion, *Les Etoiles*, Paris, 1882.

238. *Espagnole*, ca. 1922–1923, formerly A. Napier collection, Neuilly-sur-Seine.

239. *Portrait of Mlle Yvonne Picabia*, ca. 1922–1923, formerly Mme Gresse-Picabia collection, La Rochelle.

240. *Portrait of Mme Pomaret*, ca. 1922–1923, M. and Mme Pomaret collection, Nice.

241. *Portrait of Simone Breton*, 1922, private collection, Paris.

242. *Picabia par Francis*, 1922, collection unknown. Photo: Olga Picabia scrapbook, Paris.

243. *Floating Figures*, ca. 1923, as cover for *Littérature*, nos. 11–12, Paris, October 15, 1923. Location of original drawing unknown.

244. *Dresseur d'animaux (Animal Trainer)*, 1923, M. and Mme Lionel Cavalero collection.

245. *Lampe*, ca. 1923, private collection.

246. *Echynomie livide*, ca. 1922–1923, Galleria Schwarz, Milan.

247. *Breton and Initiate at the Cup of Rimbaud*, 1924, formerly Pierre de Massot collection, Paris. Photo: *391*, no. 16, Paris, May 1924.

248. *Surrealism Crucified*, ca. 1924, Musée d'Art Moderne de la Ville de Paris.

249. Drawing for Tzara's *Sept Manifestes Dada*, ca. 1924, Arturo Schwarz collection, Milan.

250. Drawing for Tzara's *Sept Manifestes Dada*, ca. 1924, Arturo Schwarz collection, Milan.

251. *Rolf de Maré*, 1924, collection unknown. Photo: *Comoedia*, Paris, December 2, 1924.

252. Page from the program of *Relâche* with statement and drawings by Picabia; location of original drawings unknown. Photo: *La Danse*, Paris, November–December 1924.

253. Page from the program of *Relâche* with Picabia's *Portrait of Erik Satie*, 1924. Photo: *La Danse*, Paris, November–December 1924. Original drawing, Dansmuseet, Stockholm.

254. *Landscape*, ca. 1923–1924, formerly Galerie Ariel, Paris.

255. *Les Rochers à St.-Honorat (Rocks at St.-Honorat)*, ca. 1924–1925, private collection.

256. *Les Amoureux (The Lovers)*, ca. 1924–1925, private collection, Paris.

257. *Femme à l'ombrelle (Woman with Parasol)*, ca. 1924–1925, private collection, Paris.

258. *Flirt*, ca. 1924–1925, The Hodes Collection.

259. *La Lecture (Reading)*, ca. 1924–1925, Troubetzkoi collection.

260. *Pailles et cure-dents (Straws and Toothpicks)*, ca. 1924, Arturo Schwarz collection, Milan.

261. *Matchwoman* I, 1920? (ca. 1923–1924), E.A. Bergman collection, Chicago.

262. *Plumes*, ca. 1923–1925, Arturo Schwarz collection, Milan.

263. *Midi*, ca. 1923–1926, Yale University Art Gallery, New Haven, Conn., Gift of Collection Société Anonyme.

264. *Retour des barques (Return of the Boats)*, ca. 1923–1927, collection unknown. Photo: Olga Picabia scrapbook, Paris.

265. *Vase of Flowers*, ca. 1924–1926, Musée d'Art Moderne de la Ville de Paris.

266. *Portrait (of Poincaré?)*, ca. 1924–1926, private collection. Remade as *Le Beau Charcutier*, fig. 267.

267. *Le Beau Charcutier (The Beauti-*

ful Pork Butcher), ca. 1924–1926 and ca. 1930–1935, private collection.

268. *Pot of Flowers*, ca. 1924–1926, Simonis collection, Turin.

269. *Centimeters*, ca. 1924–1925, Galleria Schwarz, Milan.

270. Program for "Gala du souvenir" at Les Ambassadeurs, Cannes casino (detail), 1927, collection of original drawing unknown.

271. *La Gitane* (*Gypsy*), ca. 1926, collection unknown. Photo: Cercle Nautique, Cannes, *Exposition Francis Picabia*, January–February 1927.

272. *L'Ambition*, ca. 1926, collection unknown. Photo: *This Quarter*, I, no. 3, Monte Carlo, 1927.

273, and color pl. xv. *Les Trois Grâces* (*The Three Graces*), ca. 1924–1927, private collection, Turin.

274. Peter Paul Rubens. *The Three Graces*, ca. 1639, Museo del Prado, Madrid.

275. *Idyll*, ca. 1924–1927, Musée de Peinture et de Sculpture, Grenoble.

276. *Four-footed Sibyl*, ca. 1924–1927, private collection.

277. Michelangelo. *The Libyan Sibyl*, 1511, fresco, Sistine Chapel, Vatican, Rome.

278. *Venus and Adonis*, ca. 1924–1927, Arturo Schwarz collection, Milan.

279. Titian. *Venus and Adonis*, ca. 1553, Museo del Prado, Madrid.

280. *Idyll*, ca. 1924–1927, private collection, Paris.

281. *Venus*, ca. 1924–1927, Galerie Jacques Benador, Geneva.

282. *Woman with Monocle*, ca. 1924–1927, private collection, Paris.

283. *Cyclop*, ca. 1924–1927, Paride Accetti collection, Milan.

284. Picasso. *Seated Woman*, ca. 1925–1926, collection unknown. Photo: Christian Zervos, *Pablo Picasso*, V, Paris, 1932–1942.

285. *Blue Phantoms*, ca. 1924–1927, The Hodes Collection.

286. *Phébus* (*Phoebus*), ca. 1927, private collection.

287. *Lazarus and the Lamb*, ca. 1927, collection unknown. Photo: Galerie Briant-Robert, Paris, *Francis Picabia*, November 1927.

288. Anonymous Spaniard. *Lazarus*, 12th century, fresco from the apse wall, San Clemente de Tahull, Collection Museo de Arte de Cataluña, Barcelona.

289. Anonymous Spaniard. *Apocalyptic Lamb*, 12th century, fresco from San Clemente de Tahull, Collection Museo de Arte de Cataluña, Barcelona.

290. *Barcelona*, 1924 and ca. 1927?, Seattle Art Museum, Eugene Fuller Memorial Collection.

291. *Toreador*, ca. 1927–1928, private collection, France.

292. *Female Head and Romanesque Visage of Christ*, ca. 1927–1928, formerly Sotheby Parke Bernet, New York.

293. *Totó*, ca. 1927, formerly Galerie des 4 Mouvements, Paris.

294. *Bullfight*, ca. 1925–1927, private collection, Paris.

295. *Machaon*, ca. 1926–1927, Galerie Brame et Lorenceau, Paris.

296. *Butterflies*, ca. 1926–1928, private collection, Paris.

297. *Two Heads in Biomorphic Form*, ca. 1926–1928, Mme H. Saint-Maurice collection, Paris.

298. *La Harpe de Georges* (*Harp of* [*St.*] *George*), ca. 1926–1928, formerly A. Napier collection, Neuilly-sur-Seine.

299. *Bucolic*, ca. 1924–1928, formerly Galerie Diderot, Paris.

300. *Hôtel ancien* (*Old Hotel*), ca. 1927, The Metropolitan Museum of Art, New York, The Alfred Stieglitz Collection, 1949.

301. *Chiromis*, ca. 1927, collection unknown. Photo: Chez Fabre, Cannes, *Exposition Francis Picabia*, February 1928.

302. Albrecht Dürer. *Nemesis*, ca. 1501–1502, Fogg Art Museum, Harvard University, Cambridge, Mass.

303. *Jeune Fille au paradis* (*Young Girl in Paradise*), ca. 1927–1928, private collection, Paris.

304. *Pilar*, ca. 1927–1929, formerly Sotheby's, London.

305. *Head with Cellophane*, ca. 1928, Enrico and Roberta Baj collection, Milan.

306. *L'Ombre* (*Shadow*), ca. 1928, private collection, Paris.

307. *Jésus et le dauphin* (*Jesus and the Dolphin*), ca. 1928, Mme H. Saint-Maurice collection, Paris.

308. Annibale Carracci. *Pietà*, ca. 1599–1600, Museo e Gallerie Nazionali di Capodimonte, Naples.

309. *Untitled Transparency*, ca. 1928–1929, private collection.

310. *Trifolii*, ca. 1928–1929, collection unknown.

311. *Lunaris*, ca. 1928–1929, Maurice and Rose-Marie Weinberg collection, Paris.

312, and color pl. XVI. *Dispar*, ca. 1929, Georges Marci collection.

313. Study for *Dispar*, ca. 1929, formerly Alan Auslander Gallery, New York.

314. *Hera*, ca. 1929, private collection, Paris.

315. *Catax*, ca. 1929, private collection.

316. Sandro Botticelli. *The Birth of Venus* (detail), ca. 1485, Uffizi, Florence.

317. *Briseis*, ca. 1929, formerly Léonce Rosenberg collection, Paris.

318. Anonymous Greek. *Dying Niobid*, ca. 450–440 B.C., Museo delle Terme, Rome.

319. *Untitled Drawing After the Doryphorus*, ca. 1929, private collection, Paris.

320. Anonymous Roman. Copy of Polyclitus's *Doryphorus*, ca. 450–440 B.C., Museo Nazionale, Naples.

321. *Untitled Drawing of a Head and the Doryphorus*, ca. 1929, M. and Mme Michel Perrin collection, Paris.

322. *Ino*, ca. 1929–1930, formerly Mme Dubose collection, Paris.

323. Anonymous Roman. *Perseus and Andromeda*, ca. 1st century A.D., fresco from Pompeii, Museo Nazionale, Naples.

324. Study for *Ino*, ca. 1929–1930, collection unknown. Photo: Olga Picabia scrapbook, Paris.

325. Sandro Botticelli. *Madonna and Child with St. John*, ca. 1472, The Louvre, Paris.

326. *Atrata*, ca. 1929, Maurice and Rose-Marie Weinberg collection, Paris.

327. Anonymous Roman. *Atlas*, marble, Museo Nazionale, Naples. Photo: Engraving from Solomon Reinach, *Répetoire de la statuaire greque et romaine*, I, Paris, 1930.

328. Sandro Botticelli. *Portrait of a Man with a Medal*, ca. 1473–1474, Uffizi, Florence.

329. *Villica-Caja*, 1929, Paride Accetti collection, Milan.

330. Guido Reni. *Nessus and Dejanira*, ca. 1617–1620, The Louvre, Paris.

331. Anonymous Roman. *Mars and Venus*, 1st century A.D., fresco from Pompeii, Museo Nazionale, Naples.

332. *Artemis*, ca. 1929, Mr. and Mrs. Sidney M. Ehrman collection, San Francisco.

333. Bartolommeo Schedoni. *St. Sebastian Cured by the Pious Women*, ca. 1615, Museo e Gallerie Nazionali di Capodimonte, Naples.

334. *Medea*, ca. 1929, Maurice and Rose-Marie Weinberg collection, Paris.

335. *Luscunia*, ca. 1929, Galerie Henri Bénézit, Paris.

336. *Judith*, ca. 1929, private collection, Paris.

337. *Salome*, ca. 1930, Robert Lebel collection, Paris.

338. Sandro Botticelli, school of ?. *The Redeemer*, ca. 1500, Accademia Carrara, Bergamo.

339. *Oo*, ca. 1930, formerly Jane Harper collection, Philadelphia.

340, and color pl. XVII. *Aello*, ca. 1930, Robert Lebel collection, Paris.

341. Piero della Francesca. *Baptism of Christ* (detail), ca. 1450, The National Gallery, London.

342. *Noctuelles*, ca. 1930, formerly Léonce Rosenberg collection, Paris. Photo: Chez Léonce Rosenberg, Paris, *Exposition Francis Picabia*, December 1930.

343. Piero della Francesca. *The Meeting of Solomon and the Queen of Sheba* (detail), 1453–1454, fresco, S. Francesco, Arezzo.

344. *Heads and Landscape*, ca. 1930, The Art Institute of Chicago.

345. Piero della Francesco. *The Discovery of the True Cross* (detail), ca. 1453–1454, fresco, S. Francesco, Arezzo.

346. *Genie of the Lake*, ca. 1930, Mme I. Solomon collection, Paris.

347. *L'Infinité de Dieu* (*The Infinity of God*), 1931, lithograph, illustration for André Maurois's *Le Peseur d'âmes*, Paris, 1931.

348. *Setina*, ca. 1930, collection unknown. Photo: Olga Picabia scrapbook, Paris.

349. *Mélibée*, ca. 1931, private collection, Paris.

350. *Adam and Eve*, ca. 1931, Mme H. Saint-Maurice collection, Paris.

351. Anonymous Roman copy of a Greek artist. *Orestes and Electra*, ca. 50 B.C., Museo Nazionale, Naples.

352. *Olyras*, ca. 1931, Silkeborg Kunstmuseum (The Asgar Jorn Bequest), Denmark.

353. Ambrogio Lorenzetti. *Allegory of Peace*, detail from *Good Government*, ca. 1338–1340, fresco, Sala della Pace, Palazzo Pubblico, Siena.

354. *Head*, 1932, formerly A. Napier collection, Neuilly-sur-Seine.

355. *Volupté*, ca. 1932, collection unknown. Photo: Galerie Alexandre III, Cannes, *Catalogue des aquarelles et dessins composant l'atelier de Francis Picabia*, August 1934.

356. *Portrait of Gertrude Stein*, 1933, Gertrude Stein Collection, Collection of American Literature, Beinecke Rare Books and Manuscript Library, Yale University, New Haven, Conn.

357. *Portrait of Suzy Solidor*, 1933, Arturo Schwarz collection, Milan.

358. *Portrait of Olga Mohler*, ca. 1933, Mme Olga Picabia collection.

359. *The White Lake*, ca. 1930–1934, M. and Mme Pomaret collection, Nice.

360. *Idea*, ca. 1931–1934, formerly Galerie Sept, Paris.

361. *Printemps* (*Spring*), 1935, Musée National d'Art Moderne, Paris.

362. *Man and Woman at the Seashore*, 1935, formerly Galleria Notizie, Turin.

363. *Iphigeneia*, or *Resignation*, ca. 1935, formerly M. Waismann collection, Paris.

364. Anonymous Roman. *Sacrifice of Iphigeneia*, 1st century A.D., fresco, Pompeii.

365. *Peasant Woman*, ca. 1935, collection unknown. Photo: Olga Picabia scrapbook, Paris.

366. Picabia and *Portrait of a Man with a Skull*, ca. 1935, M. Maurice Montet collection, Paris, repainted as in fig. 367.

367. *Portrait of a Doctor*, ca. 1935 and 1938?, M. Maurice Montet collection, Paris.

368. *At the Theater*, 1935 and ca. 1946?, Succession Picabia, Paris.

369. *Clowns*, 1935, Galerie de Seine, Paris.

370. *Dream*, ca. 1933–1936?, Mme Suzanne Romain collection, Paris.

371. *Hercules and His Coursers*, ca. 1933–1936?, formerly Acoris Gallery, London.

372. *Superimposition of the Madonna and Nude*, ca. 1934–1938?, formerly Galleria Schwarz, Milan.

373. *Superimposition of a Hand and Face*, 1936, collection unknown. Photo: Olga Picabia scrapbook, Paris.

374. *The Peacocks*, ca. 1937, formerly M. Daher collection, Paris.

375. *The Midnight Bath*, ca. 1937, private collection, Paris.

376. *Untitled Landscape in the Manner of the Italian "Primitives,"* ca. 1937, Mme Suzanne Romain collection, Paris.

377. *Abstract Composition*, 1937, Max H. Welti collection, Zurich.

378. *The Mask and the Mirror*, ca. 1930–1945 in two or more campaigns ?, Christine Boumeester–Henri Goetz collection, Paris.

379. *Figure and Flowers*, ca. mid-1930s and ca. 1943, Christine Boumeester–Henri Goetz collection, Paris.

380. *Landscape of the Midi*, ca. 1938, private collection, Paris.

381. *Landscape with Palm Trees*, late 1930s?, formerly Gertrude Stein Gallery, New York.

382. *Landscape with Sunset*, ca. 1938–1940, M. and Mme Pomaret collection, Nice.

383. *Asoa*, ca. 1938, collection unknown. Photo: Olga Picabia scrapbook, Paris.

384. *Portrait*, ca. 1938–1939, Mme Suzanne Romain collection, Paris.

385. *7091*, ca. 1938–1939, Mme Suzanne Romain collection, Paris.

386. *Spring Landscape*, ca. 1939–1940, Dr. and Mme Colin collection, Nice.

387. *Flower Girl*, ca. 1941, collection unknown. Photo: Olga Picabia scrapbook, Paris.

388. *The Corrida*, ca. 1941, Collection The Petit Palais, Geneva.

389. *Women and Bulldog*, ca. 1941–1942, M. and Mme Lionel Cavalero collection.

390. *Adam and Eve*, ca. 1941–1943, formerly Robert Fraser Gallery, London.

391. *Spring (M. and Mme Romain)*, ca. 1942, Mme Suzanne Romain collection, Paris.

392. *Self-Portrait with Two Women*, ca. 1940–1943, Paride Accetti collection, Milan.

393. *Little Mask*, ca. 1941–1942, M. and Mme Michel Perrin collection, Paris.

394. *Portrait*, ca. 1940–1944?, Mme Suzanne Romain collection, Paris.

395. *Portrait of Germaine Everling*, ca. 1940–1944?, Mme Germaine Everling collection, Cannes.

396. *Le Soleil dans la peinture (The Sun in Painting)*, 1945, Oeffentliche Kunstsammlung, Kunstmuseum Basel, Gift of Marguerite Arp-Hagenbach.

397. *Asoa*, 1945, collection unknown. Photo: *Journal des arts*, nos. 5–6, Zurich, January–February 1946.

398. *Suzanne*, 1945, formerly Galerie des 4 Mouvements, Paris.

399. *Viens avec moi là-bas (Come with Me There)*, 1945, Succession Picabia, Paris.

400. *Niam*, ca. 1946, private collection, Paris.

401. *La Paloma de la paz (The Dove of Peace)*, 1946, formerly Galerie Jacques Tronche, Paris.

402. *Bonheur de l'aveuglement (Happiness of Blindness)*, ca. 1946–1947, Succession Picabia, Paris.

403. *Bal nègre*, 1947, Succession Picabia, Paris.

404. *Elle danse (She Dances)*, 1948, Grandini collection, Milan.

405. *Troisième Sexe (Third Sex)*, 1948, Succession Picabia, Paris.

406. *Je vous attends (I Am Waiting for You)*, ca. 1948, collection unknown.

407. *Carte à jouer (Playing Card)*, 1949, H. Robert Greene collection, New York.

408. *Bienveillance (Benevolence)*, 1950, H. Robert Greene collection, New York.

409. *Danger de la force (Danger of Force)*, 1947–1950, Succession Picabia, Paris.

PLATES

I. *Le Pont du chemin de fer, Moret*
(*Railroad Bridge, Moret*),
1905, oil on canvas, 81 x 100 cm.,
31⅞ x 39⅜ in.

II. *Landscape*, 1909, oil on canvas,
69 x 88.5 cm., 27¼ x 34⅞ in.

III. *Dolls*, ca. 1911, oil on canvas, 51 x 72.5 cm., 20 x 29 in.

IV. *Hen Roost*, 1912, oil on canvas, 130 x 163 cm., 51¼ x 64⅛ in.

Color Plates III, IV

v. *Procession Seville*, 1912, oil on canvas, 120 x 120 cm., 47¼ x 47¼ in.

Color Plate v

VI. *Edtaonisl (ecclésiastique)* (*Edtaonisl [Ecclesiastic]*), 1913,
oil on canvas, 302 x 300.5 cm., 118¾ x 118⅜ in.

Color Plate VI

VII. *Je revois en souvenir ma chère Udnie (I See Again in Memory My Dear Udnie)*, ca. 1914, oil on canvas, 250 x 198.8 cm., 98½ x 78¼ in.

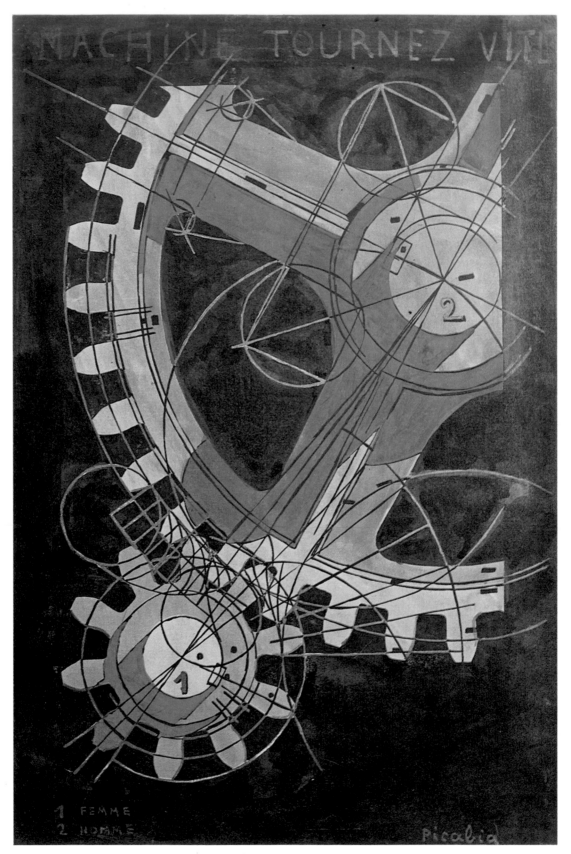

VIII. *Machine tournez vite (Machine Turn Quickly)*, ca. 1916–1918,
gouache on cardboard, 49 x 32 cm., 19¼ x 12⅝ in.

Color Plate VIII

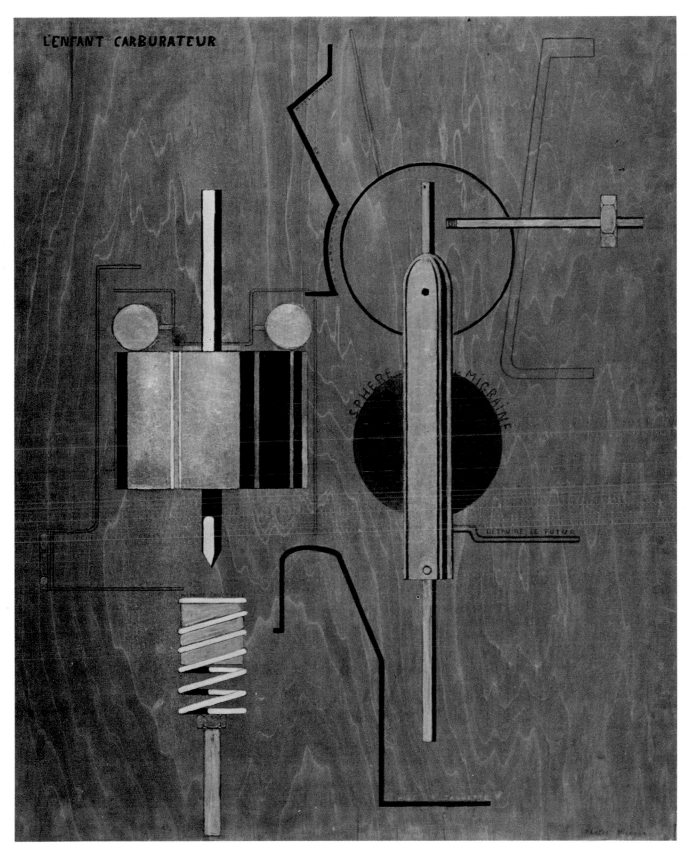

IX. *L'Enfant carburateur* (*Child Carburetor*), ca. 1919,
oil, gilt, pencil and metallic paint on plywood, 126.4 x 101.3 cm., 49¾ x 39⅞ in.

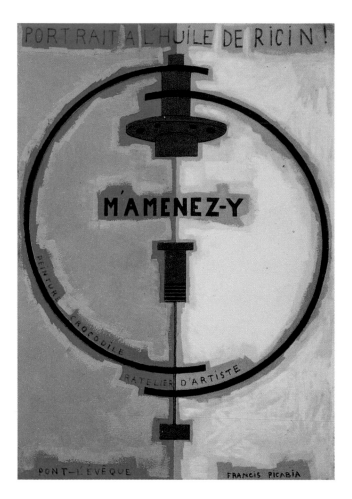

x. *M'amenez-y* (*Bring Me There*), ca. 1918–1920,
oil on cardboard, 129 x 89 cm., 50⅞ x 35⅜ in.

Color Plate x

XI. *L'Oeil cacodylate* (*The Cacodylic Eye*), 1921,
ink, gouache and collage on canvas, 146 x 115 cm., 57½ x 45¼ in.

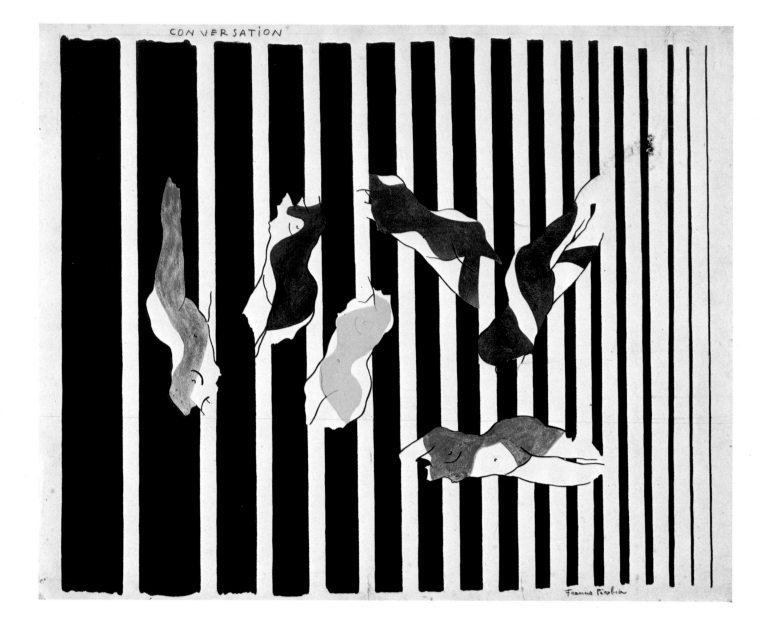

CONVERSATION

Francis Picabia

XII. *Conversation* I, ca. 1922, watercolor on paper, 60 x 72 cm., 23⅝ x 28⅜ in.

Opposite:

XIII. *Matchwoman* II, ca. 1923–1924, ripolin, matches, hairpins, leather and coins on canvas, 92 x 73 cm., 36¼ x 28¾ in.

Color Plate XII

XIV. *Le Baiser* (*The Kiss*), ca. 1924–1927, oil on canvas, 73 x 92 cm., 28¾ x 36¼ in.

Opposite:

XV. *Les Trois Grâces* (*The Three Graces*), ca. 1924–1927, oil on cardboard, 105 x 75 cm., 41⅜ x 29½ in.

Color Plate XIV

Color Plate XV

Color Plate XVI

XVII. *Aello*, ca. 1930, oil on canvas, 169 x 169 cm., 66½ x 66½ in.

XVIII. *Le Printemps* (*Spring*), ca. 1938 and ca. 1943?, oil on wood, 152.5 x 94 cm., 60 x 37 in.

Opposite:
XVI. *Dispar*, ca. 1929, oil on plywood, 150.5 x 95.3 cm., 59¼ x 37½ in.

XIX. *Adoration of the Calf*, ca. 1941–1942,
oil canvas, 106.5 x 76 cm., 42 x 30 in.

XX. *Kalinga*, ca. 1946, oil on wood, 149 x 95 cm., 58⅝ x 37⅜ in.

Color Plates XIX, XX

1. *Landscape*, ca. 1893?–1902,
oil on canvas, 33 x 24 cm., 13 x 9½ in.
2. *Landscape*, 1898,
oil on canvas, 46 x 33 cm., 18⅛ x 13 in.
3. *Sunset at St.-Tropez*, ca. 1897–1900,
oil on canvas, 33.5 x 41 cm., 13¼ x 16⅛ in.
4. *The Roofs of Paris*, 1900,
oil on canvas, 28 x 41 cm., 11 x 16⅛ in.

5. *The Banks of the Loing*, 1902, oil on wood, 23 x 32.5 cm., 9 x 12¾ in.

6. *Landscape in the Midi*, 1902,
oil on canvas, 45.7 x 63.5 cm., 18 x 25 in.

Chapter 1

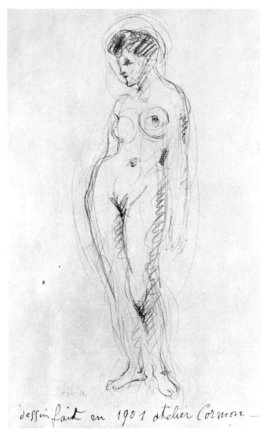

dessin fait en 1901 atelier Cormon —

7. *Study of a Nude*, ca. 1901,
pencil on paper, dimensions unknown.

F. Picabia

8. *Espagnole*, 1902, watercolor, pencil and ink on paper, 58.5 x 43 cm., 23 x 17 in.

9. *View of St.-Tropez*, 1903, oil on canvas, 73 x 92 cm., 28¾ x 36¼ in.

10. *Les Saules, effet de soleil d'automne (Willows, Effect of Autumn Sun)*, 1904, oil on canvas, dimensions unknown.

11. *Le Soleil d'avril (April Sun)*, ca. 1904, oil on canvas, dimensions unknown.

Chapter 2

12. *Banks of the Loing and Millhouses, Moret*, 1905, oil on canvas, 73 x 92 cm., 28¾ x 36¼ in.

13. Alfred Sisley. *The Bridge and Mills at Moret, Effect of Snow*, 1890, oil on canvas, 60 x 81 cm., 23⅝ x 31⅞ in.

Chapter 2

Chapter 2

Opposite:

14. *(top left) Landscape*, 1905, oil on canvas,
49 x 64 cm., 19¼ x 25¼ in. (sight)

15. *(bottom) Les Pins, effet de soleil à St.-Honorat, Cannes*
(Pine Trees, Effect of Sunlight at St.-Honorat, Cannes),
ca. 1905–1906, oil on canvas, 220 x 300 cm., 86½ x 118 in.

16. *(top right) Port de mer dans le Midi, effet de soleil*
(Seaport in the Midi, Effect of Sunlight),
ca. 1906–1907, oil on canvas, dimensions unknown.

This page:

17. *Le Pont du chemin de fer, Moret (Railroad Bridge, Moret)*, 1905,
pencil on paper, dimensions unknown.

18. *Le Pont du chemin de fer, Moret (Railroad Bridge, Moret)*, 1905,
oil on canvas, 81 x 100 cm., 31⅞ x 39⅜ in.

Chapter 2

F. Picabia   1907

19. *The Port in Martigues*, 1907, etching,
10.7 x 15.5 cm., 4⅝ x 6¼ in. (plate)
20. *Port in the Midi*, 1905, watercolor and
crayon on paper, 24 x 34 cm., 9½ x 13⅜ in.

F. Picabia 1905

Chapter 2

21. *Le Pont de Villeneuve,
effet de neige
(Bridge at Villeneuve,
Snow Effect)*, 1906, oil on canvas,
73 x 92 cm., 28¾ x 36¼ in.

22. *Le Pont de Villeneuve-sur-Yonne,
effet de soleil
(Bridge at Villeneuve-sur-Yonne,
Sunlight Effect)*, 1906, oil on
canvas, 73 x 92 cm., 28¾ x 36¼ in.

Chapter 2

23. *Lever du soleil dans la brume, Montigny* I (*Sunrise in the Mist, Montigny* I), 1905, oil on canvas, 73 x 92 cm., 28¾ x 36¼ in.

24. *Lever du soleil dans la brume, Montigny* II (*Sunrise in the Mist, Montigny* II), 1906, oil on composition board, 32.7 x 40.6 cm., 12⅞ x 16 in.

25. *Bords du Loing, effet de soleil* (*Banks of the Loing, Sunlight Effect*), ca. 1908, oil on canvas, 73 x 92 cm., 28¾ x 36¼ in.

Chapter 2

26. *View of St.-Tropez from the Citadel*, 1909, oil on canvas, 73 x 92 cm., 28¾ x 36¼ in.

27. *Tree*, ca. 1904?, oil on canvas,
55 x 38 cm., 21⅝ x 15 in.

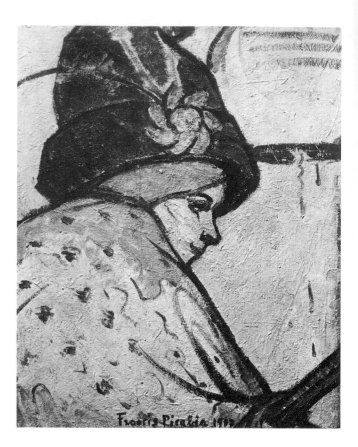

28. *Abstract Drawing*, ca. 1908?,
colored crayons on paper, 23 x 31 cm., 9 x 12¼ in.
29. *Portrait of Mistinguett*, ca. 1907–1911,
oil on canvas, 60 x 49.2 cm., 23⅝ x 19⅜ in.
30. *Port of St.-Tropez*, 1909,
oil on canvas, 73 x 60 cm., 28¾ x 23⅝ in.
31. *La Femme aux mimosas* (*Woman with Mimosas*), 1908,
oil on canvas, 116 x 89 cm., 45⅝ x 35 in.

Chapter 2

32. *Sierra Morena*, 1909,
colored crayon on paper,
23 x 30 cm., 9 x 11¾ in.

33. *Houses*, 1909, oil on canvas,
64 x 80 cm., 25¼ x 31½ in. (sight)

34. *Paysage à Cassis (Landscape at Cassis)*,
ca. 1909–1910, oil on canvas,
50.5 x 61.5 cm., 19⅞ x 24¼ in.

35. *Landscape*, 1909,
pastel and gouache on paper,
25 x 32 cm., 9⅞ x 12⅝ in.

36. *Lane*, 1909, pastel on paper,
18 x 24 cm., 7⅛ x 9½ in.

37. *Abstract Landscape*, 1909,
colored crayons on paper,
24.7 x 31.5 cm., 9¾ x 12⅜ in.

Chapter 3

38. *Caoutchouc*, ca. 1909,
gouache on paper,
45.5 x 61.5 cm., 18 x 24¼ in.

39. *Still Life with Pitcher
and Peppers*, 1909, oil on canvas,
73 x 92 cm., 28¾ x 36¼ in.

Chapter 3

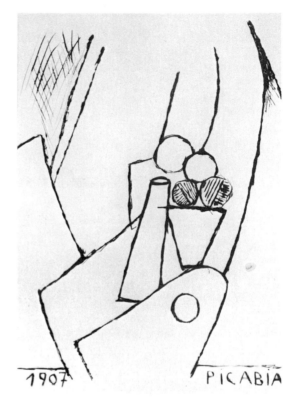

40. *Still Life*, ca. 1909?, gouache on ragboard,
57 x 45.7 cm., 22½ x 18 in.

41. *Still Life*, ca. 1947, etching,
17.8 x 14.6 cm., 7 x 5¾ in.

42. *Landscape*, 1910, oil on canvas,
73 x 92 cm., 28¾ x 36¼ in.

43. *Landscape*, 1910, oil on canvas,
54.5 x 63.5 cm., 21 x 25 in.

44. *Landscape in Jura*, 1910,
oil on canvas, dimensions unknown

45. *Le Torrent (The Torrent)*, ca. 1909–1911,
oil on canvas, 73 x 92 cm., 28¾ x 36¼ in.

46. *Regattas*, 1911, oil on canvas,
73 x 92 cm., 28¾ x 36¼ in.

47. *Adam and Eve*, 1911, oil on canvas,
100 x 81 cm., 39⅜ x 31⅞ in.

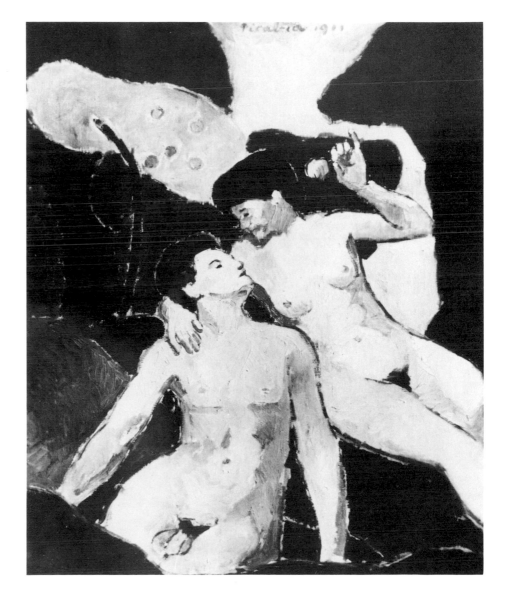

48. *Landscape*, ca. 1911, oil on canvas,
73 x 92 cm., 28¾ x 36¼ in.

50. Picasso. *The Bullfight Fan*, 1912, oil on canvas,
135 x 82 cm., 53⅛ x 32¼ in.

49. *Les Chevaux* (*Horses*), ca. 1911, oil on canvas,
73 x 92 cm., 28¾ x 36¼ in.

Chapter 3

51. *Tarentelle*, 1912, oil on canvas, 73 x 92 cm., 28¾ x 36¼ in.

52. *Port de Naples*, 1912, oil on canvas,
92 x 73 cm., 36¼ x 28¾ in.

53. *The Red Tree (Grimaldi After the Rain?)*,
ca. 1912, oil on canvas,
92 x 73 cm., 36¼ x 28¾ in.

Chapter 3

54. *Landscape, La Creuse*, ca. 1912,
oil on canvas, 73 x 92 cm.,
28¾ x 36¼ in.

55. *Paris*, 1912, oil on canvas,
73 x 92 cm., 28¾ x 36¼ in.

56. *Danses à la source* I (*Dances at the Spring* I), 1912, oil on canvas, 120.6 x 120.6 cm., 47½ x 47½ in.

Chapter 3

57. *Danses à la source* II (*Dances at the Spring* II),
1912, oil on canvas, 252 x 249 cm., 99⅛ x 98 in., prior to restoration

58. *Figure triste* (*Sad Figure*), 1912, oil on canvas, 118 x 119.5 cm., 46½ x 47 in.

59. *Musique de procession* (*Procession Music*), 1912, oil on canvas, dimensions unknown

60. *La Source (The Spring)*, 1912, oil on canvas,
249.5 x 249.2 cm., 98¼ x 98⅛ in., prior to restoration

61. Unknown cartoonist's parody
of Picabia's *The Spring*.

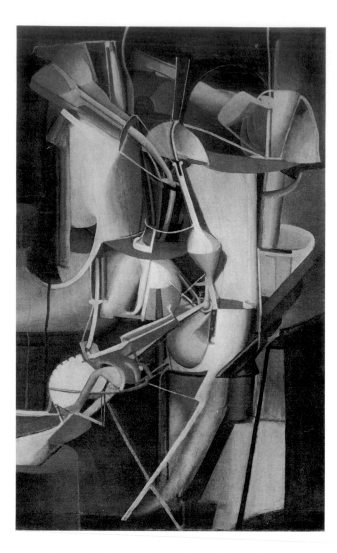

62. Marcel Duchamp. *The Bride*, 1912, oil on canvas, 90 x 55 cm., 35½ x 21⅝ in.

63. Robert Delaunay. *The Cardiff Team*, *Third Representation*, 1913, oil on canvas, 326 x 208 cm., 128⅜ x 81⅞ in.

64. *Procession*, 1912, oil on canvas, dimensions unknown

65. *Abstract Composition*, 1912,
watercolor on paper, 53.5 x 66 cm., 21 x 26 in.

66. *Mechanical Expression
Seen Through Our Own
Mechanical Expression*, 1913,
watercolor and pencil on paper,
19.7 x 16 cm., 7¾ x 6¼ in.

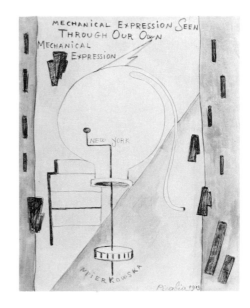

67. *New York*, 1913, watercolor on paper
mounted on board, 75 x 55 cm., 29½ x 21⅝ in.

68. *New York* (*Study for a Study of New York?*),
1913, pencil and ink on paper
mounted on cardboard, 17.8 x 15.2 cm., 7 x 6 in.

69. *New York*, 1913, watercolor and gouache on paper
mounted on cardboard, 75 x 55 cm., 29½ x 21⅝ in.

70. *New York* (*Study for a Study of New York?*), 1913,
ink on paper, dimensions unknown

71. *New York*, 1913,
gouache on paper,
56.6 x 75.8 cm., 22¼ x 29⅞ in.

72. *New York*, 1913,
watercolor and gouache on paper,
55 x 75 cm., 21⅝ x 29½ in.

Chapter 4

73. *Chanson nègre* II (*Negro Song* II), 1913,
watercolor on paper, 55.2 x 65.5 cm., 21¾ x 25¾ in.

74. *Chanson nègre* I (*Negro Song* I), 1913,
watercolor on paper, 66.3 x 55.9 cm., 26⅛ x 22 in.

75. *Danseuse étoile et son école de danse* (*Star Dancer and Her School of Dance*), 1913, watercolor on paper, 55.9 x 76.2 cm., 22 x 30 in.

76. *Danseuse étoile sur un transatlantique* (*Star Dancer on a Transatlantic Liner*), 1913, watercolor on paper, 75 x 55 cm., 29½ x 21⅝ in.

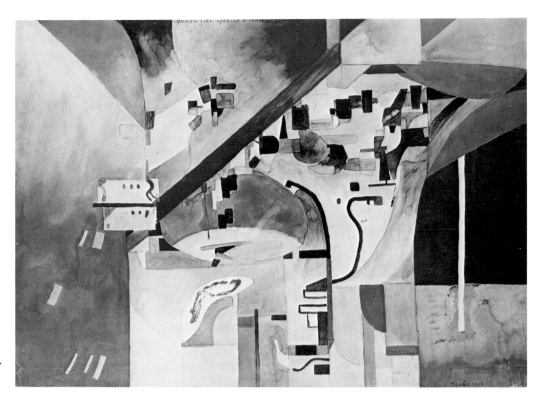

77. *La Ville de New York aperçu
à travers le corps* (*New York
Perceived Through the Body*), 1913,
watercolor on paper,
55 x 75 cm., 21⅝ x 29½ in.

78. *Abstract Composition*,
ca. 1913–1914, watercolor
and pencil on paper,
53.3 x 64.8 cm., 21 x 25½ in.

79. Morton Schamberg. *Geometrical Patterns*, 1914,
oil on canvas, 71 x 40.7 cm., 28 x 16 in.

80. Arthur Dove. *Pagan Philosophy*, 1913, pastel,
54.3 x 45.5 cm., 21⅜ x 17⅞ in.

81. Marius de Zayas. *Theodore Roosevelt*, 1913,
charcoal on paper, 63.5 x 50.8 cm., 25 x 20 in.

Chapter 4

82. *Udnie (jeune fille américaine; danse)*
(*Udnie* [*Young American Girl; Dance*]), 1913,
oil on canvas, 300 x 300 cm., 118⅛ x 118⅛ in.

83. Study for *Udnie*, ca. 1913, pencil on paper,
24 x 19.5 cm., 9½ x 7¾ in.

Chapter 5

Opposite:
84. *Catch as Catch Can*, 1913,
oil on canvas, 100.6 x 82 cm.,
39⅝ x 32¼ in.

This page:
85. *(top left) Souvenir des Luttes,
Catch as Catch Can (Memory of
Wrestling, Catch as Catch Can)*,
1913, pencil on paper,
18.5 x 14 cm., 7¼ x 5½ in.

86. *(bottom) Culture physique
(Physical Culture)*, 1913,
oil on canvas,
90 x 117 cm., 35½ x 46 in.

87. *(top right) Révérences*,
ca. 1913, watercolor
on composition board,
75 x 54.5 cm., 29½ x 21½ in.

88. *"Little" Udnie*, ca. 1913–1914, oil on canvas, 197 x 197 cm., 77½ x 77½ in.

Chapter 5

89. *Animation*, 1914, watercolor on paper, 52.8 x 64.1 cm., 20¾ x 25¼ in.

90. *Embarras* (*Predicament*), 1914, watercolor on paper, 53 x 65 cm., 20⅞ x 25½ in.

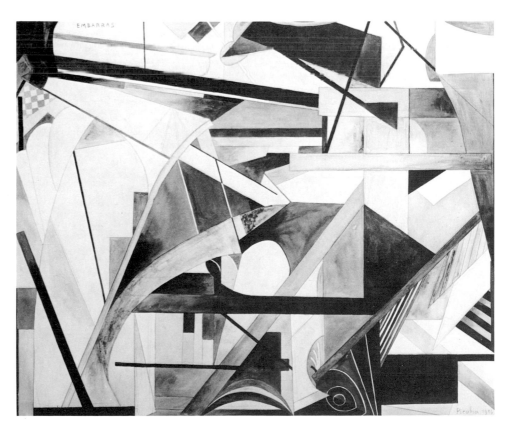

Chapter 5

91. *Une Horrible Douleur* (*A Horrible Sadness*), 1914,
watercolor and ink on paper, 54 x 65 cm., 21¼ x 25⅝ in.

92. *Moi aussi, j'ai vécu en amérique*
(*Me, Too, I Have Lived in America*), ca. 1914,
watercolor on paper, 65 x 54 cm., 25⅝ x 21¼ in.

Chapter 5

93. *Impétuosité française (French Impetuosity)*, ca. 1913–1914,
watercolor on composition board,
54 x 65 cm., 21¼ x 25⅝ in.

94. *Ad Libilum, au choix; à la volonté*
(*Ad Libilum, To the Choice of the Will*), ca. 1913–1914,
watercolor on cardboard, dimensions unknown

95. *(top left) Force comique (Comic Force)*, ca. 1914,
watercolor on paper?, 63.5 x 52.7 cm., 25 x 20¾ in.

96. *(bottom left) Chose admirable à voir (Thing Admirable to See)*,
ca. 1913–1914, tempera on composition board, 55 x 66 cm., 21¾ x 26 in.

97. *(above) Je revois en souvenir ma chère Udnie*
(I See Again in Memory My Dear Udnie), ca. 1914,
oil on canvas, 250 x 198.8 cm., 98½ x 78¼ in.

98. *C'est de moi qu'il s'agit* (*It's About Me*),
ca. 1914, oil on canvas,
199.7 x 199 cm., 78⅝ x 78⅜ in., prior to restoration

99. *Mariage comique* (*Comical Marriage*), 1914,
oil on canvas, 196.5 x 200 cm., 77⅜ x 78¾ in.,
prior to restoration

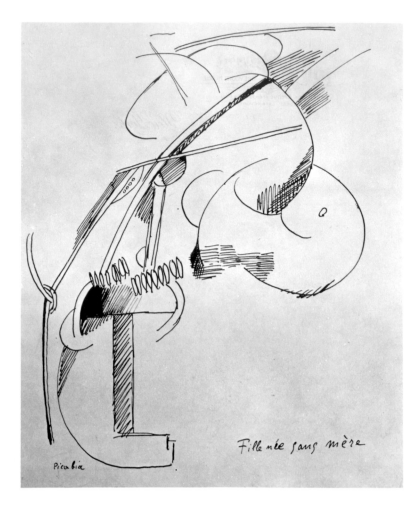

100. *Fille née sans mère*
(*Girl Born Without a Mother*),
ca. 1915, ink on paper,
26.7 x 21.6 cm., 10½ x 8½ in.

101. *Machine*, ca. 1915–1919,
ink and colored pencil on cardboard,
59 x 47.5 cm., 23¼ x 18¾ in.

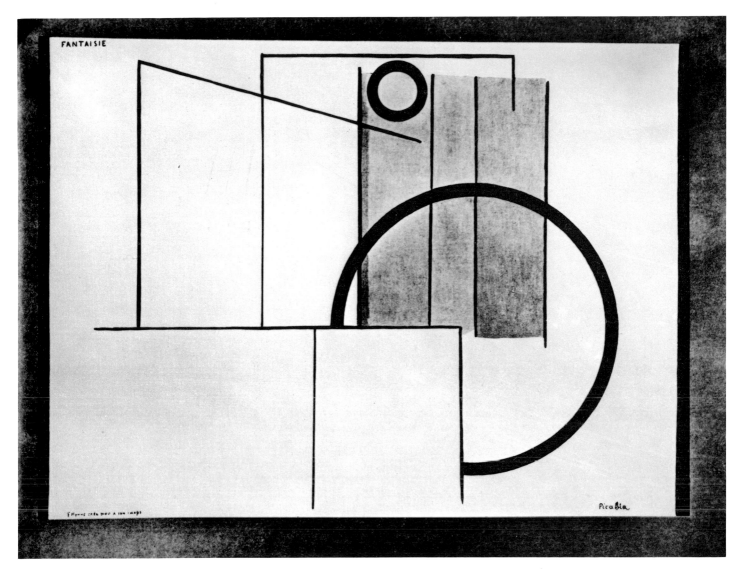

102. *Fantaisie (Fantasy)*, 1915, media, dimensions unknown

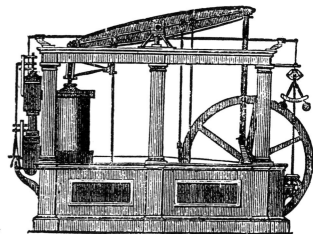

103. Illustration of a beam steam engine, mid-19th century

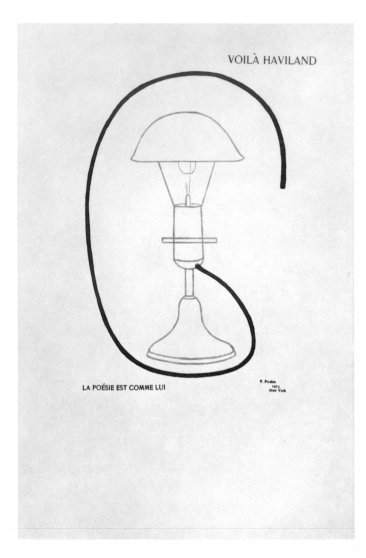

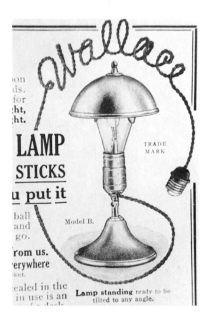

104. *Voilà Haviland* (*Here is Haviland*), 1915, ink on paper, dimensions unknown

105. Advertisement for the Wallace portable electric lamp (detail), 1915

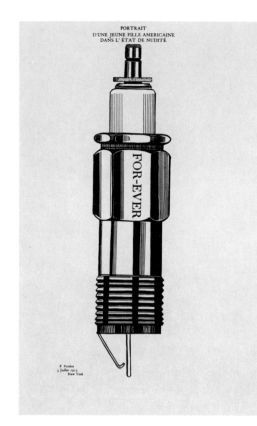

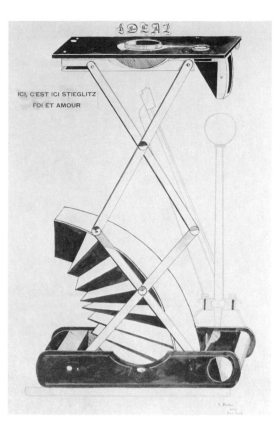

106. *Portrait d'une jeune fille américaine dans l'état de nudité*
(*Portrait of a Young American Girl in the State of Nudity*),
1915, ink on paper, dimensions unknown

107. *Ici, c'est ici Stieglitz*
(*Here, This Is Stieglitz*), 1915,
ink on paper, 75.9 x 50.8 cm., 29⅞ x 20 in.

108. *Le Saint des saints* (*The Saint of Saints*),
1915, ink on paper, dimensions unknown

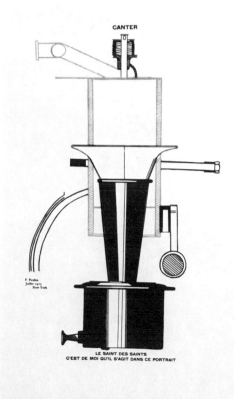

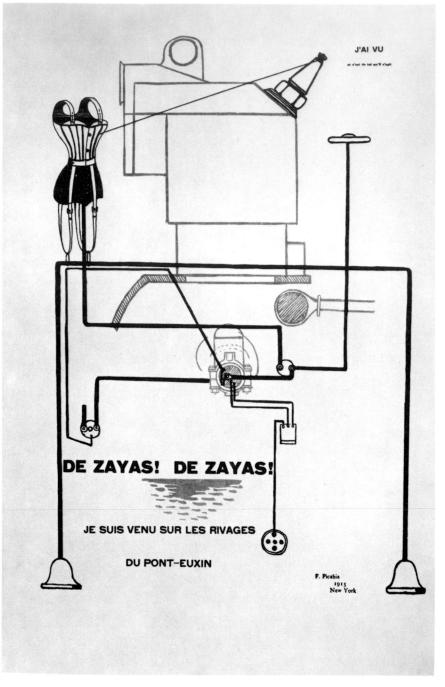

J'AI VU

DE ZAYAS! DE ZAYAS!

JE SUIS VENU SUR LES RIVAGES

DU PONT-EUXIN

F. Picabia
1915
New York

109. *De Zayas! De Zayas!*, 1915, ink on paper, dimensions unknown

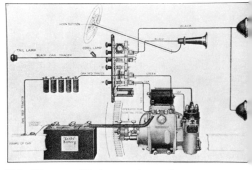

110. Diagram of Delco starting and lighting system, ca. 1915

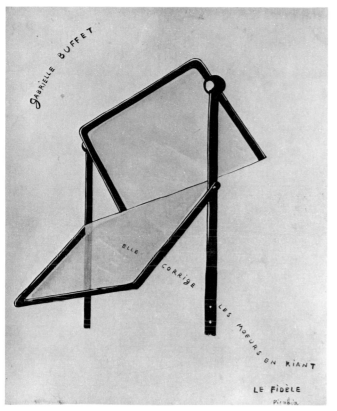

111. *Gabrielle Buffet. Elle corrige les moeurs en riant
(Gabrielle Buffet. She Corrects Manners Laughingly)*, 1915,
gouache and watercolor on cardboard, 58.5 x 47 cm., 23 x 18½ in.

112. *Portrait Max Jacob*, 1915,
ink on paper, dimensions unknown

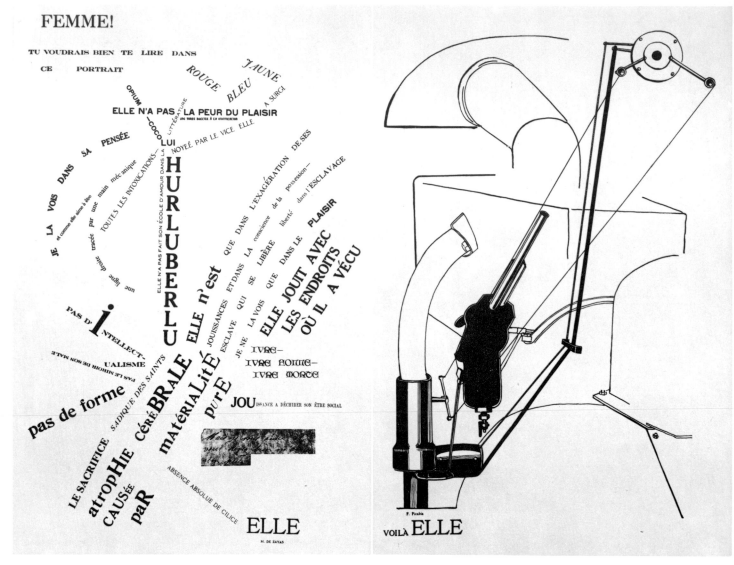

113. *Femme!* (*Woman!*), psychotype poem by Marius de Zayas, 1915, and Picabia's *Voilà elle* (*Here She Is*), 1915, ink on paper, dimensions unknown

Opposite:

114. Marcel Duchamp. *The Bride Stripped Bare by Her Bachelors, Even* (*The Large Glass*), 1915–1923, oil, lead wire, foil, dust and varnish on glass, 272 x 170 cm., 107 x 67 in.

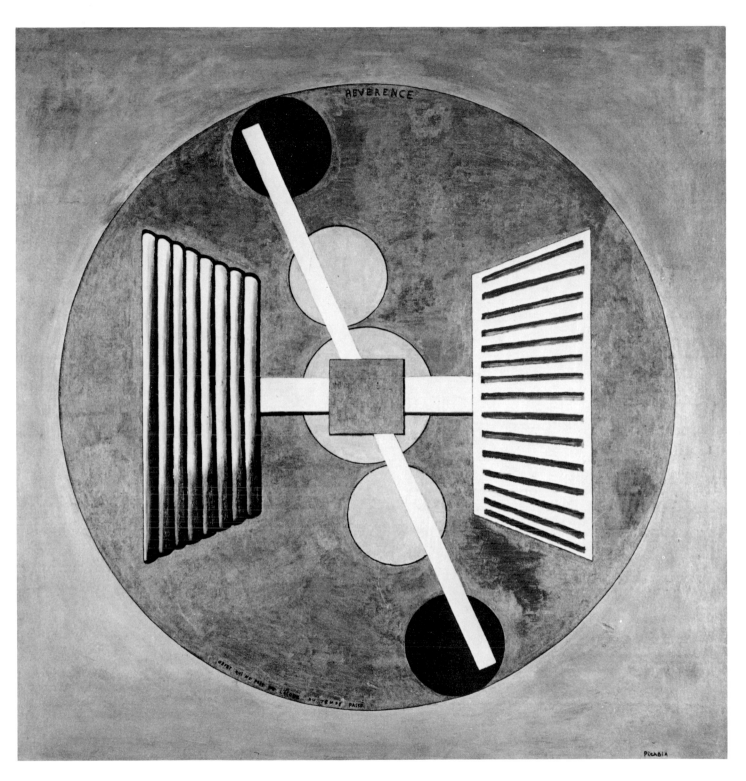

Opposite:

115. *Voilà la femme* (*Here is Woman*), 1915, watercolor,
oil and gouache on paper, 73 x 48.7 cm., 28¾ x 19¼ in.

Above:

116. *Révérence*, 1915, oil and metallic paint on cardboard,
99.7 x 99.7 cm., 39¼ x 39¼ in.

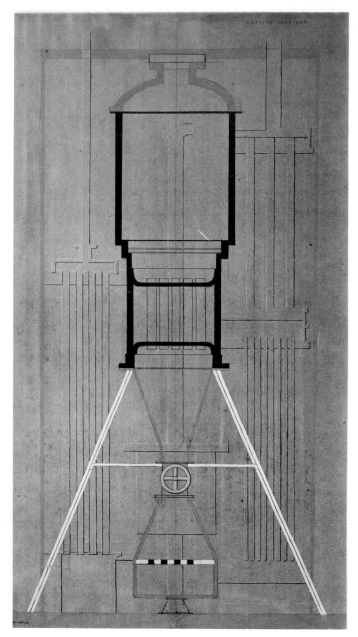

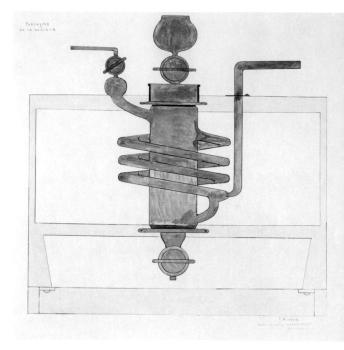

118. *Paroxyme de la douleur* (*Paroxysm of Sadness*), 1915,
oil and metallic paint on cardboard, 80 x 80 cm., 31½ x 31½ in.
Opposite:

117. *Machine sans nom* (*Machine Without Name*), 1915,
gouache and metallic paint on cardboard,
120.6 x 66 cm., 47½ x 26 in.

119. *Très rare tableau sur la terre*
(*Very Rare Painting on Earth*), 1915,
oil, wood and metallic paint
on composition board,
115 x 86.3 cm., 45½ x 34 in.

Chapter 6

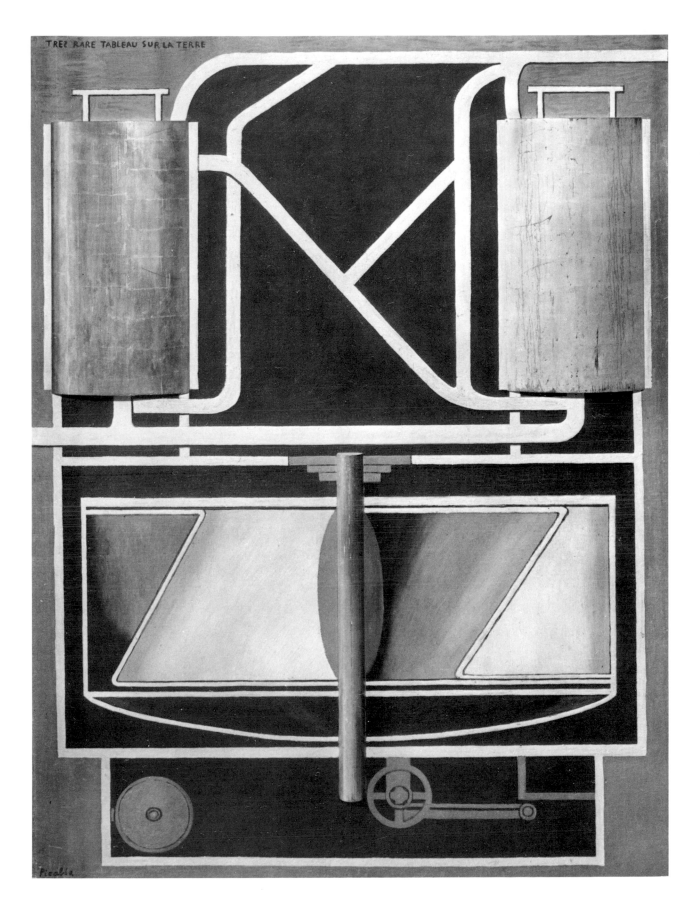

TREZ RARE TABLEAU SUR LA TERRE

Picabia

120. *Cette Chose est faite pour perpétuer mon souvenir* (*This Thing is Made to Perpetuate My Memory*), 1915,
oil and metallic paint on cardboard, 99 x 101.6 cm., 39 x 40 in.

Chapter 6

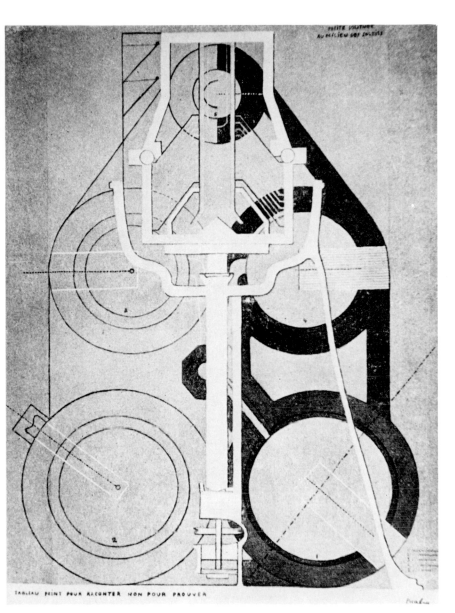

121. *Petite Solitude au milieu des soleils*
(*A Little Solitude in the Midst of Suns*),
1915, media, dimensions unknown

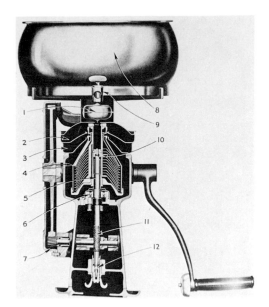

122. *(top)* Illustration for a
Deere separator, ca. 1927

123. *(center and bottom)* Illustration of a
Herschell-Spillman tractor engine,
exterior and cutaway views, ca. 1920

124. *Spanish Woman with Rose*, 1916,
watercolor and pencil on paper,
54 x 42.5 cm., 21¼ x 16¾ in. (sight)

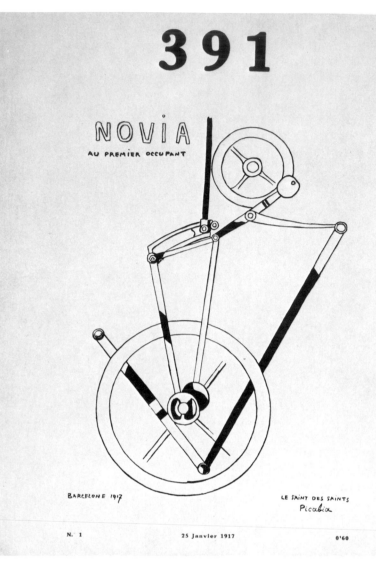

125. *Novia au premier occupant (Sweetheart of the First Occupant)*, 1917,
ink and metallized gouache, 37 x 26 cm., 14½ x 10¼ in.

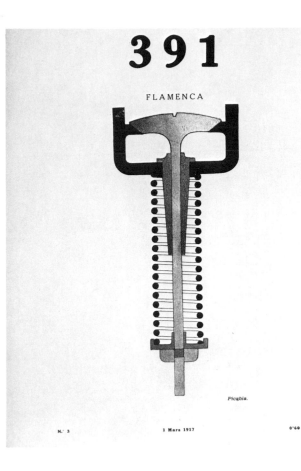

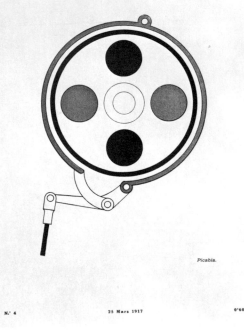

126. *Flamenca*, 1917, ink and metallized gouache,
37 x 26 cm., 14½ x 10¼ in.

127. *Roulette*, 1917, ink and gouache,
37 x 26 cm., 14½ x 10¼ in.

128. *Max Goth*, 1917, ink and photo collage,
dimensions unknown

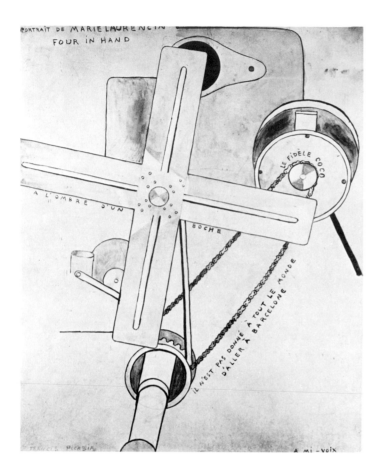

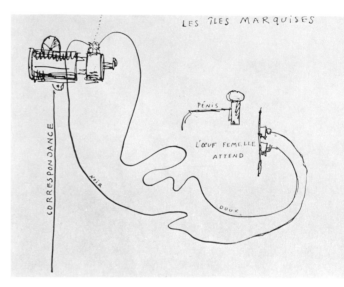

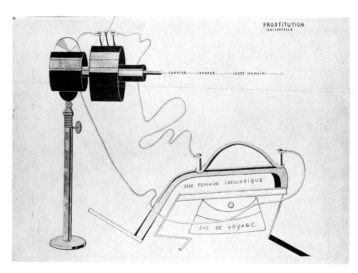

129. *Portrait de Marie Laurencin, Four in Hand*, ca. 1916–1917, ink and watercolor on cardboard, 56 x 45.5 cm., 22 x 17⅞ in.

130. *Les Iles Marquises* (*The Marquesas Islands*), ca. 1916–1917, ink on paper, 22 x 26.7 cm., 8⅝ x 10½ in.

131. *Prostitution universelle* (*Universal Prostitution*), ca. 1916–1917, ink, tempera and metallized gouache on cardboard, 74.5 x 94.3 cm., 29⅜ x 37⅛ in.

Chapter 7

132. *Parade amoureuse* (*Amorous Parade*), 1917, oil on canvas, 96.5 x 73.7 cm., 38 x 29 in.

133. *Fille née sans mère* (*Girl Born Without a Mother*), ca. 1916–1918, gouache and metallic paint on paper with a railway diagram, 50 x 65 cm., 19⅝ x 25½ in.

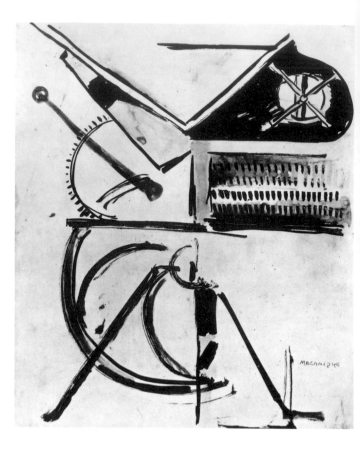

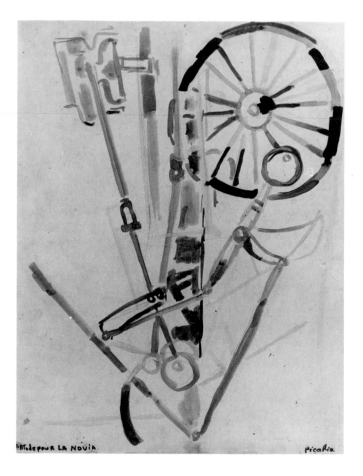

134. *(top left) Le Fiancé*, ca. 1916–1918, gouache, enamel paint and metallic paint on canvas, 25.4 x 32.3 cm., 10 x 12¾ in. (sight)

135. *(bottom left) Etude pour novia (Study for Sweetheart)*, ca. 1916–1917, watercolor on paper, 56.5 x 43.2 cm., 22¼ x 17 in.

136. *(above) Mécanique (Mechanical)*, ca. 1916–1918, ink and watercolor on cardboard, 56.5 x 46.7 cm., 22¼ x 18⅜ in. (sight)

Chapter 7

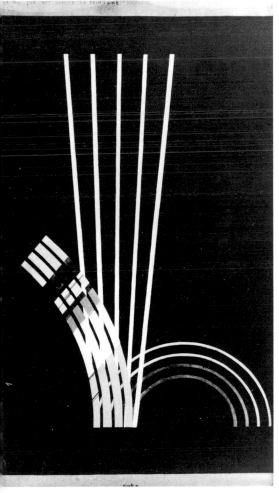

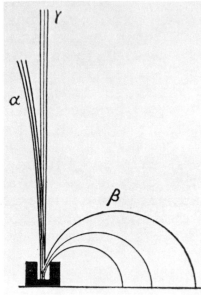

137. *(top left) Volant qui régularise le mouvement de la machine* (*Wheel Which Regulates the Movement of the Machine*), ca. 1916–1918, thinned oil on cardboard, 57 x 47 cm., 22½ x 18½ in.

138. *(top right) Novia (Sweetheart)*, ca. 1916–1917, thinned oil on cardboard, 117 x 89 cm., 45⅝ x 35 in.

139. *(bottom left) La Musique est comme la peinture* (*Music is like Painting*), ca. 1913–1917, watercolor, gouache on isorel, 122 x 66 cm., 48 x 26 in.

140. *(bottom right)* Illustration of the effect of a magnetic field on alpha, beta and gamma particles, ca. 1905

Chapter 7

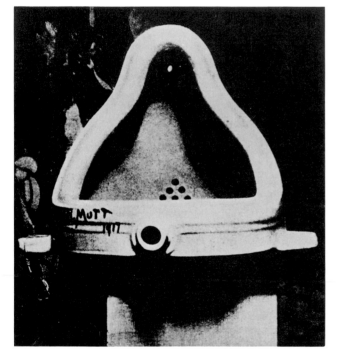

141. Marcel Duchamp. *Fountain*, 1917,
ready-made urinal in porcelain, turned on its back, about 24 in.

ÂNE

391

142. *Ane* (*Ass*, or *Donkey*), 1917, pastel or crayon on paper,
19 x 17 cm., 7½ x 6¾ in.

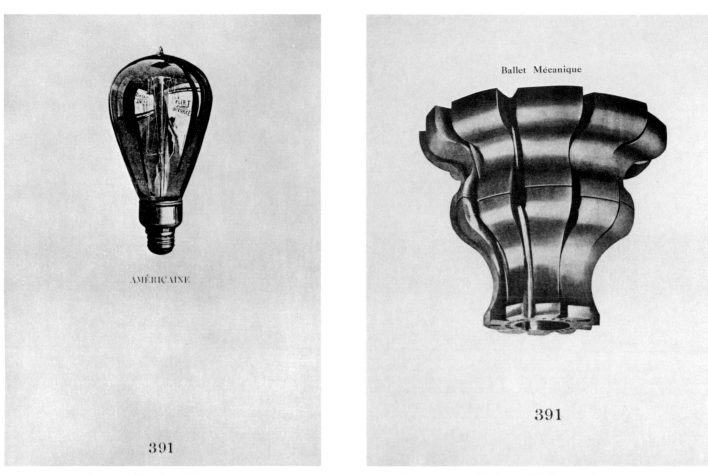

143. *Américaine* (*American* [female]), 1917,
photograph retouched in ink, 37 x 26 cm., 14½ x 10¼ in.

144. *Ballet mécanique* (*Mechanical Ballet*), 1917,
pencil or charcoal on paper, 37 x 26 cm., 14½ x 10¼ in.

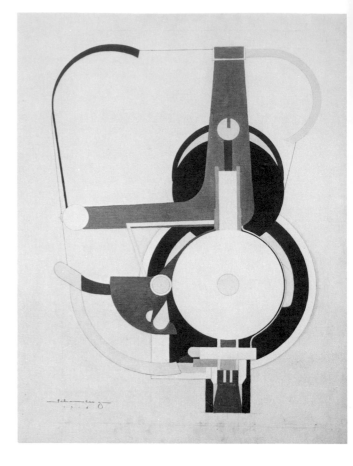

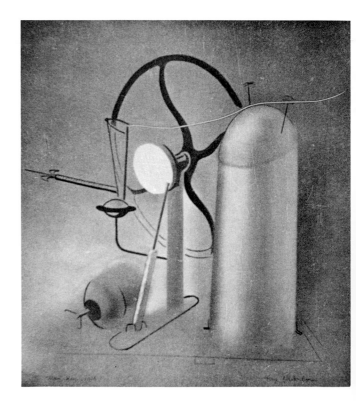

Opposite:

145. *(top left)* Charles Demuth. *Business*, 1921,
oil on canvas, 51 x 61.5 cm., 20 x 24¼ in.
146. *(top right)* Morton Schamberg. *Machine*, 1916,
oil on canvas, 76.5 x 58 cm., 30⅛ x 22⅞ in.
147. *(bottom left)* Man Ray. *The Impossibility*, or *Danger-Dancer*,
ca. 1917–1920, oil and other media on glass,
65.5 x 36 cm., 25¾ x 14⅛ in.
148. *(bottom right)* Man Ray. *My First Born*, 1919,
media and dimensions unknown

This page:

149. Jean Crotti. *The Mechanical Forces of Love in Movement*, 1916,
assemblage and oil on glass, 60 x 74 cm., 23⅝ x 29⅛ in.
150. *Esprit de jeune fille* (*Spirit of a Young Girl*), 1918, ink and
watercolor on composition board, 49 x 34.5 cm., 19¼ x 13½ in.
151. *Abstract Lausanne*, ca. 1918,
thinned oil or gouache on cardboard, 75 x 49 cm., 29½ x 19¼ in.

Chapter 8

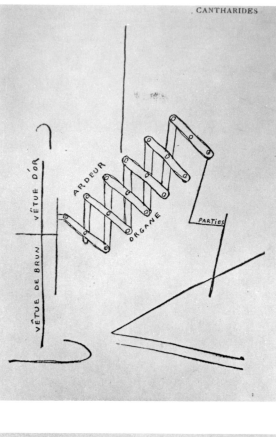

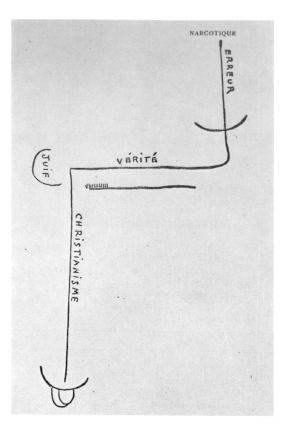

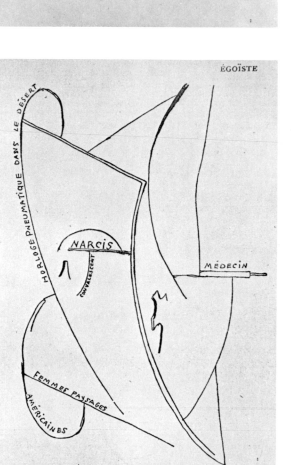

152. *Cantharides (Cantharis)*, 1918,
ink on paper, dimensions unknown

153. *Narcotique (Narcotic)*, 1918,
ink on paper, dimensions unknown

154. *Egoïste (Egoist)*, 1918,
ink on paper, dimensions unknown

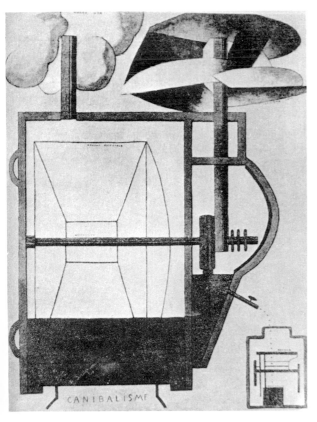

155. *(top left) Muscles brillants (Brilliant Muscles)*, ca. 1918,
media, dimensions unknown

156. *(bottom left) Cannibalisme*, ca. 1918, media, dimensions unknown

157. *(above) Voilà la fille née sans mère*
(*Here is the Girl Born Without a Mother*), ca. 1916–1918,
thinned oil on cardboard, 75 x 50 cm., 29½ x 20⅛ in.

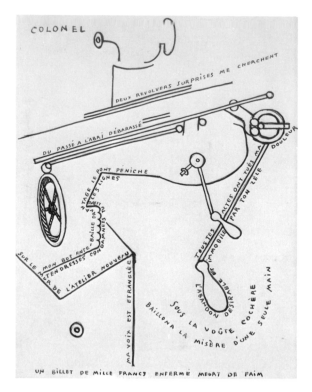

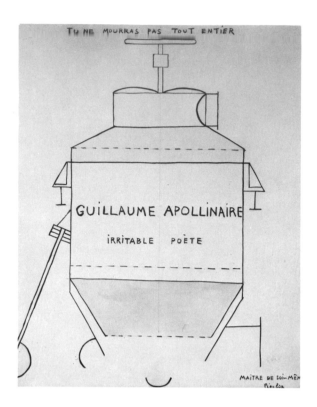

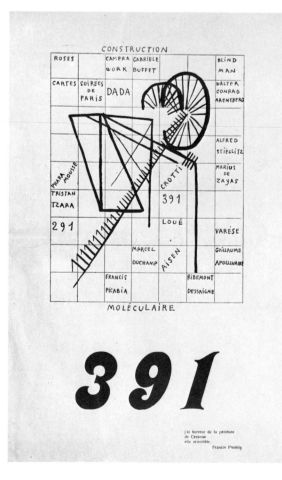

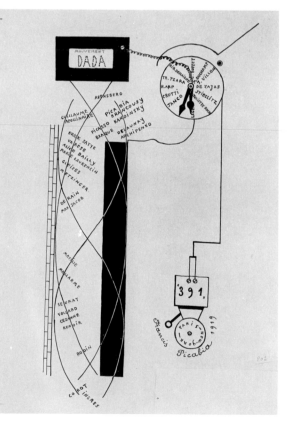

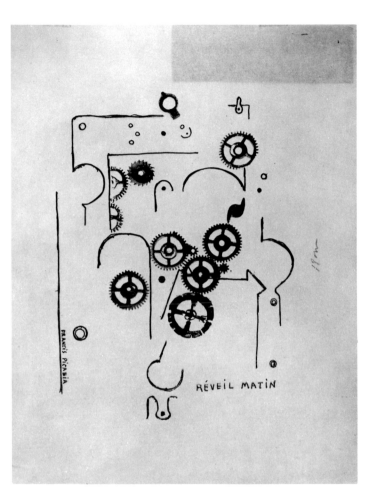

L.H.O.O.Q.

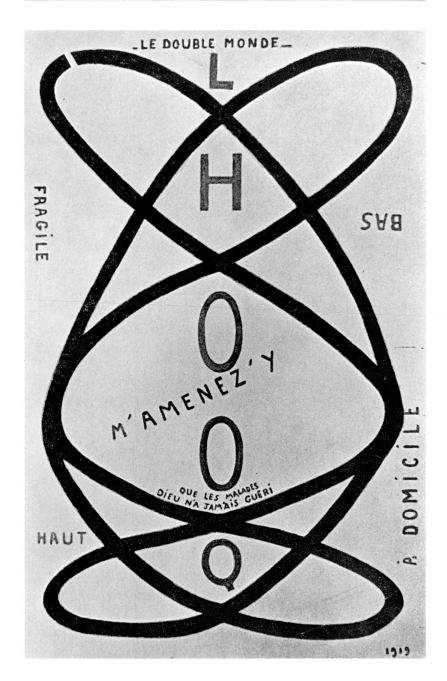

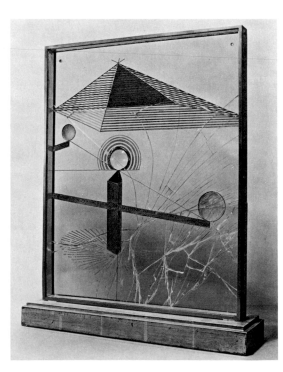

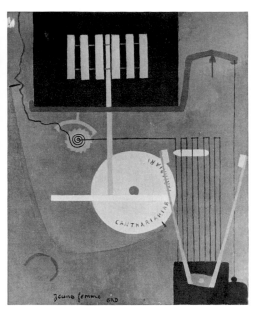

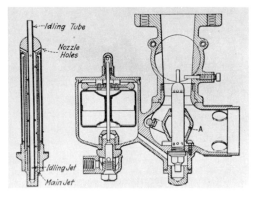

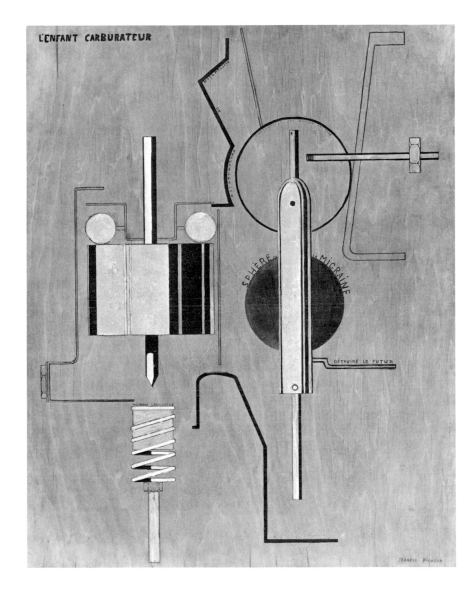

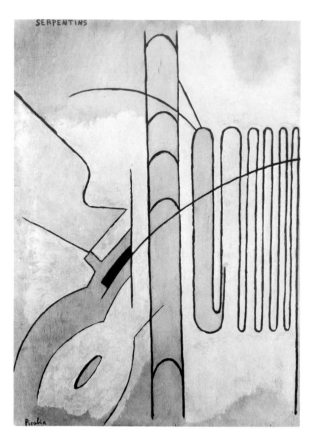

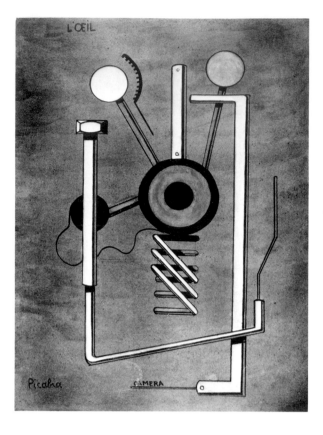

Chapter 9

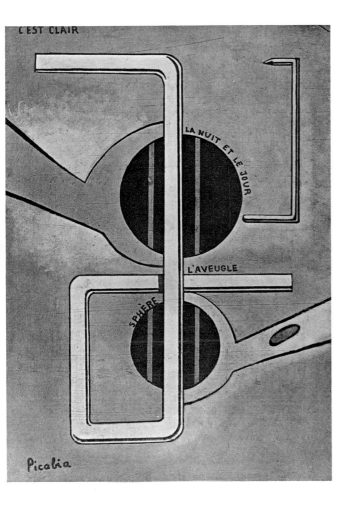

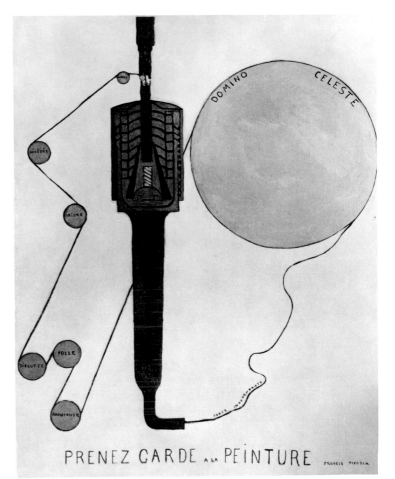

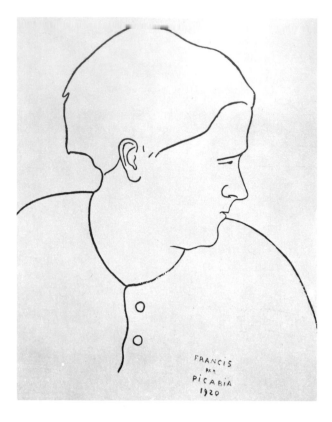

FRANCIS PICABIA

FRANCIS
PAR
PICABIA
1920

Francois Picabia
Paris 1920

RIBEMONT DESSAIGNES

FRANCIS PICABIA

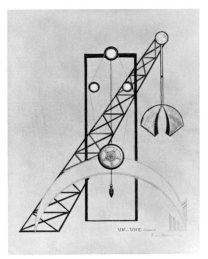

Opposite:

177. *Portrait of Tristan Tzara*, ca. 1920, ink on paper, 32 x 25 cm., 12⅝ x 9⅞ in.

178. *Francis*, 1920, ink on paper, dimensions unknown

179. *Portrait of André Breton*, 1920, ink on paper, dimensions unknown

180. *Ribemont Dessaignes*, 1920, ink on paper, dimensions unknown

This page:

181. *(top left)* Suzanne Duchamp-Crotti. *One and One Menaced*, 1916, watercolor, metallic paint and collage on paper?, dimensions unknown

182. *(above) La Sainte Vièrge (The Blessed Virgin)*, 1920, ink on paper, dimensions unknown

183. *(center left) Francis Picabia*, ca. 1920–1922, ink on paper, 32.5 x 25.5 cm, 12¾ x 10 in.

184. *(bottom left) Portrait de Cézanne, Portrait de Rembrandt, Portrait de Renoir, Natures mortes*, 1920, toy monkey and oil on cardboard?, dimensions unknown

Chapter 10

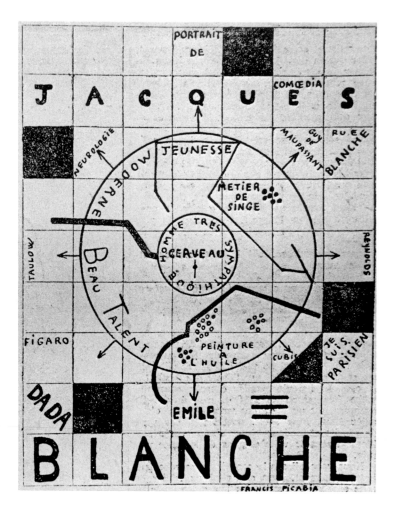

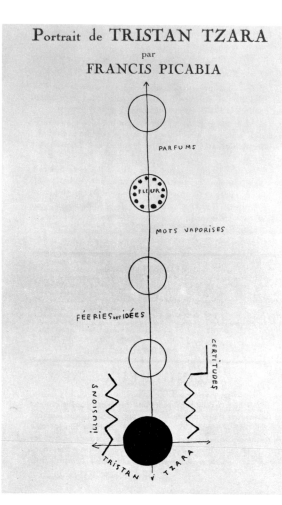

185. *Portrait de Jacques-Emile Blanche*, 1920,
ink on paper, dimensions unknown

186. *Portrait de Tristan Tzara*, ca. 1920,
ink on paper, dimensions unknown

Opposite:

187. *Far-niente beau parti (Beautiful Party of Blissful Ease)*,
1920, ink on paper, 59 x 32 cm., 23¼ x 12⅝ in.

188. *La Danseuse Jasmine (The Dancer Jasmine)*, 1920,
pencil on paper, 27.5 x 21.5 cm., 10¾ x 8½ in.

189. Study for *La Danseuse Jasmine*, 1920,
ink on cardboard, 27 x 21 cm., 10⅝ x 8¼ in.

190. *Le Rastaquouère*, ca. 1920,
oil or ripolin on canvas?, dimensions unknown

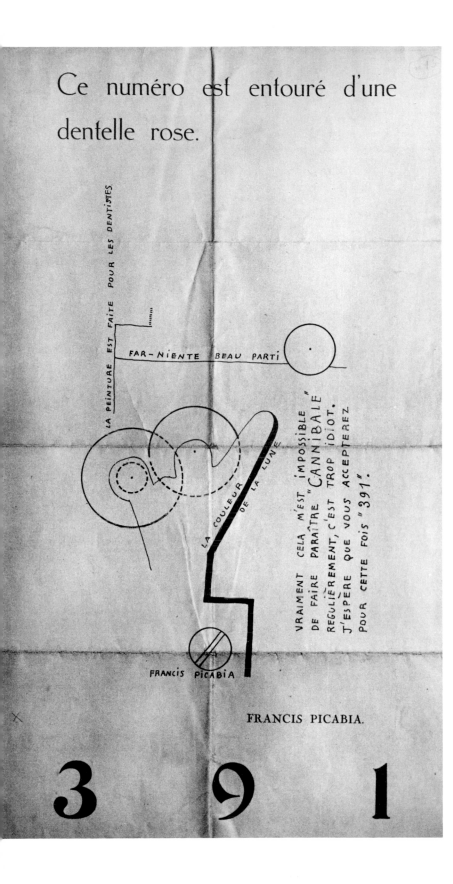

Ce numéro est entouré d'une dentelle rose.

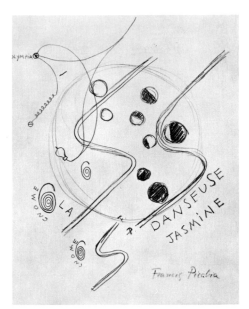

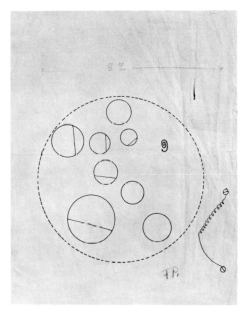

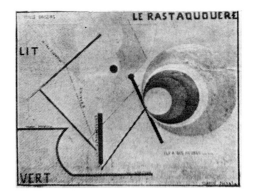

191. Cover, *391*, no. 14, Paris, November 1920, ink on paper, 59 x 32 cm., 23¼ x 12⅝ in.,
with two ready-mades: *Copy of an Ingres Letter by Francis Pacabia* and *Dada Drawing*.

192. Tristan Tzara, "A Night of Fat Chess," p. 4, *391*, no. 14, Paris, November 1920, ink on paper, 59 x 32 cm., 23¼ x 12⅝ in.

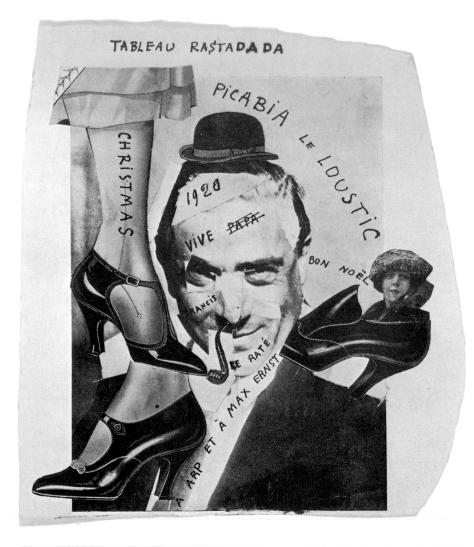

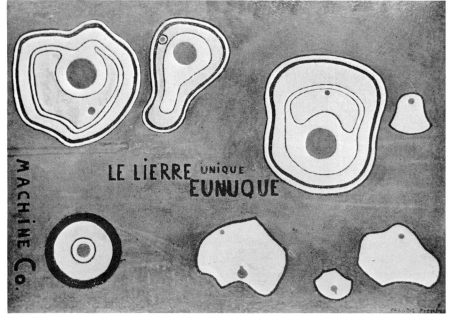

This page:

193. *Tableau rastadada (Rastadada Painting)*, 1920, collage, 19 x 17 cm., 7½ x 6⅝ in.

194. *Le Lierre unique eunuque*
(The Unique Eunuch Ivy), ca. 1920, ripolin on cardboard, 75 x 105 cm., 29½ x 41⅜ in.

Opposite:

195. Max Ernst. *Stratified Rocks, nature's gift of gneiss lava iceland moss 2 kinds of lungwort 2 kinds of ruptures of the prerineam growths of the heart (b) the same thing in a well-polished box somewhat more expensive*, 1920, anatomical engraving on paper altered with gouache and pencil, 15.2 x 20.6 cm., 6 x 8⅛ in.

196. Max Ernst. *Oedipus Rex*, 1922, oil on canvas, 89 x 116 cm., 35 x 45¾ in.

197. *Les Yeux chauds (Hot Eyes)*, 1921, ripolin? on canvas, 198 x 158 cm., 78 x 62¼ in. (sight)

198. Diagram for the governor of an airplane turbine, ca. 1921

Chapter 11

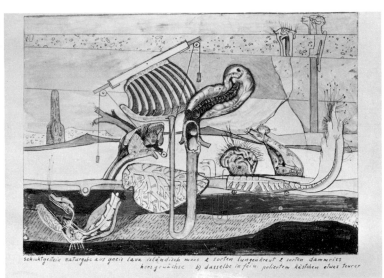

schichtgestein naturgabe aus gneis lava isländisch moos & sorten lungenkraut & sorten dammeriss
hergewächse b) dasselbe in fein poliertem kästchen etwas teurer

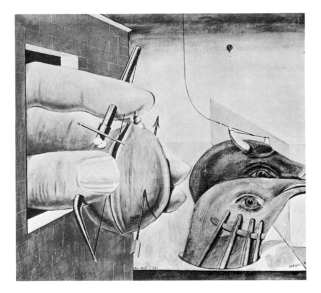

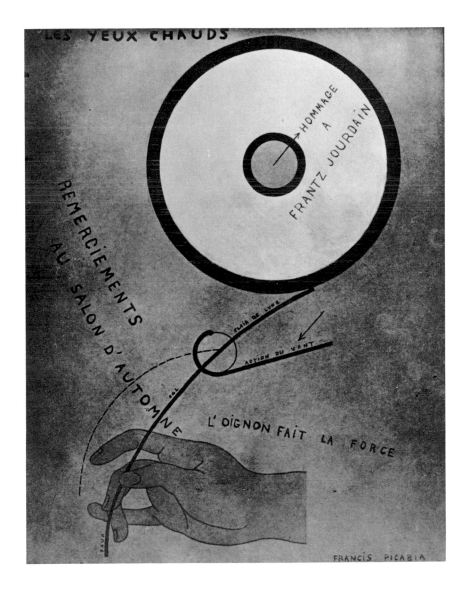

FRANCIS PICABIA

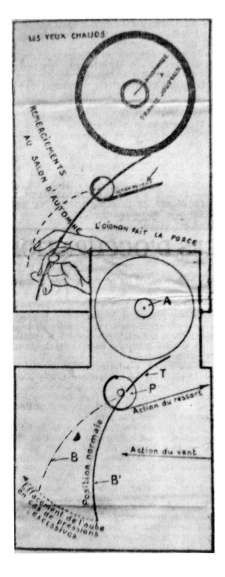

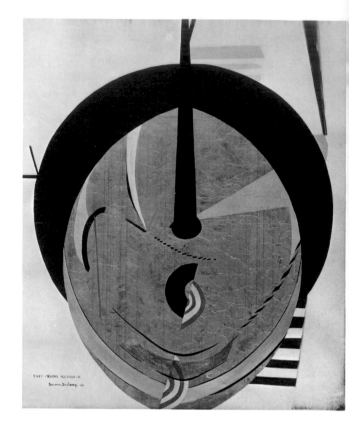

199. Jean Crotti. *Chainless Mystery*, 1921,
oil on canvas?, 116 x 89 cm., 45⅝ x 35 in.

200. Suzanne Duchamp. *Masterpiece: Accordion*, 1921, oil, gouache
and silver leaf on canvas, 100 x 81 cm., 39⅜ x 31⅞ in.

201. Man Ray. *Transatlantic*, ca. 1921, photograph and collage,
37 x 24.8 cm., 14½ x 9¾ in.

Opposite:

202. *La Veuve joyeuse (The Merry Widow)*, 1921,
oil, paper and photograph on canvas, 92 x 73 cm., 36¼ x 28¾ in.

203. *Chapeau de paille? (Straw Hat?)*, 1921,
oil, cord and paper on canvas, 92 x 73 cm., 36¼ x 28¾ in.

204. *Danse de Saint-Guy*, ca. 1919–1921,
ink, cord and cardboard in an open frame, exact original
dimensions unknown, presently reformed, as in fig. 205

205. *Tabac-Rat (Rat Tobacco)*, ca. 1919–1921 and ca. 1948–1949,
ink, cord and cardboard in open frame,
91 x 70 cm., 35⅞ x 27½ in.

Chapter 12

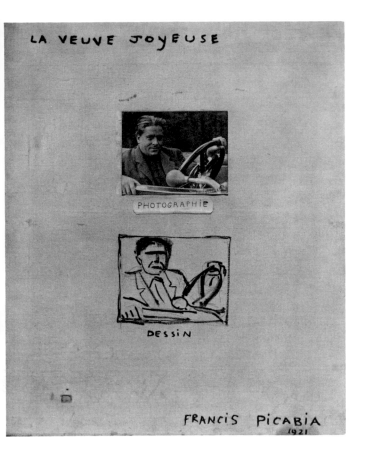

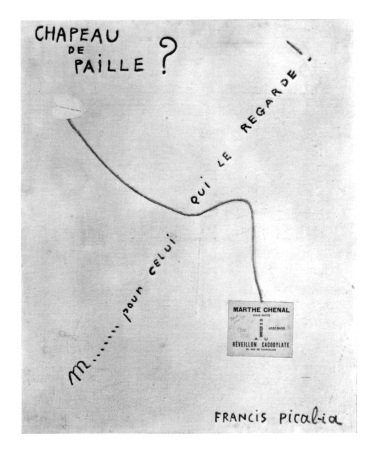

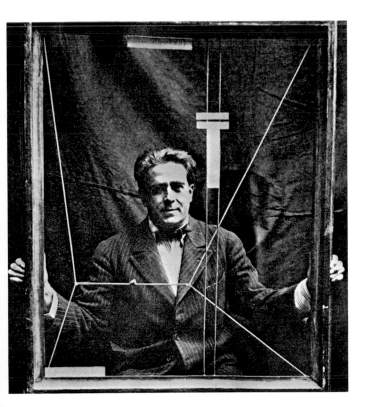

206. Jean Crotti. *Explicative*, 1921,
oil and paper on canvas?, 92 x 73 cm., 36¼ x 28¾ in.

207. Man Ray. *Boardwalk*, 1917,
oil and collage on wood, 64.8 x 71 cm., 25½ x 28 in.

208. Pablo Picasso. *Mother and Child*, 1921,
oil on canvas, 143.6 x 162.6 cm., 56½ x 64 in.

209. *La Feuille de vigne* (*Fig Leaf*), 1922,
ripolin on canvas, 198 x 158 cm.,
78 x 62¼ in. (sight)

210. *La Nuit espagnole* (*Spanish Night*), 1922,
ripolin on canvas, 160 x 130 cm., 63 x 51 in.

211. *Le Jardin (Garden)*, ca. 1921–1924, ripolin on canvas, 81 x 100 cm., 31⅞ x 39⅜ in.

212. *Sphinx*, ca. 1922, ink, gouache and watercolor on paper, 75 x 55 cm., 29½ x 21⅝ in.

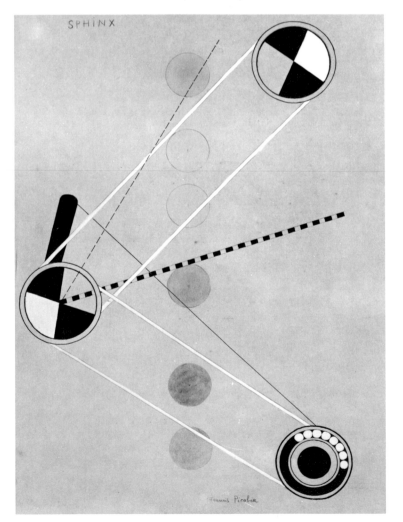

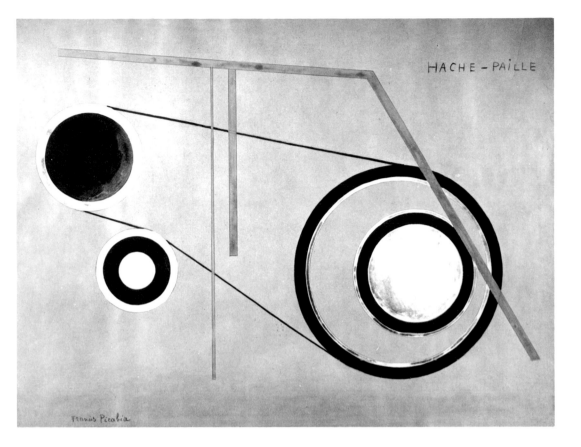

213. *Hache-paille*
(*Chaff-cutter*), ca. 1922,
watercolor and gouache
on paper, dimensions unknown

214. *Totalisateur (Totalizer)*,
ca. 1922, ink and
watercolor on paper,
55 x 75 cm., 21⅝ x 29½ in.

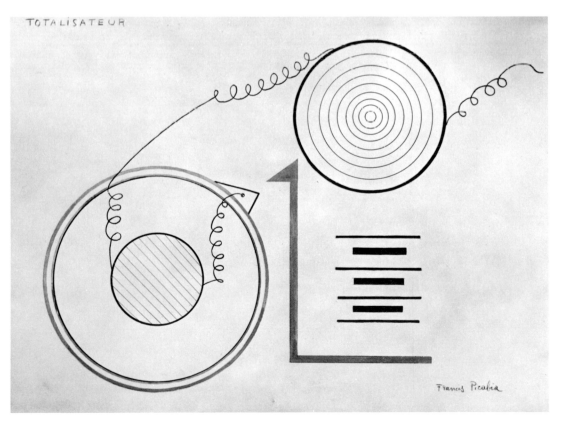

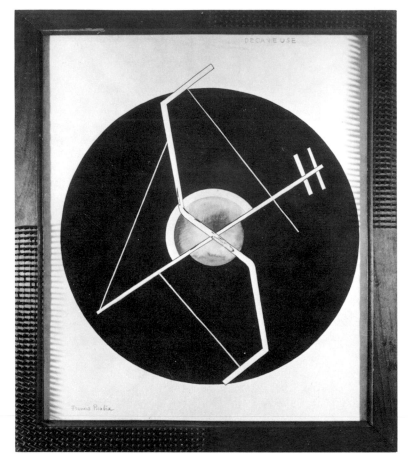

215. *Décaveuse (Digger)*, ca. 1922,
ink and watercolor on paper,
72.5 x 59.5 cm., 28½ x 23½ in.

216. *Novia (Sweetheart)*, ca. 1919–1922,
gouache on cardboard,
76 x 48.2 cm., 30 x 19 in.

Chapter 13

217. *Tickets*, ca. 1922,
ink and watercolor on paper,
75 x 56 cm., 29½ x 22 in.

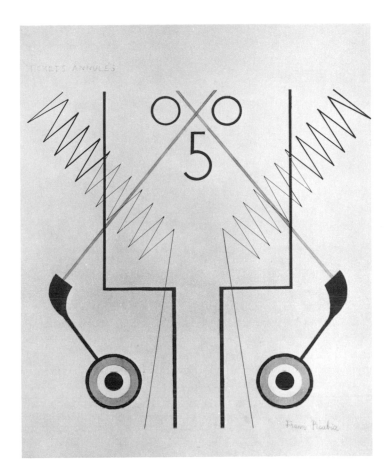

218. *Tickets annulés (Cancelled Tickets)*, ca. 1922,
ink and watercolor on paper,
71 x 58 cm., 28 x 22⅞ in. (sight)

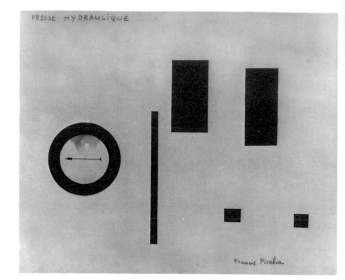

219. *Fixe*, ca. 1922, tempera and collage
on cardboard, 60 x 72 cm., 23⅝ x 28⅜ in.

220. *Radio Concerts*, ca. 1922, ink and watercolor on composition board,
72 x 59 cm., 28⅜ x 23¼ in. (sight)

221. *Presse hydraulique (Hydraulic Press)*, ca. 1922, ink and waterc[o]
on composition board, 59 x 72 cm., 23¼ x 28⅜ in. (sight)

222. Kasimir Malevich. *Supremus No. 50*, 1915,
oil on canvas, 97 x 66 cm., 38⅜ x 26 in.

Chapter 13

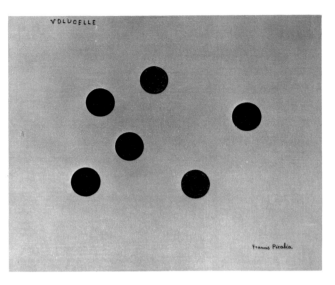

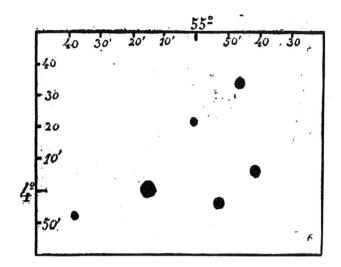

223. *Volucelle* I, ca. 1922, gouache on paper, 60 x 73 cm., 23⅝ x 28¾ in.

225. *Astrolabe*, ca. 1922, ink and watercolor on cardboard, 73 x 55 cm., 28¾ x 21⅝ in.

224. Diagram of the Pleiades of Hevelius, 1660

226. *Uranus Weighing the World System* (detail), 1651, engraving

Chapter 13

227. *Optophone* I, ca. 1922, ink and watercolor
on composition board, 72 x 60 cm., 28⅜ x 23⅝ in.

228. *Lampe cristal* (*Crystal Lamp*), ca. 1922,
watercolor on paper, 60 x 73 cm., 23⅝ x 28¾ in.

229. *Optophone* II, ca. 1922–1923, oil on canvas,
116.5 x 89 cm., 45⅝ x 35 in.

Chapter 13

230. Newton's rings

231. *Abstract Composition with Optical Patterns and Ink Spots*, ca. 1922,
ink, watercolor and collage on paper, 57 x 63 cm., 22½ x 24¾ in.

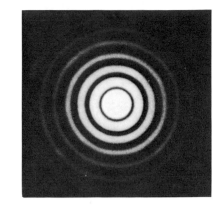

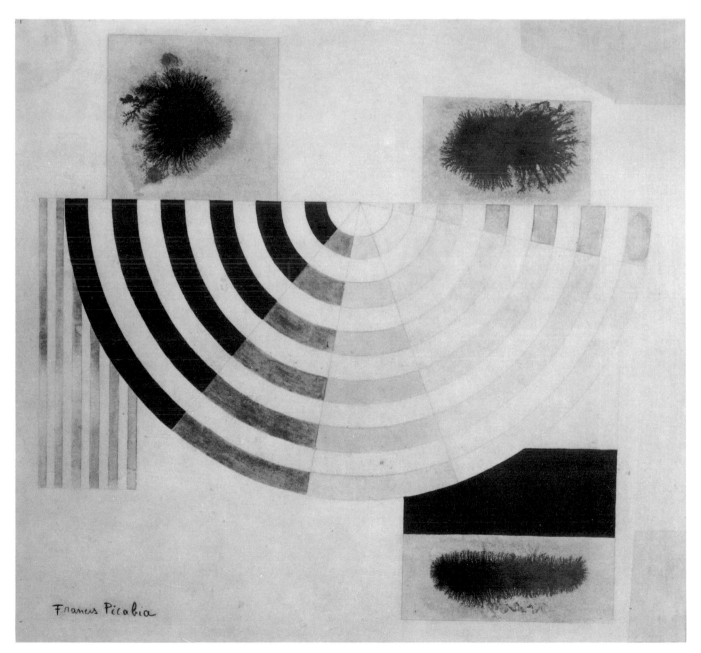

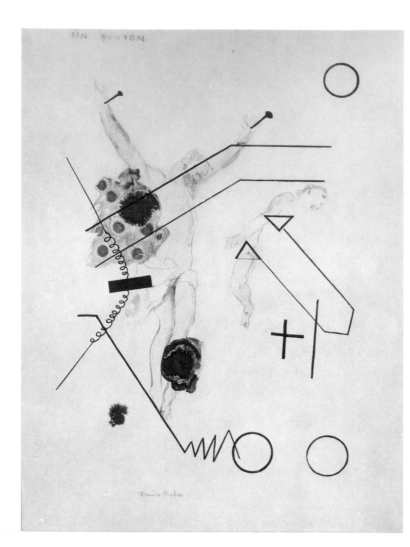

232. *(top left) Un Bouton (A Button)*, ca. 1922, ink, pencil and watercolor on paper, 62 x 47 cm., 24½ x 18½ in.

233. *(above) Chariot*, ca. 1922, watercolor on paper, 60 x 70 cm., 23⅝ x 27⅝ in.

234. *(bottom left) Volucelle* II, ca. 1922, ripolin on canvas, 198.5 x 250 cm., 78 x 98 in.

Opposite:

235. *(top left)* Diffraction fringes from a straight edge

236. *(bottom) Conversation* I, ca. 1922, watercolor on paper, 60 x 72 cm., 23⅝ x 28⅜ in.

237. *(top right) The Hercules of Hevelius*, 1660, engraving

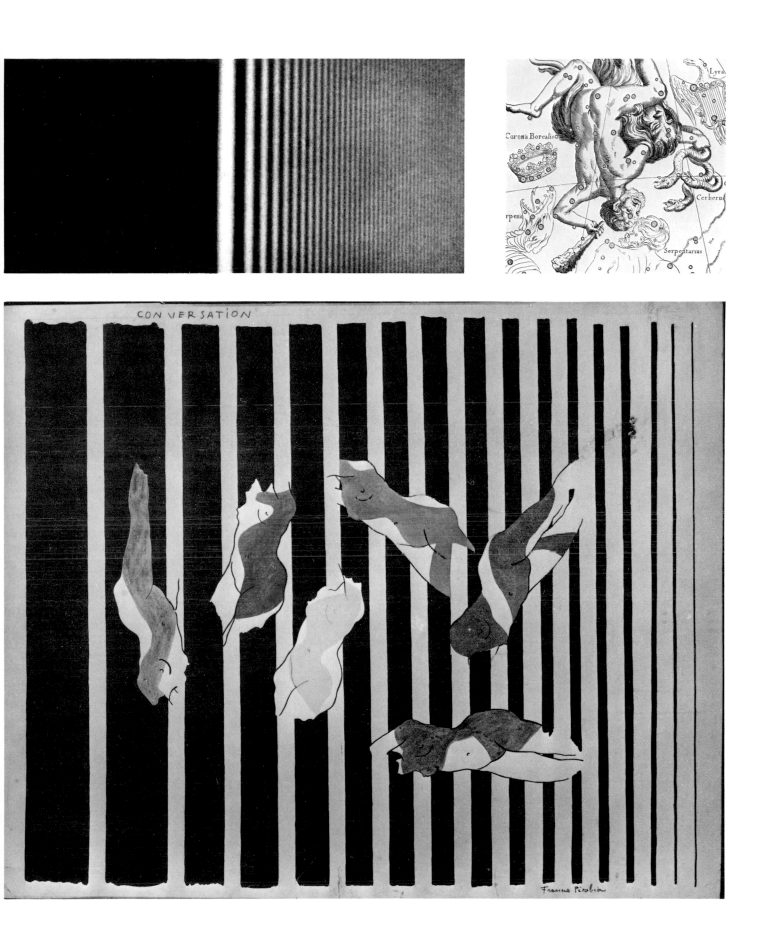

PiCABiA
PAR
FRANCiS
1922

Opposite:

238. *Espagnole*, ca. 1922–1923, ink on paper, dimensions unknown

239. *Portrait of Mlle Yvonne Picabia*, ca. 1922–1923, ink on paper, dimensions unknown

240. *Portrait of Mme Pomaret*, ca. 1922–1923,
ink, watercolor and pencil on paper, 55 x 37 cm., 21⅝ x 14½ in.

241. *Portrait of Simone Breton*, 1922,
ink and watercolor on paper, 53.5 x 40.5 cm., 21⅛ x 16 in.

This page:

242. *Picabia par Francis*, 1922, ink on paper, dimensions unknown

243. *Floating Figures*, ca. 1923, ink on paper, 23 x 18 cm., 9 x 7 in.

244. *Dresseur d'animaux (Animal Trainer)*, 1923,
ripolin on canvas, 250 x 200 cm., 98½ x 78¾ in.

FRANCiS PiCABiA

FRANCIS PICABIA

Chapter 14

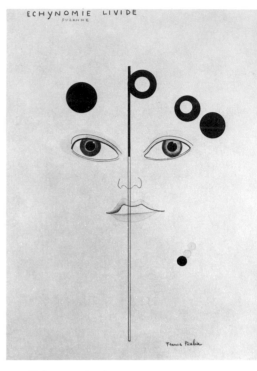

246. *Echynomie livide*, ca. 1922–1923,
watercolor and ink on paper,
63 x 48.5 cm., 24¾ x 19 in.

245. *Lampe*, ca. 1923, pencil, watercolor and gouache on paper,
62.5 x 47 cm., 24½ x 18½ in.;
frame by Pierre Legrain in wood, fabric, aluminum paper and glass tubes,
82.5 x 69.5 cm., 32½ x 27⅜ in.

247. *Breton and Initiate at the Cup of Rimbaud*, 1924,
ink on paper, dimensions unknown

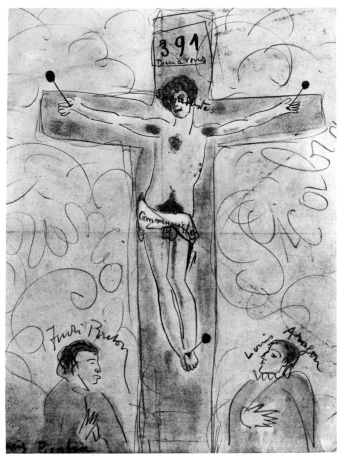

248. *Surrealism Crucified*, ca. 1924,
pencil and watercolor on paper, 31.8 x 25.2 cm., 12½ x 10 in.

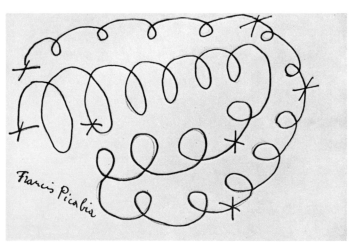

249. Drawing for Tzara's *Sept Manifestes Dada*, ca. 1924,
ink on paper, 16 x 24 cm., 6¼ x 9½ in.

250. Drawing for Tzara's *Sept Manifestes Dada*, ca. 1924,
ink on paper, 16 x 24 cm., 6¼ x 9½ in.

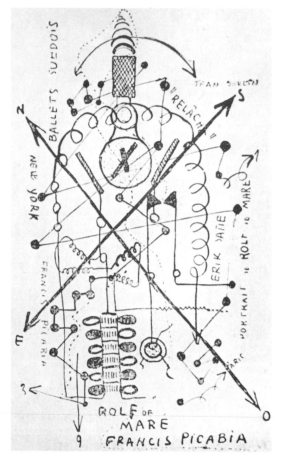

251. *Rolf de Maré*, 1924, ink on paper,
dimensions unknown

252. Page from the program of *Relâche* with statement and drawings by Picabia,
dimensions of original drawings unknown

Opposite:

253. Page from the program of *Relâche* with Picabia's *Portrait of Erik Satie*, 1924,
original drawing, ink on paper, 23 x 15 cm., 9 x 5⅞ in.

254. *Landscape*, ca. 1923–1924,
oil or ripolin on canvas,
73 x 92 cm., 28¾ x 36¼ in.

255. *Les Rochers à St.-Honorat (Rocks at St.-Honorat)*,
ca. 1924–1925, ripolin on canvas, 89.5 x 117 cm., 35¼ x 46 in.

256. *Les Amoureux* (*The Lovers*), ca. 1924–1925,
ripolin on canvas,
116 x 115 cm., 45¾ x 45¼ in.
257. *Femme à l'ombrelle* (*Woman with Parasol*), ca. 1924–1925,
ripolin on canvas, 92 x 73 cm., 36¼ x 28¾ in.
258. *Flirt*, ca. 1924–1925, ripolin, toothpicks,
straws, staples and lead wire on canvas,
92 x 73 cm., 36¼ x 28¾ in.

259. *(top left)* La Lecture *(Reading)*, ca. 1924–1925,
ripolin and drinking straws on canvas, 81 x 66 cm., 31⅞ x 26 in.

260. *(above)* Pailles et cure-dents *(Straws and Toothpicks)*, ca. 1924, oil,
cord, string, sticks and quill toothpicks on canvas, 80 x 45 cm., 31½ x 17¾ in.;
frame by Pierre Legrain in wood, aluminum paint and buttons,
92 x 73 cm., 36¼ x 28¾ in.

261. *(bottom left)* Matchwoman *I, 1920? (ca. 1923–1924)*, oil, matches, hairpins,
haircurlers, string and coins on canvas, 92 x 73 cm., 36¼ x 28¾ in.

Opposite:

262. *(top left)* Plumes, ca. 1923–1925, ripolin, feathers,
macaroni, cane and corn plasters on canvas,
92 x 70 cm., 36¼ x 27½ in. (sight);
frame in wood, 119 x 78.5 cm., 46⅞ x 30⅞ in.

263. *(bottom)* Midi, ca. 1923–1926, ripolin, feathers, macaroni
and leather on canvas, 55 x 99.7 cm., 21¾ x 39¼ in.;
frame by Pierre Legrain in snakeskin

264. *(top right)* Retour des barques *(Return of the Boats)*, ca. 1923–1927,
ripolin, shoe soles and stretcher wedges on canvas, dimensions unknown

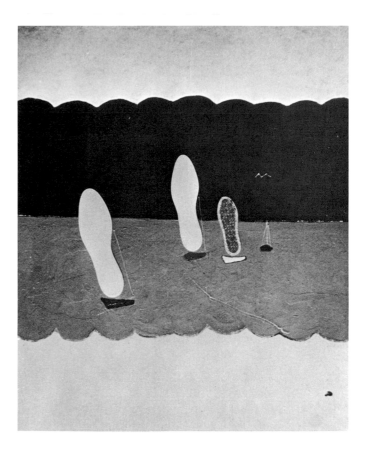

266. *Portrait (of Poincaré?)*, ca. 1924–1926, ripolin, combs, cord,
curtain rings, centimeter tape, toothpicks, pen points and erasers on canvas,
92 x 73 cm., 36¼ x 28¾ in.;
frame by Pierre Legrain in sandpaper and cardboard (missing)

265. *Vase of Flowers*, ca. 1924–1926, ripolin, straws, string
and lead wire on canvas, 61 x 50 cm., 24 x 19⅝ in.

267. *Le Beau Charcutier (The Beautiful Pork Butcher)*,
ca. 1924–1926 and ca. 1930–1935, ripolin, combs
and remnants of other materials on canvas,
92 x 73 cm., 36¼ x 28¾ in.

Chapter 15

268. *Pot of Flowers*, ca. 1924–1926, ripolin, paint-can lids, brushes, stretcher wedges, cord and pen points on canvas, 64 x 55 cm., 25⅛ x 21⅝ in.

269. *Centimeters*, ca. 1924–1925, oil, centimeter tape, matches and matchbox covers on canvas, 56 x 39 cm., 22 x 15⅜ in.

270. Program for "Gala du souvenir" at Les Ambassadeurs, Cannes casino (detail), 1927, dimensions of original drawing unknown

271. *La Gitane (Gypsy)*, ca. 1926, watercolor on paper, dimensions unknown

272. *L'Ambition*, ca. 1926, watercolor on paper, dimensions unknown

Chapter 15

273. *Les Trois Grâces* (*The Three Graces*), ca. 1924–1927,
oil on cardboard, 105 x 75 cm., 41⅜ x 29½ in.

274. Peter Paul Rubens. *The Three Graces*,
ca. 1639, oil on wood, 221 x 181 cm., 87 x 71¼ in.

275. *Idyll*, ca. 1924–1927, oil on wood, 105 x 75 cm., 41⅜ x 29½ in.

276. *Four-footed Sibyl*, ca. 1924–1927, gouache and thinned oil? on cardboard, 105 x 75 cm., 41⅜ x 29½ in.

277. Michelangelo. *The Libyan Sibyl*, 1511, fresco, Sistine Chapel, Vatican, Rome.

Chapter 15

278. *Venus and Adonis*, ca. 1924–1927,
gouache on paper, 104 x 67 cm., 41 x 26⅜ in.

279. Titian. *Venus and Adonis*, ca. 1553,
oil on canvas, 186 x 207 cm., 73⅛ x 81¾ in.

280. *Idyll*, ca. 1924–1927, gouache on
composition board, 75 x 105 cm., 29½ x 41⅜ in.

281. *Venus*, ca. 1924–1927, gouache on cardboard, 105 x 75 cm., 41⅜ x 29½ in.

282. *Woman with Monocle*, ca. 1924–1927, oil on cardboard, 105 x 75 cm., 41⅜ x 29½ in.

283. *Cyclop*, ca. 1924–1927, oil on cardboard,
105 x 75 cm., 41⅜ x 29½ in.

284. Picasso. *Seated Woman*, ca. 1925–1926,
oil on canvas, 130 x 97 cm., 51⅛ x 38⅛ in.

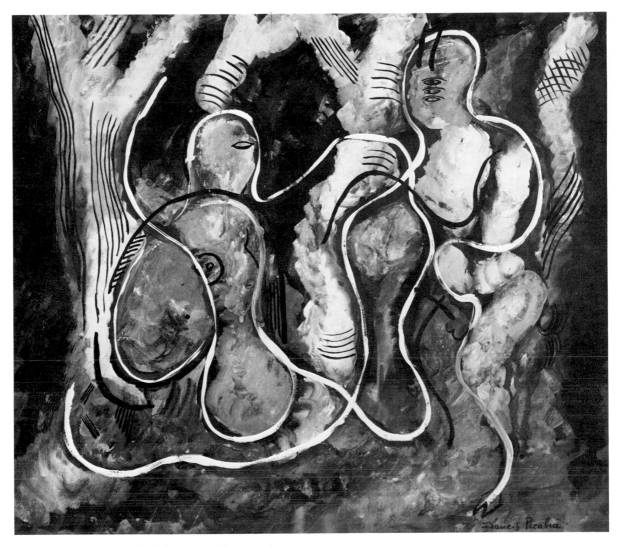

285. *Blue Phantoms*, ca. 1924–1927, gouache on cardboard,
46 x 55 cm., 18⅛ x 21¾ in. (sight)

286. *Phébus* (*Phoebus*), ca. 1927, gouache and oil on wood,
106 x 85 cm., 41¾ x 33½ in.

287. *Lazarus and the Lamb*, ca. 1927, media, dimensions unknown

288. Anonymous Spaniard. *Lazarus*, 12th century, fresco from the apse wall, San Clemente de Tahull

289. Anonymous Spaniard. *Apocalyptic Lamb*, 12th century, fresco from San Clemente de Tahull

290. *Barcelona*, 1924 and ca. 1927?, oil on cardboard, 94 x 75 cm., 41 x 29½ in.

291. *Torreador*, ca. 1927–1928, watercolor on paper, 75 x 55 cm., 29½ x 21½ in.

292. *Female Head and Romanesque Visage of Christ*, ca. 1927–1928, pencil and watercolor on paper, dimensions unknown

Chapter 15

293. *Totó*, ca. 1927,
ink and watercolor on paper,
dimensions unknown

294. *Bullfight*, ca. 1925–1927,
oil and gouache on wood,
75 x 105 cm., 29½ x 41⅜ in.

295. *Machaon*, ca. 1926–1927,
watercolor and ink on paper,
25 x 32 cm., 9⅞ x 12⅝ in.

296. *Butterflies*, ca. 1926–1928,
watercolor and pencil on paper,
38.5 x 33 cm., 15⅛ x 13 in.;
deep frame with 8 mounted butterflies,
55 x 49.5 cm., 21⅝ x 19½ in.

Chapter 15

297. *Two Heads in Biomorphic Form*, ca. 1926–1928,
ink on paper, 30.3 x 23 cm., 12 x 9 in.

298. *La Harpe de Georges (Harp of [St.] George)*,
ca, 1926–1928, watercolor on paper,
65 x 50 cm., 25⅝ x 19¾ in.

299. *Bucolic*, ca. 1924–1928, watercolor and
ink on paper, dimensions unknown

300. *Hôtel ancien (Old Hotel)*, ca. 1927, gouache on paper, 49.5 x 53.3 cm., 19½ x 21 in.

301. *Chiromis*, ca. 1927, media, dimensions unknown

302. Albrecht Dürer. *Nemesis*, ca. 1501–1502, engraving, 32.9 x 22.4 cm., 13 x 8¾ in.

Chapter 15

303. *Jeune Fille au paradis*
(*Young Girl in Paradise*),
ca. 1927–1928, watercolor and
pencil on paper, 81.5 x 73.5 cm.,
32⅛ x 29 in. (sight)

304. *Pilar*, ca. 1927–1929,
watercolor and pencil on paper,
81 x 68.5 cm., 31⅞ x 27 in.

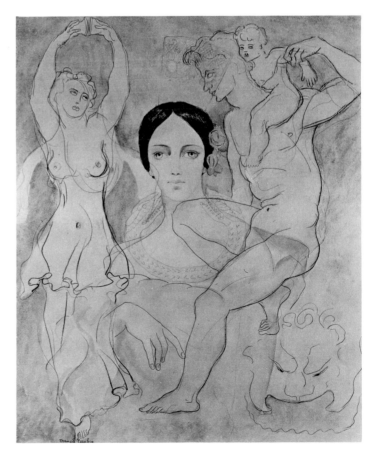

305. *Head with Cellophane*, ca. 1928,
pencil, gouache, watercolor and cellophane on paper,
32 x 25 cm., 12⅝ x 9⅞ in.

306. *L'Ombre (Shadow)*, ca. 1928,
gouache and cellophane on cardboard,
105 x 75 cm., 41¾ x 29½ in.

Chapter 16

307. *Jésus et le dauphin* (*Jesus and the Dolphin*),
a. 1928, gouache on cardboard,
14 x 75 cm., 44⅞ x 29½ in.

308. Annibale Carracci. *Pietà*, ca. 1599–1600,
oil on canvas, 156 x 149 cm., 61½ x 58⅝ in.

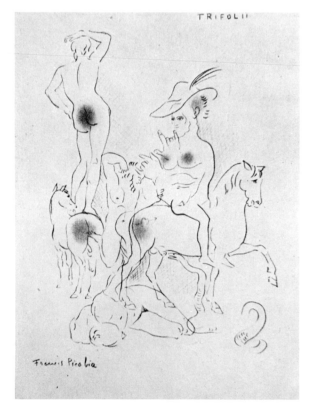

309. *(top left) Untitled Transparency*, ca. 1928–1929,
gouache and oil on cardboard, 105 x 75 cm., 41⅜ x 29½ in.

310. *(bottom left) Trifolii*, ca. 1928–1929,
ink, pencil and watercolor on paper?, dimensions unknown

311. *(above) Lunaris*, ca. 1928–1929,
oil on plywood, 119.5 x 95.3 cm., 47 x 37½ in.

312. *Dispar*, ca. 1929, oil on plywood,
150.5 x 95.3 cm., 59¼ x 37½ in.

313. Study for *Dispar*, ca. 1929, pencil on paper?, dimensions unknown

314. *Hera*, ca. 1929, thinned oil on cardboard, 105 x 75 cm., 41⅜ x 29½ in.

315. *(top left) Catax*, ca. 1929,
oil and gouache on paper,
105 x 75 cm., 41⅜ x 29½ in.

316. *(left)* Sandro Botticelli.
The Birth of Venus (detail),
ca. 1485, oil on canvas

317. *(top right) Briseis*,
ca. 1929, media and
dimensions unknown

318. *(right)* Anonymous Greek.
Dying Niobid, ca. 450–440 B.C.,
marble, height 150 cm., 59 in.

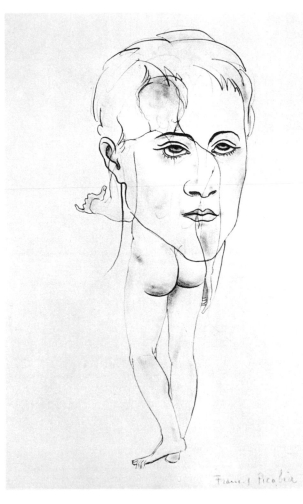

319. *(top left) Untitled Drawing After the Doryphorus*, ca. 1929,
ink, pencil and charcoal on paper,
26 x 17 cm., 10¼ x 6¾ in. (sight)

320. *(left)* Anonymous Roman. Copy of Polyclitus's *Doryphorus*,
ca. 450–440 B.C., marble, height 194 cm., 78 in.

321. *(top right) Untitled Drawing of a Head and the Doryphorus*,
ca. 1929, pencil and ink on paper,
24.5 x 18.5 cm., 9⅝ x 7¼ in.

Chapter 16

322. *Ino*, ca. 1929–1930, oil on plywood, 161.3 x 96 cm., 63½ x 37¾ in. (not verified)

323. Anonymous Roman. *Perseus and Andromeda*, ca. 1st century A.D., fresco from Pompeii

324. Study for *Ino*, ca. 1929–1930, ink on paper?, dimensions unknown

325. Sandro Botticelli. *Madonna and Child with St. John*, ca. 1472,
oil on wood, 93 x 69 cm., 36⅝ x 27⅛ in.

Chapter 16

326. *Atrata*, ca. 1929, oil on plywood, 147 x 92 cm., 57⅞ x 36¼ in.

327. Anonymous Roman. *Atlas*, marble

328. Sandro Botticelli. *Portrait of a Man with a Medal*, ca. 1473–1474, oil on wood, 57.5 x 44 cm., 22⅝ x 17⅜ in.

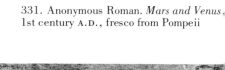

329. *Villica-Caja*, 1929, oil on canvas,
151 x 180 cm., 59½ x 70⅞ in.

330. Guido Reni. *Nessus and Dejanira*,
ca. 1617–1620, oil on canvas,
259 x 193 cm., 102 x 76 in.

331. Anonymous Roman. *Mars and Venus*,
1st century A.D., fresco from Pompeii

Chapter 16

332. *Artemis*, ca. 1929, oil on canvas, 87 x 115.5 cm., 34¼ x 45½ in.

333. Bartolommeo Schedoni.
St. Sebastian Cured by the Pious Women,
ca. 1615, oil on canvas,
187 x 126 cm., 73⅝ x 49⅝ in.

334. *Medea*, ca. 1929, watercolor on paper, 106 x 75 cm., 41⅞ x 29½ in.

Opposite:

335. *(top left) Luscunia*,
ca. 1929, oil on canvas,
147 x 138 cm., 57⅞ x 54¼ in.

336. *(top right) Judith*,
ca. 1929, oil on canvas,
200 x 150 cm., 78¾ x 59 in.

337. *(bottom left) Salome*,
ca. 1930, oil on canvas,
195 x 130 cm., 76¾ x 51¼ in.

338. *(bottom right)* Sandro
Botticelli, school of?.
The Redeemer, ca. 1500,
oil on wood, 47 x 33 cm.,
18½ x 13 in.

Chapter 16

339. *Oo*, ca. 1930, oil on canvas, 160 x 124.5 cm., 63 x 49 in.

340. *Aello*, ca. 1930, oil on canvas,
169 x 169 cm., 66½ x 66½ in.

341. Piero della Francesca. *Baptism of Christ* (detail),
ca. 1450, tempera on wood

342. *Noctuelles*, ca. 1930, oil on canvas?, dimensions unknown

343. Piero della Francesca.
The Meeting of Solomon and the Queen of Sheba (detail),
1453–1454, fresco

344. *Heads and Landscape*,
ca. 1930, oil on canvas,
60 x 81 cm., 23⅝ x 31⅞ in.

345. Piero della Francesco.
The Discovery of the True Cross
(detail), ca. 1453–1454, fresco

346. *Genie of the Lake*, ca. 1930,
oil on canvas, 80.5 x 60.5 cm.,
31½ x 25½ in.

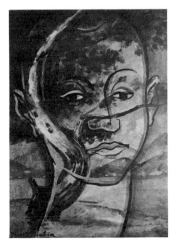

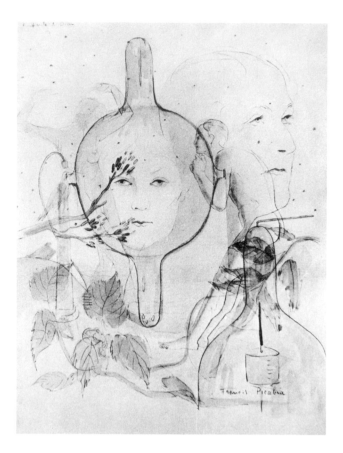

347. *(top left)* L'Infinité de Dieu (*The Infinity of God*), 1931, lithograph

348. *(left)* Setina, ca. 1930, thinned oil on canvas?, dimensions unknown

349. *(above)* Mélibée, ca. 1931, oil on canvas,
approx. 215 x 130 cm., 84¾ x 51¼ in.

Opposite:

350. *(top left)* Adam and Eve, ca. 1931, oil on canvas,
approx. 200 x 110 cm., 78¾ x 43¼ in.

351. *(bottom left)* Anonymous Roman copy of a Greek artist.
Orestes and Electra, ca. 50 B.C., marble

352. *(top right)* Olyras, ca. 1931, oil on canvas,
161.5 x 130 cm., 63¾ x 51⅛ in.

353. *(bottom right)* Ambrogio Lorenzetti. *Allegory of Peace*,
detail from *Good Government*, ca. 1338–1340, fresco

Chapter 16

Chapter 16

Opposite:

354. *Head*, 1932, watercolor and ink on paper, dimensions unknown

355. *Volupté*, ca. 1932, ink and crayons on paper, 64 x 48 cm.,
25¼ x 18⅞ in.

356. *Portrait of Gertrude Stein*, 1933,
oil on canvas, 116 x 60.4 cm., 45⅝ x 23¾ in.

357. *Portrait of Suzy Solidor*, 1933, oil on canvas,
92 x 73 cm., 36¼ x 28⅜ in.

This page:

358. *Portrait of Olga Mohler*, ca. 1933, oil on canvas, dimensions unknown

359. *The White Lake*, ca. 1930–1934,
ink and crayon on paper, 50 x 64 cm., 19¾ x 25¼ in.

360. *Idea*, ca. 1931–1934, oil on canvas, 65 x 54.5 cm., 25¾ x 21¼ in.

361. *Printemps (Spring)*, 1935, oil on canvas, 106.5 x 90 cm., 42 x 35½ in.

Chapter 17

362. *Man and Woman at the Seashore*, 1935, oil on canvas, 116 x 89 cm., 45⅝ x 35 in.

363. *Iphigeneia*, or *Resignation*, ca. 1935, oil on canvas, 73 x 60 cm., 28¾ x 23⅝ in.

364. Anonymous Roman. *Sacrifice of Iphigeneia*, 1st century A.D., fresco, Pompeii.

365. *Peasant Woman*, ca. 1935, oil on canvas?, dimensions unknown

Chapter 17

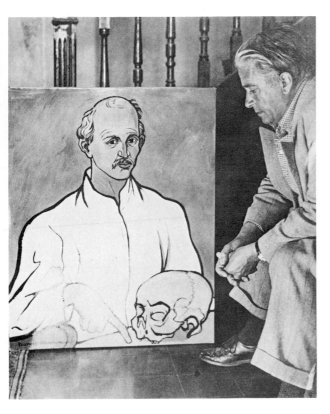

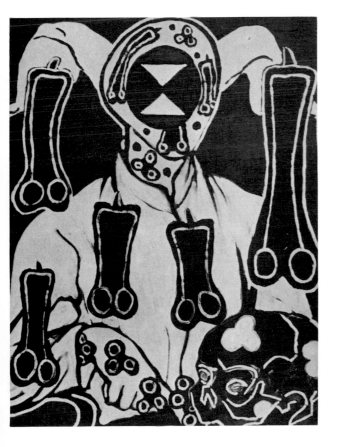

366. *(top left)* Picabia and *Portrait of a Man with a Skull*,
ca. 1935,
oil on canvas, 92 x 73 cm., 36¼ x 28¾ in.,
repainted as in fig. 367

367. *(left) Portrait of a Doctor*, ca. 1935 and 1938?,
oil on canvas, 92 x 73 cm., 36¼ x 28¾ in.

368. *(above) At the Theater*, 1935 and ca. 1946?,
oil on canvas, 116 x 89 cm., 45⅝ x 35 in.

369. *Clowns*, 1935, oil on cardboard,
116 x 89 cm., 45⅝ x 35 in.

370. *Dream*, ca. 1933–1936?, oil on wood,
74 x 51.5 cm., 29⅛ x 20¼ in. (sight)

371. *(top left) Hercules and His Coursers*, ca. 1933–1936?,
oil on canvas, 162 x 130 cm., 63¾ x 51⅛ in.

372. *(above) Superimposition of the Madonna and Nude*, ca. 1934–1938?,
oil on wood, 108.5 x 99 cm., 42¾ x 39 in. (sight)

373. *(center left) Superimposition of a Hand and Face*, 1936,
oil on canvas?, dimensions unknown

374. *(bottom left) The Peacocks*, ca. 1937, oil on canvas?, dimensions unknown

Chapter 17

375. *(top left) The Midnight Bath*, ca. 1937, oil on wood,
119 x 99.5 cm., 46⅞ x 39⅛ in. (sight)

376. *(bottom left) Untitled Landscape in the Manner of the Italian
"Primitives,"* ca. 1937, oil on wood, 59 x 51 cm., 23¼ x 20⅛ in.

377. *(top right) Abstract Composition*, 1937,
tempera on paper, 29 x 39 cm., 11½ x 15⅜ in.

378. *(bottom right) The Mask and the Mirror*, ca. 1930–1945
in two or more campaigns?, oil on wood, 85 x 70 cm., 33½ x 27½ in.

379. *(top left) Figure and Flowers*, ca. mid-1930s and ca. 1943,
oil on canvas, 100 x 73 cm., 39⅜ x 28¾ in.

380. *(bottom left) Landscape of the Midi*, ca. 1938,
oil on cardboard, 54 x 65 cm., 21¼ x 25⅝ in.

381. *(top right) Landscape with Palm Trees*, late 1930s?,
oil on canvas, 47 x 39.5 cm., 18½ x 15½ cm.

Chapter 17

382. *(top left) Landscape with Sunset*, ca. 1938–1940,
oil on canvas, 46 x 54 cm., 18⅛ x 21¼ in.

383. *(bottom left) Asoa*, ca. 1938, media, dimensions unknown

384. *(above) Portrait*, ca. 1938–1939, oil on cardboard,
62 x 52.5 cm., 24½ x 20¾ in.

385. *7091*, ca. 1938–1939, oil on cardboard, 60 x 49 cm., 23½ x 19¼ in.
386. *Spring Landscape*, ca. 1939–1940, oil on composition board,
36.5 x 43.5 cm., 14⅜ x 17⅛ in.
387. *Flower Girl*, ca. 1941, oil on canvas?, dimensions unknown

388. *The Corrida*, ca. 1941, oil on cardboard,
105.5 x 76.5 cm., 41½ x 30⅛ in.

389. *Women and Bulldog*, ca. 1941–1942, oil on cardboard,
106 x 76 cm., 41¾ x 30 in.

Chapter 18

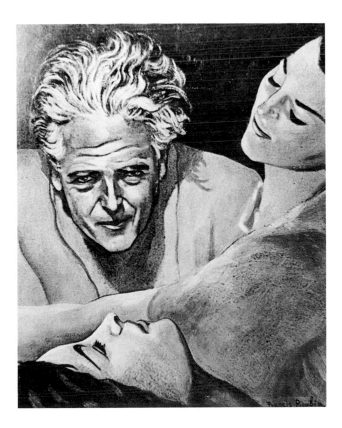

390. *Adam and Eve*, ca. 1941–1943, oil on wood,
104 x 75 cm., 41⅜ x 29½ in.

391. *Spring (M. and Mme Romain)*, ca. 1942, oil on canvas,
116 x 89 cm., 45⅝ x 35 in.

392. *Self-Portrait with Two Women*, ca. 1940–1943, oil on cardboard,
83 x 72 cm., 32⅝ x 28⅜ in.

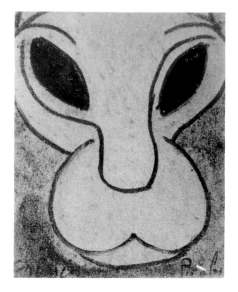

393. *Little Mask*, ca. 1941–1942,
oil on cardboard,
7.5 x 5.8 cm., 3 x 2¼ in.

394. *Portrait*, ca. 1940–1944?, pencil on paper,
38.5 x 28.5 cm., 15¼ x 11¼ in.

395. *Portrait of Germaine Everling*, ca. 1940–1944?,
pencil on paper, 28 x 18 cm., 11 x 7⅛ in. (sight)

Opposite:

396. *Le Soleil dans la peinture* (*The Sun in Painting*), 1945,
oil on composition board, 44.5 x 36.5 cm., 17½ x 14½ in. (sight)

397. *Asoa*, 1945, media, dimensions unknown

398. *Suzanne*, 1945, oil on composition board,
92 x 73 cm., 36¼ x 28¾ in.

399. *Viens avec moi là-bas* (*Come with Me There*), 1945,
oil on canvas, 65 x 54 cm., 25⅝ x 21¼ in.

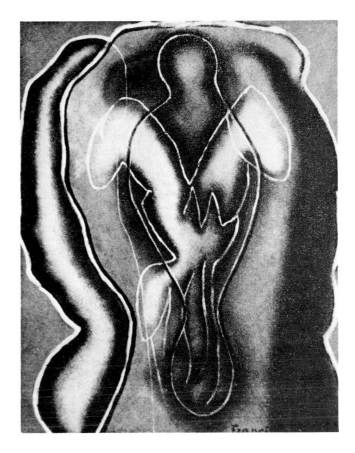

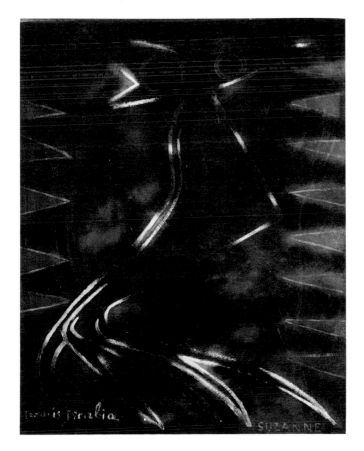

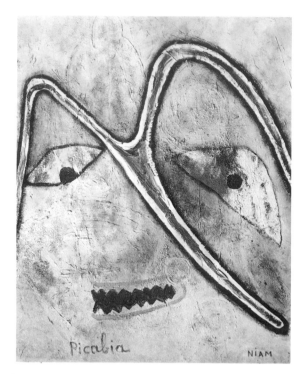

400. *Niam*, ca. 1946, oil on cardboard,
92 x 73 cm., 36¼ x 28¾ in.

401. *La Paloma de la paz* (*The Dove of Peace*),
1946, oil on wood, 84 x 68 cm.,
33 x 26¾ in. (sight)

402. *Bonheur de l'aveuglement*
(*Happiness of Blindness*), ca. 1946–1947,
oil on wood, 150 x 95 cm., 59 x 37⅜ in.

Opposite:

403. *Bal nègre*, 1947, oil on wood,
152 x 110 cm., 59¾ x 43¼ in.

404. *Elle danse* (*She Dances*), 1948,
oil on wood, 152 x 122 cm., 59⅞ x 48 in.

405. *Troisième Sexe* (*Third Sex*), 1948,
oil on canvas, 80 x 63 cm., 31½ x 24¾ in.

406. *Je vous attends* (*I Am Waiting for You*),
ca. 1948, oil on composition board,
100 x 81 cm., 39⅜ x 31⅞ in.

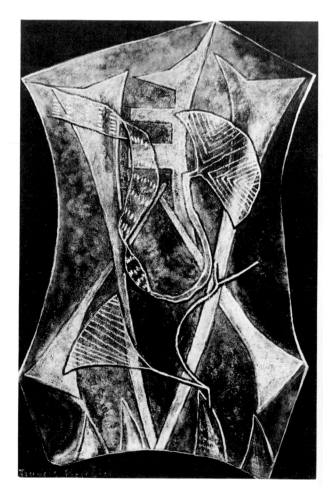

Chapter 19

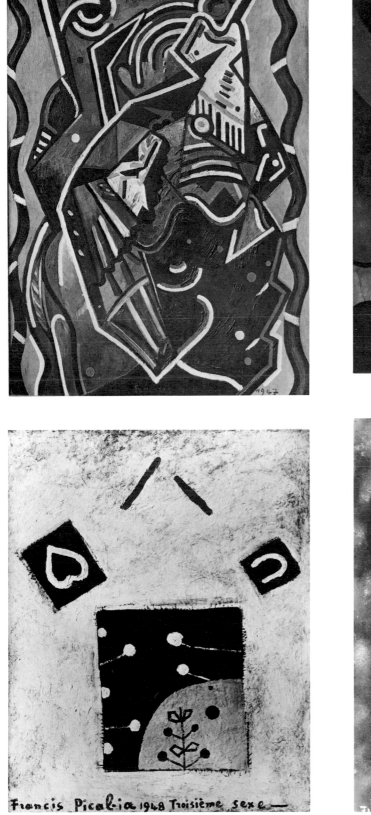

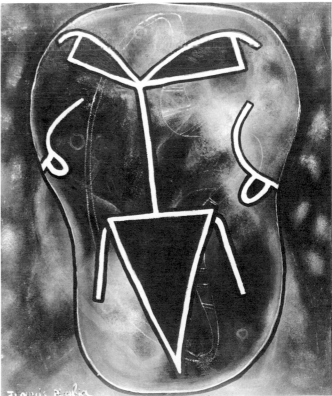

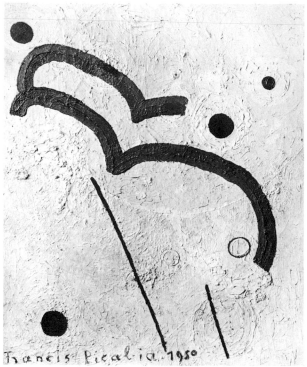

407. *(top left) Carte à jouer (Playing Card)*, 1949, oil on composition board, 76.8 x 52 cm., 30¼ x 20½ in.

408. *(left) Bienveillance (Benevolence)*, 1950, oil on composition board, 73 x 60 cm., 28¾ x 23⅝ in.

409. *(above) Danger de la force (Danger of Force)*, 1947–1950, oil on composition board, 116 x 89 cm., 45⅝ x 35 in.

Chapter 19

PHOTO CREDITS

Any reproductions not specifically credited below were provided by courtesy of the owners without identification of the photographer.

ILLUSTRATIONS

Marcel Adéma, Paris: 10; The Art Institute of Chicago: 8; Editions Cahiers d'Art, Paris: 22; William A. Camfield: 4, 5, 7, 12, 15, 26, 31-43; René Clair, Paris: 29; Dansmuseet, Stockholm: 27, 28; J. David, La Rochelle: 1, 2, 18; Mme. Yvonne Gresse-Picabia: 3; Otho St. Clair Lloyd: 16; N. Mandel, Paris: 44; Allen Mewbourn, Houston: 9, 17, 22, 27, 28, 29; Museum of Modern Art Library, New York: 20; Arturo Schwarz, Milan: 19, 30; John Lee Simons, Houston: 11, 13, 14, 21, 23, 24, 25; University Library, Newcastle-upon-Tyne: 6.

COLOR PLATES

The Art Institute of Chicago: VI; Richard L. Feigen and Co.: VIII; Galleria Schwarz, Milan: IV; The Solomon R. Guggenheim Museum, New York: IX; Allen Mewbourn, Houston: XIX; Musée National d'Art Moderne, cliché des Musées Nationaux, Paris: II, XI; The Museum of Modern Art, New York: VII, X; Succession Picabia: XX; The Tate Gallery, London: XII.

FIGURES

Acoris Gallery, London: 371; Albright-Knox Art Gallery, Buffalo: 58; Alinari/Scala: 277, 353; Archives Photographiques, Paris: 248; The Art Institute of Chicago: 72, 145, 208, 344; Bacci, Milan: 2; The Baltimore Museum of Art: 116; Centre Beaubourg, Paris. Beatrice Hatala, photographer: 124, 167, 198, 259, 367, 370, 376, 391, 394; Photo Serge Béguier: 158, 227; Rosamund Bernier: 89; Berri-Lardy et Cie., Paris: 32, 380; Bibliothèque Littéraire Jacques Doucet, Paris: 204; Gad Borel-Boissonnas, Geneva: 77; Brame et Lorenceau, Paris: 295; Jean Brown Archive, Tyringham, Mass. Remsen Wolff, photographer: 125, 126, 127, 128, 142, 144, 160, 187; Photographie Bulloz, Paris: 199, 206; Rudolph Burckhardt: 91, 174; William A. Camfield: 7, 10, 11, 16, 17, 20, 33, 39, 48, 59, 61, 64, 81, 92, 101, 102, 103, 105, 110, 121, 123, 130, 140, 147, 148, 150, 152, 153, 154, 155, 156, 170, 178, 180, 184, 185, 186, 190, 194, 242, 243, 251, 252, 253, 254, 255, 264, 267, 270, 271, 272, 287, 296, 297, 301, 310, 313, 317, 319, 321, 322, 324, 339, 342, 347, 348, 373, 383, 384, 386, 387, 392, 393, 395, 397; Carnegie Institute Museum of Art, Pittsburgh: 117; Geoffrey Clements, Staten Island: 149; A.C. Cooper, London: 52, 245, 286; Photographie Jean Dubot: 193; Suzanne Duchamp-Crotti: 181; EEVA, New York: 171, 381; Jacques Faujour, Centre Georges Pompidou, Paris: 177; Stanley M. Feuerstein, Philadelphia: 78; Augusto Fiorelli, Rome: 24; Florence, Gabinetto Fotografico, Soprintendenza alle Gallerie: 328; Fogg Art Museum, Cambridge, Mass.: 302; Fotografiretten Forbeholdes Fotografen, Silkeborg: 352; Fotopress, Turin: 273; Fratelli Alinari, Florence: 316, 318, 320, 323, 331, 338, 345, 351, 364; Galerie Henri Bénézit, Paris: 335; Galerie Cavalero, Cannes: 88, 244, 389; Galerie Jean Chauvelin, Paris: 183; Galerie Engelberts, Geneva: 36; Galerie Mona Lisa, Paris: 406; Galerie A. F. Petit, Paris: 42; Galerie des 4 Mouvements, Paris: 43, 71, 234, 293, 398; Galerie Denise René, Paris: 93; Galerie de Seine, Paris: 369; Galerie Jacques Tronche, Paris: 46; Galleria Notizie, Turin: 215, 225, 268; Galleries Maurice Sternberg, Chicago: 6, 31; Maurice Gaulmin, Cannes: 1; Hilde Gerst Galleries, New York and Miami: 12;

James Gilbert: 122; Peggy Guggenheim Foundation: 119; The Solomon R. Guggenheim Museum, New York. Robert E. Mates and Paul Katz, photographers: 8, 26, 29, 86, 90, 132, 135, 151, 169, 173, 202, 280, 291, 306, 385, 401; Bartlett Hendricks: 95; Ted Hennings, Chicago: 258, 285; B.C. Holland, Chicago: 133; Jacqueline Hyde, Paris: 196, 241; Mme. Jean Krebs: 355; Oeffentliche, Kunstsammlung, Basel: 50, 396; Libourne, Office of the Mayor: 49; Lisieux, Office of the Mayor: 21; M. de Lorenzo, Nice: 240, 359, 382; N. Mandel, Paris: 44, 45, 53, 76, 137, 282, 298, 400; Photo Marion-Valentine, Paris: 299; Marlborough, Ltd., London: 13; J. Masson, Paris: 349; Robert E. Mates and Paul Katz, New York: 34; André Melchior Foto, Zurich: 377; Claude Mercier, Geneva: 312; The Metropolitan Museum of Art, New York. The Alfred Stieglitz Collection, 1949: 74, 75, 80, 100, 107, 300; Allen Mewbourn, Houston: 55, 120, 143, 164, 175, 179, 182, 192, 197, 229, 237, 256, 284, 314, 329, 354, 358, 362, 365, 366, 374; Moderna Museet, Stockholm: 176; André Morain, Paris: 307, 350; Musées Nationaux, France: 35, 37, 38, 63, 82, 203, 325, 330, 361; Museo de Arte de Cataluña, Barcelona: 288, 289; Museo del Prado, Madrid: 274, 279; The Museum of Modern Art, New York. Soichi Sunami, photographer: 57, 60, 67, 97, 98, 99, 161, 166, 195; Marseille, Atelier Municipal de Reprographie, Palais du Pharo: 28, 47, 136, 139, 220, 399, 402, 405, 409; Naples, Laboratorio Fotografico della Soprintendenza alle Gallerie: 308, 333; The National Gallery, London: 341; O.E. Nelson, New York: 41; The Petit Palais, Geneva: 388; Philadelphia Museum of Art, A.J. Wyatt, photographer: 56, 62, 84, 85, 114; Studio Piccardy, Grenoble: 275; Fred Pillonel, Geneva: 281; John D. Schiff, New York: 40, 73, 94, 213, 360, 407, 408; Galleria Schwarz, Milan. Bacci photographer: 19, 83, 141, 163, 165, 188, 189, 191, 214, 217, 223, 246, 250, 260, 262, 269, 278, 357; Seattle Art Museum: 290; F. Wilbur Seiders, Houston: 212; John Lee Simons, Houston: 70, 104, 106, 108, 109, 112, 113, 201, 207, 224, 226, 230, 235, 238, 247, 249, 327; Sotheby's London: 292, 304; Stedelijk Museum, Amsterdam: 222; Tarica, Ltd., Paris: 134, 172, 226; The Tate Gallery, London: 236; Tooth and Sons, Ltd., London: 5; Marc Vaux, Paris: 205, 368; François Walch, Paris: 265; Photo Michel Waldberg: 210; John Webb FRPS, London: 390; Yale University Art Gallery, New Haven, Conn.: 356; Yale University Art Gallery, New Haven, Conn., Collection Société Anonyme. E. de Cusati, photographer: 131, 146, 168, 200, 263; Yale University, Beinecke Rare Book and Manuscript Library, Alfred Stieglitz Archive, Collection of American Literature, New Haven, Conn.: 68.

BIBLIOGRAPHY

THIS bibliography has been made as complete as possible for part I (Writings by Picabia), part IIA (Books on Picabia) and part IV (Exhibitions); it is selective for part IIB (Articles on Picabia) and part III (Writings on Picabia and His Milieu). One exception is claimed for unpublished, lost or incomplete writings (part IE). Unpublished notes, letters, manuscripts and poems are so numerous and diverse that only the more important items have been listed here.

Comments pertinent to specific sections of the bibliography occur under those sections in the organization below. Several general comments merit consideration here. Some of the most valuable sources for a study of Picabia are the scrapbooks of press clippings cited in part V (Archives). However, the dates and titles of the newspapers and periodicals are occasionally missing or erroneous in those clippings. The notation "attrib." indicates a writing known to exist but not verified by this author at the original source. The notation "not verified" is reserved for writings and exhibitions cited by other authors but not yet verified by any documents known to this author.

No separate publication exists for Picabia's voluminous correspondence but a number of important letters are available in the publications by Michel Sanouillet in parts IIA and IIIA of this bibliography, and *Lettres à Christine*, a publication of the Henri Goetz-Christine Boumeester collection of letters from 1946 to 1951, is in press.

I. Writings by Picabia

A. Books and Other Separately Bound Publications

Cinquante-deux Miroirs: 1914–1917. Barcelona: O. de Vilanova, October 1917.

Poèmes et dessins de la fille née sans mère. Lausanne, 1918.

L'Ilot de beau-séjour dans le canton de nudité. Lausanne, June 23, 1918.

L'Athlète des pompes funèbres. Bégnin, November 24, 1918.

Râteliers platoniques. Lausanne, 1918.

Poésie Ron-ron. Lausanne, February 24, 1919.

Pensées sans langage. Paris: Eugène Figuière, 1919. Preface by Udnie.

Unique Eunuque. Paris: Au Sans Pareil, February 20, 1920. Prefaces by Tristan Tzara and "Pascal."

Jésus-Christ Rastaquouère. Paris: Au Sans Pareil, 1920. Introduction by Gabrielle Buffet.

Thalassa dans le désert. Paris: Fontaine, collection "L'Age d'or," September 3, 1945.

Explorations. Paris: Vrille, 1947. Lithographs by Henri Goetz.

Choix de poèmes de Francis Picabia, ed. Henri Parisot. Paris: G.L.M., July 1947.

3 petits poèmes. Alès: PAB, January 1, 1949.

Un Poème de Picabia: Précaution. Alès: PAB, March 1949.

Untitled poem. Alès: PAB, September 1949.

La Raison. Alès: PAB, September 25, 1949.

Médicament. Alès: PAB, October 1949.

Innocence. Alès: PAB, November 1949. Drypoint etchings by Francis Bott.

Le Lit. Alès: PAB, November 7, 1949.

Chi-Lo-Sa. Alès: PAB, 1950.

Je n'ai jamais cru. Alès: PAB, May 1950.

Pour et contre. Alès: PAB, May 1950.

Le Moindre Effort. Alès: PAB, December 1950.

Le Dimanche. Alès: PAB, 1951.

Ce que je désire m'est indifférent. Alès: PAB, April 1951. Photograph cut by Pierre André Benoit.

Le Saint masqué. Alès: PAB, September 1951.

591. Alès: PAB, January 1952.

Ne pensez pas plus mal de moi. Alès: PAB, 1952.

Fleur montée. Alès: PAB, November 1952. Planimetric sculpture by Arp.

Oui non. Alès: PAB, 1953. Photomontage by Rose Adler.

Parlons d'autre chose. Alès: PAB, January 22, 1953.

Les Heures. Alès: PAB, January 29, 1953.

Ne sommes-nous pas trahis par l'importance. Alès: PAB, March 1953.

Demain dimanche. Alès: PAB, March 1954. Collages by PAB.

Poèmes de Dingalari. Alès: PAB, October 1955.

Maintenant. Alès: PAB, 1955.

Mon Crayon se voile. Alès: PAB, 1957.

L'Equilibre [1917]. Alès: PAB, August 1958. Engraving by Marcel Duchamp.

Dits, aphorismes réunis par Poupard-Lieussou. Paris: Le Terrain Vague, January 30, 1960.

Ou bien on ne rêve pas. Alès: PAB, February 1960.

Laissez déborder le hasard. Alès: PAB, March 19, 1962. Engraving by Gianni Bertini.

Caravansérail [1924], ed. Luc-Henri Mercié. Paris: Pierre Belfond, 1974.

Ecrits 1913–1920, ed. Olivier Revault d'Allonnes. Paris: Pierre Belfond, 1975.

Ecrits 1921–1953. Vol. II of *Ecrits 1913–1920*, forthcoming.

Lettres à Christine, ed. Maria-Lluisa Borràs. Paris: Editions Champ Libre, forthcoming.

B. Articles

"Que fais-tu 291?" *Camera Work*, no. 47 (New York, July 1914), 72.

Untitled statement, *291*, no. 12 (New York, February 1916).

"Revolver" and "Odeurs de partout" [signed Pharamousse], *391*, no. 1 (Barcelona, January 25, 1917), 2, 4.

"Convulsions frivoles," *391*, no. 2 (Barcelona, February 10, 1917), 2.

"Singulier Idéal" and "De nos envoyés spéciaux," *391*, no. 3 (Barcelona, March 1, 1917), 3, 8.

"Bossus," "Horreur du vide," "Petite Maison," "Magic City" and "D'une ville infortunée" [signed Pharamousse], *391*, no. 4 (Barcelona, March 25, 1917), 2, 7, 8.

"Medusa," *The Blind Man*, no. 2 (New York, May 1917).

"Idéal doré par l'or," "Poèmes isotropes," "Barcelone" [signed Pharamousse] and "New York," *391*, no. 5 (New York, June 1917), 2, 5, 7.

"Plafonds creux" and "Une Nuit chinoise à New York" [signed Marquis de la Torre], *Rongwrong* (New York, ca. July? 1917).

"Métal," "Délicieux," "Inférence," "Demi cons," "1093" and aphorisms, *391*, no. 6 (New York, July 1917), 2, 3, 4.

"Soldats," "Ascète," "Elle" and "Hier," *391*, no. 7 (New York, August 1917), 2.

"Salive américaine" and "Guillaume Apollinaire" [for complete publication see Picabia's untitled statement in *Temps mêlés*, nos. 31–33 (Verviers, March 1958), 67–68], *Dada 3* (Zurich, December 1918).

"Poème," *SIC*, nos. 37–39 (Paris, January 15–February 15, 1919), 19.

Aphorism, untitled poem and untitled prose-poem, "C'est assez banal," "Mousseline facile ou effet de neige," "Lèvres prolongées" and "New York-Paris-Zurich-Barcelone" [signed Pharamousse], *391*, no. 8 (Zurich, February 1919), 1, 3, 6, 7, 8.

"Carnet d'un sédentaire" [signed Pharamousse], *La Forge* (Paris: Librairie d'action de la ghilde, April 1919, May 1919, June 1919), 330–31; 402; 483–86.

Untitled poem and "Soleil sage-femme," *Dada*, no. 4–5 (Zurich, May 1919).

"Protestation," *Le Journal du peuple* [Paris], November 2, 1919, 2.

"Tombeaux et bordels," *391*, no. 9 (Paris, November 1919), 4.

"La Bicyclette archevêque," "Gutta-Percha," untitled poem and untitled statement, *391*, no. 10 (Paris, December 1919), 1, 2, 4.

"Une Protestation de Picabia," *Le Journal du peuple* [Paris], December 19, 1919, 2.

Open letter to the editor, *Comoedia* [Paris], December 22, 1919.

"Le Rat circulaire," *Proverbe*, no. 1 (Paris, February 1, 1920).

Aphorisms, an untitled poem and "Manifeste du mouvement Dada," *Bulletin Dada*, no. 6 (Paris, February 5, 1920), 1–4.

"Papa fais-moi peur," *Littérature*, I, no. 12 (Paris, February 1920), 2.

"L'Amphithéâtre chemise" and "Le Carnet du Docteur Serner," *391*, no. 11 (Paris, February 1920), 3, 4.

"Un Peu Tordu" and extracts from *Pensées sans langage* in *Die Schammade, Dadameter* (Cologne, February 1920).

"Auric-Satie à la noix de Cocteau" and aphorisms, *Z*, no. 2 (Paris, March 1920), 7.

"Je n'ai jamais pu que mettre de l'eau dans mon eau," *Proverbe*, no. 2 (Paris, March 1, 1920).

"Manifeste Dada," untitled statements and aphorisms, "¡ . — ! : , ..." and "Sperme cheminée," *391*, no. 12 (Paris, March 1920), 1, 2, 4, 5.

"Manifeste cannibale Dada" and aphorisms, *Dadaphone*, no. 7 (Paris, March 1920), 3, 4, 7.

Aphorisms and untitled statement, *Proverbe*, no. 3 (Paris, April 1, 1920).

"Origines du mouvement Dada," *Comoedia* [Paris], April 3, 1920, 2. Article signed Francis Picabia, but it appears to be by another hand or a collaborative work.

"A Madame Rachilde," "Coeur de Jésus," aphorisms,
"+ Aérophagie
0 Artériosclérose   Le refrain, de quoi?," "Carnet du Docteur Aïsen," "Carnet du Cuculin" and "Avoir le mal de mer sur un transport de joie," *Cannibale*, no. 1 (Paris, April 25, 1920), 4, 6, 7, 9, 11, 13, 15–18.

"Dada Philosophe" and "L'Art," *Littérature*, I, no. 13 (Paris, May 1920), 5–6, 12–13.

"Handicap," *Projecteur*, no. 1 (Paris, May 21, 1920), 3.

Untitled statements, " 'L'Affaire Dada,' " "Poésie pour ceux qui ne comprennent pas," "Je suis des Javanais," "Figue orgue," "Carnet du Docteur Aïsen," "Carnet du Cuculin" and "Festival-Manifeste-Presbyte," *Cannibale*, no. 2 (Paris, May 25, 1920), 3, 4, 6, 7, 9, 12–13, 17–18.

"Le 1er Mai," *Littérature*, I, no. 14 (Paris, June 1920), 26–28.

Letter to the editor, "M. Francis Picabia est son seul maître," *New York Herald* [Paris], August 4, 1920 (attrib.).

Aphorisms, "Notre-Dame-de-la-peinture" and "Carnet du Docteur Aïsen" (?), *391*, no. 14 (Paris, November 1920), 1, 3, 5, 8.

"Femmes fumigations," *Bleu*, no. 3 (Mantua, January 1921, attrib.).

"Selon M. Picabia, le 'Tactilisme' aurait été inventé par Miss Clifford-Williams en 1916," *Comoedia* [Paris], January 18, 1921, 1.

"Ninie," *La Vie des lettres* (Paris, April 1921).

"M. Picabia se sépare des Dadas," *Comoedia* [Paris], May 11, 1921, 2.

"Pourquoi je me suis séparé des Dadaïstes," *Comoedia* [Paris], May 17, 1921, 1.

"Francis Picabia et Dada," *L'Esprit nouveau*, no. 9 (Paris, June 1921), 1059–60.

"Pourquoi nous avons le cafard," *Comoedia* [Paris], June 23, 1921, 1.

"Zona," *La Vie des lettres* (Paris, July 1921).

" '391,' " "Pardon!!!" aphorisms, "Chef-d'oeuvre," "Mon cher Confucius" and "Le Pilhaou-Thibaou" [signed Funny-Guy or Francis Picabia], *Le Pilhaou-Thibaou* (Paris, July 10, 1921, 3–14; no. 15 of *391*).

"Almanach," *New York Herald* [Paris], July 12, 1921 (attrib.).

"Lutte contre la tuberculose," *Comoedia* [Paris], August 3, 1921, 1.

Open letter, *L'Intransigeant* [Paris], August 6, 1921 (attrib.).

"Fumigations," *The Little Review* (London and New York, autumn 1921), 12–14.

"Bonheur moral et bonheur physique," *Ça ira*, no. 16 (Antwerp, November 1921), 98–101.

Letter to the editor, *Le Matin* [Paris], November 10, 1921, 1.

"L'Oeil cacodylate," *Comoedia* [Paris], November 23, 1921, 2.

"Marihuana," *Comoedia* [Paris], December 21, 1921, 1.

"Trompettes de Jéricho," *Comoedia* [Paris], January 19, 1922, 1.

Letter to the editor, *New York Herald* [Paris], January 19, 1922, 3.

Letter to the editor, *Comoedia* [Paris], January 19, 1922, 3.

Open Letter to Paul Signac, *Comoedia* [Paris], January 23, 1922, 3.

"Sur les bords de la scène," *Les Potins de Paris*, February 3, 1922, 1.

"Les Arts," *Les Potins de Paris*, February 10, 1922.

"Jazz-Band," *Comoedia* [Paris], February 24, 1922, 1.

"Indifférence immobile," *Comoedia* [Paris], March 31, 1922, 1.

"Jusqu'à un certain point . . . ," *Comoedia* [Paris], April 16, 1922, 1.

"Orgue de barbarie" and "Anticoq," *The Little Review* (London, spring 1922), 3–4, 42–44.

"Cinéma," *Cinéa* (Liège, ca. May 1922, attrib.).

"Le Génie et le fox-terrier," *Comoedia* [Paris], May 16, 1922, 1.

"Ondulations cérébrales," *L'Ere nouvelle* [Paris], July 12, 1922, 1–2.

"Jardin d'acclimation," *L'Ere nouvelle* [Paris], August 5, 1922 (attrib.).

"La Bonne Peinture," *L'Ere nouvelle* [Paris], August 20, 1922, 1–2.

Letter to the journalist Clément Vautel, "Mon Film," *Le Journal* [Paris], August 23, 1922 (attrib.).

"Souvenirs sur Lénine. Le Communisme jugé par un peintre cubiste," *L'Eclair* [Paris], August 23, 1922, 1.

"Le Salon des Indépendants," *L'Ere nouvelle* [Paris], September 20, 1922, 1–2.

"Littérature," "Pensées et souvenirs" and "Picabia dit dans Littérature," *Littérature*, II, no. 4 (Paris, September 1922), 6, 13, 17–18.

"Ma Main tremble" and "Good Painting" [trans. from *L'Ere nouvelle*, August 20, 1922], *The Little Review* (London, autumn 1922), 40, 61–62.

"Un Effet facile" and "Billets de faveur," *Littérature*, II, no. 5 (Paris, October 1, 1922), 1–2, 11–12.

"Classique et merveilleux," *L'Ere nouvelle* [Paris], October 23, 1922, 1–2.

"Histoire de voir," "Condoléances," "Pithécomorphes" and "Samedi soir 16 septembre 1922," *Littérature*, II, no. 6 (Paris, November 1, 1922), 17, 19, 20, 24.

"Dactylocoque" and aphorisms, *Littérature*, II, no. 7 (Paris, December 1, 1922), 10–11.

"Souvenirs de voyage," untitled statement, "Avis" and "Francis merci," *Littérature*, II, no. 8 (Paris, January 1, 1923), 3–4, 9, 13, 16–17.

"Académisme," "Etat d'âme" and "Electrargol," *Littérature*, II, no. 9 (Paris, February 1 and March 1, 1923), 5, 13–15.

"Le Salon des Indépendants," *La Vie moderne* (Paris, February 11, 1923), 1.

"Jésus dit à ces juifs," *La Vie moderne* (Paris, February 25, 1923), 1.

"Le Petit Jeu dangereux," *La Vie moderne* (Paris, March 18, 1923), 1.

"Georges de Zayas," *L'Echo du Mexique* (Paris, March 1923), 8–9 (attrib.).

"Vues de dos," *Paris-Journal*, April 6, 1923, 1.

"Le Signe du roi" and aphorisms, *Littérature*, II, no. 10 (Paris, May 1, 1923), 13, 16.

"L'Exposition Francis Picabia," unidentified newspaper, Paris, ca. June 1923 (attrib.).

"Causes et effets," *L'Ere nouvelle* [Paris], June 14, 1923, 1–2.

"Bonheur nouveau," "Colin-Maillard" and "Irréceptif," *Littérature*, II, nos. 11–12 (Paris, October 15, 1923), 21–23.

"Ezra Pound et Georges Antheil," unidentified newspaper, Paris, ca. December 1923 (attrib.).

"Soldats" in *La Dernière Bohème*, by Paul Aressy. Paris: Jouve et Cie, 1923 (attrib.).

"Chronique du pot-pourri," *Interventions*, no. 1 (Paris, December 1923, attrib.).

"L'Enfant Jésus" [January 22, 1924], *Paris-Journal*, unknown date, 1924 (attrib.).

"Prix littéraires et Dada," *Paris-Journal*, March 21, 1924, 1.

"A Note on the Salons," *The Arts*, V, no. 4 (New York, April 1924), 191.

"André Derain," *Paris-Journal*, April 11, 1924, 6.

"Hyperpoésie trophique," "Hypertrophie poétique" and "Tabac" [signed Cattawi-Menasse], *391*, no. 16 (Paris, May 1924), 3.

"Ils n'en mourraient pas tous . . . ," *Paris-Journal*, May 23, 1924, 4.

"Réponse" and aphorisms, *391*, no. 17 (Paris, June 1924), 4.

Note in column "Courrier littéraire," *Paris-Journal*, June 13, 1924.

"Erik Satie," *Paris-Journal*, June 27, 1924, 1.

Epigrams, *391*, no. 18 (Paris, July 1924), 1, 3.

"L'Art moderne," *L'Ere nouvelle* [Paris], August 5, 1924, 2.

"Guillaume Apollinaire," *L'Esprit nouveau*, no. 26 (Paris, October 1924).

Statements, aphorisms and "Opinions et portraits," *391*, no. 19 (Paris, October 1924), 1–3.

"Première Heure," *Le Mouvement accéléré* (Paris, ca. November 20, 1924), 1.

"Instantanéisme," *Comoedia* [Paris], November 21, 1924, 4.

"Poissons volants," *L'Ere nouvelle* [Paris], November 24, 1924, 3.

"Pourquoi j'ai écrit 'Relâche,' " *Le Siècle* [Paris], November 27, 1924, 4.

"Rolf de Maré," "Relâche," aphorism and untitled statement on René Clair, *La Danse* (Paris, November–December 1924).

"Pourquoi *Relâche* a fait relâche," *Comoedia* [Paris], December 2, 1924, 1.

"Encore un péché mortel," *Paris-Journal*, December 20, 1924 (attrib.).

"Soleil," *Paris-Soir*, March 5, 1926, 1.

Letter to Christian [Georges Herbiet], July 30, 1926, transcribed by Christian as

"Copie d'une lettre-morale de Picabia" in *Cahiers Dada Surréalisme*, no. 2 (Paris, 1968), 198–99.

"A propos de bottes," "Un Peu de Picabia au Star" and "Lumière froide," *Journal des hivernants* (Cannes, January 20–30, 1927, attrib.). "Lumière froide" published as preface to Cercle Nautique, Cannes, *Exposition Francis Picabia*, January 28–February 7, 1927.

"Picabia contre Dada ou le retour à la raison," *Comoedia* [Paris], March 14, 1927, 1.

"Entr'acte," "Suzette," "Marguerite" and "Pensées," *This Quarter*, I, no. 3 (Monte Carlo, Monaco, spring 1927), 301–304.

"Jours creux," *Orbes*, no. 1 (Paris, spring–summer 1928), 29–33.

"La Fosse des anges," *Orbes*, no. 2 (Paris, spring 1929), 81–83.

"Avenue Moche," *Bifur*, no. 2 (Paris, July 25, 1929), 24–29.

"Des Perles aux pourceaux," *La Révolution surréaliste*, no. 12 (Paris, December 15, 1929), 48–49.

"Monstres délicieux" and "Entr'acte," *Orbes*, no. 3 (Paris, spring 1932), 129–32.

"Une Petite Histoire," *Orbes*, no. 4 (Paris, winter 1932–1933), 61–63.

"Dans mon pays," *Orbes*, II, no. 1 (Paris, spring 1933), 20–22.

"Avis," "A.Z." and "Vertu 'H.,' " *Orbes*, II, no. 4 (Paris, summer 1935), 20–22.

"Thalassa dans le désert" [extract], *L'Usage de la parole*, no. 3 (Paris, April 1940).

"L'Oeil froid," "Entr'acte de cinq minutes" and "L'Enfant" in *Anthologie de l'humour noir*, ed. André Breton. Paris: Le Sagittaire, June 10, 1940.

"Jeunesse," *L'Opinion* [Cannes], March 1, 1941 (attrib.).

"Under Her Little Pants" in *Art of This Century*, ed. Peggy Guggenheim. New York: Art of This Century, 1942, 60.

"Souvenir," *IIIᵉ Convoi*, no. 1 (Paris, October 1945, attrib.).

"Le Petit Monstre," *Les Quatre Vents*, no. 6 (Paris, 1946), 108–109.

"Bibliographie de Picabia" and extracts from poems in *Poètes à l'écart; Anthologie der Abseitigen*, ed. Carola Giedion-Welcker. Bern-Bümpliz: Verlag Benteli A.G., 1946.

Untitled statement, *Réalités nouvelles*, no. 1 (Paris, 1947), 65.

"Francis Bott," *Arts* (Paris, December 3, 1948, attrib.).

"En famille," "Ou bien," "Affaire de goût," "Elle" and "Logique," *Courrier*, no. 10 (Alès, December 20, 1948).

"Dans une église," *K*, no. 3 (Paris, May 1949), 23.

"Ou bien," "Affaire de goût" and "Vestiaire" in *L'Art abstrait*, by Michel Seuphor. Paris: Maeght Editeur, 1949 (attrib.).

"Ordonnance générale no. 555" in *Jean Cocteau*, eds. Robert Goffin and Herman van den Driessche. Brussels: Ecran du Monde, 68. Special issue of *Empreintes*, May–June–July 1950.

"Poème" in *Roses pour Rose*. Alès, 1951. A collection of homages to Rose Adler (attrib.).

"Christine" in *Christine Boumeester*, by Francis Picabia et al. Paris: Instance, 1951.

"Quoi," *Ma Revue*, no. 4 (Alès: PAB, April 1951).

"Francis Picabia par Francis Picabia," "Je m'entends sur elle," "Ah! la! la!,"

"La Lune sans yeux," "Pour ceux qui doivent toujours venir," "Mon Atmosphère," "Tristesse" and untitled poems and aphorisms, *La Nef*, no. 71–72 (Paris: Le Sagittaire, December 1951, attrib.).

"Extraordinaire" and poems, *Dau al Set*, IV (Barcelona, August–September 1952).

Untitled poem, *Le Peignoir de bain*, no. 1 (Alès, spring 1953, attrib.).

"Un Fou qui devient fou," *Caractères*, no. 7–8 (Paris, 1953, attrib.).

"Il faut que je rêve . . . ," *La Carotide*, no. 1 (Alès, November 1956, attrib.).

"Chant caressé par le parfum désespéré," *La Carotide*, no. 4 (Alès, February 1957).

Untitled statement on Guillaume Apollinaire dated November 26, 1918 [extract in *Dada 3*, December 1918], "Un Merle qui a perdu une plume" and "Haricots d'espagne," *Temps mêlés*, nos. 31–33 (Verviers, March 1958), 67–68.

"L'Avenir enfant" [October 27, 1948], *Panderma*, no. 1 (Basel, 1958, attrib.).

Untitled prose-poem, *691*. Alès: PAB, 1959. Contributions by Marcel Duchamp, Jean Arp, Clément Pansaers and Tristan Tzara.

"La Volonté de vie et ses complications," *Front unique*, no. 1 (Milan and Paris, spring–summer 1959), 10–12.

"Pyjama blanc" [February 1918] in *La Poésie surréaliste*, ed. Jean-Louis Bédouin. Paris: Editions Seghers, April 1964, 272.

"Mon Oncle est mort" [August 1923] in *Dada à Paris*, by Michel Sanouillet. Paris: Jean-Jacques Pauvert, 1965.

"Elle ne rougit pas" [1920] in Michel Sanouillet, "Le Dossier de 'Dadaglobe,' " *Cahiers de l'Association Internationale pour l'Etude de Dada et du Surréalisme*, no. 1 (Paris, 1966), 133–34.

"Chant du Pilhaou Thibaou" [ca. March 1921], "Manifeste du bon goût" [ca. May 1923], "Tambourin" [January 21, 1924] and "Relâche" [1924] in *Francis Picabia et "391,"* II, by Michel Sanouillet. Paris: Eric Losfeld, 1966, 140, 149, 152, 256–57.

"5 Minute Intermission," *Tracks*, I, no. 2 (New York, spring 1975), 7. Translated by Ron Padgett.

C. Prefaces

"Preface." Little Gallery of the Photo-Secession ["291"], New York. *Picabia Exhibition*, March 17–April 5, 1913.

"Préface." Pierre de Massot, *Essai de critique théâtrale*, Paris, September 1922 (not verified).

"Préface." Galerie Van Leer, Paris. *Exposition Méraud-Michael Guiness*, December 2–15, 1928.

Untitled preface. Chez Léonce Rosenberg, Paris. *Exposition Francis Picabia*, December 9–31, 1930.

"Préface." Galerie Alexandre III, Cannes. *Photographies de Man Ray*, April 13–19, 1931.

"Goetz" and "Christine." Galerie L'Esquisse, Paris. *Quelques Oeuvres de Henry Goetz et de Christine Boumeester*, March 27–April 27, 1945.

Extract from a letter to Henri Goetz. *Surindépendants*, Paris: Vrille, October 20, 1945.

"Préface illusion . . ." Galerie Colette Allendy, Paris. *Exposition Picabia*, May 30–June 23, 1947.

Untitled preface. Galerie du Luxembourg, Paris. *Francis Picabia*, April 11–May 8, 1948.

"Explications antimystiques." Galerie Colette Allendy, Paris. *HWPSMTB*, April 22, 1948.

"Les Peintres et leurs effets à distance" and aphorisms. Galerie René Drouin, Paris. *491, 50 ans de plaisir*, March 4, 1949.

Untitled preface. Galerie Colette Allendy, Paris. *Francis Picabia*, December 13, 1950–January 12, 1951.

D. Interviews and Polls

"Le Paysage contemporain: L'Opinion de quelques paysagistes. M. F. Picabia," *Le Gaulois du dimanche* [Paris], February 9–10, 1907, 2.

"French Cubist Here," *American Art News*, no. 16 (New York, January 25, 1913), 4.

"Picabia, Art Rebel, Here to Teach New Movement," *New York Times*, February 16, 1913, sec. 5, 9.

Beatty, Jerome G. "The New Delirium," *Kansas City Star*, February 23, 1913, sec. 4D.

"A Post-Cubist's Impression of New York," *New York Tribune*, March 9, 1913, pt. II, 1.

"How New York Looks to Me," *New York American*, March 30, 1913, magazine section, 11.

"Ne riez pas, c'est de la peinture et ça représente une jeune américaine," *Le Matin* [Paris], December 1, 1913, 1.

"French Artists Spur on an American Art," *New York Tribune*, October 24, 1915, pt. iv, 2.

Response to a poll, "Notre Enquête: Pourquoi écrivez-vous?" *Littérature*, 1, no. 12 (Paris, February 1920), 26.

B., M. [Marcel Boulanger?] "Le Dadaisme n'est qu'une farce inconsistante," *L'Action française* [Paris], February 14, 1920, 2.

Ch., G. "M. Paul Signac, M. Francis Picabia et Dada," *Le Figaro* [Paris], January 20, 1922, 3.

Response to a poll, *La Revue de l'époque*, no. 25 (Paris, March 1922), 643–44.

Pencil, Jack. "Vacances d'artistes," *Le Figaro* [Paris], August 20, 1922, 2.

Richard, Gaston-Ch. "Dada aux champs," *Le Petit Parisien*, October 27, 1922 (attrib.).

Response to a poll, "Le Symbolisme, a-t-il dit son dernier mot?" *Le Disque vert*, nos. 4–6 (Paris, February, March, April 1923), 91.

"Un Interview de Picabia," *Journal de Liège*, March 29, 1923 (attrib.).

Vitrac, Roger. "Francis Picabia, évêque," *Le Journal du peuple* [Paris], June 9, 1923, 3.

J., R. "Chez Francis Picabia," *Paris-Journal*, May 9, 1924, 5.

Achard, Paul. "Picabia m'a dit . . . avant 'Cinésketch' au Théâtre des Champs-Elysées," *Le Siècle* [Paris], January 1, 1925, 4.

Response to a poll, "Les Grandes Enquêtes de *L'Art vivant*. Pour un musée français d'art moderne," *L'Art vivant*, no. 16 (Paris, August 15, 1925), 37.

Gordeaux, Paul. "Hôtes d'été. Francis Picabia," *L'Eclaireur de Nice*, September 6, 1925, 3.

Christian, G[eorges]. "Interview," *Volonté* [Paris], March 4, 1926, 3.

Response to a poll, "Les Arts. Enquête: 1830–1930," *L'Intransigeant* [Paris], December 31, 1929, 6.

Colline. "Un Entretien avec Francis Picabia," *Journal des arts*, no. 3 (Zurich, November 1945), 50–51.

Response to a poll, "Enquête sur le cinéma," *Le Figaro* [Paris], October 17, 1946 (attrib.).

"Picabia nous dit," *Une Semaine de Paris*, November 15, 1946 (attrib.).

Response to a poll, *Le Savoir vivre* (Brussels, 1946, attrib.).

Guth, Paul. "Francis Picabia," *La Gazette des lettres*, no. 39 (Paris, June 28, 1947), 1–2.

Response to a poll, *Preuves*, no. 29 (Paris, July 1953), supplement, 34.

Charbonnier, Georges. *Le Monologue du peintre*. Paris: René Julliard, 1959, 131–40.

E. Unpublished, Lost or Incomplete Writings

Le Mâcheur de pétards. Volume of poetry and drawings, 1918. Lost?

"Les Yeux chauds." Musical planned in collaboration with Marthe Chenal and Igor Stravinsky, 1921. Not completed. Location unknown.

Untitled poem in manuscript. "Depuis que je suis fatigué de peindre . . ." Date unknown. Collection Enrico and Roberta Baj, Milan.

"Blum Poudding." Unpublished manuscript, December 5, 1936. Collection Librairie Robert D. Valette, Paris.

"Gertrude Stein." Unpublished manuscript, March 7, 1937. Collection Librairie Robert D. Valette, Paris.

Untitled manuscript. "J'étais le dispensateur le plus extraordinaire . . ." Date unknown. Collection Pierre André Benoit, Alès.

Untitled manuscript. "L'Amérique!" Date unknown. Collection Norma Copley, New York City.

"Préjugés des deux sexes." Poem in manuscript. Date unknown. Collection André Peeters, Louvain, Belgium.

"La Vie s'appelle 'Bonheur'? Le Bonheur est le dingalarisme." Statement, type-written carbon copy. Date unknown. Collection Christine Boumeester–Henri Goetz, Paris.

Untitled manuscript. Inscribed "ce que Francis Picabia pense du communisme." Date unknown. Olga Picabia scrapbook, 152–53. Collection Olga Picabia, Paris.

Untitled statement. Inscribed "Voilà un petit compte rendu de Francis après les interrogations de Mr Malenfant . . ." February 18, 1945. Olga Picabia scrapbook, 242. Collection Olga Picabia, Paris.

"L'Insoucience," "2^h¼," "La Vérité" and other untitled poems and statements in the letters of Francis Picabia to Christine Boumeester and Henri Goetz, ca. 1945–1951. Collection Christine Boumeester–Henri Goetz, Paris.

"Ennazus." Unpublished poem signed and dated Rubigen, September 13, 1946. Collection Christine Boumeester–Henri Goetz, Paris.

F. Magazines, Tracts and Handbills

391. Magazine founded and directed by Francis Picabia. Barcelona, New York, Zurich and Paris, nos. 1–19, January 25, 1917–November 1924. Reprinted with essay by Michel Sanouillet. Paris: Le Terrain Vague, 1960.

Cannibale. Magazine founded and directed by Francis Picabia. Paris, no. 1, April 25, 1920; no. 2, May 25, 1920.

Le Pilhaou-Thibaou. Illustrated supplement of *391* considered as *391*, no. 15 (Paris, July 10, 1921).

Funny-Guy. Tract-manifesto. Paris, autumn 1921.

Le Salon des Indépendants. Tract-manifesto. Paris, January 1922.

La Pomme de pins, ed.Francis Picabia. St. Raphael: Au Bel Exemplaire, February 25, 1922.

"La Pomme de pins dit: Merde à 'L'Oeil à Poils.' " Tract. St. Raphael, March 1922.

The Little Review. Chicago, New York, London and Paris, 1914–1929; Picabia was a co-administrator with Margaret Anderson, Jane Heap and Ezra Pound during 1922.

G. Scenarios

Relâche. Ballet produced by the Swedish Ballet, Théâtre des Champs-Elysées, Paris, 1924. Scenario, sets and costumes by Francis Picabia; music by Erik Satie; choreography by Jean Borlin; filmed intermission by Picabia and René Clair.

Entr'acte. Paris, 1924. Filmed intermission for *Relâche*. Scenario by Picabia; film by René Clair; music by Erik Satie.

Cinésketch. Spectacle by Picabia, Théâtre des Champs-Elysées, Paris, December 31, 1924.

La Loi d'accommodation chez les borgnes "Sursum corda" (Film en 3 parties). Paris: Editions Th. Briant, May 15, 1928.

"Dialogue dans la stratosphère." Skit for the municipal casino, Cannes. *Le Cancan* (Cannes, December 17, 1932), 12–13.

Réveil-Matin. Notes pour un ballet. Alès: PAB, February 1954.

H. Illustrated Books

Breton, André, and Philippe Soupault. *Les Champs magnétiques*. Paris: Au Sans Pareil, May 30, 1920.

Subscription announcement for Benjamin Péret's *La Mare aux mitrailleuses*. Paris: Librairie Gallimard, 1921.

Cendrars, Blaise. *Kodak*. Paris: Stock, 1924.

Desnos, Robert. *Deuil pour deuil*. Paris: Kra. "Cahiers nouveaux," no. 4, 1924.

Péret, Benjamin. *Immortelle Maladie*. Paris: Collection Littérature, 1924.

Tzara, Tristan. *Sept Manifestes Dada*. Paris: Jean Budry et Cie, 1924.

Maurois, André. *Le Peseur d'âmes*. Paris: Antoine Roche Editeur, 1931.

de Massot, Pierre. *5 poèmes* (privately printed). Paris, 1946.

Mendès, Murilo. *Janela do Caos*. Paris: Ambassador of Brazil, 1949.

Benoit, Pierre André. *3 mots chantés 99 fois*. Alès: P.-A. Benoit, 1950.

——— *Ma Solitude*. Alès: PAB, 1952.

de Massot, Pierre. *Le Mystère des maux* (privately printed). Paris, 1961.

II. Writings on Picabia

A. Books and Other Separately Bound Volumes, Including Prefaces and Catalogues for One-Man Exhibitions

André, Edouard. *Picabia*. Paris: Eugène Rey, 1908. Reprinted from *L'Art décoratif*, no. 101 (Paris, February 1907), 41–48.

Arnaud, Noël. *La Religion et la morale de Francis Picabia*. Verviers: Temps Mêlés, March 1958.

Arp, Jean. "Francis Picabia." Rose Fried Gallery, The Pinacotheca, New York. *Picabia*, February 15–March 31, 1950.

Benoit, P. A. *A propos des "Poèmes de la fille née sans mère."* Alès, 1958.

Bering, Myriam. "La Période dite des 'Transparences' chez Francis Picabia (1927 à 1935 environs)"; Mémoire de fin d'études à l'Ecole du Louvre, 1977.

Bibline, Myron. *Sur le chemin du calvaire.* Golfe-Juan, 1941.

Bois, Yve-Alain. *Picabia.* Paris: Flammarion, 1975. Withdrawn by publisher after publication.

Borràs, Maria-Lluisa. *Picabia.* Barcelona: Poligrafa, and Paris: Editions du Chêne, forthcoming.

Breton, André. "Préface." Galeries Dalmau, Barcelona. *Exposition Francis Picabia*, November 18–December 8, 1922

Camfield, William A. "Francis Picabia (1879–1953). A Study of His Career from 1895 to 1918." Ph.D. dissertation, Yale University, 1964.

———— *Francis Picabia.* New York: The Solomon R. Guggenheim Museum, September 1970.

———— "Picabia's Art." Galleria Schwarz, Milan. *Francis Picabia*, June 6–September 16, 1972.

———— "The Hen Roost." Galleria Schwarz, Milan. *Picabia: Le Poulailler*, October 1974.

Clémansin Du Maine, Emeran. "Francis Picabia." Cercle Nautique, Cannes. *Exposition Francis Picabia*, January 28–February 7, 1927.

———— "Prolégomènes." Chez Fabre, Cannes. *Exposition Francis Picabia*, February 20–25, 1928.

Dau al Set "Fixe." Special number devoted to Picabia. Barcelona, August–September 1952.

Desnos, Robert. "Préface." Galerie Briant-Robert, Paris. *Francis Picabia*, November 11–30, 1927.

———— "Préface." Galerie Georges Bernheim, Paris. *Exposition Francis Picabia*, November 10–25, 1931.

Duchamp, Marcel [Rrose Sélavy]. "Préface." Hôtel Drouot auction, Paris. *Tableaux, aquarelles et dessins par Francis Picabia appartenant à M. Marcel Duchamp*, March 8, 1926.

E[verling], G[ermaine]. "Préface." Chez Danthon, Paris. *Francis Picabia*, May 1923.

Everling, Germaine. "Préface." Evelyn Wyld et Eyre de Lanux, Cannes. *104 dessins par Francis Picabia*, August 19, 1932.

———— "Francis Picabia vu d'en haut." Unpublished statement dated August 1935. Olga Picabia scrapbook. Collection Olga Picabia, Paris.

———— Preface. The Lounge Library, Cannes. *Exposition Francis Picabia et Michel Sima*, July 15–31, 1942.

———— "Exposition de dessins par Francis Picabia." Office of Tourism, Monaco. *50 dessins de F. Picabia*, October 4–20, 1943.

———— "Préface." Galerie des Etats-Unis, Cannes. *Exposition Germaine Gallibert et Francis Picabia*, February 21–March 13, 1947.

———— *L'Anneau de Saturne.* Paris: Fayard, 1970.

Fabre, E. "Préface." Chez Fabre, Cannes. *Exposition Francis Picabia*, April 11–27, 1929.

Fagiolo Dell'Arco, Maurizio. "Introduction and catalogue." Galleria Civica d'Arte Moderna, Turin. *Francis Picabia*, November 28, 1974–February 2, 1975.

Flament, Albert. "Picabia vient d'épouser la nature." Galerie de Beaune, Paris. *Exposition Picabia*, November 4–17, 1938.

Goetz, Henri. Statement. Galerie Colette Allendy, Paris. *Francis Picabia, oeuvres de 1907 à 1924*, October 18–November 16, 1946.

Haguet. "Graphologie de M^r. Picabia," ca. 1940. Olga Picabia scrapbook, 211. Collection Olga Picabia, Paris.

———— Unsigned, undated manuscript (November 1940). Inscribed "Voilà ce que Mme. Haguet dit sur les 13 taches d'encre de Picabia." Olga Picabia scrapbook, 209. Collection Olga Picabia, Paris.

van Heeckeren, Jean. "Picabia, l'imprévisible." Unpublished text dated "spring 1939"; appendix dated "March 1947." Collection Olga Picabia, Paris.

———— *Francis Picabia. Seize dessins, 1930*. Paris: Collection Orbes, 1946.

———— "Picabia nom magique." Unpublished manuscript signed and dated Paris, February 1948. Collection Olga Picabia, Paris.

Hunt, Ronald. "Introduction." Hatton Gallery and Institute of Contemporary Arts, London. *Francis Picabia*, March–April 1964.

Hutin, Serge. "Picabia: Le Peinture perdue et retrouvée." Unpublished manuscript, ca. 1956.

Isarlov, Georges. *Picabia peintre*. Paris: Collection Orbes, 1929. Reprinted from *Orbes*, no. 2 (Paris, spring 1929), 85–108.

Jaguer, Edouard. "Picabia e i sortilegi." Galleria Schwarz, Milan. *Francis Picabia*, July 1–30, 1960.

La Hire, Marie de. Preface. Galerie La Cible, Paris. *Francis Picabia*, December 9, 1920.

L[atour], M-L., and J-A. C[artier]."A la découverte de Picabia." Musée Cantini, Marseille. *Picabia*, March 20–May 15, 1962.

Lebel, Jean-Jacques. "L'Ennemi des lois." Kunsthalle Bern. *Francis Picabia*, July 7–September 2, 1962.

Le Bot, Marc. *Francis Picabia et la crise des valeurs figuratives, 1900–1925*. Paris. Editions Klincksieck, 1968.

Lévesque, Jacques-Henri. "Dada." Galerie Artiste et Artisan, Paris. *Quelques Oeuvres de Picabia (époque Dada 1915–1925)*, November 20–December 4, 1951.

de Massot, Pierre. *Francis Picabia*. Paris: P. Seghers, 1966.

Mignon, Maurice. "Préface." Galerie Alexandre III, Cannes. *Catalogue des aquarelles et dessins composant l'atelier de Francis Picabia*, August 18, 1934.

Pearlstein, Philip. "The Paintings of Francis Picabia." Master's thesis, New York University, Institute of Fine Arts, 1955.

Francis Picabia 1879–1954. Homage to Picabia with texts by Jean Arp, Camille Bryen, Marcel Duchamp, B. Fricker, Jean van Heeckeren, Georges Isarlov, Jacques-Henri Lévesque, Man Ray, Pierre de Massot, Michel Perrin, H. Saint-Maurice, Pierre André Benoit. Paris: Orbes, April 20, 1955.

Picabia, Olga. "Un Quart de Siècle avec Picabia." Unpublished manuscript covering the years 1925–1953. Collection Olga Picabia, Paris.

———— *Francis Picabia*. Turin: Edizioni Notizie, 1975. Essay by Maurizio Fagiolo. Partial photo facsimile of Mme Olga Picabia's scrapbook.

Poupard-Lieussou, Y., and M. Sanouillet, eds. *Documents Dada*. Paris: Librairie Weber et Jacques Lecat, 1974.

Ribemont-Dessaignes, Georges, and Patrick Waldberg. Prefaces. Galerie Mona Lisa, Paris. *Picabia vu en transparence*, November–December 1961.

Roger-Milès, L. "Préface." Galerie Haussmann, Paris. *Picabia*, February 10–25, 1905.

———— "Préface." Galerie Haussmann, Paris. *Picabia*, February 1–15, 1907.

———— "Préface." Hôtel Drouot auction, Paris. *Tableaux, aquarelles, dessins, gravures, eaux-fortes par F. Picabia*, March 8, 1909.

———— "Préface." Galeries Georges Petit, Paris. *Exposition de tableaux par F. Picabia*, March 17–31, 1909.

Roosevelt, Mrs. André. "Recollections of Mrs. André Roosevelt, Stories and Anecdotes About Some Early Cubists." Unpublished memoirs. Archives of American Art, Smithsonian Institute, Washington, D.C.

Rosenberg, Léonce. Preface. Chez Léonce Rosenberg, Paris. *Exposition Francis Picabia*, December 9–31, 1930.

Sanouillet, Michel, ed. *391: Revue publiée de 1917 à 1924 par Francis Picabia*, I. Paris: Le Terrain Vague, 1960.

Sanouillet, Michel. *Picabia*. Paris: Editions du temps, 1964.

———— *Francis Picabia et "391,"* II. Paris: Eric Losfeld, 1966.

Seuphor, Michel. "Peinture fraîche." Galerie des Deux Iles, Paris. *Francis Picabia*, November 15–December 4, 1948.

———— "La Fin de tout." Galerie des Deux Iles, Paris. *Picabia Point*, December 12–31, 1949.

Stein, Gertrude. Preface (poem). Chez Léonce Rosenberg, Paris. *Exposition de dessins par Francis Picabia*, December 1–24, 1932. French trans. by Marcel Duchamp.

———— "Preface." Valentine Gallery, New York. *Recent Paintings by Francis Picabia*, November 5–24, 1934.

———— "Francis Picabia." La Galerie Serguy, Cannes. *Exposition Picabia*, April 1941.

Suprématie commerciale. London: De Trey and Co., Ltd., ca. 1921–1922. Dentistry booklet probably modified by Tristan Tzara but attributed to France Picabea, Frak Picabua, Francis Picabea and other variations of Francis Picabia.

Tapié, Michel, et al. Statements for *491, 50 ans de plaisir*. Paris: Galerie René Drouin, March 4–26, 1949.

Tapié, Michel. "Où il s'agit d'un corsaire de la peinture." Galerie Apollo, Brussels. *Francis Picabia*, October 18–November 3, 1950.

Tzara, Tristan. "Francis Picabia." Au Sans Pareil, Paris. *Exposition Dada: Francis Picabia*, April 16–30, 1920.

Wedewer, Rolf, et al. Texts. Städtisches Museum Schloss Morsbroich Leverkusen. *Francis Picabia*, February 7–April 2, 1967.

B. Articles

Aisen, Maurice. "The Latest Evolution in Art and Picabia," *Camera Work*, special no. (New York, June 1913), 14–21.

Alloway, Lawrence. "Art," *The Nation* (New York, October 5, 1970), 314–15.

Altmann, Robert. "Francis Picabia," *Islas*, III, no. 1 (Santa Clara, Cuba, September–December 1960), 191–207.

Arnaud, Noël. "Picabia ou la survie d'un loustic," *Cahiers du Collège de Pataphysique*, no. 18–19 (Paris, 1962), 93–101.

Arp, Jean. "Francis Picabia, Exposition Galerie des Deux-Iles, décembre 1949," *Art d'aujourd'hui*, no. 6 (Paris, January 1950).

"Les Arts, L'Oeil cacodylate," *Le Rappel* [Paris], October 30, 1921, 3.

"Les Arts, villégiature," *Le Gil Blas* [Paris], August 14, 1912.

L'Atelier. "Aquarelles de Picabia," *Paris-Journal*, May 29, 1914, 3.

B., P. "Le Vernissage de l'exposition Picabia, à Cannes," *L'Eclaireur de Nice et du Sud-Est*, February 22, 1928, 6.

Balthasar. "L'Art libre," *La Tribune de Genève*, November 3, 1923 (attrib.).

Bois, Yve-Alain. "Francis Picabia," *Art Press*, no. 21 (Paris, November–December 1975).

Breton, André. *Adieu ne plaise*. Alès: PAB, January 22, 1954. Reprinted in *La Nouvelle Revue française*, no. 15 (Paris, March 1, 1954).

Bricon, Etienne. "Salon d'Automne," *Le Gaulois* [Paris], November 5, 1921, 4.

Buffet-Picabia, Gabrielle. "On demande: 'Pourquoi 391? Qu'est-ce que 391?' " *Plastique*, no. 2 (Paris, summer 1937), 2–8.

———— "Picabia, l'inventeur," *L'Oeil*, no. 18 (Paris, June 1956), 30–35, 44–45.

Bulliet, C.J. Exhibition review, *Chicago Daily News*, January 11, 1936.

Cabanne, Pierre. "Cinquante Ans de plaisir avec Picabia, l'insaisissable," *Lectures pour tous*, no. 155 (Paris, November 1966), 16–21, 23–25.

Camfield, William A. "The Machinist Style of Francis Picabia," *The Art Bulletin*, XLVIII (New York, September–December 1966), 309–322.

Cassanyes, M.A. "Sobre l'exposició Picabia i la conferència de Breton," unidentified newspaper [Barcelona], November 1922; trans. in *Littérature*, II, no. 9 (Paris, February 1–March 1, 1923) 22–24.

Cassou, Jean. "Le Musée d'Art Moderne va exposer deux toiles anciennes de Picabia," *Arts*, no. 165 (Paris, May 7, 1948), 5.

"Ce Mois passé," *L'Esprit nouveau*, no. 17 (Paris, May 1922), 1980.

Clair, René. "Hommage à Francis Picabia," *Art d'aujourd'hui*, no. 8 (Paris, December 1953).

"Cubist Painter Paints Himself in Cubist Style," *New York Herald*, January 18, 1915, 13.

D., A. "Nous demandons qu'on reconduise Picabia à la frontière espagnole," *Le Merle blanc* [Paris], January 29, 1921, 1.

D., C. "Les Expositions," *Beaux-Arts*, no. 96 (Paris, November 2, 1934), 6.

Davenay, G. "La Vie artistique; les paysages de Monsieur Picabia," *Le Figaro* [Paris], February 14, 1905, 5.

Dermée, Paul. "Vernissage au whisky Picabia," *La Vie des lettres*, IV (Paris, April 11, 1921), 423–25 (attrib.).

Desnos, Robert. "Francis Picabia," *Paris-Journal*, January 18, 1924, 5.

D[esnos], R[obert]. "Picabia," *Paris-Soir*, March 5, 1926 (attrib.).

Dorival, Bernard. "Les Nouvelles artistiques," *Les Nouvelles littéraires* (Paris, May 20, 1948, attrib.).

d'Esparbès, A. "Autour du Dadaïsme, le vernissage Francis Picabia," *Comoedia* [Paris], December 12, 1920, 1–2.

Everling, Germaine. "Lettre à un ami," *Bref*, no. 2 (Paris, January 1956, not verified).

Everling-Picabia, Germaine. "C'était hier: Dada . . . ," *Les Oeuvres libres*, no. 109 (Paris, June 1955), 119–78.

"Les Excès de Francis Picabia ont stimulé l'art contemporain," *Beaux-Arts* (Paris, December 10–16, 1953), 7.

"L'Exposition Francis Picabia à Cannes," *L'Eclaireur de Nice et du Sud-Est*, August 22, 1930, 3.

F., M. "Picabia," *Artwork*, III, no. 12 (London, January–March 1928), 248–49.

Fagiolo, Maurizio. "Picabia," *Metro*, no. 16–17 (Venice, 1970), 57–66.

Finch, Christopher. "And Picabia," *Art and Artists*, I, no. 4 (London, July 1966), 52–53.

"Francis Picabia in His Latest Moods," *This Quarter*, I, no. 3 (Monte Carlo, 1927), 296–304.

Georges-Michel, Michel. "Journal d'un boulevardier," *Le Siècle* [Paris], February 26, 1926, 1–2.

Gsell, Paul. "Nos Echos," *La Democratie nouvelle* [Paris], February 13, 1920, 2; February 18, 1920, 2.

Gybal, A. "Le 'Truc' de M. Picabia," *Le Journal du peuple* [Paris], January 21, 1922, 2.

Hapgood, Hutchins. "A Paris Painter," *Globe and Commercial Advertiser* [New York], February 20, 1913, 8. Reprinted in *Camera Work*, nos. 42–43 (New York, April–July 1913), 49–51.

"Here is Picabia's Cubist Portrait on Going to War," *New York Herald*, January 19, 1915, 12.

Homer, William I. "Picabia's 'Jeune fille américaine dans l'état de nudité' and Her Friends," *The Art Bulletin*, LVII (New York, March 1975), 110–15.

Jean-Desthieux, F. "Dada est mort; Picabia reste," *L'Homme libre* [Paris], January 27, 1927, 1–2.

Jouffroy, Alain. "Francis Picabia, l'irréductible," *Aujourd'hui*, no. 36 (Paris, April 1962), 8–11.

Kols, Jean. "La Liberté dans l'art," *La Presse* [Paris], January 20, 1922, 1.

"Laglane du jour," *La France* [Bordeaux], October 26, 1920 (attrib.).

Legrand, Francine-Claire. "Francis Picabia, L'Eclipse, 1922," *Dix acquisitions récentes* (Brussels, February 5–March 23, 1969), 43–51.

Lévesque, Jacques-Henri. "Picabia et Dada," *Dau al Set "Fixe,"* IV (Barcelona, August–September 1952).

Magritte, René. "Francis Picabia. La peinture animée," *Le Fait*, no. 78 (Brussels, February 1973).

Martin, Jean-Hubert, and Hélène Seckel. "Francis Picabia," *La Revue du Louvre* (Paris, January 1976), 53–57.

——— "Spécial Monstres: Picabia," *L'Oeil*, nos. 246–47 (Paris, January–February 1976), 46–47, 74–75.

Du Mas, Vivian. "L'Occultisme dans l'art de Francis Picabia," *Orbes*, no. 3 (Paris, spring 1932), 113–28.

de Massot, Pierre. "Francis Picabia, Dada," *L'Ordre naturel* [Paris], February 3, 1921 (attrib.).

——— "Souvenirs," *La Nervie* [Braine-Le-Comte, Belgium], May 1921 (attrib.).

——— "Francis Picabia," *L'Ere nouvelle* [Paris], September 19, 1924.

——— "L'Oeuvre littéraire de Francis Picabia," unpublished text of lecture presented March 18, 1962, at the Musée Cantini, Marseille. Collection Olga Picabia, Paris.

Mercereau, Alexandre. "Francis Picabia," *Les Hommes du jour* (Paris, November 1920).

"Mr. Picabia Paints 'Coon Songs,' " *New York Herald*, March 18, 1913, 12.

Monda, Maurice. " 'Prenez garde à la peinture,' Quatre-vingts Picabias," unidentified newspaper [Paris], ca. March 7, 1926.

"Les Montparnos," *Le Cri de Paris*, November 18, 1938 (attrib.).

Mousseigne, Alain. "Francis Picabia et le sphinx," *Gazette des Beaux-Arts* (Paris, November 1972), 305–311.

Nantille. "Portraits d'interieurs, le Château de Mai," *La Saison de Cannes*, January 8, 1927 (attrib.).

Nora, Françoise. "Picabia Fauve et Dadaïste," *La Revue du Louvre*, no. 3 (Paris, 1973), 189–92.

Parijanine. "Une Belle 'Profession de foi,' " *L'Humanité* [Paris], February 26, 1927, 4.

———— "Petite Marché des lettres et des arts. Portrait du peintre par lui-même," *L'Humanité* [Paris], March 14, 1927, 2.

Pearlstein, Philip. "The Symbolic Language of Francis Picabia," *Arts*, XXX (New York, January 1956), 37–43.

Perrin, Michel. "Picabia," *Lettres nouvelles* (Paris, February 1954). Reprinted in *Art-Documents*, no. 43 (Geneva, April 1954), 3.

———— "L'Esprit de Picabia," *Le Crapouillot*, no. 53 [Paris], June 1961, 47–48.

"Picabia's Puzzles," *Christian Science Monitor* [Boston], January 29, 1916.

Pound, Ezra. "Literature Abroad," *The Literary Review* [London], August 13, 1921, 7.

Ravel, Gaston. "Exposition de peinture," *La Critique cinématographique* (Paris, October 29, 1929, attrib.).

Ribemont-Dessaignes, Georges. "François Picabia," *L'Esprit nouveau*, no. 1 (Paris, October 1920), 108–110.

de Sardi, Marie-Andrée. "Picabia le dynamiteur," *Jardin des arts*, no. 120 (Paris, November 1964), 44–53 (not verified).

Seuphor, Michel. "Jeunesse de Picabia," *Arts* (Paris, November 19, 1948, not verified).

———— "Epitaphe à Picabia," *Preuves* (Paris, January 1954).

Swift, Samuel. Exhibition review, *New York Sun*, March 1913. Reprinted in *Camera Work*, nos. 42–43 (New York, April–July 1913), 48–49.

Tapié, Michel. "Picabia an Explorer of Painting," *Art Review* (Paris, October 1950, not verified).

"La Turbine et le Dada," *Le Matin* [Paris], November 9, 1921, 1.

Tzara, Tristan. "Livres notes revues diversités divertissantes," section on Francis Picabia, *Anthologie Dada 4–5* (Zurich, May 15, 1919).

———— "Pic (3f9pl) bia," *Littérature*, I, no. 10 (Paris, December 1919), 28.

Vauxcelles, Louis. "Notes d'art," *Le Gil Blas* [Paris], February 10, 1905, 1.

Vitrac, Roger. "Exposition René [*sic*] Picabia," *Les Hommes du jour* (Paris, May 19, 1923), 10.

———— "Francis Picabia," *Paris-Journal*, May 20, 1923, 4.

Wescher, Herta. "Picabia peintre (1878–1953)," *Cimaise*, no. 3 (Paris, January 1954), 5–6.

"What is Happening in the World of Art," *Sun* [New York], January 23, 1916, sec. 5, 8.

Will-Levaillant, F. "Picabia et la machine: Symbole et abstraction," *Revue de l'art*, no. 4 (Paris, 1969), 74–82.

C. Radio and Television

Radio interviews and discussions with Francis Picabia recorded at the Phonethèque de l'Institut National de l'Audiovisuel, Paris.

Goetz, Henri. "Visite de l'atelier de Picabia," broadcast July 25, 1945.

Estienne, Charles, and Henri Goetz. "La Tribune de Paris," March 13, 1946.

Miró, Joan, and Lucien Coutard. "Les Peintres de la semaine," November 26, 1948.

Dumayet, Pierre. April 8, 1949.

Fromentin, Pierre. "50 ans de plaisir," 1949.

Charbonnier, Georges, with the participation of Roger Blin and Jean Topart. "Francis Picabia," January 9, 1950.

Dulls-Steiner, Mme, on Hilaire Hiler, March 17, 1950.

Charbonnier, Georges. "Francis Picabia," recorded April 18, 1950, broadcast January 1951 and published in *Le Monologue du peintre*, Paris: René Julliard, 1959.

Television program on Guillaume Apollinaire, February 19, 1952.

III. Writings on Picabia and His Milieu

A. Books and Exhibition Catalogues

Abrams, Meyer Howard. *The Milk of Paradise*, Harvard Honors Thesis in English. Cambridge, Mass.: Harvard University Press, 1934.

Adams, Henry. *The Education of Henry Adams*. Boston and New York: Houghton Mifflin Co., 1918.

Adéma, Marcel. *Apollinaire*, trans. Denise Folliot. New York: Grove Press, 1955.

Anderson, Margaret. *My Thirty Years' War*. New York: Covici, Friede Publishers, 1930.

Apollinaire, Guillaume. *Bestiaire ou cortège d'Orphée*. Paris: Deplanche, 1911.

———— *Les Peintres cubistes: Méditations esthétiques*. Paris: E. Figuière, 1913.

———— *Chroniques d'art*, ed. L.C. Breunig. Paris: Gallimard, 1960.

Aragon, Louis. *La Libertinage*. Paris: La Nouvelle Revue Française, March 1924.

———— *Aurélien*. Paris: N.R.F., 1944.

Arp, Jean. *Unsern Täglichen Traum . . .* Zurich: Verlag der Arche, 1955.

Art Institute of Chicago. *Paintings in the Art Institute of Chicago*. Chicago, 1961.

Arts Council of Great Britain. *The Almost Complete Works of Marcel Duchamp*. London: The Tate Gallery, June 18–July 31, 1966. Catalogue by Richard Hamilton.

Les Ballets suédois dans l'art contemporain. Paris: Editions du Trianon, 1931.

Banham, Reyner. *Theory and Design in the First Machine Age*. New York: Praeger, 1960.

Barzun, Henri Martin. *Orpheus, Modern Culture and the 1913 Renaissance*. New York: Liberal Press, 1960.

Bates, Scott. *Guillaume Apollinaire*. New York: Twayne Publishers, 1967.

Bergman, Pär. *"Modernolatria" et "Simultaneità."* Stockholm: Svenska bokförlaget, 1962.

Blunt, Anthony. *The Art of William Blake*. New York: Columbia University Press, 1959.

Bonnet, Marguerite. *André Breton*. Paris: Librairie José Corti, 1975.

Bragdon, Claude. *Man the Square: A Higher Space Parable*. Rochester, N.Y.: Manas Press, 1912.

Breton, André, and Philippe Soupault. *Les Champs magnétiques*. Paris: Au Sans Pareil, May 1920. Excerpts also published in *Littérature*, nos. 8, 9 and 10 (Paris, October, November, December 1919).

Breton, André. *Les Pas perdus*. Paris: La Nouvelle Revue Française, February 1924.

——— *Manifeste du Surréalisme* and *Poisson soluble*. Paris: Editions du Sagittaire, Chez Simon Kra, October 1924.

——— *Le Surréalisme et la peinture*. Paris: La Nouvelle Revue Française, 1928. 2nd ed. New York: Bretano's, 1945. Eng. ed., *Surrealism and Painting*,. trans. Simon Watson Taylor. London: MacDonald and Co., Ltd., 1972.

——— *Entretiens 1913–1952*. 10th ed. Paris: Gallimard, 1952.

Breunig, L.C., and J.-Cl. Chevalier, eds. *Les Peintres cubistes: Méditations esthétiques*, by Guillaume Apollinaire. Paris: Hermann, 1965.

Brinton, Christian. *Impressions of the Art at the Panama Pacific Exposition and an Introductory Essay on the Modern Spirit in Contemporary Painting*. New York: John Lane Company, 1916.

Brion-Guerry, L., ed. *L'Année 1913*. 3 vols. Paris: Klincksieck, 1971–1973.

Brooks, Van Wyck. *The Confident Years*. New York: E.P. Dutton and Co., Inc., 1952.

Brown, Milton. *American Painting from the Armory Show to the Depression*. Princeton: Princeton University Press, 1955.

——— *The Story of the Armory Show*. [n.p.]. Joseph H. Hirshhorn Foundation; distributed by New York Graphic Society, Greenwich, Conn., 1963.

Buffet-Picabia, Gabrielle. *Aires abstraites*. Geneva: Pierre Cailler, 1957.

Bulliet, C.J. *The Significant Moderns*. New York: Halcyon House, 1936.

Butor, Michel. *Les Mots dans la peinture*. Geneva: Skira, 1969.

Cabanne, Pierre. *Entretiens avec Marcel Duchamp*. Paris: Pierre Belfond, 1967.

——— and Pierre Restany. *L'Avant-garde au XXe siècle*. Paris: Editions André Balland, 1969.

Cagnet, Michel, et al. *Atlas of Optical Phenomena*. Englewood Cliffs, N.J.: Prentice-Hall, Inc., 1962.

Carrouges, Michel. *Les Machines célibataires*. Paris: Arcanes, 1954.

Cassou, Jean, et al. *Gateway to the Twentieth Century*. New York: McGraw-Hill, 1962.

Centre National d'Art et de Culture Georges Pompidou, Musée National d'Art Moderne, Paris. *Marcel Duchamp*, January 31–May 2, 1977, 4 vols. Contributions by multiple authors; chief curator and author, Jean Clair.

Centre National d'Art Contemporain and Le Musée National d'Art Moderne, Paris. *Charchoune*, May 7–June 21, 1971.

Clair, René. *Cinema Yesterday and Today*, trans. Stanley Appelbaum. New York: Dover Publications, Inc., 1972.

Cocteau, Jean. *Le Secret professionnel*. Paris: Librairie Stock, 1922.

——— *Opium*, trans. Ernest Boyd. London: George Allen and Unwin, Ltd.,1933.

Cocteau, Jean, Mac Ramo and Waldemar George. *Maria Lani*. Paris: Editions des Quatre Chemins, 1929.

Crespelle, Jean-Paul. *La Folle Epoque*. Paris: Editions Hachette, 1969.

Crotti, Jean. *Courants d'air sur le chemin de ma vie, 1916–1921*. Paris, 1941. Engravings by Jacques Villon.

Daniel-Rops, Henry. *Mort, où est ta victoire*. Paris: Plon, 1934.

Daulte, François. *Alfred Sisley*. Lausanne: Editions Durand-Ruel, 1959.

Décaudin, Michel. *Le Dossier d'alcools*. Geneva: Droz, 1960.

Delaunay, Robert. *Du Cubisme à l'art abstrait*. Paris: S.E.V.P.E.N., 1957. New documents published by Pierre Francastel; catalogue by Guy Habasque.

Delaware Art Museum, Wilmington. *Avant-Garde Painting and Sculpture in America 1910–1925*, April 4–May 18, 1975. General editor, William Innes Homer.

Demuth, Norman. *Vincent d'Indy, 1851–1931*. London: Rockliff, 1951.

Dorival, Bernard. *Twentieth Century Painters*, trans. W.J. Stracham. New York: Universe Books, Inc., 1958.

Duchamp, Marcel. *Marchand du sel: Ecrits de Marcel Duchamp*, ed. Michel Sanouillet. Paris: Le Terrain Vague, 1958.

———— *The Bride Stripped Bare by Her Bachelors, Even,* trans. George Heard Hamilton, typographic version Richard Hamilton. London: Percy Lund, Humphries and Co., Ltd., 1960.

Dupin, Jacques. *Joan Miró: Life and Work*. New York: Harry N. Abrams, Inc., 1962.

Eddy, Arthur Jerome. *Cubists and Post-Impressionism*. Chicago: A.C. McClurg and Co., 1914.

Edouard-Joseph, René. *Dictionnaire biographique des artistes contemporains 1910–1930*, III. Paris: Librairie Grund, 1934.

Eluard, Paul. *Mourir de ne pas mourir*. Paris: La Nouvelle Revue Française, March 1924.

Ernst, Max. *Beyond Painting*. New York: Wittenborn, Schultz, Inc., 1948.

Finch, Bernard. *Passport to Paradise . . . ?* London: Arco Publications, 1959.

Frank, Waldo, et al., eds. *America and Alfred Stieglitz*. New York: Doubleday, Doran and Co., 1934.

Fry, Edward F., ed. *Cubism*. New York: McGraw-Hill, 1966.

George, Waldemar. *Jean Crotti*. Geneva: Pierre Cailler, 1959.

Georges-Michel, Michel. *From Renoir to Picasso*, trans. Dorothy and Randolph Weaver. Boston: Houghton Mifflin Co., 1957.

Giedion, Siegfried. *Mechanization Takes Command*. New York: Oxford University Press, 1948.

———— *Space, Time and Architecture*. Cambridge, Mass.: Harvard University Press, 1962.

Gleizes, Albert, and Jean Metzinger. *Du Cubisme*. Paris: Eugène Figuière, 1912.

Gleizes, Albert. *Du Cubisme et des moyens de la comprendre*. Paris: Editions "La Cible," 1920.

Gleizes, Juliette Roche. *La Minéralisation de Dudley Craving MacAdam*. Paris: Imprimerie Croutzet et Depost, 1924.

———— "Memoires." Unpublished manuscript covering the years 1915–1923; written 1959–1963. Collection Mme Albert Gleizes, Paris.

Golding, John. *Cubism: A History and Analysis, 1907–1914*. New York: George Wittenborn, Inc., 1959.

———— and Christopher Green. *Léger and Purist Paris*. London: The Tate Gallery, November 18, 1970–January 24, 1971.

Golding, John. *Marcel Duchamp: The Bride Stripped Bare by Her Bachelors, Even*. London: Allen Lane, The Penguin Press, 1973.

Gordon, Donald E. *Modern Art Exhibitions, 1900–1916*. Munich: Prestel-Verlag, 1974.

Gregg, Frederick J., ed. *For and Against: Views on the International Exhibition Held in New York and Chicago*. New York: Association of American Painters and Sculptors, 1913.

Habasque, Guy. *Cubism*, trans. Stuart Gilbert. Paris: Skira, 1959.

Hamilton, George Heard. *Claude Monet's Paintings of Rouen Cathedral*. London: Oxford University Press, 1960.

———— *Painting and Sculpture in Europe, 1880–1940*. Baltimore: Penguin Books, 1967.

Heldt, Peter Martin. *The Gasoline Automobile, Its Design and Construction*. 4 vols. Nyack, N.Y.: P.M. Heldt, 1915–1925.

Henderson, Linda Dalrymple. "The Artist, 'The Fourth Dimension' and Non-Euclidean Geometry. 1900-1930: A Romance of Many Dimensions." Ph.D. dissertation, Yale University, 1975.

Homer, William Innes. *Alfred Stieglitz and the American Avant–Garde*. Boston: New York Graphic Society, 1977

Hope, Henry. *Georges Braque*. New York: The Museum of Modern Art, March 29–June 12, 1949.

Huelsenbeck, Richard. *En avant Dada. Eine Geschichte des Dadaismus*. Hanover: Paul Steegeman Verlag, 1920.

————*Memoirs of a Dada Drummer*, ed. Hans J. Kleinschmidt, trans. Joachim Neugroschel. New York: Viking Press, 1974.

Hugnet, Georges. *L'Aventure Dada (1916–1922)*. Paris: Galerie de l'Institut, 1957.

Hulme, Thomas Ernest. "Modern Art and Its Philosophy" in *Speculations*, ed. Herbert Read. London: K. Paul Trench, Trubner and Co., Ltd., 1954.

Jacob, Max. *Correspondance*, ed. François Garnier. 2 vols. Paris: Editions de Paris, 1953.

Jarry, Alfred. *Oeuvres complètes*. 8 vols. Lausanne: Editions du Grand-Chêne, 1948.

Jean, Marcel. *Histoire de la peinture surréaliste*. Paris: Editions du Seuil, 1959.

Kandinsky, Vasily. *Ueber das Geistige in der Kunst* [*Concerning the Spiritual in Art*]. Munich: Piper, 1912.

Krauss, Rosalind, and Margit Rowell. *Joan Miró: Magnetic Fields*. New York: The Solomon R. Guggenheim Museum, October 26, 1972–January 21, 1973.

Kreymborg, Alfred. *The Troubador*. New York: Boni and Liveright, 1925.

Lebel, Robert. *Sur Marcel Duchamp*. Paris: Editions Trianon, 1959. Eng. ed., *Marcel Duchamp*, trans. George Heard Hamilton. New York: Grove Press, 1959.

Lippard, Lucy. *Pop Art*. New York: Praeger, 1966. Contributions by Lawrence Alloway, Nicolas Calas and Nancy Mariner.

———— ed. and trans. *Surrealists on Art*. Englewood Cliffs, N.J.: Prentice-Hall, Inc., 1970.

———— ed. and trans. *Dadas on Art*. Englewood Cliffs, N.J.: Prentice-Hall, Inc., 1971.

Lissitzky, El, and Mary Whitehall. *El Lissitzky*. Greenwich, Conn.: New York Graphic Society, 1968.

Luhan, Mabel Dodge. *Movers and Shakers*. Vol. III of *Intimate Memories*. New York: Harcourt, Brace & Co., 1936.

Martin, Marianne. *Futurist Art and Theory*. Oxford: Clarendon Press, 1968.

de Massot, Pierre. *De Mallarmé à 391*. St. Raphael: Au Bel Exemplaire, 1922.

Motherwell, Robert, ed. *The Dada Painters and Poets*. New York: Wittenborn, Schultz, Inc., 1951.

Norman, Dorothy. *Alfred Stieglitz*. New York: Random House, 1973.

Parrot, Louis. *Blaise Cendrars*. Paris: P. Seghers, 1948.

Parry, Albert. *Garrets and Pretenders*. New York: Covici, Friede Publishers, 1933.

Penrose, Roland. *Man Ray*. London: Thames and Hudson, 1975.

Philadelphia Museum of Art. *The Louise and Walter Arensberg Collection*. Philadelphia, 1954.

Pissarro, Camille. *Camille Pissarro, Lettres à son fils Lucien*, ed. John Rewald with the assistance of Lucien Pissarro. Paris: Editions Albin Michel, 1943.

Ray, Man. *Self Portrait*. Boston: Little, Brown and Co., 1963.

Raynal, Maurice. *Anthologie de la peinture en France de 1906 à nos jours*. Paris: Editions Montaigne, 1927.

————— *Modern Painting*. Lausanne: Skira, 1960.

Rewald, John. *Post-Impressionism*. New York: The Museum of Modern Art, 1956.

Ribemont-Dessaignes, Georges. *Déjà jadis*. Paris: René Julliard, 1958.

Richter, Hans. *Dada: Art and Anti-Art*. New York: McGraw-Hill, 1965.

Robbins, Daniel. *Albert Gleizes*. New York: The Solomon R. Guggenheim Museum, September 15–November 1, 1964.

Rosenblum, Robert. *Cubism and Twentieth-Century Art*. New York: Harry N. Abrams, Inc., 1960.

Rourke, Constance. *Charles Sheeler*. New York: Harcourt, Brace & Co., 1938.

Roussel, Raymond. *Impressions d'Afrique*. Paris: Librairie Alphonse Lemerre, 1912.

Rubin, William S. *Dada, Surrealism and Their Heritage*. New York: The Museum of Modern Art, March 27–June 9, 1968.

————— *Dada and Surrealist Art*. New York: Harry N. Abrams, Inc., 1968.

Rudenstine, Angelica Zander. *The Guggenheim Museum Collection: Paintings 1880–1945*. 2 vols. New York: The Solomon R. Guggenheim Foundation, 1976.

Salmon, André. *La Jeune Peinture française*. Paris: Société des Trente, 1912.

Sanouillet, Michel. *Dada à Paris*. Paris: Jean-Jacques Pauvert, 1965.

Santayana, George. *The Sense of Beauty*. New York: Scribner's Sons, 1896.

Schwarz, Arturo. *The Complete Works of Marcel Duchamp*. 2nd rev. ed. New York: Harry N. Abrams, Inc., 1970.

————— *Marcel Duchamp: 66 Creative Years*. Milan: Galleria Schwarz, December 12, 1972–February 28, 1973.

Seuphor, Michel. *1910–1918: Origines et premiers maîtres*. Vol. I of *L'Art abstrait*. Paris: Maeght Editeur, 1971.

Shattuck, Roger. *The Banquet Years*. rev. ed. Garden City, N.Y.: Anchor Books, 1968.

Sima, Michel. *21 visages d'artistes*. Paris: Fernand Nathan, 1959.

The Solomon R. Guggenheim Museum, New York. *František Kupka*, October

10–December 7, 1975. Essays by Meda Mladek; essay and catalogue by Margit Rowell.

Spate, Virginia. "Orphism. Orphism, Pure Painting, Simultaneity: The Development of Non-Figurative Painting in Paris, 1908–1914." Ph.D. dissertation, Bryn Mawr College, 1970.

Stein, Gertrude. *The Autobiography of Alice B. Toklas.* New York: Harcourt, Brace & Co., 1933.

———— *Everybody's Autobiography.* New York: Random House, 1937.

———— *The Flowers of Friendship*, ed. Donald Gallup. New York: Alfred Knopf, 1953.

Temps mêlés. Parade pour Picabia-Pansaers. Verviers, Belgium, March 21, 1958. Homages by multiple authors.

Thireau, Maurice. *L'Art moderne et la graphie.* Paris: Bureau de l'Editions, 1930.

Tzara, Tristan, ed. *Le Coeur à barbe*, no. 1. Paris, April 1922.

Vaché, Jacques. *Lettres de guerre.* Paris: Au Sans Pareil, 1919. Preface by André Breton.

Vallier, Dora. *Jacques Villon.* Paris: Editions "Cahiers d'Art," 1957.

Viazzi, Glauco. *Entr'acte.* Milan: Poligono Società Editrice in Milano, 1945.

Weill, Berthe. *Pan! dans l'oeil!* . . . Paris: Librairie Lipschutz, 1933.

Yale University Art Gallery. *Collections of the Société Anonyme.* New Haven: Associates of Fine Arts at Yale University, 1950.

de Zayas, Marius, and Paul Haviland. *A Study of the Modern Evolution of Plastic Expression.* New York: 291, March 1, 1913.

Zervos, Christian. *Histoire de l'art contemporain.* Paris: Editions "Cahiers d'Art," 1938.

B. Articles

Achard, Paul. "Soirs de Paris. Chez Rolf de Maré," *Le Siècle* [Paris], November 16, 1924 (attrib.).

———— "Soirs de Paris. 'Relâche' aux ballets suédois," *Le Siècle* [Paris], December 6, 1924, 4.

———— "Soirs de Paris. Les derniers moments de 1924 . . . ," *Paris-Midi*, January 3, 1925 (attrib.).

Addington, Sarah. "Interview with M. and Mme. Gleizes," *New York Tribune*, October 9, 1915, 7.

———— "Who's Who in New York's Bohemia," *New York Tribune*, November 14, 1915, sec. 4, 2.

Agee, William. "New York Dada, 1910–1930," *Art News Annual: The Avant-Garde*, XXXIV (New York, 1968), 104–113.

"Air nouveau," *La Vie parisienne*, September 3, 1921, 751.

Alexandre, Arsène. "La Semaine artistique," *Comoedia* [Paris], November 30, 1912, 3.

Alloway, Lawrence. "London Letter," *Art International*, III, no. 9 (Zurich, 1959), 21–24.

Anonymous exhibition review. *Nebraska State Journal* [Lincoln], February 9, 1913, sec. B, 7.

Anonymous exhibition review of the Armory Show. *Chicago Daily Tribune*, March 31, 1913.

Anonymous exhibition review. *Arts and Decoration* (New York, November 1915), 35–36.

Anonymous exhibition review. *Arts and Decoration* (New York, April 1916), 286.

Anonymous exhibition review. *Bulletin de l'Effort Moderne*, no. 38 (Paris, October 1927), 8–9.

"Antologia Novisima Lirica. Effigie Liminar. Francis Picabia," *Grecia* (Seville, September 30, 1919, attrib.).

Apollinaire, Guillaume. "Du sujet dans la peinture moderne," *Les Soirées de Paris*, no. 1 (February 1912), 1–4.

Aragon, Louis. "Toutes Choses égales d'ailleurs," *La Nouvelle Revue française*, no. 84 (Paris, September 1, 1920), 346–82. Two chapters of *Anicet*.

——— "Pour arrêter les bavardages," *Le Journal littéraire*, no. 9 (Paris, June 21, 1924), 10.

Arp, Hans. "Déclaration," *Dada au grand air* (Paris, September 16, 1921, 3; no. 8 of *Dada*).

——— "Francis Picabia," *Art d'aujourd'hui*, no. 6 (Paris, January 1950).

"Les Arts—au Salon d'Automne," L'Intransigeant [Paris], October 13, 1921, 2.

Arts Magazine, Special Issue: New York Dada and the Arensberg Circle, LI, no. 9 (New York, May 1977. Multiple authors).

Ashbery, John. "Les Versions scéniques 'd'Impressions d'Afrique,' et de 'Locus Solus,' " *Bizarre*, nos. 34–35 (Paris, 2nd quarter, 1964), 19–25.

Auric, Georges. "*Relâche*, les ballets suédois," *Les Nouvelles littéraires* (Paris, December 13, 1924), 7.

Avril, Georges. "La Conversion de Picabia," *Eclaireur du Soir* [Nice], April 22, 1927.

Baur, John I.H. "The Machine and the Subconscious: Dada in America," *Magazine of Art*, XL, no. 6 (New York, October 1951), 233–37.

Begot, Jean Pierre. "L'Oeuvre de Georges Ribemont-Dessaignes de 1915 à 1930," Ph.D. dissertation, University of Paris, 1972.

Belz, Carl. "Man Ray and New York Dada," *Art Journal*, XXIII, no. 3 (New York, spring 1964), 207–213.

Bertelli, C.F. "Portrait Rejected for Salon, Bitter Art War Stirs Paris," *New York American*, October 28, 1921.

Blanche, Jacques-Emile. "La Semaine artistique," *Comoedia* [Paris], March 3, 1920, 2.

——— "La Semaine artistique," *Comoedia* [Paris], April 21, 1920, 2.

Bluemner, Oscar. "Audiator et Altera Pars: Some Plain Sense on the Modern Art Movement," *Camera Work*, special no. (New York, June 1913), 25–38.

Boisson, Marius. "Le Premier Vendredi de 'Littérature,' " *Comoedia* [Paris], January 24, 1920, 3.

Bonnet, Marguerite. "A propos de Cortège: Apollinaire et Picabia," *La Revue des lettres modernes*, special Apollinaire no. (Paris, November 1963), 62–75.

Bouche, Louis. "Art Activities in Post-War Paris," *The Arts*, I, no. 6 (New York, June–July 1921), 28–32.

Boucher, Maurice. "Les Ballets suédois. 'Relâche,' de MM. Erik Satie et Picabia. 'Entr'acte,' intermède cinématographique de M. René Clair, musique de M. E. Satie," *L'Avenir* [Paris], December 9, 1924 (attrib.).

Bouisson, Maurice. "La Musique. Relâche–Entr'acte de Picabia et Erik Satie," *L'Evénement* [Paris], December 4, 1924, 2.

Boulanger, Marcel. "De l'utilisation du mouvement Dada," *Comoedia* [Paris], March 28, 1920, 1.

———— "Herr Dada," *Le Gaulois* [Paris], April 26, 1920, 1.

Breton, André. "Pour Dada," *La Nouvelle Revue française*, no. 83 (Paris, August 1, 1920), 208–215.

[Breton, André]. "Avant le Congrès de Paris," *Comoedia* [Paris], January 3, 1922, 2.

Breton, André, et al. Open letter concerning the Congress of Paris, *Comoedia* [Paris], February 7, 1922.

Breton, André. "Après Dada," *Comoedia* [Paris], March 2, 1922, 2.

———— "Lâchez tout," *Littérature*, II, no. 2 (Paris, April 1, 1922), 8–10.

———— "Vacances d'artistes," *Littérature*, II, no. 5 (Paris, October 1, 1922), 14–15.

———— "Entrée des médiums," *Littérature*, II, no. 6 (Paris, November 1, 1922), 1–16.

———— "Francis Picabia," *The Little Review* (London and New York, winter 1922), 41–44.

———— "Caractères de l'évolution moderne et ce qui en participe" [November 1922] in *Les Pas perdus*. Paris: La Nouvelle Revue Française, February 1924, 181–212.

———— "Idées d'un peintre" in *Les Pas perdus*. Paris: La Nouvelle Revue Française, February 1924, 105–110.

———— Letter to Picabia published by Picabia as "Une Lettre de mon grand-père," *391*, no. 17 (Paris, June 1924), 4.

———— "La Querelle du Surréalisme. M. André Breton répond," *Le Journal littéraire*, no. 20 (Paris, September 6, 1924), 10.

Breunig, L.C. "Apollinaire et le Cubisme," *La Revue des lettres modernes*, nos. 69–70 (Paris, spring 1962), 7–24.

———— and J.-Cl. Chevalier. "Apollinaire et 'Les Peintres cubistes,'" *La Revue des lettres modernes*, nos. 104–107 (Paris, 1964), 89–112.

Buffet, Gabrielle. "Modern Art and the Public," *Camera Work*, special no. (New York, June 1913), 10–14.

———— "A propos de vernissage," *Les Soirées de Paris* (December 15, 1913), 5.

———— "Musique d'aujourd'hui," *Les Soirées de Paris* (March 15, 1914), 181–83.

Buffet-Picabia, Gabrielle. "A Frenchwoman's Impressions of New York and Certain American Traits," unidentified newspaper [New York], ca. March–April 1913.

———— "Arthur Cravan and American Dada," *Transition*, no. 27 (The Hague, April–May 1938), 314–21.

———— "Matières plastiques," *XXᵉ Siècle*, I–II, no. 2 (Paris, May 1, 1938), 31–35.

———— "Some Memories of Pre-Dada: Picabia and Duchamp" in *The Dada Painters and Poets*, ed. Robert Motherwell. New York: Wittenborn, Schultz, Inc., 1951, 255–67.

———— "La Section d'Or," *Art d'aujourd'hui*, IV (Paris, May 1953), 74–76.

———— "Aux temps du Futurisme," *Information et Documents* (Paris, January 1, 1957), 32–37.

Caffin, Charles. "The International—Yes—But Matisse and Picabia?" *New York American*, March 3, 1913.

Camfield, William A. "Juan Gris and the Golden Section," *The Art Bulletin*, XLVII, no. 1 (New York, March 1965), 128–34.

Candoer, Joan. "In the World of Society," *Chicago Examiner*, March 28, 1913, 9.

[Carey, Elizabeth Luther]. "Art at Home and Abroad: News and Comments," *New York Times*, January 24, 1915, sec. 5, 11. Reprinted in *Camera Work*, no. 48 (New York, October 1916), 17.

Carey, Elizabeth L. "Pictures by Chase, Some Energetic Rebels, and Others," *New York Times*, April 29, 1928, sec. 10, 18.

Carpentier, C.-A. "Dans le secteur de cabotinville," *Le Poilu* [Paris], May 1, 1920 (attrib.).

Carre, Jeffrey J. "Guillaume Apollinaire à Rouen," *La Revue des lettres modernes*, [no. 4], (Paris, 1964), 157–59.

de Casseres, Benjamin. "Modernity and the Decadence," *Camera Work*, no. 37 (New York, January 1912), 17–19.

"Ce que l'on dit," *Echo de Paris*, December 17, 1921, 2.

de Champclos, G. Davin. "Désentravons-nous!" *Comoedia* [Paris], March 20, 1912, 2.

C[harensol], G[eorges]. "Manifestation Dada," *Comoedia* [Paris], March 29, 1920, 2.

Chipp, Herschel B. "Orphism and Color Theory," *The Art Bulletin*, XL (New York, March 1958), 55–63.

Christian [Georges Herbiet]. "In the Minor Key of an Epoch," *The Little Review* (London and New York, winter 1922), 29–34.

——— "Annales du pélican," "Copie d'une lettre-morale de Picabia," "Origine" and "Moralité," *Cahiers Dada Surréalisme*, no. 2 (Paris, 1968), 185–202.

"Civitas Learns About Modern Art," *Brooklyn Daily Eagle* [New York], April 10, 1913, 7 (attrib.).

Cocteau, Jean. "Les Mariés de la Tour Eiffel," *L'Esprit nouveau*, no. 10 (Paris, July 1921).

——— "Cocteau saluant Picabia," *The Little Review* (London, spring 1922), 20.

Cogniat, R. "Pourquoi M. Signac a refusé 2 toiles à M. Picabia," *Comoedia* [Paris], January 21, 1922, 2.

Cole, Robert J. Exhibition review, *Evening Sun* [New York], October 12, 1915.

Cook, George Cram. Review of Arthur Dove exhibition. *Chicago Evening Post Literary Review*, March 29, 1912.

Cortissoz, Royal. "Exhibitions and Other Matters of Fine Art," *New York Tribune*, January 17, 1915.

——— "The Old Order and the New in the Art of Painting," *New York Tribune*, December 12, 1915, sec. 3–4, 3.

Crevel, René. "Voici . . . Tristan Tzara," *Les Nouvelles littéraires* (Paris, October 25, 1924, attrib.).

Crotti, Jean, and Suzanne Crotti. "Sous-entendu," *Le Pilhaou-Thibaou* (Paris, July 10, 1921, 3; no. 15 of *391*).

Crotti, Jean. "Tabu," *The Little Review*, VIII, no. 2 (New York, spring 1922), 45.

Croze, J.L. "Entr'acte," *Comoedia* [Paris], December 5, 1924, 4.

"Cubisme et tradition chez M. Léonce Rosenberg à Paris," *Art et industrie* (Paris, December 1930), 14–18.

Daven, André-L. "Entr'acte," *Comoedia* [Paris], October 31, 1924, 4.

Decharme, Emile. "Charlie Chaplin et le mouvement Dada," *Le Journal du peuple* [Paris], February 2, 1920, 2.

Dermée, Paul. "Premier et Dernier Rapport du secrétaire de la Section d'Or. Excommuniés," *391*, no. 12 (Paris, March 1920).

———— and Ivan Goll. Open letter "Autour du Surréalisme," *Le Journal littéraire*, no. 19 (Paris, August 30, 1924), 4.

Desnos, Robert. "L'Aumonyme," *Littérature*, II, no. 10 (Paris, May 1923), 24.

———— "Dernière Heure," *391*, no. 19 (Paris, October 1924).

———— "Après 'Relâche,' " *Paris-Journal*, December 12, 1924 (attrib.).

———— "Entr'acte par Francis Picabia, mise en scène de René Clair," *Le Journal littéraire*, no. 34 (Paris, December 13, 1924), 15.

Divoire, Fernand. "Un Nouveau Surréalisme," *Le Journal littéraire*, no. 26 (Paris, October 18, 1924), 5.

Dorival, Bernard. "Les Nouvelles artistiques. De Vallotton à Picabia," *Les Nouvelles littéraires*, no. 1129 (Paris, April 21, 1949), 6.

Dougue, Onésime. "Mouvement Fada à Marseille," *Le Merle blanc* [Paris], January 14, 1920, 3.

Dubosc, Georges. "Exposition de la Société Normande de Peinture Moderne," *Journal de Rouen*, June 17, 1912, 3.

[Duchamp, Marcel, Roché and Wood]. Editorial, *The Blind Man*, no. 2 (New York, May 1917).

Duchamp, Marcel. "Eleven Europeans in America," *The Museum of Modern Art Bulletin*, XIII, nos. 4–5 (New York, 1946), 21.

———— "Non car . . . ," *Combat-Art* [Paris], December 6, 1954, 1.

Dumont, Pierre. "Les Indépendants," *Les Hommes du jour* (Paris, April 20, 1912).

Dunan, Renée. "Gazette littéraire."/"Dada?" *Le Journal du peuple* [Paris], March 6, 1920, 3.

"Echos," *Comoedia* [Paris], February 15, 1912, 1.

"Les Éditions de 'L'Ours,' " *Le Gil Blas* [Paris], December 31, 1913, 4.

Eluard, Paul, et al. Open letter dated February 14, 1922, *Comoedia* [Paris], February 20, 1922, 2.

"Encore des Dadas," *Carnet de la semaine* (Paris, May 22, 1921), 9.

"Erotisme" and "Un Réveillon unique," *Le Journal littéraire*, no. 38 (Paris, January 10, 1925), 4.

d'E[sparbès], A[sté]. "Les 'Dadas' visitent Paris," *Comoedia* [Paris], April 14, 1921, 2.

d'Esparbès, Asté. "Les Disciples de 'Dada' à l'Eglise Saint-Julien-le-Pauvre," *Comoedia* [Paris], April 15, 1921, 2.

———— "Un Vernissage mouvementé," *Comoedia* [Paris], May 7, 1921, 2.

———— "Les Dadas ont dépassé la mesure," *Comoedia* [Paris], May 15, 1921, 1.

———— "Le Vernissage de l'exposition Dada," *Comoedia* [Paris], June 7, 1921, 2.

Estienne, Charles. "Picabia peintre et l'esprit Dada," *Combat* [Paris], August 3, 1947 (attrib.).

"L'Evolution de l'art. Vers l'Amorphisme," *Les Hommes du jour*, no. 276 (Paris, May 3, 1913).

"Les Fauves," *La Vie parisienne*, May 3, 1913, 309.

Félix. "La Potinière," *Funuusio*, no. 315 (Paris, March 1920), 433–34.

"Une Fête chez les cannibales au Château Madrid," *Cannes l'été*, August 1929 (attrib.).

"Five Picabia Works Sold to Satisfy Debt, but Don't," *New York Herald Tribune*, May 24, 1951.

de la Fouchardière, G. "Hors d'oeuvre," *Oeuvre* [Paris], January 17, 1922 (attrib.).

G[lautier], M[aximilien] [Max Goth]. "D'un certain esprit . . . ," *391*, no. 2 (Barcelona, February 10, 1917), 4.

Geffroy, Gustave. "Le Mouvement Dada," *France libre* [Paris], April 3, 1920 (attrib.).

Georges-Michel, Michel. "Le Cas Picabia et quelques autres," *L'Ordre* (Paris, May 6, 1946).

Gide, André. "Dada," *La Nouvelle Revue française*, no. 79 (Paris, April 1, 1920), 447–81.

Gir., Ch. "La Foire aux croûtes," *Paris-Journal*, ca. November 1921 (attrib.).

Gleizes, Albert. "L'Affaire Dada," *Action*, no. 3 (Paris, April 1920), 26–32.

Goll, Ivan. "Une Réhabilitation du Surréalisme," *Le Journal littéraire*, no. 17 (Paris, August 16, 1924), 8.

"Une Grave Scission chez les Dada-istes," *Carnet de la semaine* (Paris, April 18, 1920), 9.

Gros, G.-J. "La Semaine artistique," *Paris-Midi*, October 27, 1928, 2.

H., L. "Le Réveillon cacodylate," *Comoedia* [Paris], January 2, 1922, 3.

Hamilton, George Heard. "John Covert: Early American Modern," *College Art Journal*, XII, no. 1 (New York, fall 1952), 37–42.

———— "The Alfred Stieglitz Collection," *Metropolitan Museum Journal*, III (New York, 1970), 371–92.

Haviland, Paul B. Review of Gelett Burgess exhibition, *Camera Work*, no. 37 (New York, January 1912), 46–47.

———— Untitled entry, *291*, no. 1 (New York, March 1915).

———— Statement, *291*, nos. 7–8 (New York, September–October 1915).

Henderson, Linda Dalrymple. "A New Facet of Cubism: 'The Fourth Dimension' and 'Non-Euclidean Geometry' Reinterpreted," *The Art Quarterly*, XXXIV, no. 4 (Detroit, winter 1971), 410–33.

Homer, William Innes. "Stieglitz and 291," *Art in America*, no. 4 (New York, July–August 1973), 50–57.

Hugnet, Georges. "L'Esprit Dada dans la peinture," *Cahiers d'art*, VII, no. 1–2 (Paris, 1932), 57–65; no. 6–7 (Paris, 1932), 281–85; no. 8–10 (Paris, 1932), 358–64; IX, no. 1–4 (Paris, 1934), 109–114; XI, no. 8 (Paris, 1936), 267–72.

Hunt, Ronald. "The Picabia-Breton Axis," *Artforum*, V, no. 1 (Los Angeles, September 1966), 17–20.

Jacquemont, Jean. "Chronique parisienne," *Le Petit Havre*, June 14, 1921 (attrib.).

Joly, Auguste. "Sur le Futurisme," *La Belgique artistique et littéraire*, XXVIII, no. 82 (Brussels, July 1912), 68–74. Reprinted as a futurist broadsheet.

Jourdain, Frantz. Open letter in "Les Arts au Salon d'Automne," *L'Intransigeant* [Paris], October 13, 1921, 2.

Kahn, Gustave. "Réponse des Symbolistes," *L'Evénement* [Paris], September 28, 1886.

Klein, Michael. "John Covert's 'Time': Cubism, Duchamp, Einstein—a Quasi-Scientific Fantasy," *Art Journal*, XXXIII, no. 4 (New York, summer 1974), 314–20.

Laloy, Louis. "L'Antre des gnomes," *Comoedia* [Paris], July 4, 1920.

———— "Le Surréalisme," *Comoedia* [Paris], November 11, 1924, 4.

Lebel, Robert. "Picabia et Duchamp, ou le pour et le contre," *Paru*, no. 55 (Paris, November 1949).

Léger, Fernand. "L'Art moderne," *L'Ere nouvelle* [Paris], August 5, 1924, 2.

———— "Vive 'Relâche,' " *Paris-Midi*, December 17, 1924, 4.

Lemoine, Jean-Gabriel. "Le Mouvement Dada," *Le Gaulois* [Paris], March 20, 1920, literary supplement, 2.

———— "Dadaïsme," *Je sais tout* (Paris, June 1920), 588–91.

Lenormand, H.R. "Dadaïsme et psychologie," *Comoedia* [Paris], March 23, 1920, 1.

Lewis, D.B. Wyndham. "XXII—The Return," *Daily Mail* [London], March 26, 1927.

Lewis, Wyndham. "A Review of Contemporary Art," *Blast*, no. 2 (London, July 1915), 44.

Lippard, Lucy R. "Dada into Surrealism. Notes on Max Ernst as Proto-Surrealist," *Artforum*, V, no. 1 (Los Angeles, September 1966), 10–15.

M., P. "Relâche," *Paris-Journal*, December 5, 1924, 1.

"Mme. Georgette Leblanc," *Presse* [Montreal], December 15, 1923 (attrib.).

Mairol, Raphaël. "Le Grand Palais fermé au Salon d'Automne?" *Comoedia* [Paris], October 13, 1912, 2.

Malkine, Georges, et al. "Encore le Surréalisme," *Le Journal littéraire*, no. 18 (Paris, August 23, 1924), 8.

de Maré, Rolf. "La Prochaine Saison des ballets suédois," *Comoedia* [Paris], July 10, 1924, 2.

———— "A propos de 'Relâche,' ballet instantanéiste," *Comoedia* [Paris], November 27, 1924, 2.

Marinetti, F.T. "Le Tactilisme," *Comoedia* [Paris], January 16, 1921, 1.

Marson, Eugène, et al. "Relâche," unidentified newspaper [Paris], ca. December 6, 1924 (attrib.).

Martin, Marianne W. "Futurism, Unanimism and Apollinaire," *Art Journal*, XXVIII, no. 3 (New York, spring 1969), 258–68.

Martin du Gard, Maurice. "Le Surréalisme? André Breton," *Les Nouvelles littéraires* (Paris, October 10, 1924).

de Massot, Pierre. "Post-scriptum aux Mariés de la Tour Eiffel," *Le Pilhaou-Thibaou* (Paris, July 10, 1921, 14; no. 15 of *391*).

———— "Un Film 'nouveau,' " *L'Ere nouvelle* [Paris], ca. October–November, 1924 (attrib.).

———— "Relâche, ballet de plein-air," *Paris-Journal*, December 5, 1924 (not verified).

Mayr, W. "Entretien avec Erik Satie," *Le Journal littéraire*, no. 24 (Paris, October 4, 1924), 11.

McCormick, William B. "Patrons Vote to Decide Fate of Photo-Secession Gallery at No. 291 Fifth Avenue," *New York Press*, October 4, 1914, 6.

Mercure de France, Blaise Cendrars issue, no. 1185 (Paris, May 1962. Multiple authors).

Mérize, Georges. "Courrier des lettres et des arts," *Lanterne* [Paris], January 1, 1914, 2.

de Meurville, Louis. "Une Exposition tri-nationale," *Le Gaulois* [Paris], May 31, 1925, 2.

Minuit, Peter [Paul Rosenfeld]. "291 Fifth Avenue," *The Seven Arts* (New York, November 1916), 61–65.

" 'Modernist' Chef in Paris Cooks Strange Recipes," *Herald Tribune* [Paris], May 29, 1927 (attrib.).

Monroe, Harriet. "Davidson's Sculpture Proves that Artist Has Ideas," *Chicago Sunday Tribune*, March 23, 1913, sec. 8, 5.

——— "Record-Breaking Crowds See the Cubist Exhibit," *Chicago Tribune*, April 13, 1913.

"Monsieur Francis Picabia," *Le Cancan* (Cannes, May 26, 1935, attrib.).

Moussinac, Léon. "Entr'acte, par René Clair," *Le Crapouillot* [Paris], January 1, 1925, 19.

"Le Mouvement Toutou (1920)," *Le Crapouillot* [Paris], May 15, 1920, 8–9.

Naumann, Francis. "Cryptography and the Arensberg Circle" and "I Shock Myself: Excerpts from the Autobiography of Beatrice Wood," *Arts Magazine*, LI, no. 9 (New York, May 1977), 127–33, 134–39.

"The Newest 'Ism' is 'Surrealism,' " *The Art Digest*, I, no. 3 (Hopewell, N. J., May 1, 1927), 8.

"Nobody Who Has Been Drinking is Let in to See This Show," *World* [New York], February 17, 1913, 16.

Oudard, Georges. "Une Soirée chez Dada," *Le Gaulois* [Paris], May 4, 1921 (attrib.).

Padgett, Ron. "Poets and Painters in Paris, 1919–1939," *Art News Annual: The Avant-Garde*, XXXIV (New York, 1968), 88–95.

Pailleron, Marie-Louise. "Le Mouvement Dada," *L'Opinion*, no. 7 (Paris, February 14, 1920), 180–81.

Pansaers, Clément. "Une Bombe déconfiture," *Le Pilhaou-Thibaou* (Paris, July 10, 1921, 8; no. 15 of *391*).

——— "Dada et moi," *Ça ira*, no. 16 (Antwerp, November 1921), 111–15.

"Paris Autumn Salon," *Morning Post* [London], October 31, 1921 (attrib.).

"Paris Postscripts," *The Arts*, VIII, no. 1 (New York, July 1925), 51–54; no. 2 (New York, August 1925), 109.

Patin, Jacques. "Un Festival Dada," *Le Figaro* [Paris], May 27, 1920, 1 (attrib.).

"Peintres au soleil. Bonjour Picabia!" *L'Eclaireur* [Nice], February 2, 1943 (attrib.).

"Petites Nouvelles," *Le Journal du peuple* [Paris], May 3, 1924, 3.

Picabia, Francis, et al. "Les Ballets suédois. 'Relâche' de Francis Picabia," *Montparnasse* [Paris, December 1, 1924, attrib.).

Picard, Gaston. "Relâche," *Le Journal littéraire*, no. 36 (Paris, December 27, 1924), 4.

Pincus-Witten, Robert. "On Target: Symbolist Roots of American Abstraction," *Arts Magazine*, L, no. 8 (New York, April 1976), 84–91.

Prevot, Ellen. "Au Salon des Indépendants, loufoqueries," *Le Midi* [Toulouse], February 19, 1922, 1.

Rachilde, Mme. "Le Sourire silencieux," *Comoedia* [Paris], April 1, 1920, 1.

———— and André Breton. "A propos du mouvement Dada" (exchange of letters), *Comoedia* [Paris], April 4, 1920.

Rachilde, Mme. "Encore un mot sur D.A.D.A.," *Comoedia* [Paris], April 14, 1920, 1.

———— "Les qu'est-ce que nous faisons ce soir?" *Comoedia* [Paris], July 29, 1921 (attrib.).

Raynal, Maurice. "Littérature," *L'Esprit nouveau*, nos. 11–12 (Paris, August–September 1921), 1282–89.

Revel, Jean-François. "Jacques Doucet couturier et collectionneur," *L'Oeil*, no. 84 (Paris, December 1961), 44–51, 81, 106.

Rex, Margery. " 'Dada' Will Get You if You Don't Watch Out; It Is on the Way Here," *New York Evening Journal*, January 29, 1921 (attrib.).

Ribemont-Dessaignes, Georges. "Salon d'Automne," *391*, no. 9 (Paris, November 1919), 2–3.

———— "La Cravate de Dada," *Le Journal du peuple* [Paris], February 10, 1922, 1.

———— "Les Greniers du Vatican," *Les Ecrits nouveaux* [Paris], February 1922 (attrib.).

———— "Dada Painting or the Oil-Eye," *The Little Review* (London, autumn–winter 1923–1924), 10–12.

———— "A propos du Surréalisme," *Le Mouvement accéléré* (Paris, November 1924), 2.

———— "Histoire de Dada," *La Nouvelle Revue française*, no. 213 (Paris, June 1931), 867–79, and no. 214 (Paris, July 1931), 39–52.

———— "Dans la brume des souvenirs," *Mercure de France*, no. 1185 (Paris, May 1962), 113–18.

Rigaud, André. "M. Marinetti nous révèle le 'Tactilisme,' " *Comoedia* [Paris], January 15, 1921, 1.

[Rivière, Jacques]. "Mouvement Dada," *La Nouvelle Revue française*, no. 72 (Paris, September 1, 1919).

Rivière, Jacques. "Reconnaissance à Dada," *La Nouvelle Revue française*, no. 83 (Paris, August 1, 1920), 216–37.

Robbins, Daniel. "From Symbolism to Cubism: The Abbaye of Créteil," *Art Journal*, XXIII, no. 3 (New York, winter 1963–1964), 111–16.

Roland-Manuel. "La Quinzaine Musicale," *L'Eclair* [Paris], December 9, 1924 (attrib.).

Rosenberg, Léonce. "Parlons peinture," *L'Esprit nouveau*, no. 5 (Paris, February 1921), 578–84; no. 7 (April 1921), 748–50.

S., H. "Dada ou les croquemorts facétieux," *Carnet de la semaine* (Paris, June 6, 1920), 15.

Sanouillet, Michel. "Le Dossier de 'Dadaglobe,' " *Cahiers de l'Association Internationale pour l'Etude de Dada et du Surréalisme*, no. 1 (Paris, 1966), 111–43.

Satie, Erik. "Cahiers d'un mammifère," *391*, nos. 17 and 18 (Paris, June and July 1924).

Schapiro, Meyer. "Nature of Abstract Art," *Marxist Quarterly*, I, no. 1 (New York, January 1937), 77–98.

Schneider, Louis. "Theatre Proved to Be Closed and Public Suspects Joke," *New York Herald* [Paris], November 28, 1924 (attrib.).

———— "Music in Paris," *New York Herald* [Paris], December 8, 1924 (attrib.).

Scize, Pierre. "Après le concert des bruiteurs," *Bonsoir* [Paris], June 20, 1921, 3.

Severini, Gino. "Symbolisme plastique et symbolisme littéraire," *Mercure de France*, I, no. 2 (Paris, February 1, 1916), 466–76.

———— "La Peinture d'avant-garde," *Mercure de France*, I, no. 6 (Paris, June 1, 1917), 451–68.

"Sidelights of Paris, 'Mariés de la Tour Eiffel,' " *New York Herald* [Paris], June 22, 1921, 2.

Sirato, Charles. "Dimensionisme," *Plastique*, no. 2 (Paris, summer 1937), 25–28.

S[ouday], P[aul]. "Le Coq et Dada," *Le Temps* [Paris], May 28, 1920 (attrib.).

Soupault, Philippe. "La Poésie. La collection 'Poésie du Temps'—Le Surréalisme," *La Revue europénne*, no. 20 (Paris, October 1, 1924), 77–78.

———— "Dada," *Jardin des arts*, no. 89 (Paris, April 1962), 15–21.

Stieglitz, Alfred. "The First Great Clinic to Revitalize Art," *New York American*, January 26, 1913, sec. CE, 5.

Storrs, Caryl B. "Gazing at Weird Work of the Cubists is Rude Shock to One's Nervous System," unidentified newspaper [Chicago], ca. March 1913.

"Le Surréalisme en 1929," *Variétés*, special unno. ed. (Brussels, June 1929).

Trilby, T. "Lettre parisienne," *L'Alger* [Algeria], June 9, 1920 (attrib.).

" '291' The Mecca and the Mystery of Art in a Fifth Avenue Attic," *Sun* [New York], October 24, 1915, 6.

"291—A New Publication," *Camera Work*, no. 48 (New York, October 1916), 62.

Tzara, Tristan. "Marcel Janco," *Dada*, no. 1 (Zurich, July 1917).

———— "Note 2 sur l'art. H. Arp" and "Notes," *Dada 2* (Zurich, December 1917).

———— "Manifeste Dada 1918," *Dada 3* (Zurich, December 1918).

———— "Proclamation sans prétention," *Die Schammade* (Cologne, February 1920).

[Tzara, Tristan?]. Press release for the "Manifestation Dada" at the Maison de l'Oeuvre, Paris, March 23, 1920.

Tzara, Tristan, "Interview de Jean Metzinger sur le cubisme," *391*, no. 14 (Paris, November 1920), 8.

———— "Net," *Dada au grand air* (Paris, September 16, 1921, 1; no. 8 of *Dada*).

———— "A propos du Congrès de Paris," *Comoedia* [Paris], February 8, 1922.

———— Note dated February 10, 1922, quoted in "La Ville et les arts," *Paris-Midi*, February 14, 1922, 2.

———— "Les Dessous de Dada," *Comoedia* [Paris], March 7, 1922.

———— "Conférence sur Dada," *Merz*, II, no. 7 (Hanover, January 1924), 68–70. (Lecture presented at Dada Kongress, Weimar, 1922.)

Valmy-Baysse, J. "Le Carnet des lettres et des arts," *Comoedia* [Paris], February 10, 1920, 2.

———— "Le Carnet des lettres et des arts," *Comoedia* [Paris], February 27, 1920, 2.

Varagnac, André. "Dada," *Le Crapouillot* [Paris], April 1, 1920, 8–9.

Vauxcelles, Louis. "Carnet des ateliers," *Carnet de la semaine* (Paris, December 28, 1919).

Veber, Pierre. "Première Représentation," *Petit Journal* [Paris], January 29, 1925 (attrib.).

Vitrac, Roger. "Peau-Asie," *Littérature*, II, no. 9 (Paris, February–March 1923), 18.

——— "André Breton n'écrira plus," *Le Journal du peuple* [Paris], April 7, 1923.

Watson, Forbes. "Charles Demuth," *The Arts*, III, no. 1 (Brooklyn, January 1923), 74–80.

de Zayas, Marius. *Camera Work*: "Photography" and "The Evolution of Form—Introduction," no. 41 (New York, January 1913); "Photography and Artistic Photography," nos. 42–43 (New York, April–July 1913); "Modern Art—Theories and Representation," no. 44 (New York, October 1913); "Material, Relative and Abstract Caricatures," no. 45 (New York, January 1914).

——— Untitled entry, *291*, nos. 5–6 (New York, July–August 1915).

——— "Cubism?" *Arts and Decoration*, VI (New York, April 1916), 284–86, 308.

Zy, ". . . Da . . . DA . . . ," *La Tribune de Genève*, January 23, 1920, 5.

IV. Exhibitions

One-man exhibitions are marked by an asterisk. For many exhibitions, selected reviews are cited in an abbreviated form. Reviews of particular importance have also been cited in complete form in other sections of the bibliography. About twenty-five newspaper clippings, all brief and unidentified, are gathered in the Dossiers Picabia (vol. I) for exhibitions from 1899 to 1903.

Société des Artistes Français. Salon de 1899. Paris, May 1899.

Société des Artistes Français. Salon de 1901. Paris, May 1901.

Société des Artistes Français. Salon de 1902. Paris, May 1902.

Société des Artistes Indépendants. Salon de 1903. Paris, March 20–April 25, 1903.

Société des Artistes Français. Salon de 1903. Paris, May 1903.

Société du Salon d'Automne. Salon de 1903. Paris, October 31–December 6, 1903.
  La Croix [Paris], October 6, 1903; *La Politique coloniale Denonville*, October 10, 1903.

Société des Artistes Français. Salon de 1904. Paris, May 1904.
  Le Temps [Paris], April 13, 1904, 1; *L'Action quotidienne* [Paris], May 1, 1904.

Galerie Berthe Weill, Paris. Exhibition of Dufy, Girieud, Picabia, Picasso and Thiesson, October 1904.

Société du Salon d'Automne. Salon de 1904. Paris, October 15–November 15, 1904.
  Le Journal [Paris], October 1904 (attrib.).

*Galerie Haussmann, Paris. *Picabia*, February 10–25, 1905. Preface by L. Roger-Milès.
  Le Gil Blas [Paris], February 10, 1905, 1; *Le Gaulois* [Paris], February 10 and 20, 1905; *Le Journal* [Paris], February 10 and 24, 1905; *Le Figaro* [Paris], February 14, 1905, 5; *Echo de Paris*, February 14, 1905, 4.

Société des Artistes Français. Salon de 1905. Paris, May 1905.

Société du Salon d'Automne. Salon de 1905. Paris, November 1905.

Galeries Georges Petit, Paris. *Deuxième Salon de la Gravure Originale en Couleurs*, November 1905.

L'Art décoratif, no. 88 (Paris, January 1906), 20–21.

Grand Palais, Paris. *Troisième Salon de L'Ecole Française*, January 26–February 25, 1906.

Echo de Paris, January 2, 1906 (attrib.).

*Caspar's Kunst-Salon, Berlin. *Exposition Picabia*, April 1906.

Berliner Lokal Anzeiger, March 22, 1906 (attrib.).

Société des Artistes Français. Salon de 1906. Paris, May 1906.

Galeries Georges Petit, Paris. *Troisième Salon de la Gravure Originale en Couleurs*, November 1906.

Le Salon de Nancy, Nancy. *Le Grand Patis à Montjavault*, November 1906.

Est-Républicain [Nancy], November 12, 1906 (attrib.).

Ecole des Beaux-Arts, Paris. *Exposition des acquisitions de l'etat*, December 1906.

New York Herald [Paris], May 19, 1906 (attrib.); *Dépêche de Toulouse*, December 15, 1906 (attrib.).

*Exhibition of the work of Francis Picabia in his studio, Paris, 1906.

Grand Palais, Paris. *Quatrième Salon de L'Ecole Française*, February 1907.

Chronique des arts, no. 5 (Paris, February 2, 1907), 35.

*Galerie Haussmann, Paris. *Picabia*, February 1–15, 1907. Preface by L. Roger-Milès.

New York Herald [Paris], February 3, 1907; *La Chronique des arts et de la curiosité*, no. 6 (Paris, February 9, 1907), 46; *Le Gaulois* [Paris], February 10, 1907 (attrib.).

*Cremetti Gallery, London. *Picabia*, March 1907.

Daily Telegraph [London], April 17, 1907 (attrib.).

Société des Artistes Français. Salon de 1907. Paris, May 1907.

Galeries Georges Petit, Paris. *Quatrième Salon de la Gravure Originale en Couleurs*, October 22–November 17, 1907.

Le Journal [Paris], October 20, 1907 (attrib.); *Le Gaulois* [Paris], October 25, 1907 (attrib.).

*Hôtel Drouot, Paris. *Tableaux, aquarelles, dessins, gravures, eaux-fortes par F. Picabia*, public auction, March 8, 1909. Preface by L. Roger-Milès.

Journal des arts [Paris], March 3, 1909 (attrib.); *New York Herald* [Paris], March 9, 1909, 5.

*Galeries Georges Petit, Paris. *Exposition de tableaux par F. Picabia*, March 17–31, 1909. Preface by L. Roger-Milès.

L'Aurore [Paris], March 22, 1909 (attrib.); *Le Journal* [Paris], March 23, 1909 (attrib.); *New York Herald* [Paris], March 28, 1909 (attrib.); *La Revue des beaux-arts* [Paris], March 28, 1909 (attrib.).

Galerie de l'Art Contemporain, Paris. *Exposition de sculpture, peinture, art décoratif*, November 18, 1909–January 15, 1910. Preface by Louis Vauxcelles.

Salle Boieldien, Rouen. *Exposition de peinture moderne* [1st exhibit of the Société Normande de Peinture Moderne], December 20, 1909–January 20, 1910. Introduction by Elie Faure.

Journal de Rouen, November 28 and December 20, 1909, 2.

Société du Salon d'Automne. Salon de 1910. Paris, October 1–November 8, 1910.

Société des Artistes Indépendants. Salon de 1911. Paris, April 21–June 13, 1911.

Le Journal [Paris], April 20, 1911 (attrib.); *Gazette des Beaux-Arts*, 4th period, VI (Paris, July 11, 1911), 56.

Société Normande de Peinture Moderne, Rouen. *Deuxième Exposition*, May 1911.

Journal de Rouen, May 8, 1911 (attrib.).

Société du Salon d'Automne. Salon de 1911. Paris, October 1–November 8, 1911.

Le Temps [Paris], October 2, 1911 (attrib.).

Fantasie (Paris, November 1911, attrib.).

Galerie d'Art Ancien et d'Art Contemporain, Paris. *Exposition d'art contemporain*, November 20–December 16, 1911. Preface by René Blum.

La Côte [Paris], October 28, 1911, 8, and November 25; *L'Intransigeant* [Paris], November 19, 1911; *Le Journal* [Paris], November 22, 1911, 3; *Mercure de France* (Paris, December 16, 1911), 844–47.

Société des Artistes Indépendants. Salon de 1912. Paris, March 20–May 16, 1912.

Les Hommes du jour (Paris, April 6, 13 and 20, 1912).

Société Normande de Peinture Moderne, Rouen. *Salon de Juin* [Troisième Exposition], June 15–July 15, 1912. Prefaces by Elie Faure and Maurice Raynal.

Journal de Rouen, June 16 (attrib.) and 17, 1912, 3; *La Vie artistique* (Paris, June 22, 1912).

Société du Salon d'Automne. Salon de 1912. Paris, October 1–November 8, 1912.

Le Petit Parisien, September 30, 1912, 2; *L'Eclair* [Paris], September 30, 1912, 2; *Comoedia* [Paris], September 30, 1912, 2; *Comoedia illustré* (Paris, October 20, 1912), 62–63.

Galerie La Boétie, Paris. *Salon de La Section d'Or*, October 10–30, 1912. Preface by René Blum.

Comoedia [Paris], October 13, 1912, 3; *Le Temps* [Paris], October 14, 1912; *Excelsior* [Paris], October 18, 1912, 8; *Les Hommes du jour* (Paris, October 26, 1912); *Mercure de France* (Paris, November–December 1912), 181–82.

Association of American Painters and Sculptors. *International Exhibition of Modern Art* [The Armory Show]. New York, February 17–March 15, 1913; The Art Institute of Chicago, March 24–April 16, 1913; Copley Hall, Copley Society of Boston, April 28–May 19, 1913.

New York Sun, January 21 and March 3, 1913 (attrib.); *American Art News* (New York, January 25 and February 22, 1913); *New York American*, January 26 and March 3, 1913; *Nebraska State Journal* [Lincoln], February 9, 1913, sec. B, 7; *New York Times*, February 16 and 23, March 16, 1913; *World* [New York], February 17, 1913, 16; *Globe and Commercial Advertiser* [New York], February 20, 1913, 8; *Kansas City Star*, February 23, 1913, sec. 4D; *Minneapolis Morning Leib*, February 23, 1913 (attrib.); *Hartford Daily Courant*, March 17, 1913, 8; *Courrier Europe* [Paris], April 4, 1913 (attrib.); *Le Gil Blas* [Paris], April 4, 1913 (attrib.); *Chicago Tribune*, April 13, 1913.

*Little Gallery of the Photo-Secession ["291"], New York. *Picabia Exhibition at the Little Gallery of the Photo-Secession*, March 17–April 5, 1913. Preface by Francis Picabia.

New York Tribune, March 9, 11 and 14, 1913; *New York Herald*, March 18,

1913, 12; *World* [New York], March 23, 1913; *New York American*, March 24 and 30, 1913; *Camera Work*, nos. 42–43 (New York, April–July, 1913), 48–49.

Société des Artistes Indépendants. Salon de 1913. Paris, March 19–May 18, 1913.

Montjoie!, no. 3 (Paris, March 18, 1913), 4; *L'Intransigeant* [Paris], March 25, 1913.

Der Sturm Galerie, Berlin. *Erster Deutscher Herbstsalon*, September 20–December 1, 1913. Preface by Herwarth Walden.

Les Soirées de Paris, no. 18 (November 15, 1913).

Société du Salon d'Automne. Salon de 1913. Paris, November 15, 1913–January 5, 1914.

L'Intransigeant [Paris], November 14 and 19, 1913; *Les Soirées de Paris*, no. 18 (November 15, 1913); *Le Matin* [Paris], November 16 and December 1, 1913; *Montjoie!*, nos. 11–12 (Paris, November–December 1913), 9.

Société des Artistes Indépendants. Salon de 1914. Paris, March 1–April 30, 1914.

L'Intransigeant [Paris], March 2, 1914; *Les Soirées de Paris*, no. 22 (March 15, 1914), 183–88; *L'Effort libre* (Paris, April 1914); *Paris-Journal*, May 5, 1914.

De Onafhankelyken, Amsterdam. *3de Internationale Jury-Vrije Tentoonstelling*, May–June 1914.

Paris-Journal, May 29, 1914, 3.

*Little Gallery of the Photo-Secession ["291"], New York. *Picabia Exhibition*, January 12–26, 1915.

New York Tribune, January 17, 1915; *New York Herald*, January 18 and 19, 1915; *New York Times*, January 24, 1915, sec. 5, 11.

Modern Gallery, New York. *Opening Exhibition*, October 1915.

Evening Sun [New York], October 12, 1915 (attrib.); *Arts and Decoration* (New York, November 1915), 35–36; *New York Tribune*, December 12, 1915, sec. 3–4, 3; *The Forum* (New York, December 1915), 669–70.

Post-Exposition Exhibition (of the Panama-Pacific Exposition), San Francisco, January 1–May 1, 1916.

*Modern Gallery, New York. *Picabia Exhibition*, January 5–25, 1916.

American Art News, no. 14 (New York, January 8, 1916), 3; *New York Evening World*, January 9, 1916, sec. 2, 3; *Sun* [New York], January 16, 1916, sec. 3, 7, and January 23, 1916, sec. 5, 8; *Christian Science Monitor* [Boston], January 29, 1916.

J. E. McClees and Co., Philadelphia. *Exhibition of Modern Art*, May–June, 1916.

Arts and Decoration (New York, July 1916), 440.

Bourgeois Galleries, New York. *Exhibition of Modern Art*, February 10–March 10, 1917.

The Society of Independent Artists, New York. *First Annual Exhibition*, April 10–May 6, 1917.

The Society of Independent Artists, New York. *Second Annual Exhibition*, April 20–May 12, 1918.

Le Salon d'Art Wolfsberg, Zurich. *Exhibition of Modern Art*, September 1918.

Kunsthaus Zurich. *"Das Neue Leben" Erste Ausstellung*, January 12–February 5, 1919. Preface by Marcel Janco. Originated in Basel, November 1918?.

Nationalzeitung [Basel], November 26–27, 1918; *Neue Zürcher Zeitung*

[Zurich], January 12, 1919, 1; *Dada 4–5* (Zurich, May 15, 1919).

Arden Gallery, New York. *The Evolution of French Art*, April 29–May 24, 1919. Organized by Marius de Zayas.

Société du Salon d'Automne. Salon de 1919. Paris, November 1–December 10, 1919.

391, no. 9 (Paris, November 1919); *Le Matin* [Paris], November 1, 1919; *Le Journal du peuple* [Paris], November 2, 1919, 2; *France libre* [Paris], November 3, 1919; *La Petite Gironde* [Bordeaux], November 24, 1919 (attrib.); *Images de Paris*, no. 3 (December 1919), 42.

Cirque d'Hiver, Paris. *Exhibition of Modern Art*, December 1919.

Le Journal du peuple [Paris], December 19, 1919, 2; *Comoedia* [Paris], December 22, 1919, 3.

Société des Artistes Indépendants. Salon de 1920. Paris, January 28–February 29, 1920.

New York Herald [Paris], January 1920, 2; *L'Indépendance Belge* [Brussels?], February 2, 1920 (attrib.); *Mercure de France* (Paris, March 1, 1920), 506.

Salon Néri, Geneva. *Dada Exposition (Serner)*. Francis Picabia, Georges Ribemont-Dessaignes, April 1920.

*Au Sans Pareil, Paris. *Exposition Dada: Francis Picabia*, April 16–30, 1920. Preface by Tristan Tzara.

La Suisse [Geneva], April 19, 1920 (attrib.); *L'Esprit nouveau*, no. 1 (Paris, October 1920), 108–110.

Brauhaus Winter, Cologne. *Dada-Vorfrühling: Gemälde, Skulpturen, Zeichnungen, Fluidoskeptrik, Vulgardilettantismus*, April–May 1920.

Galleries of the Société Anonyme, New York. *First Exhibition*, April 30–June 15, 1920.

Kunsthandlung Dr. Otto Burchard, Berlin. *Erste Internationale Dada-Messe*, June 5–August 25, 1920.

Galleries of the Société Anonyme, New York. *Third Exhibition*, August 2–September 11, 1920.

Galerie Mauzi-Joyant, Paris. *La Jeune Peinture française*, September 1920.

Le Temps d'Asie [Saigon], September 13, 1920 (attrib.).

Galeries Dalmau, Barcelona. *Exposicio d'avantgarda*, October 1920.

Vuc de Cataluña [Barcelona], October 30, 1920 (attrib.).

Société du Salon d'Automne. Salon de 1920. Paris, October 15–December 12, 1920.

L'Avenir [Paris], October 16, 1920, 3; *Le Radical* [Paris], October 18, 1920, 2; *La France* [Bordeaux], October 26, 1920 (attrib.); *Les Hommes du jour*, no. 6 (Paris, October–November 1920), 17–29; *Le Soir* [Oran], November 10, 1920 (attrib.).

*Galerie Povolozky [Galerie La Cible], Paris. *Exposition Picabia*, December 10–25, 1920. Text by Marie de La Hire.

Le Radical [Paris], December 11, 1920; *Comoedia* [Paris], December 12, 1920, 1–2; *Carnet de la semaine* (Paris, December 20, 1920, attrib.); *The Arts*, I, no. 3 (Brooklyn, February–March 1921), 60; *De Stijl*, IV, no. 6 (Leyden, June 1921), 89–90.

Société des Artistes Indépendants. Salon de 1921. Paris, January 23–February 28, 1921.

Arts et lettres [Geneva], January 25, 1921 (attrib.); *Le Merle blanc* [Paris], January 29, 1921, 1.

*Galerie Dalpayrat, Limoges. *Exposition Picabia*, February 1–15, 1921.

Société du Salon d'Automne. Salon de 1921. Paris, November 1–December 20, 1921.

    L'Intransigeant [Paris], October 13, 1921, 2; *Comoedia* [Paris], October 28 and November 23, 1921; *Le Rappel* [Paris], October 30, 1921, 3; *Morning Post* [London], October 31, 1921 (attrib.); *Le Gaulois* [Paris], November 5, 1921, 4; *Le Matin* [Paris], November 9 and 10, 1921; *Le Canard enchaîné* [Paris], November 9, 1921, 2; *L'Eclair* [Paris], November 10, 1921 (attrib.); *Echo de Paris*, December 17, 1921, 2.

Worcester Art Museum. *Paintings by Members of the Société Anonyme*, November 3–December 5, 1921.

The Art Institute of Chicago. *The Arthur J. Eddy Collection*, 1922.

Société des Artistes Indépendants. Salon de 1922. Paris, January 28–February 28, 1922.

    Comoedia [Paris], January 19, 21 and 23, 1922; *Le Figaro* [Paris], January 20, 1922, 3; *La Presse* [Paris], January 20, 1922, 1; *Le Journal du peuple* [Paris], January 21 and 23, 1922; *Le Radical* [Marseille], January 30, 1922 (attrib.); *Le Midi* [Toulouse], February 19, 1922, 1.

MacDowell Club, New York. *Exhibition of the Collection of the Société Anonyme*, April 24–May 8, 1922.

Société du Salon d'Automne. Salon de 1922. Paris, November 1–December 17, 1922.

    L'Intransigeant [Paris], October 31, 1922, 1–2; *Montparnasse* (Paris, November 1, 1922), 3; *Le Reveil du nord* [Lille], November 21, 1922, 1.

*Galeries Dalmau, Barcelona. *Exposition Francis Picabia*, November 18–December 8, 1922. Preface by André Breton.

    [?] *Dimeores* [Barcelona], November 22, 1922 (attrib.).

Société des Artistes Indépendants. Salon de 1923. Paris, February 10–March 11, 1923.

    Oeuvre [Paris], February 13, 1923 (attrib.); *Journal de Liège*, June 21, 1923 (attrib.).

*Exposition chez Danthon, Paris. *Francis Picabia*, May 1923. Preface by G[ermaine] E[verling].

    Paris-Journal, May 6, 1923, 2; *L'Ere nouvelle* [Paris], May 15, 1923 (attrib.); *Comoedia* [Paris], May 24, 1923, 3; *Les Hommes du jour* (Paris, ca. June 1923), 10; *Le Journal* [Paris], June 14, 1923 (attrib.); *L'Eclaireur de Nice*, June 15, 1923, 3; *Telegraaf* [Amsterdam], July 21, 1923 (attrib.).

Société "Les Amis des Arts," Limoges. *Exposition*, May 10–June 3, 1923. Not listed in catalogue.

    Populaire du centre [Limoges], May 14, 1923 (attrib.).

Salon de Grenoble, Grenoble, June 30–July 30, 1923.

    Quotidien [Grenoble?], July 23, 1926 (attrib.).

Société du Salon d'Automne. Salon de 1923. Paris, November 1–December 16, 1923.

    Le Canard enchaîné [Paris], November 7, 1923, 4; *Arlequin* (Paris?, December 1, 1923, attrib.).

Société des Amateurs d'Art et des Collectionneurs, Paris. *Le Salon de la folle enchère*, November 15–30, 1923.

    Paris-Journal, November 30, 1923 (attrib.); *La Revue Européenne*, no. 13 (Paris, March 1, 1924), 65–67.

Société des Artistes Indépendants. Salon de 1924. Paris, February 9–March 12, 1924.

    Paris-Journal, February 8, 1924, 1–2; *Bonsoir* [Paris], February 9, 1924, 2; *L'Opinion* (Paris, February 15, 1924, attrib.).

Galerie Paul Guillaume, Paris. Benefit exhibition for Guillaume Apollinaire, ca. June 1924.

    Paris-Journal, June 20, 1924 (attrib.).

Galerie Mesens, Brussels, 1924 (not verified).

Galeries Durand-Ruel, Paris. *Exposition tri-nationale*, May–June 1925; London, October 1925; New York, November 1925.

    Le Gaulois [Paris], May 31, 1925, 2; *The Arts*, VIII, no. 1 (New York, July 1925), 51–54, and no. 2 (New York, August 1925), 109.

*Hôtel Drouot, Paris. *Tableaux, aquarelles et dessins par Francis Picabia appartenant à M. Marcel Duchamp*, public auction, March 8, 1926. Preface by Marcel Duchamp.

    Le Gaulois [Paris], March 9, 1924 (attrib.); *Inventaire*, no. 1 (Paris, ca. March 1924, attrib.); *Plaisir de vivre* [Paris], March 5, 1926 (attrib.); *Excelsior* [Paris], March 9, 1926 (attrib.).

Galerie Barbazanges, Paris. *Exposition*, April 1926.

    Journal des arts [Paris], April 17, 1926 (attrib.).

Galerie Detaille, Marseille. *Exposition des "Fauves,"* April 1926.

    Soleil du Midi [Marseille], April 5, 1926 (attrib.).

Hôtel Drouot, Paris. Public auction, May 31, 1926.

    Le Figaro [Paris], June 1, 1926, 7.

Dresden. *Internationale Kunstausstellung*, June–September 1926. Not listed in catalogue.

Brooklyn Museum, New York. *An International Exhibition of Modern Art*, assembled by the Société Anonyme, November 9, 1926–January 1, 1927; Anderson Galleries, New York, January 25–February 5, 1927.

Galerie au Sacre du Printemps, Paris. Benefit exhibition for Jan Sliwinski, November 30–December 11, 1926.

    Paris-Times, November 27, 1926 (attrib.).

Galerie Bernheim Jeune, Paris. *Exposition multinationale*, January 3–14, 1927.

    Impartial français [Paris], January 25, 1927 (attrib.).

*Cercle Nautique, Cannes. *Exposition Francis Picabia*, January 28–February 7, 1927. Preface by Emeran Clémansin Du Maine; statement by Emile Fabre; and "Lumière froide" by Picabia.

    L'Homme libre [Paris], January 27, 1927, 1–2; *L'Eclaireur de Nice et du Sud-Est*, January 28, 1927, 3; *Le Journal* [Paris], February 8, 1927, 2; *L'Humanité* [Paris], February 26 and March 14, 1927.

Société des Beaux-Arts de Nice. *50me Exposition*, March 1927.

    Eclaireur du soir [Nice], April 22, 1927.

*Galerie Van Leer, Paris. *Exposition Picabia*, October 24–November 5, 1927.

    Drawing and Design, III, no. 16 (London, October 1927), 168; *Cahiers d'art*, no. 7–8 (Paris, 1927), supplement, 4; *L'Art vivant* (Paris, November 1, 1927), 897–900.

*Galerie Briant-Robert, Paris. *Francis Picabia*, November 11–30, 1927. Preface by Robert Desnos.

    Bulletin de l'Effort Moderne, no. 38 (Paris, October 1927), 8–9; *Paris-Midi*, November 16, 1927, 2; *Comoedia* [Paris], November 17, 1927, 3.

*Chez Fabre, Cannes. *Exposition Francis Picabia*, February 20–25, 1928. Statement by Emile Fabre; prolegomena by Emeran Clémansin Du Maine.
L'Eclaireur de Nice et du Sud-Est, February 22, 1928, 6; *Le Littorel* [Cannes], February 26, 1928, 3; *Cannes l'hiver*, no. 1632 (1928), 17–23 (attrib.).

*The Intimate Gallery, New York. *Picabia Exhibition*, April 19–May 11, 1928.
New York Times, April 29, 1928, sec. 10, 18.

La Galerie de l'Exposition de La Renaissance, Paris. *Portraits et figures de femmes, Ingres à Picasso*, June 1–30, 1928.
La Renaissance (Paris, July 1928).

*Galerie Th[éophile] Briant, Paris. *Francis Picabia*, October 26–November 15, 1928.
Paris-Midi, October 27, 1928, 2; *L'Art vivant* (Paris, November 15, 1928), 899–900.

*Chez Fabre, Cannes. *Exposition Francis Picabia*, April 11–27, 1929. Preface by E. Fabre.
L'Eclaireur de Nice et du Sud-Est, April 8, 1929, 4.

*Galerie Théophile Briant, Paris. *Exposition Picabia*, November 12–December 7, 1929.
La Critique cinématographique (Paris, October 29, 1929, attrib.); *Comoedia* [Paris], November 21, 1929, 3; *L'Intransigeant* [Paris], November 25, 1929, 6.

Galerie Goemans, Paris. *Exposition de collages* [Louis Aragon's *La Peinture au défi*], March 1930.

*Galerie Alexandre III, Cannes. *Exposition Picabia*, August 1930.
Cannes l'été, July 1930.
L'Eclaireur de Nice et du Sud-Est, August 22, 1930, 3.

Kunstsalon Wolfsberg, Zurich. *Produktion Paris 1930*, October 8–November 15, 1930.
Das Kunstblatt (Berlin, January 1931), 27–28.

*Chez Léonce Rosenberg, Paris. *Exposition Francis Picabia*, December 9–31, 1930. Prefaces by Francis Picabia and Léonce Rosenberg.
L'Intransigeant [Paris], December 15, 1930, 5; *Art News*, XXIX (New York, January 17, 1931), 20.

New School for Social Research, New York. *Exhibition of the Collection of the Société Anonyme*, January 1–February 10, 1931.

Albright Art Gallery and Buffalo Fine Arts Academy, Buffalo.
International Exhibition Illustrating the Most Recent Developments in Abstract Art, presented by the Société Anonyme, February 18–March 8, 1931.

*Galerie Georges Bernheim, Paris. *Exposition Francis Picabia*, November 10–25, 1931. Preface by Robert Desnos.
L'Art vivant, no. 155 (Paris, December 1931), 665.

De Onafhankelijken, Amsterdam. *Hedendaagsche Schilderkunst en Beeldhouwkunst*, March 1932.

*Evelyn Wyld et Eyre de Lanux, Cannes. *104 dessins par Francis Picabia*, August 19, 1932. Preface by Germaine Everling.

*Chez Léonce Rosenberg, Paris. *Exposition de dessins par Francis Picabia*, December 1–24, 1932. Poem by Gertrude Stein; trans. by Marcel Duchamp.

The Art Institute of Chicago. *A Century of Progress, Exhibition of Painting and Sculpture*, June 1–November 1, 1933.

*Galerie Vignon, Paris. *Exposition des oeuvres de Francis Picabia*, November
9–23, 1933.
Beaux-Arts, no. 46 (Paris, November 17, 1933), 3.

*Galerie Alexandre III, Cannes. *Catalogue des aquarelles et dessins composant
l'atelier de Francis Picabia*, public sale, August 18, 1934. Preface by Maurice
Mignon.

*Galerie Vignon, Paris. *Francis Picabia, ses oeuvres récentes*, October 25–
November 6, 1934.
Beaux-Arts, no. 96 (Paris, November 2, 1934), 6; *L'Art vivant*, no. 191 (Paris,
December 1934–January 1935), 514–15.

*Valentine Gallery, New York. *Recent Paintings by Francis Picabia*, November
5–24, 1934. Preface by Gertrude Stein.
The Art Digest, IX (New York, November 15, 1934), 11.

*The Arts Club of Chicago. *Paintings by Francis Picabia*, January 3–25, 1936.
Poem by Gertrude Stein.
Chicago Daily News, January 11, 1936.

*Galerie Jeanne Bucher, Paris. *Exposition Picabia*, February 1936 (attrib.).
Le Petit Marseillais, ca. March 1935 (attrib.).

The Museum of Modern Art, New York. *Cubism and Abstract Art*, March 2–April
19, 1936. Edited by Alfred H. Barr, Jr.

The Museum of Modern Art, New York. *Fantastic Art, Dada and Surrealism*,
December 7, 1936–January 17, 1937. Edited by Alfred H. Barr, Jr.

*Galerie d'Art Duverney, Cannes. *Exposition Picabia*, February 1937.
L'Eclaireur [Nice], February 13, 1937 (attrib.); *Le Petit Marseillais*, February
13, 1937.

*La Galerie Serguy, Cannes. *Exposition Picabia*, April 1937 (not verified).
Astemposten [Oslo], October 10, 1936 (attrib.).

*Galerie de Beaune, Paris. *Francis Picabia, peintures Dada, paysages récentes*,
November 19–December 2, 1937. Excerpts from earlier statements by Marcel
Duchamp, André Breton, Jean van Heeckeren, Jean Cocteau, G. Ribemont-
Dessaignes, Vivian Du Mas, Jacques-Henri Lévesque and Gertrude Stein.
Paris-Midi, November 22, 1937 (attrib.); *Le Figaro* [Paris], November 23,
1937 (attrib.); *Beaux-Arts*, no. 256 (Paris, November 26, 1937), 4.

The London Gallery, Ltd., London. *The Impact of Machines*, ca. May–June,
1938.

*Galerie de Beaune, Paris. *Exposition Picabia*, November 4–17, 1938. Preface
by Albert Flament.
Aux Ecoutes [Paris], November 5, 1938 (attrib.); *Echo de Paris*, November 8,
1938; *Beaux-Arts*, no. 306 (Paris, November 11, 1938), 7; *Time* (New York,
November 21, 1938), 37–38; *Candide* [Paris], December 7, 1938.

The George Walter Vincent Smith Art Gallery, Springfield, Mass. *Some New
Forms of Beauty, 1909–1936. A Selection of the Collection of the Société
Anonyme–Museum of Modern Art: 1920*, November 9–December 17, 1939.

Galeria de Arte Mexico, Mexico City. *Exposicion International del Surrealismo*.
January–February 1940.

*La Galerie Serguy, Cannes. *Exposition Francis Picabia*, April 1941. Preface by
Gertrude Stein.

*Galerie Pasteur, Algiers. *Exposition Picabia*, 1941 (not verified).

Art of This Century, New York. *Art of This Century: Objects, Drawings, Photo-*

graphs, Paintings, Sculpture, Collages, 1910 to 1942, 1942. Edited by Peggy Guggenheim.

The Lounge Library, Cannes. *Exposition Francis Picabia et Michel Sima*, July 15–31, 1942. Preface by Germaine Everling.

La Galerie Serguy, Cannes. *Bonnard–Matisse–Picabia*, April 10–30, 1943.
L'Eclaireur [Nice], April 1943 (attrib.).

*Galerie Art et Artisan, Cannes. *100 dessins et 5 portraits par F. Picabia*, September 7–30, 1943.
L'Eclaireur [Nice], September 11, 1943 (attrib.); *Le Petit Niçais*, September 17, 1943 (attrib.); *Le Littorel* [Cannes], September 23, 1943 (attrib.).

*Principauté de Monaco, Office de Tourisme. *50 dessins de F. Picabia*, October 4–20, 1943. Preface by Germaine Everling.

Philadelphia Museum of Art. *History of an American, Alfred Stieglitz: "291" and After*, March 1944–January 1947.

Salon des Surindépendants, Paris, October 1945.
Arts, no. 38 (Paris, October 19, 1945), 1.

*Kunsthalle Basel. *Francis Picabia; Sammlung Nell Walden*, January 12–February 3, 1946.
Basler Nachrichten, no. 18 (January 14) and no. 39 (January 26–27, 1946); *Journal des arts*, nos. 5–6 (Zurich, January–February 1946), 20–21.

*Galerie Denise René, Paris. *Francis Picabia—Peintures sur-irréalistes*, April 26–May 20, 1946.
L'Ordre (Paris, May 6, 1946, attrib.); *France au combat* [Paris], May 9, 1946, 6; *Arts*, no. 67 (Paris, May 10, 1946), 2; *Cavalcade* (Paris, May 10, 1946, attrib.); *Les Arts et les lettres* (Paris, May 10, 1946, attrib.).

*Galerie Dellevoy, Brussels. *Exposition Picabia*, ca. May 1946 (not verified).

Premier Salon des Réalités Nouvelles, Paris, July 1946.
Arts, no. 78 (Paris, July 26, 1946), 8.

Salon des Surindépendants, Paris, October 1946.
L'Aurore [Paris], October 9, 1946; *Arts*, no. 89 (Paris, October 18, 1946), 8; *France au combat* [Paris], October 24, 1946, 8.

*Galerie Colette Allendy, Paris. *Francis Picabia, oeuvres de 1907 à 1924*, October 18–November 16, 1946. Statement by Henri Goetz.
Combat [Paris], October 23, 1946 (attrib.).

*Galerie Lhote, La Rochelle. *Exposition Francis Picabia*, January 10–20, 1947.
La Nouvelle Republique de Bordeaux et du Sud-Ouest, January 7 and 15, 1947; *Sud-Ouest* [La Rochelle?], January 15, 1947.

Galerie des Etats-Unis, Cannes. *Exposition Germaine Gallibert et Francis Picabia*, February 21–March 13, 1947. Preface by Germaine Everling.
La Liberté [Nice], February 25, 1947 (attrib.).

The London Gallery, London. *The Cubist Spirit in its Time*, March 18–May 3, 1947.

*Galerie Colette Allendy, Paris. *Exposition Picabia*, May 30–June 23, 1947. Preface by Francis Picabia.
Combat [Paris], June 4, 1947 (attrib.); *La Seine* [Paris], June 9, 1947 (attrib.); *La Gazette des lettres*, no. 39 (Paris, June 28, 1947), 1–2.

The Museum of Modern Art, New York. *Alfred Stieglitz Exhibition: His Collection*, June 10–August 31, 1947.

Salon des Réalités Nouvelles, Paris, July 1947. Statement by Picabia.

Galerie Maeght, Paris. *Exposition internationale du Surréalisme*, July–August, 1947.

*Galerie Lhote, La Rochelle. *Francis Picabia*, October 11–22, 1947.
  Sud-Ouest [La Rochelle?], October 14, 1947.

Hôtel de la Sous-Préfecture, Montbrison. *De l'impressionisme à nos jours*, October 12–November 9, 1947.

*Galerie du Luxembourg, Paris. *Francis Picabia. Peintures récentes*, April 11–May 8, 1948. Preface by Francis Picabia.
  L'age nouveau, no. 30 (Paris, 1948), 89.

Galerie Colette Allendy, Paris. *HWPSMTB*, April 22, 1948. Statement by Francis Picabia.

*Galerie des Deux Iles, Paris. *Francis Picabia, oeuvres de 1948*, November 15–December 4, 1948. Statement by Michel Seuphor.
  Arts (Paris, November 19, 1948), 4.

*Galerie René Drouin, Paris. *491, 50 ans de plaisir*, March 4–26, 1949. Exhibition catalogue edited by Michel Tapié and René Drouin. Texts contributed by A. Breton, C. Estienne, S. Ghandi, Olga Picabia, Gabrielle Buffet, H.-P. Roché, M. Seuphor, R. Desnos, C. Bryen, B. Fricker, Dédé de l'Opéra, J. van Heeckeren, M. Perrin, M. Duchamp, G. Charbonnier, H.-B. Goetz, F. Bott, F. Picabia, P. de Massot, J. Cocteau, Marie and C. Boumeester.

The Art Institute of Chicago. *20th Century Art, From the Louise and Walter Arensberg Collection*, October 20–December 18, 1949.

*Galerie des Deux Iles, Paris. *Picabia Point*, December 12–31, 1949. Statement by Michel Seuphor.
  Art d'aujourd'hui, no. 6 (Paris, January 1950).

Museu de Arte Moderna, São Paulo. *Do Figurativismo ao Abstracionismo*, 1949.

*Rose Fried Gallery, The Pinacotheca, New York. *Picabia*, February 15–March 31, 1950. Preface by Jean Arp.
  New York Times, February 19, 1950; *Time* (New York, April 10, 1950), 66; *Saturday Review* (New York, June 3, 1950).

*Galerie Apollo, Brussels. *Francis Picabia*, October 18–November 3, 1950. Preface by Michel Tapié.
  Les Beaux-Arts, no. 505 (Brussels, October 27, 1950), 3.

*Galerie Colette Allendy, Paris. *Francis Picabia*, December 13, 1950–January 12, 1951. Preface by Francis Picabia.

Rose Fried Gallery, New York. Untitled group exhibition, January 4–20, 1951.

Royal Academy of Arts, London. *L'Ecole de Paris, 1900–1950*, January 13–March 7, 1951.

Yale University, New Haven. *Gertrude Stein's "Pictures for a Picture,"* February 11–March 11, 1951.

Rose Fried Gallery, New York. *Some Areas of Search*, May–June 1951.

*Galerie Artiste et Artisan, Paris. *Quelques Oeuvres de Picabia (époque Dada 1915–1925)*, November 20–December 4, 1951. Statement by Jacques-Henri Lévesque.

*Galerie des Etats-Unis (Stoliar), Cannes. *Exposition de 100 oeuvres de Picabia*, 1951.

*Chez P.A.B., Alès. *Assortiment de dessins de F. Picabia*, January 21–28, 1952. Statement by René Char.

Galerie Marbach, Bern. *Ausstellung Francis Picabia, Christine Boumeester, Henri Goetz*, March 26–April 23, 1952.
Berner Tagblatt, April 16, 1952 (attrib.).

Kunsthalle Basel. *Phantastiche Kunst des XX Jahrhunderts*, August 30–October 12, 1952.

Rose Fried Gallery, New York. Untitled group exhibition, December 1952.

*Galerie Colette Allendy, Paris. *15 toiles récentes de Francis Picabia*, December 19, 1952–January 15, 1953. Statements by André Breton (?), Camille Bryen, Jean Cocteau, Jean van Heeckeren, Jacques-Henri Lévesque, Michel Perrin and Michel Seuphor.

Musée National d'Art Moderne, Paris. *Le Cubisme*, January 30–April 9, 1953.

Sidney Janis Gallery, New York. *Dada. 1916–1923*, April 15–May 9, 1953. Statements by Jean Arp, Tristan Tzara, Richard Huelsenbeck and Jacques-Henri Lévesque.

Walker Art Center, Minneapolis. *The Classic Tradition in Contemporary Art*, April 24–June 28, 1953.

*Galerie Cravan, Paris. *Hommage à Picabia*, October 1953. Homages by Charles Estienne, Michel Tapié, Edouard Jaguer, Roland Penrose, Christian Dotremont and Pierre Alechinsky.

Rose Fried Gallery, New York. *Marcel Duchamp and Francis Picabia*, December 7, 1953–January 8, 1954.
Christian Science Monitor [Boston], January 2, 1954.

*Galerie La Boutique d'Art, Nice. *Exposition Picabia*, January–February 1954.
L'Amateur d'art [Nantes?], October 2, 1954 (attrib.).

The Redfern Gallery, London. *Paintings, Drawings, Prints from the Movements of Cubism, Abstraction, Sur-realism, Formalism*, April 13–May 8, 1954.

Rose Fried Gallery, New York. Untitled group exhibition, November 2–December 1954.

University of Michigan, Ann Arbor. *20th Century Painting and Sculpture from the Winston Collection*, 1955.

Rose Fried Gallery, New York. *International Collage Exhibition*, February 13–March 17, 1956.

*Galerie Furstenberg, Paris. *Exposition Picabia*, June 5–July 5, 1956.
Burlington Magazine, XCVIII (London, July 1956), 250.

Château Historique de La Napoule, Henry Clews Art Foundation, La Napoule. *Exposition Picabia, les artistes au soleil et Jean-Gabriel Domergue*, September 14–October 14, 1956.
Nice-Matin, October 11, 1956.

Rose Fried Gallery, New York. *Modern Masters*, October 22–November 30, 1956.
New York Times, October 26, 1956; *Arts* (New York, November 1956).

*Villa Robioni, Nice. *30 toiles, gouaches, aquarelles, dessins de F. P. appartenant à Mme. Germaine Everling-Picabia*, December 28, 1956.

Musée d'Art et d'Industrie, St.-Etienne. *Art abstrait*, April–May 1957.

Musée des Beaux-Arts, Bordeaux. *Bosch, Goya et le fantastique*, May 20–July 31, 1957. Catalogue by Gilbert Martin-Méry; texts by multiple authors.

Detroit Institute of Arts. *Collecting Modern Art: Painting, Sculpture and Drawings from the Collection of Mr. and Mrs. Harry Lewis Winston*, September 27–November 3, 1957.

Rose Fried Gallery, New York. *50 Works by 23 Modern Masters*, October 28–
December 21, 1957.

Exposition Universelle et Internationale, Brussels. *50 ans d'art moderne*, April
17–October 19, 1958.

Galerie Knoedler, Paris. *Les Soirées de Paris*, May 16–June 30, 1958. Introduction by André Billy; catalogue by Guy Habasque.

Kunsthalle Dusseldorf. *Dada, Dokumente einer Bewegung*, September
5–October 19, 1958; Stedelijk Museum, Amsterdam, December 23, 1958–
February 2, 1959.

Arts, XXXIII, no. 5 (New York, February 1959), 30–37.

Sidney Janis Gallery, New York. *X Years of Janis*, September 29–November 1,
1958.

*The Matthiesen Gallery, London. *Francis Picabia*, October–November 1959.
Burlington Magazine, CI (London, November 1959); *Apollo*, LXIX–LXX
(London, November 1959), 131–32.

*Samlaren, Stockholm. *De Picabia tour autour*, February 1960.

Galerie Chalette, New York. *Construction and Geometry in Painting*, March
31–June 4, 1960.

*Galleria Schwarz, Milan. *Francis Picabia*, July 1–30, 1960. Brief statements by
multiple authors.

Art Associates of Lake Charles, Louisiana. *The Trojan Horse*, 1960.

Palais Barberini, Rome. *Omaggio ad Apollinaire*, December 1960–January
1961.

The Solomon R. Guggenheim Museum, New York. *Paintings from the Arensberg
and Gallatin Collections of The Philadelphia Museum of Art*, February 7–April
16, 1961.

Galerie du Dragon and Galerie Weiller, Paris. *Art Cubain contemporain*,
February 21–March 10, 1961.

Galerie de Paris, Paris. *Les Amis de St.-Tropez*, May 2–June 10, 1961.

Moderna Museet, Stockholm. *Rörelse I Konsten*, May 17–September 3, 1961.

The Museum of Modern Art, New York. *The Art of Assemblage*, October
2–November 12, 1961. Edited by William C. Seitz.

*Galerie Mona Lisa, Paris. *Picabia vu en transparence*, November–December
1961. Prefaces by Georges Ribemont-Dessaignes and Patrick Waldberg.

Palais Granvelle, Besançon. *Surréalisme et précurseurs*, 1961.

Galerie Denise René, Paris. *Art abstrait constructif*, 1961.

Detroit Institute of Arts. *French Drawings and Watercolors from Michigan
Collections*, January 1962.

*Musée Cantini, Marseille. *Picabia*, March 20–May 15, 1962. Text and catalogue
by Mme Jacques Latour and M. Jean-Albert Cartier; statements by multiple
authors from previous publications.
Combat [Paris], March 19, 1962; *La Marseillaise* [Marseille], March 19, 20
and 30, April 2, May 11, 1962; *Le Monde* [Paris], March 23 and 30, 1962;
Arts, no. 862 (Paris, March 28, 1962), 8; *Revue de Paris*, May 1962.

*Kunsthalle Bern, *Francis Picabia*, July 7–September 2, 1962. Preface by Jean-
Jacques Lebel.

Goucher College, Towson, Md. *The Epstein Collection*, January 1963.

The Alan Gallery, New York. *Duchamp, Picabia, Schwitters*, January
7–February 2, 1963.

Munson-Williams-Proctor Institute, Utica, and the Henry Street Settlement, New York. *Armory Show, 50th Anniversary Exhibition*, Utica, February 17–March 31, 1963, and New York, April 6–28, 1963. Introduction by Milton W. Brown.

The Whitney Museum of American Art, New York. *The Decade of the Armory Show*, February 27–April 14, 1963. Edited by Lloyd Goodrich.

The Solomon R. Guggenheim Museum, New York. *20th Century Master Drawings*, November 6, 1963–January 5, 1964.

Edgardo Acosta Gallery, Los Angeles. *Some Aspects of Surrealism*, 1963. *Artforum*, I, no. 6 (Los Angeles, 1963), 44, 46.

Galerie André François Petit, Paris. *Hans Bellmer, Salvador Dali, Max Ernst, René Magritte, Francis Picabia, Yves Tanguy*, 1963.

*Hatton Gallery and Institute of Contemporary Arts, London. *Francis Picabia*, March–April, 1964. Published by the Department of Fine Art, the University of Newcastle-upon-Tyne. Edited by Ronald Hunt.
Art International, VIII, no. 5–6 (Lugano, summer 1964), 72.

Michigan State University, East Lansing. *Turn of the Century Exhibition*, April 10–May 4, 1964.

*Galleria Schwarz, Milan. *Picabia*, May 5–June 1, 1964.

The Baltimore Museum of Art. *1914*, October 6–November 15, 1964.

Leonard Hutton Galleries, New York. *Albert Gleizes and the Section d'Or*, October 28–December 5, 1964. Texts by William A. Camfield and Daniel Robbins.

*Galerie Louis Carré, Paris. *Picabia, "Chapeau de Paille?"* November 4–December 4, 1964.
France-Soir [Paris], December 15, 1964.

*Galerie Furstenberg, Paris. *Francis Picabia*, November 4–December 5, 1964.
L'Express (Paris, November 2–8, 1964), 52–53; *Art International*, VIII, no. 10 (Lugano, December 1964), 58, 60–61.

Museum voor schone Kunsten, Ghent. *Figuratie Defiguratie, 1964*.

Galerie Charpentier, Paris. *Le Surréalisme: Sources, histoire, affinités*, 1964. Texts by Raymond Nacenta and Patrick Waldberg.

Museum of Fine Arts, Houston. *The Heroic Years: Paris 1908–1914*, October 20–December 8, 1965.

Moderna Museet, Stockholm. *Dada*, February 3–March 27, 1966.

La Galerie Krugier et Cie, Geneva. *Dada*, February 17–March 30, 1966. Introduction by Werner Haftmann.
Art International, X, no. 4 (Lugano, April 1966), 96–98.

Santa Barbara Museum of Art. *Harbingers of Surrealism*, February 26–March 27, 1966. Forward by William J. Hesthal.

Knoedler and Co., Inc., New York. *Seven Decades: 1895–1965, Crosscurrents in Modern Art* [Exhibition at ten New York galleries for the benefit of the Public Education Association], April–May 1966.

The Solomon R. Guggenheim Museum, New York. *Gauguin and the Decorative Style*, June 23–October 23, 1966.

Annmary Brown Memorial, Brown University and the Museum of Art, Rhode Island School of Design, Providence. *Herbert and Nannette Rothschild Collection*, October 7–November 6, 1966. Catalogue by George Downing and Daniel Robbins.

Kunsthaus Zurich. *Dada*, October 8–November 17, 1966; Musée National d'Art Moderne, Paris, November 30, 1966–January 30, 1967. Collaboration of the Association pour l'Etude du Mouvement Dada, Paris.
  La Revue du Louvre, nos. 4–5 (Paris, 1969), 269–76.
Sidney Janis Gallery, New York. *Two Generations*, January 3–27, 1967.
  Art International, XI, no. 3 (Lugano, March 20, 1967), 58–59.
*Städtisches Museum Schloss Morsbroich Leverkusen. *Francis Picabia*, February 7–April 2, 1967; Stedelijk van Abbemuseum, Eindhoven, April 21–June 4, 1967. Texts by Rolf Wedewer, Ursula Wedewer-Böcker and Lothar Romain.
The Solomon R. Guggenheim Museum, New York. *Seven Decades: Museum Collection*, June 28–October 1, 1967.
Albright-Knox Art Gallery, Buffalo. *Painters of the Section d'Or*, September 27–October 22, 1967. Text and catalogue by Richard V. West.
Galleria Civica d'Arte Moderna, Turin. *Le Muse inquietanti*, November 1967–January 1968.
Albright-Knox Art Gallery, Buffalo. *Plus by Minus: Today's Half Century*, March 3–April 14, 1968.
Grand Palais, Paris. *79ᵉ Exposition de la Société des Artistes Indépendants, Retrospective 1905–1909*, March 22–April 15, 1968.
The Museum of Modern Art, New York. *Dada, Surrealism and Their Heritage*, March 27–June 9, 1968. Catalogue by William S. Rubin.
  Art International, XII, no. 5 (Lugano, May 15, 1968), 34–39.
Ville de Strasbourg. *L'Art en Europe autour de 1918*, May 8–September 15, 1968.
National Gallery of Art, Washington, D.C. *Paintings from the Albright-Knox Art Gallery*, May 18–July 21, 1968.
The Solomon R. Guggenheim Museum, New York. *Rousseau, Redon and Fantasy*, May 31–September 8, 1968.
Casino Communal, Brussels. *Trésors du Surréalisme*, June–September 1968. Edited by André de Rache.
The Museum of Modern Art, New York. *The Machine as Seen at the End of the Mechanical Age*, November 30, 1968–February 9, 1969. Edited by K.G. Pontus Hultén.
Musée National d'Art Moderne and Minister of Cultural Affairs, Paris. *Painting in France 1900–1967*, 1968.
Musées Royaux des Beaux-Arts de Belgique, Brussels. *Dix acquisitions récentes*, February 5–March 23, 1969.
*Notizie, Turin. *Picabia. Opere dal 1917 al 1950*, October 10–November 15, 1969. Preface by Maurizio Fagiolo.
Museo Nacional de Bellas Artes, Buenos Aires. *109 Works from the Albright-Knox Art Gallery*, October 23–November 30, 1969.
*The Solomon R. Guggenheim Museum, New York. *Francis Picabia*, September 17–December 6, 1970. Text and catalogue by William A. Camfield.
  New York Times, September 27, 1970, D, 23; *Newsweek* (New York, September 28, 1970), 81; *The Nation* (New York, October 5, 1970), 314–15; *Art International*, XIV, no. 9 (Lugano, November 1970), 66, 70; *Saturday Review* (New York, November 21, 1970), 54–55; *Apollo* (London, December 1970), 490–91.

Fine Arts Gallery of San Diego. *Color and Form 1909–1914*, November 20, 1971–January 2, 1972. Essays by Henry R. Gardiner, Joshua C. Taylor, Peter Selz, Lilli Lonngren, Herschel B. Chipp and William C. Agee.

Haus der Kunst, Munich. *Der Surrealismus 1922–1942*, March 11–May 7, 1972. Preface by Patrick Waldberg.

*Galleria Schwarz, Milan. *Francis Picabia*, June 6–September 16, 1972. Preface by Marcel Duchamp; text by William A. Camfield.

Musée d'Art Moderne de la Ville de Paris, Paris. *Les Cubistes*, September 26–November 10, 1973.

Galerie de Seine, Paris. *Collection Fantôme*, October 1973. Preface by Philippe Soupault.

Städtische Galerie im Lenbachhaus, Munich. *New York Dada: Duchamp, Man Ray, Picabia*, December 15, 1973–January 27, 1974. Texts and catalogue by Arturo Schwarz.

*Galleria Schwarz, Milan. *Picabia: Le Poulailler*, October 1974. Text by William A. Camfield.

*Galleria Civica d'Arte Moderna, Turin. *Francis Picabia*, November 28, 1974–February 2, 1975. Catalogue by Maurizio Fagiolo Dell'Arco.

Kunsthalle Bern. *Junggesellenmaschinen. Les Machines célibataires*, July 5–August 17, 1975. Edited by Harald Szeemann.

Centre National d'Art et de Culture Georges Pompidou, Musée National d'Art Moderne, Paris. *Francis Picabia*, Grand Palais, January 23–March 29, 1976. Multiple contributors; text and catalogue by Jean-Hubert Martin and Hélène Seckel.

V. Archives

Access to certain material in some of these archives is very difficult. Interested students should ascertain in advance the conditions for access to the archives.

The Francis Bacon Foundation, Claremont, Calif. Photographs and letters from Mme Gabrielle Buffet-Picabia (and Francis Picabia?) to Walter Arensberg.

Bibliothèque Littéraire Jacques Doucet, in the Bibliothèque Ste.-Geneviève, Paris. Outstanding collection of published and unpublished material including the "Dossiers Picabia," the Collection Tzara, the Collection Desnos and correspondence by Jacques Doucet, Marcel Duchamp, Pierre de Massot, Georges Ribemont-Dessaignes, Georges Herbiet [Christian] and many others.

Gabrielle Buffet, Paris. Photographs of Picabia and his paintings.

Scrapbook of the Congress of Paris. Manuscript Room, Bibliothèque Nationale, Paris. Letters, clippings and manuscripts collected by André Breton.

Germaine Everling, Cannes. Folders of letters, photographs, catalogues and clippings.

Henri Goetz and Christine Boumeester, Paris. Numerous letters and some drawings by Picabia, ca. 1945–1951.

Mme Yvonne Gresse-Picabia, La Rochelle. Family legal documents and photo albums.

The Carlton Lake Collection in the Humanities Research Center, The University of Texas at Austin. Letters and manuscripts by Picabia and numerous associates, most notably Marcel Duchamp, Marie Laurencin, Clément Pansaers, Erik Satie and Tristan Tzara.

Mabel Dodge Luhan Archive. Collection of American Literature, Beinecke Rare Book and Manuscript Library, Yale University, New Haven, Conn. Scrapbooks containing clippings and miscellaneous data on Francis Picabia.

"Dossiers Picabia." Bibliothèque Littéraire Jacques Doucet, Paris. Thirteen scrapbooks of clippings, letters, photographs and drawings collected by Francis Picabia ca. 1904–1927.

"Olga Picabia scrapbook." Collection Olga Picabia, Paris. One volume of clippings, photographs and unpublished manuscripts; separate letters and manuscripts.

Collection of the Société Anonyme, Museum of Modern Art, 1920, Yale University, New Haven, Conn. Several letters of Mme Buffet-Picabia; catalogues and photographs pertaining to Francis Picabia.

Gertrude Stein Archive. Collection of American Literature, Beinecke Rare Book and Manuscript Library, Yale University, New Haven, Conn. Letters of Francis Picabia, 1913–1946.

Alfred Stieglitz Archive. Collection of American Literature, Beinecke Rare Book and Manuscript Library, Yale University, New Haven, Conn. Letters, drawings and manuscripts by Francis Picabia; letters, catalogues and scrapbooks with clippings, photographs and miscellaneous data pertaining to Francis Picabia.

Marius de Zayas Archive. In the possession of Mrs. Marius de Zayas and her son Rodrigo de Zayas, Paris, with some xerox copies at Columbia University and Yale University. Letters, invoices and catalogues relevant to Alfred Stieglitz, Francis Picabia, the Modern Gallery and various artists.

INDEX

Library of Congress Cataloging in Publication Data

Camfield, William A.
  Francis Picabia: his art, life, and times.

  Bibliography: p.
  Includes index.
  1. Picabia, Francis, 1879-1953.   2. Painters—
Frances—Biography.
ND553.P47C36   759.4 [B]   77–85533
ISBN 0–691–03932–1